HTML and CSS

Eighth Edition

ELIZABETH CASTRO • BRUCE HYSLOP

Peachpit Press

Visual QuickStart Guide
HTML and CSS, Eighth Edition
Elizabeth Castro and Bruce Hyslop

Peachpit Press
www.peachpit.com

To report errors, please send a note to errata@peachpit.com.

Peachpit Press is a division of Pearson Education.

Copyright © 2014 by Elizabeth Castro and Bruce Hyslop

Editor: Clifford Colby
Development editor: Robyn G. Thomas
Production editor: David Van Ness
Copyeditor: Scout Festa
Technical editor: Aubrey Taylor
Compositor: David Van Ness
Indexer: Valerie Haynes Perry
Cover design: RHDG / Riezebos Holzbaur Design Group, Peachpit Press
Interior design: Peachpit Press
Logo design: MINE™ www.minesf.com

Notice of Rights

css3generator.com screen shot courtesy of Randy Jensen.
css3please.com screen shot courtesy of Paul Irish.
dribbble.com screen shots courtesy of Dan Cederholm.
fontsquirrel.com screen shots courtesy of Ethan Dunham.
foodsense.is screen shots courtesy of Julie Lamba.
google.com/fonts screen shots courtesy of Google.
namecheap.com screen shots courtesy of Namecheap.
Silk icon set courtesy of Mark James (http://www.famfamfam.com/lab/icons/silk/).
Socialico font courtesy of Fontfabric (www.fontfabric.com).

Notice of Liability

Trademarks

ISBN-13:   978-0-321-92883-2
ISBN-10:   0-321-92883-0

9 8 7 6 5 4

Printed and bound in the United States of America

Dedication

To family.

To those I know who endured difficult challenges, demonstrating courage and perseverance all the way.

Acknowledgments

One of my favorite parts of working on this book has been the people I've been able to work with. All are dedicated, professional, good-natured, and good-humored folks who made it a real pleasure. The book wouldn't be the same without their contributions.

A grateful, sincere thank you goes out to:

Nancy Aldrich-Ruenzel and Nancy Davis, for their continued trust in me.

Cliff Colby, for his support, for bringing the team together, and for keeping things light.

Robyn Thomas, for making the engine go, improving copy, tracking all the details, being flexible, and providing encouragement.

Scout Festa, for her skill in simplifying language, for her watchful eye, and for helping to keep things consistent and polished.

Aubrey Taylor, for all the great suggestions and technical feedback. They were very helpful, and readers are better off for them.

David Van Ness, for leading the charge in making it all look great and for all his efforts in refining the layouts.

Valerie Haynes Perry, for compiling the all-important index, which will be the first destination for many readers in search of information.

The marketing, sales, and other folks at Peachpit, for working hard to make the book available to readers.

Natalia Ammon, for the wonderful design of the example webpage that adorns the pages of Chapters 11 and 12, and other spots. You can see more of her work at www.nataliaammon.com.

Zach Szukala, for recommending Natalia.

Scott Boms, Ian Devlin, Seth Lemoine, Erik Vorhes, and Brian Warren, for their contributions to the previous edition.

Victor Gavenda, for providing access to necessary software.

Dan Cederholm, Ethan Dunham, Paul Irish, Mark James, Randy Jensen, Julie Lamba, Fontfabric, Google, and Namecheap, for allowing me to use screen shots or design assets (as the case may be).

C.R. Freer, for working her camera magic.

My family and friends, for providing inspiration and breaks, for being patient, and for not disowning me while I was holed up writing for months.

Robert Reinhardt, as always, for getting me started in writing books and for having a swell beard.

The Boston Bruins, for providing a lot of playoffs thrills during my infrequent breaks.

The numerous folks in the web community who have shared their expertise and experiences for the betterment of others. (I've cited many of you throughout the book.)

To you readers, for inspiring me to recall when I began learning HTML and CSS so that I may explain them in ways I hope you find helpful. Thank you for choosing this book as part of your journey in contributing to the web. Happy reading!

And, lastly, I would like to give a special thank you to Elizabeth Castro, who created this title in the 1990s. She has taught countless readers how to build webpages over many editions and many years. Because the web has given me so much, I'm genuinely appreciative of the opportunity to teach readers via this title as well.

—Bruce

Contents at a Glance

Table of Contents

Introduction

Whether you are just beginning your venture into building websites or have built some before but want to ensure that your knowledge is current, you've come along at a very exciting time.

How we code and style webpages, the browsers in which we view the pages, and the devices on which we visit the web have all advanced substantially the past few years. Once limited to browsing the web from our desktop computers or laptops, we can now take the web with us on any number of devices: phones, tablets, and, yes, laptops and desktops.

Which is as it should be, because the web's promise has always been the dissolution of boundaries—the power to share and access information from any metropolis, rural community, or anywhere in between and on any web-enabled device. In short, the web's promise lies in its universality. And its reach continues to expand as technology finds its way to communities that were once shut out.

Better still, the web belongs to everyone, and anyone is free to create and launch a site. This book shows you how. It is ideal for the beginner with no knowledge of HTML or CSS who wants to begin to create webpages. You'll find clear, easy-to-follow instructions that take you through the process of creating pages step by step. And the book is a helpful guide to keep handy. You can look up topics in the table of contents or index and consult just those subjects about which you need more information.

HTML and CSS in Brief

At the root of the web's success is a simple, text-based markup language that is easy to learn and that any device with a basic web browser can read: HTML. Every webpage requires at least some HTML; it wouldn't be a webpage without it.

As you will learn in greater detail as you read this book, HTML is used to define your content, and CSS is used to control how your content and webpage will look. Both HTML pages and CSS files (*style sheets*) are text files, making them easy to edit. You can see snippets of HTML and CSS in "How This Book Works," near the end of this introduction.

You'll dive into learning a basic HTML page right off the bat in Chapter 1, and you'll begin to learn how to style your pages with CSS in Chapter 7. See "What this book will teach you" later in this introduction for an overview of the chapters and a summary of the primary topics covered.

The word *HTML* is all encompassing, representing the language in general. *HTML5* is used when referring to that specific version of HTML, such as when discussing a feature that is new in HTML5 and doesn't exist in previous versions. The same approach applies to usage of the terms *CSS* (general) and *CSS3* (specific to CSS3).

HTML and HTML5

It helps to know some basics about the origins of HTML to understand HTML5.

HTML began in the early 1990s as a short document that detailed a handful of elements used to build webpages. Many of those elements were for content such as headings, paragraphs, lists, and links to other pages. HTML's version number has increased as the language has evolved with the introduction of other elements and adjustments to its rules. The most current version is HTML5.

HTML5 is a natural evolution of earlier versions of HTML and strives to reflect the needs of both current and future websites. It inherits the vast majority of features from its predecessors, meaning that if you coded HTML before HTML5 came on the scene, you already know a lot of HTML5. This also means that much of HTML5 works in both old and new browsers; being backward compatible is a key design principle of HTML5 (see www.w3.org/TR/html-design-principles/).

HTML5 also adds a bevy of new features. Many are straightforward, such as additional elements (`article`, `main`, `figure`, and many more) that are used to describe content. Others are complex and aid in creating powerful web applications. You'll need a firm grasp of creating webpages before you can graduate to the more complicated features that HTML5 provides, which is why this book focuses on the former. HTML5 also introduces native audio and video playback to your webpages, which the book also covers.

CSS and CSS3

The first version of CSS didn't exist until after HTML had been around for a few years, becoming official in 1996. Like HTML5 and its relationship to earlier versions of HTML, CSS3 is a natural extension of the versions of CSS that preceded it.

CSS3 is more powerful than earlier versions of CSS and introduces numerous visual effects, such as drop shadows, rounded corners, gradients, and much more. (See "What this book will teach you" for details of what's covered.)

The desktop version of Firefox

Browser Version Numbers

Like HTML and CSS, browsers have version numbers. The higher the number, the more recent it is.

For instance, Safari 7 is more recent than Safari 6, which is more recent than Safari 5. Internet Explorer 10 is more recent than Internet Explorer 9. But Internet Explorer 10 is not more recent than Safari 7.

This is true because Microsoft, Apple, and the other browser vendors do not collectively coordinate either their version numbers or when they will all release new versions. Chrome and Firefox release new versions every six weeks so naturally have much higher version numbers than the other browsers, which are updated roughly once a year at best.

Regardless of who is releasing what and when, the latest version of a browser will have better support for HTML and CSS (and other) features than the previous versions do, as you would expect.

Web Browsers

We all use a web browser to visit websites, whether on a computer Ⓐ, a phone, or another device. However, the browser you use might be different than the one someone else uses.

Windows comes preinstalled with Internet Explorer, Microsoft's browser. OS X comes preinstalled with Safari, Apple's browser. There are other browsers you may download for free and use instead, such as Chrome (by Google), Firefox (by Mozilla) Ⓐ, and Opera (by Opera Software)—and that's just for the desktop.

On mobile devices, you'll find the mobile version of Safari (for iPhone, iPad, and iPod touch); various default Android browsers; Chrome for Android; Firefox for Android; Opera Mini; and more.

I'll refer to various browsers throughout the book. For the most part, the latest version of each one has similar support for the HTML and CSS features you'll learn about. But sometimes a feature doesn't work on one or more browsers (or works differently). I'll note those cases and typically offer a way to handle them. This mostly pertains to Internet Explorer 8, the oldest browser that is still relevant enough to be of concern. (Its usage is dropping, so that could change in 2014 or so.)

"Testing Your Pages" in Chapter 20 provides information about how to acquire various browsers, which ones are the most important for testing your webpages, and how to test your pages.

Web Standards and Specifications

You might be wondering who created HTML and CSS in the first place, and who continues to evolve them. The World Wide Web Consortium (W3C)—directed by the inventor of the web and HTML, Tim Berners-Lee—is the organization responsible for shepherding the development of web standards.

The W3C releases *specifications* (or *specs*, for short) that document these web standards. They define the parameters of languages like HTML and CSS. In other words, specs standardize the rules. Follow the W3C's activity at www.w3.org **Ⓐ**.

Ⓐ The W3C site is the industry's primary source of web standards specifications.

The W3C and WHATWG

For a variety of reasons, another organization—the Web Hypertext Application Technology Working Group (WHATWG)—is developing most of the HTML5 specification. The W3C incorporates WHATWG's work into its official version of the in-progress spec. You can find the WHATWG at www.whatwg.org.

If you want to dig into various specs (recommended!), here are the latest versions:

- HTML5 (W3C):
  http://www.w3.org/TR/html5/

- HTML5.1 (W3C):
  http://www.w3.org/TR/html51/

- HTML Living Standard (WHATWG):
  http://www.whatwg.org/specs/web-apps/current-work/multipage/

The HTML Living Standard includes newer features under development (and very much in flux) and informs the W3C's HTML5.1 spec.

There are too many CSS specs to list, but you can see them at http://www.w3.org/standards/techs/css#w3c_all.

Differences Between HTML4 and HTML5

If you have prior experience with HTML4 and are wondering what is different in HTML5, the W3C has created just the document for you: http://www.w3.org/TR/html5-diff/.

I call out many of the differences at various points in the book. They aren't particularly important to know for those of you who are new to HTML, because HTML5 is what virtually everyone uses now. But you might find the W3C's document interesting to peruse regardless.

With standards in place, we can build our pages from the agreed-upon set of rules, and browsers can be built to display our pages with those rules in mind. (On the whole, browsers implement the standards well. Older versions of Internet Explorer, especially Internet Explorer 8, have some issues.)

Specifications go through several stages of development before they are considered final, at which point they are dubbed a *Recommendation* (www.w3.org/2005/10/Process-20051014/tr).

Parts of the HTML5 and CSS3 specs are still being finalized, but that doesn't mean you can't use them. It just takes time (literally years) for the standardization process to run its course. Browsers begin to implement a spec's features long before it becomes a Recommendation, because that informs the spec development process itself. So browsers already include a wide variety of features in HTML5 and CSS3, even though they aren't Recommendations yet.

On the whole, the features covered in this book are well entrenched in their respective specs, so the risk of their changing prior to becoming a Recommendation is minimal. Developers have been using many HTML5 and CSS3 features for some time. So can you.

Progressive Enhancement: A Best Practice

I began the introduction by speaking of the universality of the web—the notion that the web should be accessible to all. *Progressive enhancement* helps you build sites with universality in mind. It is not a language, but rather an approach to building sites that Steve Champeon promoted beginning in 2003 (http://en.wikipedia.org/wiki/Progressive_enhancement).

The idea is simple but powerful: Start your site with HTML content and basic behavior that is accessible to all visitors **A**. To the same page, add your design with CSS **B** and additional behavior with JavaScript (a programming language). These components are kept separate but work together.

A A basic HTML page with no custom CSS applied to it. Primarily, only very old browsers would display it this way. The page may not look great, but the information is accessible—and that's what's important.

B The same page as viewed in a browser that supports CSS. It's the same information, just presented differently. (The content on the right side would be visible in **A** if you were to scroll down the page.)

More Examples

Take an early peek at Chapter 12 if you're interested in seeing how the principle of progressive enhancement helps you build a website that adapts its layout based on a device's screen size and browser capabilities. It can look great on mobile, desktop, and beyond.

Or see Chapter 14 for how older browsers can display simplified designs while modern browsers display ones enhanced with CSS3 effects.

Elsewhere in the book, you'll learn other techniques that allow you to build progressively enhanced webpages.

The result is that browsers capable of accessing basic pages will get the simplified, default experience **A**. Even browsers from the inception of the web more than 20 years ago can display this page; so too can the oldest or simplest of mobile phones with web browsers. And *screen readers*, software that reads webpages aloud to visually impaired visitors, will be able to navigate it easily.

Meanwhile, modern browsers capable of viewing more-robust sites will see the enhanced version **B**. The capabilities of yet other (somewhat older) browsers might fall somewhere in between; so, too, could the way they display the page. The experience on your site doesn't have to be the same for everyone, as long as your content is accessible.

In essence, the idea behind progressive enhancement is that everyone wins.

Is This Book for You?

This book assumes no prior knowledge of building websites. So in that sense, it is for the absolute beginner. You will learn both HTML and CSS from the ground up. In the course of doing so, you will also learn about features that are new in HTML5 and CSS3, with an emphasis on many that designers and developers are using today in their daily work.

But even if you are familiar with HTML and CSS, you still stand to learn from this book, especially if you want to get up to speed on the new elements in HTML5, several CSS3 effects, responsive web design, and various best practices.

What this book will teach you

The chapters are organized like so:

- Chapters 1 through 6 and 15 through 18 cover the principles of creating HTML pages and most of the HTML elements at your disposal, with clear examples demonstrating how and when to use each one.

- Chapters 7 through 14 dive into CSS, all the way from creating your first style rule to applying enhanced visual effects with CSS3.

- Chapter 19 shows you how to add pre-written JavaScript to your pages.

- Chapter 20 tells you how to test and debug your pages before putting them on the web.

- Chapter 21 explains how to secure your own domain name and then publish your site on the web for all to see.

Covered topics include the following:

- Creating, saving, and editing HTML and CSS files.

- What it means to write semantic HTML and why it is important.

- How to separate your page's HTML content, CSS presentation, and JavaScript behavior—a key aspect of progressive enhancement.

- Structuring your content in a meaningful way by using HTML elements that have been around for years as well as ones that are new in HTML5.

- Linking from one webpage to another, or from one part of a page to another part.

- Adding images to your pages and optimizing them for the web. This includes creating images targeted for Apple's Retina display and other high-pixel-density screens.

- Improving your site's accessibility with ARIA (Accessible Rich Internet Applications) landmark roles and other good coding practices.

- Styling text (size, color, bold, italics, and more) and adding background colors and images.

- Implementing a multi-column webpage layout.

- Building a responsive webpage. That is, a page that shrinks or expands to fit your visitor's screen and with a layout that adapts in other ways as you wish. The result is a page that's appropriate for mobile phones, tablets, laptops, desktop computers, and other web-enabled devices.

- Adding custom web fonts to your pages with **@font-face** and using fonts from services like Font Squirrel and Google Fonts.

- Using CSS3 effects such as opacity, background alpha transparency, gradients, rounded corners, drop shadows, shadows inside elements, text shadows, and multiple background images.

- Taking advantage of CSS generated content and using sprites to minimize the number of images your page needs, making it load faster for your visitors.

- Building forms to solicit input from your visitors, including using some of the new form input types in HTML5.

- Including media in your pages with the HTML5 **audio** and **video** elements for modern browsers, and a Flash fallback audio or video player for older browsers.

- And more.

These topics are complemented by many dozens of code samples that demonstrate how to implement the features based on best practices in the industry.

What this book *won't* teach you

Alas, with so many developments in the world of HTML and CSS in recent years, we had to leave out some topics. With a couple of exceptions, we stuck to omitting items that you would likely have fewer occasions to use, are still subject to change, lack widespread browser support, require JavaScript knowledge, or are advanced subjects.

Some of the topics not covered include the following:

- The HTML5 **details**, **summary**, **menu**, **command**, **output**, and **keygen** elements. The W3C has included some of these on their list of features that might not make the cut when HTML5 is finalized in 2014. The others are used infrequently at best.

- The HTML5 **canvas** element, which allows you to draw graphics, create games, and more. Also, Scalable Vector Graphics (SVG). Both are mentioned briefly in Chapter 17, with links to more information.

- The HTML5 APIs and other advanced features that require JavaScript knowledge or are otherwise not directly related to the new HTML5 elements.

- CSS3 transforms, animations, and transitions. See www.htmlcssvqs.com/resources/ for links to learn more.

- CSS3's new layout methods, such as FlexBox, Grid, and more. They are poised to change the way we lay out pages once the specs shake out and browser support is stronger. See Zoe Mickley Gillenwater's presentation at www.slideshare.net/zomigi/css3-layout, or see Peter Gasston's article at www.netmagazine.com/features/pros-guide-css-layouts.

How This Book Works

Nearly every section of the book contains practical code examples that demonstrate real-world use (Ⓐ and Ⓑ). Typically, they are coupled with screen shots that show the results of the code when you view the webpage in a browser Ⓒ.

Most of the screen shots are of the latest version of Firefox that was available at the time. However, this doesn't imply a recommendation of Firefox over any other browser. The code samples will look similar in any of the latest versions of Chrome, Internet Explorer, Opera, or Safari.

The code and screen shots are accompanied by descriptions of the HTML elements or CSS properties in question, both to increase your understanding of them and to give the samples context.

In many cases, you may find that the descriptions and code samples are enough for you to start using the HTML and CSS features. But if you need explicit guidance on how to use them, step-by-step instructions are provided as well.

Finally, most sections contain tips that relay additional usage information, best practices, references to related parts of the book, links to relevant resources, and more.

Ⓐ You'll find a snippet of HTML code on many pages, with the pertinent sections highlighted. An ellipsis (...) represents additional code or content that was omitted for brevity. Often, the omitted portion is shown in a different code figure.

```
...
<body>
<header class="masthead" role="banner">
    ...
        <nav role="navigation">
            <ul class="nav-main">
                <li><a href="/" class="current-page">Home</a></li>
                <li><a href="/about/">About</a></li>
                <li><a href="/contact/">Contact</a></li>
            </ul>
        </nav>
    ...
</header>
...
</body>
</html>
```

B If CSS code is relevant to the example, it is shown in its own box, with the pertinent sections highlighted.

```css
body {
    font-family: Georgia, "Times New Roman",
    → serif;
}

/* Site Navigation */
.nav-main {
    list-style: none;
    padding: .45em 0 .5em;
}

.nav-main li {
    border-left: 1px solid #c8c8c8;
}

.nav-main a {
    color: #292929;
    font-size: 1.125em;
    font-weight: bold;
}
```

C Screen shots of one or more browsers demonstrate how the code affects the page.

Conventions used in this book

The book uses the following conventions:

- Text that is a placeholder for a value you would create yourself is italicized. Most placeholders appear in the step-by-step instructions. For example, "Type **padding:** *x*;, where *x* is the amount of desired space to be added.

- Code that you should actually type or that represents HTML or CSS code appears in **this font**.

- An arrow (→) in a code figure indicates a continuation of the previous line—the line has been wrapped to fit in the book's column **B**. The arrow is not part of the code itself, so it's not something you would type. Instead, type the line continuously, as if it had not wrapped to another line.

- The first occurrence of a word is italicized when it is defined.

- *IE* is often used as a popular abbreviation of *Internet Explorer*. For instance, IE9 is synonymous with Internet Explorer 9.

- *Modern browsers* collectively refers to the versions of browsers with solid support for the latest HTML5 and CSS3 features. Generally, this includes recent versions of the browsers discussed in the "Web Browsers" section of this introduction, but not IE8.

- Whenever a plus sign (+) follows a browser version number, it means "the version listed plus subsequent versions." For instance, IE8+ refers to Internet Explorer 8 and all versions after it.

Companion Website

The book's companion website contains the table of contents, every complete code example featured in the book (plus some additional ones that wouldn't fit), links to resources cited in the book (as well as additional ones), a list of errata, and more.

The URLs for some of the key pages on the site follow:

- Home page:
  www.htmlcssvqs.com

- Code examples:
  www.htmlcssvqs.com/8ed/examples/

You can view the code examples directly from the site or download them to your computer—all the HTML and CSS files are yours for the taking.

In some cases, I've included additional comments in the code to explain more about what it does or how to use it. A handful of the code samples in the book are truncated for space considerations, but the complete versions are on the website.

Please feel free to use the code as you please, modifying it as needed for your own projects.

I hope you find the site helpful!

Webpage Building Blocks

Although webpages have become increasingly complex, their underlying structure remains remarkably simple. As I mentioned in the Introduction, it's impossible to create a webpage without HTML. As you will learn, HTML contains your page content and describes its meaning. In turn, web browsers display your content for users.

A webpage is primarily made up of three components:

- Text content: The bare text that appears on the page to inform visitors about your business, family vacation, products, or whatever the focus of your page may be.

- References to other files: These load items such as images, video, and audio files, as well as style sheets (which contain the CSS that controls how your page looks) and JavaScript files (which add special behavior to your page). They also link to other HTML pages and assets.

- Markup: The HTML elements that describe your text content and make the references work. (HTML stands for Hypertext *Markup* Language.)

In This Chapter

Additionally, at the beginning of each HTML page there's a bit of information that is meant primarily for browsers and search engines (that is, Bing, Duck Duck Go, Google, Yahoo, and the like). Browsers don't display it to your visitors.

It's important to note that each of these components in a webpage is made up exclusively of text. This means that pages are saved in text-only format, ensuring they are accessible via practically any browser on any platform, whether desktop, mobile, tablet, or otherwise. It also contributes to HTML pages being simple to create.

In this chapter, I will walk you through a basic HTML page, explain HTML fundamentals (including the three components I mentioned at the onset), and discuss some best practices.

Note: As mentioned in the book's introduction, I use *HTML* to refer to the language in general. For those instances in which I'm highlighting special characteristics unique to a version of the language, I will use the individual name. For example, "*HTML5* introduces several new elements and redefines or eliminates others that previously existed in *HTML 4* and *XHTML 1.0*."

Thinking in HTML

Picture this scenario: You're in a kitchen. In one hand, you have a pad of sticky notes with a word on each sheet. On some sticky notes is printed "soup," and on others "cereal," "plate," "sauce," and so on.

You open a cupboard, and as you look through it, you tag each item with the sticky note that best describes it. A yellow box of cereal gets a "cereal" sticky note. You see a red box of cereal and tag that with "cereal," too. And so on for the other items.

Writing HTML is a lot like this exercise, but instead of tagging food and dinnerware, you apply tags that describe your web-page's content. You don't make up the words on the tags—HTML has done that for you in the form of predefined elements. The **p** element is for paragraphs. The **abbr** element is for abbreviations. The **li** element is for list items. You'll learn about these and dozens more throughout the book.

Notice that the sticky notes had words like "cereal," not "yellow box of cereal" or "red box of cereal." Similarly, HTML elements describe what your content is, not how it looks. CSS, which you'll learn beginning with Chapter 7, controls your content's appearance (the fonts, colors, drop shadows, and much more). So even if you ultimately make some paragraphs green and others orange, they are all **p** elements as far as HTML is concerned.

Keep this approach in mind as you progress through the book and work on your own websites. The basic webpage that follows shows it in action.

A Basic HTML Page

Let's take a look at a basic HTML page to give you context for what's to follow in this chapter and beyond. You'll learn some bits about the code in this section, but don't worry if you don't understand it all right now. This is just to give you a taste of HTML. I'll cover more of it later in the chapter and, of course, in greater detail as you progress through the book. Also, because we all learn a little differently, some of you might find it helpful to first read "Markup: Elements, Attributes, Values, and More" (the next section) and then return here.

Every webpage begins with the simple structure shown in **Ⓐ**. It is the HTML equivalent of a blank sheet of paper **Ⓑ** because the content shown to your visitors goes in the body—the area between **<body>** and **</body>**—and so far that's empty. We'll fill it up in a minute.

First, a quick primer (the next section elaborates). HTML uses **<** and **>** to enclose each HTML tag. A *start tag*, like **<head>**, marks the beginning of an element; an *end tag*, like **</head>**, marks its end. A few elements, like **meta** **Ⓐ**, don't have an end tag.

Ⓐ Every webpage contains the DOCTYPE, as well as the **html**, **head**, and **body** elements, as its foundation. The two parts you customize in this page shell are the language code assigned to **lang** and the text between **<title>** and **</title>**.

```
<!DOCTYPE html>
<html lang="en">
<head>
    <meta charset="utf-8" />
    <title>Your page title</title>
</head>
<body>


</body>
</html>
```

Ⓑ Not a particularly exciting page unless you're a minimalist!

The Top and Head of a Webpage

I mentioned that your page content goes in the body, but what does the rest of the code do? Well, everything above the `<body>` start tag is primarily instructional information for browsers and search engines. The `<!DOCTYPE html>` portion (known as the DOCTYPE) tells browsers that this is an HTML5 page. It should always be the first line in your pages.

Next is the `html` element, which encloses the rest of the page between `<html lang="en">` and the `</html>` end tag that signals the end of the page. The `lang="en"` portion indicates that English is the default language of the page's content. You can specify a different language, as explained in "Starting Your Webpage" in Chapter 3.

Following that is the document head—the area between `<head>` and `</head>`. I cover `<meta charset="utf-8" />` a little later in "A Webpage's Text Content." The one part above the body that *is* visible to users is the text between `<title>` and `</title>`. It appears on the browser tab and as the title at the very top of the browser window (in some browsers) ⓑ. Additionally, it's typically the default name of a browser bookmark and is valuable information for search engines.

"Starting Your Webpage" and "Creating a Title" in Chapter 3 cover the DOCTYPE and head area in more detail.

So that's it for a webpage's foundation. Not too tough, right?

The Body of a Webpage: Your Content

Now let's make things a little more interesting by adding content to our page **C**. Figure **D** illustrates how a desktop browser typically renders (displays) that HTML before you make it look better with CSS.

Just as before **B**, the markup surrounding the text content doesn't appear when you view the page in a browser. But those HTML element tags—such as the **<p>** that starts a paragraph—are essential because they describe your content, as explained further in "HTML: Markup with Meaning."

C This page has the three components I mentioned at the beginning of the chapter: text content, references to other files (the image **src** and link **href** values), and markup. I've highlighted the HTML tags in the body so you can distinguish them from the page's text content. Note that some parts are separated by a blank line. This isn't mandatory and does not affect the page's display.

```
<!DOCTYPE html>
<html lang="en">
<head>
    <meta charset="utf-8" />
    <title>Blue Flax (Linum lewisii)</title>
</head>
<body>
<article>
    <h1>The Ephemeral Blue Flax</h1>

    <img src="blueflax.jpg" width="300" height="175" alt="Blue Flax" />

    <p>I am continually <em>amazed</em> at the beautiful, delicate <a href="http://en.wikipedia.
    → org/wiki/Linum_lewisii" rel="external" title="Learn more about Blue Flax">Blue Flax</a>
    → that somehow took hold in my garden. They are awash in color every morning, yet not a single
    → flower remains by the afternoon. They are the very definition of ephemeral.</p>
</article>
</body>
</html>
```

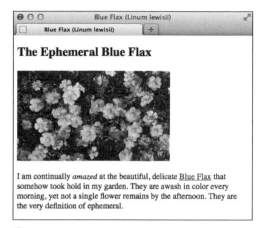

The Ephemeral Blue Flax

I am continually *amazed* at the beautiful, delicate Blue Flax that somehow took hold in my garden. They are awash in color every morning, yet not a single flower remains by the afternoon. They are the very definition of ephemeral.

D A typical default rendering of the page. Although this shows the page in Firefox, the page displays similarly in other browsers. Later in the chapter, "A Browser's Default Display of Webpages" explains why some text looks different than other text.

Indenting Your HTML

The code's indentation **C** has absolutely no bearing on how the content displays in the browser **D** (the **pre** element, which you'll learn about in Chapter 4, is the one exception). However, it's customary to indent some elements when they are contained in another element. It makes it easier to glean the hierarchy of elements as you read through and work with your code.

HTML provides numerous such elements. The example **C** demonstrates six of the most common ones: **a**, **article**, **em**, **h1**, **img**, and **p**. Each has its own meaning; for instance, **h1** is a heading, **a** is a link, and **img** is an image.

Before we get too deep into the example code, I'll cover more about HTML fundamentals such as elements in general, attributes, file names, and URLs. Once you have that foundation, I'll return to our basic page and explain further why I marked up the content the way I did. You'll also learn more about the default way that browsers display webpages.

Markup: Elements, Attributes, Values, and More

Now that you've seen some HTML, we'll take a closer look at the pieces that constitute markup: *elements*, *attributes*, and *values*. We'll also discuss what it means for an element to be a parent or child in your HTML. You've seen examples of all these in our basic page, perhaps without even realizing it. (Tricky of me, I know.)

Elements

As my sticky notes metaphor suggested, elements are like little labels that describe the different parts of a webpage: "This is a heading, that thing over there is a paragraph, and that group of links is navigation."

Some elements have one or more attributes, which further describe the element.

Most elements can contain both text and other elements (as the **p** element did in our basic page). As mentioned, these elements consist of a start tag (the element's name and attributes, if any, enclosed in less-than and greater-than signs), the content, and an end tag (a forward slash followed by the element's name, again enclosed in less-than and greater-than signs) **A**.

There are also a handful of *empty elements* (also called *void elements*), which cannot contain text or other elements. They look like a combination start and end tag, with an initial less-than sign, the element's name followed by any attributes it may have, an optional space, an optional forward slash, and the final greater-than sign, which is required **B**.

Content

Start tag   End tag

```
am continually <em>amazed</em>
```

Angle brackets   Forward slash

A Here is a typical HTML element. The start tag and end tag surround the text the element describes. It's customary to type your element tags in lowercase.

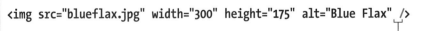

```
<img src="blueflax.jpg" width="300" height="175" alt="Blue Flax" />
```

The optional space and forward slash

B Empty elements, like **img** shown here, do not surround any text content (the **alt** attribute text is part of the element, not surrounded by it). They have a single tag that serves to both open and close the element. The space and forward slash at the end are optional in HTML5. However, the **>** that completes the element is required.

As noted, the space and forward slash before the end of an empty element are optional in HTML5. Many of us who previously coded in XHTML (which requires the forward slash to close an empty element) tend to use it in HTML5 too, though certainly others have dropped it. If you choose to omit it, the page will behave exactly the same. Whichever style you use, I recommend using it consistently.

It's customary to type your element names in all lowercase, although HTML5 isn't picky here either, allowing uppercase letters instead. However, it's now rare to find someone who codes in uppercase, so unless the rebel in you just can't resist, I don't recommend it. It's looked upon as a dated practice.

Attributes and Values

Attributes contain additional information about an element (**C** and **D**). In HTML5, an attribute's value may optionally be enclosed in quotation marks—it's customary to include them, so I recommend you always do so. (It is required when the value is more than one word.) And just as with element names, I recommend you type your attribute names in lowercase.

Although you'll find details about allowed values for most attributes in this book, let me give you an idea of the kinds of values you'll run into as you progress.

Some attributes can accept any value, while others are more limited. Perhaps the most common are those that accept

---

for *Is an attribute of* `label`

`<label for="email">Email Address</label>`

The value of the **for** *attribute*

C Here is a `label` element (which associates a text label with a form field) with a simple attribute-value pair. Attributes are always located inside an element's start tag. It's customary to enclose them in quotation marks.

href *is an attribute of* **a**   *Value for* **href**   **rel** *is also an attribute of* **a**   *Value for* **rel**

`<a href="http://en.wikipedia.org/wiki/Linum_lewisii" rel="external"`
`→title="Learn more about Blue Flax">Blue Flax</a>`

Value for **title**

title *is also an attribute of* **a**

D Some elements, like **a** (shown here) and **img** **B**, can have one or more attributes, each with its own value. The order is not important. Separate each attribute-value pair from the next with a space.

predefined (or *enumerated*) values. In other words, you must select a value from a standard list of choices **E**. Be sure to write enumerated values in all lowercase letters.

A handful of attributes require a number for their value, particularly those describing size and length. A numeric value never includes a unit type, just the number. Where units are applicable, as in the width and height of an image **B** or video, they are understood to be pixels.

Some attributes, like **href** **D** and **src** **B**, reference other files and thus must contain values in the form of a URL (uniform resource locator), a file's unique address on the web. You'll learn more about them in the "URLs" section of this chapter.

Lastly, there's a special kind of attribute called a *Boolean* attribute. Providing a value is optional, because if the attribute is present it evaluates to true **F**. If you do include a value, set it to the name of the attribute itself (the result is the same regardless). Boolean attributes are also predefined; you can't just make up your own (you really *are* a rebel, aren't you?).

```
<link rel="stylesheet" media="screen" href="style.css" />
```
                            Predefined value   *Not a predefined value*

E Some attributes accept only specific values. For example, the **media** attribute in the **link** element (Chapter 8) can be set to **all**, **screen**, or **print**, among others, but you can't just make up a value for it like you can with the **href** attribute or the **title** attribute **D**.

```
<input type="email" name="emailaddr" required />
```
                                        A Boolean attribute

F This code provides a form box for users to enter an email address (Chapter 16). The Boolean attribute **required** makes it mandatory for users to fill out. A Boolean attribute doesn't need a value, but if you were to include one in this case, the code would be **required="required"**.

Parents and Children

If one element contains another, it is considered to be the parent of the enclosed, or child, element. Any elements contained in the child element are considered descendants of the outer, parent element **G**. This underlying, family tree-like structure is a key feature of HTML code. It facilitates both styling elements with CSS (which you'll begin learning about in Chapter 7) and applying JavaScript behavior to them (which is beyond the scope of this book).

It's important to note that when elements contain other elements, each element must be properly nested—that is, fully contained within its parent. Whenever you use an end tag, it should correspond to the previous unclosed start tag. In other words, first open element 1, then open element 2, then close element 2, and then close element 1 **H**.

```
<article>
    <h1>The Ephemeral Blue Flax</h1>
    <img src="blueflax.jpg"... />
    <p>... continually <em>amazed</em> ... delicate <a ...>Blue Flax</a> ...</p>
</article>
```

G In this abbreviated HTML, the **article** element is parent to the **h1**, **img**, and **p** elements. Conversely, the **h1**, **img**, and **p** elements are children (and descendants) of the **article**. The **p** element is parent to both the **em** and **a** elements. The **em** and **a** are children of the **p** and also descendants (but not children) of the **article**. In turn, **article** is their ancestor.

Correct (no overlapping lines)

```
<p>... continually <em>amazed</em> ...</p>
<p>... continually <em>amazed ...</p></em>
```

Incorrect (the sets of tags cross over each other)

H Elements must be properly nested. If you open **p** and then **em**, you must close **em** before you close **p**.

A Webpage's Text Content

The text contained within elements is perhaps a webpage's most basic ingredient. If you've ever used a word processor, you've typed some text. Text in an HTML page, however, has some important differences.

First, when a browser renders HTML it collapses extra spaces or tabs into a single space and either converts returns and line feeds into a single space or ignores them altogether (Ⓐ and Ⓑ).

Next, HTML used to be restricted to ASCII characters—basically the letters of the English language, numerals, and a few of the most common symbols. Accented characters (common to many languages of Western Europe) and many everyday symbols had to be created with special character references like **é** (for é) or **©** (for ©). See a full list at www.elizabethcastro.com/html/extras/entities.html.

Unicode mitigates a lot of issues with special characters, so it's standard practice to encode pages in UTF-8 Ⓒ and to save HTML files with the same encoding (see "Saving Your Webpage" in Chapter 2). I recommend you do the same. Specifying **UTF-8** or **utf-8** as the **charset** value in Ⓒ yields identical results.

It's still common to use character references at times, such as for the copyright symbol since it's easy to remember and type **©** Ⓐ.

Ⓐ A page's text content (highlighted) is mostly anything besides the markup. In this example, note that each sentence in the first paragraph is separated by at least one carriage return, and some words are separated by several spaces (just to emphasize the point about collapsing returns and spaces Ⓑ). The second paragraph includes a special character reference (**©**) for the copyright symbol.

```
...
<body>
<p>I am continually <em>amazed</em> at
 the beautiful,    delicate Blue Flax
 that somehow took hold in my garden.

They are awash in        color every
 morning, yet not a single flower
 remains by the afternoon.

They are the very definition of
 ephemeral.</p>
<p><small>&copy; Blue Flax Society.</small>
 </p>
</body>
</html>
```

I am continually *amazed* at the beautiful, delicate Blue Flax that somehow took hold in my garden. They are awash in color every morning, yet not a single flower remains by the afternoon. They are the very definition of ephemeral.

© Blue Flax Society.

Ⓑ When you view the document with a browser, the extra returns and spaces are ignored and the character reference is replaced by the corresponding symbol (©).

Ⓒ Specify your document's character encoding directly after the **head** start tag. The **charset** attribute sets the encoding type (UTF-8 is the norm).

```
<!DOCTYPE html>
<html lang="en">
<head>
    <meta charset="utf-8" />
    <title>Blue Flax (Linum lewisii)</title>
</head>
<body>
...
</body>
</html>
```

A In our basic HTML document, there is a reference to an image file called **blueflax.jpg** in the **src** attribute of the **img** tag. The browser will request, load, and display it when it loads the page. The page also includes a link to a page on Wikipedia about Blue Flax, as specified in the **href** attribute of the **a** tag.

```
...
<body>
<article>
    <h1>The Ephemeral Blue Flax</h1>

    <img src="blueflax.jpg" width="300"
  → height="175" alt="Blue Flax" />

    <p>I am continually <em>amazed</em> at
  → the beautiful, delicate <a href=
  → "http://en.wikipedia.org/wiki/Linum_
  → lewisii" rel="external" title=
  → "Learn more about the Blue Flax">
  → Blue Flax</a> that somehow took
  → hold in my garden. They are awash
  → in color every morning, yet not a
  · single flower remains by the
  → afternoon. They are the very
  → definition of ephemeral.</p>
</article>
</body>
</html>
```

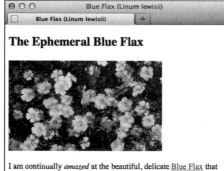

B Images and other non-text content are referenced from a webpage, and the browser displays them together with the text. As you saw earlier, linked text displays in a different color than regular text and is underlined by default.

Links, Images, and Other Non-Text Content

Of course, part of what makes the web so vibrant are the links from one page to another, and the images, videos, music, and more. Instead of actually enclosing assets such as images in the HTML file, they are saved as independent files and are simply referenced from within the page **A**.

Browsers can handle links and images without skipping a beat **B**. However, they can't necessarily handle every other kind of file. For example, some browsers require you to have Adobe Reader on your computer to view PDFs, and you may need a program like OpenOffice to view a spreadsheet.

There was a time when HTML had no built-in means to play a video or audio file. As a result, various companies created software, known as *plugins*, that you could download and install in your browser to provide missing features.

The most widespread of these is Flash, which has driven vast amounts of video on the web for years. It has some issues, however, most notably that it often demands a lot of computing power.

Thankfully, HTML5 has made strides toward remedying this by providing **audio** and **video** elements. They don't require a plugin. Instead, modern browsers have the media players built in, and you can still provide a Flash player as a fallback for older browsers. HTML5 audio and video aren't perfect either, but they are a good start toward making websites free of plugins, and they continue to evolve.

You'll learn more about images in Chapter 5, links in Chapter 6, and HTML5 audio and video in Chapter 17.

File and Folder Names

Like any other text document, a webpage has a file name. When you're assigning file and folder names, there are a few tips to keep in mind that will help you organize your files, make it easier for your visitors to find and access your pages, ensure that their browsers view the pages correctly, and improve search engine optimization (SEO) (Ⓐ and Ⓑ). (Please note that I use the words "folder" and "directory" interchangeably.)

Use Lowercase Names

Since the names you choose for your webpage can determine what your visitors will have to type in order to get to your page, you can save them from inadvertent typos by using only lowercase letters in your file and folder names. It's also a big help when you create links between your pages yourself. If all your names have only lowercase letters, it's just one less thing you'll have to worry about.

Use the Proper Extension

One way a browser knows it should read a text document as a webpage is by looking at its file name extension. Although `.htm` also works, `.html` is customary. If the page has some other extension, such as `.txt`, browsers will treat it as text and show all your nice code to visitors.

Separate Words with a Dash

Never include spaces between words in your file and folder names. Instead, use a dash; for example, `company-history.html` and `my-favorite-movies.html`. You'll come across the occasional site that uses underscores (_) instead, but don't do the same, because search engines prefer dashes.

TIP SEO pertains to getting your webpages to appear early in search engine results.

TIP Be aware that neither OS X nor Windows always reveals a document's extension. Change your folder options, if necessary, so you can see extensions (see Chapter 2).

File name, in all
lowercase letters   Extension

`buckminster-fuller.html`

Separate each word with a dash

File names with capital letters are
a pain to type and to communicate

`Buckminster_Fuller.html`

Underscores are not as good for
search engine optimization as dashes

Ⓐ Remember to use all lowercase letters for your file names, separate words with a dash, and add the .html extension. Mixing upper- and lowercase letters makes it harder to type the proper address.

Correct approach

`http://www.yoursite.com/notable-architects/20th-century/buckminster-fuller.html`
`http://www.yoursite.com/NotableArchitects/20th_CENTURY/buckminster_fuller.html`

Incorrect approach

Ⓑ Use all lowercase letters and dashes for your folders as well. The key is consistency. If you don't use uppercase letters, your visitors (and you) don't have to waste time wondering, "Now, was that a capital B or a small one?"

A Your basic URL contains a scheme, a host, and a path. The path may contain one or more directory (folder) names and a single file name at the end.

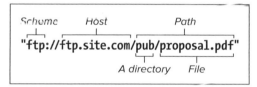

B A URL with a trailing forward slash and no file name points to the default file in the last directory named (in this case, the **tofu** directory). The most common default file name is **index.html**. So, this URL and the one in the previous example point to the same page.

C When the user clicks this URL, the browser will begin an FTP transfer of the **proposal.pdf** file. (Sometimes a username and password are required first.)

D A URL for an email address includes the **mailto** scheme followed by a colon but no forward slashes, and then the email address itself.

URLs

Uniform resource locator, or URL, is a fancy name for address. It contains information about where a file is and what a browser should do with it. Each file on the Internet has a unique URL.

The first part of the URL is called the *scheme*. It tells the browser how to deal with the file that it is about to open. The most common scheme you will see is HTTP, or Hypertext Transfer Protocol. As you are probably well aware from your own experience online, it is used to access webpages **A**. Its cousin is HTTPS, used for secure webpages such as those on e-commerce sites. The format is the same **A**, except **https** replaces **http**.

The second part of the URL is the host (or host name) where the file is located. That is followed by the path, which includes both any directory names that lead to a file and the file name itself, all of which are optional. If the path in **A** were **tofu/soft/index.html**, it would mean **index.html** is inside the **soft** directory and **soft** is inside the **tofu** directory, just like you might organize files and folders on your computer. (Though I doubt you have folders for different types of tofu!)

Sometimes, a URL path omits a file name and ends with a directory, which may or may not include a trailing forward slash **B**. In this case, the URL refers to the default file in the last directory in the path, typically named **index.html**. (Virtually all web servers are configured to recognize **index.html** as a default file name, so you don't have to change any server settings.)

Other common schemes are **ftp** (File Transfer Protocol), for downloading files **C**, and **mailto**, for sending email **D** (see Chapter 6).

A scheme is generally followed by a colon and two forward slashes; `mailto` is an exception in that it takes only a colon. Always type schemes in lowercase letters.

Of these schemes, you will use `http` (and perhaps `https`) the most, with `mailto` a distant second and `ftp` behind that. There are other schemes for specialized cases that you'll probably never face.

Absolute URLs

URLs can be either absolute or relative. An *absolute* URL contains all the information that points to a directory or file, including the scheme, the host, and the path (Ⓐ and Ⓑ). An absolute URL is analogous to a complete street address, including name, street and number, city, state or province, zip code, and country. No matter where a letter is sent from, the post office will be able to find the recipient. In terms of URLs, this means you can reference an absolute URL from any webpage on any host by using the same URL every time.

When you're referencing a file located on someone else's web server, you'll always use an absolute URL. This concept is the same as when you might have shared a URL to a news article or YouTube video via email—your friends can't access the item if you only give them part of the URL. And it's the same reason why the `href` value of the Wikipedia link in our basic webpage Ⓔ is the full URL instead of simply `Linum_lewisii`.

You'll also need to use absolute URLs for FTP sites or, generally, any kind of URL that doesn't use an HTTP protocol.

Ⓔ Because our basic page is not located at **en.wikipedia.org**, we need to include the absolute URL when linking to the page about Blue Flax (Linum lewisii in Latin). Chapter 6 gives the full scoop on links, including the **rel** attribute, which is recommended for links pointing outside your site.

```
<p>I am continually <em>amazed</em> at
→ the beautiful, delicate <a href="http://
→ en.wikipedia.org/wiki/Linum_lewisii"
→ rel="external" title="Learn more about the
→ Blue Flax">Blue Flax</a> that somehow took
→ hold in my garden . . .</p>
```

```
              Inside the current folder,
            there's a file named "history.html"...
           ┌──┴──┐
           "history.html"
```

F The relative URL to link to a file in the same folder (see **J**). Only the file's name and extension are required in the URL, rather than preceding those with **http://www.site.com/about/** (the host and folder in which both files live).

```
              Inside the current folder,
            there's a folder named "info"...
           ┌──┴──┐
           "info/data.html"
           └──┬──┘  └───┬───┘
      ...that contains...    ...a file named "data.html."
```

G To reference a file (**data.html**, in this example) that is within a folder inside the current folder (see **J**), add the sub-folder's name and a forward slash in front of the file name.

Relative URLs

To give you directions to my neighbor's house from my house, instead of giving her complete address I might just say, "it's three doors down on the right." This is a relative address—where it points to depends on where the information originates; in this case, my house. With the same information in a different city, you'd never find my neighbor. (Truth is, she's out of town a lot so you might not find her anyway.)

In the same way, a relative URL describes the location of the desired file in consideration of the location of the file that contains the URL reference itself. So, you might have the URL say something like "link to the xyz page that's in the same directory as this page."

Referencing a File in the Same Directory

The relative URL for a file that is in the same directory as the current page (that is, the one containing the URL in question) is simply the file name and extension **F**. For example, the HTML for the link would be **<a href="history.html">Take me to history.html!</a>**.

Referencing a File in a Subdirectory

You create the URL for a file in a subdirectory of the current directory by typing the name of the subdirectory followed by a forward slash and then the name and extension of the desired file **G**. For example, **<a href="info/data.html">Data supports my hypothesis</a>**.

Referencing a File in a Higher Directory

To reference a file in a directory at a higher level of the file hierarchy, use two periods and a forward slash 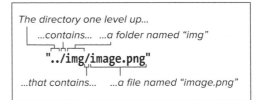. For example, `<a href="../products.html">our products</a>`. Each `../` means "go up one directory level from the current file," so `../../` would go up two levels and `../../../` would go up three.

Root Relative URLs

Alternatively, if your files are on a web server, you can avoid cumbersome file paths such as `../../img/family/vacation.jpg` by first jumping straight to your site's root and then drilling down from there to the targeted file 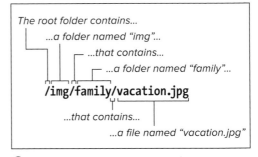. A single forward slash at the beginning achieves this, so the *root relative* URL in this case would be `/img/family/vacation.jpg` (assuming the `img` folder sits in the site's root folder, which is common). Again, this only works on a web server, like at the hosting provider that serves your site or one you're running locally on your machine (see the tips).

If you aren't developing your site on a web server on your computer, then generally you'll want to use relative URLs (except when pointing to files on someone else's server, of course). They'll make it easy to move your pages from your computer to your host's server. As long as the relative position of each file remains constant, you won't have to change any of the paths, so the links and references to files will work correctly.

TIP Apache is the most popular choice for running a development server on your computer. Search online for "set up local dev environment."

TIP Chapter 21 discusses finding a web host.

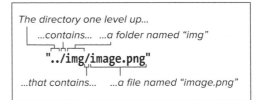

The directory one level up...
...contains... ...a folder named "img"
`"../img/image.png"`
...that contains... ...a file named "image.png"

H This file, as you can see in **J**, is in a folder (`img`) that sits alongside the current folder (`about`) in the site's root directory. In that case, you use two periods and a forward slash to go up a level, and then note the subdirectory (`img`) to go down into, followed by a forward slash, followed by the file name. (In normal practice, you'd choose a more descriptive image file name than `image.png`, which is deliberately generic for the example.)

The root folder contains...
...a folder named "img"...
...that contains...
...a folder named "family"...
`/img/family/vacation.jpg`
...that contains...
...a file named "vacation.jpg"

I The same root relative URL can be used by all pages regardless of where each page is located in your site's folder structure. For instance, with the URL shown, your homepage could locate vacation.jpg just as easily as another page six folders deep. (Not that I would advise having that many folder levels.)

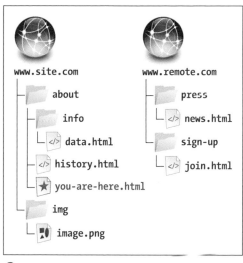

J The document that contains the URLs (**you-are-here.html** in this case) is the reference point for relative URLs. In other words, relative URLs are relative to that file's location on the server. Absolute URLs will work no matter where they are located, because they always contain the full URL to a resource.

Absolute and Relative URLs Compared

To reinforce what we've covered, **Table 1.1** and **J** work together to illustrate the difference between absolute and relative URLs. **J** shows an arrangement of files and folders on two different websites. The table describes how you could access various files from **you-are-here.html** when some of those files are on the same site (www.site.com) as that webpage and some are on another site (www.remote.com). Although you could use the absolute URLs to access the files shown in the first three rows, it's better to use relative URLs when accessing files on the same server.

TABLE 1.1 Absolute URLs vs. Relative URLs

File name	Absolute URL (can be used anywhere)	Relative URL (only works in you-are-here.html)
history.html	http://www.site.com/about/history.html	history.html
data.html	http://www.site.com/about/info/data.html	info/data.html
image.png	http://www.site.com/img/image.png	../img/image.png
news.html	http://www.remote.com/press/news.html	(none: use absolute)
join.html	http://www.remote.com/sign-up/join.html	(none: use absolute)

HTML: Markup with Meaning

I began the chapter by comparing marking up content in your webpages to tagging items in a cupboard. Subsequently, you've learned more about HTML's role and fundamental pieces.

The point of emphasis throughout has been that HTML describes the meaning of a webpage's content; that is, the *semantics*. In the web community, the term *semantic HTML* simply refers to content that is marked up with the HTML elements that best describe it and without regard for how the content should look. I'm sure you'll agree this makes more sense than choosing elements willy-nilly.

Better yet, it's easy to do, as the following exploration of our basic page demonstrates. After that, "Why Semantics Matter" reinforces why writing semantic HTML is a cornerstone of an effective website.

The Semantics of Our Basic HTML Page

Earlier in the chapter, I said we'd return to our basic webpage, and now's the time. I'll give you a minute to gather up the family.

OK, let's look a little deeper at the thought process behind marking up the content. While doing so, you'll get a taste of some of the most frequently used HTML elements Ⓐ, all of which we'll cover in greater detail in subsequent chapters. As you'll see, there's no magic to creating HTML that has good semantics. It's mostly common sense once you're familiar with the elements at your disposal.

All the content is contained in an **article** element Ⓐ. In short, **article** defines a self-contained composition that can

Ⓐ The **body** of our basic page, which contains the **article**, **h1**, **img**, **p**, **em**, and **a** elements. All the content is nested in the **article**.

```
...
<body>
<article>
    <h1>The Ephemeral Blue Flax</h1>

    <img src="blueflax.jpg" width="300"
    ⇢ height="175" alt="Blue Flax" />

    <p>I am continually <em>amazed</em> at
    ⇢ the beautiful, delicate <a href=
    ⇢ "http://en.wikipedia.org/wiki/Linum_
    ⇢ lewisii" rel="external" title="Learn
    ⇢ more about Blue Flax">Blue Flax</a>
    ⇢ that somehow took hold in my garden.
    ⇢ They are awash in color every morning,
    ⇢ yet not a single flower remains
    ⇢ by the afternoon. They are the very
    ⇢ definition of ephemeral.</p>
</article>
</body>
</html>
```

B Headings are critical elements in defining a page's structure. They make a page more accessible to users of screen readers, and search engines use them to determine the focus of a page.

```
<h1>The Ephemeral Blue Flax</h1>
```

C It's easy to add an image to a page with **img**.

```
<img src="blueflax.jpg" width="300"
→ height="175" alt="Blue Flax" />
```

D The **p** element may contain other elements that define the semantics of phrases within a paragraph. The **em** and **a** elements are two examples.

```
<p>I am continually <em>amazed</em> at
→ the beautiful, delicate <a href="http://
→ en.wikipedia.org/wiki/Linum_lewisii"
→ rel="external" title="Learn more about
→ Blue Flax">Blue Flax</a> that somehow
  took hold in my garden. They are awash in
→ color every morning, yet not a single
→ flower remains by the afternoon. They are
→ the very definition of ephemeral.</p>
```

stand on its own if reused elsewhere. The **article** element is a good choice for our basic webpage, but not necessarily for every webpage you'll write. You'll learn more about **article** in Chapter 3.

Next is a heading **B**. HTML provides you six heading levels, **h1**–**h6**, with **h1** being the most important. An **h2** is a subheading of an **h1**, an **h3** is a subheading of an **h2**, and so on, just like when you type a document with various headings in a word processor.

Every HTML page should have an **h1** (or more, depending on your content), so marking up our only heading with **h1** was the obvious choice. The heading elements **h1**–**h6** are covered more in Chapter 3.

Next, you have an image **C**. The **img** element is the primary means for displaying an image, so again, there was no debate about which element was appropriate. The **alt** attribute provides text that may display if the browser has trouble loading the image or if the page is viewed in a text-only browser (admittedly rare these days). Screen readers may also announce **alt** text (see "Accessibility" in the next section). You'll learn more about images in Chapter 5.

The paragraph is marked up with the **p** element **D**. Just as in printed materials, a paragraph can contain a single sentence or several sentences. If our page needed another paragraph, you'd simply add another **p** element after the first one.

There are two elements nested within our paragraph that define the meaning of bits (phrases) of text: **em** and **a** **D**. These are examples of the numerous *phrasing content* elements that HTML5 provides, the majority of which improve the semantics of paragraph text. Those, along with **p**, are discussed in Chapter 4.

The **em** element means "stress emphasis," sort of like you might stress words in speech. In the case of our page, it emphasizes the amazement that the flowers induced **D**. Remember that because HTML describes the meaning of content, **em** dictates semantic, not visual, emphasis even though it's common for browsers to render **em** text in italics (you can change that with CSS).

Finally, the basic page defines a link to another page with the **a** element ("anchor"). This is the most powerful element in all of HTML because it makes the web, the web: It links to other pages, specific page sections, and files. In the example, it signifies that the text "Blue Flax" is a link to a page on Wikipedia **E**.

Pretty easy, right? Once you've learned more about the HTML elements available to you, choosing the right ones for your content is usually a straightforward task. Occasionally, you'll come across a piece of content that reasonably could be marked up in more than one way, and that's OK. There isn't always a right and wrong way, just most of the time.

Besides, browsers will display your content regardless. They aren't smart enough to know that a piece of content would be more accurately described as a paragraph than some other element.

Lastly, HTML doesn't try to provide an element for every type of content imaginable, because the language would become unwieldy. Instead, it takes a practical, real-world stance, defining elements that cover the vast majority of cases.

Part of HTML's beauty is that it's simple for anyone to learn the basics, build some pages, and grow their knowledge from there. So although there are more than 100 HTML elements, don't let that number scare you. There's a core handful you'll find yourself using time and again, while the remaining ones are reserved for less common cases. And frankly, there are many you'll likely never have occasion to use.

You've learned the basics of several common elements, so you're well on your way.

E This **a** element defines a link to the Wikipedia page about Blue Flax. The optional **rel** attribute adds to the semantics by indicating that the link points to another site. The link works without it, though. The optional **title** attribute enhances the semantics of the **a** by providing information about the linked page. It appears in the browser when a user hovers over the link.

```
<a href="http://en.wikipedia.org/wiki/Linum_lewisii" rel="external" title="Learn more about Blue
   Flax">Blue Flax</a>
```

Why Semantics Matter

Here are some of the most important reasons why using good semantics in your HTML matters. This isn't an exhaustive list, and we've touched on some of these items already:

- Improved accessibility and interoperability, meaning that content is available to assistive technologies for visitors with disabilities, and to browsers on desktop, mobile, tablet, and other devices alike.
- Improved search engine optimization (SEO).
- Easier code maintenance and styling with CSS.
- (Often) lighter code and faster pages.

Accessibility

If you aren't familiar with *accessibility*, it's the practice of making your content available to all users, regardless of their capabilities (see www.w3.org/standards/webdesign/accessibility). Tim Berners-Lee, inventor of the web, famously said, "The power of the web is in its universality. Access by everyone regardless of disability is an essential aspect."

Any device with a browser is capable of displaying HTML, since it's just text. The means by which a user accesses content can vary, however. For instance, sighted users view the content, whereas some visually impaired users may use a screen reader to have the content read aloud to them (this is one example of assistive technology).

In some cases, screen readers announce the type of HTML element surrounding webpage content in order to give the user context for what's to follow. For example,

the user may be told that a list with five items has been encountered before the individual items are read aloud. Similarly, users are told when a link is encountered so they can decide whether to follow it.

Screen reader users can navigate a page in a variety of ways, such as jumping from one heading to the next via a keyboard command. This allows them to glean the key topics of a page and listen in more detail to the ones that interest them rather than having to listen to the entire page sequentially.

So you can see why good semantics makes a marked difference to users with disabilities.

Search Engine Optimization (SEO)

SEO—that is, your page's ranking in search engine results—can improve, because search engines put an emphasis on the portions of your content that are marked up in a particular way. For instance, the headings tell the search engine spider the primary topics of your page, helping the search engine determine how to catalog (or *index*) your page's content.

Easier Code Maintenance and Styling with CSS

As you'll learn, CSS makes it easy to style a particular element consistently—say, make all paragraph text display as dark gray in the Georgia font. If you mark up some paragraphs with **p** and others with an element not intended for that, you'll have to account for both in your CSS. This unnecessarily complicates styling pages.

Such deviations make it harder to work with your HTML, too. Good semantics can help you keep your webpages consistent and "clean" as a result. That often leads to smaller file sizes, which contributes to browsers loading your pages faster.

A Browser's Default Display of Webpages

All along I've insisted that HTML **A** doesn't control how your pages look, CSS does. And yet some of the text in our basic page looks larger than other text, or is bold or italicized when viewed in a browser **B**. Why is that?

The reason is that every web browser has a built-in CSS file (a *style sheet*) that dictates how each HTML element displays by default. When you write your own CSS, it overwrites these settings. The default presentation varies slightly from browser to browser, but on the whole it is fairly consistent. More importantly, the content's underlying structure and meaning as defined by your HTML remain the same.

Block-level, Inline, and HTML5

As you can see, some HTML elements (for example, **article**, **h1**, and **p**) display beginning on their own line like a paragraph does in a book. Others (for example, **a** and **em**) render in the same line as other content **B**. Again, this is a function of the browser's default style rules, not the HTML elements themselves or the blank lines I've included (or not) between elements in the code **A**.

Allow me to elaborate. Before HTML5, most elements were categorized as either *block-level* (the ones that displayed on their own line) or *inline* (the ones that

A I've added a second paragraph to our basic page so you can see that each paragraph occupies its own line when displayed in browsers **B**. By the way, the meaning of the **small** element is small (or fine) print, like a legal notice. It happens to display smaller than other text by default, but that's not why you'd use it.

```
...
<body>
<article>
    <h1>The Ephemeral Blue Flax</h1>

    <img src="blueflax.jpg" width="300"
    → height="175" alt="Blue Flax" />

    <p>I am continually <em>amazed</em> at
    → the beautiful, delicate <a href=
    → "http://en.wikipedia.org/wiki/Linum_
    → lewisii" rel="external" title="Learn
    → more about Blue Flax">Blue Flax</a>
    → that somehow took hold in my garden.
    → They are awash in color every morning,
    → yet not a single flower remains
    → by the afternoon. They are the very
    → definition of ephemeral.</p>

    <p><small>&copy; Blue Flax Society.
    → </small></p>
</article>
</body>
</html>
```

The Ephemeral Blue Flax

I am continually *amazed* at the beautiful, delicate Blue Flax that somehow took hold in my garden. They are awash in color every morning, yet not a single flower remains by the afternoon. They are the very definition of ephemeral.

© Blue Flax Society.

B A browser's default style sheet renders headings (**h1**–**h6** elements) differently than normal text, italicizes **em** text, colors and underlines links, and makes **small** text smaller. Additionally, some elements begin on their own line (**h1** and **p**, for example), and others display within surrounding content (like **a**, **em**, and **small**). It's simple to overwrite any or all of these presentation rules with your own CSS.

displayed within a line of text). HTML5 does away with these terms because they associate elements with presentation, which you've learned isn't HTML's role. (In general, the old inline elements are now categorized as phrasing content.)

With that said, browsers haven't changed the default display rules for these elements, nor should they. After all, you wouldn't want, say, the two paragraphs running into each other, or the **em** text ("amazed") to break the sentence by appearing on its own line.

So usually headings, paragraphs, and elements like `article` display on their own line, and phrasing content (like **em**, **a**, and `small`) displays on the same line as surrounding content.

And even though HTML5 no longer uses the terms "block-level" and "inline," it helps to know what they mean. It's common for tutorials to use them since they were entrenched in HTML vernacular before HTML5. I might use them occasionally in the book to quickly convey whether an element occupies its own line or shares a line by default.

We'll cover CSS in detail beginning with Chapter 7, but for now know that a style sheet, like an HTML page, is just text, so you can create one with the same text editor as your HTML...which conveniently leads to the next chapter!

Key Takeaways

The basics of HTML and some key best practices provide the foundation for building effective websites. Let's revisit the key takeaways:

- A webpage is primarily made up of three components: text content, references to other files, and markup.

- HTML markup is composed of elements, attributes, and values.

- It's customary to write your HTML in all lowercase (DOCTYPE is an exception) and surround your attribute values with quotes.

- Create file and folder names in all lowercase, and separate words with a dash instead of a space or underscore.

- Always begin your HTML documents with the DOCTYPE declaration so browsers know it's an HTML5 page:

  `<!DOCTYPE html>`

- A page's content goes in the **body** element. Instructions primarily intended for the browser and search engines are before that, mostly in the **head**.

- Mark up your content with semantic HTML. Do not consider how it should appear in a browser.

- Semantic HTML improves accessibility and can make your site more efficient, and easier to maintain and style.

- CSS controls the presentation of HTML content.

- Each browser's own style sheet dictates the default presentation of HTML. You can overwrite these rules with your own CSS.

Working with Webpage Files

Before you start writing HTML elements and attributes, you must create the file in which you'll type such code. In this chapter, you'll learn how to create, edit, save, and view webpage files. I'll also touch on some basic planning and organizational considerations.

If you can't wait any longer and already know how to create the actual files, skip ahead to Chapter 3, where I begin to explain more about the HTML code itself.

In This Chapter

Planning Your Site

Although you can jump in and start writing webpages right away, it's a good idea to first think about and plan your site. That way, you'll give yourself direction, and you'll need to make fewer changes and do less reorganizing later. There's more to creating an effective site than simply knowing how to code it. The following information is not comprehensive but does touch on some aspects to consider.

To plan your site:

- Figure out why you're creating this site. What do you want to convey?

- Think about your audience. How can you tailor your content to appeal to this audience?

- How many pages will it need? What sort of structure would you like it to have Ⓐ? Do you want visitors to go through your site in a particular sequence, or do you want to make it easy for them to explore in any direction?

- Sketch out your site on paper, and identify what components you want on each page. Among other things, this can help guide your design.

- Devise a simple, consistent naming convention for your pages, images, and other external files (see "File and Folder Names" in Chapter 1).

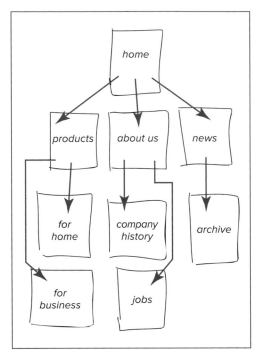

Ⓐ Sketching out your site and thinking about what it might contain can help you decide what sort of structure it needs.

TIP If you're looking for inspiration, take a look around the web to get an idea of the possibilities. You might start with the sites of some of your competitors.

TIP A List Apart (www.alistapart.com) and Smashing Magazine (www.smashingmagazine.com) are two popular resources that cover the many facets of creating sites: content strategy, user experience (UX), design, development, and more.

TIP See Erin Kissane's article "A Checklist for Content Work" (www.alistapart.com/articles/a-checklist-for-content-work/) for ideas about how you might approach crafting your site's content. It's a taste of her book, which elaborates on the subject of content strategy.

TIP Jason Beaird's *The Principles of Beautiful Web Design* (SitePoint, 2010) and Mark Boulton's *A Practical Guide to Designing for the Web* (Five Simple Steps, 2009) may interest you if you're a non-designer or novice designer looking for guidance on how to approach designing websites. Initially available only by purchase, Boulton's book now has a free version (http://designingfortheweb.co.uk/book/). In addition to explaining design theory, he provides guidance on how to work in the industry as a web designer.

TIP It's common, but not required, to map your site's folder structure to how it's organized on paper **Ⓐ**. See "Organizing Files."

Creating a New Webpage

You don't need any special tools to create a webpage. You can use any text editor, even Notepad (Ⓐ and Ⓒ), which is included with Windows, or TextWrangler (Ⓐ and Ⓑ), which is a free download for OS X (www.barebones.com/products/textwrangler). (Macs include an editor called TextEdit, but in some versions of OS X it has a bug that makes it to difficult to work with HTML files.)

To create a new webpage:

1. Open any text editor.

2. Choose File > New to create a new, blank document Ⓐ.

3. Create the HTML content as explained in the rest of this book, starting with Chapter 3.

4. Be sure to save your file as directed in "Saving Your Webpage."

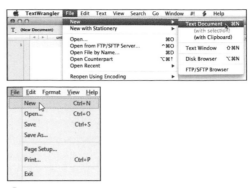

Ⓐ Open your text editor. Type your HTML in the blank document that appears, or choose File > New. The exact menu option may vary slightly. If you're using TextWrangler (Mac), it's File > New > Text Document, as shown (top). The bottom image is Notepad (Windows).

Ⓑ On a Mac, you can use TextWrangler to write the HTML code for your pages. See the tips for a list of Mac editors with more-robust features for writing code.

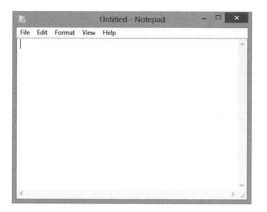

C This is Notepad, the most basic program Windows users can use to create HTML pages. Several others are available (see the tips).

TIP There are various text editors for OS X and Windows that are specifically tailored for coding HTML (and CSS). They have code-hinting and code-completion features to help you code more accurately and quickly, they highlight code to make it easier to distinguish between HTML elements and the text content you've written within them, and they have assorted other helpful features. Notepad doesn't do any of this, and TextWrangler only does some of it. Some free HTML editors are available, but the ones that aren't free are usually worth the investment and often include a free trial version you can test before making a purchase.

TIP Some popular editors for OS X are BBEdit (www.barebones.com/products/bbedit/), Coda (www.panic.com/coda/), Espresso (http://macrabbit.com/espresso/), Sublime Text (www.sublimetext.com), and TextMate (http://macromates.com). (TextWrangler is commonly thought of as "BBEdit Lite.") Sublime Text is also available on Windows, as are Notepad++ (http://notepad-plus-plus.org) and many others. Search online for "HTML editor" if you'd like to find more.

TIP The process for creating a new page is similar in all editors. And to edit an existing page, just choose File > Open in your text editor of choice and open the file (see "Editing Webpages").

TIP Don't use word processors, like Microsoft Word, to code your HTML pages. They may add unnecessary or invalid code to your files.

Saving Your Webpage

Although you create HTML pages with a text editor, they are meant to be viewable with multiple browsers on multiple platforms and devices. To be accessible to all of these, you save webpages in a universal, basic "text only" format—without any of the proprietary formatting that a word processor might apply.

HTML pages typically have the .html or .htm extension in their file names. This allows browsers to recognize them as webpages and know to interpret the code they contain. It also distinguishes these files from plain text files that are not webpages. Although both .html and .htm work, it's customary to use the .html extension (using .htm is a little dated), so I recommend you use it for your files.

Because of that extension, a webpage's icon matches your computer's default browser—not the editor with which the file was written . Indeed, when you double-click a webpage file, it is opened in a browser, not a text editor. This is great for testing a page in a browser, but does add an extra step to editing webpages (see "Editing Webpages").

To summarize, when you save your webpage, you must save it in text-only format with either the .html or .htm extension.

stuff.txt   webpage.html

Ⓐ A text file has the .txt extension and is identified with the generic text document icon on Windows (left). If you double-click it, it is displayed in Notepad (or another text editor you've associated with it). A webpage file (right), no matter the text editor you create it with, has the .html or .htm extension and is identified with the default browser's icon (Firefox, in this case). If you double-click it, it is displayed in your default browser, not in the text editor.

B Choose File > Save As from your text editor. Notepad is shown. TextWrangler has this option, too, just in a longer menu.

C In Notepad, give your file a name with the .html or .htm extension, choose Text Documents from the "Save as type" drop-down menu, make sure Encoding is set to UTF-8 (see the last tip), and click Save. The options may be different (but are similar) in another text editor.

D In TextWrangler, give your file a name and choose a location to save it. TextWrangler defaults to UTF-8 (which is what you'll want), but you can make a different choice from the Encoding drop-down menu (see the last tip). Click Save to save the file.

To save your webpage:

1. Once you've created your webpage, choose File > Save As from your text editor **B**.

2. In the dialog that appears, choose Plain Text or Text Document (or however your program words it) for the format.

3. Give the document the .html (preferably) or .htm extension. (This is very important!)

4. Choose the folder in which to save the webpage.

5. Click Save (**C** and **D**).

TIP Whether you use .html or .htm, be consistent. Using the same file extension will make it easier to remember your URLs later when you create links to your pages.

continues on next page

TIP Some text editors on Windows may add their default extension to your file name, even if you've already specified .html or .htm. (Note that this shouldn't be a problem with most editors designed specifically for editing HTML pages, such as the ones I mentioned in the previous section.) Your file, now named `webpage.html.txt`, won't be properly viewed in a browser. To make matters worse, Windows often hides extensions so that the problem is not completely obvious, especially to the uninitiated. There are two solutions. The first is to enclose your file name in double quotes when you save your document the first time. This should keep the extra extension from being added. Next, you can tell Windows to display file extensions (**E** and **F**), so you can see the offending one and remove it from your file name.

TIP When you choose a text-only format, your file is usually saved with your system's default character encoding. If you want to create webpages in another encoding, you'll have to use a text editor that lets you choose the encoding. Typically, UTF-8 is the best encoding choice. If your editor has an option to save files encoded as "UTF-8, no BOM," "UTF-8, without BOM," or something similar, choose that. Otherwise, choose UTF-8 **G**. In some cases, an editor's UTF-8 mode doesn't include the BOM even if it doesn't explicitly note that fact in its encoding menu. (See http://en.wikipedia.org/wiki/Byte_order_mark if you're *really* curious about BOM's meaning. Prepare to be enthralled!)

E The menus differ among versions of Windows **F**. If you use Windows 8, from Windows Explorer choose the View tab to display this menu. Select "File name extensions" (so the box is checked) if you want to be able to see a file's extension (like .html) on the Desktop and in folders.

F Earlier versions of Windows have a menu like this one from Windows 7 (it may look a little different depending on your version). From Windows Explorer, choose either Organize > Folder and Search Options, or Tools > Folder Options (depending on your version of Windows) to view it. Click the View tab and scroll down until you see "Hide extensions for known file types." Make sure it is *unselected* to show a file's extension on the Desktop and in folders.

G Many text editors let you choose the encoding for your file. UTF-8 is the recommended encoding. Choose the UTF-8, no BOM option if it's available in your editor. Otherwise, choose UTF-8. Some editors (like TextWrangler, shown here) default to it.

Save As: index.html

B When the visitor types the path to the directory but omits the file name itself, the file with the default name is used. I typed http://htmlcssvqs.com/gaudi/ in this case. If I had typed http://htmlcssvqs.com/gaudi/index.html instead, the same page would have loaded.

When a Default Page Doesn't Exist

If you don't have a default page in each directory, some servers may show a list of the directory's contents (which you may or may not want to reveal to your visitors). To keep those prying eyes out, create a default page for every directory on your site that contains HTML pages. Alternatively, you can change the server setting so the list of files is hidden (you can also show it if it's already hidden). Hiding the list is advisable for folders that contain assets, such as your images, media files, style sheets, and JavaScript files. Ask your web hosting provider for instructions on how to do this.

Specifying a Default Page or Homepage

Most web servers have a system for recognizing a default page in each folder, based on the name of the file. In almost all cases, **index.html** is recognized as the default page **A**, though if **index.html** doesn't exist, servers will typically look for file names like **index.htm** and **default.htm**. If your visitors type a URL with a directory name but don't specify a file name, the default file is used **B**. (A directory is just a folder, like the ones you have on your computer.)

The default page that you create at the top level of your site's folder structure (often called the *root*) is your site's home page. This is the page that will appear when your visitors type your domain with no additional path information: www.*yourdomain*.com. It's the same as typing www.*yourdomain*.com/index.html, assuming that's what you named your homepage.

Similarly, you can (and usually should) create a default page for any and every directory on your site. For instance, the landing page (that is, the main page) for a **/products/** or **/about-us/** directory in your site would also be called **index.html**, but it would exist in its specific folder. Visitors typically access these sections of your site from your homepage or via main navigation that exists on every page.

To specify a homepage for your site or a landing page for a directory within it:

Save your file as **index.html** in the desired folder. (If **index.html** doesn't work as the default page on your site's server, consult your web hosting provider per Chapter 21.)

Editing Webpages

Because webpages are most often viewed with a web browser, when you double-click them on the desktop, the default browser cheerily opens and displays them. So if you want to edit the page, you'll have to manually open it in your text editor.

To edit webpages:

1. Open your text editor.

2. Choose File > Open.

3. Navigate to the directory that contains the desired file.

4. If you don't see your file listed, choose All Files (or a similar option) (**A** and **B**). The name and location may vary slightly from program to program and platform to platform.

5. Click Open. Your file is ready to edit.

> **TIP** You can also open a file directly from its folder (or the Desktop if that's where it is) **C**.

> **TIP** Once you've made changes to an already saved document, choose File > Save to save the changes without having to worry about the format (as described in "Saving Your Webpage"). An even quicker way is to use a keyboard shortcut. Typically, editors save files via Command-S on OS X and Ctrl-S on Windows.

A Some text editors in Windows, like Notepad, can't automatically see HTML files. Choose All Files to reveal files with any extension.

B Once files with any extension are displayed, you can choose the desired HTML file and click Open.

C In Windows (shown), you can also right-click the document's icon or file name and choose Edit or Open With to choose the desired text editor (the options that appear may vary). On a Mac, right-click the icon or file name, select Open With, and choose the desired text editor. On both systems, the editor will start up if it had been closed.

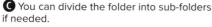

A On a Mac, choose New Folder and then give the folder a name. Create a separate folder for each section of your site.

B In Windows, from the desktop or Windows Explorer, right-click and choose New > Folder.

C You can divide the folder into sub-folders if needed.

Organizing Files

Before you have too many files, it's a good idea to figure out where you're going to put them. It's customary (but not required) to create a folder for each main section within your site, allowing you to group related HTML pages.

To organize your files:

1. Create a central folder or directory to hold everything that will be available on your website. On the Mac, choose File > New Folder in the Finder **A**. In Windows, from the desktop (or within Windows Explorer), right-click and choose New > Folder **B**. Give the folder a name.

2. Create sub-folders in a way that reflects the organization of your website (**A** and **C**). For instance, you may decide to create a separate folder for each section of your site, along with individual sub-folders within those as necessary.

3. Create one or more folders for your site's images, style sheets (CSS files), and JavaScript files, each optionally with sub-folders of their own. There are many ways to organize files; it's entirely up to you. One approach is shown in **A** and **C**. Another is to place your CSS and JavaScript folders at the root with your images folder (and other folders), or to group them in a root-level assets folder

TIP Steps 2 and 3 are optional but recommended.

TIP Use short, descriptive names for your files and folders, preferably separating words in a name with a dash (*not* a space). Use all lower-case letters so that your URLs are easier to type and thus your pages are easier to reach. For more details on how to create good file names, consult "File and Folder Names" in Chapter 1.

Viewing Your Page in a Browser

Once you've created a page, you'll want to see what it looks like in a browser. In fact, since you don't know which browser your visitors will be using—and browsers don't always render pages exactly the same way—it's recommended to look at the page in several browsers (see "Testing Your Pages" in Chapter 20).

To view your page in a browser:

1. Open a browser.

2. If the browser has a File menu, you may choose File > Open File (the second term may vary depending on the browser; regardless, don't choose Open Location) **A**. Or use the keyboard shortcut Command-O (OS X) or Ctrl-O (Windows), both of which take you straight to step 3 except in Internet Explorer—it displays an intermediary Open dialog **A**.

3. In the dialog box that appears, navigate to the folder on your computer that contains the desired webpage, select the page, and click Open **B**. The page is displayed in the browser **C** just as it will appear when you actually publish it on your web server (see Chapter 21). These steps may vary slightly in different browsers.

A On OS X, choose File > Open File from the desired browser (Chrome is at top). If you use Ctrl-O in Internet Explorer (bottom), click Browse in the Open dialog box to move to the next step.

B Choose the file that you want to open, and click the Open button. (This is OS X, but the Windows dialog is comparable.)

C The page appears in the browser. Check it over carefully to see if it's displaying the way you planned.

Disabling Chrome's Cache

Chrome's cache can be a little finicky. Even if you use Command-R (OS X) or Ctrl-F5 (Windows) to refresh the page, sometimes it will use files from its cache rather than the latest versions you've saved. This can be misleading and frustrating when checking your pages. Fortunately, it's possible to disable the cache so Chrome will always use the latest versions. Here's how:

1. With Chrome open, press Command-Option-I (OS X) or Ctrl-Shift-I (Windows) to open Chrome's Developer Tools.

2. Click the gear icon in the lower-right corner.

3. Under Settings > General, select Disable Cache.

4. Close the Settings panel but do not close Developer Tools. The cache will remain disabled as long as Developer Tools is open (or until you deselect Disable Cache).

By the way, to undock Developer Tools from the main Chrome window and display it in its own window, click the icon in the lower-left corner of Developer Tools.

TIP You can (usually) double-click a webpage's file name or icon to view it in a browser. Or, if you already have a browser open, drag the file name or icon and drop it in the browser window. That's often the easiest way to view a page in a browser once you get the hang of it.

TIP Some modern browsers don't have a menu option equivalent to File > Open File for opening a page. Try the keyboard shortcut in step 2 or the drag-and-drop method described in the previous tip instead.

TIP If your webpage does not appear in the dialog for choosing a file **B**, make sure that you have saved it as text-only and given it the .html or .htm extension (see "Saving Your Webpage").

TIP You don't have to close the document in the text editor before you view it with a browser, but you do have to save it. If you make a change to the page in your text editor after you've opened it in a browser, save the file again and use the browser's reload button to refresh the page. Better yet, use the browser's keyboard shortcuts: Command-R (OS X) or Ctrl-F5 (Windows). Those shortcuts refresh the webpage without using files in the browser's cache (see the sidebar regarding Chrome).

TIP Your visitors won't be able to view your website until you publish it to your web server (see Chapter 21).

The Inspiration of Others

One of the easiest ways to expand your HTML fluency is by looking at how other people have created *their* pages. Luckily, HTML code is easy to view and learn from. However, text content, graphics, sounds, videos, and other external files may be copyrighted. Use other's pages for inspiration for your HTML, and then create your own content.

To view others' HTML code with View Source:

1. Open a webpage with any browser.

2. Choose View Source (or the appropriate choice for a particular browser) via one of the methods shown in and 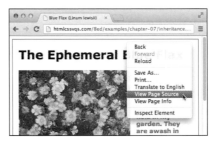. The HTML code will be displayed .

3. If desired, save the file for further study (see the tips).

To view other designers' HTML code with developer tools:

Another way to view a page's source is with a browser's developer tools. The tools are different for each browser vendor, but they all have some features that overlap.

These tools show a more interactive view of the source code. You can inspect the HTML and CSS for specific parts of a page, edit it in the browser, and see the changes reflected in the page immediately. And you can use the tools on any site, not just your own. The changes are temporary—they don't write over the actual HTML and CSS files the page loaded. This is valuable for learning, because you can see how a particular effect was achieved or fiddle with

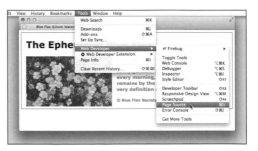

A All desktop browsers have a menu command that lets you view a page's HTML code. The name varies from View Source to Page Source (in Firefox, shown) to similar names. (In Chrome, it's Tools > View Page Source.)

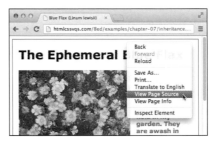

B Most browsers will also let you right-click the page and then choose the View Source command (whatever it's called) from the menu that appears. Chrome is shown. This is often the easiest way to view source, because it can be hard to find the option in the main menu or sub-menu.

C Modern browsers display the code in their own tab or window (as shown), whereas older browsers may show it in a specified text editor. Colors distinguish page content from HTML elements, attributes, and attribute values. This is called syntax highlighting. The line numbers on the left are not part of the HTML code, and not all browsers show them in their View Source modes.

the code to see what happens with no fear of damaging anything.

See the "Browser Developer Tools" sidebar in Chapter 20 for information about the tools available for both modern and older browsers.

TIP There's no rule about who gets to put a site on the web. That's what's so great about it—it's an open medium with a relatively low barrier to entry. You can be a novice, an expert, or anywhere in between. Keep this in mind when you review the code from other sites. If some of the code looks fishy, don't assume its author knows better than you just because their site is on the web. There are plenty of sites that serve as great examples of coding best practices, and there are plenty of others that are, shall we say, less than ideal. So keep a critical eye, and check this book and other resources when in doubt about the appropriateness of a particular technique.

TIP You can also save the source code by copying it from the View Source window and pasting it into your text editor. Then you can save the file. On OS X, use Command-A to select all the code and Command-C to copy it. Then switch over to your editor and paste it with Command-V. The process is the same for Windows, but use the Ctrl key instead of the Command key.

TIP You can also save the source code and typically many of its assets (such as images) by selecting File > Save As (or File > Save Page As) in most browsers. However, the browser may rewrite portions of the code when saving the page, so it won't be exactly the same as if you'd saved it using the previous tip.

TIP For viewing the CSS in a webpage, see "The Inspiration of Others: CSS" in Chapter 8.

Basic HTML Structure

This chapter covers the HTML elements you need to establish the foundation and structure of your documents; that is, the primary semantic containers for your content.

You'll learn about:

- Starting a webpage
- Using the **h1–h6**, **header**, **nav**, **main**, **article**, **section**, **aside**, **footer**, and **div** elements (most of which are new in HTML5)
- Improving your page's accessibility with ARIA **role** attributes
- Applying a class or ID to elements
- Applying the **title** attribute to elements
- Adding comments to your code

Creating a clear and consistent structure not only sets up a good semantic foundation for your page but also makes it that much easier to apply styles to your document with Cascading Style Sheets (CSS) (coverage begins in Chapter 7).

In This Chapter

Starting Your Webpage

At its most basic level, each of your HTML documents should contain the following components, as shown in  **A**:

- The DOCTYPE
- The **html** element (with the **lang** attribute, which is optional but recommended)
- The **head** element
- The character encoding in a **meta** element
- The **title** element (you'll add its content in a bit)
- The **body** element

As I noted in Chapter 1, these HTML components create the equivalent of a blank sheet of paper, since there is no content in the **body** **B**.

Before you add content or other information, you need to set up the foundation of your page.

To start an HTML5 page:

1. Type **<!DOCTYPE html>** to declare your page as an HTML5 document. (See the "HTML5's Improved DOCTYPE" sidebar.)

2. Type **<html lang="*language-code*">** to begin the actual HTML portion of your document, where *language-code* is the language code that matches the primary language of your page's content. For instance, **<html lang="es">** for Spanish or **<html lang="fr">** for French. You can also be more specific, such as **<html lang="en-US">** for American English versus **<html lang="en-GB">** for British English.

A Here's the foundation of every HTML page. The indentation of the code doesn't matter, but the structure is crucial. The **html** element, which follows the DOCTYPE, must enclose all other elements in your page. In this example, the default language (per the **lang** attribute) is set to **en** for English. The character encoding is set to UTF-8.

```
<!DOCTYPE html>
<html lang="en">
<head>
    <meta charset="utf-8" />
    <title></title>
</head>
<body>


</body>
</html>
```

B The minimal HTML foundation code viewed in Firefox. As you can see, there's nothing to see! However, you'll start adding content soon enough.

Reviewing Chapter 1

If you haven't done so already, I strongly suggest you read Chapter 1 before continuing. It shows a simple HTML page and explains some of the basic concepts. Since that is your first glimpse at a webpage, I'll repeat some (but not all) of the information and assume you're familiar with the rest so you can build on those ideas.

3. Type **`<head>`** to begin the document head of your page.

4. Type **`<meta charset="utf-8" />`** or **`<meta charset="UTF-8" />`** to declare the character encoding of your document as UTF-8. Also, the space and forward slash are optional, so **`<meta charset="utf-8">`** and **`<meta charset="UTF-8">`** work the same as the others. (Character encodings besides UTF-8 are valid too, but UTF-8 is the most versatile, and it's rare that you'd need to deviate.)

5. Type **`<title></title>`**. This will contain your page's title. You'll add title text in the "Creating a Title" section.

6. Type **`</head>`** to end the document head of your page.

7. Type **`<body>`** to start the body of your page. This is where your content will go (eventually).

8. If desired, leave a few blank lines for creating your page content, which you'll do throughout the rest of this book.

9. Type **`</body>`** to end the body.

10. Type **`</html>`** to end your page.

That's a pretty healthy number of steps, but since all your pages will start that way, you could use a single HTML page as the template from which to begin every page, saving yourself some typing. In fact, most code editors allow you to specify the starter code for each new page, making it even easier. If you don't find a Settings or Preferences menu in your editor, search its Help section.

A page's two sections: head and body

Just as a quick recap of what you learned in Chapter 1, pages are divided into two sections within the **html** element: the **head** and the **body** Ⓐ. The DOCTYPE, which starts each page, is a preamble of sorts. It tells the browser the HTML version of the page. You should include it in all your pages.

The document **head** is where you define the title of your page, include information about your page for search engines, load style sheets, and occasionally load JavaScript files (see Chapter 19 for why to avoid loading JavaScript here most of the time). You'll see examples of these as you progress through the book. Except for the **title**, the content of the **head** is not visible to users when they visit your page.

The **body** element encloses your page's content, including text, images, forms, audio, video, and more. There are several chapters dedicated to HTML's content-related elements, some of which you'll get an early look at in this chapter.

A Note About the Word "Section"

Both here and in the pages to follow, I'll often use "section" as a generic term to mean a distinct part of a page, as opposed to the **section** element specifically. When I am referring to the **section** element, the word will be styled as code, just like it is in this sentence.

HTML5's Improved DOCTYPE

Oh, how much simpler it is to start your webpage now that HTML5 is here. HTML5's DOCTYPE is refreshingly short, especially when compared to the DOCTYPEs of yore.

In the days of HTML 4 and XHTML 1.0, there were several DOCTYPEs from which to choose. You invariably had to copy them from somewhere else because they were too convoluted to remember.

For instance, here's the DOCTYPE for XHTML Strict documents.

```
<!DOCTYPE html PUBLIC "-//W3C//DTD XHTML 1.0 Transitional//EN"
→ "http://www.w3.org/ TR/xhtml1/DTD/xhtml1-strict.dtd">
```

Gobbledygook.

Luckily, all browsers—both old and new—understand HTML5s DOCTYPE, so you can stick with it for all your pages and forget the other ones ever existed.

TIP The HTML5 DOCTYPE makes sure browsers display pages in a reliable mode and tells the HTML validators to judge your code against HTML5's allowed elements and syntax. HTML validators are discussed in Chapter 20.

TIP HTML5's DOCTYPE isn't case sensitive. For Instance, some choose to type it as `<!doctype html>`, but it's probably more common to use `<!DOCTYPE html>` **A**.

TIP A search engine could use the language specified in `lang` to categorize search results and display only those that match the language of the searched phrase. Screen readers might adjust the pronunciation of a word based on the language code specified.

TIP Richard Ishida's language subtag lookup tool (http://rishida.net/utils/subtags/) helps you look up language codes.

TIP Be sure your code editor is configured to save files as UTF-8 to match the character encoding specified in the code by `<meta charset="utf-8" />` **A**. (Or if you've specified a different `charset`, save your files in that.) Not all code editors will save your pages as UTF-8 by default, but most do allow you to choose the encoding from a menu or in a panel (see "Saving Your Webpage" in Chapter 2). If you don't use UTF-8, you may occasionally see funny characters in your content rather than the intended letter, such as an accented *i* or an *n* with a tilde (~).

TIP You don't have to indent the code that is nested in the head element **A**. However, the benefit of doing so is that you can see at a glance where the head begins, what's in it, and where it ends. It's not unusual for the head to become very long in some pages.

Creating a Title

The HTML foundation code in the previous section had **<title></title>** as a place-holder until it was time to discuss **title** further. Now's the time!

Each HTML page must have a **title** element. A title should be short, descriptive, and unique to each page (A). In most browsers, the title appears in the title bar of the window (Chrome is one exception) and on the browser tab (B). The title also shows in your visitors' browser history lists and bookmarks (C).

Perhaps most importantly, the title is used by search engines like Google, Bing, DuckDuckGo, and Yahoo to get a sense of your page's content and typically as the link that appears in their search results (D).

In short, make your **title** unique and relevant to each page to improve search engine results and make your visitors' experience better.

(A) The **title** element must be placed in the **head** section. Place it after the **meta** element that specifies the character encoding.

```
<!DOCTYPE html>
<html lang="en">
<head>
    <meta charset="UTF-8" />
    <title>Antoni Gaudí - Introduction
    → </title>
</head>
<body>
</body>
</html>
```

```
⊗ ⊖ ⊕   Antoni Gaudí – Introduction           ⤢
  ⬚    Antoni Gaudí – Introduction        +
```

```
⊖ ○ ○    🗋 Antoni Gaudí – Introductio  ×         ⤢
```

(B) In most browsers, like Firefox, the title of a webpage is displayed both in the title bar of the window and on the tab. However, Chrome (bottom) displays the title only on the tab.

Show All History	Ctrl+Shift+H
Clear Recent History...	Ctrl+Shift+Del
Restore Previous Session	
Recently Closed Tabs	▸
Recently Closed Windows	▸
🌐 Antoni Gaudí - Introduction ⬚	

(C) The title also appears in your visitor's History pane (shown), Favorites list, and Bookmarks list.

Antoni Gaudí - Introduction
Antoni Gaudí. Many tourists are drawn to Barcelona to see
Antoni Gaudí's incredible architecture. **Gaudí**'s non-conformity,
already visible in his teenage years, coupled with his quiet but

(D) The title is typically used as the linked text pointing to your page in search results. It's also an important factor for determining a page's relevance in search results. Typically, search engines display the title and part of the copy from your page's **body**.

A Deeper Look at Page Titles

Many developers—even well-intentioned, fairly experienced ones—give little consideration to the **title** element. They'll simply input the name of their site and then copy it across all HTML pages. Or even worse, they'll leave the **title** text that their code editor may insert by default. If one of your goals is to drive traffic to your site, you'd be doing yourself and your potential readers a huge disservice by following suit.

Search engines have different algorithms that determine a page's rank and how its content is indexed. Universally, though, **title** plays a key role. Search engines may look to the **title** for an indication of what a page is about, and index a page's content in search of related text. An effective **title** focuses on a handful of key words that are central to a page's content.

As a best practice, choose **title** text that briefly summarizes a page's content. In addition to benefiting your search engine rankings, it helps screen reader users learn the focus of your page quickly (the title may be read aloud).

Secondarily, and optionally, indicate your site's name in the **title**. Although it's *common* to see a site's name at the beginning of the **title**, it's *better* to put the unique, page-specific **title** text at the beginning instead.

I recommend you get your **title**'s core message into the first 60 characters, including spaces, because search engines often cut them off in their results at around that number (as a baseline). Browsers display a varying number of characters in the title bar at the top of the browser before cutting off the text. Browser tabs cut off the title even sooner because there's less real estate.

To create a title:

1. Place the cursor between **<title>** and **</title>** in the document **head**.

2. Enter the title of your webpage.

TIP The **title** element is required.

TIP A title cannot contain any formatting, HTML, images, or links to other pages.

TIP Some code editors pre-populate the **title** with default text when you start a new page unless you've configured it to use specific starter template code, as described in "Starting Your Webpage." So be on the lookout for that, and be sure to replace any default text with a **title** of your own making.

Creating Headings

HTML provides six heading levels for describing the hierarchy of information in your pages. Mark up each heading with an **h1**, **h2**, **h3**, **h4**, **h5**, or **h6** element. Organizationally, **h1** is a top-level heading, **h2** is a heading beneath **h1**, **h3** is a heading beneath **h2**, and so on. For brevity, I'll refer to them collectively as **h1**–**h6** rather than listing them.

Think of **h1**–**h6** like headings within a non-HTML document you might write, such as a term paper, sales report, news article, product manual—you get the idea. When you write those types of documents, you start each major section of content with a heading. Each subsection gets a subheading, as do sub-subsections, and so on. Collectively, those headings represent the outline of your document. The same is true for your webpages (Ⓐ and Ⓑ).

The importance of headings

Headings are among the most important HTML elements in any page. Because headings typically convey your page's topic(s), search engines weigh them heavily when matching your pages against search terms. This is particularly true for the likes of **h1**, the heading of the highest rank. (Which is not to say to load your page up with **h1**s; search engines are wise to that!)

Humans love good headings, too. Sighted users scan a page's headings to determine its content. Screen reader users do the same, but with their hands and ears. They'll often navigate a page by headings via the keyboard. Listening to the headings allows them to quickly assess a page's content and find areas of interest without having to listen to the whole page. Once they find an interesting heading, they can

Ⓐ Use headings to define your document structure, just like an outline. Here, "La Sagrada Família" and "Park Guell"—marked up as **h2** elements—represent sections under the top-level heading, "Barcelona's Architect," because it's an **h1**. If "Park Guell" were an **h3** instead, then it would fall under "La Sagrada Família" (and be a sub-subheading of the **h1**). If I were coding the rest of the page right now, the related content (paragraphs, images, video, and so on) would follow each heading.

```
<!DOCTYPE html>
<html lang="en">
<head>
    <meta charset="UTF-8" />
    <title>Antoni Gaudí - Introduction
    ↪ </title>
</head>
<body>
<h1>Barcelona's Architect</h1>
<h2 lang="es">La Sagrada Família</h2>
<h2>Park Guell</h2>
</body>
</html>
```

Ⓑ In this example, there are three main areas within the product guide, each with varying degrees of subheadings. I've included spaces and indentation only to make the hierarchy clear to you—I wouldn't indent them like this in practice, though you could with no effect on how they display in browsers.

```
...
<body>
<h1>Product User Guide</h1>
    <h2>Setting it up</h2>

    <h2>Basic Features</h2>
        <h3>Video Playback</h3>
            <h4>Basic Controls</h4>
            <h4>Jumping to Markers</h4>

        <h3>Recording Video</h3>
            <h4>Manual Recording</h4>
            <h4>Scheduling a Recording</h4>

    <h2>Advanced Features</h2>
        <h3>Sharing Video</h3>
        <h3>Compressing Video</h3>
</body>
</html>
```

C While all headings display in boldface by default, **h1** is in a larger font than **h2**, which is larger than **h3**, and so on. The space between each heading is also a product of the default browser CSS, not any blank lines you might include in your HTML document.

choose to listen to the associated content that follows. The usability and accessibility benefits of **h1–h6** are big.

In short, a good structure of headings helps both you and your visitors.

To organize your webpage with headings:

1. In the **body** section of your HTML document, type **<hn>**, where *n* is a number from 1 to 6, depending on the rank of the heading that you want to create. **h1** has the highest rank, and **h6** has the lowest rank.

2. Type the contents of the header.

3. Type **</hn>** where *n* is the same number used in step 1.

TIP By default, browsers typically display headings progressively smaller moving from h1 to h6 **C**. (In some browsers, h1 and h2 look the same by default when nested in certain elements.) But don't forget to choose your heading levels solely based on what hierarchy is appropriate for your content, not on how big or small you want the text to appear. You can style the headings as you please with a particular font, size, color, and more. For details about achieving this with CSS, consult Chapter 10.

TIP Avoid skipping a level when creating headings; for example, from h3 to h5. However, you *can* move from a lower ranked heading to a higher ranked heading, as appropriate. For instance, in **B** we have <h4>Scheduling a Recording</h4> and then <h2>Advanced Features</h2>. That sequence makes sense—just like it might if this were a printed product guide—because the Basic Features (also an h2) section containing Scheduling a Recording has ended and Advanced Features is beginning.

continues on next page

TIP Don't use an h1–h6 to markup a subtitle, tagline, or a subheading that isn't a heading for its own section. For example, think of a news story that has a main heading and then a subheading immediately after it. In that case, use a paragraph **D** or other non-heading element.

TIP Previously, HTML5 included an element named hgroup for grouping consecutive headings, but the W3C removed it from the HTML5 spec.

TIP As a side note, in **A** I used the lang attribute on each h2 to indicate that its text is in a different language (Spanish, represented by the language code es) than the page's default (English, as declared by <html lang="en">).

TIP At the time of this writing, there is talk about possibly adding a subhead element to HTML for marking up subheadings, subtitles, taglines, and bylines. It's too early to tell if it will be adopted.

D Here is one approach to marking up a subheading or subtitle of an article, a blog entry, or the like. You could include a **class** (named **subhead** or whatever you prefer) to facilitate styling it with CSS.

```
...
    <h1>Giraffe Escapes from Zoo</h1>
    <p class="subhead">Animals Worldwide
    ⤷ Rejoice</p>

    <p>... story content ...</p>
...
```

HTML5's Document Outline

At the time of this writing, HTML5 includes an algorithm for how it treats any of **h1–h6** when nested in the **article**, **aside**, **nav**, and **section** elements. The algorithm is often referred to as the *HTML5 document outline*. No browser has implemented it, however, and signs point to that remaining the case. Furthermore, among screen readers, only JAWS (a screen reader for Windows) accounts for it, but its implementation is faulty.

With this in mind, the W3C has included the document outline on the list of features at risk of being removed from the spec by the time it goes final in 2014. Even if it happens to remain in the spec or browsers implement it, you can continue to mark up your headings as I've shown here. It reflects current practices and is future-proof—the document outline won't break your pages.

In other words, nothing to see here! I'm mentioning all this just in case you come across the document outline elsewhere and wonder if you need to learn how it works.

Common Page Constructs

A A common layout with main navigation along the top, main content on the left, a sidebar on the right, and the footer at the bottom. CSS is required to make the page look like this.

Masthead/header with navigation	
Main page content	Related, but tangential information
Footer	

B The types of information commonly found in a page. This is just one type of arrangement, though a common one.

No doubt you've visited dozens of sites arranged like the one shown in **A**. Stripping away the content, you can see that there are four main components: a masthead with navigation, an article in the main content area, a sidebar with tangential information, and a footer **B**.

Now, you can't style a page like this or arrange it as shown without CSS. You'll start learning CSS in Chapter 7, learn how to format text and add colors beginning in Chapter 10, and do a multi-column layout in Chapter 11.

However, the semantics that apply to these common page constructs are similar no matter the layout. You'll explore them for most of the remaining pages of this chapter. You'll see how to use the **header**, **nav**, **main**, **article**, **section**, **aside**, and **footer** elements to define the structure of your pages, and then how to use **div** as a generic container for additional styling and other purposes. Except for **div**, none of these elements existed until HTML5.

As you learn about these elements, don't get too attached to where they display in the sample layouts, and instead focus on their semantic meaning.

In the ensuing pages, you'll get an early look at some other elements, such as the **ul** (unordered list), which is used for structuring most lists of links (**a** elements), among other lists. Those will be explained in later chapters.

Creating a Header

If a section of your page has a group of introductory or navigational content, mark it up with the **header** element.

A page can have any number of **header** elements, and their meaning can vary depending on their context. For instance, a **header** at or near the top of a page may represent the header (sometimes called a masthead) for the whole page Ⓐ. Typically, the page header includes the site's logo, the main navigation Ⓑ, other global links, and possibly even a search box Ⓒ. Undoubtedly, this is the **header** element's most common use, but don't mistake it for its only one.

A **header** can also appear deeper within a page, as long as it fits the bill. One example is a section's table of contents Ⓓ.

A **header** often includes its section's heading (an **h1**–**h6**), but this isn't mandatory. For example, you see headings in Ⓒ but not in Ⓐ.

Ⓐ This **header** represents the header for the whole page. It contains a list of links in a **nav** element to indicate it's a primary set of navigation on the page. The optional **role="banner"** portion is not appropriate for every header. It improves accessibility by explicitly marking the page-level header. See Ⓓ for another example and "Improving Accessibility with ARIA" to learn more. (See "Marking Navigation" for the **role** value that's specific to the **nav** element.)

```
...
<body>
<header role="banner">
    <nav>
        <ul>
            <li><a href="#gaudi">Barcelona's
            → Architect</a></li>
            <li lang="es"><a href="#sagrada-
            → familia">La Sagrada Família</a>
            → </li>
            <li><a href="#park-guell">Park
            → Guell</a></li>
        </ul>
    </nav>
</header>
</body>
</html>
```

Ⓑ The page-level header containing the navigation.

Ⓒ Here's a styled header for another site. This type of page-level header is common across the web. It has the name of the site (usually a logo), links to navigate the primary areas of the site, and a search box.

D This page has two **header**s: one serving as the whole page's header and another as the header for the Frequently Asked Questions parent **article** element. Note that the first one doesn't have any **h1–h6** headings, but the second one does. Also, only the first **header** includes **role="banner"** because it is the page-level header.

```
...
<body>
<header role="banner">
    ... [site logo, navigation, etc.] ...
</header>

<main role="main">
<article>
    <header>
        <h1>Frequently Asked Questions</h1>
        <nav>
            <ul>
                <li><a href="#answer1">What is
                → your return policy?</a><li>
                <li><a href="#answer2">How do I
                → find a location?</a><li>
                ...
            </ul>
        </nav>
    </header>

    <!-- links in 2nd header point to
    → these -->
    <article id="answer1">
        <h2>What is your return policy?</h2>
        <p> ... [answer] ... </p>
    </article>

    <article id="answer2">
        <h2>How do I find a location?</h2>
        <p> ... [answer] ... </p>
    </article>
    ...
</article> <!-- end parent article -->
</main>
</body>
</html>
```

To create a header:

1. Place the cursor within the element for which you want to create a header.

2. Type **<header>**.

3. Type the contents of the header, which can include a variety of content types marked up with their respective HTML elements (most of which you'll learn about in the coming chapters). For instance, a **header** might contain **h1–h6** headings, a logo or series of logos, navigation, a search box, and more.

4. Type **</header>**.

TIP Don't use **header** unnecessarily. If all you have is an **h1–h6**, there's no need to wrap it in a **header** in most cases.

TIP A **header** is not interchangeable with a heading, as in the **h1–h6** elements (see "Creating Headings"). Each has its own semantic purpose.

TIP You may not nest a **footer** element or another **header** within a **header**, nor may you nest a **header** within a **footer** or **address** element.

TIP A **header** doesn't always have to contain a **nav** element as the examples do (**A** and **D**), but in most cases, it likely will if the **header** contains navigational links. In the case of **D**, **nav** is appropriate around the list of Frequently Asked Questions links, since it's a major navigation group within the page, as discussed in "Marking Navigation."

TIP See "Creating Generic Containers" to learn about how **header** has replaced one of the **div** element's roles from its pre-HTML5 days.

Marking Navigation

Earlier versions of HTML didn't have an element that explicitly represents a section of major navigation links, but HTML5 does: the **nav** element. Links in a **nav** may point to content within the page , to other pages or resources, or both. Whatever the case may be, use **nav** only for your page's most important groups of links, not all of them.

If you looked closely at the code in the previous section, you got a look at the **nav** element in action. I've carried that code sample over to this page, while highlighting **nav**. The **nav** element doesn't impose any default formatting on its contents **B**.

To designate a group of links as important navigation:

1. Type **<nav>**.

2. Type your list of links structured as a **ul** (unordered list) **A** unless the order of the links is meaningful (like breadcrumb navigation), in which case you could structure them as an **ol** (ordered list). (See Chapters 6 and 15 to learn about links and lists, respectively.)

3. Type **</nav>**.

A These links (the **a** elements) represent an important set of navigation, so I've nested them in a **nav** element. The **role** attribute is not required but improves accessibility. See the last tip in this section for information about applying **role="navigation"** to **nav**.

```
...
<body>
<header role="banner">
    <nav role="navigation">
        <ul>
            <li><a href="#gaudi">Barcelona's
            → Architect</a></li>
            <li lang="es"><a href="#sagrada-
            → familia">La Sagrada Família</a>
            → </li>
            <li><a href="#park-guell">Park
            → Guell</a></li>
        </ul>
    </nav>
</header>
</body>
</html>
```

B Our navigation looks rather plain by default. The bullets are not a product of the **nav** element, which has no default styling other than starting on its own line. The bullets display because each link is in an **li** element (a list item). With CSS, you can turn off the bullets or show different ones, as well as lay out the links horizontally, change their color, make them look like buttons, and more. Chapters 11 and 15 have examples of styled lists of links.

TIP If you have some experience with HTML or XHTML, you're probably accustomed to structuring your links in a ul or ol element, as appropriate. In HTML5, nav doesn't replace that best practice; continue to use those elements, and simply wrap a nav around them Ⓐ.

TIP Although screen readers on the whole are still catching up with the new semantics in HTML5, the nav element can help them identify your page's important navigation and allow users to jump to them via the keyboard. This makes your page more accessible, improving your visitors' experience. Don't go overboard, though—if too many groups of links are marked with nav, the page becomes noisier for screen readers and the importance of each group is diminished.

TIP The HTML5 spec recommends not wrapping ancillary page footer links like "Terms of Use" and "Privacy Policy" in a nav, which makes sense. Sometimes, though, your page footer might include a series of links you consider very important, such as for "Store Locator," "Careers," and the like. If these are not grouped in a nav elsewhere in your page, you could consider putting those types of footer links in a nav.

TIP HTML5 doesn't allow nesting a nav within an address element.

TIP See "Improving Accessibility with ARIA" to learn how to use role="navigation" with nav Ⓐ.

A Deeper Look at nav

As I mentioned earlier, just because you have a group of links in your page doesn't mean it should be contained in a **nav**.

Suppose you have a news page like the one in Ⓒ. It's an article about a gallery opening in the Arts & Entertainment section of a paper. The page includes four lists of links, only two of which are considered major enough to warrant being wrapped in a **nav**. (I've abbreviated portions of the code.)

The secondary navigation in the **aside** allows the user to navigate to category pages in Arts & Entertainment (such as Movies and Music), so I felt it constitutes a major navigational section of the page. However, the Other Stories **aside** with links does not, nor do the **footer** links. (See "Specifying an Aside" regarding the **aside** element.)

So how do you decide when a group of links deserves a **nav**? Ultimately, it's a judgment call based on your content. At a minimum, mark up your site's global navigation (that is, what allows users to jump to sections of the site) with **nav**. Usually, that particular **nav** appears within a **header** for the whole page (see "Creating a Header").

Ⓒ Only two of this page's groups of links are wrapped in **nav**. The other two aren't considered major groups of navigation.

```
...
<body>
    <!-- ==== Start Page Header ==== -->
    <header role="banner">
        <!-- site logo could go here -->
        <!-- site global navigation -->
        <nav role="navigation">
            <ul> ... </ul>
        </nav>
    </header>

    <!-- ==== Start Main Content ==== -->
    <main role="main">
        <h1>Arts & Entertainment: Museums
        ⇥ </h1>

        <article>
            <h2>Gallery Opening Features the
            ⇥ Inspired, Inspiring</h2>
            <p>... [story content] ... </p>
        </article>

        <aside>
            <h2>Other Stories</h2>
            <!-- not wrapped in nav -->
            <ul> ... [story links] ... </ul>
```

```
        </aside>
    </main>

    <!-- ==== Start Sidebar ==== -->
    <aside>
        <!-- secondary navigation -->
        <nav role="navigation">
            <ul>
                <li><a href="/arts/movies/">
                ⇥ Movies</a></li>
                <li><a href="/arts/music/">
                ⇥ Music</a></li>
                ...
            </ul>
        </nav>
    </aside>

    <!-- ==== Start Page Footer ==== -->
    <footer role="contentinfo">
        <!-- Ancillary links not wrapped
        ⇥ in nav. -->
        <ul> ... </ul>
    </footer>
</body>
</html>
```

code continues in next column

(A) Here is a look ahead at the completed page we are evolving throughout the chapter. Some of the elements will look unfamiliar to you, but we'll cover them shortly. The `main` element surrounds the content for the page's central topic. It's good practice to include `role="main"` in the `main` start tag (see the last tip).

```
...
<body>
<header role="banner">
    <nav role="navigation">
        ... [ul with links] ...
    </nav>
</header>

<main role="main">
    <article>
        <h1 id="gaudi">Barcelona's Architect
        → </h1>
        <p>Antoni Gaudí's incredible
        → buildings bring millions ...</p>

        ... [rest of main page content] ...
    </article>
</main>

<aside role="complementary">
    <h1>Architectural Wonders of Barcelona
    → </h1>

    ... [rest of aside] ...
</aside>

<footer role="contentinfo">
    ... [copyright] ...
</footer>
</body>
</html>
```

Marking the Main Area of a Webpage

Most webpages have a variety of sections: a header, a footer, perhaps a sidebar with additional information or links to other sites, and more. However, only one part of a page represents its main content—that is, its primary focus. Wrap this content with the aptly named `main` element, using it only once per page (**(A)** and **(B)**).

TIP `main` is one of the newest elements in HTML5. Remember to use it only once in each page.

TIP If you're creating a web application, wrap `main` around its main functionality.

TIP You cannot place `main` inside an `article`, `aside`, `footer`, `header`, or `nav` element.

TIP The `role="main"` attribute-value pair **(A)** can help screen readers locate the main content of your pages. See "Improving Accessibility with ARIA" to learn more about ARIA landmarks like this one.

(B) The display of the `main` element begins on its own line, just like a `p`, `header`, `footer`, and some other elements, but otherwise does not affect the style of your page at all. (The layout you see here is because of CSS, not `main`.) I've added a blue outline to help you see what part of the styled, completed page `main` encompasses.

Creating an Article

Another element that's new thanks to HTML5 is **article** (Ⓐ and Ⓑ). You've seen some examples of it in play already. Now let's learn more about what makes it tick.

Based on its name, you'd rightly guess that you can use **article** to contain content like a newspaper article. However, it isn't limited to that. In HTML5, "article" isn't meant literally.

Here's how HTML5 defines it:

> The **article** element represents a complete, or self-contained, composition in a document, page, application, or site and that is, in principle, independently distributable or reusable, for example in syndication. This could be a forum post, a magazine or newspaper article, a blog entry, a user-submitted comment, an interactive widget or gadget, or any other independent item of content.

Other **article** examples could include a movie or music review, a case study, a product description, and more. You might have been surprised to learn that it also can be an interactive widget or gadget, but those too are independent, reusable items of content.

Ⓐ I've abbreviated the article contents and the **nav** code from the previous section to keep it simple. You can see the complete version of the page code on the book site at www.htmlcssvqs.com/8ed/structure-final. Although this example includes only paragraphs and images, an **article** can contain a variety of content types.

```
...
<body>
<header role="banner">
    <nav role="navigation">
        ... [ul with links] ...
    </nav>
</header>

<main role="main">
    <article>
        <h1 id="gaudi">Barcelona's Architect
        ⟶ </h1>

        <p>Antoni Gaudí's incredible buildings
        ⟶ bring millions of tourists to
        ⟶ Barcelona each year.</p>

        <p>Gaudí's non-conformity, already
        ⟶ visible in his teenage years,
        ⟶ coupled with his quiet but firm
        ⟶ devotion to the church, made a
        ⟶ unique foundation for his thoughts
        ⟶ and ideas. His search for simplicity
        ⟶ ...is quite apparent in his work,
        ⟶ from the <a href="#park-guell">Park
        ⟶ Guell</a> and its incredible
        ⟶ sculptures and mosaics, to...</p>

        <h2 id="sagrada-familia" lang="es">
        ⟶ La Sagrada Família</h2>

        <p><img src="img/towers.jpg"
        ⟶ width="75" height="100" alt="Sagrada
        ⟶ Família Towers" /> The
        ⟶ complicatedly named and curiously
        ⟶ unfinished masterpiece...</p>

        <h2 id="park-guell">Park Guell</h2>

        ... [image and paragraphs] ...
    </article>
</main>
</body>
</html>
```

Browser window

Antoni Gaudí, Barcelona's architect

Antoni Gaudí, Barcelona's archit... +

- Barcelona's Architect
- La Sagrada Família
- Park Guell

Barcelona's Architect

Antoni Gaudí's incredible buildings bring millions of tourists to Barcelona each year.

Gaudí's non-conformity, already visible in his teenage years, coupled with his quiet but firm devotion to the church, made a unique foundation for his thoughts and ideas. His search for simplicity, based on his careful observations of nature, is quite apparent in his work, from the Park Guell and its incredible sculptures and mosaics, to the Church of the Sacred Family and its organic, bulbous towers.

La Sagrada Família

The complicatedly named and curiously unfinished masterpiece that is the Expiatory Temple of the Sacred Family is the most visited building in Barcelona. In it, Gaudí combines his vision of nature and architecture with his devotion to his faith. The Sagrada Família attracts even the non-religious to its doors in large part due to its tragic story and its still unfinished state, of which the everpresent scaffolding and cranes are permanent reminders.

Park Guell

The Park Guell always reminds me of Howard Roark in Ayn Rand's *The Fountainhead*. Gaudí's

B Now the page has **header**, **nav**, **main**, and **article** elements, as well as their contents. The **article** headings may be a different size by default depending on the browser. You can standardize their look across browsers with CSS (see Chapter 10).

To create an article:

1. Type `<article>`.

2. Type the article's contents, which could include any number of elements, such as paragraphs, lists, audio, video, images, and figures.

3. Type `</article>`.

TIP You can nest an `article` inside another one as long as the inner `article` is related to the `article` on the whole. See the sidebar for an example.

TIP A page may contain several `article` elements (or none at all). For example, a blog's homepage typically includes a few of the most recent postings; each could be its own `article`.

TIP An `article` may have one or more `section` elements (covered next). It's also perfectly valid to let the h1–h6 elements alone indicate the parts within your `article`, as I did here.

More article Examples

The previous example **Ⓐ** is just one way to use **article**. Let's take a look at some more possibilities.

Figure **Ⓒ** illustrates how you could mark up a basic news story or report. Note the use of the **footer** and **address** elements (see discussions about them in this chapter and Chapter 4, respectively). Here, **address** applies only to its parent **article** (the one shown), not to the page or any **article** elements nested within that **article**, such as the reader comments in **Ⓓ**.

Figure **Ⓓ** demonstrates nested **article** elements in the form of user-submitted comments to the parent **article**, just like you see in the comments section of blogs or news sites. It also shows one use for the **section** element (see "Defining a **Section**") and the **time** element, covered in Chapter 4.

These are just a couple of more common ways to leverage **article** and its companion elements.

Ⓒ A common way to mark up an article that includes information about the author.

```
...
<article>
    <h1>The Diversity of Papua New Guinea
    → </h1>
    <p>Papua New Guinea is home to more than
    → 800 tribes and languages ...</p>

    ... [rest of story content] ...

    <!-- article's footer, not the page's -->
    <footer>
        <p>Leandra Allen is a freelance
        → journalist who earned her degree
        → in anthropology from the University
        → of Copenhagen.</p>

        <address>
        You may reach her at <a href="mailto:
        → leandra@therunningwriter.com">
        → leandra@therunningwriter.com</a>.
        </address>
    </footer>
</article>
...
```

Ⓓ Each reader comment is an **article** nested in the main **article**.

```
...
<article>
    <h1>The Diversity of Papua New Guinea
    → </h1>
    ... [parent article content] ...

    <footer>
        ... [parent article footer] ...
    </footer>

    <section>
        <h2>Reader Comments</h2>
        <article>
            <footer>travelgal wrote on
            → <time datetime="2014-02-26">
            → February 26, 2014</time>:
            → </footer>
            <p>Great article! I've always
            → been curious about Papua New
            → Guinea.</p>
        </article>

        <article>
            ... [next reader comment] ...
        </article>
    </section>
</article>
...
```

Take a look at virtually any news site and you're likely to see news headlines grouped in various categories. Each group could be marked with a **section**.

```
...
<body>
...
<main role="main">
    <h1>Latest World News</h1>
    <section>
        <h2>Breaking News</h2>
        <ul>... [list of headlines] ...</ul>
    </section>

    <section>
        <h2>Business</h2>
        <ul>... [list of headlines] ...</ul>
    </section>

    <section>
        <h2>Arts</h2>
        <ul>... [list of headlines] ...</ul>
    </section>
</main>
...
</body>
</html>
```

Ⓑ In this slightly modified example from the HTML5 spec, you see **section** used to demarcate the sections of a graduation program Ⓒ.

```
...
<h1>Graduation Program</h1>
<section>
    <h2>Ceremony</h2>
    <ol>
        <li>Opening Procession</li>
        <li>Speech by Valedictorian</li>
        <li>Speech by Class President</li>
        ...
    </ol>
</section>

<section>
    <h2>Graduates (alphabetical)</h2>
    <ol>
        <li>Molly Carpenter</li>
        ...
    </ol>
</section>
...
```

Defining a Section

Another of the new elements in HTML5 is **section** (Ⓐ through Ⓒ). In part, HTML5 defines it as follows:

The **section** element represents a generic section of a document or application. A section, in this context, is a thematic grouping of content, typically with a heading.

Examples of sections would be chapters, the various tabbed pages in a tabbed dialog box, or the numbered sections of a thesis. A website's home page could be split into sections for an introduction, news items, and contact information.

Although **section** is partly defined as a "generic" section, don't confuse it with the truly generic **div** element (see "Creating Generic Containers"). Semantically, **section** marks a distinct section of your page, whereas **div** conveys no meaning whatsoever.

To define a section:

1. Type `<section>`.

2. Type the section's contents, which could include any number of elements, such as paragraphs, lists, audio, video, images, figures, and more.

3. Type `</section>`.

TIP You may nest `section` elements in an `article` to explicitly mark the various sections or chapters of a report, a story, a manual, and so on. For example, I could use it in the Antoni Gaudí example shown in this chapter—one `section` surrounding the La Sagrada Família h2 and related paragraph and another `section` around the Park Guell h2 and related paragraphs.

TIP If you need to add a container around content solely for styling purposes, use `div` instead of `section`.

Graduation Program

Ceremony

1. Opening Procession
2. Speech by Valedictorian
3. Speech by Class President
4. Presentation of Diplomas
5. Closing Speech by Headmaster

Graduates (alphabetical)

1. Molly Carpenter
2. Anastasia Luccio
3. Ebenezar McCoy
4. Karrin Murphy
5. Thomas Raith

C Like most elements in this chapter, `section` doesn't affect a page's display. The numbers appear because of the ordered lists (`ol`) in **B**. (Please see lists in Chapter 15.)

Getting a Feel for the `section` Element

I quoted HTML5's definition of **section** so you'd get it straight from the source. The **section** element has been the subject of a fair amount of discussion in the web community because its usage seems open to interpretation.

When considering when to use **section**, it can help to keep the "thematic grouping" part of its definition in mind. It's another reason why **section** is different than the likes of **div**. To differentiate between **section** and **article**, consider that **section** is more organizational and structural in nature, whereas **article** represents a self-contained composition.

As mentioned in Chapter 1, there isn't always a right choice and wrong choice when it comes to marking up your content—just most of the time. The other times come down to personal decisions about which HTML elements you feel best describe your content.

So think carefully when you're deciding when to use **section**, but don't wring your hands worrying about whether you get it and other elements exactly right every time. Sometimes it's a little subjective, and in any case, your page will continue to work. Plus, no one's going to come knocking at your door in the middle of the night.

Well, *I* might, but that's just because it's dark and scary outside.

Specifying an Aside

Sometimes you have a section of content that is tangentially related to the content around it but that is sufficient on its own (conceptually, if not visually) (**A** and **B**). How would you indicate the semantics for that?

A This **aside**, featuring information about Barcelona's architectural wonders, is tangentially related to the Antoni Gaudí content that's the focus of the page, but it also would work fine by itself without that context. I could have nested it within the **article** since they are related, but I decided to put it after the **article** in order to treat it visually like a sidebar with CSS **C**. The **role="complementary"** on the **aside** is optional but can improve accessibility. See the last tip for more information.

```
...
<body>
<header role="banner">
    <nav role="navigation">
        ... [ul with links] ...
    </nav>
</header>

<main role="main">
    <article>
        <h1 id="gaudi">Barcelona's Architect</h1>

    ... [rest of article] ...
    </article>
</main>

<aside role="complementary">
    <h1>Architectural Wonders of Barcelona</h1>

    <p>Barcelona is home to many architectural wonders in addition to Gaudí's work. Some of them
    → include:</p>
    <ul>
        <li lang="es">Arc de Triomf</li>
        <li>The cathedral <span lang="es">(La Seu)</span></li>
        <li lang="es">Gran Teatre del Liceu</li>
        <li lang="es">Pavilion Mies van der Rohe</li>
        <li lang="es">Santa Maria del Mar</li>
    </ul>

    <p><small>Credit: <a href="http://www.barcelona.de/en/barcelona-architecture-buildings.html"
    → rel="external"><cite>Barcelona.de</cite></a>.</small></p>
</aside>
</body>
</html>
```

Until HTML5, there was no way to do this explicitly. Now, you have the **aside** element.

Examples of **aside** include a pull quote, a sidebar , a box of links to related articles on a news site, advertising, groups of **nav** elements (for instance, a blog roll), a Twitter feed, and a list of related products on a commerce site.

Although it's common to think of an **aside** as a sidebar, you can place an **aside** element in a variety of places in your page, depending on the context. An **aside** nested within the primary content of a page (instead of placed outside as with sidebars) should be related to that content specifically, rather than to only the page on the whole. Example 1 in the sidebar "Other **aside** Examples" demonstrates this.

story and its still unfinished state, of which the everpresent scaffolding and cranes are permanent reminders.

Park Guell

The Park Guell always reminds me of Howard Roark in Ayn Rand's *The Fountainhead*. Gaudí's project in the Park Guell was to build a residential community whose residents would love where they lived. It was never finished.

Perhaps that is for the best, since now we *all* get to enjoy it. The Park Guell is set on a hill overlooking practically all of Barcelona. Its beautiful and even comfortable serpentine bench is filled with foreigners and locals alike every day of the week. Its mosaic lizards have become synonymous with the city itself.

Architectural Wonders of Barcelona

Barcelona is home to many architectural wonders in addition to Gaudí's work. Some of them include:

- Arc de Triomf
- The cathedral (La Seu)
- Gran Teatre del Liceu
- Pavilion Mies van der Rohe
- Santa Maria del Mar

Credit: *Barcelona.de*.

B The **aside** appears below the article because it follows it in the HTML itself **A**. As you can see, browsers don't apply any special formatting to an **aside** by default (except starting them on their own line). However, you have complete control over its appearance with CSS **C**.

C When you apply CSS to the finished page, you can make the **aside** (which begins with "Architectural Wonders of Barcelona") appear alongside the main content instead of below it. So in this case, you've treated the **aside** like a sidebar. (You'll learn how to do a two-column CSS layout in Chapter 11.)

To specify an aside:

1. Type **<aside>**.

2. Type the content for the **aside**, which could include any number of elements, such as paragraphs, lists, audio, video, images, figures, and more.

3. Type **</aside>**.

TIP Place sidebar content after your page's main content in the HTML A. It's better for SEO and accessibility purposes to place the most important content first. You can change the order in which they display in the browser with CSS.

TIP Use the **figure** element (see Chapter 4), not **aside**, to mark up figures that are related to and referenced from your content, such as a chart, a graph, or an inset photo with a caption.

TIP HTML5 disallows nesting an **aside** inside an **address** element.

TIP See "Improving Accessibility with ARIA" to learn how you may use **role="complementary"** with **aside**.

Other aside Examples

As mentioned, **aside** can appear within your primary content or outside it

Example 1 (nested in related primary content):

```
...
<body>
<main role="main">
    <article>
        <h1>The Diversity of Papua New Guinea</h1>
        ... [article content] ...
        <aside>
            <h2>Papua New Guinea Quick Facts</h2>
            <ul>
                <li>The country has 38 of the 43 known birds of paradise</li>
                <li>Though quite tropical in some regions, others occasionally
                → experience snowfall.</li>
                ...
            </ul>
        </aside>
    ... [more article content] ...
    </article>
</main>
</body>
</html>
```

That same story might include a pull quote from the article text. That, too, would be in an **aside**. Or it could have a "Related Stories" **aside** containing a list of links to other essays about the country. Alternatively, that **aside** could be in a different page section instead of nested in the **article** in **main**.

You've already seen one example of an **aside** in a sidebar (Ⓐ and Ⓒ). Now, let's consider an example of a design portfolio or set of case studies, in which each HTML page focuses on a single project and you provide links (nested in a **nav**) to the other project pages in an adjacent column (as controlled by CSS, not simply by virtue of arranging the code as shown in Example 2).

Other aside Examples *(continued)*

Example 2 (aside not nested in main content and containing a nav):

```
...
<body>
<main role="main">
    <article>
        <h1>... [name of project] ...</h1>
        <figure>... [project photo] ...</figure>
        <p>... [project write-up] ...</p>
    </article>
</main>


<!-- this aside is not nested in the main content -->
<aside>
    <h2>Other Projects</h2>
    <nav>
        <ul>
            <li><a href="habitat-for-humanity.html">Habitat for Humanity
            → brochure</a></li>
            <li><a href="royal-philharmonic.html">Royal Philharmonic Orchestra
            → website</a></li>

            ...

        </ul>
    </nav>
</aside>
</body>
</html>
```

This **aside** is outside the **article** because it is tangentially related to the page on the whole, but it is not about the **article** content specifically.

Creating a Footer

When you think of a footer, you probably think of a page footer—the part of a page that often contains a copyright notice and maybe links to a privacy policy and the like. HTML5's **footer** element is appropriate for that, but like **header**, it can also be used elsewhere.

The **footer** element represents a footer for the nearest **article**, **aside**, **blockquote**, **body**, **details**, **fieldset**, **figure**, **nav**, **section**, or **td** element in which it is nested. It's the footer for the *whole* page only when its nearest ancestor from that list of elements is the **body** (Ⓐ and Ⓑ).

And if a **footer** wraps *all* the content in its section (an **article**, for example), it represents the likes of an appendix, index, long colophon, or long license agreement, depending on its content.

Ⓐ This **footer** represents the footer for the whole page, since its nearest ancestor is the **body** element. Our page now has **header**, **nav**, **main**, **article**, **aside**, and **footer** elements. Not every page requires them all, but, along with **section**, they do represent the primary page constructs available in HTML.

```
...
<body>
<header role="banner">
    <nav role="navigation">
        ... [ul with links] ...
    </nav>
</header>

<main role="main">
    <article>
        <h1 id="gaudi">Barcelona's Architect
        → </h1>
        ... [rest of article] ...

        <h2 id="sagrada-familia" lang="es">
        → La Sagrada Família</h2>
         ... [image and paragraph] ...

        <h2 id="park-guell">Park Guell</h2>
        ... [another image and paragraphs] ...
    </article>
</main>

<aside role="complementary">
    <h1>Architectural Wonders of Barcelona
    → </h1>
    ... [rest of aside] ...
</aside>

<footer>
    <p><small>&copy; Copyright All About
    → Gaudí</small></p>
</footer>
</body>
</html>
```

B This footer appears at the very bottom of the page, after the `aside`. The `footer` element itself doesn't impose any formatting on the text by default. Here, the copyright notice is smaller than normal text because it's nested in a `small` element to represent legal print semantically (see Chapter 4). Like everything else, the font size can be changed with CSS.

To create a footer:

1. Place the cursor within the element for which you want to create a footer.

2. Type `<footer>`.

3. Type the contents of the footer.

4. Type `</footer>`.

TIP A `footer` typically includes information about its section, such as links to related documents, copyright information, its author, and similar items. See the first two examples in the "Other `footer` Examples" sidebar.

TIP A `footer` doesn't need to be at the end of its containing element, though usually it is.

TIP It's invalid to nest a `header` or another `footer` within a `footer`. Also, you can't nest a `footer` within a `header` or `address` element.

TIP See "Creating Generic Containers" to learn how `footer` has replaced one of the `div` element's roles from its pre-HTML5 days.

TIP See "Improving Accessibility with ARIA" to learn why to use `role="contentinfo"` on the `footer` for a whole page. It would be appropriate to include it on the `footer` in **A** because it is a page-level footer, but I omitted it to avoid giving the impression that `role="contentinfo"` is right for all `footer` elements. See "Other `footer` Examples" for an example that shows the distinction and uses the role properly.

Other footer Examples

You saw one small example of a footer for the whole page (Ⓐ and Ⓑ). Figure Ⓒ is another example of a page footer, but with more content.

Figure Ⓓ demonstrates a **footer** in the context of a page section (in this case an **article**), and a second **footer** for the whole page. (See "More **article** Examples" for an explanation of the **address** element's scope here.)

Note that only the page **footer** is given the optional (but recommended) `role="contentinfo"`. See "Improving Accessibility with ARIA" to learn more about this role.

Ⓒ The footer for a whole page often has a copyright notice and links that aren't part of the global navigation in the **header** for the whole page.

```
...
<body>
... [page header with global navigation] ...
... [page content] ...

<!-- this is a page footer because body is
→ its nearest ancestor -->
<footer role="contentinfo">
    <p><small>&copy; Copyright 2014 The
    → Corporation, Inc.</small></p>

    <ul>
        <li><a href="terms-of-use.html">
        → Terms of Use</a></li>
        <li><a href="privacy-policy.html">
        → Privacy Policy</a></li>
    </ul>
</footer>
</body>
</html>
```

Ⓓ The first **footer** is for the **article**, by virtue of being nested within it. The second **footer** is for the whole page. Use `role="contentinfo"` only on the page footer, and thus only once per page.

```
...
<body>
...
<article>
    <h1>... [article heading] ...</h1>
    <p>... [article content] ...</p>

    <!-- the article footer -->
    <footer>
        <p>Leandra Allen is a freelance
        → journalist who earned her
        → degree in anthropology from the
        → University of Copenhagen.</p>
        <address>
            You may reach her at
            → <a href="mailto:leandra@
            → therunningwriter.com">
            → leandra@therunningwriter.com
            → </a>.
        </address>
    </footer>
</article>

<!-- the page footer -->
<footer role="contentinfo">
    ... [copyright and so on] ...
</footer>
</body>
</html>
```

A I achieved this design without any **div** elements. But by adding a **div** around the whole page **B**, I now have a generic container to which I can apply more styles (see the results in **C**).

Creating Generic Containers

Sometimes you need to wrap a container around a segment of content because you want to apply some styling with CSS or maybe an effect with JavaScript. Your page just wouldn't be the same without it **A**. But maybe when you assess the content, you determine that using **article**, **section**, **aside**, **nav**, or other elements wouldn't be appropriate semantically.

continues on next page

What you really need is a generic container, one without any semantic meaning at all. That container is the **div** element (think of a "division") **B**. With a **div** in place, you can apply the desired style **C** or JavaScript to it. Be sure to read the sidebar "About **div** and When to Use It in HTML5" to learn more about when to use **div** in your pages.

C A **div** element doesn't have any of its own styling by default except that it starts on a new line **D**. However, you can apply styles to **div** to implement your designs. Here, I added the light background and a drop shadow to the **div**. That allowed me to change the **body** element's background to a red gradient so the content pops. You can see how I achieved this in the page's HTML and CSS (www.htmlcssvqs.com/8ed/structure-final).

B Now a **div** surrounds all the content. The page's semantics are unchanged, but now I have a generic container I can hook some styles onto with CSS **C**.

```
...
<body>
<div>
    <header role="banner">
        <nav role="navigation">
            ... [ul with links] ...
        </nav>
    </header>

    <main role="main">
        <article>
            <h1 id="gaudi">Barcelona's
            → Architect</h1>
            ... [rest of article] ...

            <h2 id="sagrada-familia" lang="es">
            → La Sagrada Família</h2>
            ... [image and paragraph] ...

            <h2 id="park-guell">Park Guell</h2>
            ... [another image and
            → paragraphs] ...
        </article>
    </main>

    <aside role="complementary">
        <h1>Architectural Wonders of
        → Barcelona</h1>
        ... [rest of aside] ...
    </aside>

    <footer role="contentinfo">
        <p><small>&copy; Copyright All About
        → Gaudí</small></p>
    </footer>
</div>
</body>
</html>
```

D The same page with no CSS applied to the **div**, the headings, the paragraphs, or any other element. As you can see, the **div** doesn't make anything look fancy on its own.

To create a generic container:

1. Type `<div>`.

2. Create the contents of the container, which could include any number of elements.

3. At the end of the container, type `</div>`.

TIP Like `header`, `footer`, `main`, `article`, `section`, `aside`, `nav`, `h1-h6`, `p`, and many others, `div` automatically displays on a new line by default **D**.

TIP `div` is also helpful when implementing certain interactions or effects with JavaScript. For instance, displaying a photo or dialog box in an overlay that covers the page (the overlay is typically a `div`).

TIP For all of my stressing the point that HTML describes the meaning of your content, `div` isn't the only element that has no semantic value. The `span` element is `div`'s counterpart. Whereas `div` is a semantic-less container for blocks of content, `span` (written as `<span>content is here</span>`) is one for phrases, like within a p element for paragraphs. See more about `span` in Chapter 4.

TIP See "Improving Accessibility with ARIA" to learn how you may use landmark roles with `div`.

About `div` and When to Use It in HTML5

Of the structural elements featured in this chapter, **div** is the only one besides **h1–h6** that predates HTML5. Until HTML5, **div** was the de facto choice for surrounding chunks of content such as a page's header, footer, main content, insets, and sidebars so you could style them with CSS. But **div** had no semantic meaning then, and it still doesn't today.

That's why HTML5 introduced **header**, **footer**, **main**, **article**, **section**, **aside**, and **nav**. These types of building blocks were so prevalent on webpages that they deserved their own elements *with* meaning. **div** doesn't go away in HTML5, you'll just have fewer occasions to use it than in the past.

Let's look at a couple of common instances in which **div** is the right choice.

You've seen one already: to wrap a whole page with a container for styling purposes (**B** and **C**).

How did I get the two-column layout with **div**? I applied some CSS to the **main** element to make it display as column one and to the **aside** element to make it display as column two.

Much of the time, however, each of your columns has more than one section of content. For instance, maybe you want another **article** (or **section**, or **aside**, and so on) in the main content area below the first **article**. And maybe you want an additional **aside** in the second column, say, with a list of links to other sites about Gaudí. Or perhaps you'd like yet another type of element in that column.

You'd need to group together the sidebar content in a **div** **E** and then style that **div** accordingly. (If you were thinking **section** would be an option instead, it isn't intended as a generic container for styling.) I've provided a diagram **F** to help you visualize the relationship between the code and a potential CSS layout. Keep in mind that it's just one layout possibility for this HTML; CSS is quite powerful.

So, it's very common to have a **div** around a group of content that you want to style as a column or even a module within a column. In terms of what goes *in* the **div** elements, well that can vary wildly, based on what content you want in your pages. Don't forget that, as your primary semantic containers for sections of content, **article**, **section**, **aside**, and **nav** can go nearly anywhere. As can **header** and **footer**. Don't read too much into the fact that the example (**E** and **F**) shows only **article** **element**s in the **main** content area and **aside** elements in the sidebar.

To be sure, though, **div** should be your last resort as a container due to its lack of semantic value. Most of the time, it'll be right to use **header**, **footer**, **main** (once), **article**, **section**, **aside**, and possibly **nav** instead. However, *don't* use one of those just to avoid **div** if it's not semantically appropriate to do so. **div** has its place; you just want to limit its use.

Having said that, there is a valid situation in which it is fine to use **div** for all (or most, it's up to you) containers in a page instead of the new HTML5 elements. See "Styling HTML5 Elements in Older Browsers" in Chapter 11 for more information.

```
...
<body>
<!-- Start page container -->
<div class="container">
    <header role="banner">
       ...
    </header>

    <!-- Column One when CSS applied -->
    <main role="main">
       <article>
          ...
       </article>

       <article>
          ...
       </article>

       ... [more sections as desired] ...
    </main>
    <!-- end column one -->

    <!-- Column Two when CSS applied -->
    <div class="sidebar">
       <aside role="complementary">
          ...
       </aside>

       <aside role="complementary">
          ...
       </aside>

       ... [more sections as desired] ...
    </div>
    <!-- end column two -->

    <footer role="contentinfo">
       ...
    </footer>
</div>
<!-- end page container -->
</body>
</html>
```

This diagram illustrates how the code in (minus the **role** attributes) could map to a CSS layout conceptually. It's a very common arrangement, but just one of many possibilities that CSS affords you with the same HTML. Be sure to see the next section, "Improving Accessibility with ARIA," to learn how to enhance the semantics and accessibility of your pages.

Improving Accessibility with ARIA

WAI-ARIA (Web Accessibility Initiative's Accessible Rich Internet Applications), or ARIA for short, is a specification that declares itself "a bridging technology." That is, it fills semantic gaps with attributes you can use in your pages until languages like HTML provide their own equivalent semantics.

You've likely noticed that most examples in this chapter include one or more ARIA **role** attributes, along with a note pointing you to this section to learn more. Here we go! Oh, wait. I'll get to **role** in a second, but first let's review what we know about accessibility so far.

Accessibility is about making your site's content available to all visitors. Some visitors to your sites will rely on assistive technologies such as screen readers to access your page content (see the sidebar "Trying Screen Readers").

Making your sites accessible is part of being a thoughtful, responsible citizen of the web. Plus, it's good for you—why *wouldn't* you want visitors to be able to access your content?

Fortunately, it's simple to make your pages accessible in most cases. You can improve your site's accessibility simply by marking up your content with the HTML that best describes it. So if you're already doing that, you're doing great. In this section, I'll tell you how adding a few simple attributes to your HTML can help your visitors even more.

Trying Screen Readers

The following screen readers are among the popular ones available. All but VoiceOver are for Windows.

- JAWS: Free demo version available at www.freedomscientific.com.

- NVDA: Free at www.nvda-project.org.

- VoiceOver: Free as part of OS X and iOS 4+. Type Command-F5 to start or stop it in OS X. See https://support.apple.com/kb/HT3598 to learn how to use it on iOS devices.

- Window-Eyes: Free demo version available at www.gwmicro.com.

I can't recommend strongly enough that you try at least one of these. I think you'll come away with an even greater appreciation for the screen reader user experience. Plus, you will learn first-hand how your semantic HTML choices influence that experience. Better yet, you can test your pages in a screen reader as part of your normal process of building sites.

Landmark roles

A bit ago I mentioned that ARIA fills semantic gaps in HTML. For instance, what HTML markup would you use to let a screen reader know how to jump to the footer for your whole page? Marking it with **footer** isn't sufficient—remember, your pages can contain more than one **footer**.

HTML doesn't have a solution for this—but ARIA's *landmark roles* do. Landmark roles identify a set of important webpage regions so screen reader users can navigate directly to them. Naturally, you specify them with the **role** attribute.

As **Table 3.1** illustrates, there is some overlap between ARIA and HTML5, which has also tried to fill some of the gaps with the new elements covered in this chapter. Where there is overlap, screen reader support is currently further along for ARIA. So you can continue to create HTML as you always would (including the new elements) and add ARIA roles to enhance the accessibility of your pages.

TABLE 3.1 Some of the Available ARIA Landmark Roles

Landmark Role	How and When to Use it
role="banner"	
Site oriented content [that] typically includes things such as the logo or identity of the site sponsor, and a site-specific search tool. A banner usually appears at the top of the page and typically spans the full width.	Apply it to the **header** element that contains the header for your whole page, using it only once per page.
role="navigation"	
A collection of navigational elements (usually links) for navigating the document or related documents.	This mirrors the **nav** element. Add it to each **nav** element (or alternative element if you don't use **nav**) that surrounds a major group of navigation. You can use this role more than once on each page, but just as with **nav**, don't overuse it.
role="main"	
The main content of a document.	This mirrors the **main** element. Add it to **main** (preferably) or the element you use in its place (such as a **div**). Use it once per page.
role="complementary"	
A supporting section of the document, designed to be complementary to the main content ... but that remains meaningful when separated from the main content.	This mirrors the **aside** element. Add it to an **aside** or **div** (as long as it contains complementary content only). You can include more than one **complementary** role in each page, but do not overuse it.
role="contentinfo"	
A large perceivable region that contains information about the parent document. Examples of information included in this region of the page are copyrights and links to privacy statements.	Add it to the footer for your whole page (typically a **footer** element), using it only once per page.

It's very simple to do. **Ⓐ** is the same as the example from "Creating Generic Containers" except I've added a **nav** element and highlighted the landmark roles.

Table 3.1 includes excerpts from some of the landmark role definitions found in the ARIA spec (www.w3.org/TR/wai-aria/roles#landmark_roles), along with usage recommendations. (See the first tip regarding the other three roles.) The descriptions will sound familiar because of their similarity to how you use certain HTML elements (**Ⓐ** and **Ⓑ**).

To be clear, your pages will work without ARIA landmark roles, but including them can improve the experience for users of assistive technology. For that reason, I recommend them. I've included them in some other examples throughout the book, as well as on the book site.

TIP Table 3.1 does not include three of the landmark roles. The `form` role is redundant semantically with the `form` element, `search` marks a search `form`, and `application` is for advanced use. See "Creating Email, Search, Telephone, and URL Boxes" in Chapter 16 for an example that uses `role="search"`.

Ⓐ This page uses all five landmark roles from Table 3.1 and six in all.

```
...
<body>
<!-- Start page container -->
<div class="container">
    <header role="banner">
        ...
        <nav role="navigation">
            ... [ul with links] ...
        </nav>
    </header>

    <!-- Column One when CSS applied -->
    <main role="main">
        <article>
            ...
        </article>

        <article>
            ...
        </article>

        ... [more sections as desired] ...
    </main>
    <!-- end column one -->

    <!-- Column Two when CSS applied -->
    <div class="sidebar">
        <aside role="complementary">
            ...
        </aside>

        <aside role="complementary">
            ...
        </aside>

        ... [more sections as desired] ...
    </div>
    <!-- end column two -->

    <footer role="contentinfo">
        ...
    </footer>
</div>
<!-- end page container -->
</body>
</html>
```

TIP Don't go crazy with landmark roles in your pages. Too many makes the page verbose for screen reader users, diminishing the value of the landmarks and the overall experience.

TIP Accessibility expert Steve Faulkner elaborates on landmark roles at blog.paciellogroup.com/2013/02/using-wai-aria-landmarks-2013/. (Any similarities between Table 3.1 and his table are unintentional.) He also includes a short video by fellow expert Léonie Watson that demonstrates how a screen reader user navigates a page. Recommended viewing!

TIP WebAIM periodically conducts a survey of screen reader users to better understand their preferences and challenges when visiting sites. The latest results are well worth a read: webaim.org/projects/screenreadersurvey4/.

TIP Landmark roles are just one of many features of the ARIA spec (www.w3.org/TR/wai-aria/). You may also be interested in the implementation guide at www.w3.org/WAI/PF/aria-practices/.

TIP You can use ARIA role attributes in your CSS selectors to style the elements marked with them. See Chapter 11 for details.

```
<header role="banner">
    Page header
    <nav role="navigation">
        Global navigation
    </nav>
</header>

<main role="main">
    <article>
        Main page content (article 1)
    </article>

    <article>
        Main page content (article 2)
    </article>
</main>

<div class="sidebar">
    <aside
    role="complementary">
        Related,
        but tangential
        information
    </aside>

    <aside
    role="complementary">
        More related, but
        tangential information
    </aside>
</div>

<footer role="contentinfo">
    Page Footer
</footer>
```

B This diagram is similar to the one in "Creating Generic Containers." It aims to help you visualize common uses for some landmark roles, *no*t to suggest they affect layout at all. For instance, in the **main** element, you could have local navigation in a **nav** with **role="navigation"**. Unrelated, the **div** with **class="sidebar"** could have **role="complementary"** *instead of* the **aside** elements if the entire sidebar qualifies as complementary content.

Naming Elements with a Class or ID

Although it isn't required, you can give your HTML elements a unique identifier, assign them a particular class (or classes), or both **Ⓐ**.

After doing so, you can apply styles to all elements with a given **class** name or **id** (though I discourage using **id**s for styling). Or link directly to each element with a particular **id** **Ⓐ**. Or use JavaScript to access **id** and **class** attributes to apply custom behavior to particular elements. (See the second tip.)

To name an element with a unique ID:

Within the start tag of the element, type **id="*name*"**, where *name* uniquely identifies the element **Ⓐ**. *name* can be almost anything, as long as it doesn't start with a number or contain any spaces.

To assign an element a class:

Within the start tag of the element, type **class="*name*"**, where *name* is the identifying name of the class **Ⓐ**. If you want to assign more than one class, separate each one with a space, as in **class="*name anothername*"**. (You may assign more than two class names.)

> **TIP** For information about applying styles to an element with a particular class or ID, consult "Selecting Elements by Class or ID" in Chapter 9. However, as I explain there, I recommend sticking with classes for styling.

Ⓐ The links in the **nav** point to the **id**s on the **h1** and **h2**s. Add a **class** attribute to one or more elements to be able to style them all in one fell swoop. For example, the **architect** class could be applied to content about other architects for consistent formatting. The **gaudi** class could provide additional styling for the content about him.

```
...
<body>
<div class="container">
    <header role="banner">
        <nav role="navigation">
            <ul>
                <li><a href="#gaudi">Barcelona's
                → Architect</a></li>
                <li><a href="#sagrada-familia"
                → lang="es">La Sagrada Família
                → </a></li>
                <li><a href="#park-guell">Park
                → Guell</a></li>
            </ul>
        </nav>
    </header>

    <main role="main">
        <article class="architect gaudi">
            <h1 id="gaudi">Barcelona's
            → Architect</h1>

            <p>Antoni Gaudí's incredible
            → buildings...</p>
            ...

            <h2 id="sagrada-familia" lang=
            → "es">La Sagrada Família</h2>
            ...

            <h2 id="park-guell">Park Guell
            → </h2>
            ...
        </article>
    </main>
    ...
</div>
</body>
</html>
```

TIP See "Creating and Linking to Anchors" in Chapter 6 for more details about linking to an element with an `id`. Explaining how to use JavaScript on elements with an `id` or `class` is beyond the scope of this book, but you can see an example in Chapter 19.

TIP Each `id` in an HTML document must be unique. In other words, no two elements in the same page can be named with the same `id`, and each element may have only one `id`. The same `id` can appear on multiple pages and doesn't have to be assigned to the same element each time, though it is customary to do so.

TIP Conversely, a particular `class` name can be assigned to any number of elements in a page, and an element may have more than one `class`.

TIP The `class` and `id` attributes may be added to any HTML element. An element may have both an `id` and any number of `classes`.

TIP It's customary to separate multi-word `class` and `id` names with a dash, for example, `class="footer-page"`.

TIP Choose meaningful names for your `ids` and `classes`, regardless of how you intend to use them. For instance, if you use a `class` for styling, avoid names that describe the presentation, like `class="red"`—that's a cardinal sin (get it, red, cardinal?). In all seriousness, `class="red"` is a poor choice because you might decide next week to change your site's color scheme to blue. Changing the color assigned to a `class` in CSS is incredibly simple, but then your HTML would have a `class` called red that really renders in a different color. Changing all the `class` names in your HTML usually isn't trivial. This will become more evident to you as you begin to learn CSS later.

TIP You can use the `class` attribute to implement what are known as *microformats*. See http://microformats.org to learn more.

Adding the Title Attribute to Elements

You can use the **title** attribute—not to be confused with the **title** *element*—to add a tool tip label to practically any part of your website ( **A** through **C**). They aren't just for tool tips, though. Screen readers may read title text to users, improving accessibility.

To add a title to elements in a webpage:

In the start tag of the desired HTML element, add **title="*label*"**, where *label* is the brief descriptive text that should appear as a tool tip or that will be read aloud by a screen reader.

> **TIP** Old versions of Internet Explorer (IE7 and earlier) also make tool tips out of the **alt** attribute used in **img** elements (see Chapter 5). However, if both the **title** and **alt** attributes are present in an **img** element, the tool tip is set to the contents of the **title** attribute, not the **alt** attribute.

A You can add titles to any elements you wish, though it's most common to use them on links.

```
...
<ul title="Table of Contents">
    <li><a href="#gaudi" title="Learn about
    → Antoni Gaudí">Barcelona's Architect
    → </a></li>
    <li><a href="#sagrada-familia" lang="es">
    → La Sagrada Família</a></li>
    <li><a href="#park-guell">Park Guell</a>
    → </li>
</ul>
...
</body>
</html>
```

B When your visitors point at the labeled element, the title will appear as a tool tip. If you were pointing at the Barcelona's Architect link...

C ...you'd see "Learn about Antoni Gaudí," since it has its own **title** attribute.

(A) This sample includes five comments. Four combine to mark the beginning and end of two sections of the page (main and sidebar). Another "comments out" the first paragraph so it won't be displayed in the page (if you want the paragraph to be removed long-term, it would be best to delete it from the HTML).

```
...

<!-- ==== START MAIN CONTENT ==== -->
<main role="main">
    <article class="architect">
        <h1 id="gaudi">Barcelona's Architect
        → </h1>

        <!-- This paragraph doesn't display
        → because it's commented out.
        <p>Antoni Gaudí's incredible
        → buildings bring millions of
        → tourists to Barcelona each year.
        → </p>
        -->

        <p>Gaudí's non-conformity, already
        → visible in his teenage years...</p>
        ...
    </article>
</main>
<!-- end main content -->

<!-- ==== START SIDEBAR ==== -->
... [sidebar content] ...
<!-- end sidebar -->

...
```

Adding Comments

You can add comments to your HTML documents to note where sections begin or end, to comment to yourself (or future coders) the purpose of a particular piece of code, to prevent content from displaying, and more **(A)**. These comments only appear when the document is opened with a text editor or via a browser's View Source option. They are invisible to visitors in the browser otherwise **(B)**.

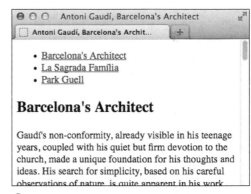

(B) Comments are invisible in the page. Similarly, if you wrap a comment around some of your content, it won't display. Here, the first paragraph in the code doesn't show.

To add a comment to your HTML:

1. In your HTML page, where you wish to insert a comment, type `<!--`.

2. Type the comments.

3. Type `-->` to complete the comment.

TIP It's common to comment the beginning and end of major sections of code to make it easier for you or fellow coders to modify later (pages can get long). I like to use a different, more prominent format for a starting comment than for one signifying the end of a block so my eye can easily distinguish between the two points as I scan the code **A**.

TIP You should view your commented page with a browser before publishing. This will help you avoid displaying your (possibly) private comments to the public because you accidentally formatted a comment wrong.

TIP Beware, however, of comments that are too private. Although invisible when visiting your page normally in the browser, they can be seen via a browser's View Source feature or if the user saves the page as HTML code.

TIP Comments may not be nested within other comments.

Text

Unless a site is heavy on videos or photo galleries, most content on webpages is text. This chapter explains which HTML semantics are appropriate for different types of text, especially (but not solely) for text within a sentence or phrase.

For example, the **em** element is specifically designed for indicating emphasized text, and the **cite** element's purpose is to cite works of art, movies, books, and more.

Browsers typically style many text elements differently than normal text. For instance, both the **em** and **cite** elements are italicized. Another element, **code**, which is specifically designed for formatting lines of code from a script or program, displays in a monospace font by default.

How content will look is irrelevant when deciding how to mark it up. So, you shouldn't use **em** or **cite** just because you want to italicize text. That's the job of CSS.

Instead, focus on choosing HTML elements that describe the content. If by default a browser styles it as you would yourself with CSS, that's a bonus. If not, just override the default formatting with your own CSS.

In This Chapter

Adding a Paragraph

HTML does not recognize the returns or other extra whitespace that you enter in your text editor. To start a new paragraph in your webpage, you use the **p** element (Ⓐ and Ⓑ).

To create a new paragraph:

1. Type **<p>**.

2. Type the contents of the new paragraph.

3. Type **</p>** to end the paragraph.

TIP You can use styles to format paragraphs (and other page text) with a particular font, size, or color (and more). For details, consult Chapter 10.

TIP To control the amount of space between lines within a paragraph, consult "Setting the Line Height" in Chapter 10. To control the amount of space before or after a paragraph, consult "Setting the Margins Around an Element" or "Adding Padding Around an Element," both of which are in Chapter 11.

TIP You can justify paragraph text or align it to the left, right, or center with CSS (see "Aligning Text" in Chapter 10).

Ⓐ Unsurprisingly, **p** is one of the most frequently used HTML elements. (Note: In practice, I would wrap an **article** around this particular content. I omitted it to make the example generic and to avoid giving the impression that **p** elements must always be nested in an **article**.)

```
...
<body>

<h1>Antoni Gaudí</h1>
<p>Many tourists are drawn to Barcelona
→ to see Antoni Gaudí's incredible
→ architecture.</p>

<p>Barcelona celebrated the 150th
→ anniversary of Gaudí's birth in
→ 2002.</p>

<h2 lang="es">La Casa Milà</h2>
<p>Gaudí's work was essentially useful.
→ <span lang="es">La Casa Milà</span> is
→ an apartment building and real people
→ live there.</p>

<h2 lang="es">La Sagrada Família</h2>
<p>The complicatedly named and curiously
→ unfinished Expiatory Temple of the
→ Sacred Family is the most visited
→ building in Barcelona.</p>

</body>
</html>
```

Ⓑ Here you see the typical default rendering of paragraphs. By default, browsers provide vertical space between headings and paragraphs, and between paragraphs themselves. As with all content elements, you have full control over the formatting with CSS.

A The **small** element denotes brief legal notices in both instances shown. The second one is a copyright notice contained in a page-level **footer**, a common convention.

```
...
<body>

<p>Order now to receive free shipping.
<small>(Some restrictions may apply.)
→ </small></p>

...

<footer role="contentinfo">
    <p><small>&copy; 2013 The Super
    → Store. All Rights Reserved.
    → </small></p>
</footer>

</body>
</html>
```

```
●●●              Specifying Fine Print
   ⬜   Specifying Fine Print          +
Order now to receive free shipping. (Some restrictions may apply.)

© 2013 The Super Store. All Rights Reserved.
```

B The **small** element may render smaller than normal text in some browsers, but the visual size is immaterial to whether you should mark up your content with it.

Specifying Fine Print

The **small** element represents side comments such as fine print, which, according to the HTML5 spec, "typically features disclaimers, caveats, legal restrictions, or copyrights. Small print is also sometimes used for attribution or for satisfying licensing requirements."

The **small** element is intended for brief portions of inline text, not for text spanning multiple paragraphs or other elements (**A** and **B**).

To specify fine print:

1. Type **<small>**.

2. Type the text that represents a legal disclaimer, note, attribution, and so on.

3. Type **</small>**.

TIP Be sure to use **small** only because it's appropriate for your content, not because you want to reduce the text size, as happens in some browsers **B**. You can always adjust the size with CSS (even making it larger if you'd like). See "Setting the Font Size" in Chapter 10 for more information.

TIP The **small** element is a common choice for marking up your page's copyright notice (**A** and **B**). It's meant for short phrases like that, so don't wrap it around long legal notices, such as your Terms of Use or Privacy Policy pages. Those should be marked up with paragraphs and other semantics, as necessary.

Marking Important and Emphasized Text

The **strong** element denotes important text, whereas **em** represents stress emphasis. You can use them individually or together, as your content requires (**A** and **B**).

To mark important text:

1. Type ****.

2. Type the text that you want to mark as important.

3. Type ****.

To emphasize text:

1. Type ****.

2. Type the text that you want to emphasize.

3. Type ****.

TIP Do not use the b and i elements as replacements for strong and em, respectively. Although they may look similar in a browser, their meanings are very different (see the sidebar "The b and i Elements: Redefined in HTML5").

TIP Just as when you emphasize words in speech, where you place em in a sentence affects its meaning. For example, `<p><em>Run</em> over here.</p>` and `<p>Run over <em>here</em>.</p>` convey different messages.

TIP The importance of strong text increases each time it's a child of another strong. The same is true of the level of emphasis for em text in another em. For example, "due by April 12th" is marked as more important semantically than the other strong text in this sentence: `<p><strong>Remember that entries are <strong>due by March 12th</strong>.</strong></p>`.

A The first sentence has both **strong** and em, whereas the second has em only.

```
...
<body>

<p><strong>Warning: Do not approach the
→ zombies <em>under any circumstances</em>
→ </strong>. They may <em>look</em>
→ friendly, but that's just because they want
→ to eat your arm.</p>

</body>
</html>
```

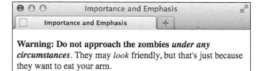

Warning: Do not approach the zombies *under any circumstances*. They may *look* friendly, but that's just because they want to eat your arm.

B Browsers typically display **strong** text in boldface and em text in italics. If em is a child of a **strong** element (see the first sentence in **A**), its text will be both italicized and bold.

TIP You can style any text as bold or italic with CSS, as well as negate the browser's default styling of elements like strong and em **B**. For details, consult "Creating Italics" and "Applying Bold Formatting" in Chapter 10.

TIP If you had experience with HTML before HTML5, you may know that at that time strong represented text with stronger emphasis than em text. In HTML5, however, em is the only element that indicates emphasis, and strong has shifted to importance.

The b and i Elements: Redefined in HTML5

HTML5 focuses on semantics, not on an element's presentation. The **b** and **i** elements are hold-overs from the earliest days of HTML, when they were used to make text bold or italic (CSS didn't exist yet). They fell out of favor in HTML 4 and XHTML 1 because of their presentational nature. Coders were encouraged to use **strong** instead of **b**, and em instead of **i**. It turns out, though, that em and **strong** are not always semantically appropriate. HTML5 addresses this by redefining **b** and **i**.

Some typographic conventions in traditional publishing fall through the cracks of available HTML semantics. Among them are italicizing certain scientific names (for example, "The *Ulmus americana* is the Massachusetts state tree."), named vehicles (for example, "We rode the *Orient Express*."), and foreign (to English) language phrases (for example, "The couple exhibited a *joie de vivre* that was infectious."). These terms aren't italicized for emphasis, just stylized per convention.

Rather than create several new semantic elements to address cases like these (and further muddy the waters), HTML5 takes a practical stance by trying to make do with what is available: em for all levels of stress emphasis, **strong** for importance, and **b** and **i** for the through-the-cracks cases. HTML5 emphasizes that you use **b** and **i** only as a last resort when another element (such as **strong**, em, **cite**, and others) won't do.

The b Element in Brief

HTML5 redefines the **b** element this way:

The **b** element represents a span of text to which attention is being drawn for utilitarian purposes without conveying any extra importance and with no implication of an alternate voice or mood, such as key words in a document abstract, product names in a review, actionable words in interactive text-driven software, or an article lede.

For example:

```
<p>The <b>XR-5</b>, also dubbed the <b>Extreme Robot 5</b>, is the best robot we've ever
→ tested.</p>
```

The **b** element renders as bold by default.

The i Element in Brief

HTML5 redefines the **i** element this way:

The **i** element represents a span of text in an alternate voice or mood, or otherwise offset from the normal prose in a manner indicating a different quality of text, such as a taxonomic designation, a technical term, an idiomatic phrase or short span of transliterated prose from another language, a thought, or a ship name in Western texts.

Here are some examples:

```
<p>The <i lang="la">Ulmus americana</i> is the Massachusetts state tree.</p>
<p>We rode the <i>Orient Express</i>.<p>
<p>The couple exhibited a <i lang="fr">joie de vivre</i> that was infectious.<p>
```

The **i** element displays in italics by default.

Creating a Figure

No doubt you've seen figures in printed newspapers, magazines, reports, and more. Typically, figures are referenced from the main text on a page (like a news story). This very book has them on most pages.

Prior to HTML5, there wasn't an element designed for this use, so developers cobbled together solutions on their own. This often involved the less-than-ideal, non-semantic **div** element. HTML5 has changed that with **figure** and **figcaption** (**A** and **B**). A **figure** element may contain a chart, a photo, a graph, an illustration, a code segment, or similar self-contained content.

You may refer to a **figure** from other content on your page (as shown in **A** and **B**), but it isn't required. The optional **figcaption** is a **figure**'s caption or legend and may appear either at the beginning or at the end of a **figure**'s content.

To create a figure and figure caption:

1. Type **<figure>**.

2. Optionally, type **<figcaption>** to begin the figure's caption.

3. Type the caption text.

4. Type **</figcaption>** if you created a caption in steps 2 and 3.

5. Create your figure by adding code for images, videos, data tables, and so on.

6. If you didn't include a **figcaption** before your **figure**'s content, optionally follow steps 2–4 to add one after the content.

7. Type **</figure>**.

A This **figure** has a chart image, though more than one image or other types of content (such as a data table or video) are allowed as well. The **figcaption** element isn't required, but it must be the first or last element in a **figure** if you do include it. A **figure** doesn't have a default styling aside from starting on its own line in modern browsers **B**. (Note: **figure**s aren't required to be in an **article**, but it's probably suitable in most cases.)

```
...
<body>
...
<article>
    <h1>2013 Revenue by Industry</h1>

    <p>... [report content] ...</p>

    <figure>
      <figcaption><b>Figure 3:</b>
    → Breakdown of Revenue by
    → Industry</figcaption>

      <img src="chart-revenue.png"
    → width="180" height="143" alt=
    → "Revenue chart: Clothing 42%,
    → Toys 36%, Food 22%" />
    </figure>

    <p>As Figure 3 illustrates, ... </p>

    <p>... [more report content] ...</p>
</article>
...
</body>
</html>
```

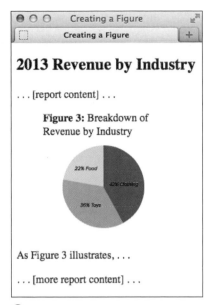

2013 Revenue by Industry

. . . [report content] . . .

Figure 3: Breakdown of
Revenue by Industry

22% Food

42% Clothing

36% Toys

As Figure 3 illustrates, . . .

. . . [more report content] . . .

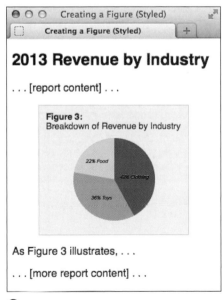

2013 Revenue by Industry

. . . [report content] . . .

Figure 3:
Breakdown of Revenue by Industry

22% Food

42% Clothing

36% Toys

As Figure 3 illustrates, . . .

. . . [more report content] . . .

Ⓐ The `figure` of the chart and caption appears within the `article` text. The figure is indented because of the browser's default styling (see the last tip).

Ⓒ You can differentiate your `figure` from the surrounding text with just a little bit of CSS. This simple example is available at www.htmlcssvqs. com/8ed/figure-styled/.

TIP Typically, `figure` is part of the content that refers to it Ⓐ, but it could also live elsewhere on the page or on another page, such as in an appendix.

TIP The `figure` element may include multiple pieces of content. For instance, Ⓐ could include two charts: one for revenue and another for profits. You can even nest one `figure` inside another one. Keep in mind, though, that regardless of how much content a `figure` has, only one `figcaption` is allowed per `figure`.

TIP Don't use `figure` simply as a means to embed all instances of self-contained bits of content within text. Oftentimes, the `aside` element may be appropriate instead (see "Specifying an Aside" in Chapter 3).

TIP See "Quoting Text" to learn how to use `figure` with a `blockquote` element.

TIP You can't use the `figcaption` element unless it's in a `figure` with other content.

TIP `figcaption` text doesn't have to begin with "Figure 3" or "Exhibit B." It could just as well be a brief description of the content, like a photo caption.

TIP Modern browsers apply left and right margins of 40px to a `figure` by default Ⓒ. You can change that with the `margin-left` and `margin-right` CSS properties. For example, `margin-left: 0;` would make the figure flush left. Also, you can make the text containing a `figure` wrap around it with `figure { float: left;}` (so the text will wrap around the right side) or `figure { float: right;}` (so the text will wrap around the left side). You may need to set a `width` to the `figure` as well so it doesn't occupy too much horizontal real estate. CSS coverage begins in Chapter 7, and the `float` and `width` properties are demonstrated in Chapter 11.

Indicating a Citation or Reference

Use the **cite** element for a citation or reference to a source. Examples include the title of a play, script, or book; the name of a song, movie, photo, or sculpture; a concert or musical tour; a specification; a newspaper or legal paper; and more (**Ⓐ** and **Ⓑ**).

To cite a reference:

1. Type **\<cite\>**.

2. Type the reference's name.

3. Type **\</cite\>**.

TIP For instances in which you are quoting from the cited source, use the **blockquote** or q elements, as appropriate, to mark up the quoted text (see "Quoting Text"). To be clear, **cite** is only for the source, not for what you are quoting from it.

Ⓐ In this example, the **cite** element marks up the titles of an album, a movie, a book, and a work of art. (Note: The **lang="it"** in the last instance declares that the language of the **cite** text is Italian.)

```
...
<body>

<p>He listened to <cite>Abbey Road</cite>
→ while watching <cite>A Hard Day's Night
→ </cite> and reading <cite>The Beatles
→ Anthology</cite>.

<p>When he went to The Louvre, he learned
→ that <cite>Mona Lisa</cite> is also
→ known as <cite lang="it">La Gioconda
→ </cite>.</p>

</body>
</html>
```

He listened to *Abbey Road* while watching *A Hard Day's Night* and reading *The Beatles Anthology*.

When he went to The Louvre, he learned that *Mona Lisa* is also known as *La Gioconda*.

Ⓑ The **cite** element renders in italics by default.

HTML5 and Using the `cite` Element for Names

Amid a good amount of disagreement from the development community, HTML5 explicitly declares that using **cite** for a reference to a person's name is invalid, even though previous versions of HTML allowed it and many developers and designers used it that way.

The HTML 4 spec provides the following example (I've changed the element names from uppercase to lowercase):

```
As <cite>Harry S. Truman</cite> said,

<q lang="en-us">The buck stops here.</q>
```

In addition to instances like that, sites have often used **cite** for the name of people who leave comments in blog postings and articles (the default WordPress theme does, too).

Many developers have made it clear that they intend to continue to use **cite** on names associated with quotes in their HTML5 pages, because they find the alternatives that HTML5 provides unacceptable (namely, the **span** and **b** elements). Jeremy Keith made the case vociferously in http://24ways.org/2009/incite-a-riot/.

```
...
<body>

<p>He especially enjoyed this selection from
→ <cite>The Adventures of Huckleberry Finn
→ </cite> by Mark Twain:</p>

<blockquote cite="http://www.
→ marktwainbooks.edu/the-adventures-of-
→ huckleberry-finn/">
        <p>We said there warn't no home like a
        → raft, after all. Other places do seem
        → so cramped up and smothery, but a
        → raft don't. You feel mighty free and
        → easy and comfortable on a raft.</p>
</blockquote>

<p>It reminded him of his own youth exploring
→ the county by river in the summertime.</p>

</body>
</html>
```

B If you'd like to provide attribution, it must be outside the **blockquote**. You could place the attribution in a **p**, but the most explicit way to associate a quote with its source is with a **figure** and **figcaption**, as shown (see "Creating a Figure").

```
...

<figure>
        <blockquote>
        I want all my senses engaged. Let
        → me absorb the world's variety and
        → uniqueness.
        </blockquote>
        <figcaption>– Maya Angelou</figcaption>
</figure>

...
```

Quoting Text

There are two special elements for marking text quoted from a source. The **blockquote** element represents a standalone quote (generally a longer one, but not necessarily) (**A** and **B**) and displays on its own line by default **C**. Meanwhile, the **q** element is for short quotes, like those within a sentence **D**.

continues on next page

He especially enjoyed this selection from *The Adventures of Huckleberry Finn* by Mark Twain:

> We said there warn't no home like a raft, after all. Other places do seem so cramped up and smothery, but a raft don't. You feel mighty free and easy and comfortable on a raft.

It reminded him of his own youth exploring the county by river in the summertime.

C Browsers typically indent **blockquote** text by default, and don't display the **cite** attribute value. (See the second tip for a related recommendation.) The **cite** element, on the other hand, is supported by all browsers and typically renders in italics, as shown. All of these defaults can be overridden with CSS.

D Here we see two **q** examples. Add the **lang** attribute to the **q** element if the quoted text is in a different language than the page's default (as specified by the **lang** attribute on the **html** element).

```
...
<body>

<p>And then she said, <q>Have you read
→ Barbara Kingsolver's <cite>High Tide in
→ Tucson</cite>? It's inspiring.</q></p>

<p>She tried again, this time in French:
→ <q lang="fr">Avez-vous lu le livre <cite
→ lang="en">High Tide in Tucson</cite> de
→ Kingsolver? C'est inspirational.</q></p>

</body>
</html>
```

Browsers are supposed to enclose **q** element text in language-specific quotation marks automatically, but the results are mixed 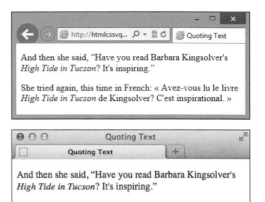. Be sure to read the tips to learn about alternatives to using the **q** element.

To quote a block of text:

1. Type `<blockquote` to begin a block quote.

2. If desired, type `cite="`*url*`"`, where *url* is the address of the source of the quote.

3. Type `>` to complete the start tag.

4. Type the text you wish to quote, surrounding it with paragraphs and other elements as appropriate.

5. Type `</blockquote>`.

To quote a short phrase:

1. Type `<q` to begin quoting a word or phrase.

2. If desired, type `cite="`*url*`"`, where *url* is the address of the source of the quote.

3. If the quote's language is different than the page's default language (as specified by the **lang** attribute on the **html** element), type `lang="`*xx*`"`, where *xx* is the code for the language the quote will be in. This code is *supposed* to determine the type of quote marks that will be used (" " for English, « » for many European languages, and so on), though browser support for this rendering can vary.

4. Type `>` to complete the start tag.

5. Type the text that should be quoted.

6. Type `</q>`.

And then she said, "Have you read Barbara Kingsolver's *High Tide in Tucson*? It's inspiring."

She tried again, this time in French: « Avez-vous lu le livre *High Tide in Tucson* de Kingsolver? C'est inspirational. »

And then she said, "Have you read Barbara Kingsolver's *High Tide in Tucson*? It's inspiring."

She tried again, this time in French: "Avez-vous lu le livre *High Tide in Tucson* de Kingsolver? C'est inspirational."

E Browsers are supposed to add language-specific quotation marks around **q** elements automatically. In this example, that means curly double quotes for English and guillemets for French. IE (shown on top) and Chrome do this correctly. Firefox (shown on bottom) is correct for English but not French. Opera and Safari do neither, rendering straight quotes instead, including for French. Inconsistencies like these limit the usefulness of the **q** element.

TIP If your blockquote contains only a single paragraph or phrase, you don't have to enclose it in a p within the blockquote.

TIP You can use the optional cite attribute on blockquote and q to provide a URL to the source you are quoting. Although historically browsers haven't displayed the cite attribute's URL **C**, in theory it can be handy for search engines or other automated tools that gather quotes and their references. If you would like visitors to have access to it, you could repeat the URL in a link (via the a element) in your content. Less effectively, you could expose cite's value via JavaScript (search online for sample code).

TIP The q element is invalid for a quote that extends beyond one paragraph. Instead, use blockquote.

TIP Be sure you don't use q simply because you want quotation marks around a word or phrase. For instance, `<p>Every time I hear the word <q>soy</q>, I jump for joy.</p>` is improper because "soy" isn't a quote from a source. In that case, simply type quotation marks around the word.

TIP You can nest blockquote and q elements. For example, `<p>The short story began, <q>When she was a child, she would say, <q>Howdy, stranger!</q> to everyone she passed.</q></p>`. Nested q elements should display the appropriate quotation marks automatically—for example, in English the outer quotes should be double and the inner ones should be single. Since outer and inner quotations are treated differently in languages, add the lang attribute to q as needed **D**. Unfortunately, browsers are inconsistent with nested q elements much like they are for non-nested ones **E**.

TIP Because of cross-browser issues with q **E**, many (most likely the majority of) coders choose to simply type the desired quotation marks or use character entities instead of the q element.

Specifying Time

You can mark up a time, date, or duration with the **time** element, which is new in HTML5. It allows you to represent this information in a variety of ways (**A** and **C**).

The text content inside **time** (that is, `<time>text</time>`) appears on the screen for us humans (**B** and **D**), whereas the value of the optional **datetime** attribute is intended for the machines among us. It requires a specific format; the sidebar "Understanding the Valid Time Format" covers the basics, and the first tip explains another case when the format is required.

To specify a time, date, or duration:

1. Type **<time** to begin a **time** element.

2. If desired, type **datetime="*time*"** where *time* is in the approved machine-readable format (see the sidebar) that represents the text you'll enter in step 4.

3. Type **>** to complete the start tag.

4. Type the text that reflects the time, the date, or the duration that you want to display in the browser. (See the first tip if you did not include **datetime** in step 2.)

5. Type **</time>**.

A As shown in the first example, the simplest form of the **time** element lacks a **datetime** attribute. But it does provide the times and date in the valid machine-readable format as required when **datetime** is omitted. The remaining examples show that the text between the **time** tags doesn't need to match the valid format when **datetime** is present (the last example shows one case of each approach).

```
...
<body>

<p>The train arrives at <time>08:45</time>
→ and <time>16:20</time> on <time>
→ 2017-03-19</time>.</p>

<p>They made their dinner reservation for
→ <time datetime="2013-11-20T18:30:00">
→ tonight at 6:30</time>.</p>

<p>We began our descent from the peak of
→ Everest on <time datetime="1952-06-12T
→ 11:05:00">June 12, 1952 at 11:05 a.m.
→ </time></p>

<p>The film festival is <time datetime=
→ "2014-07-13">July 13</time>-<time
→ datetime="2014-07-16">16</time>.</p>

<!-- Example with no year -->
<p>Her birthday is <time datetime="03-29">
→ March 29th</time>.</p>

<!-- Example of durations -->
<p>The meeting lasted <time>2h 41m 3s
→ </time> instead of the scheduled <time
→ datetime="2h 30m">two hours and thirty
→ minutes</time>.</p>

</body>
</html>
```

The train arrives at 08:45 and 16:20 on 2017-03-19.

They made their dinner reservation for tonight at 6:30.

We began our descent from the peak of Everest on June 12, 1952 at 11:05 a.m.

The film festival is July 13-16.

Her birthday is March 29th.

The meeting lasted 2h 41m 3s instead of the scheduled two hours and thirty minutes.

B Only the **time** text displays in browsers, not the **datetime** value.

C This shows how you might include a date for a blog post or news article. As is required for all cases of **datetime**, its value represents the text content in a machine-readable format.

```
...
<body>

<article>
        <h1>Cheetah and Gazelle Make Fast
        → Friends</h1>
        <p><time datetime="2014-10-15">October
        → 15, 2014</time></p>

        ... [article content] ...
</article>

</body>
</html>
```

Cheetah and Gazelle Make Fast Friends

October 15, 2014

. . . [article content] . . .

D As expected, the date is below the heading.

TIP If you omit the **datetime** attribute, the text content inside **time** must follow the machine-friendly format rather than being "free-form." In other words, the first example in **A** could not be coded as <p>The train arrives at <time>8:45 a.m.</time> and <time>4:20 p.m.</time> on <time>April 20th, 2015</time>.</p> because the **time** text doesn't follow the format in any of the three instances. However, when you do include **datetime**, you're free to represent the date, time, or duration in the text content as you wish, as seen in the other examples in **A**.

TIP The **datetime** attribute doesn't do anything on its own but could be used for syncing dates and times between web applications and the like (for example, think of a calendar application). That's why it requires a standard, machine-readable format; it allows these programs to share information by speaking the same "language."

TIP You may not nest a **time** element inside another one or place any other elements (just text) in a **time** element that lacks a **datetime** attribute.

TIP The **time** element allowed an optional attribute named **pubdate** in an earlier iteration of HTML5 (remember that the language is still evolving). However, **pubdate** is no longer part of HTML5. I mention this in case you come across it in an older tutorial or book (such as the seventh edition of this book!) and wonder if you should use it (you shouldn't).

Understanding the Valid Time Format

The **datetime** attribute—or a **time** element without **datetime**—must provide the desired date and/or time in a specific machine-readable format. I've simplified it below:

YYYY-MM-DDThh:mm:ss

For example (local time):

1985-11-03T17:19:10

This means "November 3, 1985, at 10 seconds after 5:19 p.m. local time." The hours portion uses a 24-hour clock, hence **17** instead of **05** for 5 p.m. If you include a time, the seconds are optional. (You may also provide time with milliseconds in the format of **hh:mm.sss**. Note the period before the milliseconds.)

The format is a little different when representing a duration. There are a couple of syntax options, but this is the simplest to follow:

*n*h *n*m *n*s

(Where *n* is the number of hours, minutes, and seconds, respectively.)

The last example in Ⓐ shows it in action.

Global Dates and Times and Time Zone Offsets

If you'd like, you can represent your dates and times in a global context instead of a local one. (Or simply the time by omitting the date.) Add a **Z** at the end to mark the time zone as UTC (Coordinated Universal Time), the primary global time standard. (See https://en.wikipedia.org/wiki/Coordinated_Universal_Time.)

For example (global date and time in UTC):

1985-11-03T17:19:10Z

Or, you can specify a time-zone offset from UTC by omitting **Z** and preceding the offset with **–** (minus) or **+** (plus).

For example (global date and time with offset from UTC):

1985-11-03T17:19:10-03:30

This means "November 3, 1985, at 10 seconds after 5:19 p.m. Newfoundland Standard Time (NST)," because NST is minus three and a half hours from UTC. A list of time zones by UTC offsets is available at http://en.wikipedia.org/wiki/List_of_time_zones_by_UTC_offset.

Just as a reminder, if you do include **datetime**, it doesn't require the full complement of information I just described, as the examples in Ⓐ show.

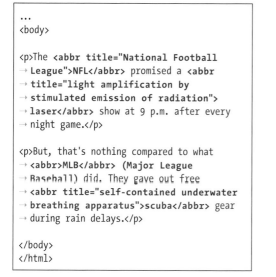

Ⓐ Use the optional **title** attribute to provide the expanded version of an abbreviation. Alternatively, and arguably preferably, you could place the expansion in parentheses after the abbreviation. Or mix and match. Most people will be familiar with words like laser and scuba, so marking them up with **abbr** and providing titles isn't really necessary, but I've done it here for demonstration purposes.

```
...
<body>

<p>The <abbr title="National Football
→ League">NFL</abbr> promised a <abbr
→ title="light amplification by
→ stimulated emission of radiation">
→ laser</abbr> show at 9 p.m. after every
→ night game.</p>

<p>But, that's nothing compared to what
→ <abbr>MLB</abbr> (Major League
→ Baseball) did. They gave out free
→ <abbr title="self-contained underwater
→ breathing apparatus">scuba</abbr> gear
→ during rain delays.</p>

</body>
</html>
```

Ⓑ When abbreviations have a **title** attribute, Firefox and Opera draw attention to them with dots underneath the text. You can instruct other browsers Ⓒ to do the same with CSS; see the tips.

Explaining Abbreviations

Abbreviations abound, whether as Jr., M.D., or even good ol' HTML. You can use the **abbr** element to mark up abbreviations and explain their meaning (Ⓐ through Ⓒ). You don't have to wrap every abbreviation in **abbr**, only when you think it would be helpful for visitors to be given the expanded meaning.

To explain abbreviations:

1. Type **<abbr**.

2. Optionally, next type **title="*expansion*"**, where *expansion* is the words represented by the abbreviation.

3. Type **>**.

4. Then type the abbreviation itself.

5. Finally, finish up with **</abbr>**.

6. Optionally, type a space and **(*expansion*)**, where *expansion* is the words represented by the abbreviation.

TIP It's common practice to include an abbreviation's expansion (by way of a **title** or a parenthetical) only the first time it appears on a page.

TIP A parenthetical abbreviation expansion is the most explicit way to describe an abbreviation, making it available to the widest set of visitors Ⓐ. For instance, users on touchscreen devices like smartphones and tablets may not be able to hover on an **abbr** element to see a **title** tool tip. So if you provide an expansion, consider putting it in parentheses whenever possible.

TIP If you use an abbreviation in its plural form, make the expansion plural as well.

continues on next page

TIP As a visual cue to sighted users, Firefox and Opera display `abbr` with a dotted bottom border if it has a `title` **B**. If you'd like to replicate that effect in other browsers, add the following to your style sheet: `abbr[title] { border-bottom: 1px dotted #000; }`. Browsers provide the `title` attribute's contents as a tool tip **C** regardless of whether the `abbr` is styled with a border.

TIP If you don't see the dotted bottom border under your `abbr`, try adjusting the parent element's CSS `line-height` property (see Chapter 10).

TIP HTML had an `acronym` element before HTML5, but coders were often confused by the difference between an abbreviation and an acronym, so HTML5 eliminated the `acronym` element in favor of `abbr` for all instances.

C Browsers display the `title` of abbreviations as a tool tip when you hover the pointer over text marked up with `abbr`. (This figure also demonstrates an example of a browser—Chrome in this case—that doesn't style abbreviations with a `title` any differently than regular text by default.)

A Note that although *pleonasm* appears twice in the example, **dfn** marks only the second one, because that's when I defined the term. Similarly, if I were to use pleonasm subsequently in the document, I wouldn't use **dfn**. Although browsers style **dfn** text differently than normal text **B**, what's important is that the term is marked up differently. Also, you don't have to use the **cite** element each time you use **dfn**, just when you reference a source.

```
...
<body>

<p>The contestant was asked to spell
→ "pleonasm." She requested the definition
→ and was told that <dfn>pleonasm</dfn>
→ means "a redundant word or expression"
→ (Ref: <cite><a href="http://dictionary.
→ reference.com/browse/pleonasm" rel=
→ "external">dictionary.com</a></cite>).</p>

</body>
</html>
```

```
●○○          Defining Instance of a Term
[  ]    Defining Instance of a Term         +

The contestant was asked to spell "pleonasm." She requested
the definition and was told that pleonasm means "a redundant
word or expression" (Ref: dictionary.com).
```

B Typically, the **dfn** element renders in italics by default, as does **cite**.

Proximity of a Term and Its Definition

The location of a term marked with **dfn** relative to the location of its definition is important. HTML5 states, "The paragraph, description list group, or section that is the nearest ancestor of the **dfn** element must also contain the definition(s) for the term given by the **dfn** element." Simplified, this means that the **dfn** and its definition should be near each other, which makes sense. This is the case in both **A** and the example given in the fourth tip; the **dfn** and its definition are in the same paragraph.

Defining a Term

In the print world, it's customary to differentiate a term visually when you define it. Typically, this is done with italics; subsequent uses of the term are not italicized.

In HTML, when you define a term, you differentiate it *semantically* with the **dfn** element. You wrap its tags only around the term you're defining, not around the definition **A**. And just as in print convention, subsequent uses of the term are not marked with **dfn**, because you aren't defining them again. (HTML refers to the point where you define a term as the "defining instance of a term.")

To mark the defining instance of a term:

1. Type **<dfn>**.
2. Type the term you wish to define.
3. Type **</dfn>**.

TIP You can also use **dfn** in a description list (the **dl** element). See "Creating Description Lists" in Chapter 15.

TIP Use **dfn** only when defining a term, not simply because you want to italicize text. CSS allows you to style any text in italics (see "Creating Italics" in Chapter 10).

TIP **dfn** may also enclose another phrasing element, like **abbr**, when appropriate. For example, **<p>A <dfn><abbr title="Junior">Jr.</abbr></dfn> is a son with the same full name as his father.</p>**.

TIP If you use the optional **title** attribute on a **dfn**, it should have the same value as the **dfn** term. If you nest a single **abbr** in **dfn** and the **dfn** has no text of its own, the optional **title** should be on the **abbr** only, as in the previous tip.

Creating Superscripts and Subscripts

Letters or numbers that are raised or lowered slightly relative to the main body text are called superscripts and subscripts, respectively **Ⓐ**. HTML includes elements for defining both kinds of text. Common uses for superscripts include marking trademark symbols, exponents, and footnotes **Ⓑ**. Subscripts are common in chemical notation.

To create superscripts or subscripts:

1. Type **<sub>** to create a subscript or **<sup>** to create a superscript.

2. Type the characters or symbols that represent the subscript or superscript.

3. Type **</sub>** or **</sup>**, depending on what you used in step 1, to complete the element.

TIP Most browsers automatically reduce the font size of sub- or superscripted text by a few points.

TIP Superscripts are the ideal way to mark up certain foreign-language abbreviations—such as M[lle] for *Mademoiselle* in French or 3[a] for tercera in Spanish—or to mark up numerics like 2nd and 5th.

TIP One proper use of subscripts is for writing out chemical molecules, such as H_2O. For example, **<p>I'm parched. Could I please have a glass of H₂O?</p>**.

TIP Super- and subscripted characters gently spoil the even spacing between lines. In **Ⓑ**, for example, notice that there is more space between lines 4 and 5 of the first paragraph and lines 2 and 3 of the second than between the other lines. CSS comes to the rescue, though; see the sidebar to learn how to fix this.

Ⓐ One use of the **sup** element is to indicate footnotes. I placed the footnotes in a **footer** within the **article** rather than in the page at large because they are associated. I also linked each footnote number within the text to its footnote in the footer so visitors can access them more easily. Note, too, that the **title** attribute on the links provides another cue.

```
...
<body>

<article>
     <h1>Famous Catalans</h1>
     <p>... Actually, Pablo Casals' real
  → name was <i>Pau</i> Casals, Pau
  → being the Catalan equivalent of Pablo
  → <a href="#footnote-1" title="Read
  → footnote 1"><sup>1</sup></a>.</p>

     <p>... Pau Casals is remembered in this
  → country for his empassioned speech
  → against nuclear proliferation at the
  → United Nations <a href="#footnote-2"
  → title="Read footnote 2"><sup>2</sup>
  → </a> ...</p>

     <footer>
          <p id="footnote-1"><sup>1</sup>It
       → means Paul in English.</p>
          <p id="footnote-2"><sup>2</sup>In
       → 1963, I believe.</p>
     </footer>
</article>

</body>
</html>
```

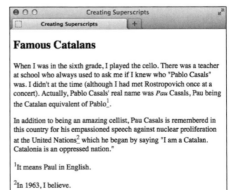

Ⓑ The **sup** elements display higher than text in the same line. In the process, unfortunately, they change the spacing between lines (see the last tip).

Fixing the Spacing Between Lines When Using sub or sup

With a little bit of CSS, you can fix the line height discrepancies caused by the **sub** and **sup** elements. The code below comes from Nicolas Gallagher and Jonathan Neal's excellent **normalize.css** (http://necolas.github.com/normalize.css/). They didn't invent the method that follows; they borrowed it from https://gist.github.com/413930, which includes a full explanation of what this CSS does, so I encourage you to give it a look.

I also recommend checking out **normalize.css**, which you can use on your own projects. It helps you achieve a consistent baseline display of elements across browsers and is documented thoroughly (see "Resetting or Normalizing Default Styles" in Chapter 11).

```
/*
 * Prevents sub and sup affecting line-height in all browsers
 * gist.github.com/413930
 */
sub,
sup {
    font-size: 75%;
    line-height: 0;
    position: relative;
    vertical-align: baseline;
}
sup {
    top: -0.5em;
}
sub {
    bottom: -0.25em;
}
```

You may need to adjust this CSS a bit to level out the line heights, depending on your content's font size, but this should give you a very good start at the least. You'll learn about creating style sheets and how to add this CSS to your site in Chapter 8.

Adding Author Contact Information

You might think the **address** element is for marking up a postal or street address, but it isn't (except for one circumstance; see the first tip). In fact, there isn't an HTML element explicitly designed for that purpose.

Instead, **address** defines the contact information for the author, people, or organization responsible for either a part of a webpage (such as a news article, product review, or report) or a whole page (**A** and **B**). Which of those is true depends on where **address** appears. The first step describes each scenario.

To provide the author's contact information:

1. If you want to provide author contact information for an **article**, place the cursor within that **article** (see the first instance in **A**). Alternatively, place the cursor within the **body** (or, more commonly, the page-level **footer**) if you want to provide author contact information for the page at large (see the second instance in **A**).

2. Type **<address>**.

3. Type the author's email address, a link to a page with contact information, and so on.

4. Type **</address>**.

A This page has two **address** elements: one for the **article**'s author and the other in a page-level **footer** for the people who maintain the whole page. Note that the **address** for the **article** contains only contact information. Although the background information about Tracey Wong is also in the **article**'s **footer**, it's outside the **address** element.

```
...
<body>
<main role="main">
<article>
    <h1>Museum Opens on the Waterfront</h1>
    <p>The new art museum not only
    → introduces a range of contemporary
    → works to the city, it's part of
    → larger development effort on the
    → waterfront.</p>

    ... [rest of story content] ...

    <!-- the article's footer with address
    → information for the article -->
    <footer>
        <p>Tracey Wong has written for
        → <cite>The Paper of Papers</cite>
        → since receiving her MFA in art
        → history three years ago.</p>
        <address>
        Email her at <a href="mailto:
        → traceyw@thepaperofpapers.com">
        → traceyw@thepaperofpapers.com
        → </a>.
        </address>
    </footer>
</article>
</main>

<!-- the page's footer with address
→ information for the whole page -->
<footer role="contentinfo">
        <p><small>&copy; 2014 The Paper of
        → Papers, Inc.</small></p>
        <address>
        Have a question or comment about the
        → site? <a href="site-feedback.html">
        → Contact our web team</a>.
        </address>
</footer>
</body>
</html>
```

The new art museum not only introduces a range of contemporary works to the city, it's part of a larger development effort on the waterfront.

. . . [rest of story content] . . .

Tracey Wong has written for *The Paper of Papers* since receiving her MFA in Art History three years ago.

Email her at traceyw@thepaperofpapers.com.

© 2014 The Paper of Papers, Inc.

Have a question or comment about the site? Contact our web team

B The **address** element renders in italics by default. (The text "The Paper of Papers" is also italicized, but it is enclosed in the **cite** element, covered in "Indicating a Citation or Reference" in this chapter.)

TIP Most of the time, contact information takes the form of the author's email address or a link to a page with more contact information. The contact information could very well be the author's postal address, in which case marking it up with address would be valid. But if you're creating the Contact Us page for your business and want to include your office locations, it would be incorrect to code those with address. The example in "Creating a Line Break" shows one way to mark up a postal or street address.

TIP The address element pertains to the nearest article it is contained in, or to the page's body if address isn't nested within an article. It's customary to place address in a footer element when noting author contact information for the page at large, like the second instance of address in **A**.

TIP An address in an article provides contact information for the author of that article **A**, not for any articles nested within that article, such as user comments.

TIP The address element may contain only author contact information, not anything else such as the document or article's last modified date **A**. Additionally, HTML5 forbids nesting any of the following elements inside address: h1–h6, article, address, aside, footer, header, hgroup, nav, and section.

TIP See Chapter 3 to learn more about the article and footer elements.

Noting Edits and Inaccurate Text

Sometimes you may want to indicate content edits that have occurred since the previous version of your page. There are two elements for noting edits: the **ins** element represents content that has been added, and the **del** element marks content that has been removed (Ⓐ through Ⓓ). You may use them together or individually.

Meanwhile, the **s** element notes content that is no longer accurate or relevant (it's not for edits) (Ⓔ and Ⓕ).

To mark newly inserted text:

1. Type **<ins>**.

2. Type the new content.

3. Type **</ins>**.

To mark deleted text:

1. Place the cursor before the text or element you wish to mark as deleted.

2. Type **<del>**.

3. Place the cursor after the text or element you wish to mark as deleted.

4. Type **</del>**.

Ⓐ One item (the bicycle) has been added to this gift list since it was previously published, and purchased items have been removed, as noted by the **del** elements. You are not required to use **del** each time you use **ins**, or vice versa. Browsers differentiate the contents of each element visually by default Ⓑ.

```
...
<body>

<h1>Charitable Gifts Wishlist</h1>

<p>Please consider donating one or more
→ of the following items to the village's
→ community center:</p>

<ul>
    <li><del>2 desks</del></li>
    <li>1 chalkboard</li>
    <li><del>4 solar-powered tablets
    → </del></li>
    <li><ins>1 bicycle</ins></li>
</ul>

</body>
</html>
```

Charitable Gifts Wishlist

Please consider donating one or more of the following items to the village's community center:

- 2 desks
- 1 chalkboard
- 4 solar-powered tablets
- 1 bicycle

Ⓑ Browsers typically display a line through deleted text, and they typically underline inserted text. You can change these treatments with CSS.

C Both **del** and **ins** are rare in that they can surround both phrasing content ("inline" content, in pre-HTML5 parlance) and blocks of content like entire paragraphs or lists, as shown here.

```
...
<body>

<h1>Charitable Gifts Wishlist</h1>
<del>
    <p>Please consider donating one or more of the following items to the village's community
    → center:</p>
</del>

<ins>
    <p>Please note that all gifts have been purchased.</p>
    <p>Thank you <em>so much</em> for your generous donations!</p>
</ins>

<del>
    <ul>
        <li><del>2 desks</del></li>
        <li>1 chalkboard</li>
        <li><del>4 solar-powered tablets</del></li>
        <li><ins>1 bicycle</ins></li>
    </ul>
</del>

</body>
</html>
```

D Just as before, browsers indicate which content has been deleted or inserted.

To mark text that is no longer accurate or relevant:

1. Place the cursor before the text you wish to mark as no longer accurate or relevant.

2. Type `<s>`.

3. Place the cursor after the text you wish to mark.

4. Type `</s>`.

TIP Both `del` and `ins` support two attributes: cite and datetime. The cite attribute (not the same as the `cite` *element*) is for providing a URL to a source that explains why an edit was made. For example, `<ins cite="http://www.movienews.com/ticket-demand-high.html">2 p.m. (this show just added!)</ins>`. Use the `datetime` attribute to indicate the time of the edit. (See "Specifying Time" to learn about `datetime`'s acceptable format.) Browsers don't display the values you assign to either of these attributes, so their use isn't widespread with `del` and `ins`, but feel free to include them to add context to your content. The values could be extracted with JavaScript or a program that parses through your page.

TIP Use `del` and `ins` anytime you want to inform your visitors of your content's evolution. For instance, you'll often see them used in a web development or design tutorial to indicate information that was learned since it was initially posted, while maintaining the copy as it originally stood for completeness. The same is true of blogs, news sites, and so on.

E This example shows an ordered list (the `ol` element) of show times. The time slots for which ticket availability is no longer relevant have been marked with the **s** element. You can use **s** around any phrases, not just around text within list items (`li` elements), but you cannot use it around a whole paragraph or other "block-level" element like you can with `del` and `ins`.

```
...
<body>

<h1>Today's Showtimes</h1>
<p>Tickets are available for the following
→ times today:</p>

<ol>
    <li><ins>2 p.m. (this show just added!)
    → </ins></li>
    <li><s>5 p.m.</s> SOLD OUT</li>
    <li><s>8:30 p.m.</s> SOLD OUT</li>
</ol>

</body>
</html>
```

Today's Showtimes

Tickets are available for the following times today:

1. 2 p.m. (this show just added!)
2. ~~5 p.m.~~ SOLD OUT
3. ~~8:30 p.m.~~ SOLD OUT

F The **s** element renders as a strikethrough by default in browsers.

TIP Text marked with the `ins` element is generally underlined by default **B**. Since links are often underlined as well (if not in your site, then in many others), this may be confusing to visitors. You may want to use CSS to change how inserted passages (or links) are displayed (see Chapter 10).

TIP Text marked with the `del` element is generally struck out **B**. Why not just erase it and be done with it? It depends on whether you think it's important to indicate what's been removed. Striking out content makes it easy for sighted users to know what has changed. (Also, screen readers could announce the content as having been removed, but their support for doing so has historically been lacking.)

TIP Only use `del`, `ins`, and `s` for their semantic value. If you wish to underline or strike out text purely for cosmetic reasons, you can do so with CSS (see "Decorating Text" in Chapter 10).

TIP HTML5 notes that "The `s` element is not appropriate when indicating document edits; to mark a span of text as having been removed from a document, use the `del` element." You may find the distinction a little subtle at times. It's up to you to decide which is the appropriate semantic choice for your content.

Marking Up Code

If your content contains code samples or file names, the **code** element is for you (Ⓐ and Ⓑ).

The examples show **code** used in a sentence. To show a standalone block of code (outside of a sentence), wrap the **code** element with a **pre** element to maintain its formatting (see "Using Preformatted Text" for an example).

To mark up code or a file name:

1. Type **\<code\>**.

2. Type the code or file name.

3. Type **\</code\>**.

> **TIP** You can change the default monospaced font applied to code Ⓑ with CSS (see Chapter 10).

> **TIP** See "A Webpage's Text Content" in Chapter 1 regarding character entities Ⓐ.

Ⓐ The **code** element indicates that the text is code or a file name. If your code needs to display **<** or **>** signs, use the **<** and **>** character entities, respectively (see the last tip). Here, the second instance of **code** demonstrates this. If you were to use **<** and **>**, the browser would treat your code as an HTML element, not as text to display.

```
...
<body>

<p>The <code>showPhoto()</code> function
→ displays the full-size photo of the
→ thumbnail in our <code>&lt;ul id=
→ "thumbnail"&gt;</code> carousel list.</p>

<p>This CSS shorthand example applies a
→ margin to all sides of paragraphs: <code>p
→ { margin: 1.25em; }</code>. Take a look
→ at <code>base.css</code> to see more
→ examples.</p>

</body>
</html>
```

```
●○○                 Marking up Code
 ☐        Marking up Code                     +
```

The showPhoto() function displays the full-size photo of the thumbnail in our <ul id="thumbnails"> carousel list.

This CSS shorthand example applies a margin to all sides of paragraphs: p { margin: 1.25em; }. Take a look at base.css to see more examples.

Ⓑ The **code** element's text even looks like code because of the monospaced default font.

Other Computer and Related Elements: kbd, samp, and var

The **kbd**, **samp**, and **var** elements see infrequent use, but you may have occasion to take advantage of them in your content.

The kbd Element

Use **kbd** to mark up user input instructions.

```
<p>To log into the demo:</p>
<ol>
    <li>Type <kbd>tryDemo</kbd> in the User Name field</li>
    <li><kbd>TAB</kbd> to the Password field and type <kbd>demoPass</kbd></li>
    <li>Hit <kbd>RETURN</kbd> or <kbd>ENTER</kbd></li>
</ol>
```

Like **code**, **kbd** renders as a monospaced font by default.

The samp Element

The **samp** element indicates sample output from a program or system.

```
<p>Once the payment went through, the site returned a message reading,
→ <samp>Thanks for your order!</samp></p>
```

samp also renders as a monospaced font by default.

The var Element

The **var** element represents a variable or placeholder value.

```
<p>Einstein is best known for <var>E</var>=<var>m</var><var>c</var><sup>2</sup>.</p>
```

var can also be a placeholder value in content, like a Mad Libs sheet in which you'd put `<var>adjective</var>`, `<var>verb</var>`, and so on.

var renders in italics by default.

Note that you can use **math** and other **MathML** elements in your HTML5 pages for advanced math-related markup. See http://dev.w3.org/html5/spec-author-view/mathml.html for more information.

Using Preformatted Text

Usually, browsers collapse all extra returns and spaces and automatically break lines of text according to the width of the browser window. Preformatted text lets you maintain and display the original line breaks and spacing that you've inserted in the text. It is ideal for computer code examples **A**, though you can also use it for text (hello, ASCII art!).

To use preformatted text:

1. Type **<pre>**.

2. Type or paste the text that you wish to display as is, with all the necessary spaces, returns, and line breaks. Unless it is code, do not mark up the text with any HTML, such as **p** elements.

3. Type **</pre>**.

A The **pre** element is ideal for text that contains important spaces and line breaks, like the bit of CSS code shown here. Note, too, the use of the **code** element to mark up pieces of code or code-related text outside of **pre** (see "Marking Up Code" for more details).

```
...
<body>

<p>Add this to your style sheet if you want
→ to display a dotted border underneath the
→ <code>abbr</code> element whenever it has
→ a <code>title</code> attribute.</p>

<pre>
    <code>
    abbr[title] {
        border-bottom: 1px dotted #000;
    }
    </code>
</pre>

</body>
</html>
```

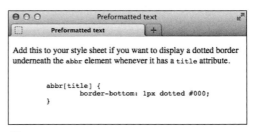

B Notice that the indentation and line breaks are maintained in the **pre** content.

Presentation Considerations with pre

Be aware that browsers typically disable automatic word wrapping of content inside a **pre**, so if the text is too wide, it might affect your layout or force a horizontal scrollbar. The following CSS rule enables wrapping within **pre** in many browsers, but not in Internet Explorer 7 and below. (In the vast majority of cases, those versions are too old to worry about.)

```
pre {

    white-space: pre-wrap;

}
```

On a related note, in most cases I don't recommend you use the **white-space: pre;** CSS declaration on an element such as **div** as a substitute for **pre**. Whitespace can be crucial to the semantics of content, especially code, and only **pre** always preserves it. (Also, if the user has disabled CSS in his or her browser, the formatting will be lost.)

Please see CSS coverage beginning in Chapter 7. Text formatting, in particular, is discussed in Chapter 10.

TIP Preformatted text is typically displayed with a monospaced font like Courier or Courier New **B**. You can use CSS to change the font, if you like (see Chapter 10).

TIP If what you want to display—such as a code sample in a tutorial—contains HTML elements, you'll have to substitute each < and > around the element name with their appropriate character entities: < and > respectively (see "Marking Up Code" for an example). Otherwise the browser may try to display those elements.

TIP Be sure to validate your pages to see if you've nested HTML elements in **pre** when you shouldn't have (see "Validating Your Code" in Chapter 20).

TIP The **pre** element isn't a shortcut for avoiding marking up your content with proper semantics and then styling the way it looks with CSS. For instance, if you want to post a news article you wrote in a word processor, don't simply copy and paste it into a **pre** because you like the spacing the way it is. Instead, wrap your content in p (and other relevant text elements) and write CSS to control the layout as desired.

TIP **pre**, like a paragraph, always displays on a new line by default **B**.

Highlighting Text

We've all used a highlighter pen at some point or another. Maybe it was when studying for an exam or going through a contract. Whatever the case, you used the highlighter to mark key words or phrases.

HTML5 replicates this with the new **mark** element. Think of **mark** as a semantic version of a highlighter pen. In other words, what's important is that you're noting certain words; how they appear isn't important. Style its text with CSS as you please (or not at all), but use **mark** only when it's pertinent to do so.

No matter when you use **mark**, it's to draw the reader's attention to a particular text segment. Here are some use cases for it:

- To highlight a search term when it appears in a search results page or an article. When people talk about **mark**, this is the most common context. Suppose you used a site's search feature to look for "solar panels." The search results or each resulting article could use `<mark>solar panels</mark>` to highlight the term throughout the text.

- To call attention to part of a quote that wasn't highlighted by the author in its original form (**A** and **B**). This is akin to the real-world task of highlighting a textbook or contract.

- To draw attention to a code fragment (**C** and **D**).

A Although **mark** may see its most widespread use in search results, here's another valid use of it. The phrase "15 minutes" was not highlighted in the instructions on the packaging. Instead, the author of this HTML used **mark** to call out the phrase as part of the story.

```
...
<body>

<p>So, I went back and read the instructions
→ myself to see what I'd done wrong. They
→ said:</p>

<blockquote>
    <p>Remove the tray from the box. Pierce
    → the overwrap several times with a
    → fork and cook on High for <mark>15
    → minutes</mark>, rotating it half way
    → through.</p>
</blockquote>

<p>I thought he'd told me <em>fifty</em>. No
→ wonder it exploded in my microwave.</p>

</body>
</html>
```

So, I went back and read the instructions myself to see what I'd done wrong. They said:

> Remove the tray from the box. Pierce the overwrap several times with a fork and cook on High for 15 minutes, rotating it half way through.

I thought he'd told me *fifty*. No wonder it exploded in my microwave.

B Browsers with native support of the **mark** element display a yellow background behind the text by default. Older browsers don't, but you can tell them to do so with a simple rule in your style sheet (see the tips).

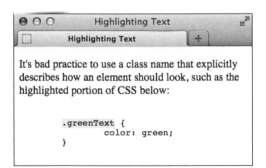
 This example uses **mark** to draw attention to a code segment.

```
...
<body>

<p>It's usually bad practice to use a class
→ name that explicitly describes how an
→ element should look, such as the
→ highlighted portion of CSS below:</p>

<pre>
    <code>
        <mark>.greenText</mark> {
            color: green;
        }
    </code>
</pre>

</body>
</html>
```

```
It's bad practice to use a class name that explicitly
describes how an element should look, such as the
highlighted portion of CSS below:

        .greenText {
                color: green;
        }
```

 The code noted with **mark** is called out.

To highlight text:

1. Type **<mark>**.

2. Type the word or words to which you want to call attention.

3. Type **</mark>**.

TIP The **mark** element is not the same as either **em** (which represents stress emphasis) or **strong** (which represents importance). Both are covered earlier in this chapter.

TIP Since **mark** is new in HTML5, older browsers don't render a background color by default. You can instruct them to do so by adding **mark { background-color: yellow; }** to your style sheet.

TIP Be sure not to use **mark** simply to give text a background color or other visual treatment. If all you're looking for is a means to style text and there's no proper semantic HTML element to contain it, use the **span** element (covered later in this chapter), perhaps with a **class** assigned to it, and style it with CSS.

Creating a Line Break

Browsers automatically wrap text according to the width of the block or window that contains content. It's best to let content flow like this in most cases, but sometimes you'll want to force a line break manually. You achieve this with the **br** element.

Using **br** is a last resort tactic because it mixes presentation with your HTML instead of leaving all display control to your CSS. For instance, never use **br** to simulate spacing between paragraphs. Instead, mark up the two paragraphs with **p** elements and define the spacing between the two with the CSS `margin` property (see the second tip).

So when might **br** be OK? Well, the **br** element is suitable for creating line breaks in poems, in a street address (Ⓐ and Ⓑ), and occasionally in other short lines of text that should appear one after another.

Ⓐ The same address appears twice, but I coded them a little differently for demonstration purposes. Remember that the returns in your code are always ignored, so both paragraphs shown display the same way Ⓑ.

```
...
<body>

<p>53 North Railway Street<br />
Okotoks, Alberta<br />
Canada T1Q 4H5</p>

<p>53 North Railway Street <br />Okotoks,
↪ Alberta <br />Canada T1Q 4H5</p>

</body>
</html>
```

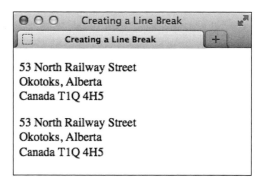

Ⓑ Each **br** element forces the subsequent content to a new line. Without them, the entire address would display on one line, unless the browser were narrow enough to force wrapping.

To insert a line break:

Type **\<br /\>** (or **\<br\>**) where the line break should occur. There is no separate end **br** tag because it's what's known as an *empty* (or *void*) *element*; it lacks content.

TIP Typing **br** as either **\<br /\>** or **\<br\>** is perfectly valid in HTML5.

TIP CSS allows you to control the space between lines in a paragraph (see "Setting the Line Height" in Chapter 10) and between the paragraphs themselves (see "Setting the Margins Around an Element" in Chapter 11).

TIP The hCard microformat (http://microformats.org/wiki/hcard) is for representing people, companies, organizations, and places in a semantic manner that's human- and machine-readable. You could use it to represent a street address instead of using the provided example **A**.

Creating Spans

The **span** element, like **div**, has absolutely no semantic meaning. The difference is that **span** is appropriate around a word or phrase only, whereas **div** is for blocks of content (see "Creating Generic Containers" in Chapter 3).

The **span** element is useful when you want to apply any of the following to a snippet of content for which HTML doesn't provide an appropriate semantic element:

- Attributes, like **class**, **dir**, **id**, **lang**, **title**, and more (**A** and **B**)
- Styling with CSS
- Behavior with JavaScript

Because **span** has no semantic meaning, use it as a last resort when no other element will do.

A In this case, I want to specify the language of a portion of text, but there isn't an HTML element whose semantics are a fit for "La Casa Milà" in the context of a sentence. The **h1** that contains "La Casa Milà" before the paragraph is appropriate semantically because the text is the heading for the content that follows. So for the heading, I simply added the **lang** attribute to the **h1** rather than wrap a **span** around the heading text unnecessarily for that purpose. (The **lang** attribute allows you to declare the language of the element's text.)

```
...
<body>

<h1 lang="es">La Casa Milà</h1>

<p>Gaudí's work was essentially useful.
→ <span lang="es">La Casa Milà</span> is
→ an apartment building and <em>real people
→ </em> live there.</p>

</body>
</html>
```

Creating Spans

La Casa Milà

Gaudí's work was essentially useful. La Casa Milà is an apartment building and *real people* live there.

B The span element has no default styling.

To add a span:

1. Type **<span**.

2. If desired, type **id="*name*"**, where *name* uniquely identifies the spanned content.

3. If desired, type **class="*name*"**, where *name* is the name of the class that the spanned content belongs to.

4. If desired, type other attributes (such as **dir**, **lang**, or **title**) and their values.

5. Type **>** to complete the start **span** tag.

6. Create the content you wish to contain in the **span**.

7. Type **</span>**.

TIP A span doesn't have default formatting **B**, but just as with other HTML elements, you can apply your own with **CSS**.

TIP You may apply both a **class** and **id** attribute to the same **span** element, although it's more common to apply one or the other, if at all. The principal difference is that **class** is for a group of elements, whereas **id** is for identifying individual, unique elements on a page.

TIP Microformats often use **span** to attach semantic class names to content as a way of filling the gaps where HTML doesn't provide a suitable semantic element. You can learn more about them at http://microformats.org.

Text **121**

Other Elements

This section covers other elements that you can include within your text, but which typically have fewer occasions to be used or have limited browser support (or both).

The u element

Like **b**, **i**, **s**, and `small`, the **u** element has been redefined in HTML5 to disassociate it from its past as a non-semantic, presentational element. In those days, the **u** element was for underlining text. Now, it's for unarticulated annotations (sounds a little befuddling, I know). HTML5 defines it thus:

> The **u** element represents a span of text with an unarticulated, though explicitly rendered, non-textual annotation, such as labeling the text as being a proper name in Chinese text (a Chinese proper name mark), or labeling the text as being misspelt.

Here is an example of how you could use **u** to note misspelled words:

```
<p>When they <u class="spelling">
→recieved</u> the package, they put
→it with <u class="spelling">there
→</u> other ones with the intention
→of opening them all later.</p>
```

The **class** is entirely optional, and its value (which can be whatever you'd like) doesn't render with the content to explicitly indicate a spelling error. But you could use it to style misspelled words differently (though **u** still renders as underlined text by default). Or you could add a **title** attribute with a note such as "[sic]"—a convention in some languages to indicate a misspelling.

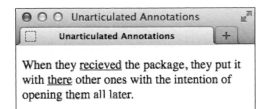

When they <u>recieved</u> the package, they put it with <u>there</u> other ones with the intention of opening them all later.

A Like links, **u** elements are underlined by default, which can cause confusion unless you change one or both with CSS.

Use **u** only when an element like **cite**, **em**, or **mark** doesn't fit your desired semantics. Also, it's best to change its styling if **u** text will be confused with linked text, which is also underlined by default **A**.

The **wbr** element

HTML5 introduces a cousin of **br** named **wbr**. It represents "a line break opportunity." Use it in between words or letters in a long, unbroken phrase (or, say, a URL) to indicate where it could wrap if necessary to fit the text in the available space in a readable fashion. So unlike **br**, **wbr** doesn't force a wrap; it just lets the browser know where it *can* force a line break if needed.

Here are a couple of examples:

```
<p>They liked to say, "FriendlyFleas
→ andFireFlies<wbr /> FriendlyFleasa
→ ndFireFlies<wbr />FriendlyFleasand
→ FireFlies<wbr />" as fast as they
→ could over and over.</p>
```

```
<p>His favorite site is this<wbr />
→ is<wbr />a<wbr />really<wbr />
→ really<wbr />longurl.com.</p>
```

You can type **wbr** as either **<wbr />** or **<wbr>**. As you might have guessed, you won't find many occasions to use **wbr**. Additionally, browser support is inconsistent as of this writing. Although **wbr** works in current versions of Chrome and Firefox, Internet Explorer and Opera simply ignore it.

The `ruby`, `rp`, and `rt` elements

A *ruby annotation* is a convention in East Asian languages, such as Chinese and Japanese, and is typically used to show the pronunciation of lesser-known characters. These small annotative characters appear either above or to the right of the characters they annotate. They are often called simply *ruby* or *rubi*, and the Japanese ruby characters are known as *furigana*.

The **ruby** element, as well as its **rt** and **rp** child elements, is HTML5's mechanism for adding them to your content. **rt** specifies the ruby characters that annotate the base characters. The optional **rp** element allows you to display parentheses around the ruby text in browsers that don't support **ruby**.

The following example demonstrates this structure with English placeholder copy to help you understand the arrangement of information both in the code and in supporting **B** and non-supporting **C** browsers. The area for ruby text is highlighted:

```
<ruby>
    base <rp>(</rp><rt>ruby chars
    → </rt><rp>)</rp>
    base <rp>(</rp><rt>ruby chars
    → </rt><rp>)</rp>
</ruby>
```

Now, a real-world example with the two Chinese base characters for "Beijing," and their accompanying ruby characters **D**:

```
<ruby>
    北 <rp>(</rp><rt>ㄅㄟˇ</rt><rp>)
    → </rp>
    京 <rp>(</rp><rt>ㄐㄧㄥ</rt><rp>)
    → </rp>
</ruby>
```

B A supporting browser will display the ruby text above the base (or possibly on the side) without parentheses because it ignores the **rp** elements.

> base (ruby chars) base (ruby chars)

C A non-supporting browser displays the **rt** content in parentheses in the normal flow of content.

ㄅㄟˇ ㄐㄧㄥ
北 京

D Now, the ruby markup for "Beijing" as seen in a supporting browser.

北(ㄅㄟ)京(ㄐㄧㄥ)

You can see how important the parentheses are for browsers that don't support **ruby** **E**. Without them, the base and ruby text would run together, clouding the message.

TIP At the time of this writing, Firefox and Opera lack basic **ruby** support (all the more reason to use **rp** in your markup). The Firefox add-on HTML Ruby (https://addons.mozilla.org/en-US/firefox/addon/html-ruby/) provides support for Firefox in the meantime.

TIP You can learn more about ruby characters at http://en.wikipedia.org/wiki/Ruby_character.

The **bdi** and **bdo** elements

If your HTML pages ever mix left-to-right characters (like Latin characters in most languages) and right-to-left characters (like characters in Arabic or Hebrew), the **bdi** and **bdo** elements may be of interest.

But first, a little backstory. The base directionality of your content defaults to left-to-right unless you set the **dir** attribute on the **html** element to **rtl**. For instance, **<html dir="rtl" lang="he">** specifies that the base directionality of your content is right-to-left and that the base language is Hebrew.

Just as I've done with **lang** in several examples throughout the book, you may also set **dir** on elements within the page when the content deviates from the page's base setting. So if the base were set to English (**<html lang="en">**) and you wanted to include a paragraph in Hebrew, you'd mark it up as **<p dir="rtl" lang="he">...</p>**.

With those settings in place, the content will display in the desired directionality most of the time; Unicode's bidirectional ("bidi") algorithm takes care of figuring it out.

The **bdo** ("bidirectional override") element is for those occasions when the algorithm *doesn't* display the content as intended, and you need to override it. Typically, that's the case when the content in the HTML source is in visual order instead of logical order.

Visual order is just what it sounds like—the HTML source code content is in the same order in which you want it displayed. *Logical order* is the opposite for a right-to-left language like Hebrew; the first character going right to left is typed first, then the second character (in other words, the one to the left of it), and so on.

In line with best practices, Unicode expects bidirectional text in logical order. So if it's visual instead, the algorithm will still reverse the characters, displaying them opposite of what is intended. If you aren't able to change the text in the HTML source to logical order (for instance, maybe it's coming from a database or a feed), your only recourse is to wrap it in a **bdo**.

To use **bdo**, you must include the `dir` attribute and set it to either `ltr` (left-to-right) or `rtl` (right-to-left) to specify the direction you want. Continuing our earlier example of a Hebrew paragraph within an otherwise English page, you would type `<p lang="he"><bdo dir="rtl">...</bdo></p>`. The **bdo** element is appropriate for phrases or sentences within a paragraph. You wouldn't wrap it around several paragraphs.

The **bdi** element, new in HTML5, is for cases when the content's directionality is unknown. You don't have to include the **dir** attribute, because it's set to auto by default. HTML5 provides the following example, which I've modified slightly:

> This element is especially useful when embedding user-generated content with an unknown directionality.

In this example, usernames are shown along with the number of posts that the user has submitted. If the **bdi** element were not used, the username of the Arabic user would end up confusing the text (the bidirectional algorithm would put the colon and the number "3" next to the word "User" rather than next to the word "posts").

```
<ul>
    <li>User <bdi>jcranmer</bdi>:
    → 12 posts.</li>
    <li>User <bdi>hober</bdi>:
    → 5 posts.</li>
    <li>User <bdi>ايان</bdi>:
    → 3 posts.</li>
</ul>
```

TIP If you want to learn more on the subject of incorporating right-to-left languages, I recommend reading the W3C's article "Creating HTML Pages in Arabic, Hebrew, and Other Right-to-Left Scripts" (www.w3.org/International/tutorials/bidi-xhtml/).

The meter element

The **meter** element is another that is new thanks to HTML5. At first glance, it seems very similar to the **progress** element, covered next, which is for indicating "the completion progress of a task" (to quote the spec).

In contrast, you can use **meter** to indicate a fractional value or a measurement within a known range. In plain language, it's the type of gauge you use for the likes of voting results (for example, "30% Smith, 37% Garcia, 33% Hawkins"), the number of tickets sold (for example, "811 out of 850"), a numerical test grade (for example, "91 out of 100"), and disk usage (for example, "74 GB out of 256 GB").

HTML5 suggests (but doesn't require) that browsers could render a **meter** not unlike a thermometer on its side—a horizontal bar with the measured value colored differently than the maximum value (unless they're the same, of course). Firefox, one of the browsers that supports **meter** so far, does just that 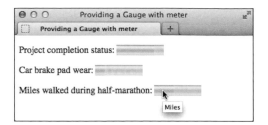. For non-supporting browsers, you can style **meter** to some extent with CSS or enhance it further with JavaScript.

Although it's not required, it's best to include text inside **meter** that reflects the current measurement for non-supporting browsers to display **G**.

Here are some **meter** examples (as seen in **F** and **G**):

```
<p>Project completion status: <meter
→ value="0.80">80% completed</meter>
→ </p>

<p>Car brake pad wear: <meter low=
→ "0.25" high="0.75" optimum="0"
→ value="0.21">21% worn</meter></p>

<p>Miles walked during half-marathon:
→ <meter min="0" max="13.1" value="5.5"
→ title="Miles">4.5</meter></p>
```

F A browser, like Firefox, that supports **meter** displays the gauge automatically, coloring it based on the attribute values. It doesn't display the text in between **<meter>** and **</meter>**. As seen in the last example, if you include **title** text, it displays when you hover over the meter.

G IE9 doesn't support **meter**, so instead of a colored bar, it displays the text content inside the **meter** element. You can change the look with CSS.

The meter element doesn't have defined units of measure, but you can use the title attribute to specify text of your choosing, as in the last example. As is usual with title text, browsers display it as a tooltip **F**.

TIP meter supports several attributes. The value attribute is the only one that's required. The min and max attributes default to 0 and 1.0, respectively, if omitted. The low, high, and optimum attributes work together to split the range into low, medium, and high segments. The number assigned to optimum indicates the optimum position within the range, such as "0 brake pad wear" in one of the examples. Set optimum in between if neither a low nor a high value is optimal.

TIP At the time of this writing, browser support of meter is still evolving: It's not supported by Internet Explorer, mobile Safari (iOS devices), or Android's browser. This partially explains why you don't yet see it much in the wild. Feel free to use it, but just understand that these browsers will render the meter text rather than the visual gauge by default **G**. See http://caniuse.com/#feat=progressmeter for the latest browser support.

TIP The style of the gauge that each supporting browser displays may vary.

TIP Some people have experimented with styling meter CSS for both supporting and non-supporting browsers. Search online for "style HTML5 meter with CSS" to see some of the results (note that some use JavaScript).

TIP The meter element is not for marking up general measurements—such as height, weight, distance, or circumference—that have no known range. For example, you cannot use it for the following because the number of miles walked isn't gauged against a range: `<p>I walked <meter value="4.5">4.5 </meter> miles yesterday.</p>`.

TIP Be sure not to mix up your uses of the meter and progress elements.

The progress element

The **progress** element is yet another of the new elements in HTML5. As stated earlier, it indicates the completion progress of a task. Think of a progress bar, like the kind you might see in a web application to indicate progress while it is saving or loading a large amount of data.

As with **meter**, supporting browsers automatically display a progress bar based on the values of the attributes 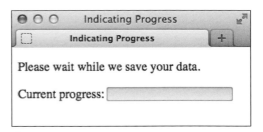. And again like **meter**, it's usually best to include text (for example, "0% saved," as shown in the example) inside **progress** to reflect the current progress for older browsers to display ❶, even though it's not required.

Here's an example:

```
<p>Please wait while we save your
→ data.</p>

<p>Current progress: <progress
→ max="100" value="0">0% saved
→ </progress></p>
```

A full discussion of **progress** is beyond the scope of this book, since typically you would dynamically update both the **value** attribute and the inner text with JavaScript as the task progresses (for example, to indicate that it's 37% completed). The visual results are the same whether you do that with JavaScript or code it that way in the HTML initially; for example, `<progress max="100" value="37">37% saved</progress>` ❶. Of course, non-supporting browsers would display it similarly to ❶.

❶ A browser, like Firefox, that supports **progress** displays the progress bar automatically, coloring it based on the value. It doesn't display the text in between **<progress>** and **</progress>**. The **value** attribute is set to **0** in this example, so the bar indicates no progress.

❶ IE9 doesn't support **progress**, so instead of a colored bar, it displays the text content inside the element. You can change the look with CSS.

❶ The **progress** bar in Firefox when the **value** attribute is set to **37** programmatically with JavaScript (or directly in the HTML), assuming **max="100"**. The blue area reflects the amount of progress.

TIP The `progress` element supports three attributes, all of which are optional: `max`, `value`, and `form`. The `max` attribute specifies the total amount of work for the task and must be greater than 0. The `value` attribute specifies the amount completed relative to the task. Assign the `form` attribute to the `id` of a `form` element on the page if you want to associate the `progress` element with a `form` it isn't nested within.

TIP Here's a small taste of how to modify a `progress` element with JavaScript. Let's assume that the element had been coded with an `id` of your choosing, like this:

```
<progress max="100" value="0" id=
→ "progressBar">0% saved</progress>
```

JavaScript such as the following would give you access to the element:

```
var bar = document.getElementById
→ ('progressBar');
```

Then you could get or set the value via `bar.value` as needed. For example, `bar.value = 37;` would set it to 37, and the appearance of the `progress` element would change accordingly.

TIP The `progress` element is supported by the most current version of all desktop browsers as of this writing. IE9 and prior, mobile Safari, and Android browsers don't support it. See http://caniuse.com/#feat=progressmeter for the latest support information.

TIP The style of the `progress` bar that each supporting browser displays may vary, though you can style it yourself to some extent with CSS.

Images

Creating images for the web is a bit different from creating images for output on paper. Although the basic characteristics of web images and printable images are the same, six main factors distinguish them: format, download speed, color, size (dimensions), transparency, and animation.

This chapter will discuss the important aspects of these six factors and explain how to use that knowledge to create effective images for your website. You'll also learn how to insert images on a webpage.

In This Chapter

Images for the Web

Let's look at the six factors you should keep in mind as you create web images. If you're in a hurry or want to avoid the details, you can skip to "Summary" at the end of this section.

Format and download speed

People who print images on paper don't have to worry about what their readers will use to look at the images. And their readers don't have to wait for images to appear when they turn a page in a magazine or newspaper. It's a different story on the web.

The web is accessed every day by millions of Macs, Windows-based PCs, Linux machines, phones, tablets, and other kinds of devices. The graphics you use in your webpage should be in a format that any of these devices can recognize. Currently, the three formats that are most widely supported by browsers are JPEG, PNG, and GIF. Your goal is to choose a format that gives you the best quality with the smallest file size for each image.

🅐 Full-color photographs are typically saved in the JPEG format. PNG-24 also works but usually results in much larger files.

TABLE 5.1 Comparison of Image Formats

Format	Usage	Colors	Index (Basic) Transparency	Alpha Transparency
JPEG	Most photos and other images with many colors when some loss of fidelity is acceptable.	16 million +	-	-
PNG-8	Logos, patterns, and other graphics with fewer or continuous colors.	256	Y	Y
PNG-24	The same as PNG-8 but for images with more colors. Some color-rich graphics or photos when no loss of clarity is crucial.	16 million +	Y	-
PNG-32	The same as PNG-24 but for images with alpha transparency.	16 million +	-	Y
GIF	Similar usage as PNG-8, but use PNG-8 instead in most cases.	256	Y	-

JPEG

The JPEG format is great for color photographs because it handles large amounts of color and compresses well, reducing your file sizes **Ⓐ**. When an image's file size is smaller—regardless of the format—it downloads faster, so your visitors don't have to wait as long to view it.

However, JPEG is a *lossy* format, meaning you lose some of the image's original clarity when you save it as a JPEG. Usually this is a worthy compromise, because you can choose a difference in quality that isn't very noticeable yet still make your pages load more quickly.

Be aware that uncompressing a JPEG will not restore the lost image details. So if you plan to edit the image in the future, you should keep a copy in an uncompressed format (for example, PSD or TIFF) and only save it as a JPEG after you have made your final edits.

PNG and GIF

PNG and GIF are *lossless* formats, so they can compress your images without losing quality. GIF is limited to 256 colors, but PNG can support millions. Unlike JPEG, PNG and GIF both support transparency and are better for saving non-photographic graphics. Images that have large areas of a single color, like logos, patterns, illustrations, and rendered text are the best candidates.

You may use PNG for photos, but because the image quality isn't altered, the file sizes will be (often considerably) larger than JPEG. So typically you'll use PNG for photos only if it's essential that the image not have any artifacts introduced by compression.

PNG has a few flavors: PNG-8, PNG-24, and PNG-32. PNG is usually preferred over GIF, partly because it has superior transparency support and a better compression algorithm for smaller file sizes.

See **Table 5.1** for a quick comparison of all formats, including the PNG variations. "Saving Your Images" contains examples of images with various compression settings and formats.

The WebP Image Format

Google has created another image format, named WebP. This format supports both lossy and lossless compression and can result in significant file-size savings over JPEG and PNG. It also features alpha transparency, like PNG.

WebP is still evolving, and browser support is limited at the time of this writing: Chrome, Opera 12+, and some Android browsers are the only ones with full support, and it's uncertain if other browsers will adopt it. But it is worth keeping an eye on its progress, and before long there may be a way to deliver WebP images to supporting browsers while other browsers fall back to one of the other formats. You can learn more about WebP at https://developers.google.com/speed/webp/, and you can track the latest browser support at http://caniuse.com/#search=webp.

Color

Most computer monitors can display millions of colors, but this wasn't always the case. Some image formats have a limited color palette. GIF and PNG-8 images can have only 256 colors, which is often fine for icons and logos .

JPEG, PNG-24, and PNG-32 all support more than 16 million colors, which is why they represent photographs and complex illustrations well. But, as noted, you'll use JPEG in most cases for these types of images.

Size (dimensions)

Have you ever been emailed a photo that looks enormous on your screen? Chances are it was taken with a digital camera and whoever sent it to you didn't reduce the size before emailing it. But why was it so large to begin with, and how large should images be for your websites?

Digital images are measured in pixels. Nowadays, digital cameras in excess of 8 megapixels are common, but let's consider a 3-megapixel capability as an example. A 3-megapixel digital camera can take pictures that are 2048 pixels wide by 1536 pixels high. How big is that in a browser? It depends on your display, but in most cases, *much* too big , just like when viewed in your email.

B Logos and other graphics with few colors are often saved in the PNG-8 format (or its less desirable counterpart, GIF).

C This image is 2048 pixels wide and 1536 pixels tall, which means scrolling both vertically and horizontally is required to see the rest of it. Blech. Not to mention that the file size is enormous, so it takes a long time for the image to display. Talk about not seeing the forest for the trees (ba dum-bum).

Yellowstone National Park's multi-colored pools seem like they are from another planet.

D Behold, there's more to our image after all! I reduced the size to make it easy to see all of it (see "Scaling Images with an Image Editor"). This version is 400 pixels wide and 300 pixels high, maintaining the 4:3 aspect ratio of the original image so it's not distorted. As you will learn in Chapter 12, it's possible to control the width and height of your images with CSS to shrink or expand them for optimal viewing on everything from mobile phones to big screens.

So how large should images be for your website? The short answer is that, generally speaking, you should keep your images to within a few hundred pixels wide at most **D**. The larger the image size, the larger the file size, and the slower your webpages will load. Choosing your image sizes is about finding a balance. Plus, as we've seen, if your images are really large, visitors may need to scroll horizontally to see the full width **C**.

Of course, your image's dimensions will vary depending on its purpose. Icons will naturally be small. Logos, a little bigger. Photos, usually bigger still. And sometimes you'll want to make a big impact with an image that occupies the full width of your site's content or beyond. Those are often a maximum of about 960 pixels wide.

Lastly, images typically print smaller than they appear on a display. Printers print more dots per inch (dpi) than most displays have pixels per inch (ppi). The screen resolution of your display plays into this, too. That's why the same image can look much larger on a monitor or laptop than on paper.

Scalable Vector Graphics (SVG)

The SVG graphics language allows you to create graphics that can scale up or down without compromising quality (and more). Also, the file size is consistent for a particular SVG graphic no matter how large or small you display it in a page. You can include SVG in your webpages; gradually, we're seeing more of that, because all modern browsers provide basic support. However, IE8 does not. You can use the JavaScript libraries SVG Web (http://code.google.com/p/svgweb/) or Raphaël (http://raphaeljs.com/) to realize similar effects in IE8. See "Coupling video with SVG" in Chapter 17 for more information about SVG in general and using it with HTML video in particular.

Transparency

You can take advantage of transparency to give an image a non-rectangular outline, allowing it to blend in with a background color or texture behind the image. Both PNG and GIF allow transparency; JPEG does not.

In the GIF format, a pixel can be transparent or not. This is known as *index transparency*. PNG supports both index transparency and *alpha transparency*, the latter of which allows you to control the degree to which a pixel is transparent. In other words, a pixel can be partially transparent—it's not all or nothing. This means that images with transparency look better as a PNG **E** than as a GIF no matter what kind of background is behind them—the edges appear smooth instead of jagged.

PNG-8 supports both index and alpha transparencies, but you'll need a program like Fireworks to save an alpha PNG-8. Photoshop doesn't support alpha transparency for PNG-8, but it does support it for PNG-32. (See the "Photoshop, PNG-24, and PNG-32" sidebar.) This is one reason why most transparent PNGs on the web are PNG-32.

In short, use PNG-8 or PNG-32 for transparent images. The latter is required if your image has more than 256 colors.

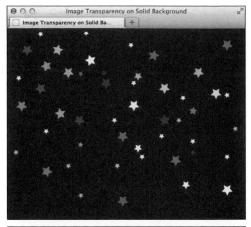

E Neither the solid blue background nor the black-to-red gradient background is part of the stars PNG image. Instead, they are colors I applied to the **body** of the pages with CSS. The stars image has alpha transparency, which allows the background to show through and look "clean" no matter what is in the background (colors, gradients, another image, or text). You cannot do this with a JPEG, and GIF supports a simpler form of transparency that doesn't look good except on solid backgrounds.

Photoshop, PNG-24, and PNG-32

PNG-24 and PNG-32 are essentially the same except the latter supports alpha transparency. Just to keep things interesting, Photoshop refers to both PNG-24 and PNG-32 as PNG-24, so it's common to think PNG-24 has alpha transparency. In truth, when you select the Transparency option for a PNG-24 in Photoshop, it creates a PNG-32 behind the scenes.

But it's probably safe to say that most people don't know this. Many haven't even heard of PNG-32. As a result, the term "PNG-24" is often used when speaking of alpha transparent images, even though it isn't technically accurate.

Animation

Animated images can be saved as GIFs but not as JPEGs or PNGs. Even so, using an image for animation is becoming increasingly uncommon. (Notable exceptions are the popular and often funny animated GIFs that get circulated in places like Tumblr.) Nowadays, animation is generally created using CSS Animations, JavaScript, HTML5 Canvas, SVG (the dark horse of the bunch), and Flash. In recent years, the use of Flash for animations on the web has declined significantly. Primarily, this is due to iOS's lack of Flash support and the increasing capabilities of, and browser support for, the other standard web technologies.

Summary

Let's review the key takeaways for working with images for the web:

- Save most photographs in the JPEG format; save most images that have fewer colors, like logos and icons, in the PNG format.

- Create alpha transparent images with PNG-8 or PNG-32 (often incorrectly referred to as PNG-24).

- Reasonable image sizes (dimensions) make your image file sizes smaller. Keep your image file sizes as small as possible to minimize the load time of your pages.

Getting Images

So how do you get an image that you can use for your webpage? You can buy or download ready-made images, use a digital camera, digitize traditional photographs or hand-drawn images with a scanner, or draw images from scratch in an image editing program like Adobe Photoshop. Once you've got them in your computer, you can adapt them for use on the web by saving them in one of the formats discussed earlier.

To get images:

- Use a search engine to find images on the web. Select the Images link in the top navigation bar, and enter search criteria as usual. Be aware that, generally, even free images found on the web are restricted in one form or another (see the "Creative Commons Licenses" sidebar). Images you buy can usually be used for any purpose (except reselling the images themselves). Read any disclaimers or licenses carefully.

- Many companies sell stock photography and images for a very reasonable price. They often have several versions of each image for different purposes and resolutions.

- Digital cameras (including those in smartphones) are probably the most popular way to create your own images.

Creative Commons Licenses

CreativeCommons.org is a non-profit organization that has developed a system of copyright templates that let artists share their work in specified ways without giving up all rights over their work. Website designers, musicians, and photographers are some of the many artists who use Creative Commons licenses to get their work out in the marketplace without fear that it will be used in a way they don't agree with.

Flickr, the popular photo-sharing web application (www.flickr.com), asks its users to designate a Creative Commons license for each photo they upload. Flickr then lets visitors search for photos according to the licenses assigned to them. It can be a great place to find photos for your website.

You can also use Google to restrict searches based on usage rights. (Go to www.google.com/advanced_search and then choose the desired option from the Usage Rights drop-down menu near the bottom.)

Alternatives to Photoshop and Fireworks

You aren't limited to using either Photoshop or Fireworks to create your images. Some of the alternatives include the following:

- Gimp
  (Linux or OS X: www.gimp.org;
  Windows: http://gimp-win.source
  forge.net/stable.html) free
- Acorn
  (OS X; http://flyingmeat.com/acorn/)
- Pixelmator
  (OS X; www.pixelmator.com)
- Paint.NET
  (Windows; www.getpaint.net) free
- PaintShop Pro
  (Windows; www.corel.com)

Each has its own way of working with images, so your decision is just a matter of personal preference.

Choosing an Image Editor

There are many, many different software programs that you can use to create and save images for the web. Most modern image editors have special tools for creating web images, which take into account the factors discussed earlier in this chapter.

The industry standard is no doubt Adobe Photoshop (www.adobe.com). Adobe Fireworks also has a dedicated following. Both programs are available for OS X and Windows, although in the spring of 2013, Adobe announced they will continue to sell Fireworks but won't be adding new features—something to consider before making a purchase. There are many alternatives to Photoshop and Fireworks (and much cheaper ones at that); see the sidebar.

All of them are capable of at least the most common tasks related to preparing images for a website, such as resizing, cropping, adjusting colors, applying effects, and optimizing. There are free trial versions available for the ones that aren't free. OS X comes with a very basic image editor named Preview. You can find others by searching online for "image editors."

Let me stress, however, that the basic strategies for optimizing images for the web are the same regardless of the software you choose. The command names may be slightly different and there may be more or fewer steps, but the ideas remain the same.

Saving Your Images

Now that you have your images, it's time to save them. This process is a balancing act between the visual quality of the image and its file size.

You can use a trial version of Photoshop if you don't have the software installed on your computer.

Adobe Photoshop

Photoshop offers the Save for Web command on the File menu. It lets you visually compare the original image with up to three versions that you can optimize while keeping an eye on any resulting savings in file size and download time.

To use Photoshop's Save for Web command:

1. Open Photoshop and create your image. Or open an existing image, and prepare it for publishing by cropping, sizing, and editing it as desired.

2. Choose File > Save for Web. (This was named Save for Web & Devices in earlier versions.) The Save for Web dialog appears **Ⓐ**.

3. Click the Optimized tab to see one optimized version, click the 2-Up tab to see one optimized version next to the original, or click the 4-Up tab to see three next to the original **Ⓑ**.

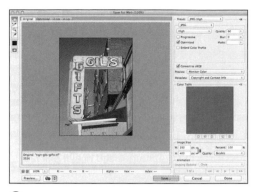

Ⓐ The Save for Web dialog defaults to the Original tab, showing the original image.

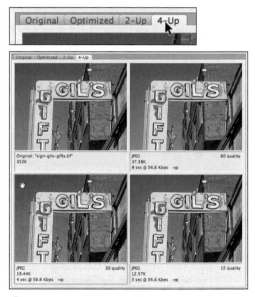

Ⓑ By selecting the 4-Up tab (top), you can compare the original to three versions with optimization settings of your choosing. I've selected the lower-left square so I can change its settings **Ⓒ**.

4. Click an optimized version, if necessary **B**.

5. Choose the desired format **C**.

In general, images that have been created on a computer—including logos, charts, graphs, line art, and any graphic with large areas of a single color and sharp detail—should be saved in PNG-8 format.

Images like photographs, should be saved in either JPEG or (sometimes) PNG-24 format.

6. Adjust the additional settings that appear until you get the smallest file possible with an acceptable quality **D**.

continues on next page

C The right side of the Save for Web dialog has controls for changing the optimization settings. Select an image format from the drop-down menu (top) and then specify a quality by either typing directly in the Quality box or dragging the slider (bottom). The higher the number, the better the quality but the larger the file size. (Alternatively, choose a preset such as "Very High" from the drop-down menu to the left of Quality.) Although JPEG is usually the best choice for photographs, large sections of a color (like the blue sky in this photo) can appear a little smudgy if you set the quality too low

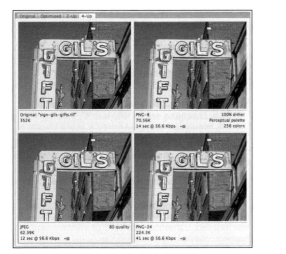

D My changes are reflected in the lower-left square. If I were to save it, it would be 62.39K now as opposed to the 19.44K it was in **B**, but the improved sharpness is worth it in this case. I've changed the settings for the other two squares as well. The PNG-8 (upper right) compression pixelates the photograph in spots, plus the file size (70.56K) is larger than the JPEG. The PNG-24 (lower right) offers a high-quality image but at a much larger file size (224.3K). Clearly, JPEG is the best choice for this photo.

7. Click Save. Choose a directory, and name the new file. It will automatically carry the extension of the selected format (and thus normally will not replace the original image).

The steps are the same for outputting PNG images (**E** and **F**).

TIP Images should be created in RGB, not CMYK (which is for print).

TIP There is no single right or wrong setting when it comes to optimizing and outputting an image. Just remember that your main objective is to get the smallest file size possible while maintaining acceptable image quality.

TIP Various tools are available for shrinking your image file sizes further even after optimizing them with an image editor. Some, like ImageOptim (http://imageoptim.com, OS X only) and JPEGmini (www.jpegmini.com), run on your machine, whereas others, like www.smushit.com, are web-based. Search online for "image optimization tools" to find others. I encourage you to use one of them.

TIP If you're not sure which format to choose, compare two optimizations and see which format compresses better. Also, not all image editors generate optimized images of the same file size.

TIP The Save for Web command creates a new image and leaves the original image intact—unless you save the new image with the same name and extension, and in the same folder, as the old.

TIP PSDs (Photoshop documents) allow you to design parts of your image on different layers that you can turn on or off. Typically, only an image's visible layers are saved in the optimized version. Fireworks allows you to save additional data in a PNG so it can have layers. Note that Photoshop cannot show those layers.

E This image (I've zoomed in) has a lot of flat color, as well as text, that should be kept sharp. Note that the PNG-8 format (lower left) compresses the image the best, to just over 5.5K. Reducing the number of colors would make it even smaller. PNG-24, with more colors available, is 11.17K. JPEG at maximum quality is 19.76k. If you cut the JPEG quality to 50 (not shown), it's slightly smaller than PNG-8 but looks terrible.

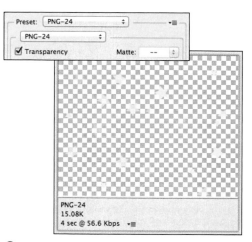

F Choose PNG-24 with Transparency selected (top) to save an image with alpha transparency, like our stars image (bottom) from earlier in the chapter. Other image editors might label this choice as PNG-32. (Note: You have to give the image transparent areas prior to opening Save for Web.)

A The URL for this image—since it contains only the file name and no folder name before it—indicates that the image is located in the same folder as this webpage. See the first tip regarding how to reference the image if it is in a different folder.

```
...
<body>
<h1>Barcelona's Market</h1>

<img src="corner-market.jpg" />

<p>This first picture shows one of the fruit
→ stands in the <span lang="es">Mercat de la
→ Boquería</span>, the central market that
→ is just off the Rambles. It's an incredible
→ place, full of every kind of food you
→ might happen to need. It took me a long
→ time to get up the nerve to actually take
→ a picture there. You might say I'm kind
→ of a chicken, but since I lived there,
→ it was just sort of strange. Do you take
→ pictures of your supermarket?</p>
</body>
</html>
```

Inserting Images on a Page

You can place all kinds of images on your webpage, from logos to photographs. Images placed in your HTML as described here A appear automatically when the visitor goes to your page B. However, the time it takes for each image to appear depends on the strength of your visitor's Internet connection, the file size of the images, and how many images your page contains.

To insert an image on a page:

1. Place the cursor in the HTML code where you want the image to appear.

2. Type `<img src="image.url"`, where `image.url` indicates the location of the image file on the server.

3. Type a space and then the final `>` or `/>` (either is fine in HTML5).

continues on next page

Barcelona's Market

Barcelona's Market

The Mercat de la Boquería is the central market that is just off the Rambles. It's an incredible place, full of every kind of food you might happen to need. It took me a long time to get up the nerve to actually

B By default, images are aligned to the left side of the page to match the alignment of the text. You can change the alignment or wrap text around an image by using CSS properties such as **float** (see "Making Elements Float" in Chapter 11).

TIP The example in **A** shows the simplest form of an image path: just the file name. However, it's common practice to store your images in their own folder to keep your files organized. The `src` URL in your `img` tags needs to reflect this. Suppose the webpage in **A** were located in a folder that itself contains a folder named `images`. Assuming the market image is in `images`, the HTML for displaying it would be `<img src="images/corner-market.jpg" />`. See "URLs" in Chapter 1 for more information about how to reference files.

TIP Images must be uploaded to a web server before visitors will be able to see them. You upload them the same way you do HTML, CSS, JavaScript, and other files. See "Transferring Files to the Server" in Chapter 21.

TIP Don't expect your visitors to wait very long for your page to load so they can view it. Test it (keeping in mind that you may have a faster connection than your visitors). If you can't wait, they won't either. If your page has a lot of images or even a few very large ones, one alternative is to create miniatures (*thumbnails*) of large images and let visitors choose to view the larger images through a link. See "Creating Other Kinds of Links" in Chapter 6 to learn how to do this. Charles (www.charlesproxy.com) and Fiddler (http://fiddler2.com) are two good tools for simulating slower connections.

TIP You can apply a border to images with the CSS `border` shorthand property (and related properties), covered in Chapter 11. Older browsers add a border to linked images automatically. You can remove it with `img { border: none; }` in your CSS.

A I referenced an image (`market.jpg`) that doesn't exist in my site to demonstrate the effect of including **alt** text **B**.

```
...
<body>
<h1>Barcelona's Market</h1>

<img src="market.jpg" alt="Oranges,
 bananas, apples, and other fruit abound
 at the Mercat de la Boquería." />

<p>The <span lang="es">Mercat de la Boquería
 </span> is the central market that is just
 off the Rambles. It's an incredible place,
 full of every kind of food you might
 happen to need....</p>
</body>
</html>
```

B In Internet Explorer 10, the **alt** text appears alongside an icon in a box. In other browsers, like Firefox and Opera, the **alt** text appears alone. In Chrome and Safari, a missing-image icon displays instead of the **alt** text.

Offering Alternative Text

With the **alt** attribute, you can add text that will appear if the image, for whatever reason, does not appear. Screen readers may also read this text aloud, helping visually impaired visitors understand the content of the image in a different manner. The HTML5 spec encourages you to think of **alt** text as a replacement for the image: "In general, alternative text can be written by considering what one would have written had one not been able to include the image." Usually, this means writing **alt** text that works in the flow of the surrounding text; it is not meant for describing the image in most cases.

To offer alternative text when images don't appear:

1. Within the **img** tag, after the **src** attribute and value, type **alt="**.

2. Type the text that should act as a replacement for the image (**A** and **B**).

3. Type **"**.

continues on next page

TIP The HTML5 spec contains an extensive discussion with examples of how to use alt effectively in a variety of scenarios (www.w3.org/TR/html5/embedded-content-0.html#alt). I encourage you to take a look.

TIP If the image does not add value to the content and thus is not particularly useful to nonvisual users, provide blank alternative text with alt="". Images with nearby text that communicate similar information as the image can have blank alt text as well. (You could make an argument that the example in Ⓐ fits this criterion, especially if the paragraph mentioned the type of fruit.)

TIP Do not place an image's caption in the alt text. Instead, consider including the img in a figure and with a figcaption. "Creating a Figure" in Chapter 4 has an example.

TIP If an image is part of your page design instead of being content, include it in your page with the CSS background-image property instead of an img tag. See "Setting the Background" in Chapter 10 to learn how.

Why Images Might Not Appear

An image may not appear for a variety of reasons. Perhaps you coded the wrong URL in the **src** attribute Ⓐ or you forgot to upload the image to the web server. Other reasons are beyond your control. For example, your visitor might have a poor connection. Also, did you know you can instruct your browser not to load images? Most browsers contain a setting in a preferences menu to toggle image loading. Typically, a visitor would do this to speed up pages (try it some time!) or, in the case of a mobile or tablet browser, to prevent eating into their data plan limit by downloading images. Not all devices allow this.

Specifying Image Sizes

(A) Right-click the image in the browser to make the menu appear. The browser will offer a way to inspect the image, show its properties, or get the dimensions.

Type:	JPEG Image
Size:	Unknown (not cached)
Dimensions:	300px × 399px

(B) A box appears (its appearance varies depending on the browser you're using) that shows the size of the image in pixels.

Sometimes when you load a webpage, you see the text first, and then when the images load a few moments later, the text jumps around to accommodate them. This happens because the size of the image is not specified in the HTML. It is more likely to happen on older browsers or when a visitor's connection is slow.

If you specify the image's dimensions in your code, the browser will reserve the space and can fill in the text around the image as the image loads, so that your layout will remain stable as your page loads.

You can use either your browser or your image editing program to get the exact dimensions of your image.

To find the size of your image with your browser:

1. Right-click the image. A context menu appears **(A)**.

2. Choose Properties or View Image Info (depending on your browser). A box appears that shows the dimensions of your image in pixels **(B)**.

To find the size of your image with Photoshop:

1. Open the image in Photoshop.

2. Choose Image > Image Size **C**.
   The Image Size dialog displays **D**.

To specify the size of your image in HTML:

1. Determine the size of your image using one of the techniques described in "To find the size of your image with your browser" or "To find the size of your image with Photoshop."

2. Within the **img** tag, after the **src** attribute, type **width="x" height="y"**, using the values you found in step 1 to specify the values for **x** and **y** (the width and height of your image) in pixels **E**.

C In Photoshop, choose Image Size from the Image menu.

D The Image Size dialog box indicates this image is 300 x 399 pixels. (You can change the size with this dialog box. Make sure you have selected Pixels from the drop-down menu next to either Width or Height. Then type in a new Width value. The Height will change automatically to maintain the image's proportions. See the last tip for more.)

E It's common to specify the width and height in the HTML to save the browser the work of determining the dimensions. One case in which you should omit **width** and **height** attributes is when displaying responsive images, as discussed in Chapter 12 ("Making Images Flexible").

```
...
<body>
<h1>Barcelona's Market</h1>

<img src="corner-market.jpg" width="300"
→ height="399" alt="Oranges, bananas, apples,
→ and other fruit abound at the Mercat de la
→ Boquería." />

<p>The <span lang="es">Mercat de la Boquería
→ </span> is the central market that is just
→ off the Rambles. It's an incredible place
→ ...</p>

</body>
</html>
```

TIP The **width** and **height** attributes don't necessarily have to reflect the actual size of the image.

TIP If you have several images that are the same size, you can set their height and width all at the same time with CSS. Of course, you can do it for a single image too.

TIP You can also find the size of an image in a browser by opening the image in its own window **F**.

TIP In Photoshop, you can select the entire image and then view the Info panel for the image's dimensions.

TIP If you use the Image Size dialog **D** to change an image's size, make sure the Resample check box is selected. The Resolution check box is irrelevant for web images. See "Scaling Images with an Image Editor" for another way to change an image's size in Photoshop.

F If you drag and drop or open an image directly in a browser, its dimensions are displayed in the title bar.

Scaling Images with the Browser

You can change the display size of an image just by specifying a new height and width in pixels (Ⓐ through Ⓒ). This can help provide sharper images to visitors using Retina displays while presenting the image at the same size in all displays. See the sidebar "Creating and Sizing Images for Retina Displays" for details.

To scale an image with the browser:

1. Type **<img src="*image.url*"**, where *image.url* is the location on the server of the image.

2. Type **width="*x*" height="*y*"** where *x* and *y* are the desired width and height, respectively, in pixels, of your image.

3. Add any other image attributes as desired, and then type the final **/>**.

> **TIP** With Retina images as a noted exception, using the **width** and **height** attributes is a quick and dirty way to change how the image displays on a webpage. Since the file itself is not changed, the visitor always gets cheated—reduced images take longer to load than images that are really that size; enlarged images lose sharpness. A better solution is to use your image editor to change the size of the image.

> **TIP** Thomas Fuchs (http://retinafy.me) and Daan Jobsis (http://blog.netvlies.nl/design-interactie/retina-revolution/) discuss an interesting technique for creating images for Retina and similar displays while keeping the file sizes reasonable: Double the image size, but use a high compression setting (or in Photoshop terms, a *low* Quality setting). When you display the image at half its size, most artifacts resulting from the high compression aren't perceptible. Results vary depending on an image's content.

Ⓐ I intend to display this image at half the size (220 x 170 pixels) in a page, but I created it at double the size (440 x 340 pixels) to improve its sharpness on Retina displays and others with high pixel density. (The black outline is from the browser, not the image itself.)

Ⓑ I've set the **width** and **height** to half their respective sizes in the image. The aspect ratio remains the same, ensuring the image won't look distorted.

```
...
<figure>
    <img src="stupas.jpg" alt="Two Stupas"
    → width="220" height="170" alt="" />

    <figcaption>These stupas in Yunnan,
    → China, are Buddhist monuments used as
    → a place for worship.</figcaption>
</figure>
...
```

These stupas in Yunnan, China, are Buddhist monuments used as a place for worship.

Ⓒ The image appears at half its original size. It's important to note, however, that it takes the same time to load as before. After all, it's the same file.

Creating and Sizing Images for Retina Displays

You've likely heard the term *Retina display* associated with some of Apple's iPhones, iPads, and MacBooks. What is it?

Well, imagine you make a painting using only dots of paint, like Claude Monet or George Seurat. Now imagine you do the same painting on the *same size* canvas, but with four dots for every one dot in the first painting. The second painting would be more detailed, and it would be harder to see the individual dots.

Apple's Retina display is similar to that second painting. It has four times as many pixels in the same amount of space **D** as in an otherwise comparable normal display, resulting in sharper images. Or, in more technical terms, it has more pixels per inch (PPI), or greater *pixel density*. There are also other displays with high pixel density besides Apple's.

There is a catch. In some cases, images need to be made with the Retina display and similar displays in mind, otherwise they might look a little blurry in a browser. If you don't care about why that happens, here's all you need to know to avoid it: Double the size of your images, but display them at half that size.

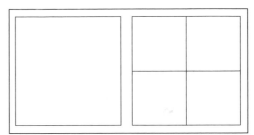

D This diagram might help you visualize that Retina displays (right) fit four pixels in the space used by one pixel on most displays (left). This isn't to scale; actual pixels are much smaller, as I'm sure you know.

For example, if you want your image to be 40×30 on all displays (not just Retina), create it at 80×60 and code the dimensions at the desired display size: `<img src="photo.jpg" width="40" height="30" alt="" />`. Browsers will shrink the 80×60 image down and show it at 40×30. (Figures **A** through **C** demonstrate this approach with different dimensions.)

Here's why that works. At 4800 total pixels (80×60), the image has four times as many pixels as the desired size (1200, which is 40×30). This gives the Retina display the extra pixels it needs to render a sharp image. If you use a 40×30 image instead, Retina displays will stretch those pixels to fill the space, which reduces the sharpness. How obvious this is varies from one image to the next.

Although it's up to you, coders and designers often don't double the resolution of every image on a site. If the images are particularly important—like on a photographer's portfolio site, for instance—then, yes, it's highly recommended. The file sizes may be larger—see the second tip for a possible way to avoid this—and keep in mind that double-resolution images consume much more memory on devices. (Primarily an issue for mobile devices.) Testing on at least one mobile device is recommended.

Icon fonts and SVG

Icon fonts and SVG scale without losing fidelity. I recommend you use an icon font instead of an image for single-color icons whenever possible. (See "Where to Find Web Fonts" in Chapter 13.) For logos and other non-photographic images, you may want to consider using SVG. (See the sidebar about SVG in "Images for the Web.")

Scaling Images with an Image Editor

Most images are too big for a webpage. While an image destined for print might measure 1800 pixels across (to print at 300 dpi and be six inches wide), images for webpages should rarely be wider than 600 pixels or so, and are typically much smaller.

You can scale images down or up from their original size with an image editor. However, an image that is scaled up usually doesn't look as sharp and can look downright awful. Also, it will increase the image's file size and your page's load time.

To scale an image with Photoshop:

1. In the lower-right portion of the Save for Web window, click the W (Width) box or the H (Height) box in the Image Size section 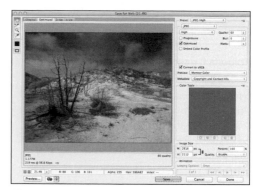.

2. Enter a new width or height in pixels, or a percentage, and then press the Tab key to resize the image **B**.

3. You can continue to adjust the size up or down until you're satisfied. The image is not resampled until you press Save.

TIP You can also change the size of an image before you Save for Web by using the Image Size command under the Image menu item. See Figures **C** and **D** in "Specifying Image Sizes."

TIP Another great way to reduce the size of an image is to crop out unwanted areas.

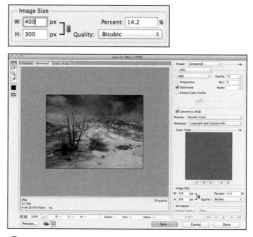

A The original photograph, snapped with a digital camera's default settings, measured 2816 by 2112 pixels, which (besides being far too big for a typical webpage) weighed in at a whopping 1.177MB when compressed as a high-quality JPEG! Using that would be a surefire way to see your visitors scurrying for another website.

B Type the new width, such as 400 pixels, in the W field (top). The height value in the H field will change proportionally. The reduced image (bottom) will fit properly in a webpage and, by changing the compression settings, the file size is dropped to a friendly 37.75k.

(A) The favicon is typically shown in tabs (as it is here), among other places within the browser. Internet Explorer is the only one that shows it in the address bar, before the URL. Because the browser often displays your icon over gray or other colors, you may want to make your icon's background transparent **(B)**.

(B) Favicons, in real life, are small: a measly 16×16 pixels at their smallest.

(C) The `apple-touch-icon` is used when you add your website to the home screen of iOS devices from mobile Safari.

Adding Icons for Your Website

The small icon (associated with a website) that you see in browser tabs **(A)**, history, bookmarks, favorites, and address bars is known as a *favicon*, which is short for favorites icon. At a minimum, you should create a 16×16 icon (all icon sizes are in pixels). If you don't, browsers will try to load it anyway.

You can also create one or more icons— commonly dubbed *touch icons*—that will display when a site is added to the home screens of Apple and other touch devices. Apple's specified sizes are 57×57 and 114×114 (Retina) for iPhone and iPod touch, and 72×72 and 144×144 (Retina) for iPad. The Android operating system supports these icons as well.

To add an icon for your website:

1. Create a 16×16 image, and save it in the ICO format as `favicon.ico` **(B)**. Optionally, include a 32×32 image for Retina displays. ICO files allow more than one size in the same file.

2. (Recommended) Create at least one image for touch devices **(C)**. Save it in the PNG format, and if you create only one, name it `apple-touch-icon.png`. Create additional touch favicons as desired.

4. Place the icon images at the root of your website. Browsers look for those specific file names at the root automatically.

continues on next page

TIP X-Icon Editor (http://xiconeditor.com) is one of many ICO-format editors available. There are Photoshop plug-ins available, too (search online for these).

TIP It is possible to put your icons in a location other than the root, although you will need to add `link` elements to your HTML so browsers can locate them. See the resources in the sidebar for more details.

TIP HTML5 Boilerplate (h5bp.com) comes with a good example of the various touch icon sizes.

More About Favicons

See www.netmagazine.com/features/create-perfect-favicon for more about creating favicons. (Note that some of its information is out of date.) Thomas Fuchs covers favicons at http://davidwalsh.name/retina-favicons.

6

Links

Links are the lifeblood of the web. Without them, every webpage would just exist on its own, completely disconnected from all the others. That makes for sad webpages.

A link has two main parts: a destination and a label. You use the *destination* to specify what will happen when the visitor triggers the link. You can create links that go to another page or website, jump within a page, show an image, download files, prompt a phone call, and more. The most common links, however, connect to other webpages, and sometimes to specific locations on webpages, which are called *anchors*. Destinations are defined by writing a URL and are generally visible to the visitor only in the browser's status bar (on desktop browsers).

The second part of the link is the *label*, the part the visitor sees in a webpage or hears in a screen reader. It is the part you interact with to reach the link's destination. For instance, a link on an airline site might be labeled Book a Flight. A label can be text, an image, or both. Browsers typically show label text as underlined and in blue by default. It's easy to change this with CSS.

In This Chapter

Creating a Link to Another Webpage (and Other Link Basics)

The **a** element is your key to creating links **Ⓐ**. If you have more than one webpage, you will probably want to create links from one page to the next (**Ⓑ** through **Ⓓ**) and possibly back again. You can also link to pages on other sites, whether they are your own or someone else's (**Ⓔ** through **Ⓖ**).

To create a link to another webpage:

1. Type `<a href="page.html">`, where *page.html* is the URL of the destination webpage.

2. Type the label text; that is, the text that is usually blue and underlined by default **Ⓒ** and that when triggered will take the user to the page referenced in step 1. Alternatively (or in addition to label text), add an `img` element as the label. (See "Creating Other Kinds of Links" and the sidebar "Linking Thumbnail Images.")

3. Type `</a>` to complete the definition of the link.

Navigating Links with a Keyboard

You may navigate through a webpage with the keyboard. In fact, some people do so out of necessity because they lack the motor skills to use devices like a mouse.

Each time you press Tab, the focus shifts to the next (or, with Shift-Tab, previous) link, form control, or image map link as it appears *in the HTML code*. This is not necessarily the same as where it appears onscreen, because a page's CSS layout may arrange items differently. HTML's `tabindex` attribute allows you to change the tabbing sequence, but I discourage you from using it, because it's unnecessary in most instances and can present accessibility issues. Namely, screen reader users may become disoriented. ("Effects with Generated Content" in Chapter 14 shows a use of `tabindex` that is helpful.)

Instead, take care to mark up your content so the tabbing sequence is logical. Test this by tabbing through your own pages to see how you like it as a user, and adjust the HTML accordingly. (Note that this might be disabled if you are on a Mac. Search online for "Enabling keyboard navigation in OS X browsers" if you want to turn it on.)

The **a** element

`<a href="cats.html">Cookie and Woody</a>`

Link destination   Link label

Ⓐ Each link has a destination (indicated by the **href** attribute) and a label. The label is text in this example, but it can be (or include) an image.

B Since there is only a file name (and no domain or directories) referenced in the **href** attribute, the file **pioneer-valley.html** must be in the same directory as the page that contains the link to it. Otherwise, the browser won't be able to find **pioneer-valley.html** when the user activates the link.

```
...
<body>

<h1>Cookie and Woody</h1>
<img src="img/cookie.jpg" width="143" height="131" alt="Cookie" />

<img src="img/woody.jpg" width="202" height="131" alt="Woody" />

<p>Generally considered the sweetest and yet most independent cats in the <a href="pioneer-valley.
→ html">Pioneer Valley</a>, Cookie and Woody are consistently underestimated by their humble
→ humans.</p>

</body>
</html>
```

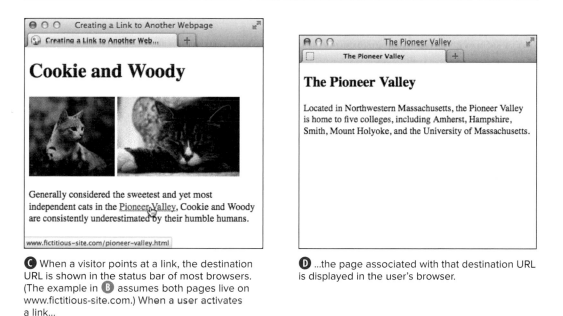

C When a visitor points at a link, the destination URL is shown in the status bar of most browsers. (The example in **B** assumes both pages live on www.fictitious-site.com.) When a user activates a link...

D ...the page associated with that destination URL is displayed in the user's browser.

You can link to a page at another site too. For example, **`<a href="http://www.site.com/directory/page.html" rel="external">Label text</a>`** (E) through (G). Replace the **`href`** value with the URL of the destination. The **`rel`** attribute is optional, since the link works the same without it, but I recommend including it for links that point to another website. It describes the relationship between the page containing the link and the page to which you're linking, and it is yet another way of improving the semantics of your HTML. Search engines may leverage the information too. Additionally, as a cue to visitors, you could style links with **`rel="external"`** differently than links that point within your site. (See "Selecting Elements Based on Attributes" in Chapter 9.)

(E) If you're creating links to someone else's website, you'll have to use an absolute URL, with the **`http://`**, host, and (if necessary) full path. Like **`rel`**, the **`title`** attribute is optional. (See Chapter 4 to learn about the **`cite`** element.)

```
...
<body>

<h1>The Glory of Cats</h1>

<p><a href="http://en.wikipedia.org/wiki/
→ Cat" rel="external" title="Cat entry
→ on Wikipedia">Cats</a> are wonderful
→ companions. Whether it's a bottle cap,
→ long string, or your legs, they always
→ find something to chase around.</p>

<p>In fact, cats are so great they even have
→ <a href="http://www.catsthemusical.com"
→ rel="external" title="Official site of
→ Andrew Lloyd Webber's musical">their own
→ musical</a>. It was inspired by T.S. Eliot's
→ <cite>Old Possum's Book of Practical Cats
→ </cite>.</p>

</body>
</html>
```

(F) Just as with a link to a page within your site, when a visitor points at a link to another site, the destination URL is shown in the status bar and the **`title`** text, if specified, displays near the link. When the visitor activates a link...

(G) ...the page associated with that destination URL is displayed in the visitor's browser.

(H) We've all probably visited sites with story snippets that link to a full article. This is a good use of a block-level link if you want to link both the snippet and the prompt (like "Read more") to the story page. You can style the link with CSS so that not all (or none) of the text is underlined.

```
...
<a href="giraffe-escapes.html">
    <p>A giraffe escaped from the zoo today,
    → and animals rejoiced worldwide.</p>
    <p>Read more</p>
</a>

... [more headlines] ...
```

(I) Don't go overboard. Avoid doing what is shown here, which is to wrap a link around a large chunk of content. Although the link will work and it's valid HTML5, a screen reader may read all the content more than once, and even that much content once is more link information than a visitor typically wants to hear. It's better to narrow the focus of your link to the most relevant content.

```
...
<body>
<a href="pioneer-valley.html">
    <h1>Cookie and Woody</h1>
    <img src="img/cookiefora.jpg" width=
    → "143" height="131" alt="Cookie" />

    <img src="img/woodygran.jpg" width="202"
    → height="131" alt="Woody" />

    <p>Generally considered the sweetest
    → and yet most independent cats in the
    → Pioneer Valley, Cookie and Woody are
    → consistently underestimated by their
    → humble humans.</p>
</a>
...
</body>
</html>
```

Linking blocks of content

So far, I've shown you examples of links around brief text phrases within an element. But HTML5 allows wrapping a link *around* nearly any kind of element or group of elements **(H)**. Examples include paragraphs, lists, entire articles—pretty much anything except interactive content such as other links, audio, video, form elements, `iframes`, and so on. (Most of these were known as block-level elements prior to HTML5.) Testing your pages in an HTML validator (see "Validating Your Code" in Chapter 20) will reveal when you've wrapped a link around an element that isn't allowed.

These *block-level* links, as they often are called unofficially, are a big departure from previous versions of HTML, which only allowed linking images, text phrases, and elements that mark up text phrases (such as `em`, `strong`, and `cite`).

The funny thing is that although block-level links were disallowed in the previous HTML specifications, browsers supported them anyway. This means you can use them now and they'll work in all browsers, both new and old. But use them with care (**(H)** and **(I)**).

There are some accessibility concerns to consider, particularly pertaining to how different screen readers treat block-level links. Two articles, by accessibility experts Derek Featherstone and Steve Faulkner, respectively, discuss the issues in more depth: http://simplyaccessible.com/article/html5-block-links/ and http://blog.pacellogroup.com/2011/06/html5-accessibility-chops-block-links/. They advise putting the most pertinent content at the beginning of a link and not putting too much content in one link. As Featherstone notes, the accessibility issues are likely temporary as screen readers and browsers catch up with supporting block-level links.

Most of the time, you'll want to stick with the simpler, traditional style of link **A**, but know that smartly crafted block-level links are available to you as well.

TIP You can change the default styling of the label text (see "Selecting Links Based on Their State" in Chapter 9) or even use an image as a label (see "Creating Other Kinds of Links" in this chapter).

TIP `href` stands for hypertext reference. As a general rule, use relative URLs for links to webpages on your site, and use absolute URLs for links to webpages on other sites. For more details, consult "URLs" in Chapter 1.

TIP Omit the file name from the path to link to the default file for a directory, which is typically index.html: `http://www.site.com/directory/`. Omit the path entirely to link to a site's default (home) page: `http://www.site.com`.

TIP Use all lowercase letters for your URLs unless you're pointing to a page or directory name that has uppercase letters. (For your own sites, name all folders and files in lowercase and match your link URLs accordingly.) See "File Names" in Chapter 1 for more information.

TIP Don't make the link's label too long. If the link is part of a sentence, use only the key words as the label within the link.

TIP Whatever you do, avoid using "click here" as a label. This type of linked text is unfortunately all too common on the web, and it's bad for usability, for accessibility, and for you as a site owner. When users quickly scan links on a page (whether visually or via a screen reader), "click here" lacks context ("Click here? Why?"). There's little incentive to trigger the link, and it relies on the visitor reading the link's surrounding text in hopes that it will explain the link's purpose. Understandably, your visitor is probably more likely to skip it. Also, the word "click" doesn't always apply to how users activate links. Instead, identify the link by using the key words that already exist in your text. For example, "Learn about our sale" instead of "Click here to learn about our sale."

TIP This is getting ahead of ourselves a bit, but if you'd like to apply style properties such as `background`, `border`, `margin`, or `padding` to a block-level link, you may also have to set `display: block` on the link in your style sheet. See "Controlling the Display Type and Visibility of Elements" in Chapter 11 concerning the CSS `display` property.

TIP Although used rarely, image maps allow you to add a link to one or more regions of a single image. You can learn more about them by searching online for "HTML image maps."

TIP An ever-evolving list of `rel` values is maintained at http://microformats.org/wiki/existing-rel-values.

TIP Be sure each page on your site contains navigation to the key sections of your site, including the home page. This allows visitors to browse your site freely, whether they came to your site directly or via a link from another site. You never know where visitors will enter your site. It might be via a link that "deep links" to one of your inner pages, so you'll typically want to allow them to access the rest of the site from there.

How to Use and Why Not to Use the `target` Attribute (Most of the Time)

It's possible to make a link open in a new window (or tab, depending on the browser), but it's considered bad practice in most cases. There are a few arguments against it.

Primarily, it should be the user's decision to open a link in a different window or tab, not yours or mine as HTML developers. Otherwise, we're dictating the browsing behavior on our users' behalf.

There are usability and accessibility concerns as well. Less-experienced users may be confused when they activate a link and don't see the results display in their current window. Using a browser isn't straightforward for everyone; I've shown browser tabs to people of various ages who previously had no idea that they could have more than one page open at a time. Similarly, users of assistive devices such as screen readers will have to negotiate their way over to that new window or tab, assuming it's even clear which one loaded the new content.

If all this hasn't convinced you to avoid loading links in other windows, or your boss or client won't listen to your reasoned argument against it, here's how to do it: Type **`target="window"`** in your link code, where **`window`** is the name (of your own choosing) of the window where the corresponding page should be displayed.

For instance, **`<a href="some-page.html" target="doodad">Some page</a>`** opens **`some-page.html`** in a new window or tab named doodad. (Visitors don't see the name. It just helps the browser differentiate one window or tab from another.)

If you target several links to the same name, the links will all open in that same window or tab. Or, if you always want a link to open in a different window or tab (even if you triggered the same link more than once), use HTML's predefined name, **`_blank`**, as in **`target="_blank"`**.

But remember, you didn't read any of that here.

There is one other use for **`target`**, which is to open a link in an **`iframe`**. You code the **`target`** the same way, except its value should match the **`id`** of the **`iframe`**. You'll rarely have occasion to use this, especially since **`iframe`**s are generally discouraged (sometimes they have their place, though). Learn more about the **`iframe`** element at https://developer.mozilla.org/en/HTML/Element/iframe.

Creating and Linking to Anchors

Generally, activating a link brings the user to the *top* of the corresponding webpage. If you want to have the user jump to a specific section of the webpage, create an *anchor* and reference that anchor in the link (Ⓐ, Ⓑ, and Ⓒ). FAQ pages are perhaps the most common use for anchor links.

Ⓐ Each link **href** value that begins with **#** anchors to the element with the corresponding **id** (without the **#**). For instance, **<a href="#question-03">...</a>** anchors to **<h2 id="question-03">...</h2>**. You may apply an **id** to any element as long as any given **id** exists in a page only once (see "Naming Elements with a Class or ID" in Chapter 3). This example also gives you an early look at an unordered list (**ul**), by far the most frequently used list type on the web. (Lists are covered extensively in Chapter 15.)

```
...
<body>

<article>
    <header>
        <h1>Frequently Asked Questions (FAQ)</h1>

        <nav>
          <ul>
            <li><a href="#question-01">Can an id have more than word?</a></li>
            <li><a href="#question-02">Can visitors bookmark anchor links?</a></li>
            <li><a href="#question-03">My anchor link isn't working. What am I doing wrong?</a></li>
            ...
          </ul>
        </nav>
    </header>

    <h2 id="question-01">Can an id have more than word?</h2>
    <p>Yes, your ids can have more than one word as long as there are no spaces. Separate each word
  → with a dash instead.</p>

    <h2 id="question-02">Can visitors bookmark anchor links?</h2>
    <p>Yes, they can! And when they visit that link, the browser will jump down to the anchor as
  → expected. Visitors can share the link with others, too, so all the more reason to choose
  → meaningful anchor names.</p>

    <h2 id="question-03">My anchor link isn't working. What am I doing wrong?</h2>
    <p>The problem could be a few things. First, double-check that you added an id (without "#") to
  → the element your link should point to. Also, be sure that the anchor in your link <em>is</em>
  → preceded by "#" and that it matches the anchor id.</p>

    ...
</article>

</body>
</html>
```

Creating and Linking to Anchors

Creating and Linking to Anchors +

Frequently Asked Questions (FAQ)

- Can an id have more than one word?
- Can visitors bookmark anchor links?
- My anchor link isn't working. What am I doing wrong?
- How do I link to a specific part of someone else's webpage?

Can an id have more than one word?

Yes, your ids can have more than one word as long as there are no spaces. Separate each word with a dash instead.

Can visitors bookmark anchor links?

www.allaboutlinks.info/anchor-links.html#question-03

B When the visitor points at a link that refers to an anchor, the URL and the anchor name appear in the status bar (in the lower-left corner of the window) on desktop browsers.

Creating and Linking to Anchors

Creating and Linking to Anchors +

My anchor link isn't working. What am I doing wrong?

The problem could be a few things. First, double-check that you added an id (without "#") to the element your link should point to. Also, be sure that the anchor in your link *is* preceded by "#" and that it matches the anchor id.

How do I link to a specific part of someone else's webpage?

Although you obviously can't add anchors to other people's pages, you can take advantage of the ones that they have already created. View the source code of their webpage to see if they've included

C Once the visitor activates the link, the particular part of the page that the anchor references is displayed at the top of the browser window. (Ironically, in this case, it links to information about what to do when an anchor link *doesn't* work!)

To create an anchor:

1. Place the cursor in the start tag of the element that you wish the user to jump to.

2. Type `id="anchor-name"`, where *anchor-name* is the text you will use internally to identify that section of the webpage. Be sure there is a space between the element's name and the `id`; for example, `<h2 id="features">`.

To create a link to an anchor:

1. Type `<a href="#anchor-name">`, where *anchor-name* is the value of the destination's `id` attribute (per step 2 in "To create an anchor"). For example, `<a href="#features">`.

2. Type the label text; that is, the text that is highlighted (usually blue and under-lined by default) and that when acti-vated will take the user to the section referenced in step 1. As usual, images are allowed too.

3. Type `</a>` to complete the definition of the link.

TIP Give each anchor an `id` with a meaning-ful name to increase the semantic richness of your HTML document. In other words, avoid a generic `id` like `anchor3`.

TIP If the anchor is in a separate document, use `<a href="page.html#anchor-name">` to reference the section. (There should be no space between the URL and the #.) If the anchor is on a page on a different site, you'll have to type `<a href="http://www.site.com/directory/page.html#anchor-name">` (with no spaces).

TIP If an anchor is near the bottom of the page and the content below it isn't at least as tall as the viewable area in the browser, the anchor may not display at the top of the window, but rather toward the middle.

Creating Other Kinds of Links

You are not limited to creating links to other webpages. You can create a link to any URL: RSS feeds, images, files that you want visitors to be able to download, email addresses, phone numbers, and more **Ⓐ**.

To create other kinds of links:

1. Type **<a href="**.

2. Type the URL.

   For a link to any file on the web, including images, ZIP files, programs, PDFs, or whatever, type **http://www.site.com/dir/file.ext**, where **www.site.com** is the name of the host and **/dir/file.ext** is the path to the desired file. The latter includes the directory or directories that lead to the file, as well as the file name itself (with its extension).

   For an email address, type **mailto:name@domain.com**, (*not* preceded by **http://**), where **name@domain.com** is the email address. (But see the tips for a reason to avoid linking to email addresses.)

   For a phone number, type **tel:+** (*not* preceded by **http://**) followed by the country code and then the phone number, all without dashes. The total number of digits will vary from country to country. For example, 1 is the country code for the United States, so a number could be **tel:+18889995555** (whereas the UK's country code is 44, Kenya's is 254, and so on).

Ⓐ You can create links to many different kinds of URLs. This page includes six links. The link around the image may not be obvious in all browsers **Ⓑ**.

```
...
<h1>Other Types of Links</h1>

<p>There are lots of different kinds of
→ links that you can create on a webpage.
→ Following are some examples.</p>

<h2>Images</h2>
<p>You can link directly to <a href=
→ "img/blueflax.jpg">a photo</a> or
→ even make links out of photos. For
→ example, the following image is linked
→ to a flowers photo gallery page.
→ <a href="gallery-flowers.html" title=
→ "More flower images"><img src="img/
→ blueflax.jpg" width="165" height="105"
→ alt="Blue Flax" /></a></p>

<h2>Other Assets</h2>
<p><a href="media/piano.mp3">Listen to
→ tickling of the ivories</a> (MP3, 1.3 MB)
→ or <a href="media/paddle-steamer.mp4">
→ watch a paddle steamer</a> (MP4, 2.4 MB).
→ These link directly to the files (handy for
→ downloading).</p>

<h2>Email Addresses</h2>
<p>Send feedback to <a href="mailto:
→ someone@somedomain.com">someone@
→ somedomain.com</a>.</p>

<h2>Phone Numbers</h2>
<p>Call now for free things!
→ <a href="tel:+18001234567">1
→ (800) 123-4567</a></p>
...
```

Other Types of Links

There are lots of different kinds of links that you can create on a webpage. Following are some examples.

Images

You can link directly to <u>a photo</u> or even make links out of photos. For example, the following image is linked to a photo gallery page.

Other Assets

<u>Listen to tickling of the ivories</u> (MP3, 1.3 MB) or <u>watch a paddle steamer</u> (MP4, 2.4 MB). These link directly to the files (handy for downloading).

Email Addresses

Send feedback to <u>someone@somedomain.com</u>.

Phone Numbers

Call now for free things! <u>1 (800) 123-4567</u>

B No matter where a link points, it looks similar by default in browsers unless you wrap it around a photo (some browsers show a border around the image, and some don't). Notice that I've created labels that read naturally with the text, instead of using "click me."

3. Type **">**.

4. Type the label for the link; that is, the text that will be underlined and a different color by default and that when activated will take the visitor to the URL referenced in step 2. Alternatively (or in addition to label text), add an `img` element as the label. (See **A** and the "Linking Thumbnail Images" sidebar.)

5. Type **</a>**.

TIP If you create a link to a file that a browser doesn't know how to handle (an Excel file, for example), the browser will either try to open a helper program to view the file or try to download it to the visitor's drive.

TIP I recommend you avoid linking email addresses, because spambots grab them from webpages and bombard them with spam. It's better to offer an email address in a descriptive way, like "someone at somedomain," although that isn't always foolproof either.

TIP A smartphone that understands `tel:` links will ask if you want to call the number when you trigger a link. Some non-phone devices, like the iPad, will ask if you'd like to add the number to one of your contacts. Finally, some desktop browsers may initiate Google Voice or Skype, but others won't know what to do with a `tel:` link when it's triggered.

continues on next page

TIP Although you can link to PDFs and other non-HTML documents (Word, Excel, and so on), try to avoid it whenever possible. Instead, link to an HTML page that contains the information. PDFs can take a long time to load, and some browsers can get sluggish while trying to display them. For those times when a PDF is your only option, make it clear to users that the link points to a PDF rather than to another HTML page so they won't be surprised (users don't appreciate being tricked into time-consuming downloads). That advice goes for most other non-HTML documents, too. You can message this simply by putting the file type and size in parentheses; showing an icon helps as well. Here's an example (without an icon): `<p><a href="q2-sales-report.pdf">Q2 Sales Report</a> (PDF, 725kb)</p>`. You may also want to include a `title` attribute (such as `title="View PDF"`) on the link.

TIP It's a good idea to compress large files and groups of files that you want visitors to download. For instance, a set of Photoshop templates saved as PSD files. Search online for "ZIP and RAR" to find tools for creating and opening file archives using these popular compression formats.

TIP If you want to "create links to content on the iTunes Store, the App Store, the iBookstore, and the Mac App Store" (per the URL that follows), you can use Apple's Link Maker (http://itunes.apple.com/linkmaker) to generate the URL to include in your HTML. If you are an affiliate (www.apple.com/itunes/affiliates/), Apple pays you a commission on items people buy through your links.

Linking Thumbnail Images

No doubt you've visited a photo gallery page that shows several thumbnails (miniature versions of your images) linked to larger versions. This allows you to see a lot of photos at a glance before choosing which ones to view full size.

Implementing a basic version of this would be similar to the example code that links the flower image to another page **A**. Each of those pages could contain a full-size photo, plus a link back to the thumbnails page. (Advanced approaches beyond the capabilities of HTML alone could allow for a single dynamic page.)

Be careful not to go crazy with the number of thumbnails on any given page. They may be small, but each thumbnail is a separate request to the web server, and those add up, slowing down your page. There's no set rule for how many is appropriate. It partially depends on the number and size of other assets your page loads, as well as your intended audience. For instance, mobile phones typically load images more slowly.

If you have a lot of thumbnails, consider splitting them up into more than one page. Test your pages to determine what works best.

Lastly, I recommend marking up your list of thumbnails with an unordered list (**ul**), covered in Chapter 15.

CSS Building Blocks

Let's face it—most of the webpages I've shown you so far aren't particularly compelling visually. That's because we've been focusing on defining our content with HTML, not on styling our webpages with CSS (Cascading Style Sheets). But that's about to change. Over the next handful of chapters, you'll learn how to style text and backgrounds, implement multi-column layouts, build a layout that looks good on everything from phones to desktops (and beyond), and more. In this chapter, we'll lay the groundwork by covering the basic CSS concepts.

A style sheet is simply text that contains one or more rules that determine—through properties and values—how certain elements in your webpage should be displayed. There are CSS properties for controlling basic formatting (such as **font-size** and **color**), layout properties (such as **position** and **float**), and printing (such as deciding where page breaks should appear when visitors print a page). CSS also has a number of dynamic properties that allow items to look different when a

In This Chapter

user interacts with them, to appear and disappear, and much more.

CSS2 is the version of CSS that is best supported across browsers both new and old, so this book will cover it extensively. CSS3, which is still evolving as a specification, encapsulates and builds upon CSS2 to provide features that designers and developers desired for years; these include rounded corners, drop shadows, text shadows, custom fonts, rotated text, semitransparent background colors, multiple background images, gradients, and much more. The great news is that modern browsers have already implemented these and other CSS3 features (and continue to add more), so you can use them today.

In fact, there have been so many features added to CSS in recent years that we can't possibly fit them all in this book. Heck, even CSS4 is already underway. But you'll learn some of the most useful CSS3 features, and I'll point you to resources you can use to learn about some features not covered in this book.

The wonderful thing about CSS is that your styles can be created in a different text file than your HTML pages and then be applied to all the pages on your site. This simplifies styling your site both when you build it and as you make changes over time. And when it comes time to redesign a site, if your content and structure remain the same, it's even possible to give it an entirely new look without having to change the HTML.

To get the full benefit of CSS, consistently mark up your webpages according to the recommendations in the HTML chapters.

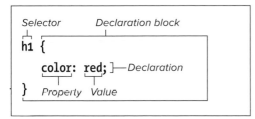

Selector   *Declaration block*

```
h1 {
    color: red; }—Declaration
}   Property  Value
```

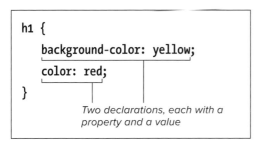

A A style rule is made up of a selector (which indicates what will be formatted) and a declaration block (which describes the formatting that should be executed). Each declaration within the block is a property-value pair separated by a colon and ending with a semicolon. A left curly brace begins a declaration block, and a right curly brace ends it.

```
h1 {
    background-color: yellow;
    color: red;
}
            Two declarations, each with a
            property and a value
```

B The order of declarations doesn't matter unless the same property is defined twice. In this example, **color: red** could be before **background-color: yellow** and have the same effect. Note the spacing and indenting (optional, but customary and recommended), which keeps everything readable.

C When a style rule like the one in **B** is applied to this simple bit of HTML …

```
...
<body>
    <h1>Hey, I've got style!</h1>
</body>
</html>
```

D … the heading colors change from the default browser styling of black text on a white background.

Constructing a Style Rule

A style sheet contains the rules that define how a webpage looks. Each rule has two main parts: the *selector*, which determines which part of your page is affected, and the *declaration block*, which is made up of one or more property-value pairs (each constitutes a *declaration*) that specifies the design treatments to apply (**A** through **D**).

To construct a style rule:

1. Type *selector*, where *selector* identifies the part or parts of your page you wish to format. You'll learn how to create all sorts of selectors in Chapter 9.

2. Type { (an opening curly bracket) to begin the declaration block.

3. Type *property*: *value*;, where *property* is the name of the CSS property that describes the sort of formatting you'd like to apply and *value* is one of a list of allowable options for that property. Descriptions of CSS properties and values begin in earnest in Chapter 10.

4. Repeat step 3 as needed. It's common practice to enter each property-value pair (a declaration) on its own line **B**, but this isn't required.

5. Type } to complete the declaration block and the style rule.

TIP You may add extra spaces, tabs, or returns in a style rule to keep the style sheet readable **B**. The format in the example is perhaps the most common among coders.

TIP Technically, you may omit the semicolon that follows the last declaration in a style rule, but it's a best practice to include it.

Adding Comments to Style Rules

It's a good idea to add comments to your CSS to note the primary sections of your style sheets or simply to explain something about a particular rule or declaration. Comments do not display in your webpages, so you don't have to worry about them distracting your visitors. CSS comments help not only you but also others who are viewing and possibly contributing to your code. And even if you're the only one working on a site, you'll be happy that you left yourself comments if you revisit the code months later.

To add comments to a style sheet:

1. In your style sheet, type **/*** to begin your comment.

2. Type the comment.

3. Type ***/** to signal the end of the comment.

TIP Comments may include returns and thus span several lines. Similarly, the /* and */ may appear on their own lines or alongside your comment text **A**. You may also put comments inside a declaration block or after a rule **B**.

TIP You may not put comments inside other comments. This is incorrect:
**/* Wrong because /* this comment */ is
→ inside a comment. */.**

TIP Comments are extremely helpful as an organizational tool. Style sheets can quickly get long, so organizing them is critical to making your CSS easy to maintain. It's common practice to group related rules together and precede them with a descriptive comment **C**.

TIP However you format your comments, decide on a convention and use it consistently, especially if you're working with a team.

A Comments can be long or short, though they tend to be short. Use them as you see fit to describe the purpose of a style rule or a group of related rules.

```
/*
This is a CSS comment. It can be one line
→ long or span several lines. This one
→ is much longer than most. Regardless, a
→ CSS comment never displays in the
→ browser with your site's HTML content.

Of course, you wouldn't really write a
→ silly comment like this that merely
→ talks about comments. The next comment
→ is more in line with a comment's
→ typical use.
*/

/* Set default rendering of certain HTML5
→ elements for older browsers. */
article,
aside,
figcaption,
figure,
footer,
header,
main,
nav,
section {
    display: block;
}
```

B You can also insert comments within the declaration block or after a rule.

```
.byline {
    color: green;
    font-size: .875em;
    text-shadow: 2px 1px 5px orange; /* IE9
    → and earlier don't support */
} /* You can put comments here, too! */
```

C Comment primary sections of rules within your style sheets to keep them organized. I find that using a format like this (all-caps and an underline) makes it clear where each major grouping begins.

```
/* GLOBAL NAVIGATION
------------------------------- */
... rules for global nav ...


/* MAIN CONTENT
------------------------------- */
... rules for main content ...


/* SIGN-UP FORM
------------------------------- */
... rules for sign-up form ...


/* PAGE FOOTER
------------------------------- */
... rules for page footer ...
```

D You can "comment out" a declaration that you don't want to affect the page. Here, all images will get a 4-pixel solid red border but not a right margin treatment, because **margin-right: 12px;** is inside a comment.

```
img {
    border: 4px solid red;
    /* margin-right: 12px; */
}
```

TIP You can put comments within **D** or around **E** style rules to hide them from the browser. This is a good way to test a style sheet change without permanently removing the commented portion until you are ready to do so. It's also helpful when debugging; comment out something you think might be causing a problem, refresh the page in the browser, and see if the problem is fixed.

TIP Although these examples are heavy on comments for demonstration purposes, don't feel the need to comment everything. Style sheets can be harder to read if they have too many comments. You'll probably find that a good mix entails organizational comments coupled with descriptive ones as needed. Find the balance that works for you and the others on your team.

E A comment can go around an entire rule or multiple rules. In this style sheet, only the **line-height** for paragraphs is applied, because the rules for **.byline** and **img** are commented out. Note that I removed their comments (shown in **B** and **D**) so I could place a comment around them without creating an error.

```
p {
    line-height: 1.2;
}

/*
.byline {
    color: black;
    font-size: .875em;
    text-shadow: 2px 1px 5px orange;
}

img {
    border: 4px solid red;
    margin-right: 12px;
}
*/
```

Understanding Inheritance

Inheritance is one of the key concepts behind CSS. Take a look at the webpage in 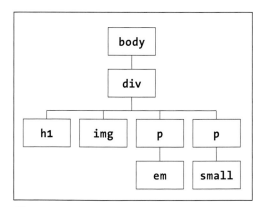 **A**. Behind the scenes, browsers look at your HTML as a document tree **B**. Doing the same can help you understand CSS. Here's why: When you apply certain CSS properties to an element, they not only affect that element but also flow down the branch or branches beneath them. These lower elements are said to *inherit* from their ancestors. Except they inherit things like colors and font sizes instead of cold hard cash (a raw deal?).

A All content elements are descendants of the **body** element, and in this case, a **div** wraps around everything inside that. Digging deeper, the **em** and **small** elements are contained within a **p** element and thus are descendants of **p** (and **div** and **body**), as the diagram illustrates **B**.

```
...
<body>
<div>
    <h1>The Ephemeral Blue Flax</h1>

    <img src="img/blueflax.jpg" width="300"
    → height="175" alt="Blue Flax (Linum
    → lewisii)" />

    <p>I am continually <em>amazed</em>
    → at the beautiful, delicate Blue Flax
    → that somehow took hold in my garden.
    → They are awash in color every morning,
    → yet not a single flower remains
    → by the afternoon. They are the very
    → definition of ephemeral.</p>

    <p><small>&copy; Blue Flax Society.
    → </small></p>
</div>
</body>
</html>
```

B It's easy to see which elements are descendants of others when you visualize an HTML page as a tree structure. Each element that is inside another immediate element in your code—for example, as **img** is inside **div** in **A**—is a branch of its parent.

C This style sheet for the HTML document in **A** takes advantage of inheritance to apply certain styles to the page. Don't worry too much about the details right now, but do notice that there are rules for the **body**, **div**, and **p** elements, but not for the **h1**, **em**, and **small** elements.

```
body {
    font-family: Verdana, Geneva,
    → sans-serif;
}

div {
    border: 1px solid #000;
    overflow: hidden;
    padding: 0 1em .25em;
}

p {
    color: #36c; /* a blue color */
    font-weight: bold;
}

img {
    float: left; /* makes text wrap it */
    margin-right: 1em;
}
```

Figures **A**, **C**, and **D** demonstrate inheritance at work. Remember, not all properties are inherited. For instance, **font-family** is inherited, but **border** and **padding** are not. That is why all text on the page displays in Verdana, but only the **div**—and none of its descendants—has a border (the thin black box) and padding (the space between the border and content inside) **D**. The **color** and **font-weight** properties are inherited, too,

continues on next page

D Here we see inheritance (and the lack thereof) in action. The **h1** inherits the Verdana **font-family** styling from **body**. But it does not have its own style rule defined in **C**, so it otherwise displays in accordance with the browser defaults, which make headings bold and black. Similarly, in the absence of a rule specified explicitly for the **em** and **small** elements, they also inherit Verdana from the **body**, and their **font-weight** and **color** from the **p** rule. The italics come from the browser's default styling of **em**. The slightly reduced size of the legal notice marked up with **small** (that is, legal "fine print") is also due to a browser default style. Finally, the **div** surrounding the content shows a thin border and padding inside it, but as expected, no other elements inside the **div** do because those properties aren't inherited.

which explains why the text in the **em** and **small** elements is blue and bold like the other paragraph text instead of black and not bold per the default browser styles. I've listed other properties that are inherited in the aptly titled sidebar "Which Properties Are Inherited?"

As you can see, inheritance helps simplify your style sheets. Imagine if you had to define the font for each element on your page individually! Keep this in mind while writing your own CSS and take advantage of inheritance whenever it makes sense.

You can also use a CSS value of **inherit** with most properties to force inheritance (see the section, "A Property's Value").

Which Properties Are Inherited?

Following are the CSS display properties that are inherited, grouped by type. Most of them are covered later in the book, but I bet you can guess from their names what many of them do.

Text
- **color** (except by the **a** element)
- **direction**
- **font**
- **font-family**
- **font-size**
- **font-style**
- **font-variant**
- **font-weight**
- **letter-spacing**
- **line-height**
- **text-align**
- **text-indent**
- **text-transform**
- **visibility**
- **white-space**
- **word-spacing**

Lists
- **list-style**
- **list-style-image**
- **list-style-position**
- **list-style-type**

Tables
- **border-collapse**
- **border-spacing**
- **caption-side**
- **empty-cells**

Paged Media (as in printing)
- **orphans**
- **page-break-inside**
- **widows**

Other
- **cursor**
- **quotes**

A In this example, there are four rules of varying specificity. The first affects any **p** element, the second affects only those elements with a class equal to **example** in the HTML **B**, and the third and fourth affect any element with both the **example** and **example-2** classes. The order of these rules is not important—except for the last two relative to one another, because they have the same selector.

```
p {
    color: red;
}

.example {
    color: blue;
}

.example.example-2 {
    color: magenta;
    /* negated by next rule */
}

.example.example-2 {
    color: green;
}
```

The Cascade: When Rules Collide

Styles come from many sources. As you learned in Chapter 1, every browser has its own default styles. But you can apply your own styles to override or complement those in three ways: You can load one or more from an external style sheet file (the recommended method) **A**, insert them at the top of an HTML document, or apply them to a specific HTML element right in the code (though this is to be avoided whenever possible). See the next chapter for specifics about each method.

What happens when there is more than one style rule that applies to a given element? Well, if one rule defines, say, an element's **color** and another its **width**, those rules are effectively combined and both properties are applied.

B Three paragraphs: one generic one, one with a single class, and one with two classes. Note that when an element has more than one class, you separate each one with a space in the HTML, but not in a CSS selector that targets the element. Also, class names are preceded by a period in CSS. (The style sheet in **A** is in a file named **style.css**. The **link** tag in line two loads it into the page. The next chapter elaborates.)

```
...
    <link rel="stylesheet" href="style.css" />
</head>
<body>

<p>Here's a generic <code>p</code> element. It will be red.</p>

<p class="example">Here's a <code>p</code> element with a <code>class</code> of <code>example
 ›</code>. There are two rules that could apply, but since the <code>.example</code> selector is
→ more specific, this paragraph will be blue.</p>

<p class="example example-2">Here's a <code>p</code> element with two classes: <code>example
→ </code> and <code>example-2</code>. There are four rules that could apply to this paragraph. The
→ first two are overruled by the more specific last two. However, because the last two have the
→ same selector, the order breaks the tie between them: the one that appears later wins, and thus
→ this paragraph will be green instead of magenta.</p>

</body>
</html>
```

However, sometimes multiple rules define the *same* property on an element Ⓐ. What then? CSS uses the principle of *the cascade* to determine which of a group of conflicting style declarations should win out. First, any style you write takes precedence over a conflicting browser default style. Beyond that, the cascade takes into account a style's *specificity*, *order*, and *importance* to determine winners. Don't be put off by all the lingo. The way CSS decides which styles are applied—and when—will make sense once you try it out.

Let's take a closer look at specificity, order, and importance.

Specificity

The law of *specificity* states that the more specific the selector Ⓐ, the stronger the rule—and the conflicting style in the stronger rule wins (Ⓒ and Ⓓ). Makes sense, right?

You aren't limited to defining styles with the basic selectors shown in the examples. Chapter 9 covers other selector types of varying specificity weights. Among those, note that **id** selectors are considered the most specific by a vast margin (since each **id** must be unique in an HTML page) Ⓓ. On the flip side, inherited styles are considered the most general of all styles (besides

Here's a generic p element. It will be red.

Here's a p element with a class of example. There are two rules that could apply, but since the .example selector is more specific, this paragraph will be blue.

Here's a p element with two classes: example and example-2. There are four rules that could apply to this paragraph. The first two are overruled by the more specific last two. However, because the last two have the same selector, the order breaks the tie between them: the one that appears later wins, and thus this paragraph will be green instead of magenta.

Ⓒ The second paragraph is blue because it has the **example** class. For the third paragraph, since the third and fourth rules have the same specificity, their order in the style sheet becomes a factor—and thus the fourth rule wins out since it appears last.

Selector	Corresponding HTML
p { ... }	<p>...</p>
.someClass { ... }	<p class="someClass">...</p>
.someClass.someOtherClass { ... }	<p class="someClass someOtherClass">...</p>
#someID { ... }	<p id="someID">...</p>
	<p id="someID" class="someClass">...</p>
	<p id="someID" class="someOtherClass">...</p>
	<p id="someID" class="someClass someOtherClass">...</p>

Ⓓ This table lists a few selectors, from least specific (an element name, at the top) to most specific (an ID, at the bottom). The behavior played out in Ⓐ through Ⓒ reflects this.

browser defaults) and thus are overruled by any other rule.

I cover **id** selectors further in Chapter 9 ("Selecting Elements by Class or ID"), but for now, I'll mention that I recommend you favor classes and avoid IDs in your style sheets. Using IDs for styling is typically overkill and does not allow for as much flexibility.

Order

Sometimes, the specificity is the same for competing rules, so it can't determine a winner. In that case, the *order* of the rules breaks the tie: Rules that appear later take precedence (as exemplified by the styling of the third HTML paragraph in Ⓐ through Ⓒ). Also, rules that are applied inline right in the HTML element (not recommended) are considered to appear after (and thus take precedence over) rules applied in either an external style sheet or one embedded in the HTML document.

Importance

If all that isn't enough, you can override the whole system by declaring that a particular style should be more important than the others, regardless of the rule's specificity or order. You do so by adding **!important** at the end of the declaration. For example, **p { color: orange !important; }**. (This isn't recommended except in uncommon cases.)

For more details, consult "The Cascade and the Order of Styles" in Chapter 8.

Recap

The styles you write override browser defaults. With two or more competing styles, the style declaration in the more specific rule takes precedence, regardless of its order in your style sheets. With two or more rules of equal specificity, the one that

appears last wins unless one of the others is marked with **!important**.

And, in the absence of a rule targeting an element directly, the element's inherited value (if any) is used.

If any of this sounds confusing, don't worry too much about it right now. Once you start playing with CSS and different selectors, I think you'll find that in most cases the cascade operates just as you'd expect it to.

TIP If you need a refresher on classes and IDs in HTML, see "Naming Elements with a Class or ID" in Chapter 3.

TIP If you're interested in the nitty-gritty of how browsers calculate specificity weight, see Section 9 of the CSS specifications (www.w3.org/TR/selectors/#specificity). Keep in mind that a lot of it will look foreign to you unless you've skipped ahead to Chapter 9. You absolutely do *not* have to commit the formula to memory to write CSS. The truth is that very few coders—even those with years of experience—can recite those specificity rules. They (and you) don't need to, because CSS specificity works intuitively. And if a style you've written doesn't work, it could be because it isn't specific enough, so you'll learn by doing.

TIP At the onset, I mentioned that style sheets may originate from the browser and from you. There is a third potential, although unlikely, source: Your visitors. Some browsers let users create and apply their own style sheets to pages they visit—including yours—so they can customize their experience to their liking. For instance, a vision-impaired user might prefer a specific amount of contrast between the text and background colors. In truth, very few people know about this browser feature and even fewer take advantage of it. These styles do affect the cascade. They are given precedence over default browser styles, but not over the style sheets you create for your site unless a user style sheet declaration is marked with **!important**. I mention this primarily in case it is helpful for you to know as a user. It doesn't change how you go about styling your own webpages for others to visit.

A Property's Value

Each CSS property has different rules about what values it can accept. Some properties accept only one of a list of predefined values. Others accept numbers, integers, relative values, percentages, URLs, or colors. Some can accept more than one type of value. The acceptable values for each property are listed throughout this book in the section describing that property (Chapters 10, 11, and 14), but you'll learn the basic systems here.

Inherit

Use the **inherit** value when you want to explicitly specify that the value of a property be the same as that of the element's parent. For example, suppose a couple of paragraphs are inside an **article** element that has a border setting. Borders aren't normally inherited, so the rule **p { border: inherit; }** would apply the same border to those paragraphs. (Versions of Internet Explorer prior to IE8 don't support the **inherit** value for most properties, but it's unlikely you'll need to support browsers that old for most sites.)

Predefined values

Most CSS properties have a few predefined values that can be used. For example, the **float** property can be set to **left**, **right**, or **none**. In contrast with HTML, you don't need to—and indeed *must not*—enclose predefined values in quotation marks **Ⓐ**. In fact, that's true of most CSS values, predefined or not. (Some exemptions include **font-family** names that are more than one word, and what's known as generated content.)

Lengths and percentages

Many CSS properties take a length as their value. All length values must contain a quantity and a unit, with no spaces between them; for example, **3em** or **10px Ⓑ**. The only exception is **0**, which may be used with or without units. The effect is the same regardless, so it's customary to leave off the unit for a **0** value.

There are length types that are relative to other values. An em is equal to the element's font size. For example, setting **margin-left: 2em** on an element would mean, "set a left margin that's twice the font size" of the element. (When the em

---

A preset value

```
border: none;
```

Ⓐ Many CSS properties will accept only values from a predefined list. Type them exactly, and do not enclose them in quotation marks.

A length

```
font-size: .875em;
```

Ⓑ Lengths must always explicitly state the unit. There should be no space between the unit and the measurement.

is used to set the element's **font-size** property itself, as shown in Chapter 10, its value is relative to the font size of the element's parent.) The relative nature of an em makes it an essential part of building sites today, especially those designed to adjust for screen sizes. (This practice is known as *responsive web design*, which is covered in Chapter 12.) Meanwhile, a rem unit is relative to the font size of the **html** element. See "Setting the Font Size" in Chapter 10.

If you've used software such as Adobe Photoshop, you're no doubt familiar with pixels. Unlike ems, CSS pixels (**px**) are not relative to other style rules. So values in **px** aren't affected by the font size of an element. However, in today's broad device landscape (phones, tablets, and so on), a pixel isn't considered the predictable unit of measure it once was. That's because a pixel isn't necessarily the same size on one type of device as it is on another. (See Peter-Paul Koch's detailed description at www.quirksmode.org/blog/archives/2010/04/a_pixel_is_not.html. Warning: It can be a confusing topic!) You'll still have occasion to use **px**, just not as frequently.

There are also absolute units, such as points (**pt**), which is a unit that typically is reserved for print style sheets. In general, you should use absolute lengths only when the size of the output is known (as with **pt** and the printed page).

A percentage value—**65%**, for example— works much like an em, in that it is relative to some other value **C**. For this reason, percentage values are another powerful tool for building responsive websites, as you will learn.

Of all these, you will use ems, percentages, and pixels the most, with rem gaining steam. Your style sheets can use any combination of them; they can be combined even within the same style rule. There are other units, too, but they see little use.

Bare numbers

A very few CSS properties accept a value in the form of a number without a unit, like **3** or **.65**. The most common are **line-height** **D**, **opacity**, and **z-index** (see "Setting the Line Height" in Chapter 10, "Setting the Opacity of Elements" in Chapter 14, and "Positioning Elements in a Stack" in Chapter 11, respectively).

```
             A percentage
                 ┬
 width: 80%;
```

C Percentages are generally relative to the parent element. So in this example, the width would be set to 80 percent of the parent's width.

```
             A number
                 ┬
 line-height: 1.5;
```

D Don't confuse numbers and integers with length. A number or integer has no unit (like **px**). In this case, the value shown here is a factor that will be multiplied by the font size to get the line height.

URLs

Some CSS properties allow you to specify the URL of another file, particularly images (**background-image** is one such property). In that case, use **url(*file.ext*)**, where ***file.ext*** is the path and file name of the desired asset **E**. Note that relative URLs should be relative *to the location of the style sheet* in your site's folder structure and not to the HTML file. I've provided an example in "Setting the Background" in Chapter 10.

You can use quotation marks around the file name, but they're not required. There should be no space between the word **url** and the opening parenthesis. White space between the parenthesis and the address to the file is allowed but not required (or customary).

For more information on writing the URLs themselves, consult "URLs" in Chapter 1.

CSS colors

You can specify colors for CSS properties by using a predefined color keyword or by using a value represented in hexadecimal (usually called *hex*), RGB, HSL, RGBA, or HSLA. Those last two are for colors with a level of alpha transparency, and they, along with HSL, were introduced in CSS3.

CSS3 specifies a basic list of 16 color keywords carried over from CSS2.1 **F** and adds 131 more. The full list is available at www.w3.org/TR/css3-color/#svg-color.

I'd wager that few people remember any but the most obvious color keywords, but you'll see them used occasionally. And you typically grab colors from tools like Adobe Photoshop, which gives you the RGB and hex value rather than the CSS color name. Besides, the color keywords cover only a fraction of the colors available to you. So

---

A URL

background: url(bg-pattern.png);

E URLs in CSS properties do not need to be enclosed in quotation marks.

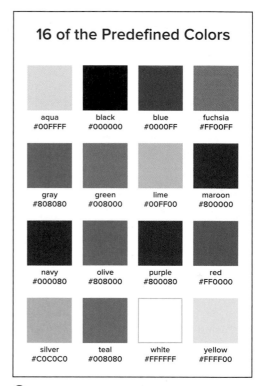

16 of the Predefined Colors

aqua #00FFFF	black #000000	blue #0000FF	fuchsia #FF00FF
gray #808080	green #008000	lime #00FF00	maroon #800000
navy #000080	olive #808000	purple #800080	red #FF0000
silver #C0C0C0	teal #008080	white #FFFFFF	yellow #FFFF00

F The 16 basic color keywords, along with their hex equivalents. CSS3 provides 131 additional keywords, but you can define far more colors using hex, RGB, or HSL.

in practice, it's more common to define your CSS colors with the hex format (the most common) or the RGB format—unless you want to specify alpha transparency, in which case either RGBA or HSLA will do.

RGB

You can construct your own color by specifying its amount of red, green, and blue (hence the name *RGB*). You can give the value of each contributing color as a number from 0–255 or a percentage. For example, if you wanted to create a dark purple, you might use 89 red, no green, and 127 blue. That color could be written **rgb(89, 0, 127)** 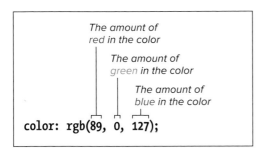.

Alternatively, you could represent each value as a percentage, though it is far less common to do so, likely because image editors like Photoshop provide you numerical RGB values. But if you do want to use percentages, you would write the same color as **rgb(35%, 0%, 50%)**, since 89 is 35% of 255 and 127 is 50% of 255.

Hexadecimal

I've saved the most common method for last . Convert those numerical values to hexadecimal, join them together, and prefix the value with a #, as in **#59007F**. If you're saying to yourself, "*what*adecimal?," don't fret. Photoshop and the like include tools for choosing colors and displaying their hex values, just as they do for RGB. You can also find free tools by searching online for "rgb to hex converter" (or vice versa).

For the example of **#59007F**, 59 is the hex equivalent of 89, 00 is the hex equivalent of 0, and 7F is the hex equivalent of 127. You can also write the letters in lowercase; for example, **7F** as **7f** (my preference, but plenty of others like to capitalize them).

When a hex color is composed of three pairs of repeating digits, as in **#ff3344**, you may abbreviate the color to **#f34**. In fact, it's a best practice to do so, since there's no reason to make your code longer than it needs to be.

The amount of
red in the color

The amount of
green in the color

The amount of
blue in the color

`color: rgb(89, 0, 127);`

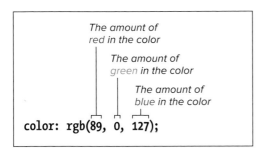 Another way to express color in CSS is with RGB numeric values from 0–255. Define red first, followed by green and then blue.

The amount of
red in the color

The amount of
green in the color

The amount of
blue in the color

`color: #59007f;`

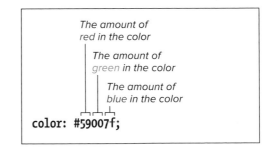 The most common way to define a color in CSS is by using hexadecimal numbers to specify the amounts of red, green, and blue that it contains.

More color options in CSS3: RGBA, HSLA, and HSL

Thanks to CSS3, we now have another way to specify colors—HSL—and the ability to set alpha transparency via RGBA and HSLA. (You can't indicate alpha transparency with hex notation.)

RGBA

RGBA is the same as RGB except the *A* stands for *alpha transparency*. It's common to leverage alpha transparency on the **background-color** (or **background**) of an element (**I** and **J**) because alpha transparency allows whatever is behind the element—an image, other colors, text, and more—to peek through and blend with it **K**. To be clear, though, you can also set alpha transparency on other color-based properties, such as **border**, **border-color**, **box-shadow**, **color**, and **text-shadow**. All modern browsers support it, but versions of Internet Explorer prior to IE9 do not **L**.

You specify the amount of transparency with a decimal from 0 to 1 after the red, green, and blue values. So the syntax is as follows:

property: rgba(red, green, blue, alpha
→ transparency);

The closer to 0 the alpha setting, the more transparent the color becomes. If it *is* 0, it's completely transparent, as if you hadn't set a color at all. Similarly, 1 is completely opaque, meaning it's not transparent at all.

I This style sheet applies a repeating background image and default text formatting to the whole page, with slightly different **background-color** treatments for the paragraphs depending on what class they have (if any) **J**. Modern browsers display the result shown in **K**. IE9 and later support RGBA, but older versions ignore the declarations on **.test-1** and **.test-2**, showing the RGB style assigned to **p** instead **L**.

```
/* Set repeating page background image, and
→ default color, font, and size for all text.
*/
body {
    background: url(../img/bg-pattern.png);

    /* Because of inheritance, these text
    → styles cascade down to all text on
    → a page unless overridden by styles
    → elsewhere. */
    color: #ff0; /* Hex yellow */
    font-family: arial, helvetica,
    → sans-serif;
    font-size: 100%;
}

/* Solid background (not transparent) for all
→ paragraphs unless given one of the classes
→ below. Versions of IE older than IE9 will
→ show this background color regardless. */
p {
    background-color: rgb(60,143,0);
    font-size: 1.75em;
    padding: .5em;
}

/* 25% transparent */
.test-1 {
    background-color: rgba(60,143,0,.75);
}

/* 60% transparent */
.test-2 {
    background-color: rgba(60,143,0,.4);
}
```

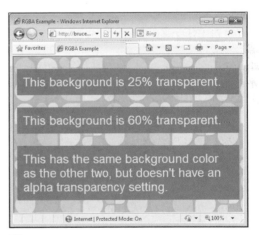

J The first paragraph is given a class of **test-1**, so it will have a 25% transparent background color according to the style sheet. The second is assigned **test-2** for 60% transparency. The final paragraph does not have a class, so its background color will be solid, as specified in the default styling for all **p** elements by the second rule in **I**.

```
...
<body>

<p class="test-1">This background is 25%
→ transparent.</p>

<p class="test-2">This background is 60%
→ transparent.</p>

<p>This has the same background color as
→ the other two, but doesn't have an alpha
→ transparency setting.</p>

</body>
</html>
```

Here are some example declarations to illustrate the point:

```
/* no transparency, so the same as
→ rgb(89, 0, 127); */
background-color: rgba(89,0,127,1);

/* completely transparent */
background-color: rgba(89,0,127,0);

/* 25% transparent */
background-color: rgba(89,0,127,0.75);

/* 60% transparent */
background-color: rgba(89,0,127,0.4);
```

Of course, to make those work, you'll need to include them in one or more rules **I**. As you can see, the RGB color values are the same throughout the style sheet, but the colors themselves appear different in the browser because of their different levels of transparency **K**.

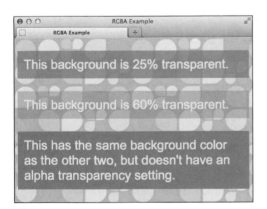

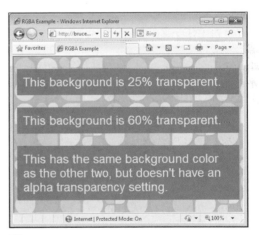

K You can see the background pattern peeking through the background color of the top two paragraphs but not of the bottom one. The background color for all three is the same, but they look like three different shades of green because of their different alpha transparency settings. (See the CSS comment in the **body** rule in **I** to learn how the text styling was achieved.)

L IE didn't start supporting alpha transparency (RGBA or HSLA) until IE9. This screen shot shows IE8, which ignores the RGBA declarations in the style sheet because it doesn't understand them. So all paragraphs have the solid background color defined for **p** elements in the second rule; without that, the paragraphs wouldn't have a background color. (The text in the paragraphs is now misleading, because there is no transparency.)

HSL and HSLA

HSL and HSLA are the other new additions in CSS3. The latter is the alternative to RGBA for setting alpha transparency on a color. You specify the alpha the same way you do with RGBA. You'll see that in a second, but first take a look at how HSL works.

HSL stands for *hue*, *saturation*, and *lightness*, where hue is a number from 0–360, and both saturation and lightness are percentages from 0 to 100. You can think of the hue value as a degree on a color circle 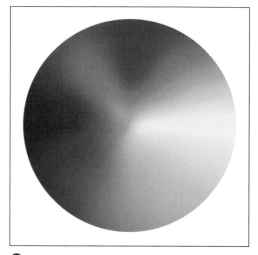, with 0 and 360 meeting at the top. (This means that both 0 and 360 are the same color: red.) The saturation and lightness settings are applied to that color. (Don't confuse HSL with HSB or HSV. They are similar but not the same, and CSS doesn't allow expressing colors in HSB or HSV.)

In CSS 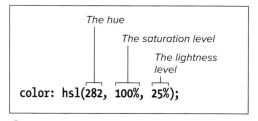, the HSL syntax is:

```
property: hsl(hue, saturation,
→ lightness);
```

And the HSLA format is this:

```
property: hsla(hue, saturation,
→ lightness, alpha transparency);
```

M HSL hue values run clockwise on the circle. So **90** is the rightmost point, **180** is at the bottom, **270** is the leftmost point, and **360** meets **0** at the top. See the sidebar "How to Think in HSL" for a list of standard colors and their hue values.

N The breakdown of the HSL format.

O The same style sheet as **I** except it uses HSL and HSLA. Plus, I've defined a fallback hex **background-color** for styling paragraphs in older browsers. The order of the declarations in the **p** rule is important. Older versions of IE use the first line because they understand it, and modern browsers understand both lines but apply the second because it's last.

```
body {
       ... same styles as before ...
}

/* Solid background (not transparent) for
→ all paragraphs unless given one of the
→ classes below, with the exception of older
→ versions of IE, which will show the hex
→ color always. */
p {
      background-color: #3c8f00; /* for IE
      → before IE9 */
      background-color: hsl(95,100%,28%);
      ...
}

/* 25% transparent */
.test-1 {
      background-color:
      → hsla(95,100%,28%,.75);
}

/* 60% transparent */
.test-2 {
      background-color: hsla(95,100%,28%,.4);
}
```

Take a look at the updated (and slightly abbreviated) style sheet **O**, which defines the same green from the RGB and RGBA example in HSL and HSLA.

If you look closely, you'll notice something a bit curious in the rule that styles **p** elements. Namely, I defined a **background-color** in hex and then in HSL immediately after it. This is necessary because all versions of Internet Explorer understand hex colors, but they didn't support either HSL or HSLA until IE9. Those older browsers ignore HSL and HSLA styles, just like they ignore RGBA, but other browsers display them. The result of this new style sheet is the same in modern browsers **K** and IE8 **L** as before.

Not all image editors specify HSL out of the box (Photoshop doesn't support it at the time of this writing, but you can search online for a plugin). But Brandon Mathis's HSL Color Picker (hslpicker.com) is a free online tool that allows you to pick a color and get its HSL, hex, and RGB values. Or, you can type in values for any of those formats to see the color change. You can find other color tools by searching online.

TIP As noted, versions of IE prior to IE9 don't understand RGBA, HSL, or HSLA. You can define a fallback solid color for those older browsers in separate rules ❶ or in the same rule ❷.

TIP If you *really* want to show alpha transparency background colors in old versions of IE, you have a couple of options. One is to use a 1-pixel semi-transparent PNG as a repeating background (see "Setting the Background" in Chapter 10). Define this fallback `background` property before the one that uses RGBA or HSLA (similar to ❷). The site rgbapng.com can create the image for you; just be sure to save it without the .part filename extension it defaults to. Or, you can use IE's proprietary Gradient filter. The syntax will make you dizzy, but luckily there's a tool that writes it for you: Michael Bester's RGBA & HSLA CSS Generator for Internet Explorer (http://kimili.com/journal/rgba-hsla-css-generator-for-internet-explorer). Keep in mind that too many filters can slow down your pages in these versions of IE.

How to Think in HSL

Learning HSL's logic takes some time, but once you get a feel for it you may find it easier to work with than other formats. In the "Why?" section of his HSL Color Picker site, Mathis provides a nice explanation of HSL. He writes, "Pick a hue from 0 to 360, and with saturation at 100 and luminosity at 50 you'll have the purest form of that color. Reduce the saturation and you move toward gray. Increasing the luminosity moves you toward white; decreasing it moves you toward black."

For example, here are some core colors as you move around the circle:

- Red is `hsl(0,100%,50%);`
- Yellow is `hsl(60,100%,50%);`
- Green is `hsl(120,100%,50%);`
- Cyan is `hsl(180,100%,50%);`
- Blue is `hsl(240,100%,50%);`
- Magenta is `hsl(300,100%,50%);`

8

Working with Style Sheets

Before you start defining your style sheets, it's important to know how to create and use the files that will contain them. In this chapter, you'll learn how to create a style sheet file and then how to apply CSS to multiple webpages (including a whole site), a single page, or an individual HTML element. You achieve these via three methods: external style sheets (the preferred choice), embedded style sheets, and inline styles (the least desirable).

You'll learn how to create the content of your style sheets in the chapters that follow.

Creating an External Style Sheet

External style sheets are ideal for giving the pages on your website a consistent look. You can define all your styles in an external style sheet and then tell each page on your site to load the external sheet, thus ensuring that each page will have consistent design elements. Later you will learn about two other methods of applying CSS: embedded styles and inline styles. Loading CSS via an external style sheet is a best practice and the recommended method (with a few exceptions).

To create an external style sheet:

1. Create a new text document in your text editor of choice (see the first tip). Most people use the same editor to create both HTML and CSS documents.

2. Define as many style rules for your webpages as desired. Also, include CSS comments as you see fit (see "Constructing a Style Rule" and "Adding Comments to Style Rules" in Chapter 7) **A**.

3. Save the document in a text-only format in the desired directory of your website. Any file name will do as long as you include the extension **.css** to designate it as a Cascading Style Sheet **B**.

In the next section, you'll learn how to load the style sheet in your HTML pages so the style rules are applied to them.

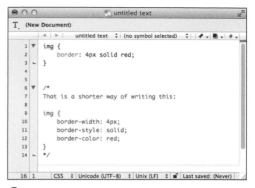

A Use any text editor you like to create a style sheet. This is TextWrangler on a Mac. I included a CSS comment at the bottom so you'd understand how the **border** property works; this becomes relevant in "The Cascade and the Order of Styles" later in the chapter. I absolutely don't suggest you explain every rule in your own style sheets!

B Be sure to save the CSS file with the .css extension and with UTF-8 encoding. Although TextWrangler doesn't, your editor may require you to specify that you want the file saved in text-only format (as a Text Document or Plain Text or ASCII or whatever your text editor calls it). Notepad does this; see "Saving Your Webpage" in Chapter 2 for more information. Note that I am saving **style.css** alongside the HTML page (**example.html**) that will use it. I did this to keep the example simple, but in practice, it's best to save your style sheets in a separate folder so your site is organized.

TIP See "Creating a New Webpage" in Chapter 2 for more information about text editors you can use for writing CSS.

TIP Don't worry too much about the intricacies of the CSS Ⓐ at this point; you'll learn more about creating rules like this in the chapters to follow. But as you likely figured out, this one means, "add a solid red border that's four pixels wide around all img elements in the page."

TIP You can name your style sheets however you like. The names style.css and styles.css are commonly used by websites that have a single style sheet. For larger sites, it's not uncommon to have more than one style sheet. In those cases, base.css, global.css, and main.css are popular names for the style sheet that contains the display rules intended for all or most of the pages on a site. Section-specific style sheets complement those base styles (both are loaded into relevant pages). For instance, if you're building a commerce site, products.css could contain the rules for your product-related pages. Regardless of the file names you choose, make sure they end in .css and don't contain any spaces.

TIP External style sheets can be either linked to (as demonstrated in "Linking to External Style Sheets") or imported (via @import), but I don't recommend you import them. The @import directive negatively affects the speed at which pages download and display, particularly in Internet Explorer. Steve Souders, a web performance expert, discusses this at www.stevesouders.com/blog/2009/04/09/dont-use-import/. If you're still curious about @import, see http://reference.sitepoint.com/css/at-import for the basics.

TIP CSS comments Ⓐ neither affect your webpage's display nor appear in your webpage, but they are visible if a visitor views your source code (see "The Inspiration of Others: CSS" later in this chapter).

Linking to External Style Sheets

Now that you've created a style sheet **A**, you need to load it into your HTML pages so the style rules are applied to the content. The best way to do this is to link to the style sheet **B**.

To link an external style sheet:

1. Type **<link rel="stylesheet"** in the **head** section of each HTML page in which you wish to use the style sheet.

2. Type a space, and then type **href="*url.css*"**, where *url.css* is the location and name of your CSS style sheet.

3. Type a space and the final **/>**. (Or, if you prefer, type **>** without the leading space. HTML5 allows both approaches, and they work exactly the same.)

TIP When you make a change to an external style sheet, all the pages that reference it are automatically updated as well (**C** and **D**). That is the awesome power of an external style sheet!

TIP Another benefit of an external style sheet is that once a browser has loaded it for one page, it typically doesn't need to retrieve it from the web server for subsequent pages. The browser *caches* the file, which means it saves it on the user's computer and uses that version, speeding up the load time of your pages. If later you make changes to your style sheet and upload it to your web server, browsers will download your updated file rather than use the cached one (technically there are exceptions, but none that you're likely to face often).

A The **style.css** external style sheet created earlier in the chapter, minus the CSS comment for brevity.

```
img {
    border: 4px solid red;
}
```

B The **link** element goes inside the **head** section of your HTML document. Your page may contain more than one **link** element, but it's best to keep the total to a minimum so your page loads faster.

```
<!DOCTYPE html>
<html lang="en">
<head>
    <meta charset="UTF-8" />
    <title>El Palau de la Música</title>
    <link rel="stylesheet"
    → href="style.css" />
</head>
<body>
<article>
    <h1>El Palau de la Música</h1>

    <img src="img/palau.jpg" width="250"
    → height="163" alt="El Palau de la
    → Música" />

    <img src="img/tickets.jpg" width="87"
    → height="163" alt="The Ticket Window" />

    <p>I love the <span lang="es">Palau de la
    → Música</span>. It is ornate and gaudy
    → and everything that was wonderful
    → about modernism. It's also the home
    → of the <span lang="es">Orfeó Català
    → </span>, where I learned the benefits
    → of Moscatell.</p>
</article>
</body>
</html>
```

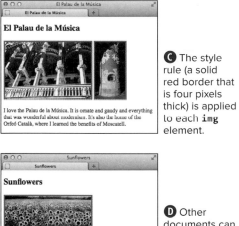

El Palau de la Música

I love the Palau de la Música. It is ornate and gaudy and everything that was wonderful about modernism. It's also the home of the Orfeó Català, where I learned the benefits of Moscatell.

C The style rule (a solid red border that is four pixels thick) is applied to each **img** element.

Sunflowers

There are fields and fields of sunflowers, that turn with the passing of the sun.

D Other documents can link to the very same external style sheet to have the same styles applied.

Name	Size	Kind
▶ 📁 css	--	Folder
▶ 📁 img	--	Folder
📄 example.html	647 bytes	HTML Document

Name	Size	Kind
▼ 📁 css	--	Folder
🖼 style.css	171 bytes	CSS
▼ 📁 img	--	Folder
🖼 palau.jpg	23 KB	JPEG image
🖼 sunflowers.jpg	16 KB	JPEG image
📄 tickets.jpg	4 KB	JPEG image
📄 example.html	647 bytes	HTML Document

E These screen shots show one common way to organize a site. The first is a bird's-eye view of the structure, followed by all folders open so you can see all the files.

F Because **style.css** is located in a subfolder named **css**, the path in **example.html** needs to be updated when linking to the style sheet.

```
...
<head>
    <meta charset="UTF-8" />
    <title>El Palau de la Música</title>
    <link rel="stylesheet"
    → href="css/style.css" />
</head>
...
```

TIP For simplicity's sake, the `link` example shown here assumes that the HTML page lives in the same directory as `style.css` **B**. In practice it is best to organize your style sheets in a subfolder rather than mix them with your HTML pages. Popular style sheet folder names include `css` and `styles`, but you can name it whatever you like as long as you refer to it properly in the `link`'s `href` value. For example, if `style.css` is in a folder named `css` and your HTML page is in the folder above it **E**, the `link` element would read as shown in **F**.

TIP URLs *within* an external style sheet are relative to the location of the style sheet file on the server, not to the HTML page's location. You'll see this in action when you learn about CSS background images in Chapter 10 ("Setting the Background").

TIP You can load more than one style sheet in your page by using multiple `link` elements. In the event that a competing display declaration appears in more than one file, the one in the later file takes precedence over the earlier ones.

TIP An external style sheet's rules may be overridden by styles within an HTML document. The relative influence of styles applied in different ways is summarized in "The Cascade and the Order of Styles" later in this chapter.

TIP You can limit style sheets to a particular kind of output by setting the `media` attribute. For more details, see "Using Media-Specific Style Sheets," later in this chapter.

TIP Previous versions of HTML asked you to include `type="text/css"` in your `link` elements, but HTML5 doesn't require it. You can omit it, as I have in the code examples throughout the book.

Creating an Embedded Style Sheet

An embedded style sheet is the second way to apply CSS to a page. You create one with the **style** element, which contains your style sheet and goes in the **head** section of the HTML page you want to affect Ⓐ. Because the styles are in only that HTML file, they won't apply to other pages (like the styles in a linked external style sheet do), and you won't get the caching benefits described in the previous section either. As mentioned, an external style sheet is the recommended approach for most cases, but it's important to understand your options for the times you'll need to deviate.

Ⓐ When you embed a style sheet, the **style** element and its enclosed style rules go in the **head** section of your document. The browser renders your page the same way it would had the styles been loaded from an external style sheet Ⓑ.

```
<!DOCTYPE html>
<html lang="en">
<head>
    <meta charset="UTF-8" />
    <title>El Palau de la Música</title>
    <style>
    img {
        border: 4px solid red;
    }
    </style>
</head>
<body>
<article>
    <h1>El Palau de la Música</h1>

    <img src="img/palau.jpg" width="250"
    → height="163" alt="El Palau de la
    → Música" />

    <img src="img/tickets.jpg" width="87"
    → height="163" alt="The Ticket Window" />

    <p>I love the <span lang="es">Palau de
    → la Música</span>. It is ornate and
    → gaudy and everything that was
    → wonderful about modernism. It's also
    → the home of the <span lang="es">Orfeó
    → Català </span>, where I learned the
    → benefits of Moscatell.</p>
</article>
</body>
</html>
```

El Palau de la Música

I love the Palau de la Música. It is ornate and gaudy and everything that was wonderful about modernism. It's also the home of the Orfeó Català, where I learned the benefits of Moscatell.

B The result is exactly the same as if you had linked to the styles in an external style sheet. The difference is that no other webpage can take advantage of the styles used on this page.

To create an embedded style sheet:

1. Type `<style>` in the **head** section of your HTML document.

2. Define as many style rules for your web-pages as desired, including CSS comments as you see fit (see "Constructing a Style Rule" and "Adding Comments to Style Rules" in Chapter 7).

3. Type `</style>` to complete the embedded style sheet **A**.

TIP Conflicting styles applied in an embedded style sheet override those in external style sheets if the `style` element comes after the `link` element. For more details, see "The Cascade and the Order of Styles" later in this chapter.

TIP Embedded style sheets are the second-best way to add CSS to your page. (There are rare exceptions, such as very high-trafficked sites under certain conditions.)

TIP Previous versions of HTML asked you to include `type="text/css"` as an attribute in your `style` start tags, but HTML5 doesn't require it. You can omit it, as I have in the code examples throughout the book.

Applying Inline Styles

Inline styles are the third way to apply CSS to HTML. However, they are by far the least desirable option because they intertwine your content (HTML) and your presentation (CSS), a cruel slap in the face to best practices **Ⓐ**. An inline style affects only one element **Ⓑ**, so you lose one of the key benefits an external style sheet provides: Write once and see everywhere. Imagine having to sift through a slew of HTML pages to make the same font-color change over and over, and you can see why inline styles aren't intended for regular use.

However, an inline style can be helpful if you want to try something quickly as a test before removing it from your HTML and placing it in your external style sheet (assuming you were happy with the test results), where it'll be easier to maintain moving forward.

To apply inline styles:

1. Type `style="` within the start tag of the HTML element that you want to format (or simply within *the* tag of void elements like `img`, which don't have an end tag.)

2. Create a style rule without a selector or curly brackets. The selector isn't necessary since you're placing the rule directly inside the desired element. If your rule has more than one declaration, separate each one by typing `;` (a semicolon).

3. Type the final quote mark `"` **Ⓐ**.

Ⓐ Rules applied inline affect only a single element; in this case, the first `img`.

```
<!DOCTYPE html>
<html lang="en">
<head>
    <meta charset="UTF-8" />
    <title>El Palau de la Música</title>
</head>
<body>
...
    <img src="img/palau.jpg" width="250"
    → height="163" alt="El Palau de la Música"
    → style="border: 4px solid red" />

    <img src="img/tickets.jpg" width="87"
    → height="163" alt="The Ticket Window" />
...
</body>
</html>
```

Ⓑ Only the first image has a border. If you wanted to apply the border to images in your website via inline styles, you'd have to add `style="border: 4px solid red"` to every single `img` element individually. As you can see, inline styles are not particularly efficient and would be a headache to apply and update across a site. A better way to do this is shown in **Ⓒ** and **Ⓓ**.

C Here's a preferred approach to achieve the look of **B**. Assign a class—instead of an inline style—to the first **img**. Then, create a rule in an external style sheet that targets that class **D**. If you want other elements to have the same style, just add **class="frame"** to them, too. Any class name will do; **frame** is just an example.

```
...
<body>
...
    <img src="img/palau.jpg" width="250"
    → height="163" alt="El Palau de la Música"
    → class="frame" />

    <img src="img/tickets.jpg" width="87"
    → height="163" alt="The Ticket Window" />
...
</body>
</html>
```

D By using a *class selector*, this rule adds a red border to any element (not just **img**) with **class="frame"** assigned to it in the HTML. Include it in an external style sheet to make it easy to apply across your site. You'll learn about this and other selector types in the next chapter.

```
.frame {
    border: 4px solid red;
}
```

TIP Be careful not to confuse the equal sign with the colon. Since they both assign values, it's easy to interchange them without thinking.

TIP Don't forget to enclose your style definitions in straight quote marks (") and to separate multiple property definitions with a semicolon (;).

TIP Styles applied inline take precedence over all other styles unless a conflicting style elsewhere is marked with !important (see "The Cascade and the Order of Styles" in this chapter).

TIP If you specify the font family (Chapter 10) in an inline style declaration, you'll have to enclose multi-word font names with single quotes to avoid conflict with the style element's double quotes. You can't use the same type of quotes in both places.

TIP Probably the most common use of inline styles is applying them to elements from JavaScript functions as part of making portions of a page dynamic. You may notice these generated inline styles when looking at the source of a page in, say, Firebug or Chrome's Developer Tools. The inline styles aren't part of the HTML file itself; JavaScript adds them. And in most cases, the JavaScript that applies them is in a different file than the HTML, so it still maintains the desired separation of content (HTML), presentation (CSS), and behavior (JavaScript).

The Cascade and the Order of Styles

It's not unusual for more than one style rule to apply to the same element, particularly on larger sites that require more effort to manage the CSS. Sometimes these rules address the same property. As mentioned in "The Cascade: When Rules Collide" in Chapter 7, in these cases a style's order can break a tie when the specificity of the rules is the same. The basic tenet is that, with all else equal, the later the style appears, the more precedence it has (**Ⓐ** through **Ⓔ**). Here is how that plays out when considering different orders:

- The relationship between an embedded style sheet (you'll recall that that's one in a **style** element) and any linked external style sheets depends on their relative positions in your HTML. If the **link** element comes earlier in the code **Ⓑ**, the **style** element (and any **@import** style sheets it contains) overrides the linked style sheet where they conflict **Ⓒ**. If the **link** element comes later **Ⓓ**, conflicting styles in it (and any **@import** style sheets it contains) override any in the **style** element **Ⓔ**.

- Inline styles—by virtue of being applied directly to elements—come after external and embedded style sheets. By being last, they have the most precedence and will override any conflicting styles applied elsewhere.

Ⓐ Here is our familiar external style sheet, **style.css**, from earlier examples.

```
img {
    border: 4px solid red;
}


/*
That is a shorter way of writing this:

img {
    border-width: 4px;
    border-style: solid;
    border-color: red;
}
*/
```

Ⓑ In this example, the embedded style sheet comes last. Therefore, its styles will have precedence over the ones in **style.css** (as long as the conflicting rules have the same inheritance and specificity factors). The embedded style sheet overrides the style of border in **style.css**, making it dashed instead of solid, but doesn't affect the width or color **Ⓒ**.

```
...
<head>
    <title>El Palau de la Música</title>

    <link rel="stylesheet" href="style.
css" />

    <style>
    img {
       border-style: dashed;
    }
    </style>
</head>
...
```

C The **style** element's dashed border wins out over the solid border from the linked **style.css**, but the border width and color specified in **style.css** remain.

D Here, the linked style sheet comes last and has precedence over rules in the **style** element (all else being equal).

```
...
<head>
        <title>El Palau de la Música</title>
        <style>
        img {
            border-style: dashed;
        }
        </style>
        <link rel="stylesheet"
 → href="style.css" />
</head>
...
```

E The solid border from the **style.css** style sheet wins out over the internal **style** element's dashed border.

- There is one exception to how the order of conflicting styles affects which one wins out. A style marked with **!important** always wins, whether it's first in the order, last, or somewhere in between. Here's an example:

  p { margin-top: 1em !important; }

  You should avoid using it, though (although there are exceptions). You can achieve the same result with a selector almost every time. Meanwhile, **!important** makes your declarations too strong, and your CSS will get bogged down with additional **!important** declarations if you need to override any.

Got all that? The goods news is—because you're going to use only external style sheets and avoid using **!important** (you are, right?)—you don't even have to worry about the rules I just explained. But it still helps to understand them in case you come across someone else's code that is different.

The order rule that will matter the most to you is this: If a webpage contains more than one **link** element, conflicting styles in the external style sheet linked later take precedence.

TIP I advise not using @import, for performance reasons. But if it is used, imported styles will lose out to any conflicting styles that appear later than them, as you would expect.

TIP Here is one valid reason to use !important. Sometimes a webpage contains HTML that you can't change; for instance, a news feed that comes from a third-party service. Suppose that HTML has inline styles that don't fit in with your design. You can override them with !important in your style sheet.

Using Media-Specific Style Sheets

You can designate a style sheet to be used only for a particular output, such as only for printing or only for viewing onscreen in a browser. For example, you might create one general style sheet with features common to both the print and screen versions, and then create individual print and screen style sheets with properties to be used only for print or screen, respectively.

To designate media-specific style sheets:

- Add media="*output*" to the **link** or **style** element start tags, where *output* is one or more of the following: **print**, **screen**, or **all** (these are the most common types, though others exist; see the tips) **A**. Separate multiple values with commas.

- Alternatively, use the **@media** at-rule in your style sheet **B**. This method does not require specifying a media type in the **link** element.

TIP The default value for the media attribute is all, so declaring media="all" is redundant. In other words, you can leave out the media attribute unless you need to be specific. Some coders prefer to be explicit by always including media="all".

TIP See Christian Krammer's article at www.smashingmagazine.com/2011/11/24/how-to-set-up-a-print-style-sheet/ to learn more about creating a print style sheet.

A Limit the style sheet to a particular output by adding the **media** attribute to the **link** element. In this example, **style.css** affects the page when viewed in the browser (due to **media="screen"**), while **print.css** affects how the page prints (due to **media="print"**). If the first link element had **media="all"** or no **media** attribute at all, the rules in **style.css** would apply to printed pages, too.

```
<!DOCTYPE html>
<html lang="en">
<head>
    <meta charset="UTF-8" />
    <title>El Palau de la Música</title>
    <link rel="stylesheet" href="style.css"
    → media="screen" />
    <link rel="stylesheet" href="print.css"
    → media="print" />
</head>
<body>
<article>
    <h1>El Palau de la Música</h1>

    <img src="img/palau.jpg" width="250"
    → height="163" alt="El Palau de la
    → Música" />

    <img src="img/tickets.jpg" width="87"
    → height="163" alt="The Ticket Window" />

    <p>I love the <span lang="es">Palau de
    → la Música</span>. It is ornate and
    → gaudy and everything that was
    → wonderful about modernism. It's also
    → the home of the <span lang="es">Orfeó
    → Català</span>, where I learned the
    → benefits of Moscatell.</p>
</article>
</body>
</html>
```

B The `@media` at-rule in a style sheet is another way to target other media types (see Chapter 12 for more discussion). This example shows styles affecting all media types (including print) on top, and print-specific styles at the bottom contained within `@media print { }`. Viewed in a browser, this page would look similar to other figures in this chapter, except the text would be orange and italicized. The print version of this page is shown in **C**.

```
/* Styles for all media */
img {
    border: 4px solid red;
}

p {
    color: orange;
    font-style: italic;
}

/* Print Style Sheet */
@media print {

    body {
        /* make text larger */
        font-size: 25pt;
    }

    p {
        /* hex for black */
        color: #000;
    }

    img {
        /* don't show images */
        display: none;
    }

}
```

TIP There are nine possible output types: `all`, `aural`, `braille`, `handheld`, `print`, `projection`, `screen`, `tty`, and `tv`. They have varying degrees of browser support (most have modest support). Practically speaking, the ones you will likely ever use are `screen` and `print` (and perhaps `all`); each has very wide browser support. The `handheld` type never got much support from devices, so you'll typically use `screen` instead when designing for mobile (Chapter 12). Opera's projection mode, Opera Show, supports the `projection` type, which is geared toward projectors and similar views.

TIP Media queries, introduced by CSS3, combine with the media output types discussed here to grant you more styling power. They allow you to specify which styles are applied to a page based on characteristics of the output devices. For example, you can make your page look one way on a narrow screen like a smartphone, and another way on a wider screen like a laptop. With the vast array of devices in the wild nowadays, media queries are an essential tool for coders. Chapter 12 shows you how to build a site that works across devices. The discussion on media queries begins in "Understanding and Implementing Media Queries."

C The Chrome browser's print preview feature shows how the page in **A** would print. The text is enlarged, images are omitted, and paragraph text is italicized and black instead of orange. The `font-style: italic` declaration applies to print mode, too, since the print style sheet doesn't specify a different `font-style`.

The Inspiration of Others: CSS

In Chapter 2, you learned how to see the source code for a webpage. Viewing someone's CSS is not much more difficult.

To view others' CSS code:

1. First view the page's HTML code . For more details on viewing HTML source code, see "The Inspiration of Others" in Chapter 2.

   If the CSS code is in an embedded style sheet, you'll be able to see it already.

2. If the CSS is in an external style sheet, locate the reference to it in the HTML and click the file name Ⓐ. The style sheet displays in the browser window Ⓑ. You can copy it from there and paste it into your text editor if you like.

> **TIP** As with HTML, use others' code for inspiration, then write your own style sheets. View their code with a careful eye, though. Just because it's on the web doesn't mean it's always an example of the best way to code a particular design or effect, despite the author's best intentions.

> **TIP** Modern browsers allow you to click the style sheet name in the HTML source, as shown in Ⓐ. To view a style sheet in an older browser, you may need to copy the URL shown in the `link` element, paste it in the address bar of your browser (replacing the HTML file name), and press Enter. If the style sheet's URL is a relative address (see "URLs" in Chapter 1), you may have to reconstruct the style sheet's URL by combining the webpage's URL with the style sheet's relative URL.

> **TIP** The developer tools offered in modern browsers also allow quick access to viewing a page's CSS. They come bundled with most browsers, and there's an extension called Firebug for Firefox (Chapter 20).

Ⓐ View the source code for the HTML page that contains the style sheet you want to view, and click the style sheet file name.

Ⓑ The style sheet displays in the browser window, including the CSS comment below the **img** rule (so make sure you keep it clean in your comments!).

Defining Selectors

As you saw in "Constructing a Style Rule" in Chapter 7, there are two principal parts of a CSS style rule. The *selector* determines which elements the formatting will be applied to, and the *declarations* define just what formatting will be applied. In this chapter, you'll learn how to define CSS selectors.

Whereas the simplest selectors let you format all the elements of a given type—say, all the **h2** headings—other selectors let you apply formatting rules to elements based on their class, context, state, and more. As you progress through the chapter and learn about numerous selector types, please keep in mind that they can be combined in a single selector. For instance, you can write a selector that combines a class selector and an attribute selector.

Once you've defined the selectors, you can go on to create the declarations (with actual properties and values) explained in Chapters 10–16. Until then, you'll use the very simple and relatively obvious **color: red** in most examples.

Constructing Selectors

The selector determines which elements a style rule is applied to. For example, if you want to format all **p** elements with the Georgia font, 12 pixels high, you'd need to create a selector that identifies just the **p** elements and leaves the other elements in your code alone. If you want to format the first **p** in each section with a special indent, you'll need to create a slightly more specific selector that identifies only those **p** elements that are the first element in their section of the page.

A selector can define up to five different criteria for choosing the elements that should be formatted:

- The type or name of the element **A**.
- The context in which the element is found **B**.
- The class or ID of an element (**C** and **D**).
- A pseudo-element or the pseudo-class of an element **E** (I'll explain both of those later, I promise).
- Whether or not an element has certain attributes and values **F**.

Selectors can include any combination of these to pinpoint the desired elements. Mostly, you use one or two at a time. In addition, you can apply the same declarations to several selectors at once if you need to apply the same style rules to different groups of elements (see "Specifying Groups of Elements," later in this chapter).

The rest of this chapter explains exactly how to define selectors.

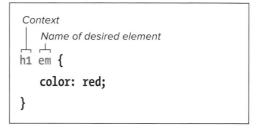

A The simplest kind of selector is simply the name of the type of element that should be formatted—in this case, the **h1** element.

B This selector uses context. The style will be applied only to the **em** elements within **h1** elements. The **em** elements found elsewhere are not affected.

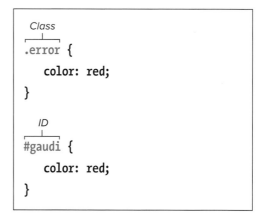

C The first selector chooses all elements that belong to the **error** class; in other words, any element with **class="error"** in its HTML start tag. The second selector chooses the one element with an **id** of **gaudi**, as specified by **id="gaudi"** in its HTML start tag. You'll recall that an ID may appear only once in each page, whereas a class may appear any number of times. This is the main reason why class selectors are recommended (and ID selectors are not)—you can reuse their styles on as many elements as you like.

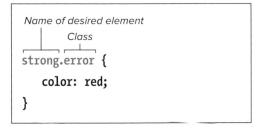

Name of desired element
Class

```
strong.error {
    color: red;
}
```

D You can be more specific by prefixing a class selector (or ID selector) with the element name to target. In this case, the selector chooses only the **strong** elements with the **error** class rather than every element with the **error** class. In general, don't use this approach unless you have to; the less specific class selector in the previous example **C** is typically preferred, because of its flexibility.

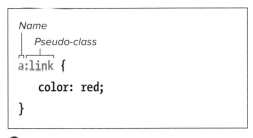

Name
Pseudo-class

```
a:link {
    color: red;
}
```

E In this example, the selector chooses **a** elements that belong to the **link** pseudo-class (that is, the links on your page that haven't yet been visited).

TIP I recommend that you avoid ID selectors **C**. I'll elaborate in "Selecting Elements by Class or ID."

TIP As you will learn in "Selecting Elements Based on Attributes," your selectors are not limited to targeting an attribute's exact value, as in the diagram in **F**.

TIP A key goal when writing CSS is to keep your selectors as simple as you can while making them only as specific as necessary. Take advantage of the fact that many styles cascade down to an element's descendants. Also, identify common design elements in your pages and write a selector (like a class) that allows you to share the styles across various elements. Style sheets are typically smaller and easier to manage as a result. These tips will become more obvious as you gain experience building pages, but I'm mentioning them now to plant the seed.

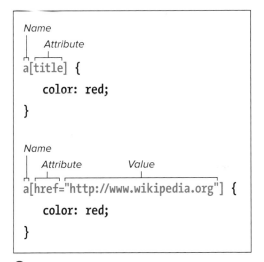

Name
Attribute

```
a[title] {
    color: red;
}
```

Name
Attribute   Value

```
a[href="http://www.wikipedia.org"] {
    color: red;
}
```

F You can use the square brackets to add to a selector information about the desired element's attributes (or attributes and values). The first example targets all **a** elements with a **title** attribute, and the second targets only those that point to Wikipedia.

Selecting Elements by Name

One of the most common criteria for choosing which elements **A** to format is the element's name (known as a *type selector*, because you specify what type of element to style). For example, you might want to make all the **h1** elements big and green and format all the **p** elements with the Verdana font.

A This HTML code has two **h2** elements. (In case you're wondering, placing the `lang` attribute on an element indicates that the content is in a different language than the page's default language, which is specified on the **html** element that follows the DOCTYPE at the beginning of each page. In this case, `lang="es"` on each **h2** indicates that their content is in Spanish.)

```
<!DOCTYPE html>
<html lang="en">
<head>
...
</head>
<body>
...
<article class="architect">
    <h1>Antoni Gaudí</h1>
    <p>Many tourists are drawn to Barcelona to see Antoni Gaudí's incredible architecture.</p>

    <p>Barcelona <a href="http://www.gaudi2002.bcn.es/english/" rel="external">celebrated the 150th
    → anniversary</a> of Gaudí's birth in 2002.</p>

    <h2 lang="es">La Casa Milà</h2>
    <p>Gaudí's work was essentially useful. <span lang="es">La Casa Milà</span> is an apartment
    → building and <em>real people</em> live there.</p>

    <h2 lang="es">La Sagrada Família</h2>
    <p>The complicatedly named and curiously unfinished Expiatory Temple of the Sacred Family is
    → the <em>most visited</em> building in Barcelona.</p>
</article>
...
```

B This selector will choose all the **h2** elements in the document and make them red **C** .

```
h2 {
    color: red;
}
```

Antoni Gaudí

Many tourists are drawn to Barcelona to see Antoni Gaudí's incredible architecture.

Barcelona celebrated the 150th anniversary of Gaudí's birth in 2002.

La Casa Milà

Gaudí's work was essentially useful. La Casa Milà is an apartment building and *real people* live there.

La Sagrada Família

The complicatedly named and curiously unfinished Expiatory Temple of the Sacred Family is the *most visited* building in Barcelona.

C All the **h2** elements are colored red.

To select elements to format based on their type:

1. Type *selector*, where *selector* is the name of the desired type of element, without any attributes **B** .

2. Type { .

3. Type the styles you'd like to apply to the selected element, expressed in **property**: **value** pairs. Descriptions of CSS properties and values begin in earnest in the next chapter.

4. Type } to finish your style rule.

Please note that I won't repeat steps 2–4 in the steps of the remaining sections in this chapter, but they are required to build a complete style rule. See "Constructing a Style Rule" in Chapter 7 for more information.

TIP Unless you specify otherwise (using the techniques in the rest of this chapter), all the elements of the specified type will be formatted, no matter where they appear in your document.

TIP Not all selectors need to specify an element's name. If you want to apply formatting to an entire class of elements, regardless of which type of elements have been identified with that class, leave the name out of the selector. The next section explains how to do this.

TIP The wildcard, * (asterisk), matches any element name in your code. For example, * { border: 2px solid green; } gives every element a two-pixel, green, solid border! Because it has a wide reach and takes browsers longer to apply, be careful about using a wildcard. In practice, you won't have many occasions where it's appropriate anyway.

TIP You can choose a group of element names for a selector by using the comma to separate them. For more details, consult "Specifying Groups of Elements," later in this chapter.

Selecting Elements by Class or ID

If you've labeled elements with a class Ⓐ or an ID (see the last tip), you can use that criterion in a selector to apply formatting to only those elements that are so labeled Ⓑ. However, using a class is preferred, as I'll explain.

Ⓐ There are two **article** elements with a **class** of **architect**. A short paragraph without the **class** is between them.

```
...
<article id="gaudi" class="architect">
    <h1>Antoni Gaudí</h1>
    <p>Many tourists are drawn to Barcelona to see Antoni Gaudí's incredible architecture.</p>

    <p>Barcelona <a href="http://www.gaudi2002.bcn.es/english/" rel="external">celebrated the 150th
    → anniversary</a> of Gaudí's birth in 2002.</p>

    <h2 lang="es">La Casa Milà</h2>
    <p>Gaudí's work was essentially useful. <span lang="es">La Casa Milà</span> is an apartment
    → building and <em>real people</em> live there.</p>
    ...
</article>

<p>This paragraph doesn't have <code>class="architect"</code>, so it isn't red when the CSS is
→ applied.</p>

<article class="architect">
    <h1>Lluís Domènech i Montaner</h1>
    <p>Lluís Domènech i Montaner was a contemporary of Gaudí.</p>
    ...
</article>
...
```

B This selector will choose the elements with a **class** equal to **architect**. In this case, they're both **article** elements, but you could apply the classes to any elements. If you wanted to apply the style *only* when an **article** element has this class, you would write the selector as **article.architect**. But that's more specific than you'll usually need to be.

```
.architect {
    color: red;
}
```

Antoni Gaudí – Introduction

Antoni Gaudí – Introduction +

Antoni Gaudí

Many tourists are drawn to Barcelona to see Antoni Gaudí's incredible architecture.

Barcelona celebrated the 150th anniversary of Gaudí's birth in 2002.

La Casa Milà

Gaudí's work was essentially useful. La Casa Milà is an apartment building and *real people* live there.

La Sagrada Família

The complicatedly named and curiously unfinished Expiatory Temple of the Sacred Family is the *most visited* building in Barcelona.

This paragraph doesn't have class="architect", **so it isn't red when the CSS is applied.**

Lluís Domènech i Montaner

Lluís Domènech i Montaner was a contemporary of Gaudí.

C The **article** elements with the **architect** class are displayed in red, but the **p** element between those elements is not. (In case you're wondering, the link is blue because of the browser's default link style, but you can write your own rule to override it.)

To select elements to format based on their class:

1. Type **.** (a period).

2. With no intervening space, immediately type *classname*, where *classname* identifies the class to which you'd like to apply the styles.

To select elements to format based on their ID:

1. Type **#** (a hash, or pound, sign).

2. With no intervening space, immediately type *id*, where *id* uniquely identifies the element to which you'd like to apply the styles.

continues on next page

TIP You can use class and ID selectors alone or with other selector criteria. For example, `.news { color: red; }` would affect all elements with the news class, while `h1.news { color: red; }` would affect only the h1 elements with the news class. It's best to omit the element name from an ID or class selector unless you have to target it specifically.

TIP Notice in Ⓐ and Ⓑ that I used a class name (`architect`) that conveys the meaning of the content to which it's applied rather than calling it `red`. Though there are exceptions, it's generally best to avoid creating a class name that describes how something looks (often called *presentational* class names), because you might change the styles later, like making the text green in this case.

TIP If you want to target an element that has multiple classes, you can chain together the class names in your selector, like this: `.architect.bio { color: blue; }`. Any rules with `.architect` or `.bio` selectors would still apply to the element, but a rule with `.architect.bio` is more specific, so any competing styles it has would take precedence. Please note that there is *not* a space between the class names. If there were, it would style any element with the `bio` class that is nested inside any element with the `architect` class, as described in "Selecting Elements by Context."

TIP If the example in Ⓑ were written instead as `#gaudi { color: red; }`, only the text in the first `article` would be red, because it's the only one with `id="gaudi"`. Each ID must be unique, so you can't reuse that ID on the `article` about Lluís Domènech i Montaner.

TIP For more information on assigning classes to elements in the HTML code, consult "Naming Elements with a Class or ID" in Chapter 3.

Class Selectors vs. ID Selectors

When deciding between class selectors and ID selectors, I suggest using class selectors whenever possible, in large part because you can reuse them. Many advocate not using ID selectors at all, an argument I agree with and adhere to in my own work, although ultimately the choice comes down to you as you develop your sites. Here are two of the issues that ID selectors introduce:

- Their associated styles can't be reused on other elements (remember, an ID may appear on only one element in a page). This can lead to repeating styles on other elements, rather than sharing them via a class.

- They are far more specific than class selectors. It's sort of like using a sledgehammer instead of your fingers to press a tack into a corkboard—a stronger tool than is necessary for the job and harder to undo. In CSS, it means that if you ever need to override styling that was defined with an ID selector, you'll need to write a CSS rule that's even more specific. A few of these might not be hard to manage, but once you're working on a site of a decent size, your selectors and your CSS overall can get longer and more complicated than necessary. The problems can compound if you are working with a team—using ID selectors or other selectors that create a very high specificity can be a big headache for all involved.

Those two points probably will become more clear to you as you work with CSS more. (On the flip side, one reason some people like using IDs is so they'll know at a glance if an element is unique. However, in my own experience, I don't think the trade-off is worth it. Besides, if your site design changes and makes an element no longer unique, the ID selector won't suffice.)

So, I recommend looking for opportunities to combine shared styles into one or more class selectors so you can reuse them, and to keep ID selectors to a minimum if you do use them. I think you'll find your style sheets shorter and easier to manage.

To be clear, though, ID selectors still play a role in your HTML. They identify link anchors within a page (see "Creating and Linking to Anchors" in Chapter 6) and are invaluable when you're writing JavaScript to apply special behavior to a specific page element (JavaScript is a subject all its own, so I won't dive into it in this book).

Selecting Elements by Context

In CSS, you can pinpoint elements depending on their ancestors, their parent, or their siblings (see "Parents and Children" in Chapter 1) (Ⓐ through Ⓓ).

An *ancestor* is any element that contains the desired element (the *descendant*), regardless of the number of generations that separate them. (A *parent* is an element that directly contains another element [a *child*], meaning they are only one generation away.) It's common practice to indent elements that are children of another element so you can see their relationship at a glance Ⓑ. The indentation has no bearing on how your page looks.

There is often more than one way to craft your selectors to get the desired effect. It comes down to how specific you need to be Ⓒ.

Ⓐ I've added a **section** element around part of the **article** so I can demonstrate a page with a few generations. I've also shortened the text to make the relationships between elements easier to see. Note that in this snippet there are two second-generation **p** elements directly within the **article** with the **architect** class, and one third-generation **p** element within the first **section** (within the **article**). There's another third-generation **p** in the full code, not shown. The **h2** instances are also third generation.

```
...
<article class="architect">
     <h1>Antoni Gaudí</h1>
     <p>Many tourists ... </p>
     <p>Barcelona ... </p>

     <section>
        <h2 lang="es">La Casa Milà</h2>
        <p>Gaudí's work ... </p>
     </section>

     <section>
        <h2 lang="es">La Sagrada Família</h2>
        ...
     </section>
</article>
...
```

Ⓑ This combines a class selector with a type selector. The space between **.architect** and **p** means that this selector will find any **p** element that is a descendant of any element with the **architect** class, regardless of its generation. See the results in Ⓓ and other ways to create the same effect in Ⓒ.

```
.architect p {
    color: red;
}
```

C The selector in the first example here (**article p { }**) is less specific than the one in **B** and the one that follows it (**article.architect p { }**). The second example here is more specific than all of them, but prefixing a class (or especially an ID) with the element name is usually more specific than you need to be in practice.

```
/* Other ways to get the same effect
------------------------------------ */
/* Any p that is a descendant of any article.
→ The least specific of the three. */
article p {
    color: red;
}

/* Any p that is a descendant of article
→ elements with the architect class. The most
→ specific of the three. */
article.architect p {
    color: red;
}
```

Antoni Gaudí

Many tourists are drawn to Barcelona to see Antoni Gaudí's incredible architecture.

Barcelona celebrated the 150th anniversary of Gaudí's birth in 2002.

La Casa Milà

Gaudí's work was essentially useful. La Casa Milà is an apartment building and *real people* live there.

La Sagrada Família

The complicatedly named and curiously unfinished Expiatory Temple of the Sacred Family is the *most visited* building in Barcelona.

D All the **p** elements that are contained within the element with the **architect** class are red even if they're also within other elements that are within the element with the **architect** class. The style rules in **B** and **C** yield the result shown here.

To select an element to format based on its ancestor:

1. Type *ancestor*, where *ancestor* is the selector for the element that contains the element you wish to format.

2. Type a space. (This is critical.)

3. If necessary, repeat steps 1 and 2 for each successive generation of ancestors.

4. Type *descendant*, where *descendant* is the selector for the element you wish to format.

TIP If you're keeping score at home, a selector based on an element's ancestor had been known as a *descendant selector*, but CSS3 renamed it a *descendant combinator*. (Some people still say "selector.")

TIP Don't be thrown off by the **article.architect** portion of the second example in **C**. Remember that it simply means "the **article** whose **class** is equal to **architect**." So **article.architect p** means "any p element that is contained in the **article** element whose **class** is equal to **architect**." By comparison, the less-specific **.architect p** means "any p element that is contained in *any* element whose **class** is equal to **architect**" **C**.

To select an element to format based on its parent:

The previous examples showed descendant combinators. CSS also has *child combinators*, which allow you to define a rule for an *immediate* descendant (in other words, a *child*) of a parent element. You may know them as *child selectors*, the pre-CSS3 terminology.

1. Type *parent*, where *parent* is the selector for the element that directly contains the element you wish to format.

2. Type > (the greater-than sign) Ⓔ.

3. If necessary, repeat steps 1 and 2 for each successive generation of parents.

4. Type *child*, where *child* is the selector for the element you wish to format.

TIP Just as you saw with the descendant combinator, you can add the element name before the class. For example, `article. architect > p { color: red; }` yields the same effect in this case, but it is more specific. Or, to be less specific than either this or Ⓔ, leave out the class entirely, as in `article > p { color: red; }`. Some of the examples that follow in the rest of the chapter could be simplified in a similar manner. Now that you have a taste for how it's done, I won't call out these alternatives. As I've mentioned before, but just to reinforce the point, use simpler forms when appropriate before resorting to more-specific ones.

TIP You may also use ID selectors in child combinators, but as you know by now, I recommend using less-specific selectors, like those with a class, whenever possible.

TIP Also see "Parents and Children" in Chapter 1.

Ⓔ This selector will choose only those **p** elements that are children (not grandchildren, not great-grandchildren, and so on) of elements with the **architect** class. To qualify, they may not be contained within any other element Ⓕ.

```
.architect > p {
    color: red;
}
```

Ⓕ Only the first two **p** elements are children of the element with the **architect** class. The two other **p** elements are children of the **section** elements within the **article** element. For the HTML code used in this example, see Ⓐ.

G This adjacent sibling combinator chooses only those **p** elements that directly follow a sibling **p** element.

```
.architect p+p {
    color: red;
}
```

Antoni Gaudí

Many tourists are drawn to Barcelona to see Antoni Gaudí's incredible architecture.

Barcelona celebrated the 150th anniversary of Gaudí's birth in 2002.

La Casa Milà

Gaudí's work was essentially useful. La Casa Milà

H Only the **p** elements that *directly* follow a sibling **p** element are red. If there were a third, fourth, or more consecutive paragraphs, they too would be red. For example, an adjacent sibling combinator would be useful for indenting all paragraphs except the first.

TIP You may also use a *general sibling combinator*, which allows you to select a sibling that is not necessarily immediately preceded by another sibling. The only difference in syntax from an adjacent sibling combinator is that you use a ~ (tilde) instead of a + to separate the siblings. For instance, h1~h2 { color: red; } would make any h2 element red as long as it is preceded by a sibling h1 somewhere within the parent (it could be immediately adjacent, but it doesn't have to be).

To select an element to format based on an adjacent sibling:

Continuing with the familial theme, *sibling* elements are elements of any kind that are children of the same parent. *Adjacent siblings* are elements that are next to each other directly, meaning no other sibling sits between them. In the following crude example, the **h1** and **p** are adjacent siblings, and the **p** and **h2** are adjacent siblings, but the **h1** and **h2** are not. However, they are all siblings (and children of the **body** element):

```
...
<body>
      <h1>...</h1>
      <p>...</p>
      <h2>...</h2>
</body>
</html>
```

The CSS *adjacent sibling combinator* allows you to target a sibling element that is preceded immediately by a sibling you specify (**G** and **H**). (See the tip regarding the *general sibling combinator*, new in CSS3.)

1. Type *sibling*, where *sibling* is the selector for the element that directly precedes the desired element within the same parent element. (As long as they are directly next to each other, they don't have to be the same element type, as explained previously.)

2. Type + (a plus sign).

3. If necessary, repeat steps 1 and 2 for each successive sibling.

4. Type *element*, where *element* is the selector for the element you wish to format.

Selecting an Element That Is the First or Last Child

The previous section explained how to select an element that is the child of another element. The example given was **.architect > p**, which selects all paragraphs that are children of the element with the **architect** class. But it's sometimes useful to be able to select an element only when it is the first or last child of an element. The **:first-child** (**A** through **C**) and **:last-child** (**A**, **D**, and **E**) *pseudo-classes* are what you need to achieve this.

Initially, some people get a little tripped up by how they work. They think that a selector such as **li:first-child** will select the **li** element's first child and that **li:last-child** will select its last child. If that were true, "(Colegio Teresiano)" would be red in both cases (**C** and **E**), because the **span** it is in is both the first and last child of an **li** **A**. What actually happens is that those pseudo-classes select an element—in this case, an **li**—when *it* is the first child or the last child.

A We'll cover lists extensively in Chapter 15, but this is an unordered list (**ul**), and each list item (**li**) is a child of it. It is common to use **:first-child** and **:last-child** to style list items, though often it is to apply or remove a border rather than to make a simple text color change.

```
...
<p>A partial list of Gaudí's projects
→ follows:</p>

<ul>
    <li lang="es">La Casa Milà</li>
    <li lang="es">La Sagrada Família</li>
    <li>College of the Teresians <span lang=
    → "es">(Colegio Teresiano)</span></li>
    <li>Park Güell</li>
</ul>
...
```

B This selector chooses only the **li** element that is the first child of its parent.

```
li:first-child {
    color: red;
}
```

A partial list of Gaudí's projects follows:

- La Casa Milà
- La Sagrada Família
- College of the Teresians (Colegio Teresiano)
- Park Güell

C By virtue of being the first child of the **ul**, the first **li** is red. (The indentation and bullets are due to the browser's default styling of unordered lists.)

D This selector chooses only the `li` element that is the last child of its parent.

```
li:last-child {
    color: red;
}
```

A partial list of Gaudí's projects follows:

- La Casa Milà
- La Sagrada Família
- College of the Teresians (Colegio Teresiano)
- Park Güell

E As you would expect, only the last `li` is red in this case.

To select an element to format that is the first or last child of its parent:

1. Optionally, type the selector that represents the first child or last child you want to style (for example, **p** or **.news**). (See the last tip.) Do *not* follow it with a space.

2. Type `:first-child` **B** or `:last-child` **D**, as desired.

TIP I discuss pseudo-classes more in the sidebar of the next section.

TIP The `:last-child` pseudo-class was added to CSS later than was `:first-child`. As a result, it is not supported in versions of Internet Explorer prior to IE9. The good news is that you can work often around this, because IE8 and later do support `:first-child`. Here's a common scenario, although it does get ahead of us by touching on margins (Chapter 11). Suppose you want a margin of 20px *below* every list item except the last one. Set `li { margin-bottom: 0; margin-top: 20px; }` so the list items have space at the *top* instead of the bottom. Then use `li:first-child { margin-top: 0; }` to negate the top margin on the first item. It's sort of like coding in reverse to get the same effect.

TIP You can target pseudo-classes more specifically by adding another selector before them. For example, `.architect h1:first-child { color: red; }` would style only those h1 elements that are the first child of an element with the `.architect` class.

TIP Although it's common to do so, you do not have to specify a selector in step 1. For instance, simply `:first-child { color: red; }` would apply to each element that is a first child of another element. In the case of our example **A**, that would result in the paragraph (it is the first child of body), the first `li` (it is the first child of the `ul`), and "(Colegio Teresiano)" (the `span` it's in is the first child of an `li`) all being red.

Selecting the First Letter or First Line of an Element

You can select just the first letter (**A**
through **C**) or first line (**A**, **D**, and **E**) of
an element with the **:first-letter** and
:first-line *pseudo-elements*, respectively. (See the sidebar for more info.)

To select the first letter of an element:

1. Type *element*, where *element* is the
   selector for the element whose first
   letter you'd like to format.

2. Type **:first-letter** to select the first
   letter of the element referenced in
   step 1.

To select the first line of an element:

1. Type *element*, where *element* is the
   selector for the element whose first line
   you'd like to format.

2. Type **:first-line** to select the entire
   first line of the element referenced in
   step 1.

A It's easy to tell which are the first letters that
:first-letter will target, but there's no telling
which words will be affected by **:first-line** until
you view the page in the browser and see how the
content flows **E**. It's not determined by what line
the words are on in the HTML itself.

```
...
<article class="architect">
    <h1>Antoni Gaudí</h1>
    <p>Many tourists are drawn to Barcelona
    → to see Antoni Gaudí's incredible
    → architecture.</p>
    <p>Barcelona <a href="http://
    → www.gaudi2002.bcn.es/english/"
    → rel="external">celebrated the 150th
    → anniversary</a> of Gaudí's birth in
    → 2002.</p>

    <h2 lang="es">La Casa Milà</h2>
    <p>Gaudí's work was essentially
    → useful...</p>
    ...
</article>
...
```

B Here the selector will choose just the first letter
of each **p** element.

```
p:first-letter {
    color: red;
    font-size: 1.4em; /* make letter
    → larger */
    font-weight: bold;
}
```

C The **first-letter** selector can be used
to create a drop-cap effect.

D Here the selector will choose the first line of each **p** element.

```
p:first-line {
    color: red;
}
```

E Adjusting the width of the window changes the content of the first lines (and thus, what is formatted).

TIP You may combine the `:first-letter` or `:first-line` pseudo-elements with more-complicated selectors than those used in this example. For example, if you wanted to select just the first letter of each paragraph contained in elements with a class named `project`, your selector would be `.project p:first-letter`.

TIP Only certain CSS properties can be applied to `:first-letter` pseudo-elements: font, color, background, text-decoration, vertical-align (as long as the `:first-letter` is not floated), text-transform, line-height, margin, padding, border, float, and clear. You'll learn about all these in Chapters 10 and 11.

TIP Punctuation (like a quotation mark) that precedes the first letter is formatted as if it is part of the first letter. Modern browsers support this, but versions of IE prior to IE8 don't. Instead, they consider the punctuation itself as the first letter.

Pseudo-Elements, Pseudo-Classes, and CSS3's Syntax

In CSS3, the syntax of `:first-line` is `::first-line` and the syntax of `:first-letter` is `::first-letter`. Note the double, rather than single, colons. The intent of this change was to distinguish the four pseudo-elements—`::first-line`, `::first-letter`, `::before`, and `::after`—from pseudo-classes like `:first-child`, `:last-child`, `:link`, `:hover`, and others.

A *pseudo-element* is one that doesn't exist as an element in the HTML. For instance, you don't mark up your first letter or first line of text with HTML that defines it as such. Instead, it represents content that's part of other elements, like the **p** elements in the example.

A *pseudo-class* identifies a group of elements without your having to mark them with a class in the HTML code. You saw that with `:first-child`—I didn't have to add `class="first-child"` to an element for it to work. You will learn more pseudo-classes in the next section.

The double-colon syntax of `::first-line` and `::first-letter` is preferred moving forward, and modern browsers support it. The original, single-colon syntax is deprecated, but browsers continue to support it for backward compatibility. However, no version of Internet Explorer prior to IE9 supports the double colon, so you may decide to continue using the single-colon syntax unless you serve different CSS to IE8 and below (see http://reference.sitepoint.com/css/conditionalcomments).

Selecting Links Based on Their State

CSS lets you apply formatting to links **A** based on their current state; that is, whether the visitor is hovering their cursor on top of one, whether a link has been visited, or whatever. You achieve these with a series of pseudo-classes.

To select links to format based on their state:

1. Type **a** (since **a** is the name of the element for links).

2. Optionally, type **:** (a colon) with no spaces before or after it.

3. If you did step 2, do one of the following to indicate the link state you wish to affect **B**:

   ▸ Type **link** to change the appearance of links that haven't yet been or aren't currently being activated or pointed at **C**.

   ▸ Type **visited** to change links that the visitor has already activated **D**.

   ▸ Type **focus** if the link is selected via the keyboard and is ready to be activated **E**. (Note: Focus also happens when a link is active.)

   ▸ Type **hover** to change the appearance of links when they're pointed to with the cursor **F**. (See the last tip.)

   ▸ Type **active** to change the appearance of links as they are activated **G**.

A You can't specify in the HTML what state a link will have; it's controlled by your visitors. Pseudo-classes allow you to access the state and change the display as you please.

```
...
    <p>Many tourists are drawn to Barcelona
→ to see Antoni Gaudí's incredible
→ architecture.</p>

    <p>Barcelona <a href="http://www.
→ gaudi2002.bcn.es/english/">
→ celebrated</a> the 150th anniversary
→ of Gaudí's birth in 2002.</p>
...
```

B Styles for links should always be defined in this order, to avoid overriding properties when a link is in more than one state (say, focused and active, which happens whenever you activate a link).

```
a:link {
    color: red;
}

a:visited {
    color: orange;
}

a:focus {
    color: purple;
}

a:hover {
    color: green;
}

a:active {
    color: blue;
}
```

C Links will be red when new and not visited.

D Once the link has been visited, it turns orange.

E If the link gets the focus (such as with the Tab key), it is purple.

F When the visitor hovers over the link with the pointer, it is green.

G As the visitor activates the link, it turns blue.

TIP You do not have to specify a pseudo-class to style links (this is why steps 2 and 3 are optional). For example, a { color: red; } styles all link states the same way. However, it is good practice to differentiate the states for your visitors' benefit by using the pseudo-classes.

TIP You may also apply the :active and :hover pseudo-classes to other elements. For instance, p:hover { color: red; } would change the color of each paragraph to red when it is hovered over.

TIP Since a link can be in more than one state at a time (say, simultaneously active and hovered above) and later rules override earlier ones, it's important to define the rules in the following order: link, visited, focus, hover, active (LVFHA). One popular way to remember this is the mnemonic "Lord Vader's Former Handle Anakin." Some argue for ordering the rules LVHFA instead; it works too.

TIP Browsers on touch devices like smartphones and tablets don't have a hover state like desktop browsers do. That's because a device such as an iPad doesn't detect when your finger is "hovering" above a link, only when you tap it to activate it. However, iPhones and iPads do display what you specify with :hover when a visitor *activates* the link. Other touch devices vary in behavior.

Selecting Elements Based on Attributes

You can also apply formatting to elements with specific attributes or attribute values **A**. CSS provides numerous ways to match these, including checking for just the attribute name, or for a whole or partial value (see **Table 9.1** for more information). If you omit the value from your selector **B**, you can style an element with a given attribute regardless of its value **C**.

To select elements to format based on their attributes:

1. Type *element*, where *element* is the selector for the element whose attributes you want to target.

2. Type [*attribute*, where *attribute* is the name of the attribute that an element must have to be selected.

3. Optionally, do one of the following:

   ▸ Type =*"value"* if you want to specify the *value* that the attribute's value must equal for its element to be selected.

   ▸ Type ~=*"value"* to specify an exact *value* that the attribute's value must contain (among any other space-separated values) for its element to be selected. It matches a complete word, not part of a word.

   ▸ Type |=*"value"* (that was the pipe symbol, not a "1" or the letter "I") to specify that the attribute's value must be equal to *value* or begin with *value* and be followed by a hyphen for its element to be selected. Don't type the hyphen; browsers know to look for it. (This is most common when searching for elements containing the lang

A For demonstration purposes, I've added a **class** on two paragraphs.

```
...
<article class="architect">
    <h1>Antoni Gaudí</h1>

    <p class="intro">Many tourists are
    → drawn to Barcelona to see Antoni
    → Gaudí's incredible architecture.</p>

    <p>Barcelona <a href="http://www.
    → gaudi2002.bcn.es/english/" rel=
    → "external">celebrated the 150th
    → anniversary</a> of Gaudí's birth
    → in 2002.</p>

    <h2 lang="es">La Casa Milà</h2>
    <p class="highlight">Gaudí's work was
    → essentially useful. <span lang="es">La
    → Casa Milà</span> is an apartment
    → building and <em>real people</em> live
    → there.</p>

    <h2 lang="es">La Sagrada Família</h2>
    <p>The complicatedly named and curiously
    → unfinished Expiatory Temple of the
    → Sacred Family is the <em>most visited
    → </em> building in Barcelona.</p>
</article>
...
```

B The square brackets enclose the desired attribute and any desired value. In this case, the value is omitted to select any paragraph with any **class** attribute.

```
p[class] {
    color: red;
}
```

Antoni Gaudí

Many tourists are drawn to Barcelona to see Antoni Gaudí's incredible architecture.

Barcelona celebrated the 150th anniversary of Gaudí's birth in 2002.

La Casa Milà

Gaudí's work was essentially useful. La Casa Milà is an apartment building and *real people* live there.

La Sagrada Família

The complicatedly named and curiously unfinished Expiatory Temple of the Sacred Family is the *most visited* building in Barcelona.

C Every **p** element that contains a **class** attribute, regardless of the class's value, is red. If the selector had been **p[class="intro"]**, only the first paragraph would be red. And if the selector had been **p[class^="intro"]**, the first paragraph would be red as well as any paragraph with **class="introduction"**, **class="introductory"**, and so on.

attribute; for example, **[lang|="en"]** would match both **lang="en"** and **lang="en-US"** in the HTML.)

- ▸ Type **^="***value***"** to specify that the attribute's value must begin with **value** as either a full word or part of a word (new in CSS3; see the tip in this section).
- ▸ Type **$="***value***"** to specify that the attribute's value must end with **value** as either a full word or part of a word for its element to be selected (new in CSS3; see the tip in this section).
- ▸ Type ***="***value***"** to specify that the attribute's value must contain at least one instance of the **value** substring for its element to be selected. In other words, **value** doesn't need to be a complete word in the attribute's value (new in CSS3; see the tip in this section).

4. Type **]**. If you would like to specify additional attributes or attribute values for **element**, repeat beginning with step 2.

TIP Selecting elements based on the attributes (and values) they contain is supported by all current major browsers. IE7 and IE8 have a few quirks related to the three new CSS3 attribute selectors noted in step 3. See http://reference.sitepoint.com/css/css3attributeselectors for more information.

TABLE 9.1 Attribute Selector Options

Selector	Attribute value
[attribute]	Matches attribute regardless of its value
[attribute="value"]	Is an exact match of *value*
[attribute~="value"]	Is an exact match of any complete word (*value*) in a space-separated list of words
[attribute|="value"]	Is exactly *value* or begins with *value* followed immediately by a –
[attribute^="value"]	Begins with *value* as a full word or part of a word
[attribute$="value"]	Ends with *value* as a full word or part of a word
[attribute*="value"]	Contains *value* substring (part of a word within a word)

More Attribute Selector Examples

Attribute selectors can be a little funny-looking (Table 9.1), but they give you a lot of flexibility to match attributes and their values. Here are a few more examples to demonstrate some of the diverse ways in which you can use them.

- This example selects any **a** element with a **rel** attribute equal to **external** (it has to be an exact match). It's good practice to include **rel="external"** on any **a** element that links to a page outside your website (an *external* link). By using the following rule, you can style external links differently to give your visitors a cue that the link leaves your site.

```
a[rel="external"] {
   color: red;
}
```

- Imagine you have one **article** element with two classes, such as **<article class="project barcelona">**, and another that has one, **<article class="barcelona">**. The **~=** syntax tests for a partial match of a complete word within a whitespace-separated list of words, making both elements red in the following example.

```
article[class~="barcelona"] {
   color: red;
}

/* This would also match because this selector matches partial
strings (complete words not required). */
article[class*="barc"] {
   color: red;
}

/* This would NOT match because barc is not a complete word in the
whitespace-separated list, as required by ~=. */
article[class~="barc"] {
   color: red;
}
```

- This example selects any **h2** with a **lang** attribute that is **es** or **es** followed by a – (such as **es-ES** for Spanish in Spain or **es-PE** for Spanish in Peru). There are two instances of these in the HTML code in Ⓐ.

```
h2[lang|="es"] {
   color: red;
}
```

continues on next page

More Attribute Selector Examples *(continued)*

- By using the universal selector, this example selects *any* element with a **lang** attribute that begins with **es** or **es** followed by a **-**. There are three instances of these in the HTML code in Ⓐ.

```css
*[lang|="es"] {
    color: red;
}
```

- Combining a couple of the methods, this example selects any **a** element with both any **href** attribute and any **title** attribute containing the word **howdy**.

```css
a[href][title~="howdy"] {
    color: red;
}
```

- As a less precise variation of the previous one, this example selects any **a** element with both any **href** attribute and any **title** attribute containing **how** as a complete word or a substring (it matches if the title's value is **how**, **howdy**, **show**, and so on, regardless of where in the value **how** appears).

```css
a[href][title*="how"] {
    color: red;
}
```

- This example matches any **a** element with an **href** attribute value that begins with **http://**.

```css
a[href^="http://"] {
    color: orange;
}
```

- This example matches any **img** element with a **src** attribute value of exactly **logo.png**.

```css
img[src="logo.png"] {
    border: 1px solid green;
}
```

- This example is less specific than the previous one, matching any **img** element with a **src** attribute value that ends with **.png**.

```css
img[src$=".png"] {
    border: 1px solid green;
}
```

That's by no means the limit of what you can do, but hopefully it inspires you to explore further.

Specifying Groups of Elements

It's often necessary to apply the same style rules to more than one element. You can either reiterate the rules for each element, or you can combine selectors and apply the rules in one fell swoop (**A** through **C**). Of course, the latter approach is more efficient and generally makes your style sheets easier to maintain.

To apply styles to groups of elements:

1. Type *selector1*, where *selector1* is the name of the first element that should be affected by the style rule.

2. Type **,** (a comma).

3. Type *selector2*, where *selector2* is the next element that should be affected by the style rule.

4. Repeat steps 2 and 3 for each additional element.

TIP Styling elements as a group is nothing more than a handy shortcut. The rule in **B** is precisely the same as these two rules: h1 { color: red; } and h2 { color: red; }.

TIP You can group any kind of selector, from the simplest **B** to the most complex. For example, you could use h2, .project p:first-letter to choose the level two headings and the first letter of the p elements in elements whose class is equal to project.

TIP Each selector doesn't have to be on its own line (as in **B**), but many coders use this convention to make it easier to read.

TIP It is sometimes useful to create a single style rule with the common styles that apply to several selectors and then create individual style rules with the styles they do not share. Remember that rules specified later override rules specified earlier in the style sheet.

A The code contains one **h1** and two **h2** elements.

```
...
<article class="architect">
    <h1>Antoni Gaudí</h1>
    <p>Many tourists are drawn ...</p>
    <p>Barcelona ...</p>

    <h2 lang="es">La Casa Milà</h2>
    <p>Gaudí's work was ...</p>

    <h2 lang="es">La Sagrada Família</h2>
    <p>The complicatedly named ...</p>
</article>
...
```

B You can list any number of individual selectors (whether they include element names, classes, pseudo-elements, and more), as long as you separate each with a comma.

```
h1,
h2 {
    color: red;
}
```

Antoni Gaudí

Many tourists are drawn to Barcelona to see Antoni Gaudí's incredible architecture.

Barcelona celebrated the 150th anniversary of Gaudí's birth in 2002.

La Casa Milà

Gaudí's work was essentially useful. La Casa Milà is an apartment building and *real people* live there.

La Sagrada Família

The complicatedly named and curiously unfinished Expiatory Temple of the Sacred Family is the *most visited* building in Barcelona.

C The **h1** and **h2** elements are colored red with a single rule.

A Here's a doozy for you. Moving right to left, it says "choose only the **em** elements that are found within **p** elements that are immediately adjacent siblings to **h2** elements that have a `lang` attribute whose value begins with **es** inside of any element with a **class** equal to **project**." Got that? I hope you never feel compelled to write something that complicated, but at least you know what's possible.

```
.project h2[lang|="es"] + p em {
    color: red;
}
```

Antoni Gaudí – Introduction

Antoni Gaudí – Introduction

Gaudí's birth in 2002.

La Casa Milà

Gaudí's work was essentially useful. La Casa Milà is an apartment building and *real people* live there.

La Sagrada Família

The complicatedly named and curiously unfinished Expiatory Temple of the Sacred Family is the *most visited* building in Barcelona.

B All that code **A** just to turn the **em** elements red? If you're thinking it would be much better (and easier) to simply write something like **em { color: red; }** or **.architect em { color: red; }**, you're absolutely right—unless you need to be more specific.

Combining Selectors

The examples throughout the chapter have been simple to help you get a feel for various selector types. However, the real power lies in the fact that you can combine any of the techniques to pinpoint the elements that you want to format.

An extreme example is shown in **A** to demonstrate what's possible (though not recommended in this case). Here are a few ways you could achieve the same results **B**, moving from least specific to most specific:

```
em {
    color: red;
}

.project em {
    color: red;
}

.architect .project em {
    color: red;
}
```

continues on next page

It doesn't require a lot of crazy selectors to implement most designs, no matter how intricate they may appear in a browser. So combine selectors when it makes sense to, but to reiterate, I recommend making your style rules only as specific as necessary. For instance, if you just want to target **em** elements inside elements with **class="project"**, go with **.project em { color: red; }**. Even though the **em** elements are nested inside **p** elements in the HTML, there's no point in writing **.project p em { color: red; }** unless there are **em** elements *outside of* paragraphs you want to leave alone. In short, start simple and get more specific as needed.

More Selectors in CSS3

CSS3 adds a lot of new selectors to your toolbox. You saw some of them in this chapter. Most of the other new ones are pseudo-classes, some of which are fairly complex, but powerful as a result. You can find a table of CSS3 selectors and full descriptions at www.w3.org/TR/css3-selectors/#selectors, and brief descriptions and examples at www.w3.org/wiki/CSS/Selectors.

Browser support is solid except in Internet Explorer, which didn't begin supporting most of the new CSS3 selectors (particularly the new pseudo-classes and pseudo-elements) until IE9.

In many cases, it's just fine if your site is a little different in older browsers than in modern ones. But if you really want IE8 and prior to honor some of these selectors, you might want to consider Keith Clark's Selectivizr (http://selectivizr.com). In his words, it is "a JavaScript utility that emulates CSS3 pseudo-classes and attribute selectors in Internet Explorer 6–8." As he notes, Selectivizr has some limitations. I recommend doing without it if you can, which I don't at all mean as a slight on his tool. It's just that the more JavaScript your webpage uses, the longer it takes to load and display (see Chapter 19), and older browsers (like IE8) are not as efficient at processing it.

Formatting Text with Styles

With CSS, you can change the font, size, weight, slant, line height, foreground and background, spacing, and alignment of text. You can decide whether text should be underlined or struck through, and you can convert it to all uppercase, all lowercase, or small caps. And you can apply those changes to an entire page or an entire site in just a handful of lines of code. In this chapter, you'll learn how.

While most properties discussed in this chapter apply solely to text, the section "Setting the Background" also applies to non-text elements. Additionally, there are a couple of text-related topics covered elsewhere: web fonts in Chapter 13, and "Adding Drop Shadows to Text" in Chapter 14.

All these CSS features are integral parts of designing your webpages. We'll continue in that vein with CSS layout in Chapter 11.

In This Chapter

Before and After

Browsers apply minimal styling to a page by default **A**. Throughout the chapter, we'll attempt to spruce up this page a bit **B** by applying our own CSS for the text and background. You may want to refer to the abbreviated HTML **C** as you progress through the chapter, paying particular attention to how some of the classes are utilized in the CSS. The complete HTML and all examples from the chapter are available on the companion website at www.htmlcssvqs.com/8ed/10.

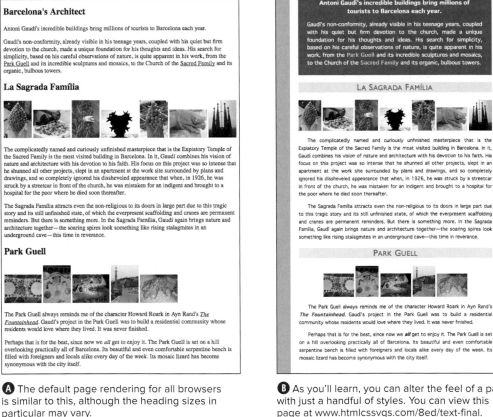

A The default page rendering for all browsers is similar to this, although the heading sizes in particular may vary.

B As you'll learn, you can alter the feel of a page with just a handful of styles. You can view this page at www.htmlcssvqs.com/8ed/text-final.

C The HTML contains various classes for targeting specific areas with CSS.

```
...
<body>
<article class="architect">
    <div class="intro">
        <h1>Barcelona's Architect</h1>

        <p class="subhead">Antoni Gaudí's incredible buildings bring...</p>

        <p>Gaudí's...search for simplicity...is quite apparent in his work, from the <a href=
        → "#park-guell">Park Guell</a> ... to the Church of the <a href="#sagrada-familia">Sacred
        → Family</a> ...</p>
    </div>

    <section class="project family">
        <h2 id="sagrada-familia">La Sagrada Família</h2>

        <div class="photos">
            <img src="img/red-bubbles.jpg" ... />
            ... 6 more images ...
        </div>

        <p>The complicatedly named...</p>
        <p>The Sagrada Família attracts...</p>
    </section>

    <section class="project guell">
        <h2 id="park-guell">Park Guell</h2>

        <div class="photos">
            ... 5 images ...
        </div>

        <p>The Park Guell always reminds me of ... Howard Roark in ... <a href="http://..."><cite>The
        → Fountainhead</cite></a>...</p>
        <p>...now we <em>all</em> get to enjoy it...</p>
    </section>
</article>
</body>
</html>
```

Choosing a Font Family

One of the most important choices you'll make for your website is the font for the body text and headlines. As you'll learn, not every system has the same fonts by default, so you should define alternate fonts as fallbacks. But first let's see how to define a single font family (Ⓐ and Ⓑ) and the ramifications of not providing the alternates Ⓒ.

To set the font family:

After the desired selector in your style sheet, type **font-family:** *name*, where *name* is your first choice of font.

TIP Surround multi-word font names with quotes (single or double) Ⓐ.

TIP You can specify font names in lowercase as well. For example, **font-family: geneva;**.

TIP While you can specify any font you want, your visitor will see only the fonts that they already have installed on their system. (The exception to this is when you load a web font, as described in Chapter 13.) See the next section for more details about standard fonts shared by OS X and Windows.

TIP Although the **font-family** property is inherited, a few elements are stubborn and don't take on their parent's font setting. Among these are form **select**, **textarea**, and **input** elements (Chapter 16). You can force them to inherit with **input, select, textarea { font-family: inherit; }**.

TIP You can set the font family, font size, and line height all at once by using the general **font** property. See "Setting All Font Values at Once," later in this chapter.

Ⓐ Because **font-family** is an inherited property, I specified Geneva on the **body** element so that all elements in the page take on the style. I overrode that setting for the **h1** and **h2** elements by setting their font to Gill Sans.

```
body {
    font-family: Geneva;
}

h1, h2 {
    font-family: "Gill Sans";
}
```

Ⓑ Both Geneva and Gill Sans are common on OS X, so they display properly here. The **p** and **a** elements inherit the **body font-family** setting, so all text except for the headings is styled in Geneva. The **h1** and **h2** headings would show it, too, if we hadn't specified Gill Sans for them.

Ⓒ Typically, Geneva and Gill Sans do not come installed on Windows systems. If you choose a font that is not installed on your visitor's system, their browser will use the default browser font instead. Times New Roman is the default on Windows, as shown here.

A The first font stack tells the browser to look for Tahoma on systems that don't have Geneva, and then fall back to a standard sans-serif font if neither is installed. The font stack for the headings provides three fallbacks. Your alternates might not match your first choice exactly, but the goal is to specify a font that's as close as possible **C**.

```
body {
    font-family: Geneva, Tahoma, sans-serif;
}

h1,
h2 {
    font-family: "Gill Sans", "Gill Sans MT",
    → Calibri, sans-serif;
}
```

Specifying Alternate Fonts

Although you can specify whichever font you want, it might not display on every system (as shown in the previous section). To combat this, the **font-family** property lets you list more than one font **A**. The browser will use the first listed font that's available on the visitor's system (**B** and **C**) or loaded as a web font (Chapter 13).

A list of fonts is known as a *font stack*. Typically, a font stack will include at least three fonts: the preferred font, one or more alternates, and a generic standard font for "if all else fails, use this" situations (see the first tip).

continues on next page

B Systems that have Geneva and Gill Sans installed—like this OS X one—will continue to use those fonts. Consequently, the fonts are identical to figure **B** in the previous section (the screen shots look different because the browser is narrower here).

C Systems that don't have Geneva will use Tahoma for the main text if they have it (as most Windows systems do, like this one). If they don't have Tahoma either, the browser will use the font mapped to sans-serif. The same goes for the headings. This Windows machine doesn't have either Gill Sans or Gill Sans MT, so the headings are shown in Calibri, the third choice.

The sidebar "Default Fonts Shared by OS X and Windows" discusses the small set of fonts that both systems share out of the box. It's common to use one or more of these or a web font so visitors see the same font.

To specify alternate fonts:

1. Type **font-family:** *name*, where *name* is your first choice of font.

2. Type **,** *name2*, where *name2* is your second font choice. Separate each choice with a comma and a space.

3. Repeat step 2 as desired, and finish your list of fonts with a generic font name (**serif**, **sans-serif**, **cursive**, **fantasy**, or **monospace**; whichever style is most appropriate based on your preferred font).

Default Fonts Shared by OS X and Windows

There is a very limited list of fonts to choose from that both OS X and Windows have by default: Arial, Comic Sans MS, Courier New, Georgia, Impact, Trebuchet MS, Times New Roman, and Verdana. Consequently, the majority of sites on the web use one of these fonts in some capacity. They might not render in exactly the same way in browsers on OS X and Windows, but you can be confident that they will display.

You also have options beyond these, as shown in Ⓐ. Both OS X and Windows include more (but different) system fonts you can use in your font stacks. Search online for "font stacks" to see a range of **font-family** declarations that you can copy and paste into your style sheets to provide each visitor a similar font.

Lastly, you also can load a font that systems don't have by default. Web designers fantasized about this for eons, and it finally became possible in recent years. *Web fonts*, as they are known, are common on sites now that more quality fonts are available. You'll learn how to use web fonts in Chapter 13.

Showing Arial on Windows and Helvetica on OS X

Here's a neat trick. But first, a little background.

Arial is almost certainly the most used font on the web—the `font-family: arial`, `helvetica`, `sans-serif;` declaration is everywhere. Problem is, designers would often prefer to use Helvetica when it's available, but most OS X machines have Arial, so Helvetica is ignored in that font stack.

All OS X machines have Helvetica, but it's not common on Windows. Even if a user has installed it on Windows, sometimes it displays quite poorly. That's why listing Helvetica before Arial in a font stack isn't ideal.

What to do? The solution is deceptively simple: Use `font-family: sans-serif;`. Because of the way each operating system maps to `sans-serif`, Windows browsers will show Arial and OS X browsers will show Helvetica.

TIP Systems typically have a font that maps to the following generic font names: serif, sans-serif, cursive, fantasy, and monospace—which is why it's standard practice to specify one at the end of your font stack. Of these, you'll use serif and sans-serif the most (by far), since they correspond to the most commonly used font types. Typically, serif maps to Times New Roman on Windows and Times on OS X. And sans-serif typically maps to Arial on Windows and Helvetica on OS X.

TIP Geneva font stacks typically include `Verdana` in the third slot before `sans-serif` to account for the small percentage of systems that don't have either Geneva or Tahoma. I left it out to demonstrate that font stacks can have different numbers of fonts, but I've included it in subsequent examples.

TIP You can specify fonts for different alphabets (such as Japanese and English) in the same `font-family` declaration to format a chunk of text that contains different languages and writing systems.

Creating Italics

In traditional publishing, italics are used often to set off quotations, emphasized text, words that are foreign relative to a language (for example, *de rigueur*), some scientific names (for example, *Homo sapiens*), movie titles, and much more.

Browsers typically italicize some HTML elements (such as **cite**, **em**, and **i**) by default, so you don't need to italicize them in your CSS. However, sometimes none of those elements is the proper semantic choice for marking up your content, yet you still want to make some text italic. The CSS **font-style** property allows you to do this.

Just as an example, let's see how to do this to paragraphs **A**. (We won't leave them this way because they'd be exceedingly difficult to read **B**, so we'll omit the rule from subsequent examples.)

A In this example, I've made the paragraphs display in italics.

```
body {
    font-family: Geneva, Tahoma, Verdana,
    → sans-serif;
}

h1,
h2 {
    font-family: "Gill Sans", "Gill Sans MT",
    → Calibri, sans-serif;
}

p {
    font-style: italic;
}
```

Barcelona's Architect

Antoni Gaudí's incredible buildings bring millions of tourists to Barcelona each year.

Gaudí's non-conformity, already visible in his teenage years, coupled with his quiet but firm devotion to the church, made a unique foundation for his thoughts and ideas. His search for simplicity, based on his careful observations of nature are quite apparent in his work, from the Park Guell and its incredible sculptures and mosaics, to the Church of the Sacred Family and its organic, bulbous towers.

La Sagrada Família

B The paragraphs and the links within them are italicized, but the headings are not.

To create italics:

1. Type **font-style:**.

2. After the colon (:), type **italic** for italic text, or **oblique** for oblique text. (You'll probably use **italic** 99 percent of the time. You might not notice a difference with **oblique** in all instances.)

To remove italics:

Type **font-style: normal**.

TIP One reason you might want to remove italics is to emphasize some text in a paragraph that has inherited italic formatting from a parent element. For more details about inheritance, consult "Understanding Inheritance" in Chapter 7.

TIP See "HTML: Markup with Meaning" in Chapter 1 regarding the importance of writing semantic HTML.

TIP The **font-style** property is inherited.

Real Italics vs. Faux Italics, plus Oblique Text

A font designer often creates the italic version of a font from scratch, especially for serif fonts. It is not merely a slanted version of the normal text, but instead includes differences appropriate to the form. For example, Palatino Linotype has a true italic font face ⓒ. The letter "a" in particular is clearly not just slanted to mimic italics.

But a font may not have an italic version. That is the case with Geneva. If you set text in that font to **font-style: italic**, the browser may display a computer-simulated, faux italic that *does* simply slant the normal letters to mimic the style ⓒ. However, the quality isn't the same as if the characters had been tailored for italic.

Additionally, a font designer may create an oblique version of a font, which typically *is* the normal letters slanted, perhaps with some adjustments to spacing and the like, but with the same letters. You can set **font-style: oblique;**, though it's uncommon to do so. Faux italic may show in the absence of an oblique or italic version of the font.

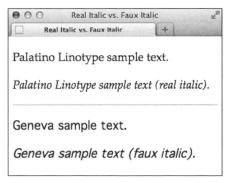

ⓒ Here is a line of normal text followed by one styled with **font-style: italic;** for two fonts. If you look closely, you can see that Palatino Linotype has characters specifically for italic display. The difference between normal and italic text is especially clear in letters such as "a," "p," and "y." Because Geneva lacks italic characters, the browser merely slants the normal characters to simulate italic styling.

Applying Bold Formatting

Bold formatting is probably the most common and effective way to make text stand out. For instance, browsers typically style the **h1**–**h6** headings in bold by default. Just as with italics, you may style any text in bold or turn it off. To do so, use the `font-weight` property (Ⓐ and Ⓑ).

To apply bold formatting:

1. Type `font-weight:`.

2. Type **bold** to give a regular bold weight to the text. You'll likely use this value the majority of the time.

   Or type a multiple of **100** (up to **900**), where **400** typically represents normal weight (that is, not bold) and **700** is the same as typing **bold**. This approach is useful when you're working with fonts that have numerous weights available (for example, you'll encounter this with some web fonts).

   Or type **bolder** or **lighter** to use a value relative to the current weight (it's uncommon to use these).

To remove bold formatting:

Type `font-weight: normal`. (Some web font services, like Google Fonts, ask you to use `font-weight: 400` instead.)

Ⓐ Browsers add bold formatting to **h1**–**h6** headings automatically. I applied a normal font weight to remove it from all **h1** and **h2** elements. I've also added bold formatting to **em** text, links, and the `.subhead` paragraph below the **h1** Ⓑ.

```
body {
    font-family: Geneva, Tahoma, Verdana,
    → sans-serif;
}

h1,
h2 {
    font-family: "Gill Sans", "Gill Sans MT",
    → Calibri, sans-serif;
    font-weight: normal;
}

em,
a:link,
.intro .subhead {
    font-weight: bold;
}
```

Ⓑ The headings have a normal weight instead of their default bold (as seen in figure Ⓑ of "Creating Italics"). The paragraph with the `.subhead` class is bold, as are all links.

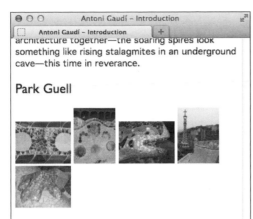

Park Guell

The Park Guell always reminds me of Howard Roark in Ayn Rand's *The Fountainhead*. Gaudí's project in the Park Guell was to build a residential community whose residents would love where they lived. It was never finished.

Perhaps that is for the best, since now we *all* get to enjoy it. The Park Guell is set on a hill overlooking practically all of Barcelona. Its beautiful

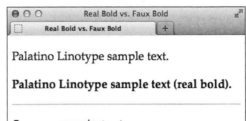

C At the bottom of the page, you see a link ("The Fountainhead") and the word "all." Both are bold because of our new style rule, but they're also italic because of the default browser styles. The phrases are marked up with `cite` and `em`, respectively, to reflect their meaning. (You'll also notice that the "Park Guell" `h2` has a normal weight, not bold.)

Helvetica at 100.

Helvetica at 200.

Helvetica at 300.

Helvetica at 400.

Helvetica at 500.

Helvetica at 600.

Helvetica at 700.

Helvetica at 800.

Helvetica at 900.

D Some of the weights look the same because Helvetica doesn't have a different set of characters for each relative weight.

TIP Since the way weights are defined varies from font to font, the predefined values may not be relative from font to font. They are designed to be relative *within* a given font family, so 700 in one font might look heavier than in another.

TIP Fonts themselves don't always include different weights that map to relative values. If the font family has fewer than nine weights, or if they are concentrated on one end of the scale, some numeric values will correspond to the same font weight, making them look the same **C**.

TIP For the reasons noted in the previous two tips, it's customary to assign bold simply with `font-weight: bold`.

TIP Some fonts do not contain a set of bold letters. To compensate, browsers will create a faux bold effect when you declare `font-weight: bold`; with such a font (**D** and **E**). See a related discussion of faux italics in "Creating Italics."

TIP What can you remove bold formatting from? Any element where it's been applied automatically (`strong`, `h1`–`h6`, and `b` come to mind) or where it's been inherited from a parent element (see "Understanding Inheritance" in Chapter 7).

TIP The `font-weight` property is inherited.

Palatino Linotype sample text.

Palatino Linotype sample text (real bold).

Geneva sample text.

Geneva sample text (faux bold).

E Just as with italic styling, Palatino Linotype has bold letters but Geneva doesn't. Consequently, the browser fattens Geneva to simulate bold, but the result lacks the sharpness, elegance, and attention to spacing found in a font with bold letters.

Setting the Font Size

There are two primary ways to set the font size for the text in your webpage. You can mandate that a specific size be defined in pixels (**A** through **C**), or you can have the size be relative to the element's parent font size by using percentage, em (**D** and **E**), or rem values (see the "Sizing Fonts with rem" sidebar).

Pixels are often easier for beginners to use, but I really encourage you to learn and use a relative unit like ems. They allow for greater flexibility and for sizing various parts of your page designs—such as spacing and padding—relative to font sizes. Relative units have become even more valuable with the explosion of devices of various sizes (smartphones, tablets, and so on); relative units can help you build sites that display nicely across that spectrum. (This is what *responsive web design* is all about; see Chapter 12.)

A Here I use pixel values to dictate the size of the text (**B** and **C**).

```
... [previous CSS] ...

em,
a:link,
.intro .subhead {
    font-weight: bold;
}

h1 {
    font-size: 35px;
}

h2 {
    font-size: 28px;
}

.intro .subhead {
    font-size: 18px;
}

.intro p {
    font-size: 17px;
}

.project p {
    font-size: 15px;
}
```

Barcelona's Architect

Antoni Gaudí's incredible buildings bring millions of tourists to Barcelona each year.

Gaudí's non-conformity, already visible in his teenage years, coupled with his quiet but firm devotion to the church, made a unique foundation for his thoughts and ideas. His search for simplicity, based on his careful observations of nature, is quite apparent in his work, from the **Park Guell** and its incredible sculptures and mosaics, to the Church of the **Sacred Family** and its organic, bulbous towers.

La Sagrada Família

B The font sizes I've specified are displayed in the browser. The different heading sizes reflect the hierarchy of information. The paragraph text in the introductory area below the main heading is larger than ...

mosaics, to the Church of the **Sacred Family** and its organic, bulbous towers.

La Sagrada Família

The complicatedly named and curiously unfinished masterpiece that is the Expiatory Temple of the Sacred Family is the most visited building in Barcelona. In it, Gaudí combines his vision of nature and architecture with his devotion to his faith. His focus on this project was so intense that he shunned all other

C ... the paragraph text in the rest of the page.

D The **font-size: 100%** declaration on **body** sets a baseline from which the em font sizes are based. That **100%** translates to an equivalent default text size of 16 pixels on most systems. So this style sheet result will be equivalent to the one shown in **A**. The comment following each **font-size** value explains how it was calculated, showing the typical pixel equivalents.

```
body {
    font-family: Geneva, Tahoma, Verdana,
    → sans-serif;
    font-size: 100%; /* 16px */
}

h1,
h2 {
    font-family: "Gill Sans", "Gill Sans MT",
    → Calibri, sans-serif;
    font-weight: normal;
}

h1 {
    font-size: 2.1875em; /* 35px/16px */
}

h2 {
    font-size: 1.75em; /* 28px/16px */
}

em,
a:link,
.intro .subhead {
    font-weight: bold;
}

.intro .subhead {
    font-size: 1.125em; /* 18px/16px */
}

.intro p {
    font-size: 1.0625em; /* 17px/16px */
}

.project p {
    font-size: .9375em; /* 15px/16px */
}
```

Understanding em and percentage font sizes

Setting the size relative to the parent takes a little getting used to; you need to understand how the browser treats these units relative to their parents. I'll explain that in a minute.

But first, when you use relative font sizes it's best to establish a baseline on the **body** element; you do that by declaring **body { font-size: 100%; } D**. Most of the time, this sets the size to the equivalent of 16px, because that is the default font size in most browsers. As usual, that value flows

continues on next page

E On most systems with default settings, the em-based font sizes match those from the pixel-based version (**B** and **C**).

down to the other elements—remember, **font-size** is an inherited property—unless they are given their own **font-size** by a browser default or by you in your style sheet. (Most elements will be 16px, but **h1**–**h6** headings are larger by default.)

So how do you figure out what em values to specify? Well, 1em is *always* equal to the parent's size; that's how ems work. In this case, 1em is equivalent to 16px because we've established that as the default for elements. From there you can determine the em (or percentage) values with just a tiny bit of division:

desired size / parent's size = value

Let's look at how to apply that to change some of our pixel values from figure Ⓐ to ems. For example, you want the **h1** to resemble 35px, and you already know that the parent's size is 16px. So:

35 / 16 = 2.1875

So by defining **h1 { font-size: 2.1875em; }**, you're all set Ⓓ. What this says is, "Make the **h1** text 2.1875 times as large as its parent's text." Another way to write the rule would be **h1 { font-size: 218.75%; }**. However, aside from setting the base **font-size** on **body** with a percentage, it's more common to size type in ems rather than percentages.

Here's another one. You want the paragraphs in the sections with the **project** class to be 15px, and:

15 / 16 = .9375

So you set **.project p { font-size: .9375em; }** Ⓓ. (Alternatively, this could be **93.75%**.)

Let's discuss one more example, since this is where you can get tripped up with relative values. The second paragraph on the page ("Gaudí's non-conformity...") contains two links (Ⓔ and Ⓕ). The paragraph itself is styled with **.intro p { font-size: 1.0625em; }** Ⓓ, which makes it 17 pixels because 17/16 = 1.0625.

Now suppose you want to make the links 16px while leaving the other paragraph text at 17px. You might be inclined to set the links with **.intro a { font-size: 1em; }**, thinking that 1em = 16px.

But remember that these values are relative to their parent, and the parent in this case is the **p**. And that paragraph's size is 17px, not 16px, making 1em equivalent to 17px (as I said earlier, 1em always equals the parent's font size).

So in order to make the links 16px, you need to use an em value smaller than 1em. We'll use the same handy formula as

Ⓕ Part of the HTML, which has two **a** elements nested in their parent **p**. The **intro** class on the **div** container allows for styling the paragraphs and links for this part of the page (Ⓐ and Ⓓ) without affecting the same elements elsewhere.

```
...
<div class="intro">
    <h1>Barcelona's Architect</h1>
    ...
    <p>Gaudí's non-conformity...His search for simplicity...is quite apparent in his work, from
    → the <a href="#park-guell">Park Guell</a> ... to the Church of the <a href="#sagrada-
    → familia">Sacred Family</a> and its organic, bulbous towers.</p>
</div>
...
```

before: **desired size / parent's size = value**.

16 / 17 = .941176

So the slightly verbose **.intro a { font-size: .941176em; }** gives us the desired result. (I truncated the number a bit so as not to frighten you too much.)

One final point regarding relative font sizes: Remember that a **body font-size** of **100%** maps to a default of 16px most of the time. One case in which that can deviate is when a user overrides the default in their browser settings; for instance, making it 22px if they prefer (or require) larger text. With **body** set to **100%**, your page respects this and sizes the rest of the text accordingly, er, *relatively*! That's the beauty of sizing your text with the likes of ems and percentages. (The same is true of rem units when you set the **html** element to **100%**; see the "Sizing Fonts with Rem" sidebar.) See the last tip for more reasons to use ems.

Sizing Fonts with rem

CSS3 introduces some new units. One of the most interesting ones is rem, short for *root em*. It's like em, but it sizes everything relative to the root **G** instead of to the parent element. The root is the **html** element (because it contains **body**, which in turn contains the rest of your content).

This simplifies matters because the font size of **html** won't vary, unlike a parent's size can, as I demonstrated with the example of sizing links in a paragraph. (See "Understanding em and percentage font sizes.") This means our formula (adjusted from earlier) is:

desired size / root size = value

Which is really:

desired size / 16 = value

Easier, right? I can hear you rejoicing already.

Hold your horses. Support for rem is strong in modern browsers, but unfortunately Internet Explorer didn't support it until version 9 (http://caniuse.com/#search=rem). IE8 still has a large enough market share in most parts of the world that it is usually worth accommodating when building a site. This is one reason why more coders haven't used rems.

G With rems, only the root element's font size matters, not the size of the links' parent **p**. Since the root (**html**) is set to **100%**, which typically maps to 16px, setting the **a** elements to **1rem** makes the links the equivalent of 16px, too. Separately, the styles marked **/* optional */** show how you can provide pixel sizes as a fallback for IE8 and other browsers that don't support rem.

```
html {
    font-size: 100%; /* 16px usually */
}

.intro p {
    font-size: 17px; /* optional */
    font-size: 1.0625rem; /* 17px/16px */
}

.intro a {
    font-size: 16px; /* optional */
    font-size: 1rem; /* was .941176em */
}
```

However, one strategy you can use is to provide a default px value for earlier versions of IE, followed by the rem equivalent for modern browsers **G**. Of course, one drawback to that is that it's extra code for you to manage and for browsers to load. Another is that users cannot resize text in IE8 if it is pixel-based (see the tips); admittedly, this affects a small percentage of users. You might decide that the trade-offs are worth it.

To mandate a specific font size:

1. Type `font-size:`.

2. Type a specific size after the colon (:), such as **13px**. (See Ⓐ for pixel examples.)

   Or use a keyword to specify the size:

   `xx-small`, `x-small`, `small`, `medium`, `large`, `x-large`, or `xx-large`.

   See "A Property's Value" in Chapter 7 for details about units.

   TIP There shouldn't be any spaces between the number and the unit.

   TIP If you set the font size with pixels, visitors using IE8 or earlier versions will not be able to make the text bigger or smaller with the browser's text size option. That's one argument for sizing your fonts with ems or percentages. Beginning with IE7, visitors can zoom the *entire* page in and out, though it isn't the same as changing only the text size. Nowadays, coders don't worry about IE6 and IE7 for most sites because their user base is so low. One exception is China, where IE6 still represents roughly **25** percent of users at the time of this writing. You can check approximate worldwide numbers at www.ie6countdown.com.

   TIP Different browsers may interpret the keywords in different ways.

   TIP Use points (pt) as the unit type in print style sheets.

   TIP The `font-size` property is inherited.

To set a size that depends on the parent element's size:

1. Type `font-size:`.

2. Type the relative value following the colon (:), such as **1.5em** or **150%**. (See Ⓓ for em and percentage examples.)

   Or use a relative keyword: `larger` or `smaller`. (These are less common to use than percentages, which are themselves less common than ems.)

To set a size that depends on the root element's size:

1. Type `font-size:`.

2. Type the root relative value following the colon (:), such as **.875rem**. (See Ⓖ for rem examples.)

   TIP The parent element's size may be set by the user (pretty uncommon) or by you as the coder, may be inherited from its parent, or may come from the browser's defaults. As mentioned, on most current browsers the default font size for the `body` element is 16 pixels.

   TIP The child of an element with a relative size inherits the size, not the relative factor. So, the `a` elements in the `p` Ⓕ inherit a size of 15 pixels Ⓓ, not a relative value of .9375em. The links display as 15px just like the paragraph text unless you override it.

   TIP You can set font size together with other font values. See "Setting All Font Values at Once," later in this chapter.

   TIP Chris Coyier notes a variety of reasons why ems are preferable to pixels at http://css-tricks.com/why-ems/.

Assuming a default **body** element font size of 16 pixels, the font size of the paragraphs within **.project** typically will equal 15 pixels when set to **.9375em** (15/16 = .9375). The line height will be 1.65 times those 15 pixels, or about 24.75 pixels. I also set the **.intro** container's **line-height**, which is inherited by its descendants.

```
... previous CSS ...

.intro {
    line-height: 1.45;
}

.intro .subhead {
    font-size: 1.125em;
}

.intro p {
    font-size: 1.0625em;
}

.project p {
    font-size: .9375em; /* 15px/16px */
    line-height: 1.65; /* 15px*1.65 =
    → 24.75px */
}
```

The complicatedly named and curiously unfinished masterpiece that is the Expiatory Temple of the Sacred Family is the most visited building in Barcelona. In it, Gaudí combines his vision of nature and architecture with his devotion to his faith. His focus

B Spacing out lines with **line-height** can make them easier to read. The difference in this case is more obvious for the main text (at the bottom) than for the intro text (at the top).

Setting the Line Height

Line height refers to a paragraph's leading, which is the amount of space between each line in a paragraph (A and B). Using a large line height can sometimes make your body text easier to read. A small line height for headings with more than one line often makes them look more cohesive.

To set the line height:

1. Type **line-height:**.

2. Type *n*, where *n* is a number that will be multiplied by the element's font size to obtain the desired line height. (This is the most common approach; just a number with no unit.)

   Or type *a*, where *a* is a value in ems, pixels, or points that *does* include the unit type (**em**, **px**, or **pt**). (Use points only for print.)

   Or type *p%*, where *p%* is a percentage of the font size.

TIP If you use a number to determine the line height (as is common), this factor is inherited by all child items. So if a parent's font size is set to **16px** (or the equivalent in ems or such) and the line height is 1.5, the parent's line height will be 24 (16 × 1.5). If the child's font size is 10, its line height will be 15 (10 × 1.5).

TIP If you use a percentage or em value, only the resulting size (or "computed value") is inherited. So given a parent at 16 pixels with a line height of 150%, the parent's line height will still be 24 pixels; however, all child elements will also inherit a line height of 24 pixels, regardless of their font size.

TIP You can specify the line height together with the font family, size, weight, style, and variant, as described in the next section.

Setting All Font Values at Once

You can set the font style, weight, variant, size, line height, and family all at once with the **font** shorthand property (Ⓐ and Ⓑ). This is more efficient than declaring the properties separately, so it can help keep your style sheets lean.

You don't have to specify all font properties, but each use of **font** shorthand *must* include the font size and family at a minimum (hence the two comments in Ⓐ noting where shorthand cannot be used).

To set all font values at once:

1. Type **font:**.

2. Optionally type **normal**, **italic**, or **oblique** to set the font style (see "Creating Italics").

3. Optionally type **normal**, **bold**, **bolder**, **lighter**, or a multiple of **100** (up to **900**) to set the font weight (see "Applying Bold Formatting").

4. Optionally type **normal** or **small-caps** to remove or set small caps as the font variant (see "Using Small Caps").

5. Type the desired font size (see "Setting the Font Size").

6. If desired, type **/line-height**, where **line-height** is the amount of space there should be between lines (see "Setting the Line Height").

7. Type a space followed by the desired font family or families in order of preference, separated by commas, as described in "Choosing a Font Family."

Ⓐ This style sheet is equivalent to the one shown in Ⓐ in "Setting the Line Height," as is the resulting display Ⓑ. I've simply consolidated the **font** properties for the **body**. I couldn't consolidate either the **h1** or **h2** font styles or those for **.project p** because **font** shorthand requires both the family and size properties at a minimum. See Ⓒ and Ⓓ for more examples.

```
body {
    font: 100% Geneva, Tahoma, Verdana,
    → sans-serif;
}

h1,
h2 {
    /* Can't combine these into
    font shorthand unless you include
    font size in the shorthand. */
    font-family: "Gill Sans", "Gill Sans MT",
    → Calibri, sans-serif;
    font-weight: normal;
}

h1 { font-size: 2.1875em; }

h2 { font-size: 1.75em; }

em,
a:link,
.intro .subhead {
    font-weight: bold;
}

.intro {
    line-height: 1.45;
}

.intro .subhead {
    font-size: 1.125em;
}

.intro p {
    font-size: 1.0625em;
}

.project p {
    /* Can't combine these into
    font shorthand unless you include
    font family in the shorthand. */
    font-size: .9375em;
    line-height: 1.65;
}
```

Antoni Gaudí – Introduction

Barcelona's Architect

Antoni Gaudí's incredible buildings bring millions of tourists to Barcelona each year.

Gaudí's non-conformity, already visible in his teenage years, coupled with his quiet but firm devotion to the church, made a unique foundation for his thoughts and ideas. His search for simplicity, based on his careful observations of nature, is quite apparent in his work, from the Park Güell and its incredible sculptures and mosaics, to the Church of the Sacred Family and its organic, bulbous towers.

La Sagrada Família

The complicatedly named and curiously unfinished masterpiece that is the Expiatory Temple of the Sacred Family is the most visited building in Barcelona. In it, Gaudí combines his vision of nature and architecture with his devotion to his faith. His focus on this project was so intense that he shunned all other projects, slept in an apartment at the work site surrounded by

B This page is identical to the one shown in **B** in "Setting the Line Height."

C This example combines the **font-size**, **line-height**, and **font-family** declarations into **font** shorthand. The line height follows the size and forward slash. You can also include the **font-style**, **font-variant**, and **font-weight** **D**.

```
.example-2 {
    font: .875em/1.3 "Palatino Linotype",
    → Palatino, serif;
}
```

TIP The size and family properties must always be specified in this order: first the size, then the family.

TIP The line height, which is optional, must come directly after the size and the forward slash and before the family (**C** and **D**).

TIP The properties in steps 2–4 may be specified in any order **D** or omitted (**A** and **C**). If you omit them, they are set to normal—which may not be what you expected.

TIP The font property is inherited.

D This example has all possible properties in a **font** declaration. You can use any combination of the properties as long as both the size and family are declared. The order of the first three properties is not important.

```
.example-3 {
    font: italic small-caps bold .875em/1.3
    → "Palatino Linotype", Palatino, serif;
}
```

Setting the Color

You can also change the color of the text on your webpage. Your style sheets can contain any combination of color name, hexadecimal, RGB, HSL, RGBA, and HSLA values to define your colors (Ⓐ and Ⓑ). (See "CSS colors" in the Chapter 7 section "A Property's Value" for more about these various color values.)

To set the color:

1. Type **color:**.

2. Type ***colorname***, where ***colorname*** is one of the predefined colors.

   Or type **#*rrggbb***, where ***rrggbb*** is the color's hexadecimal representation. This is the most common way to specify colors.

   Or type **rgb(*r, g, b*)**, where ***r, g***, and ***b*** are integers from 0–255 that specify the amount of red, green, and blue, respectively, in the desired color.

   Or type **rgb(*r%, g%, b%*)**, where ***r, g***, and ***b*** give the percentage of red, green, and blue in the desired color.

   Or type **hsl(*h, s, l*)**, where ***h*** is an integer from 0–360 that specifies the hue, and ***s*** and ***l*** are percentages from 0 to 100 that specify the amount of saturation and lightness, respectively, in the desired color. (Generally, it's better to instead use hex or RGB for non-transparent colors.)

   Or type **rgba(*r, g, b, a*)**, where ***r, g***, and ***b*** are integers from 0–255 that specify the amount of red, green, and blue, and ***a*** is a decimal from 0 to 1 that specifies the amount of alpha transparency in the desired color.

Ⓐ Set your page's default text color on **body** so all elements (except links) will inherit it. Then declare other colors directly on elements as desired, like I've done with **h2**. Note that the **a:hover** color (**#f00**) uses the abbreviation discussed in the first tip. (I've used the blue on **body** just to show the effect; I won't leave it this way.)

```
body {
    color: blue;
    font: 100% Geneva, Tahoma, Verdana,
    → sans-serif;
}

...

h2 {
    color: #7d717c;
    font-size: 1.75em;
}

...

/* :::: Links :::: */
a:link {
    color: #e10000; /* a red */
}

a:visited {
    color: #b44f4f;
}

a:hover {
    color: #f00;
}

.intro a {
    color: #fdb09d; /* a little pinkish */
}

.intro a:hover {
    color: #fec4b6;
}
```

Barcelona's Architect

Antoni Gaudí's incredible buildings bring millions of tourists to Barcelona each year.

Gaudí's non-conformity, already visible in his teenage years, coupled with his quiet but firm devotion to the church, made a unique foundation for his thoughts and ideas. His search for simplicity, based on his careful observations of nature are quite apparent in his work, from the Park Guell and its incredible sculptures and mosaics, to the Church of the Sacred Family and its organic, bulbous towers.

La Sagrada Família

The complicatedly named and curiously unfinished masterpiece that is the Expiatory Temple of the Sacred Family is the most visited building in Barcelona. In it, Gaudí combines his vision of nature and architecture with his devotion to his faith. His focus on this project was so intense that he shunned all other projects, slept in an apartment at the work site surrounded by plans and drawings, and so completely ignored his disheveled appearance that when, in 1926, he was struck by a streetcar in front of the church, he was mistaken for an indigent and brought to a hospital for the poor where he died soon thereafter.

The Sagrada Família attracts even the non-religious to its doors in large part due to this tragic story and its still unfinished state, of which the everpresent scaffolding and cranes are permanent reminders. But there is something more. In the Sagrada Família, Gaudí again brings nature and architecture together—the soaring spires look something like rising stalagmites in an underground cave—this time in reverance.

Park Guell

The Park Guell always reminds me of the character Howard Roark in Ayn Rand's *The Fountainhead*. Gaudí's project in the Park Guell was to build a residential community whose residents would love where they lived. It was never finished.

Perhaps that is for the best, since now we *all* get to enjoy it. The Park Guell is set on a hill overlooking practically all of Barcelona. Its beautiful and even comfortable serpentine bench is filled with foreigners and locals alike every day of the week. Its mosaic lizard has become synonymous with the city itself.

Or type `hsla(h, s, l, a)`, where *h* is an integer from 0–360 that specifies the hue, *s* and *l* are percentages from 0 to 100 that specify the amount of saturation and lightness, respectively, and *a* is a decimal from 0 to 1 that specifies the amount of alpha transparency in the desired color.

If you type a value higher than 255 for **r**, **g**, or **b**, 255 will be used. Similarly, a percentage higher than 100 will be substituted with 100.

TIP You can abbreviate hexadecimal notation when a hex value contains three pairs of repeated digits. In fact, I recommend it. So you could (and should) write #FF0099 as #F09 or #f09. Similarly, #CC0000 would become #C00 or #c00. However, a value like #31AA55 contains only two pairs that repeat, so it cannot be shortened to #31a5.

TIP Keep in mind that Internet Explorer didn't support HSL, RGBA, and HSLA until IE9, so if you use any of those in your color declarations you'll have to define fallback colors for older versions of IE. See "CSS colors" in the Chapter 7 section "A Property's Value" for details.

TIP Figure **B** in "Decorating Text" shows the `:hover` link colors in action.

TIP The `color` property is inherited by all text elements except links (the a element). Links must be styled explicitly, as shown in **A**.

B As expected, the, umm, rather obvious blue is applied to most text. The **h2** headings override that with a medium gray (**#7d717c**). The default link color is red (**#e10000**) but is overridden by the setting for the pinkish (**#fdb09d**) link color in the **.intro** area at the top. I'll be setting some text to white in the next section when I apply background colors—if I were to do it now, you wouldn't see it!

Setting the Background

You have a lot of options when styling backgrounds. You can set the background of individual elements, the whole page, or any combination of the two. In so doing, you can change the background of just a few paragraphs or words, links in their different states, sections of content, and more. In short, you can apply backgrounds to nearly every element, even forms and images (yes, an image can have a background image!).

You also have a lot of properties to leverage. Some of them are **background-color**, **background-image**, **background-repeat**, **background-attachment**, and **background-position**. Better still, the **background** shorthand property allows you to save a lot of typing by combining the properties. We'll cover all of these in this section.

We'll start out by adding background colors to our evolving page before deviating for a bit with additional background-related examples.

To change the background color:

1. Type **background-color:**.

2. Type **transparent** (to let the parent element's background show through) or *color*, where *color* is a color name or a hex, RGB, RGBA, HSL, or HSLA color value (see step 2 in "Setting the Color") (**A** through **F**). Hex colors are the most common.

A Setting the background color of the **body** element colors the whole page except where other elements are given their own backgrounds. The background set on the **div** element with the **intro** class distinguishes that area from other parts of the page **B**.

```
body {
      background-color: #88b2d2;
      font: 100% Geneva, Tahoma, Verdana,
    → sans-serif;
}

...

h2 {
      background-color: #eaebef;
      color: #7d717c;
      font-size: 1.75em;
}

.intro {
      background-color: #686a63;
      color: #fff;
      line-height: 1.45;
}

...
```

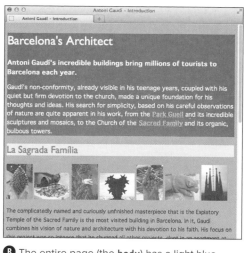

B The entire page (the **body**) has a light blue background. It is overridden in two cases: the brown background of the **intro div** and the light gray background of the level 2 heading.

C The **article** element that contains all content has **class="architect"** assigned to it, so this CSS will give it a white background except in a couple of spots **D**.

```
.architect {
    background-color: #fff;
}
```

D The white fills out the content area. The **.intro** area and the **h2** are also descendants of the **article** with the **architect** class, so their backgrounds would also be white if not for the different backgrounds we gave them earlier **A**. We still see some of the light blue **body** background around the **.architect article** because of the browser's default margin setting on **body**.

E I'm cheating a little bit by using a property we won't cover until the next chapter (see "Adding Padding Around an Element"). Hopefully, you'll forgive me.

```
...

.architect {
    background-color: #fff;
    padding: 1.5em 1.75em;
}

.intro {
    background-color: #686a63;
    color: #fff;
    line-height: 1.45;
    padding: 1px 1.875em .7em;
}

...
```

F Amazing what a little padding can do—the page is actually looking respectable now.

To use a background image:

1. Type **background-image:**.

2. Then type **url(*image.png*)**, where ***image.png*** is the location and file name of the background image relative to the location of the style sheet 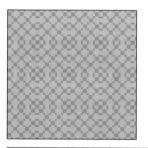. Or type **none** to use no image at all, as in **background-image: none;** (you'd only use this when overriding another style rule that's applying a background image to the element).

G The image URL reflects the location of the style sheet relative to the image. I've kept it simple here; see the second tip. I want the image to fill out the entire page, but I don't have to set **background-repeat**, because background images repeat by default **H**. Visitors will see the background *color* only if the image loads slowly (like on a mobile connection) or if the image fails to load for some reason.

```
body {
    background-color: #ccc;
    background-image: url(bg-pattern.png);
    ...
}
```

H The background image (top) contains a nice pattern. When added to the page **body**, it repeats infinitely both horizontally and vertically. I made the content narrower so you could see the effect.

This time we want the image to repeat only horizontally (the x-axis). Its starting position will be the lower-left corner of the page. Notice that I didn't provide a background color.

```
body {
    background-image: url(sky.png);
    background-repeat: repeat-x;
    background-position: left bottom;
    ...
}
```

J This background image (top) goes from black to blue to green, so it's better suited for tiling horizontally. But it isn't tall enough to fill the page, making the downside of not specifying a background color obvious. The text isn't cut off, we just can't see it because it's the same color as the default white background.

To repeat a background image:

Type **background-repeat: *direction***, where ***direction*** is either **repeat** to tile the image both horizontally and vertically **H**, **repeat-x** to tile the image only horizontally (**I** through **L**), **repeat-y** to tile the image only vertically, or **no-repeat** to not tile the image at all. (Leaving out **background-repeat** defaults to **repeat** **G**.)

K Building on figure **I**, the background color will fill in the spots that the image doesn't cover. I've also added a rule that forces the **html** element to have a minimum height of 100% of the browser window's height **L**. (Note: This **html** rule isn't necessary when **background-attachment** is set to **fixed**, as you'll see shortly.)

```
html {
    min-height: 100%;
}

body {
    background-color: #000;
    ...
}
```

L The black (**#000**) background color blends perfectly with the black at the top of the image. And now you can see the text! This composite image shows two snapshots of the page in browser windows of identical height. The sliver on the left shows what happens when you *don't* include the rule in **K** for the **html** element—the background image stops a little below the text because that's where the page ends, revealing the black background color below it.

To control whether the background image is attached:

1. Type **background-attachment:**.

2. Then type **fixed** to stick the background image to the browser window (meaning it will continue to show even if the visitor scrolls the page), **scroll** to let it move when the visitor scrolls the whole page , or **local** so it scrolls only when the visitor scrolls its *element* (not the whole page). (Leaving out **background-attachment**, as is usually the case, defaults to **scroll**.)

When combined with our **background-position** setting, the **fixed** value will ensure that our background image is attached to the lower-left corner of the browser window.

```
body {
    background-color: #000;
    background-image: url(sky.png);
    background-repeat: repeat-x;
    background-attachment: fixed;
    background-position: left bottom;
    ...
}
```

The background image stays fixed in place no matter how much content there is or how much you scroll.

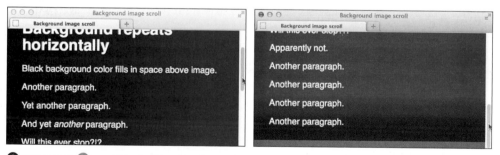

This is how would look without **background-attachment: fixed;**. (Leaving it out is the same as setting **background-attachment: scroll;**, because **scroll** is the default.) The background image moves with the content, so you can't see all of it until you scroll to the bottom of the page (shown at right).

P It's high time we condensed all those individual declarations into the **background** shorthand notation. In doing so, instead of using **background-position**, I've tacked the horizontal and vertical position values at the end. Note the use of **no-repeat** to make the image appear only once **Q**.

```
body {
    background: #004 url(../img/ufo.png)
    → no-repeat 170px 20px;
    color: greenyellow;
    ...
}
```

Q The UFO appears 170 pixels from the left edge of the page and 20 pixels from the top, making room for our Martian-green text. The image is transparent around the shape (and the tractor beam has alpha transparency), so it blends right in with the dark blue **body** background color.

R With the structure shown, **style.css** would need a declaration like **background: url(../img/pattern.png)**; to show **pattern.bg**. See "URLs" in Chapter 7 for more information.

To specify the position of an element's background image:

Type **background-position:** *x y*, where *x* and *y* can be expressed as a percentage or as an absolute distance **P**, such as **20px 147px** (negative values are also allowed). Or use the values **left**, **center**, or **right** for *x* and **top**, **center**, or **bottom** for *y* **M**. (If both values are keywords, they can be in either order; for example, **top right** is the same as **right top**).

To change all the background properties at once:

1. Type **background:**.

2. Specify any of the accepted background property values (as described beginning with "To change the background color" and continuing through "To specify the position of an element's background image") in any order **P**.

TIP Although most examples involve styling the body, don't forget you can apply backgrounds to nearly every HTML element.

TIP I used basic background image URLs to simplify most examples. In practice, your URLs will be something like **../img/ufo.png** **P** because it's better to avoid putting your images in the same folder as your style sheets. This chapter's examples on the book's site use a folder structure similar to **R**, with CSS background image paths adjusted accordingly.

TIP The default for **background-color** is **transparent**. The default for **background-image** is **none**. The default for **background-repeat** is **repeat**. The default for **background-attachment** is **scroll**. The default for **background-position** is **0 0** (this is the same as **top left**). You only need to explicitly set default values when you want to override another style rule.

continues on next page

TIP It's common to use the background shorthand whenever possible. You needn't specify all the properties with it. For example, in practice I would usually rewrite the rule in ⑥ as background: #ccc url(bg-pattern.png);. But be aware that if any non-specified properties are set to their defaults, they may override earlier style rules.

TIP By default, an element's background fills its content and padding areas (🅔 and 🅕) and extends behind its border (see "The Box Model" in Chapter 11). You can change this with background-clip (see the sidebar "More Background Control with CSS3").

TIP The local value for background-attachment is new in CSS3. Lea Verou demonstrates it at http://lea.verou.me/2012/04/background-attachment-local/. Browser support is limited to IE9+, Chrome, Safari, and Opera—no Firefox.

TIP You can use negative values with the background-position property. For example, background-position: -45px 80px positions the image to the left—not *from* the left—45 pixels (so you won't see the first 45 horizontal pixels of the image) and 80 pixels down from the top of the element.

TIP Be sure to create enough contrast between the text and background. Not only does this help the average user, but it's important for vision-impaired visitors. (See http://contrastrebellion.com.) Lea Verou comes through again here, having created a tool (http://leaverou.github.com/contrast-ratio/) that helps you choose colors with sufficient contrast to meet accessibility guidelines.

TIP If we had not used background-position: left bottom; for ⑩, the effect would be reversed. We'd see the image repeat across the *top* of the page (the default position). As you scroll down, the image would scroll out of view along with the content.

More Background Control with CSS3

CSS3 provides more background effects. I cover gradients and multiple backgrounds in Chapter 14.

The **background-clip** and **background-origin** properties control where an element's background displays and begins, respectively. Both properties accept the same values: **content-box** encompasses the content; **padding-box** encompasses the content and padding; and **border-box** encompasses the content, padding, and border. (See "The Box Model" in Chapter 11.) The defaults are **background-clip**: **border-box;** and **background-origin**: **padding-box;**. Learn more at http://css-tricks.com/transparent-borders-with-background-clip/.

The **background-size** property controls a background image's size via the following values:

- **contain**—Makes the image as large as possible while showing its full width and height. It might not fill the entire background area.

- **cover**—Makes the image as small as possible while filling the element's entire background area. Part of the image might be scaled out of view.

- A length, percentage, or **auto**—For example, **background-size: 250px 400px;** or **background-size: 50% 50%;**.

Learn more at www.css3.info/background-size/. The property is especially handy with sprites (see the last page of "Putting It All Together" in Chapter 12).

Most of the new background styles are covered at www.sitepoint.com/new-properties-and-values-in-backgrounds-with-css3/.

A I've added seven pixels of extra space between each heading letter to make the effect of **letter-spacing** more clear **B**. I'll reduce this value to **1px** in subsequent examples.

```
body {
    background-color: #88b2d2;
    font: 100% Geneva, Tahoma, Verdana,
    → sans-serif;
}

h1,
h2 {
    font-family: "Gill Sans", "Gill Sans MT",
    → Calibri, sans-serif;
    font-weight: normal;

    /* temporary for demo purposes */
    letter-spacing: 7px;
}

h1 {
    font-size: 2.1875em;
}

... rest of CSS ...
```

B The letters in all headings now have more space between them. Compare the spacing here with figure **F** in "Setting the Background." This is temporary, however; I'll reduce it in the next section.

Controlling Spacing

You can add or reduce space between words (which is called tracking) or between letters (which is called kerning) **A**.

To specify tracking:

Type **word-spacing:** *length*, where *length* is a number with units, as in **0.4em** or **5px**.

To specify kerning:

Type **letter-spacing:** *length*, where *length* is a number with units, as in **0.4em** or **5px**.

TIP You may use negative values for word and letter spacing.

TIP Word and letter spacing values may also be affected by your choice of alignment (via the **text-align** property) and font family.

TIP Use a value of **normal** or 0 to set the letter and word spacing back to their defaults (that is, to add no extra space).

TIP If you use an em value, only the resulting size (or "computed value") is inherited. So a parent at **16** pixels with .1em of extra **word-spacing** will have **1.6** pixels of extra space between each word (16 x 0.1). And all child elements will also have **1.6** pixels of extra space between words, regardless of their font size. Set the extra spacing explicitly for the child elements if you need to override such a value.

TIP The **word-spacing** and **letter-spacing** properties are inherited.

Adding Indents

You can determine how much space should precede the first line of a paragraph by setting the **text-indent** property (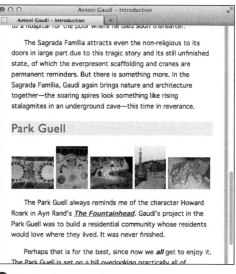**A** and **B**).

To add indents:

Type **text-indent: *length***, where ***length*** is a number with units, as in **1.5em** or **18px**.

> **TIP** You can apply **text-indent** to other elements, not only paragraphs. However, it has no effect on inline elements like em, strong, and cite by default. You can force it to apply if you set them to display: block; or display: inline-block;.

> **TIP** A negative value creates a hanging indent. You may need to increase the padding or margins around a text box with a hanging indent in order to accommodate the overhanging text. (See "Adding Padding Around an Element" and "Setting the Margins Around an Element" in Chapter 11.)

> **TIP** Em values for **text-indent** are calculated with respect to the *element's* font size (not its parent's) **A**. Percentages are calculated with respect to the width of the parent element.

> **TIP** The **text-indent** property is inherited.

> **TIP** If you use a percentage or an em value, only the resulting size (or "computed value") is inherited. So if the parent is 300 pixels wide, a **text-indent** of 10% will be 30 pixels; and child elements will also have their first lines indented 30 pixels, regardless of the width of their respective parents.

> **TIP** Use a value of 0 to remove an inherited indent.

A This code adds a 2em indent to the **p** elements. Since their **.9375em** font size is equivalent to 15 pixels (15/16 = .9375), the indent will be 30 pixels (15 × 2) **B**.

```
...

h1,
h2 {
    font-family: "Gill Sans", "Gill Sans MT",
    → Calibri, sans-serif;
    font-weight: normal;
    letter-spacing: 1px;
}

...

.project p {
    font-size: .9375em; /* 15px/16px */
    line-height: 1.65;
    text-indent: 2em; /* 30px */
}

... rest of CSS ...
```

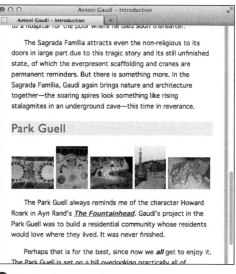

B The first line in each paragraph is indented 30 pixels.

A Some text is centered, but most is justified (meaning it will align with both the left and right sides) **B**.

```
...

h1, h2 {
    font-family: "Gill Sans", "Gill Sans MT",
    → Calibri, sans-serif;
    font-weight: normal;
    letter-spacing: 1px;
    text-align: center;
}

...

p {
    text-align: justify;
}

.intro .subhead {
    font-size: 1.125em;
    text-align: center;
}

... rest of CSS ...
```

B After the changes, the headings and `.subhead` paragraph are centered, while all other paragraph text is justified. The `text-indent` value set on paragraphs earlier remains. (Note: I removed the images below the second heading so you could see more text in this figure.)

Aligning Text

You can set up text so that it always aligns right, left, center, or justified, as desired **A**.

To align text:

1. Type `text-align:`.

2. Type `left` to align the text to the left.

   Or type `right` to align the text to the right.

   Or type `center` to center the text in the middle of the screen.

   Or type `justify` to align the text on both the right and the left.

TIP If you choose to justify the text, be aware that the word spacing and letter spacing may be adversely affected. For related information, see "Controlling Spacing."

TIP The `text-align` property works great out of the box for elements, like h1–h6 and p, that display on their own line by default. But unless you force it, `text-align` doesn't work on phrasing content elements—such as strong, em, a, cite, and others—that display *within* lines. (These were known as "inline" elements before HTML5; see the Chapter 1 section "A Browser's Default Display of Web-pages.") To align the text in these elements separate from their surrounding text, you must first override their default `display: inline;` style with either `display: block;` (to make them display on their own line like paragraphs) or `display: inline-block;` and then set `text-align` accordingly. For those with `display: inline-block;`, you may also need to add a `width` to see the alignment effect. In truth, the occasions you'll have a need to set `text-align` on "inline" content are pretty limited.

TIP The `text-align` property is inherited. Its default value is supposed to depend on the page's language and writing system (meaning right-to-left or left-to-right), but in most cases it's indiscriminately set to `left`.

Changing the Text Case

You can define the text case for your style by using the **text-transform** property 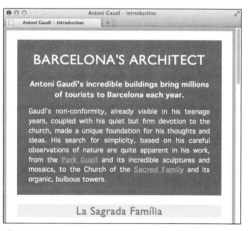. In this way, you can display the text with initial capital letters, with all capital letters B, with all lowercase letters, or as it was typed.

To change the text case:

1. Type **text-transform:**.

2. Type **capitalize** after the colon (:) to put the first character of each word in uppercase.

   Or type **uppercase** to change all the letters to uppercase.

   Or type **lowercase** to change all the letters to lowercase.

   Or type **none** to leave the text as is (possibly canceling out an inherited value).

TIP The capitalize value has its limitations. It doesn't know when a language's word shouldn't be capitalized by convention; it just capitalizes every word. So, text in your HTML like "Jim Rice enters the Hall of Fame" would render as "Jim Rice Enters The Hall Of Fame."

TIP Why use text-transform if you can just change the text in the HTML? Well, sometimes the content is beyond your reach. For example, it could be stored in a database or pulled from another site's news feed. In those cases, you're dependent on adjusting the text case with CSS. Also, search engines typically index the text as it's typed in the HTML, and the text may be more legible in search results in standard case.

TIP The lowercase value can be useful for creating stylish headings (or if you're e.e. cummings).

TIP The text-transform property is inherited.

Ⓐ I've decided to display the level 1 heading in all uppercase letters for emphasis Ⓑ.

```
body {
    background-color: #88b2d2;
    font: 100% Geneva, Tahoma, Verdana,
    → sans-serif;
}

h1,
h2 {
    font-family: "Gill Sans", "Gill Sans MT",
    → Calibri, sans-serif;
    font-weight: normal;
    letter-spacing: 1px;
    text-align: center;
}

h1 {
    font-size: 2.1875em;
    text-transform: uppercase;
}

... rest of CSS ...
```

Ⓑ Now the main heading really stands out. The **h2** headings are unchanged.

Ⓐ I've changed the level 2 headings to **small-caps** Ⓑ. Don't forget the hyphen in both **font-variant** and **small-caps**.

```
...

h1,
h2 {
     font-family: "Gill Sans", "Gill Sans MT",
     → Calibri, sans-serif;
     font-weight: normal;
     letter-spacing: 1px;
     text-align: center;
}

h1 {
     font-size: 2.1875em;
     text-transform: uppercase;
}

h2 {
     background-color: #eaebef;
     color: #7d717c;
     font-size: 1.75em;
     font-variant: small-caps;
}

... rest of CSS ...
```

LA SAGRADA FAMÍLIA

PARK GUELL

Ⓑ Now the **h2** letters are in small caps. The rendering of small caps may vary a tiny bit from browser to browser.

Using Small Caps

Many fonts have a corresponding small caps variant that includes uppercase versions of the letters proportionately reduced to small caps size. You can invoke the small caps variant with the **font-variant** property Ⓐ.

To use a small caps font:

Type **font-variant: small-caps**.

To remove small caps:

Type **font-variant: none**.

TIP Small caps are not quite as heavy as uppercase letters that have simply been reduced in size.

TIP Not all fonts have a corresponding small caps face. In these cases, browsers often fake small caps by simply reducing the size of uppercase letters (which tends to make them look a bit squat). Alternatively, they may display the text in all uppercase (similar to **text-transform: uppercase**, as described earlier).

TIP The **font-variant** property is inherited.

Decorating Text

CSS lets you adorn your text with underlines and other types of lines via the **text-decoration** property. By far, its most common use is for styling link states (**A** and **B**).

A Here's the entire style sheet from the chapter, including the **text-decoration** changes to the links **B**. The version on the companion website has more comments.

```
body {
    background-color: #88b2d2;
    font: 100% Geneva, Tahoma, Verdana,
    → sans-serif;
}

h1, h2 {
    font-family: "Gill Sans", "Gill Sans MT",
    → Calibri, sans-serif;
    font-weight: normal;
    letter-spacing: 1px;
    text-align: center;
}

h1 {
    font-size: 2.1875em; /* 35px/16px */
    text-transform: uppercase;
}

h2 {
    background-color: #eaebef;
    color: #7d717c;
    font-size: 1.75em; /* 28px/16px */
    font-variant: small-caps;
}

p { text-align: justify; }

em,
a:link,
.intro .subhead {
    font-weight: bold;
}

.architect {
    background-color: #fff;
    padding: 1.5em 1.75em;
}
```

```
.intro {
    background-color: #686a63;
    color: #fff;
    line-height: 1.45;
    padding: 1px 1.875em .7em;
}

.intro .subhead {
    font-size: 1.125em; /* 18px/16px */
    text-align: center;
}

.intro p {
    font-size: 1.0625em; /* 17px/16px */
}

.project p {
    text-indent: 2em;
    font-size: .9375em; /* 15px/16px */
    line-height: 1.65;
}

a:link {
    color: #e10000;
    text-decoration: none;
}

a:visited { color: #b44f4f; }

a:hover {
    color: #f00;
    text-decoration: underline;
}

.intro a { color: #fdb09d; }
.intro a:hover { color: #fec4b6; }
```

code continues in next column

To decorate text:

1. Type `text-decoration:`.

2. Type `underline` after the colon (:) to underline text.

   Or type `overline` for a line above the text.

   Or type `line-through` to strike out the text.

To get rid of decorations:

Type `text-decoration: none;`.

TIP You can apply `text-decoration` to other elements, not just a elements as in the example.

TIP You can eliminate decorations from elements that normally have them (like a, `del`, or `ins`) or from elements that inherit decorations from their parents.

TIP Although it's perfectly fine to remove underlines from links, be sure to distinguish them sufficiently from surrounding text another way (Ⓐ and Ⓑ), or visitors may not realize they're actionable.

Ⓑ You can see that the underline is removed from all links in their default state. When they are being hovered over, the underline returns and the link colors get slightly lighter. These effects reinforce to users that they are interacting with a link and encourage them to take action.

Setting Whitespace Properties

By default, multiple spaces and returns in an HTML document are either displayed as a single space or ignored. If you want to change the way they are treated, use the **white-space** property (🅐 and 🅑).

To set whitespace properties:

1. Type **white-space:**.

2. Type **pre** to have browsers display all the spaces and returns in the original text.

    Or type **nowrap** to treat all spaces as non-breaking, meaning the text won't wrap to the next line.

    Or type **normal** to treat whitespace as usual.

TIP The value of pre for the white-space property gets its name from the pre element (Chapter 4), which displays text in a mono-space font while maintaining all of its spaces and returns. However, white-space: pre; does not display text in a monospace font.

TIP If you were to add overflow: hidden; text-overflow: ellipses; to the .intro .subhead rule in 🅐, an ellipsis would show instead of the text that breaks out of the box in 🅑.

TIP You may use the br element to manually create line breaks in an element styled with white-space: nowrap. Having said that, it's best to avoid using br unless you have no alternative, because it mixes presentation with your HTML instead of letting CSS take care of it. For details about the br element, consult "Creating a Line Break" in Chapter 4.

🅐 I've prevented the **.subhead** paragraph text from wrapping and styled it so the impact of **nowrap** is obvious against both dark and light backgrounds 🅑. The **text-shadow** property is covered in Chapter 14 ("Adding Drop Shadows to Text").

```
...

.intro {
    background-color: #686a63;
    color: #fff;
    line-height: 1.45;
    padding: 1px 1.875em .7em;
}

.intro .subhead {
    font-size: 1.125em;

    /* temporary for demo only */
    color: lime;
    text-shadow: 3px 2px 2px black;
    white-space: nowrap;
}

... rest of CSS ...
```

🅑 The **.subhead** text won't wrap, even when the browser window is too narrow to display the entire line. As a result, a horizontal scrollbar appears so you can scroll over to see the rest of the text.

Layout with Styles

You can create a wide variety of layouts with CSS. This chapter demonstrates how to build a common layout type: a masthead (page header) on top, two columns of content, and a footer on the bottom **A** (on the next page). However, you can apply the CSS properties you'll learn about to make vastly different layouts.

This chapter and the next are companion pieces. As a way of easing you into layouts, this chapter shows you how to create a *fixed-width* layout. But most of what you will learn applies to any layout. In Chapter 12, you will see how to lay out the same page but make it *responsive*. The next section explains these terms.

I won't show every line of CSS needed for the page in this chapter. For instance, the text formatting was done ahead of time (per lessons from Chapters 10 and 13). Please see the complete code at www.htmlcssvqs.com/8ed/11/finished-page. I've included comments in all of the files (especially the style sheets) to help explain the code.

In This Chapter

Considerations When Beginning a Layout

Here are a few things to help you along as you lay out your own sites and hone them before releasing them into the wild.

Separating content and presentation

I've mentioned this before, but it bears repeating because it's so fundamental to building webpages. As a best practice, always separate your content (HTML) and presentation (CSS). You learned how (and why) to do this in Chapter 8 by linking to an external style sheet. If you do so from all your pages, they can all share the same layout and overall style, with page-specific differences as desired.

Layout approaches

There are two main types of website designs: fixed-width and responsive.

- A *fixed-width* page has pixel-based widths for the whole page and for each column of content within it. As its name suggests, its width doesn't change when viewed on smaller devices like mobile phones and tablets or when a desktop browser window is reduced. Chances are, the majority of sites you've visited have fixed widths. This is how most sites were built until responsive web design became possible. So even though their numbers may be diminishing, fixed-width layouts are still common, particularly on corporate and big-brand sites. Also, fixed-width layouts are the easiest to get the hang of when learning CSS, which is why this chapter shows you how to build one.

- A *responsive* webpage is known to be *fluid* (or liquid) because it uses

A This page, with two columns, a header, and a footer, was laid out with CSS. CSS gives you tremendous versatility in how your pages look. This particular page design aims to be clean and content-focused. Building this layout is explained step by step throughout this chapter, and the layout is made responsive in Chapter 12.

The Origins of Responsive Web Design

Ethan Marcotte coined the term *responsive web design* and made known the group of techniques behind creating a responsive site. The approach first gained wide attention from his article on *A List Apart*: www.alistapart.com/articles/responsive-web-design/. He went into greater detail in his outstanding book *Responsive Web Design* (A Book Apart, 2011), which I highly recommend.

Chapter 12 of *this* book echoes the techniques he has popularized and that others in the web community have evolved.

percentages instead of pixels for widths, allowing the page to shrink and expand depending on the viewing conditions. In addition to having fluid columns, responsive webpages can shift their design in specific ways based on the screen size. For instance, images can change sizes and columns can be rearranged to fit better. This allows for tailoring the experience to mobile, tablet, and desktop users independently—but with the same HTML, not with three different sites.

There is no single layout approach that is right for every circumstance. However, given the explosion of smartphones and tablets—not to mention the inevitable arrival of devices of all sizes we haven't even conceived of yet—it stands to reason that making your site responsive is probably in your best interest. It also explains why more responsive sites turn up seemingly every day. As mentioned, you will build upon what you learn here to create a responsive webpage in the next chapter.

Browser considerations

Not all visitors will use the same browser, operating system, or even device when accessing your site. So in most cases, you will want to test your pages on a range of browsers before making them live on your web server. I recommend testing each page in a few browsers periodically as you develop it so you'll have fewer issues to address at the end when you perform comprehensive testing. See "Testing Your Page" in Chapter 20 for information about both how to test your pages and the browsers in which to check them.

Structuring Your Pages

CSS brings your content to life, allowing you to work your design magic. You can style the content containers that represent a page's primary structural elements (which you learned about in Chapter 3) as well as the content within them (covered in Chapters 4–5 and 15–18). But first, at the heart of any effective webpage is well-structured, semantic HTML **Ⓐ**.

To structure your page:

1. Divide sections of your page into **article**, **aside**, **main**, **nav**, **section**, **header**, **footer**, and **div** elements, as appropriate. Also apply ARIA landmark roles as appropriate. See Chapter 3 for more details on both. In **Ⓐ**, you have a fictitious blog named *Le Journal* with:

- ▸ A **div** that wraps around the whole page and another one that contains two main parts to apply some design

- ▸ A **header** for the masthead, which contains the logo, links to social media sites, and main navigation

- ▸ A **main** element divided into multiple blog post **section** elements, each with their own **footer**

- ▸ A sidebar **div** (that also uses **article** and **aside**) to provide information about the blog author and links to blog posts in the right column (once CSS is applied)

- ▸ A page-level **footer** element for copyright info

continues on page 271

Ⓐ This is the HTML page I use throughout this chapter and the next. There are four main sections (masthead, main, sidebar, and page footer). The main and sidebar areas are wrapped in a **div** with **class="container"**. The entire page is wrapped in a **div** with **class="page"**. You can find the complete file at www.htmlcssvqs.com/ 8ed/11/finished-page. By default, the page is plain but still functional Ⓑ.

```
...
<body>
<div class="page">
    <!-- ==== START MASTHEAD ==== -->
    <header class="masthead" role="banner">
        <p class="logo"><a href="/"><img ... /></a></p>

        <ul class="social-sites">
            ... [social icons links] ...
        </ul>

        <nav role="navigation">
            ... [list of main navigation links] ...
        </nav>
    </header>
    <!-- end masthead -->

    <div class="container">
        <!-- ==== START MAIN ==== -->
        <main role="main">
            <section class="post">
                <h1>Sunny East Garden at the Getty Villa</h1>

                <img ... class="post-photo-full" />

                <div class="post-blurb">
                    <p>It is hard to believe ...</p>
                </div>

                <footer class="footer">
                    ... [blog post snippet footer] ...
                </footer>
            </section>

            <section class="post">
                <h1>The City Named After Queen Victoria</h1>

                <img ... class="post-photo" />

                <div class="post-blurb">
                    <p>An hour and a half aboard ...</p>
                </div>

                <footer class="footer">
                    ... [blog post snippet footer] ...
                </footer>
            </section>
```

code continues on next page

Ⓐ continued

```
            <nav role="navigation">
                <ol class="pagination">
                    ... [links list items] ...
                </ol>
            </nav>
        </main>
        <!-- end main -->

        <!-- ==== START SIDEBAR ==== -->
        <div class="sidebar">
            <article class="about">
                <h2>About Me</h2>
                ...
            </article>

            <div class="mod">
                <h2>My Travels</h2>
                ... [map image] ...
            </div>

            <aside class="mod">
                <h2>Popular Posts</h2>
                <ul class="links">
                    ... [links list items] ...
                </ul>
            </aside>

            <aside class="mod">
                <h2>Recently Shared</h2>
                <ul class="links">
                    ... [links list items] ...
                </ul>
            </aside>
        </div>
        <!-- end sidebar -->
    </div>
    <!-- end container -->

    <!-- ==== START PAGE FOOTER ==== -->
    <footer role="contentinfo" class="footer">
        <p class="legal"><small>&copy; 2013 Le Journal ...</small></p>
    </footer>
    <!-- end page footer -->
</div>
<!-- end page -->
</body>
</html>
```

- facebook
- twitter
- flickr

- Home
- About
- Contact

Sunny East Garden at the Getty Villa

It is hard to believe, but there are about 300 varieties of plants at the East Garden at the Getty, making the experience truly remarkable. This area is one of the most tranquil spaces at the Villa. As I wandered around, enjoying shade provided by sycamore and laurel trees and serenaded by splashing water from two sculptural fountains, I couldn't help but think of ancient Rome and the role of the garden 20 centuries ago. It was a place of peace and … Read More

Posted in California, Los Angeles and Garden May 17, 2013 at 11:20am

The City Named After Queen Victoria

B Here's what some of our example page looks like with no styles except the browser defaults. The page is all in one column. Thanks to its solid semantics, it is perfectly usable and intelligible, if a bit spare.

A Note About the Semantics

You may have noticed I used **section** elements in the example A to contain each partial blog post (B shows one). Had they been complete posts, I would have marked them up with **article** instead, just as I would for pages dedicated to individual complete blog entries. Using **article** for these instead of **section** wouldn't be wrong, just an indication that the snippets are sufficient as self-contained compositions. See Chapter 3 for a variety of examples that use **article** and **section**.

2. Put your content in an order that would be the most useful if the CSS were not used B. For example, the masthead, followed by the main content, followed by one or more sidebars, followed by the page-level footer. This can make it easier for you to provide the most important content on top for visitors on smaller screens like smartphones and tablets. In addition, search engines "see" your page as if CSS weren't applied, so if you prioritize your main content, they'll be better able to properly index your site. It benefits screen-reader users as well.

3. Use heading elements (**h1–h6**) consistently to identify and prioritize information on your page within the sections.

4. Mark up the rest of your content with the appropriate semantics, such as paragraphs, figures, and lists.

5. Use comments as desired to identify different areas of your page and their contents. As A shows, my preference is to use a different format for comments that mark the start, rather than the end, of a section.

TIP You don't have to mark up your entire page before you apply CSS. In practice, it's not uncommon to do the HTML for a section and then some or all of its CSS, then the same for the next section, and so on. It's really a matter of personal preference and what process works best for you.

Styling HTML5 Elements in Older Browsers

As you know, HTML5 has introduced several new semantic elements, most of which you learned about in Chapters 3 and 4. In most cases, modern browsers support those elements natively. From a styling point of view, that means these browsers apply default styles to the new elements just as they do for HTML elements that have existed since the earliest days of the language. For example, **article**, **footer**, **header**, **nav**, and some others display on their own line, just like **div**, **blockquote**, **p**, and others that were defined as block-level elements in versions of HTML before HTML5.

You might be wondering, "What about older browsers? How can I use the new HTML5 elements if they didn't exist when those browsers were created?"

Well, the good news is that most browsers allow you to style elements that they don't yet support natively. Internet Explorer 8 (and previous versions) is the exception, but there's an easy workaround that I describe in step 2. So follow these three easy steps to begin styling pages that use the new HTML5 elements.

To style new HTML5 elements in all browsers:

1. Add the code in Ⓐ to your site's main style sheet (the one that all pages use). Note: You can skip this step if you use a CSS reset or **normalize.css** (see the next section). They include the code.

2. There are two ways to get the styling of new HTML5 elements to work in Internet Explorer prior to version 9. (Do one or the other, not both.) They both use

Ⓐ Most browsers treat elements they don't recognize as inline elements by default. So this bit of CSS forces certain new HTML5 semantics to render on their own line. **display: block;** is the same declaration applied to **div**, **blockquote**, **p**, and others by each browser's built-in default style sheet. See "Controlling the Display Type and Visibility of Elements" to learn more about it.

```
article, aside, figcaption, figure, footer,
→ header, main, nav, section {
    display: block;
}
```

Ⓑ The **script** element is wrapped in what's known as a *conditional comment*. Place it after your **link**(s) to style sheets. The part of the code that reads **[if lt IE 9]** means that only versions *less than* Internet Explorer 9 load the file. Usually it's best to load JavaScript at the end of your page (you'll see why in Chapter 19). However, loading the HTML5 shiv is one of the few instances in which it's necessary to place JavaScript in the **head**. It won't work otherwise.

```
<!DOCTYPE html>
<html lang="en">
<head>
<meta charset="utf-8" />
<title>Le Journal</title>
<link rel="stylesheet"
→ href="css/lejournal.css" />
<!--[if lt IE 9]>
    <script src="http://html5shiv.
    → googlecode.com/svn/trunk/
    → html5.js"></script>
<![endif]-->
</head>
<body>
...
```

C Save the HTML5 shiv ZIP file to your computer so you can extract the JavaScript file you will use **D**.

D When you open the ZIP on your computer, you'll see that it contains several folders (shown). You can ignore all of them except **dist**, which has the **html5shiv.js** file you will use. Copy the file into one of your website's folders, such as one named **js**. (Alternatively, you can use **html5shiv-printshiv.js**. It's the same as **html5shiv.js**, but it allows IE8 and prior versions to print the new HTML5 elements accurately.)

E The highlighted code goes in the **head** of your webpages after your **link**(s) to style sheets. The only difference between this and **B** is the **src** value. It should reference the JavaScript file in the location you pasted it among the other files in your site. The code shown assumes you put it in a folder named **js** that is itself in the folder containing the HTML page (see "URLs" in Chapter 1). Modify the **src** path to match your site's structure as necessary.

```
...
<link rel="stylesheet"
→ href="css/lejournal.css" />
<!--[if lt IE 9]>
    <script src="js/html5shiv.js">
    → </script>
<![endif]-->
</head>
<body>
...
```

the HTML5 shiv JavaScript file (see the sidebar "The HTML5 Shiv").

Of the two, the *easier* way is to add the highlighted code in **B** to the **head** element (*not* the **header** element) of each of your pages. That loads the file from another website (googlecode.com).

The *better* way is to host the JavaScript file on *your* website. I recommend you go this route. It prevents your site from breaking in the older versions of IE if anything should happen to the file at googlecode.com (unlikely, but not unimaginable). Download the HTML5 shiv ZIP file from https://github.com/aFarkas/html5shiv/ **C** (this is where the code is maintained), and include the enclosed JavaScript file in your site (**D** and **E**).

3. Now, style away with CSS as you please!

The HTML5 Shiv

Unlike other mainstream browsers, Internet Explorer 8 and older *ignore* CSS on elements they don't support natively. The HTML5 shiv is a bit of JavaScript that fixes that. (It's also referred to as the HTML5 shim.) The script was created by several members of the web community based on a discovery about IE made by Sjoerd Visscher.

The HTML5 shiv has been bundled into some JavaScript libraries, like Modernizr (www.modernizr.com). So if you add Modernizr to your pages, you won't need to load the HTML5 shiv separately. In other words, you can skip step 2 on the previous page. Incidentally, Modernizr is a handy library that allows you to detect whether a browser supports various HTML5 and CSS3 features.

Resetting or Normalizing Default Styles

By now, you know that each browser has a built-in style sheet that dictates the look of your HTML unless you write your own CSS to override it. The default browser styles are pretty similar on the whole, but they have enough differences that it's common for developers to level the playing field before they apply their own CSS.

There are two main ways to level the playing field (you would use one, not both):

- Begin the main style sheet with a CSS reset, like the Meyer reset created by Eric Meyer (http://meyerweb.com/eric/tools/css/reset/). There are also other reset style sheets available.

- Begin the main style sheet with **normalize.css**, created by Nicolas Gallagher and Jonathan Neal. Find it at http://necolas.github.io/normalize.css/ (use the Download button for the latest version).

To do so, you copy the CSS from the appropriate URL above and paste it into your own style sheet.

A CSS reset effectively sets all the default element styles to "zero" . The second method, **normalize.css**, takes a different approach. Instead of resetting everything, it tweaks the default styles so they are more consistent across browsers 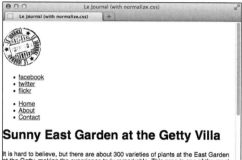. (Important note: I removed the large images from those two figures so you could see more text. Neither a reset nor **normalize.css** will hide your images!)

You aren't required to use either of these approaches, although doing so is common. It's perfectly fine if you just let the

A Here's our example page with a reset applied to it. The most obvious differences are that all font sizes are the same, any bolding of text and styling of lists are removed, and all margins and padding are set to zero.

B Here's the example page using **normalize.css** instead of the reset. It's similar to the unstyled, default rendering, but there are differences. More to the point, this version would look very similar if you were to view it in today's browsers.

 Here's what remains of my version of **normalize.css** after I removed the rules the site won't need.

```
/*! normalize.css v2.1.2 | MIT License |
→ git.io/normalize */

article, aside, figcaption, figure, footer,
→ header, main, nav, section {
    display: block;
}

html {
    -ms-text-size-adjust: 100%;
    -webkit-text-size-adjust: 100%;
}

body {
    margin: 0;
}

a:focus {
    outline: thin dotted;
}

a:active,
a:hover {
    outline: 0;
}

small {
    font-size: 80%;
}

img {
    border: 0;
}
```

browser defaults remain and write your CSS accordingly.

And if you do use **normalize.css** or a reset, you don't have to keep all the CSS they provide. Some of their style rules may apply to HTML elements your site doesn't use. In that case, there's no point in including extra CSS in your style sheet.

For this chapter, I have used a portion of **normalize.css**  and have styled the text to get the page started. So before applying the remaining styling described in this chapter, the page looks like **D**. You can see the full page, as well as those for **A** and **B**, at www.htmlcssvqs.com/8ed/11.

D Here's the example page with the reset and text formatting applied. You'll begin styling the rest of the page from here, evolving it as you step through the chapter.

The Box Model

CSS treats your webpage as if every element it contains were enclosed in an invisible box. The *box model*, as it is known, is made up of a content area, the space surrounding that area (*padding*), the *border* around the padding, and the space around the border that separates one element from the next (*margin*) **A**. It's akin to a framed picture on a wall, where the picture is the content, the matting is the padding, the frame is the border, and the distance between that picture frame and the next one is the margin.

You can use CSS to determine the appearance of each element's box, and in so doing, you have considerable control over the layout of your webpage **B**. Throughout the chapter, you will learn in depth about the `width`, `padding`, `border`, `margin`, and other properties that facilitate this. But it helps to understand the fundamentals of the box model first.

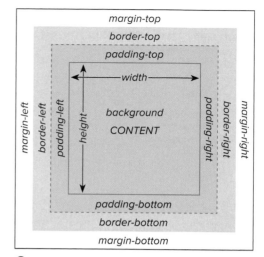

A Each element's box has the same components that determine how much space it occupies and how it looks. You can control each component individually with CSS. Note that the width and height define only the content area dimensions by default. The background (the blue area) extends *behind* the border, so it is only visible as far out as the padding extends unless you make the border color transparent or semi-transparent.

The space around content is the padding. (Here, there is padding on all four sides.) The background color fills both the content and padding areas

The margin is the space that separates an element from others. (Sometimes padding can be used for the same effect.)

The sidebar content area. It is set to a width of 300 pixels. No explicit height is specified, so it is set automatically based on the content flow.

Each element may have a visible border. (In this case, the image has a border of 5 pixels on each side.)

B The box model in the context of the sidebar in our page. Remember, each element has its own box. For example, the `img` element shown has a border, but the space on the left and right of it is padding applied to the `article` element that contains the image.

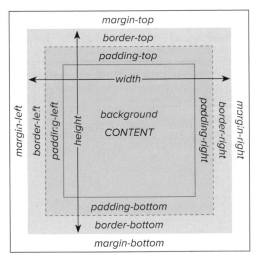

C When **box-sizing: border-box;** is set, the width and height encompass everything but the margins. Otherwise, the box behaves the same as **A**.

Default box model

border-width: 10px;
padding: 15px;
width: 300px;

Content width is 300 pixels

Display width is 350 pixels

box-sizing: border-box;
border-width: 10px;
padding: 15px;
width: 300px;

Display width is 300 pixels

D Both **div**s have the same **border-width** (the lighter green), **padding**, and **width** settings. The top one renders per the default box model **A**. The bottom one is set to **box-sizing: border-box;** **C** to make its display width the same as the **width** property (**300px**). Both boxes are set to **height: 170px;** (not shown), but the first one is taller due to the top and bottom padding and border sizes being added to the height. (Note: The black strips are superimposed; they are not part of the **div**s and so don't affect their height.)

Width, height, and the box model

The box model can operate in one of two ways regarding how the CSS **width** property affects how wide an element displays. (Not including any margin separating it from adjacent elements.)

The default behavior—which maps to figure **A**—is actually a little counterintuitive. An element's width in browsers does not match its **width** property value (unless it doesn't have padding or borders). The **width** only dictates the width of the *content* area inside the padding, as reflected in **A**. Instead, an element's display width is determined by the total of the **width**, the padding on left and right, and the border on left and right. The display height works similarly, taking into account top and bottom padding and border values.

The second way it can operate is more intuitive for most coders. In this case, the display width of an element *does* match the value of the **width** property. The content width, padding, and border fall within it **C**. The **height** property works similarly. You trigger this model by setting **box-sizing: border-box;** on an element.

All this might seem too abstract, so let's see an example that uses both approaches **D**. Be aware that the **padding** and **border-width** values shown are applied to each side. For example, **padding: 15px;** results in 30 pixels of total horizontal padding (15 on the left and 15 on the right) and 30 pixels of total vertical padding (15 on top and 15 on bottom).

> **TIP** The illustration in **A** was inspired by Rich Hauck's box model diagram (which is itself inspired by the one in the CSS spec).

> **TIP** See "Setting the Height or Width for an Element" for more about **box-sizing: border-box;**, why you won't usually set a **height** value, and more.

Controlling the Display Type and Visibility of Elements

As discussed in Chapter 1, by default each element displays either on its own line (like **h1-h6** and **p**) or within a line (like **em**, **strong**, and **cite**) **A**. I also explained in Chapter 1 that, unofficially, the former are referred to as block-level elements and the latter are referred to as inline elements.

The source of those terms is their default **display** property setting: Block-level elements are set to **display: block** (or **display: list-item** in the case of the **li** element), and inline elements are set to **display: inline**.

Of course, with CSS being all-powerful, you can change an element's natural display, such as changing it from **block** to **inline** **B** or vice versa **C**. There is also a hybrid display type called **inline-block**, which allows an element to appear on the same line as other content while other- wise behaving like a block-level element (**D** through **F**). Lastly, you may also set an element to not display at all **G**.

A These simple paragraphs with nested **em** elements demonstrate the difference between **display: block** and **display: inline**.

```
<p>This is the <em>first</em> paragraph.</p>
<p>This is the <em>second</em> paragraph.</p>
```

Browser default

This is the *first* paragraph.

This is the *second* paragraph.

B The two paragraphs look like one.

```
p {
    display: inline;
}
```

Paragraphs set to display: inline

This is the *first* paragraph. This is the *second* paragraph.

C The **em**s display on their own lines like paragraphs.

```
em {
    display: block;
}
```

---

em elements set to display: block

This is the
first
paragraph.

This is the
second
paragraph.

The Document Flow

By default, elements are displayed in the same order as they appear in the HTML code from top to bottom—this is known as the *document flow*—with line breaks at the beginning and end of each element that isn't inline. For a longer example than the ones shown here, see the example page in figures **A** and **B** of "Structuring Your Pages."

D Elements set to `inline` ignore any `width`, `height`, `margin-top`, and `margin-bottom` settings. However, those properties *are* applied to elements set to `inline-block`, like the `em`s shown here that have a `width`. So, if they were set to `display: inline;` instead, this example would look just like **A**—minus the background color—even with the `width` specified. (All `display` types accept a `background` style. I made it green here so the width of the `em`s would be evident.)

```
em {
    background: lightgreen;
    display: inline-block;
    width: 300px;
}
```

`em` **elements set to** `display: inline-block`

This is the *first*   paragraph.

This is the *second*   paragraph.

E I set the main navigation links and their parent list items to `inline-block` to allow me to add some top and bottom padding to the links later (see "Adding Padding Around an Element"). The social icons won't need further adjustments that can only be achieved when elements behave like a block, so setting them to `inline` is sufficient.

```
.social-sites li {
    display: inline;
}

.nav-main li {
    display: inline-block;
}

.nav-main a {
    color: #292929;
    display: inline-block;
    font-family: 'Open Sans', sans-serif;
    font-size: 1.125em;
    font-weight: 700;
    text-transform: uppercase;
}
```

F Here's a practical example of how changing the display setting can be advantageous. By default, the social icon links and main navigation links are stacked (as shown in the figure on the left) because they are contained in list items (`li`). By overriding their default `display: list-item;` setting **E**, the items in each list of links appear in a single row.

G The `em` text neither displays nor occupies any visual space. Instead, the words that follow it in the HTML shift over, leaving no hint the `em` text was ever there.

```
em {
    display: none;
}
```

`em` **elements set to** `display: none`

This is the paragraph.

This is the paragraph.

To specify how elements should be displayed:

1. In your style sheet rule, type **display:**.

2. Type **block** to display the element as block-level (thus like starting a new paragraph) **C**.

   Or type **inline** to display the element as inline (not like starting a new paragraph) **B**.

   Or type **inline-block** to display the element as inline but with block-level characteristics, meaning you can also assign the element properties, such as **width**, **height**, **margin**, and **padding**, on all four sides (**D** through **F**).

   Or type **none** to hide the given element and completely remove it from the document flow **G**.

   See the tips for a link to other **display** values.

To control an element's visibility:

Meanwhile, the **visibility** property's primary purpose is to control whether an element is, well, visible. Unlike the **display** property, when you hide an element with **visibility**, a blank space shows where the element and its content would appear otherwise **H**. The space that the hidden element would have taken up still remains in the document flow.

1. In your style sheet rule, type **visibility:**.

2. Type **hidden** to make the element invisible without removing it from the document flow **H**.

   Or type **visible** to reveal the element.

H An empty space remains where the hidden **em** text used to be. It's as if we made the **em** text white—the size of the space matches the size of the text (or whatever content you hide).

```
em {
    visibility: hidden;
}
```

em elements set to visibility: hidden

This is the   paragraph.

This is the   paragraph.

TIP An element set to `display: inline;` does accept padding, but `padding-top` and `padding-bottom` will cross into the territory of adjacent elements rather than remain confined to the element. You can see what I mean if you also add `background: red;` to the element as a test.

TIP Chapter 12 shows a practical example of setting a naturally inline element to `display: block;` for narrow screens (like phones) and back to `display: inline;` for wider ones (like desktops).

TIP All content (including any descendants) within an element set to `display: none;` or `visibility: hidden;` is also affected. For instance, if you set `display: none;` to an `article` that contains several p, `figure`, and `img` elements, none of them would display. If you set `visibility: hidden;` to the `article` instead, a blank space (probably large!) would show.

TIP The `display` property has several other values as well, with varying degrees of maturity and browser support. For example, the `grid` and `flex` properties are for additional layout techniques that are still being finalized in the specs. See more information at https://developer.mozilla.org/CSS/display.

TIP The `visibility` property has another value (apart from `inherit`): `collapse`, which you use with certain parts of `table` elements. Browser support varies. Learn more about `collapse` at https://developer.mozilla.org/CSS/visibility.

Setting the Height or Width for an Element

You can set a height and width on elements such as sectioning content, paragraphs, list items, **div**s, images, **video**, form elements, and more (**A** through **C**).

Also, you can set phrasing content elements (which display as inline by default) to **display: block;** or **display: inline-block;** and then apply a width or height to them too. (See "Controlling the Display Type and Visibility of Elements" for more information about the **display** property.)

To set the height or width for an element:

1. Type **width: w**, where **w** is the width of the element's content area and can be expressed either as a length (with units like **px** and **em**) or as a percentage of the parent element. Or use **auto** to let the browser calculate the width (this is the default).

2. Type **height: h**, where **h** is the height of the element and can be expressed only as a length (with units like **px** and **em**). Or use **auto** to let the browser calculate the height (this is the default).

A Eventually, our page will have two columns: One with the content in **main** and one with the content in the **div** with **class="sidebar"**. The rules set their respective fixed widths (**B** and **C**).

```
main {
    width: 600px;  /* 62.5% = 600px/960px */
}

.sidebar {
    width: 300px;  /* 31.25% = 300px/960px */
}
```

B I set the width of **main** to **600px** to match the width of the image. Now, the main area remains at 600 pixels wide no matter how wide you make the browser window. As a result, the text wraps instead of continuing beyond the width of the image.

C The sidebar begins with the About Me module. Currently, our page is one long column, so you can see the end of the **main** content above the sidebar. This also demonstrates that the sidebar (now set to **300px**) is half the width of **main**.

D You can apply **border-box** to every element using the * wildcard. Alternatively, you can apply it to elements individually just like any other style (replace * with the selector of your choice). The funny-looking property prefixes **-webkit-** and **-moz-** make it work in older Android and iOS devices and in Firefox, respectively.

```
* {
    -webkit-box-sizing: border-box;
    -moz-box-sizing: border-box;
    box-sizing: border-box;
}
```

Pixels for Fixed-Width Pages, Percentages for Responsive Web Designs

This chapter uses pixels for widths as a way of introducing you to laying out webpages. In the code comments, I have included the equivalent percentages of the pixel widths, and how I arrived at those values **A**. I will use the percentages instead of the pixels in Chapter 12 when I show you how to make this layout responsive.

TIP The padding, borders, and margin are not included in the value of **width** or **height** (see "The Box Model" and "Width, margins, and auto"). "The Box Model" also shows how applying **box-sizing: border-box;** to an element **D** *will* make the values of **width** and **height** include the padding and borders.

TIP A percentage width value is relative to the width of the element's parent. For example, assume a **div** is 100 pixels wide and you set an element within it to **width: 70%;**. The child element will be 70 pixels wide (70% of 100). You will see this in the next chapter.

TIP You can't set a **height** or **width** on elements that display as inline elements (like phrasing content) unless you set them to **display: inline-block** or **display: block**. See "Controlling the Display Type and Visibility of Elements" for more information about the **display** property.

TIP There are also **min-width**, **min-height**, **max-width**, and **max-height** properties for setting minimum and maximum sizes. The **max-width** property is ideal for setting the outside limit of a fluid layout, like the one you'll see in the next chapter. In that case, I set the **.page div** that wraps around the whole page to **max-width: 960px;**. When combined with percentage-based widths for **main** and **.sidebar**, this allows the page to be narrower on smaller screens but no wider than 960 pixels, even if visitors have huge displays. See also "Why **min-height** Is Often Preferable to **height**."

TIP **widths** and **heights** are not inherited.

Width, margins, and auto

If you don't explicitly set the **width** or **height**, **auto** is used as the value. For elements that display as a block, the **auto** value for **width** is calculated from the width of the *containing block* minus the element's padding, borders, and margins (**E** and **F**). In simple terms, the containing block in this context is the content area of the parent element that contains the element.

For example, a **p** contained in a space that is 200 pixels wide automatically will be 200 pixels wide as well. But if it has **padding-right: 10px**, the **auto** width will be 190 pixels.

E In this example, I've set the **width** of the parent **div** to 300 pixels. This will be our containing block. Then, both paragraphs have 10-pixel margins, 3-pixel borders, and 8-pixel padding on all sides. The first paragraph has the **width** set automatically, since **auto** is the default **width** value unless you specify otherwise. The second paragraph (which has **class="second"** in the HTML) is set at **200px**.

```
div { /* containing block */
    background: khaki; /* tan */
    width: 300px;
}

p,
.second {
    background: white;
    border: 3px solid royalblue;
    margin: 10px;
    padding: 8px;
}

.second { /* the second paragraph */
    border-color: orangered;
    width: 200px;
}
```

Why min-height Is Often Preferable to height

Unless you're certain an element's content won't get taller, it's almost always best to avoid giving it a **height** in your style sheet. In most cases, you'll let the content and browser dictate the height automatically. This lets content flow as needed on the range of browsers and devices.

If you do set a **height** and the content grows, it could break out of the element's box, which might not be what you'd expect. Browsers do *not* expand the height automatically in this circumstance; they take your word for it when you specify a height, and they stick to it. See "Determining How to Treat Overflow" for an example.

However, if you always want the element to be *at least* a certain height, set a **min-height**. If the content later grows, the element's height will grow automatically as desired. That is the difference between **height** and **min-height**, as well as between **width** and **min-width**.

And in case you're wondering, there are a variety of reasons beyond your control that content might grow. Your content might come from a database or a feed from a third party or be user-generated. Also, your visitor may increase the font size in his or her browser, overriding the style you specified.

This paragraph has an automatic width, 10px margins, 3px blue borders, and 8px padding. Since the containing block is 300px wide, this paragraph has a width of 300-10-10-3-3-8-8 (that is, 300-42), or 258 pixels, as determined by the browser automatically. Don't forget you have to subtract the margin, border, and padding from both the left and right sides!

This paragraph has class="second" applied to it, so its width is set to 200 pixels, with the same 10px margins, 3px borders (though red), and 8px padding as the first paragraph. So, the total amount of horizontal space it occupies is 200+10+10+3+3+5+5 (that is, 200+42), or 242 pixels. Because it has an explicit width set, the paragraph isn't stretched by the browser automatically to fill the remaining space of the containing block.

58 pixels of space

|◄—— width: 200px ——►|

width: 300px
(containing block)

F If the **width** is **auto**, as in the top paragraph, its value is derived from the width of the containing block (tan area) minus its own margins, border, and padding. If the **width** is set manually (as in the bottom paragraph), the right margin is usually adjusted to pick up the slack.

Elements like images have an **auto** width equal to their intrinsic value; that is, the actual dimensions of the external file (like the example page's largest image, which is 600 x 365). Inline elements ignore the **width** property altogether (meaning you can't set a width on elements like **em** and **cite** unless you set them to **display: inline-block** or **display: block**). See "Controlling the Display Type and Visibility of Elements" for more information about **display**.

If you manually set the **width**, **margin-left**, and **margin-right** values, but together with the border and padding they don't equal the size of the containing block, something's got to give. And indeed, the browser will honor the **width**, making the space to the right larger than your **margin-right** setting (see the bottom paragraph in **F**).

If you manually set the **width** but set one of the margins to **auto**, then that margin will stretch or shrink to make up the difference.

However, if you manually set the **width** but leave *both* margins set to **auto**, *both* margins will be set to the same maximum value, resulting in your element being centered. For example, **.page { margin: 0 auto; }** centers the page. That's precisely what I've done for the example page, as shown in figures **F** and **G** of "Setting the Margins Around an Element."

Adding Padding Around an Element

Padding is just what it sounds like: extra space around the contents of an element but inside the outer edge (the border). You might recall my analogy from before—padding is like the matting between a photo (the content) and a picture frame (the border). You can change the padding's thickness (**A** through **D**) but not its color or texture. The color or texture that shows in the padded area is the element's background, as set via `background`, `background-color` **A**, or `background-image`.

Shorthand Notation for `padding`

As with the `border` and `margin` properties, you can use shorthand notation instead of defining padding for each side with `padding-top`, `padding-right`, and so on.

- **`padding: 5px;`**—With one value, it applies to all sides.

- **`padding: 5px 9px;`**—With two values, the first value applies to the top and bottom and the second value applies to the right and left.

- **`padding: 5px 9px 11px;`**—With three values, the first applies to the top, the second to the right and left, and the third to the bottom (**A** and **B**).

- **`padding: 5px 9px 11px 0;`**—With four values, they are applied to the top, right, bottom, and left, in clockwise order (**C** and **D**).

Padding can be expressed in any combination of pixels, percentages, ems, or rems.

A As with setting margins, when you set three values for **padding** they are assigned, in clockwise order, to the top, right and left, and bottom. So here, there will be padding on all four sides **B**.

```
.about {
    background-color: #2b2b2b;
    padding: .3125em .625em .625em;
}

/*
Similar to
    padding: 5px 10px 10px;
because font-size is 16px and
.3125 = 5px/16px
.625 = 10px/16px
*/
```

B Without the padding (left), the content touches the edges. When you add padding, space is created inside the element and around its content (right). Also, the background color shows through the padding. (If we were to add `.about { border: 1px solid red; }`, a red border would be around the whole box, *outside* the padding.) You'll notice there is more space at the top and bottom of the module than is specified by the padding. This happens in part because the browser applies a default top margin to headings ("ABOUT ME") and bottom margin to paragraphs (like the one below the image). The padding on the surrounding `.about` box forces the margins to take effect inside the box.

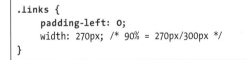

C Now I've added padding to all sides of the main navigation links. The top and bottom padding will be more evident when I add borders in the next section.

```
.nav-main a {
    color: #292929;
    display: inline-block;
    font-family: 'Open Sans', sans-serif;
    font-size: 1.125em; /* 18px/16px */
    font-weight: 700;
    padding: .5em 1.15em .5em 1.4em;
    text-transform: uppercase;
}

/*
Similar to
    padding: 9px 20.7px 9px 25.2px;
because font-size is 18px and
.5   = 9px/18px
1.15 = 20.7px/18px
1.4  = 25.2px/18px
*/
```

D The links were cramped before (top), but thanks to the padding, they now have room to breathe (bottom).

E The sidebar contains two groups of links, each of which is contained in an unordered list (**ul**) that has **class="links"**. I set the padding to **0** to override the browser default of **40px** **F**. The width style ensures that the links wrap 30 pixels before the right edge of the sidebar, which is **300px** wide, as defined earlier. (See Chapter 15 for more about lists, and specifically "Using Custom Markers" regarding the default left padding.)

```
.links {
    padding-left: 0;
    width: 270px; /* 90% = 270px/300px */
}
```

To add padding around an element:

Type **padding: *x*;**, where ***x*** is the amount of desired space to be added, expressed in units (typically in ems or pixels) or as a percentage of the width of the parent element (for example, **20%**).

Or apply padding to a single side by typing **padding-top: *x*;**, **padding-right: *x*;**, **padding-bottom: *x*;**, or **padding-left: *x*;** (**E** and **F**).

TIP See the "Understanding em Values for Padding and Margin" sidebar for more about how I determined the em values in **A** and **C**.

TIP By default, your **width** and **height** settings for an element do not include its padding size. See "Width, margins, and auto" (in the previous section) and "The Box Model," which also shows how to override the default.

TIP Background styling is covered in the Chapter 10 section "Setting the Background" and the Chapter 14 sections "Applying Multiple Backgrounds" and "Using Gradient Backgrounds."

TIP Padding is not inherited.

POPULAR POSTS

The City Named After Queen Victoria »

Heaven on Earth? Let's Have

POPULAR POSTS

The City Named After Queen Victoria »
Heaven on Earth? Let's Have Dinner in Paris »
Enjoying Strauss at the Volksoper in Vienna »

RECENTLY SHARED

Heaven on Earth? Let's Have Dinner in Paris »
Experiencing Ramadan in

F The default list indentation was unsightly (top), but now the links line up with their heading because I negated the padding (bottom).

Setting the Border

You can create a border around an element (Ⓐ and Ⓑ) or on individual sides of an element (Ⓒ through Ⓓ) and set its thickness, style, and color. If you've specified any padding (see "Adding Padding Around an Element"), the border encloses both the padding and the contents of the element (Ⓔ through Ⓙ). Figures Ⓚ and Ⓛ demonstrate all border style options available to you.

To define the border style:

Type **border-style:** *type*, where *type* is **none**, **dotted**, **dashed**, **solid**, **double**, **groove**, **ridge**, **inset**, or **outset**.

To set the width of the border:

Type **border-width:** *n*, where *n* is the desired width, including units (for example, **4px**).

To set the color of the border:

Type **border-color:** *color*, where *color* is a color name, hex value, or RGB, HSL, RGBA, or HSLA color (see "CSS colors" in Chapter 7).

Ⓐ Borders may be applied to any element, including images. If you intend to use the same border treatment on more than one element, it would be best to apply it with a class so it's easy to reuse. For example, **.frame { border: 5px solid #bebebe; }**

```
.about img {
    border: 5px solid #bebebe;
}
```

Ⓑ The border frames the image nicely.

C These simple borders give both the main navigation and the page masthead overall a little more definition **D**. As is customary, each navigation link is contained in a list item (**li**). Notice that I turned off the left border of the first one with **border-left: none;**, which resets it to the default.

```
.nav-main {
     /* green */
     border-top: 5px solid #019443;
     /* gray */
     border-bottom: 1px solid #c8c8c8;
}

.nav-main li {
     border-left: 1px solid #c8c8c8;
     display: inline-block;
}

.nav-main li:first-child {
     border-left: none;
}
```

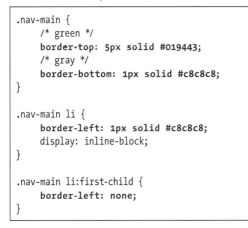

D The borders make the main navigation more prominent, distinguish each navigation link, and help separate the masthead from the page content below it (not shown). The horizontal borders stretch across the width of the page.

E A little padding on the top and bottom of the navigation container adds a subtle touch **F**.

```
.nav-main {
     padding: .45em 0 .5em; /* 7px 0 8px */
}
```

F Now space separates the horizontal lines from the vertical lines.

To set one or more border properties at once with a shortcut:

1. Type **border**.

2. If desired, type **-top**, **-right**, **-bottom**, or **-left** to limit the effect to a single side.

3. If desired, type **-property**, where **property** is **style**, **width**, or **color**, to limit the effect to a single property.

4. Type **:** (a colon).

5. Type the appropriate values (as described in the three previous techniques). If you skipped step 3, you can specify any or all of the three types of border properties (for example, **border: 1px solid** or **border-right: 2px dashed green;**). If you specified a property type in step 3, use an accepted value for just that property (for example, **border-right-style: dotted;**).

TIP By default, Internet Explorer shows a blue border around images that are linked. To negate this, include img { border: none; } in your style sheet. I've done this for the example page because the site logo is contained in an a element that links to the homepage. (The example *is* the homepage, but the same logo code would be used throughout the site.)

TIP The border shorthand property or individual properties (border-width, border-style, and border-color) can have from one to four values. If you use one value, it is applied to all four sides. If you use two, the first is used for the top and bottom, and the second for the right and left. If you use three, the first is used for the top, the second for the right and left, and the third for the bottom. And if you use four, they are applied to the top, right, bottom, and left, in clockwise order.

continues on next page

TIP You must define at least the style for a border to display. If there's no style, there will be no border. The default is `border-style: none`.

TIP If you use a shortcut, like `border` or `border-left` (and so on), the properties you don't give values for are set to their defaults. So `border: 1px black;` means `border: 1px black none;`, which means you won't get a border (even if you specified a style earlier with `border-style`).

TIP The default border color is the value of the element's `color` property (see "Setting the Color" in Chapter 10).

TIP The `border` property can be used for tables and their cells (see "Structuring Tables" in Chapter 18 for an example).

TIP By default, your `width` and `height` settings for an element do not include the size of its borders. The first tip in "Setting the Height or Width for an Element" explains how to override this.

TIP CSS3 introduces the `border-image` property. Browser support is good outside of Internet Explorer (see http://caniuse.com/#search=border-image). You can learn about `border-image` at www.sitepoint.com/css3-border-image and css-tricks.com/understanding-border-image.

TIP Borders are not inherited.

G I add a border to several headings at once with a single rule **H**. (The class name **mod** represents a generic module on my page.)

```
.about h2,
.mod h2 {
    font-size: 0.875em;
}

.about h2,
.mod h2,
.nav-main a {
    font-family: 'Open Sans',sans-serif;
    font-weight: 700;
    text-transform: uppercase;
}

.mod h2 {
    border-bottom: 1px solid #dbdbdb;
    padding-bottom: 0.75em;
}
```

MY TRAVELS

POPULAR POSTS

The City Named After Queen Victoria »

RECENTLY SHARED

Heaven on Earth? Let's Have Dinner in Paris »

H The same treatment is applied to three headings in the sidebar. The bottom padding gave the border a little distance from the heading text.

I I apply a similar effect to the footers below each blog post snippet, except they get a top border as well **H**. Each one is a paragraph with `class="post-footer"`.

```
.footer p {
    font-size: .6875em; /* 11px/16px */
}

.post-footer {
    border-bottom: 1px solid #dbdbdb;
    border-top: 1px solid #dbdbdb;
    padding-bottom: .7em; /* 7.7px/11px */
    padding-top: .7em;
}
```

Posted in **California, Los Angeles** and **Garden** • May 17, 2013 at 11:20am

Posted in **California, Los Angeles** and **Garden** • May 17, 2013 at 11:20am

J Without the top and bottom padding **G**, the borders almost touch the text (top). It looks much better with the padding (bottom).

K In this example, I set the padding and default border for each paragraph. Then for the first paragraph, I set the border width for all four sides, and then the style for each side. For the four remaining paragraphs, I define only their styles and colors because the border width of **10px** is taken from the first rule that covered all paragraphs.

```
p {
    border: 10px solid red;
    padding: 15px;
}

.ddd {
    border-width: 4px;
    border-style: dotted dashed double;
}

.ridge {
    border-style: ridge;
    border-color: orange;
}

.groove {
    border-style: groove;
    border-color: purple;
}

.inset {
    border-style: inset;
    border-color: blue;
}

.outset {
    border-style: outset;
    border-color: green;
}
```

L Border styles aren't treated consistently across browsers, but this view of Firefox gives you a sense of the differences between the style types.

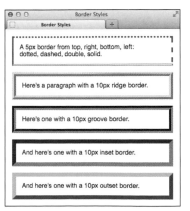

Setting the Margins Around an Element

The margin is the amount of transparent space between one element and the next (**A** and **B**). See "The Box Model" for how it relates to an element's border and padding.

To set an element's margins:

Type `margin: x`, where *x* is the amount of desired space to be added, expressed as a length, a percentage of the width of the parent element, or `auto`.

Or apply a margin to a single side by typing `margin-top: x;`, `margin-right: x;`, `margin-bottom: x;` (**A** and **C**), or `margin-left: x;`.

A I have overridden the default bottom margin with my own setting, which is smaller. See the sidebar for an explanation of how to use ems for margins.

```
h1 {
    color: #212121;
    font-family: "Lato", sans-serif;
    font-size: 3.25em; /* 36px/16px */
    font-weight: 300;
    letter-spacing: -2px;
    line-height: .975;
    margin-bottom: .4125em; /* 21.45px */
}
```

B The default space between each blog post heading and image seemed too large for this design (top). Now the space is a little tighter and feels more appropriate (bottom).

C These rules tackle the space between a few elements. The first one allows the map to breathe **D**. The final two rules affect the links in the sidebar **E**.

```
.map {
    margin: 1.4375em 0 .8125em;
    /* 23px 0 13px */
}

.links {
    margin: 1.5em 0 4.125em;
    /* 24px 0 66px */
    padding: 0;
}

.links li {
    margin-bottom: 1.1em;
}
```

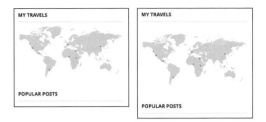

D The map was crowded between the two headings (left), but the margins solved that (right).

POPULAR POSTS

The City Named After Queen Victoria »

Heaven on Earth? Let's Have Dinner in Paris »

Enjoying Strauss at the Volksoper in Vienna »

RECENTLY SHARED

Heaven on Earth? Let's Have Dinner in Paris »

Experiencing Ramadan in

E There is more space between each group of links, as well as between the links themselves. (You can see how it was before in figure **F** of "Adding Padding Around an Element.")

F It's common to center a webpage horizontally in browsers. It's also simple to implement. First, give its container a `width` (`max-width` works, too). Then set the left and right margins to `auto`. That tells the browser to figure out those margins based on the difference between the width of the browser window and the width specified for the container. In our example, a `div` with `class="page"` contains the entire page **G**.

```
.page {
    border: 1px solid red; /* temporary */
    margin: 0 auto;
    width: 960px;
}
```

TIP If you use one value for `margin`, that value is applied to all four sides equally. If you use two values **B**, the first value applies to the top and bottom and the second value applies to the right and left. If you use three values **C**, the first applies to the top, the second to the right and left, and the third to the bottom. If you use four values, they are applied to the top, right, bottom, and left, in clockwise order.

TIP The `margin` property's `auto` value depends on the value of the element's `width` property **F**. (See "Setting the Height or Width for an Element.")

TIP If one element is placed above another, only the greater of the two touching margins—that is, the touching bottom and top margins of the elements—is used. The other margin is said to *collapse*. Left and right margins don't collapse.

TIP You may want to keep a calculator handy for determining em values, or you can use a tool like http://pxtoem.com, which calculates the values for you.

TIP Margins are not inherited.

G The content within the page may be left-aligned, but the page *itself* is centered in the browser window. I added a temporary red border to the `.page div` to make this clear. I made the same `div`'s width **960px** to make room for the sidebar, which will occupy the space on the right once we learn how to show it there in the next section.

Understanding em Values for Padding and Margin

When used for padding and margins, em values are relative to the *element's* font size, *not* to its parent's font size as you might think (see "Setting the Font Size" in Chapter 10). The formula to determine a margin or padding em value is

desired size / element's font size = value

Consider a simple example in which paragraphs are styled with **p { font-size: 14px; padding: .5em; }**. The padding on all sides would be 7 pixels, because 7/14 = .5. If the font size were changed to **20px**, the padding would automatically change to 10 pixels (10/20 = .5). That is the power of a relative unit like em—a layout's proportions remain as the layout scales up and down.

The same applies to margins. As shown in Ⓐ, the **h1**'s font size is roughly the equivalent of 36 pixels (3.25em = 36px/16px). So, the bottom margin of **.4125em** is about 21.45 pixels (21.45/36 = .4125).

The advantages of relative units like ems, percentages, and rems are more evident in responsive web pages, which you will learn about in the next chapter. But they can benefit fixed-width layouts, too. Trent Walton makes a strong case for using relative units at http://trentwalton.com/2013/01/07/flexible-foundations.

I recommend using relative units such as ems for padding and margins, as I have in the examples. However, I know they can take some time to get used to when you're new to building sites. That's why I've given you values in both ems and pixels. Initially, you might feel more comfortable using pixels for padding and margins, and that's OK. You can switch to ems and the like when you're ready.

One quick note: If you use percentages for padding and margin, typically you won't want to use them for top or bottom values, because they are based on the containing block's *width*.

An hour and a half aboard a comfortable car ferry is all it takes to transport you from the modern, urban space that is Greater Vancouver to colonial Vancouver Island, seemingly stuck in the 18th century. The main town of Victoria showcases all the

A This is one of the blog post snippets. By default, the paragraph appears below the image. I haven't applied a width to the paragraph; the text wraps because the paragraph (and the image) is inside the `main` element, which I set to 600 pixels wide earlier (and as seen in **C**). The image's width (370) is specified in the HTML. How can we make the text wrap around the image?

B Easy! When you float an element that *has a* width set, the content that would normally display below it flows around it—as long as that content does *not* have a width set. Our image (which has `class="post-photo"`) and paragraph meet these criteria, which is why floating the image to the left works **C**. The margins add a little space between the image and text.

```
.post-photo {
    float: left;
    margin-bottom: 2px;
    margin-right: 22px;
}
```

The City Named After Queen Victoria

An hour and a half aboard a comfortable car ferry is all it takes to transport you from the modern, urban space that is Greater Vancouver to colonial Vancouver Island, seemingly stuck in the 18th century. The main town of Victoria showcases all the picturesque gems the British Empire was so proud of at the height of its spanning expansion. Representative yet inviting Victorian style municipal buildings, a protected harbor and cobblestone streets populated with small shops and artisanal ... Read More »

Posted in Island, Canada and Roadtrip • May 02, 2013 at 5:45pm

C When the image is floated left, the text scoots up alongside it and wraps around it when it's taller. This example uses an image, but you could apply the same approach to float a `figure`, an `aside`, or other elements.

Making Elements Float

You can make elements float in a sea of text (or other elements) with the **float** property. You can use this technique to make text wrap around images (**A** through **C**) or other elements, to create multi-column layouts (**D** and **E**), and more.

To wrap text around elements:

1. Type **float:**.

2. Type **left** if you want the element on the left and the rest of the content to flow to its right.

   Or type **right** if you want the element on the right and the rest of the content to flow to its left.

   Or type **none** if you don't want the element to float at all. (**none** is the default value, so you'd only set it explicitly if you were overriding another rule that made an element float.)

continues on next page

3. Use the **width** property to explicitly set the width of the floated element (see "Setting the Height and Width for an Element") so there's room for content to flow next to it.

TIP Remember, the direction you choose applies to the element you're floating, not to the elements that flow around it. When you **float: left**, the following content flows to the right, and vice versa.

TIP The **float** property is not inherited.

E Voilà, a two-column layout! But what is that sitting between the left and right columns? Let's take a closer look... **F**

D You can use a similar approach to make two elements appear next to each other, such as the main content and sidebar. Both have explicit widths, so I'll float both of them.

```
main {
    float: left;
    width: 600px; /* 62.5% = 600px/960px */
}

.sidebar {
    float: right;
    margin-top: 1.875em; /* 30px/16px */
    width: 300px; /* 31.25% = 300px/960px */
}
```

F It's the footer! How did it get up there? First, remember that our page is 960 pixels wide, **main** is 600 pixels wide, and the sidebar is 300 pixels wide. With the columns floated to opposite sides, that leaves 60 pixels of space between them. Second, if you look at the HTML, the code for **main** is directly before the sidebar, which is directly before the footer. Because the columns are floated, the footer content flows in between them, just like the paragraph text flowed around the image in **C**. You'll learn how to get the footer back down where it belongs in the next section.

Ⓐ This simple structure keeps all blog post introductory content in a **section**. In the real page shown throughout the chapter, **<h1>The City Named After Queen Victoria</h1>** is directly before the **img** inside the **section**.

```
<section class="post">
    <img ... class="post-photo" />

    <div class="post-blurb">
        <p>An hour and a half ...</p>
    </div>

    <footer class="footer">
        <p class="post-footer">Posted ...</p>
    </footer>
</section>
```

An hour and a half aboard a comfortable car ferry is all it takes to transport you from the modern, urban space that is Greater Vancouver to colonial Vancouver Island, seemingly stuck in the 18th century. The main town of Victoria showcases all the picturesque gems the British Empire was so proud of at the height of its spanning expansion. Representative yet inviting Victorian style municipal buildings, a protected harbor and cobblestone streets populated with small shops and artisanal ... Read More »

Posted in Island, Canada and Roadtrip May 02, 2013 at 5:45pm

Ⓑ The image has **float: left;** applied to it, forcing the text to flow around it. The height of the **section** element (the yellow area) seems to be affected by the image, but looks can be deceiving.

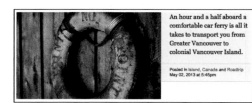

An hour and a half aboard a comfortable car ferry is all it takes to transport you from Greater Vancouver to colonial Vancouver Island.

Posted in Island, Canada and Roadtrip May 02, 2013 at 5:45pm

Ⓒ Now you can really see how a floated element affects the document flow—it doesn't affect the parent element's height at all.

Controlling Where Elements Float

You can control when floating stops, but before I show you how, it helps to understand more about how the **float** property affects your pages.

Consider the HTML in **Ⓐ**, which represents one of the blog post introductions (minus the heading). As you can see, the **section** element contains all associated content. Assume the styling is the same as shown earlier, except you add a garish background color to the **section** so its height is evident **Ⓑ**.

A floated element affects the document flow differently than a non-floated element. As you've seen, a floated element (like the image) forces subsequent content to wrap around it **Ⓑ**. However, it does not factor into the height of its parent or other ancestors, so in this sense it is taken out of the document flow.

To illustrate this, I've removed some of the text from the blog post snippet **Ⓒ**. You may be surprised to see that the **section** is *shorter* than the image, even though the image is a child of the **section**! Only the content in the normal document flow affects the parent's height. In this case, that includes the blog snippet text and the blog post footer, but not the image.

And what about that footer? It makes sense that it scooted up next to the image when the text before it became shorter. But clearly, this is undesirable. After all, you might have a blog post snippet with short text sometimes. How can you guard against this?

continues on next page

Fortunately, you can stop the floating effect with the **clear** property (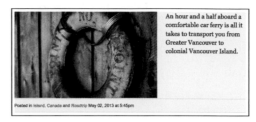 **D** and **E**). When applied to an element, it and subsequent elements display after the floated element.

Making a parent of a float "self-clearing"

Looking back at "Making Elements Float" (figure **F**), we still have a layout issue to resolve. The page footer doesn't display after the **main** and sidebar columns, even though it appears after them in the HTML **F**.

Remember that, from styles applied earlier, the **main** element has **float: left;** and the sidebar has **float: right;**. Now that you know that floated elements don't contribute to the height of their parents, it makes more sense that the page footer appears near the top of the page. The height of the columns' parent—the container **div**—is 0! Don't believe it? Take a look at **G**.

You could solve the footer issue by applying **clear: both;** to it. This is the same approach used in **D** to stop the floating effect, except that it clears both left and right floats.

That would make the page footer appear below the floated columns, but the container **div** would still have a height of 0. Unlike the **.post-footer** that was cleared *inside* the same parent as the float (the **section** in **A** and as seen in **E**), the *page* footer is *outside* the container parent **F**. This means it can't possibly affect the container's height, floats or no floats.

D Use **clear: left;** to make content display after (or *clear* of) an element that is floated left **E**.

```
.post-footer {
    clear: left;
}
```

An hour and a half aboard a comfortable car ferry is all it takes to transport you from Greater Vancouver to colonial Vancouver Island.

Posted in Island, Canada and Roadtrip May 02, 2013 at 5:45pm

E Now the post footer won't appear next to the image, no matter how short the text preceding it may be. The parent's height has expanded accordingly. You could add a **margin-top** style to the footer so it doesn't sit so close to the image. Also, once you've cleared a float, the effect is gone, so you don't have to apply it to every element you want to appear after the image.

F The basic structure of our page. The **div** with **class="container"** is the parent of the **main** and sidebar areas. The page footer is after it.

```
...
<body>
<div class="page">
    ... [masthead] ...

    <div class="container">
      <main role="main">
        ...
      </main>

      <div class="sidebar">
        ...
      </div>
    </div> <!-- end container -->

    <footer role="contentinfo" ...>
      <p class="legal"><small>&copy; 2013
      → Le Journal. All Rights Reserved.
      → </small></p>
    </footer>
</div>
</body>
</html>
```

Sunny East Garden at the

G If you apply `.container { border: 1px solid red; }`, you don't see a border around both child columns as you might expect. Instead, the border looks like a single line at the top because all the container **div**'s content is floated either left or right, giving it a height of 0. That's why the page footer is directly below the container.

H Websites far and wide use this **clearfix** class or one very similar to it to clear floats. I won't explain what all the code means since it's a little involved. But keep it handy; paste it into a style sheet for each website that needs it.

```
.clearfix:before,
.clearfix:after {
    content: " ";
    display: table;
}

.clearfix:after {
    clear: both;
}

.clearfix {
    *zoom: 1;
}
```

I Adding **clearfix** to the container will clear the floated **main** and sidebar elements and make the container height equal to the taller of the two columns.

```
...
<div class="container clearfix">
    <main role="main">
        ...
    </main>

    <div class="sidebar">
        ...
    </div>
</div>
...
```

This might not be a problem most of the time. But I want to add a background to the container, and it won't show if the container has no height. The solution is to make the container clear the floats itself.

There are a few ways to do this, but the most reliable is to use what's known as the *clearfix* method. To do so, include the `.clearfix` rules in your style sheet **H**, and add the **clearfix** class to the parent of the floated element(s) you wish to clear **I** so the parent grows taller and can be styled as desired (**J** and **K**).

J When positioned 629 pixels from the left and repeated vertically, the simple 5 x 20 background image provides a subtle divider between the two columns. You can also add a border across the top of the page footer to separate the footer **K**.

```
.container {
    background: url(../img/bg.png)
    ➜ repeat-y 629px 0;
    padding-bottom: 1.9375em;
}

footer[role="contentinfo"] {
    border-top: 1px solid #cacbcb;
}
```

K The page footer border is perpendicular to the column divider background image. The padding that was added to the bottom of the container provides some space between the pagination links and the page footer below them.

To control where elements float:

1. Type `clear:` **D**.

2. Type **left** to keep elements from floating to the left of the element you're styling.

   Or type **right** to keep elements from floating to the right of the element you're styling.

   Or type **both** to keep elements from floating to either side of the element you're styling.

   Or type **none** (the default) to let elements float to either side of the element you're styling.

3. Or, to make an ancestor of a float include the floated element in its height and stop floating behavior after it, use the clearfix (**H** and **I**) or **overflow** methods instead of steps 1 and 2. (See the sidebar "Using **overflow** for Self-Clearing Floats.")

TIP You add the `clear` property to the element whose sides you want to be clear of floating objects (**D** through **F**). So if you want an element not to be displayed until the right side is clear of floating elements, add `clear: right;` to it (and *not* to the floating elements). By comparison, the clearfix and `overflow` methods are applied to a parent or ancestor of a float.

TIP Many people have refined the clearfix code over the years. The version shown **H** is by Nicolas Gallagher (http://nicolasgallagher.com/micro-clearfix-hack/, but be warned that the discussion is pretty technical) and is taken from the very helpful HTML5 Boilerplate (www.h5bp.com), a project started by Paul Irish.

TIP The `display` property of a floated element becomes `display: block;` even if it had been set previously to `display: inline;` either via a browser default or by you explicitly.

Using `overflow` for Self-Clearing Floats

Often, you can use the **overflow** property on the parent of a float instead of the clearfix method (**H** and **I**). For example, this would yield the same result in our example page:

```
.container {
    overflow: hidden;
}
```

Sometimes **overflow: hidden;** will cut off content, so keep an eye out for that. Using **overflow: auto;** instead also works and doesn't cut off content, but sometimes you might see a scroll bar, which is obviously undesirable in its own way. Consequently, some coders choose to use **overflow** to solve float issues when it's able to do the job, and use clearfix for the rest. Others prefer to use clearfix all the time.

Incidentally, you can apply either clearfix or **overflow** to a non-parent ancestor of a float. That won't make the parent taller, but the ancestor's height will encompass the float.

See "Determining How to Treat Overflow" for more about the **overflow** property.

A The span text I'll position in a moment.

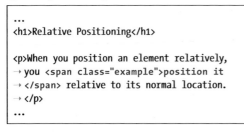

```
...
<h1>Relative Positioning</h1>

<p>When you position an element relatively,
→ you <span class="example">position it
→ </span> relative to its normal location.
→ </p>
...
```

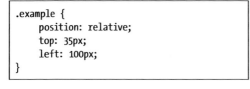

B This is a normal paragraph, so there are no surprises in the rendering here.

C Remember to specify the relative positioning and also declare at least one offset. It can be either a positive or negative value. I used pixels to simplify the example, but using ems would keep the offset in proportion with the size of the text, even if the text got smaller or larger. Because 1em is equal to an element's font size and text is typically 16 pixels by default, in this example **top: -3em;** would move the text up the equivalent of 48 pixels.

```
.example {
    position: relative;
    top: 35px;
    left: 100px;
}
```

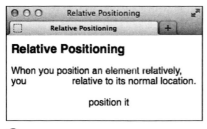

D The text displays 35 pixels from the top and 100 pixels from the left of its normal location, which is left as a blank space. If I had set it to **top: -55px;**, the text would sit on top of the **h1** text.

Positioning Elements Relatively

Each element has a natural location in a page's flow (**A** and **B**). Moving the element with respect to this original location is called relative positioning (**C** and **D**). The surrounding content and elements are not affected at all **D**.

To offset elements within the natural flow:

1. Type **position: relative;**.

2. Type **top**, **right**, **bottom**, or **left**.

   Then type **:d**, where **d** is the desired distance that you want to offset the element from its natural location, expressed either as an absolute or relative value (**10px** or **2em**, for example) or as a percentage. The value can be positive or negative. Repeat this step as desired for additional offsets.

TIP The other elements flow as usual with respect to the original containing block of the element. Depending on your **top**, **right**, **bottom**, or **left** values, your relatively positioned content may overlap other content.

TIP Use the **z-index** property to specify the stacking order of elements that overlap each other when positioned with **relative**, **absolute**, or **fixed**. See "Positioning Elements in a Stack" for details.

TIP Set an element to **position: static** to override a **position: relative** setting. **static** is the default value for elements, which is why they appear in the normal document flow. See an example in "Positioning Elements in a Stack."

TIP Positioning is not inherited.

Positioning Elements Absolutely

As noted, the elements in your webpage flow in the order in which they appear in the HTML source code (**A** and **B**), unless you instruct them to do otherwise with CSS. That is, if an **img** element comes before a **p** in the code, that image displays before that paragraph in browsers.

You can position elements absolutely—which takes them out of the normal flow entirely—by specifying their precise position with respect to the **body** (**C** and **D**) or to their nearest positioned ancestor element (**E** and **F**).

This is different than relative positioning in that no space is left where an absolutely positioned element would have appeared normally. It's also different than when you float an element. Other elements do not flow around an absolutely positioned element. In fact, they don't even know it exists, and vice versa.

To position elements absolutely:

1. Type **position: absolute;**.

2. If desired, type **top**, **right**, **bottom**, or **left**.

   Then type **: d;**, where *d* is expressed as the desired distance that you want to offset the element from its ancestor (**10px** or **2em**, for example) or as a percentage of the ancestor. (See the second tip for a related note.)

A Our page masthead (or header, if your prefer) contains the site logo, the social icon links, and main navigation, in that order. Their default display follows suit **B**. Soon you'll see how to position the icons absolutely within the masthead by leveraging the two highlighted classes.

```
...
<header class="masthead" role="banner">
    <p class="logo"><a href="/"><img ... />
    → </a></p>

    <ul class="social-sites">
        ...
    </ul>

    <nav role="navigation">
        <ul class="nav-main">
            ...
        </ul>
    </nav>
</header>
...
```

B Our list of social icons sits between the logo and navigation as a result of the normal document flow. I want it to display about halfway down from the top and on the far right side of the masthead **header** that contains it **A**.

 By positioning the list of icons absolutely, I've taken it completely out of the document flow. This code alone doesn't achieve our desired results because, unless you specify otherwise, an element with **position: absolute** is positioned relative to the **body** element, as you can see in .

```
.masthead .social-sites {
    position: absolute;
    top: 41px;
    right: 0;
}
```

 The icons display 41 pixels from the top of the **body** and 0 from the right. Clearly, this isn't good, because the wider you make the browser window, the more the icons run away from the rest of the page!

 I set the **header** that contains the list of icons  to **position: relative** so the icons will be positioned absolutely relative to the **header**, not to the **body** element. This gets the icons where you want them .

```
.masthead {
    position: relative;
}

.masthead .social-sites {
    position: absolute;
    top: 41px;
    right: 0;
}
```

 Perfection!

3. If desired, repeat step 2 for additional offsets.

4. If desired, add **position: relative;** to the ancestor element to which you want your absolutely positioned element to be offset ( and ). If you skip this step (as in ), the element will be offset with respect to the **body** .

TIP Because absolutely positioned elements are taken out of the flow of the document, they can overlap each other and other elements. (This is not always bad.)

TIP If you don't specify an offset for an absolutely positioned item, the item appears in its natural position but does not affect the flow of subsequent items.

TIP There is also a fixed positioning type. When a visitor scrolls in the browser window, the contents of the page usually move up or down. When you set an element to **position: fixed;**, it is affixed to the browser window so that it doesn't move when the visitor scrolls up or down. The rest of the page does scroll as usual. It's much like the way fixed background images work (see "Setting the Background" in Chapter 10). Fixed positioning is notoriously buggy in many mobile browsers, so it's best to avoid using it for sites you expect to be viewed with mobile devices.

TIP Use the **z-index** property to specify the stacking order of elements that overlap each other when positioned with **relative**, **absolute**, or **fixed**. See "Positioning Elements in a Stack" for details.

TIP Set an element to **position: static;** to override a **position: absolute;** setting. **static** is the default value for elements, which is why they appear in the normal document flow. See an example in "Positioning Elements in a Stack."

TIP Positioning is not inherited.

Positioning Elements in a Stack

Once you start using relative, absolute, or fixed positioning, it's quite possible that you'll find that your elements have overlapped. You can choose which element should display on top (Ⓐ through Ⓒ).

To position elements in a stack:

Type **z-index:** *n*, where *n* is a number that indicates the element's level in the stack of positioned objects.

TIP The higher the value of the **z-index** property, the higher up the element will be in the stack (Ⓑ and Ⓒ).

TIP The **z-index** property only works on positioned elements (that is, **absolute**, **relative**, or **fixed**). The example Ⓐ shows **absolute** elements only, but you can mix and match, and the **z-index** settings will apply collectively, not separately within the **absolute**, **relative**, and **fixed** elements.

TIP The **z-index** property is not inherited.

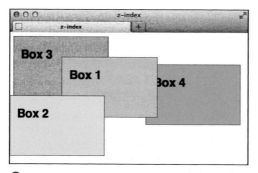

Ⓒ The positioned boxes are stacked from highest **z-index** down to lowest. The third box is below all of them because it's in the normal document flow.

Ⓐ The order of the **div**s in the HTML.

```
<div class="box1"><p>Box 1</p></div>
<div class="box2"><p>Box 2</p></div>
<div class="box3"><p>Box 3</p></div>
<div class="box4"><p>Box 4</p></div>
```

Ⓑ The positioned element with the highest **z-index** number always shows on top Ⓒ, regardless of where it is in the HTML Ⓐ. The first rule sets all four **div**s to **position: absolute;**, but then I set **.box3** back to the default value of **static**. So, even though it has the highest **z-index**, that has no effect and **.box3** will always be on the bottom.

```
div {
    border: 1px solid #666;
    height: 125px;
    position: absolute;
    width: 200px;
}

.box1 {
    background: pink;
    left: 110px;
    top: 50px;
    z-index: 120;
}

.box2 {
    background: yellow;
    left: 0;
    top: 130px;
    z-index: 530;
}

.box3 {
    background: #ccc;
    position: static;
    /* Static, so has no effect. */
    z-index: 1000;
}

.box4 {
    background: orange;
    left: 285px;
    top: 65px;
    z-index: 3;
}
```

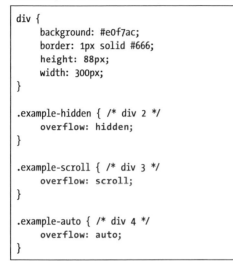

A Usually it's best not to set a **height** on an element, as I have done here with **div**. I added a background color and border so you can see why. The three classes demonstrate your options for controlling content that overflows its container **B**.

```
div {
    background: #e0f7ac;
    border: 1px solid #666;
    height: 88px;
    width: 300px;
}

.example-hidden { /* div 2 */
    overflow: hidden;
}

.example-scroll { /* div 3 */
    overflow: scroll;
}

.example-auto { /* div 4 */
    overflow: auto;
}
```

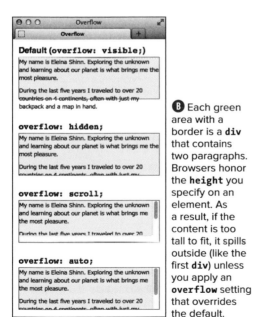

B Each green area with a border is a **div** that contains two paragraphs. Browsers honor the **height** you specify on an element. As a result, if the content is too tall to fit, it spills outside (like the first **div**) unless you apply an **overflow** setting that overrides the default.

Determining How to Treat Overflow

Elements are not always contained in their boxes. Sometimes the box is simply not big enough. For example, an image that is wider than its container will spill out of it. Or perhaps you've positioned the content outside of the box, either with negative margins or absolute positioning. Or maybe you set an explicit height on an element and its content is too tall to fit. Regardless of the cause, you can control the area outside of the element's box with the **overflow** property (**A** and **B**).

To determine how the browser should treat overflow:

1. Type **overflow:**.

2. Type **visible** to let the content show. This is the default option.

   Or type **hidden** to hide any contents that don't fit in the element's box.

   Or type **scroll** to always add scroll bars to the element, even if they aren't needed.

   Or type **auto** to have scroll bars appear only when necessary for visitors to access the overflow content.

> **TIP** If the div in **A** had **min-height: 88px;** *instead of* height 88px;, the divs in **B** would grow to fit the content. If the content were shorter than 88 pixels, the div would still be 88 pixels tall because **min-height** sets the minimum height.

> **TIP** The **overflow** property is also handy for stopping **floats**. See the sidebar in "Controlling Where Elements Float."

> **TIP** The **overflow** property is not inherited.

Aligning Elements Vertically

You can align elements vertically in many ways to make them look better than the default alignment (**A** through **D**).

To align elements vertically:

1. Type **vertical-align:**.

2. Type **baseline** to align the element's baseline with the parent's baseline.

   Or type **middle** to align the middle of the element slightly above the parent's baseline.

   Or type **sub** to position the element as a subscript of the parent's baseline.

   Or type **super** to position the element as a superscript of the parent's baseline.

A Here is a simple form with a text label, text input field, and image submit button. For more information on forms, see Chapter 16.

```
...
<form action="results.php" method="get"
→ role="search">
      <label for="search">Search</label>
      <input type="search" id="search"
      → name="search" />
      <input type="image" src="img/btn-go.png"
      → alt="Submit search" />
</form>
...
```

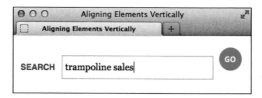

B By default, inline content is vertically aligned according to the text baseline. I entered text in the form field to illustrate this—the **label** text ("Search"), the text in the field, and the bottom of the image all sit at the baseline.

C There is an invisible box—the *line box*—around each entire line of content. It represents the height of the line. In this case, the text input field dictates the bottom of the line box because it's the lowest part of the line **B**. With the CSS shown, the image will align to the bottom of the line box **D**.

```
input[type="image"] {
      vertical-align: bottom;
}
```

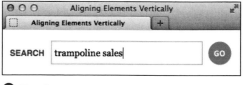

D Bingo!

More About vertical-align

You may also use **vertical-align** to align content in table cells. Typically, the default setting is **middle** in this context, as opposed to **baseline** for content not in a table. Tables are covered in Chapter 18. Beyond tables, the **vertical-align** property works only on elements displayed inline, not on elements that display as a block. See Chris Coyier's explanation at http://css-tricks.com/what-is-vertical-align/ for more details.

Or type **text-top** to align the top of the element with the top of the parent's content.

Or type **text-bottom** to align the bottom of the element with the bottom of the parent's content.

Or type **top** to align the top of the element with the top of the line box.

Or type **bottom** to align the bottom of the element to the bottom of the line box (explained in Ⓒ).

Or type a percentage of the line height of the element, which may be positive or negative.

Or type a positive or negative value (such as in pixels or ems) to shift the element up or down, respectively, by that amount.

Changing the Cursor

Normally, the browser takes care of the cursor shape for you, using an arrow most of the time and a pointing finger to highlight links , as well as some others. CSS lets you take the reins (**B** and **C**).

To change the cursor:

1. Type **cursor:**.

2. Type **pointer** for the cursor that usually appears over links (🖑), type **default** for an arrow (↖), or type **crosshair** (+), **move** (✛), **wait** (⧗), **help** (↖?), **text** (I), or **progress** (↖⧗).

   Or type **auto** to get whatever cursor usually appears in that situation.

   Or type **x-resize** to get a double-sided arrow, where **x** is the cardinal direction one of the arrows should point—that is, **n** (north), **nw** (northwest), **e** (east), and so on. For example, the **e-resize** cursor might look like this: ↦.

TIP The cursors vary slightly from browser to browser and system to system.

A When you point to the Home link, the cursor changes to a pointing hand and the link is highlighted, just as for any other main navigation link.

B I've assigned **class="current-page"** to the Home link when the visitor is on the homepage. By doing so, I can then change the default color, the hover state color, and the cursor so the Home link doesn't look like a link. (Alternatively, you could remove the **a** element around the Home link from the navigation in this instance.)

```
.nav-main .current-page,
.nav-main .current-page:hover {
    color: #747474;
    cursor: default;
}
```

C Although this continues to be a real, live link, it no longer looks like one. Since you are already on the page to which this link goes, that makes sense.

Building Responsive Webpages

A last-minute decision to go to the movies. A bet about the official language of Andorra. The phone number for a company where you're fifteen minutes late for a meeting. A map to the company, because the reason you're late is that you can't find it.

We want information immediately, and with the proliferation of powerful mobile devices of all shapes and sizes, the web can be in your pocket, purse, or backpack just as easily as it's at your desk or kitchen table or in your living room.

So now it's up to you and me to build sites that make it possible for visitors to access information from any mobile phone, smartphone, tablet, laptop, desktop computer, game console, TV, or future web-enabled devices that don't exist yet. Responsive web design facilitates this.

In this chapter, you'll learn how to build a page that works on the entire range of devices, adapting its layout according to the device's capabilities and characteristics.

In This Chapter

Responsive Web Design: An Overview

It wasn't too long ago that if you wanted to cater to mobile users, you'd build a separate site specifically for mobile. Some companies still do this today, although that is becoming less common. A few may even have a third site for tablets.

There is no single correct approach that applies to every situation. However, with new devices seemingly hitting the market each week and new types of devices no doubt being envisioned behind company walls, is it realistic—or even desirable—to build and maintain separate sites? We can't know what's around the corner.

Thankfully, we can build a single site that will work on devices now and in the future. Better yet, we can make it look different on small screens than on large screens or anywhere in between (**A** through **C**).

A Believe it or not, the versions of the Food Sense home page shown here and in the next two figures are all from the same site, www. foodsense.is, not separate sites hosted at their own URLs. The site uses the responsive web design approach, so its layout changes based on the viewing conditions. The iPhone (shown here) and devices with similar screen sizes display the layout according to specific CSS rules. Different CSS rules target other, larger browser views (**B** and **C**), adjusting the layout accordingly. The HTML never changes.

Components of a responsive page

With responsive web design, Ethan Marcotte has given us a blueprint for doing this. (See "Considerations When Beginning a Layout" in Chapter 11 for some history.) His approach is rooted in three things:

- Flexible images and media. Assets are sized with percentages so that they scale up and down in the space available to them.

- A flexible (fluid), grid-based layout. A responsive webpage has all **width** properties set in percentages so that layout components can shrink or expand. Other horizontal properties typically use a relative unit too (em, percentage, or rem).

- Media queries. Adding these to your style sheet allows you to adjust your page design based on the width of the browser's viewable page area and other characteristics.

We'll cover each of these in the coming sections. Then you'll learn how to build a responsive version of Chapter 11's example page from scratch.

> **TIP** John Allsopp's article "A Dao of Web Design" (http://alistapart.com/article/dao), written all the way back in 2000, made the argument for designing and building flexible websites. It was a precursor to responsive web design, and Marcotte and many others have cited it as a big influence. It's well worth a read.

> **TIP** Jeremy Keith summed up the value in building one site for all devices in his "One Web" presentation (www.vimeo.com/27484362/). The transcript is available at www.adactio.com/articles/4938/.

B Here is Food Sense as seen on the iPad and other devices with similar screen sizes. The CSS for this view changes the logo and navigation since the browser has more space to display content.

C This is the widest view of the site, shown on a desktop browser. The site has two other layouts not shown in these figures. You can view them by visiting www.foodsense.is on your computer and dragging the corner of the browser to make it narrower or wider.

Making Images Flexible

As you learned in Chapter 5, an image displays by default according to the **width** and **height** attribute values you specify in the HTML **Ⓐ**. If you omit those attributes, it will show at its normal size automatically. Alternatively, you could set the **width** and **height** in pixels in CSS.

Clearly, showing an image at its normal size isn't always suitable when screen real estate is limited **Ⓑ**. With the flexible images technique (**Ⓒ** and **Ⓓ**), you can make images scale up or down in the available space but never get wider than their normal width (**Ⓔ** and **Ⓕ**). The available space is determined by the element that contains the image (see the first tip). In **Ⓔ**, it is the **body** element, and in **Ⓕ** it is the **main** element in our example page.

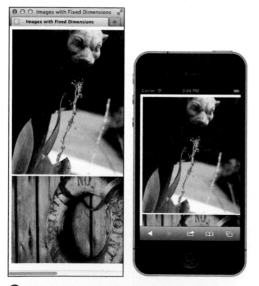

Ⓑ With fixed **width** and **height** values, the images stay the same size even if the viewable area is reduced. Desktop browsers show a scroll bar (left). On a phone (right), they can take up the whole screen or more.

Ⓐ A couple of typical **img** tags with **width** and **height** specified **Ⓑ**. These appeared in the code for Chapter 11. (Note: I've left the **alt** text blank to keep the code samples short.)

```
    ...
        <meta name="viewport"
        → content="width=device-width,
        → initial-scale=1" />
</head>
<body>
<img src="img/gettyvilla.jpg" width="600"
→ height="365" alt="" class="post-photo-full"
→ />

<img src="img/victoria.jpg" width="370"
height="220" alt="" class="post-photo" />
</body>
</html>
```

Ⓒ Images can't be made flexible unless you omit the **width** and **height**. If you like, you can include a class to facilitate styling the images.

```
...
<img src="img/gettyvilla.jpg" alt=""
→ class="post-photo-full" />

<img src="img/victoria.jpg" alt=""
→ class="post-photo" />
...
```

Ⓓ The magic bit of CSS that makes flexible images work.

```
.post-photo,
.post-photo-full {
    max-width: 100%;
}
```

E Flexible images scale proportionally to fit in the element that contains them (**body**, in this case). They will never be wider than their natural width, as the bottom image demonstrates. In this case, one is a maximum of 600 pixels wide and the other is 370.

To make your images flexible:

1. For each image you wish to make flexible, omit the **width** and **height** attributes from the **img** tag in your HTML **C**.

2. In your style sheet, apply **max-width: 100%;** to each image you want to be flexible **D**.

TIP Specifically, the space an image fits within is the containing block established by its parent. If the parent has horizontal padding, the available space would be reduced. See "Setting the Height or Width for an Element" in Chapter 11 for a refresher on the containing block.

TIP Be sure to use max-width: 100% and *not* width: 100%;. They both scale an image within its container. However, width: 100%; tells the image to be as wide as its containing element at all costs. If that element is wider than the image, the image will scale up beyond its normal size, possibly making it look a little fuzzier than you'd like.

TIP Icon fonts and SVG allow you to include graphics that scale up and down with no loss in fidelity. See "Where to Find Web Fonts" in Chapter 13 and "Images for the Web" in Chapter 5, respectively.

continues on next page

F The responsive page we'll build later in the chapter as viewed at 320 pixels wide (left) and 480 pixels wide (right). The image scales to fit!

TIP Don't forget to optimize your images so their file sizes are as small as possible. See "Saving Your Images" in Chapter 5.

TIP This technique also works for images you've made twice as large for the benefit of Retina displays. Of course, double-resolution images can have much larger file sizes too. See "Scaling Images with the Browser" in Chapter 5 regarding preparing images for Retina displays, including a tip that could help you reduce the file sizes quite a bit.

TIP Except in IE8, you can make background images scale with the `background-size` property. See www.css3.info/preview/background-size/ for more information.

TIP You also can make HTML5 video and other media flexible with `video, embed, object { max-width: 100%; }` (and by not including `width` and `height` for them in the HTML). Jonathan Nicol's article may help in cases where videos don't scale as expected (http://f6design.com/journal/2011/10/18/responsive-elements-that-retain-their-aspect-ratio/).

Responsive Design and the Images Conundrum

Flexible images are pretty sweet, right? "But wait," I can hear you saying, "isn't it bad to load a larger image than what you'll show on a page? *Especially* on mobile devices that have slower connections?"

You are absolutely correct, and therein lies the biggest issue people are trying to tackle regarding responsive web design.

Ideally, we want to use images that are only as large as necessary for a particular device. Mobile phones get small images, tablets get larger ones, and so on. This keeps file sizes down and reduces the amount of memory a device uses to display the image (which is especially important on phones). Typically, this results in faster pages. It's also friendlier to visitors who are paying for a mobile data plan that limits how much they can download from the web each month.

Additionally, sometimes you may want a different image to appear rather than simply a smaller version. A common example of this is a photo of a person. Small screens could be served a photo of the person's face. Larger screens could show the person head to toe.

A lot of sharp folks have been working on a way to facilitate this, but there is no simple solution at the time of this writing.

Two proposals in the mix suggest adding features to HTML. One proposes a new **img** attribute named **srcset**, and the other proposes a new element named **picture** (www.w3.org/community/respimg/). They look to solve similar but not identical issues, so it's possible there could be room for both ideas. Stay tuned!

In the meantime, try to be smart about the images you include in your pages. At 600 pixels wide, the biggest image in our example page ❻ is larger than desired for smartphones (most are 320 pixels wide)—visitors would likely notice it taking a bit too long to load. Fortunately, the page has only one image that large. See also the second tip above regarding images for Retina displays.

Ⓐ Our entire page from Chapter 11 is contained in a **div** that has the **page** class. The basic structure within that is made up of the masthead (header), main and sidebar areas wrapped in a **div** (with the **container** class), and the page footer.

```
...
<body>
<div class="page">
    <header class="masthead" role="banner">
        ...
    </header>

    <div class="container">
        <main role="main">
            ...
        </main>

        <div class="sidebar">
            ...
        </div>
    </div>

    <footer role="contentinfo"
    → class="footer">
        ...
    </footer>
</div>
</body>
</html>
```

Ⓑ These are the fixed widths we set on the containers in Chapter 11 **Ⓐ**. We didn't set widths for the header, footer, and **container div** around the main and sidebar content. Instead, we left them at the browser default, **width: auto;**, so they'd be as wide as their parent. Their parent is the **page div Ⓐ**, so they are 960 pixels wide too **Ⓒ**.

```
.page {
    width: 960px;
}

main {
    width: 600px;
}

.sidebar {
    width: 300px;
}
```

Creating a Flexible Layout Grid

A webpage that has fixed-width containers is rigid. Such is the case with the sample page from the previous chapter (**Ⓐ** through **Ⓒ**). If you make a desktop browser narrower than the page width, a horizontal scroll bar appears **Ⓓ**.

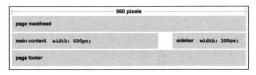

Ⓒ At its most basic level, the page has four primary sections of content. The **.page** and **.container divs** are not shown explicitly because they are merely wrappers with no content of their own. With no widths specified **Ⓑ**, the **.container div**, masthead, and footer automatically are the same width as the **.page div**. (Note: The CSS in **Ⓑ** and **Ⓕ** does not cause the main and sidebar areas to sit next to each other. See "Making Elements Float" in Chapter 11 to see how that is done.)

Ⓓ The width remains the same even if you make the browser narrower.

A mobile browser could show the full width, but the page would be tiny and not very friendly **E**.

This isn't suitable for a responsive webpage. You want its width to shrink or expand to fit in the viewable area in browsers, just like flexible images. A fluid or flexible layout achieves this.

It is simple to create a flexible layout once you get the hang of it. You use percentage-based widths, applying them to the main sections of your page (**A** and **F**). It requires a tiny bit of math, but fear not, it's no more complicated than what you learned in elementary school. When in doubt, keep a calculator handy!

So how do you know what percentages to use? Well, an element's percentage width is based on the space available within its parent; that is, its containing block. If that sounds familiar, it's because it's the same as for flexible images. You can use this formula to determine the value you'll use for the percentage:

desired width in pixels / containing
→ block width in pixels = value

(This the same as Ethan Marcotte's formula **target / context = value**, just with more explicit terminology.) You take the pixel values you would use if you were making a fixed-width layout, and you plug them into the formula.

E Phones like the iPhone can shrink the page if you want them to, but visitors would have to zoom in a lot to read any of the content.

F This is the fluid equivalent of the fixed-width layout in **B**. The rigid **width: 960px;** of the **.page div** has been replaced by **max-width: 960px;**. This allows it to shrink but never expand beyond 960 pixels. I used the formula shown earlier to determine the percentage widths for **main** and **.sidebar**.

```
.page {
    max-width: 960px;
}

main {
    /*
    desired width / containing block width
    using 600px/960px
    */
    width: 62.5%;
}

.sidebar {
    width: 31.25%; /* 300px/960px */
}
```

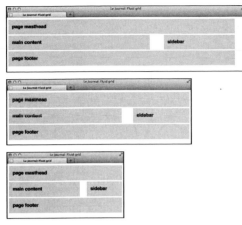

G The columns keep their proportions regardless of how wide you view the page. The page stops growing wider at 960 pixels, as the top image shows.

H When applied to the responsive page built later in the chapter, the styles from **F** allow the layout to shrink and expand. But it never gets wider than 960 pixels, no matter how wide you make the browser window (bottom).

A real-world example

Let's consider the layout for the sample page I'll build later in the chapter. I'll show you how to arrive at 62.5% for the **width** of **main F**. Using the formula, here's the quick explanation:

```
desired width in pixels (600) /
→ containing block width in pixels
→ (960) = value (.625)
```

Then you convert the value to a percentage by moving the decimal point two spots to the right, giving you 62.5%. You use that number as the **width F**. Done!

I'll elaborate in case you're still a little fuzzy on the numbers. The layout is 960 pixels at its widest, as determined by the rule on **.page F**. With no width of its own specified, the **.container div A** that is the parent of **main** has an automatic width of 960 pixels too. (The **.container div**'s parent is the **.page div**.)

At most, I want **main** to occupy 600 of those 960 pixels. Using the formula from earlier gives me 600/960 = .625. As a percentage, that is 62.5%. I used the same approach for **.sidebar**, except I never want it to exceed 300 pixels in width. The calculation was 300/960, and .3125 becomes 31.25% **F**.

When combined with flexible images, a flexible grid allows a whole page to expand and contract (**G** and **H**).

To make your layout flexible:

1. For elements requiring a width to achieve your desired layout, set **width: percentage;**, where **percentage** represents the percentage of horizontal space you want the element to occupy within its containing block **F**. Generally speaking, avoid setting elements to **width: 100%;**. Elements set to **display: block;** by default (like **p** and many others) or manually will fill the entire space available to them by default.

2. Optionally, apply **max-width: value;** to the element that contains your whole page, where **value** represents the maximum width to which your page can grow (**F**, **G**, and **H**). Typically, **value** is specified in pixels, but it can be expressed as a percentage or in ems or another unit value.

TIP If the parent has horizontal padding, it establishes a smaller containing block for its children. See "Setting the Height or Width for an Element" in Chapter 11 for a refresher on the containing block.

TIP You may also apply percentage-based horizontal **margin** and **padding** values to an element. I use ems for these properties in the sample page, which is pretty common. Padding and margins set in ems are relative to the element's **font-size** while percentage-based values are relative to the element's containing block.

TIP One neat advantage to using ems for **font-size**, **margin**, **padding**, and **max-width** with body { **font-size: 100%;** } is the page scales up and down in proportion if the user changes the browser's default font size. For example, in Firefox, you can change the default font size in the Content tab of Preferences. Give it a try while viewing **www.htmlcssvqs.com/8ed/examples/12/ finished-page.html**!

TIP Don't forget that when you use the formula to calculate a percentage width for an element, its containing block comes from its immediate ancestor (that is the context).

TIP Setting the **box-sizing** property to **border-box** allows you to define percentage widths on elements that have horizontal padding in ems or another unit without having to do complicated math to get the percentages right. This is very handy for responsive pages. See "The Box Model" in Chapter 11 for more information.

Setting a Relative max-width

The **.page div** that contains the whole page **A** was given a **max-width** in pixels (960) **F**. How could you express this as a flexible, relative unit instead? Well, **.page { max-width: 60em; }** would do the trick. Here's why:

An em width is based on the element's font size. For example, if its font size is the equivalent of 14 pixels, **width: 10em;** would make it 140 pixels wide.

The **.page div** wasn't given a **font-size** so it inherits it from its parent, the **body** element. As you know, **body** has a default font size that is typically the equivalent of 16 pixels. So, with a target maximum width of 960 pixels for **.page**, 960/16 = 60em.

Setting **.page { max-width: 60em; }** is similar to using **960px** with one notable exception: it will scale according to the browser's default font size. The third tip explains how to see this.

```
...
<head>
    ...
    <link rel="stylesheet" href=
    ,"your-styles.css" media="screen" />
</head>
...
```

B The **@media print** rule allows you to define styles in your style sheet specifically for printing pages from the browser. They may be alongside styles for other media.

```
/* Styles shared by screen and print */
...

/* Styles for print only */
@media print {
    header[role="banner"] nav,
    .ad {
        display: none;
    }
}
```

C The styles in **base.css** are used for all output devices. The styles in **styles-480.css** are used only in browsers that support media queries and when the viewport is at least 480 pixels wide.

```
...
<head>
    <meta charset="utf-8" />
    <title>Media query in link</title>
    <meta name="viewport" content="width=
    → device-width, initial-scale=1.0" />
    <link rel="stylesheet" href="base.css"
    → media="all" />

    <!--
    The logic is only.
    The type is screen.
    The feature: value is min-width: 480px.
    -->
    <link rel="stylesheet" media="only
    → screen and (min-width: 480px)"
    → href="styles-480.css" />
</head>
...
```

Understanding and Implementing Media Queries

As you learned in the Chapter 8 section "Using Media-Specific Style Sheets," you can target your CSS to specific media types in two ways. (There is a third way, the **@import** rule, but we didn't cover it because it affects performance.) To recap, the first way is via the **media** attribute of the **link** element, which goes in your page's **head** **A**. The second way is with an **@media** rule in your style sheet **B**.

Media queries enhance the media type methods, allowing you to target your styles to specific device features **C**. They're particularly handy for changing how your site looks on different screen sizes, as you will learn. The following is a list of media features you can include in media queries:

- **width**
- **height**
- **device-width**
- **device-height**
- **orientation**
- **aspect-ratio**
- **device-aspect-ratio**
- **color**
- **color-index**
- **monochrome**
- **resolution**
- **scan**
- **grid**

There are some non-standard media features too, such as

- **-webkit-device-pixel-ratio**
- **-moz-device-pixel-ratio**

For all but **orientation**, **scan**, and **grid**, you can include **min-** and **max-** prefixes. The **min-** prefix targets values that are "greater than or equal to," and **max-** targets values that are "smaller than or equal to."

We'll focus on **min-width** and **max-width** in this chapter, because they're the ones you'll use over and over for responsive webpages.

Media queries enjoy great support among modern desktop and smartphone browsers. However, Internet Explorer 8 and below does not support them. See "Accommodating Older Versions of Internet Explorer" for a couple of solutions.

Media query syntax and examples

With a large nod to Peter Gasston's *The Book of CSS3* (No Starch Press, 2011), which summarizes this very well, here's the basic syntax for media queries.

- For a link to an external style sheet:

  ```
  <link rel="stylesheet" media="logic
  ↪ type and (feature: value)"
  ↪ href="your-stylesheet.css" />
  ```

- For a media query within a style sheet:

  ```
  @media logic type and (feature:
  ↪ value) {

      /* your targeted CSS rules go
      ↪ here */

  }
  ```

I'll explain the syntax shortly, but a couple of quick examples (**C** and **D**) will help put everything in context. The queries in the examples are identical, but the means by which they deliver the styles are different.

D This crude example contains default paragraph styling followed by changes to the paragraph text when the media query is true. I've saved this style sheet in **basic-media-query.css**, and I've loaded it into the page shown in **E**. You can see the results in **F** through **H**.

```
/* Your regular styles go here. Every device
↪ gets them unless they are overridden by
↪ rules in the media queries. */
body {
    font: 200%/1.3 sans-serif;
}

p {
    color: green;
}

/*
The logic is only.
The type is screen.
The feature: value is min-width: 480px.
*/
@media only screen and (min-width:
↪ 480px) {
    p {
        color: red;
        font-weight: bold;
    }
}
```

E The style sheet containing the media query is loaded just like any other style sheet.

```
<!DOCTYPE html>
<html lang="en">
<head>
    <meta charset="utf-8" />
    <title>Basic media query example</title>
    <meta name="viewport" content="width=
    ↪ device-width, initial-scale=1.0" />
    <link rel="stylesheet" href="assets/
    ↪ css/basic-media-query.css" />
</head>
<body>
    <p>Hi, I'm a paragraph. By default, I'm
    ↪ green and normal. But get me in a
    ↪ viewport that's at least 480px wide,
    ↪ and I get red and bold!</p>
</body>
</html>
```

Hi, I'm a paragraph. By default, I'm green and normal. But get me in a viewport that's at least 480px wide, and I get red and bold!

F Mobile Safari's viewport in portrait mode is 320 pixels wide, so the text remains green per the base styles in the style sheet. (I made the `font-size` twice as big as normal for legibility.) However, when the page is viewed on an iPad...

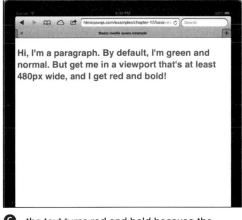

Hi, I'm a paragraph. By default, I'm green and normal. But get me in a viewport that's at least 480px wide, and I get red and bold!

G ...the text turns red and bold because the browser's viewport is 768 pixels wide in portrait view on the iPad, and the media query triggers when the width is 480 pixels or greater. It also takes effect on the iPhone in landscape mode, which has a viewport width of exactly 480 pixels.

Hi, I'm a paragraph. By default, I'm green and normal. But get me in a viewport that's at least 480px wide, and I get red and bold!

H Modern desktop browsers understand media queries too. Here is Firefox with the lower-right corner dragged in to make the viewport narrower than 480 pixels, so the text is green with a normal `font-weight`. If I were to stretch the window so it's at least 480 pixels, the text would turn bold and red immediately—no page refresh required.

The example in **C** translates to "Load and use the rules in **styles-480.css** only when the media type is **screen** and the minimum width of the viewport is 480 pixels." The example in **D** translates to "Use the following rules only when the media type is **screen** and the minimum width of the viewport is 480 pixels." (See the sidebar "The Viewport and Using the Viewport **meta** Element" to learn the meaning of viewport.) For responsive pages, you will place the media queries in your style sheet most of the time.

I've created a test page **E** that links to a style sheet that contains the code from **D**. You can see the results on an iPhone **F**, an iPad **G**, and a narrow desktop browser **H**.

Returning to the syntax, let's explore its components:

- The *logic* portion is optional and can have a value of either **only** or **not**. The **only** keyword ensures that older browsers don't try to read the rest of the media query. The **not** keyword negates the result of the media query, making the opposite true. For example, when used on the **link** element, **media="not screen"** will load the style sheet if the media type is anything other than **screen**.

- The *type* portion is the media type, such as **screen** or **print**.

- A *feature: value* pair is optional, but if present it must be enclosed in parentheses and preceded by the word **and**. The *feature* is one of the predefined media features, such as **min-width**, **max-width**, or **resolution**. The *value* is optional for the **color**, **color-index**, and **monochrome** features.

You can chain together sets of features and values with **and**, as well as create a list of media queries by separating each media query with a comma. A whole media query list is true if any one of the media queries in the comma-separated list is true. **I** and **J** show a variety of media queries.

Summary

Media queries let you apply styles to a page based on specific media features of a device. Although there are several features media queries can include, **min-width** and **max-width** are what you will use the most for responsive webpages.

Using Ems in Media Queries

So far I've used pixels for **min-width** and **max-width** values in the media query examples (**C**, **D**, **I**, and **J**), because I thought that would help you get the hang of how media queries work. In practice, it's better to use ems, because your media queries will trigger in relation to the font size in your visitor's browser. Lyza Gardner explains the benefits further in http://blog.cloudfour.com/the-ems-have-it-proportional-media-queries-ftw/.

I use em values in the media queries for building the sample responsive page in the next section. For context, I include comments that note what pixel values they generally approximate.

I Examples of other media queries used to load external style sheets when true.

```
...
    <link rel="stylesheet" media="only screen and (min-width: 480px) and (max-width: 767px)"
    → href="styles.css" />

    <link rel="stylesheet" media="only screen and (orientation: landscape)" href="styles.css" />

    <link rel="stylesheet" media="only print and (color)" href="color-pages.css" />

    <link rel="stylesheet" media="only print and (monochrome)" href="monochrome-pages.css" />

    <link rel="stylesheet" media="only screen and (color), projection and (color)"
    → href="styles.css" />
</head>
<body>
...
```

TIP Any base style rules you include outside the media queries are applied to all devices. You can override those as desired with media queries. To clarify, declarations within media query rules only write over *conflicting* declarations in the regular styles, such as `color: green;` in the case of **C**. If the p rule before the media query had included `font-style: italic;`, paragraph text would still be italicized when the media query is true, because the p rule within the media query doesn't specify `font-style`.

TIP If you own a Mac, you can use Apple's free iOS Simulator to test the example pages on the iPhone and iPad. See "Testing Your Pages" in Chapter 20 for more information.

TIP Descriptions for all media features are available in the CSS3 Media Queries spec (www.w3.org/TR/css3-mediaqueries/#media1).

J These are the same media queries as in **I**, but they appear directly in a style sheet.

```
/* Base Styles
--------------------------------------- */

/* your base rules for all devices */
...


/* Begin Media Queries
--------------------------------------- */
@media only screen and (min-width: 480px) and (max-width: 767px) {
    /* your rules */
}

@media only screen and (orientation: landscape) {
    /* your rules */
}

@media only print and (color) {
    /* your rules */
}

@media only print and (monochrome) {
    /* your rules */
}

@media only screen and (color), projection and (color) {
    /* your rules */
}
```

The Viewport and Using the Viewport meta Element

The viewport is the area within a desktop or mobile browser that displays your page. It doesn't include things like the browser's address bar or buttons, just the browsing area. The media query **width** feature maps to the viewport width. However, this is different than the **device-width** media feature, which is the width of the screen.

These values are often different by default on mobile devices such as the iPhone. The viewport of Mobile Safari, which is the iPhone's browser, is 980 pixels wide by default, but the iPhone device width is only 320 pixels wide. (Retina display iPhones have a screen resolution of 640 pixels wide, but they squeeze twice as many pixels in the same amount of space, so the device width is still 320.)

So the iPhone takes what is akin to a desktop browser set to 980 pixels wide and scales it down to fit in the screen width of 320 pixels in portrait mode Ⓚ. As a result, when you navigate in Mobile Safari to most websites that have been built for desktop browsers, it displays a small, zoomed-out view of them. It does the same thing in landscape mode, but the width is 480 pixels (or 568 for iPhone 5). As you can see in Ⓚ, pages are often hard to read without zooming in. (Be aware that the default viewport width varies among devices.)

Ⓚ My test page contains a green **div** that is 320×480. By default, Mobile Safari's viewport is 980 pixels wide, so the iPhone shrinks it to display it within the 320-pixel-wide screen. That's why the green box occupies roughly a third of the screen's width (that is, 320/980).

Fortunately, there's a quick solution. Simply add the viewport **meta** element to the **head** of your pages.

(continues on next page)

The Viewport and Using the Viewport meta Element *(continued)*

```
<!DOCTYPE html>
<html lang="en">
<head>
    <meta charset="utf-8" />
    <title>Your page title</title>
    <meta name="viewport" content="width=device-width, initial-scale=1" />
    ...
</head>
<body>
...
```

The important part of this code is **width=device-width**. With that in place, the viewport width is set to be the same as the device width (for the iPhone, that's 320 pixels), so page content of that width fills the screen in portrait mode ⬤. Without including this, you won't get the results you expect from your media queries that leverage **min-width** and **max-width**.

The **initial-scale=1** portion of the code has no bearing on the **width** and **device-width** values. It sets the page zoom level to 100%, even with an orientation change to landscape. (Note that there is a bug in versions of iOS prior to 6 that crops some content; see http://adactio.com/journal/5802/.) If you omit **initial-scale=1**, the iPhone will scale the page up in landscape mode so the layout is the same as in portrait mode but larger.

L This test page's code is exactly the same as in ⓚ except it has the viewport **meta** element set to **width=device-width**. As you can see, the viewport width and the screen width are the same now.

Putting It All Together

Now that you understand flexible images, flexible layouts, and media queries, it's time to put them together to build a responsive webpage.

I'm not going to show you all the style rules I apply. Instead, I will focus on the kinds of decisions you might make to shift your content's display as a page expands or shrinks. Overall, the important thing is to know how to approach building a responsive site, and the types of media queries used in the process. You can access the finished page and its code at www.htmlcssvqs.com/8ed/12.

Just to clarify, you don't build a fixed-width design and then convert it to be responsive. Chapter 11 showed you how to build a fixed-width page; this chapter (and this section in particular) shows you how to build a responsive page from the ground up, as if you hadn't built the fixed-width page.

Creating your content and HTML

Everything should begin with carefully considered content. If you attempt to design and build your site with placeholder text (the vaunted lorem ipsum), you may find that it doesn't hold together well when you drop in real content. So if possible, do the legwork up front so you can be confident you're designing and developing a site that will serve your visitors (and you) well.

The underlying HTML for the example page is the same as that of the page in Chapter 11, but I added `<meta name="viewport" content="width=device-width, initial-scale=1" />` to the **head** element. See the earlier sidebar "The Viewport and Using the Viewport **meta** Element" for why this is important.

Ⓐ A sampling of the base styling I apply for all viewports, both small and large. The rules are just like others you've seen leading up to this chapter—they are not encased in media query blocks. Notice that I gave the entire page a maximum width of 60em (typically the equivalent 960 pixels) and center it with **auto** margins. I also set all elements to use **box-sizing: border-box;**, and I made most images flexible.

```css
/* Base Styles
--------------------------------- */
body {
    font: 100%/1.2 Georgia, "Times New
    → Roman", serif;
    margin: 0;
    ...
}

* { /* See Chapter 11 */
    -webkit-box-sizing: border-box;
     -moz-box-sizing: border-box;
          box-sizing: border-box;
}

.page {
    margin: 0 auto;
    max-width: 60em; /* 960px */
}

h1 {
    font-family: "Lato", sans-serif;
    font-size: 2.25em; /* 36px/16px */
    font-weight: 300;
    ...
}

.about h2, .mod h2 {
    font-size: .875em; /* 15px/16px */
}

.logo,
.social-sites,
.nav-main li {
    text-align: center;
}

/* Make images flexible */
.post-photo, .post-photo-full,
.about img, .map {
    max-width: 100%;
}
...
```

The mobile first approach

I will follow the *mobile first* approach to style the page, and I recommend you do the same for yours. Here's how:

1. Provide baseline styles for all devices **A**. This is also the version that old browsers and less capable devices will display. This baseline usually includes basic styles for text (fonts, colors, sizes), padding, borders, margins, and backgrounds (as appropriate), and styles for making images flexible. Typically, at this stage you will want to avoid floating content left or right, or defining widths on containers, because the smallest screens aren't wide enough. Content will run top to bottom according to the normal document flow. The goal is for your site to be legible and presentable in a single column **B**. As a result, the site will be accessible to all devices, new and old. It might look a little different from device to device, but that is to be expected and is perfectly fine.

2. Work your way up from there, using media queries to define styles for progressively larger screen sizes (or other media features, like `orientation`). The `min-width` and `max-width` media query features will be your main tools most of the time.

This is progressive enhancement in action. (Please see "Progressive Enhancement: A Best Practice" in the book's introduction for a refresher.) Less capable (usually older) devices and browsers will show a simpler version of the site per the CSS they understand. More-capable devices and browsers show the enhanced version. Everyone has access to the content.

B The starting point of the page with the base styles applied. The page layout is linear on all browsers (the portion in the image on the right appears below the part on the left). These screen shots are representative of what older mobile browsers that don't support media queries will render. It is perfectly usable in this state. If you were to view this in a desktop browser, the content would stretch out as wide as the browser window because I haven't applied column widths yet.

Evolving your layout: step by step

In responsive web design lingo, you leverage media queries to define styles for each *breakpoint* in your page—that is, each width at which your content would benefit from adjustments. In the case of the example, after applying the base styles **A**, I created style rules for the breakpoints in the list that follows. Keep in mind that for each `min-width` case with no `max-width` counterpart, the styles target devices at that `min-width` and *all the way up*, including the desktop and beyond.

- A minimum width of **20em** (which generally is 320 pixels) (**C** and **D**). This targets the iPhone, the iPod touch, and numerous Android and other mobile phones in portrait mode.

- A minimum width of **30em** (which generally is 480 pixels) (**E** through **H**). This targets larger mobile phones, as well as many of the 320-pixel devices when in landscape mode (the iPhone, the iPod touch, and certain Android models among them).

- Within the range of a minimum width of **30em** (generally 480 pixels) and a maximum width of **47.9375em** (generally 767 pixels) (**I** and **J**). The changes here are viewable on some phones in landscape mode and tablets like certain versions of the Galaxy Tab and Kindle Fire, and when a desktop browser is a little narrower than usual.

- A minimum width of **48em** (which generally is 768 pixels) (**K** through **M**). This suits the iPad and other tablets, desktop browsers at typical widths, and everything wider.

continues on page 331

C I modify the main navigation for browsers with a viewport that is at least **20em** wide. (Usually this translates to 320 pixels because 20 * 16 = 320, assuming your **body** element's font size is the equivalent of 16 pixels). This makes the links appear on a single line instead of stacked **D**. I didn't do this in the base styles because some phones have narrower screens that would have made the links look cramped or would have forced one to wrap to a second line.

```
/* Base Styles
--------------------------------- */
...

/* 20em (320px and up)
--------------------------------- */
@media only screen and (min-width: 20em) {
    .nav-main li {
        border-left: 1px solid #c8c8c8;
        display: inline-block;
        text-align: left;
    }

    .nav-main li:first-child {
        border-left: none;
    }

    .nav-main a {
        display: inline-block;
        font-size: 1em;
        padding: .5em .9em .5em 1.15em;
    }
}
```

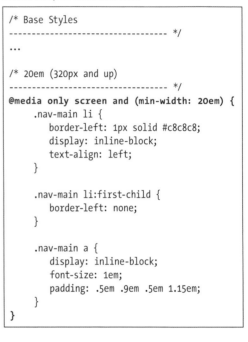

D The main navigation is on a single line, with the links separated by a gray vertical border, thanks to the media query in **C**. The style takes effect in the iPhone (and many others) because the viewport is 320 pixels wide in portrait mode. If you wanted to shorten the masthead area more, you could add rules to move the logo to the left and place the social icons to the right. But I've saved that for the next media query (**E** and **F**).

E Now the style sheet has a media query that targets a viewport of at least **30em**, which is typically 480 pixels. This represents larger phones as well as phones like the iPhone in landscape mode **F**. These styles adjust the masthead once again. The first two rules are the same ones we used in Chapter 11 for the same effect.

```
/* Base Styles
---------------------------------- */
...

/* 20em (320px and up)
---------------------------------- */
@media only screen and (min-width: 20em) {
    ...
}

/* 30em (480px and up)
---------------------------------- */
@media only screen and (min-width: 30em) {
    .masthead { position: relative; }

    .social-sites {
        position: absolute;
        right: -3px;
        top: 41px;
    }

    .logo {
        margin-bottom: 8px;
        text-align: left;
    }

    .nav-main {
        margin-top: 0;
    }
}
```

G Continuing with styles in the same media query block, I float an image to the left and reduce its **max-width** to allow more text to flow to its side than would fit otherwise. "Controlling Where Elements Float" in Chapter 11 explains why I set **clear: left;** on the footer below the blog post snippet.

```
...

/* 30em (480px and up)
---------------------------------- */
@media only screen and (min-width: 30em) {

    ... masthead styles ...

    .post-photo {
        float: left;
        margin-bottom: 2px;
        margin-right: 22px;
        max-width: 61.667%;
    }

    .post-footer {
        clear: left;
    }

}
```

H The text wraps around the floated image.

F Here's the top of the page viewed at 30em (480 pixels) wide. The masthead is complete. It will grow wider automatically in larger viewports.

I Now I float the About Me image, but only when the viewport is from 30em **J** to 47.9375em wide. Beyond that width, I'll make the layout switch to two columns, and the About Me text will display underneath the image again. I'll do that next.

```
/* Base Styles
--------------------------------- */
...

/* 20em (320px and up)
--------------------------------- */
@media only screen and (min-width: 20em) {
    ...
}

/* 30em (480px and up)
--------------------------------- */
@media only screen and (min-width: 30em) {
    ...
}

/* 30em – 47.9375em
    (From 480px–767px, not beyond)
--------------------------------- */
@media only screen and (min-width: 30em)
→ and (max-width: 47.9375em) {
    .about { /* self-clear float */
        overflow: hidden;
    }

    .about img {
        float: left;
        margin-right: 15px;
    }
}
```

J The floated About Me image is displaying at its normal width (270 pixels) already, which is plenty narrow for text to fit next to it comfortably. That's why I didn't reduce its **max-width** like I did for the previous image (**G** and **H**).

K This is the final media query, targeting viewports that are at least **48em** wide. This is true for most desktop browsers **M** (unless the user has made it narrower), but it also maps to the width of the iPad and some other tablets in portrait mode **L**.

```
/* Base Styles
--------------------------------- */
...

/* 20em (320px and up)
--------------------------------- */
@media only screen and (min-width: 20em) {
    ...
}

/* 30em (480px and up)
--------------------------------- */
@media only screen and (min-width: 30em) {
    ...
}

/* 30em – 47.9375em
    (From 480px–767px, not beyond)
--------------------------------- */
@media only screen and (min-width: 30em) and
→ (max-width: 47.9375em) {
    ...
}

/* 48em (768px and up)
--------------------------------- */
@media only screen and (min-width: 48em) {
    .container {
        background: url(../img/bg.png)
        → repeat-y 65.9375% 0;
        padding-bottom: 1.875em;
    }

    main {
        float: left;
        width: 62.5%; /* 600px/960px */
    }

    .sidebar {
        float: right;
        margin-top: 1.875em;
        width: 31.25%; /* 300px/960px */
    }

    .nav-main { margin-bottom: 0; }
}
```

Your breakpoints may be different from the ones I used. It depends on what is right for your content and design. It's not unusual to see breakpoints beyond **48em** to adapt a layout more for wider viewports. You also can stray from the breakpoints that align with the exact device viewport widths. If a media query based on **(min-width: 36em)** is best for presenting your content, use it.

To build a responsive webpage:

1. Create your content and HTML.

2. In the **head** element of your HTML page, type **<meta name="viewport"** → **content="width=device-width" />** or **<meta name="viewport" content=** → **"width=device-width, initial-** → **scale=1" />**.

3. Apply your baseline styles for all devices (see "The mobile first approach"). Make sure you set images to shrink and expand (see "Making Images Flexible").

4. Identify breakpoints that are appropriate for your content. Create associated media queries to adapt your layout for the different viewport widths, moving from small-screen to large-screen. (See "Evolving your layout: step by step.")

5. If you need to assign widths to parts of your page in step 4, use percentages (see "Creating a Flexible Layout Grid").

6. Choose how you would like older versions of IE to display your page. (See "Accommodating Older Versions of Internet Explorer.")

7. Test away! (See the "Testing a Responsive Page" sidebar.)

8. Refine your CSS in steps 3–5 as necessary, and test until the page renders as desired across a range of devices.

L The page is complete. The iPad's rendering is shown here, but it looks similar on desktop browsers (though wider if the visitor has expanded the browser). The columns automatically stretch, because their widths are percentage values.

M In a browser of at least 960 pixels wide, it looks just like our fixed-width layout from Chapter 11. If you make the browser narrower, the layout scales and shifts just like it does on mobile devices.

TIP Eivind Uggedal's http://mediaqueri.es site is an ever-expanding gallery of responsive sites in the wild. It's worth a look for inspiration.

TIP The Screen Sizes website (http://screensiz.es) provides screen resolution and device width information for popular devices and monitors. The information may be helpful when crafting media queries.

TIP Maximiliano Firtman maintains a matrix of HTML5 and CSS3 support among modern mobile devices at http://mobilehtml5.org. (Most of the information pertains to advanced features not covered in this book.)

Testing a Responsive Page

You will want to check your responsive page on mobile devices and desktop browsers before releasing it in the wild.

While you are building a responsive page, you can resize your desktop browser to approximate the viewport size of various mobile phones and tablets. Then you can adjust your styles accordingly. This is a crude method to be sure, but it can help you get your styles in the ballpark so you'll have less refining to do after you've done proper testing on devices. You might find Malte Wasserman's Viewport Resizer (http://lab.maltewassermann.com/viewport-resizer/) helpful for this.

But don't stop there. Resize your browser all the way in and out to test how your layout adjusts when viewed at any width on the desktop. You may find other breakpoints that need attention with additional media queries.

I describe proper ways to do mobile and desktop testing in "Testing Your Pages" in Chapter 20.

Media Query for Retina and Similar Displays

Sometimes you may want to target styles for high-pixel-density devices. (See "Scaling Images with the Browser" in Chapter 5.) A common use case is to serve them a double-sized (*2x*) sprite so your images look sharp. (See "Combining Images in a Sprite" in Chapter 14.)

Suppose your normal-sized sprite is 200×150 and each image within it is separated by one pixel. You create a double-sized version that is 400×300 and that has *two* pixels between each image. Also, each image in the sprite should be twice its normal size. Use the following media query to target the high-pixel-density devices:

```
@media (-o-min-device-pixel-
→ratio: 5/4),
(-webkit-min-device-pixel-ratio:
→1.25),
(min-resolution: 120dpi) {
    .your-class {
        background-image:
        →url(sprite-2x.png);
        background-size: 200px
        →150px;
    }
}
```

Note that **background-size** is set to the *normal* dimensions, not **400px 300px**. That shrinks it so the styles you create for the normal sprite work for the 2x version too.

Ⓐ There's a lot of weird-looking code here. The parts you probably don't recognize are called *conditional comments* (www.quirksmode.org/css/condcom.html). The first one goes around the `link` to the style sheet intended for all browsers except IE8 and older. The second one goes around the style sheet meant only for IE lower than IE9.

```
...
<head>
    ...

    <!--[if gt IE 8]><!-->
    <link rel="stylesheet"
    → href="css/styles.css" />
    <!--<![endif]-->

    <!--[if lt IE 9]>
    <link rel="stylesheet"
    → href="css/old-ie.css" />
    <![endif]-->
</head>
...
```

Accommodating Older Versions of Internet Explorer

There's one caveat to the mobile first approach: Internet Explorer 8 and lower don't support media queries. That means they render only the styles you define outside of media queries; namely, the baseline styles. IE6 and IE7 have very low market share in most parts of the world, so the real decision for you to make is for IE8. Its share is less than 9 percent of users worldwide, and that's going down. (See http://gs.statcounter.com.)

You have at least three options for IE8 (and earlier versions):

- Do nothing. Let them display the basic version of your site.

- Create a separate style sheet specifically for them so they display the widest version of the site (it won't be responsive). One way to do this is to start with *a copy* of your regular style sheet. Name it something similar to **old-ie.css**. Remove the media queries but *not* the style rules inside them. Add conditional comments to your HTML to deliver the right style sheets to the right browsers **Ⓐ**.

continues on next page

- If you want them to display your page responsively, load **respond.min.js** in your page **B**. Scott Jehl created this lightweight script, which makes **min-width** and **max-width** media queries work in the older versions of IE. See the sidebar.

The second option is the more reliable and gives IE8 users the full layout version of the site.

TIP You can automate creating a style sheet for older IE versions if you use a CSS preprocessor like Sass, LESS, or Stylus. Nicolas Gallagher shares an approach that uses Sass (http://nicolasgallagher.com/mobile-first-css-sass-and-ie/).

B Replace the **js** part of the **src** value with the location (if different) of the file in your site. When all is set, IE8 and below will understand your **min-width** and **max-width** media queries and render the styles accordingly. There's no need for a separate IE style sheet with this option. The conditional comment around the **script** element is optional, but if you include it, only IE8 and below will load **respond.min.js**.

```
...
<head>
...

    <link rel="stylesheet"
    → href="css/styles.css" />

    <!--[if lt IE 9]>
    <script src="js/respond.min.js">
    → </script>
    <![endif]-->
</head>
...
```

Using Respond.js

You can download Respond.js at https://github.com/scottjehl/Respond by clicking the ZIP button. Open the zip file on your computer, and copy **respond.min.js** into a folder in your website. Take a look at the "Support & Caveats" section at the github link if the script isn't working. Respond.js isn't a perfect solution for all sites.

Working with Web Fonts

Over the past handful of years, we have observed a renaissance in using fonts on the web. We used to have a very limited choice of typefaces. As Chapter 10 explains, we had to stick to the fonts you could expect users to have installed on their computers. This is the reason most websites have their **body** copy set in Arial, Georgia, Verdana, or Trebuchet MS.

Now, thanks to web fonts, we have myriad options for choosing typefaces for web projects. Consequently, web designers can create better-crafted experiences for visitors. Watching this change unfold has been extremely exciting.

This chapter explains web font basics, how to use self-hosted web fonts (with fonts from Font Squirrel as an example), and how to use fonts hosted by Google Fonts. It takes a little longer to learn how to use self-hosted fonts. If you want to fast-track your usage of web fonts, you might consider hopping to "Using Web Fonts from Google Fonts," at the end of this chapter.

In This Chapter

What Is a Web Font?

Web fonts are made possible thanks to the **@font-face** CSS rule, which allows CSS to link to a font on a server for use in a webpage.

Many people think web fonts are new. In fact, web fonts have been around since 1998. Netscape Navigator 4 and Internet Explorer 4 both adopted this technology, but neither of their implementations supported standard font file formats, so they didn't see much use. It wasn't until nearly a decade later that browsers started adopting this standard with more common font file types. Consequently, the use of web fonts started to become commonplace.

Web font file formats and browser support

Web fonts come in an array of file types. In particular, the first three types described below are used regularly today.

- Embedded OpenType (.eot). Internet Explorer 8 and earlier support only Embedded OpenType for use with **@font-face**. A Microsoft proprietary format, Embedded OpenType uses digital rights management technology to prevent unlicensed use of the font.

- TrueType (.ttf) and OpenType (.otf). The standard font file types used for desktop computers, TrueType and OpenType are widely supported by Mozilla Firefox (3.5 and later), Opera (10 and later), Safari (3.1 and later), Mobile Safari (iOS 4.2 and later), Google Chrome (4.0 and later), and Internet Explorer (9 and later). These formats do not use digital rights management.

- Web Open Font Format (.woff). This newer standard is designed specifically for use as a web font. A Web Open Font Format font is a TrueType or OpenType font that has been compressed. The WOFF format also allows additional metadata to be attached to the file; this can be used by font designers or vendors to include licensing or other information beyond what is present in the original font. Such metadata does not affect the rendering of the font in any way, but it may be displayed to the user on request. Web Open Font Format is supported by Mozilla Firefox (3.6 and later), Opera (11.1 and later), Safari (5.1 and later), Google Chrome (6.0 and later), and Internet Explorer (9 and later).

- Scalable Vector Graphics (.svg). In short, avoid using SVG for web font files. It was used more in the early days of web fonts because it was the only format that mobile Safari on iOS 4.1 supported (it also caused some crashes). Mobile Safari began supporting TrueType in iOS 4.2, which gained wide usage in early 2011.

As you can see, the support for web fonts across browsers is robust, so there is nothing holding you back from using them on your websites today.

Legal issues

Fonts are, at a technical level, little pieces of software. There are people who make their living designing and building fonts, and it's a painstaking and detailed creative process that is not for the faint of heart.

For this reason, it's understandable that it might ruffle some feathers that the `@font-face` feature even exists in the first place. After all, if a browser can link to and download a font, then that means anybody can download and install that font onto their computers, whether they've purchased It or not.

This is why we, as web designers and developers, must make sure that any fonts we use in our websites are properly licensed for use on the web. Most font foundries and font services offer this licensing as a part of the purchase of a font or as an à la carte option.

However you proceed, make sure you're solidly in the right when it comes to using web fonts in a project. You can do this by taking a look at the license for any fonts you purchase. Some fonts may be used for desktop applications like Adobe Photoshop and Adobe Illustrator, but not as web fonts on your site. This information is often mentioned on the website of the font foundry you are purchasing from. When in doubt, contact the foundry to see what is allowed.

If you have purchased a font and know for sure that you can use it as a web font, one tool that might come in handy is Font Squirrel's free `@font-face` generator (www.fontsquirrel.com/tools/webfont-generator). This tool converts your font to all the web font file types you will need for using it on the web.

The real boon is the numerous web font services that have surfaced. Combined, they offer thousands of fonts with licenses that allow web usage (see "Where to Find Web Fonts"). Many of these fonts are free.

Managing file size

One potential risk with web fonts, especially when you're using more than a couple of them, is that they can start to weigh down the page. I'm not talking about French fries and doughnuts here—I'm talking about kilobytes and megabytes.

All the fonts used on a webpage need to be downloaded to the user's computer before they can be rendered on the page. This can slow down the website considerably, especially for mobile users. My recommendation to you is to be prudent with your web font choices. If you find yourself using more than a couple of web fonts, look for ways to consolidate your font choices.

Subsetting

One way to save some page weight is through subsetting. Subsetting is a way to trim the size of the actual font by including only the characters you know you will use. For instance, if you are using League Gothic for headlines but the design of the site requires that the headlines are always in all caps, then there is no need for lowercase letters. Using subsetting, you can remove those letters from the font, and the font's file size will be measurably smaller.

Additionally, you can select language-specific subsets for many fonts. I show you how to do this at Font Squirrel in "Downloading Your First Web Font."

Explaining the nuts and bolts of subsetting is beyond the scope of this book, but Font Squirrel's `@font-face` generator (mentioned earlier) can help you do expert-level subsetting.

Where to Find Web Fonts

You have two options for using web fonts in a website: self-hosting and web font services. Both are perfectly valid options and have pros and cons to consider. Regardless of which option you choose, you will find that not all web fonts are available everywhere. You may find that even though you want to go with self-hosting, the font you need is available only from a web font service. Or, you may find that the service you prefer does not have a particular font you want. This may require finding a close substitute or rethinking your approach. It pays to be flexible and to weigh all your options before you commit to a direction.

Self-hosting

With self-hosting, the web fonts are served up from your own server much like any other asset, such as an image or a CSS file. If there's a cost associated with the font, it's usually a one-time purchase, and it's up to you to upload the font files and create the CSS for displaying the font on your site. In the sections that follow, we will cover self-hosting step by step, using a free web font downloaded from Font Squirrel.

It's pretty easy to find web fonts for self-hosting, because there are plenty of them out there. And they come in a wide range of qualities and prices (some are even free). Some of the more popular ones are:

- Font Squirrel (www.fontsquirrel.com) free
- MyFonts (http://myfonts.com)
- The League of Moveable Type (www.theleagueofmoveabletype.com) free
- FontShop (www.fontshop.com)

A Font Squirrel is a popular destination for finding free web fonts you can host yourself. You will learn how to use it across the next four sections of this chapter. You don't need to know everything they cover to use a web font service like Google Fonts, but they will give you a better understanding of how web fonts work and some pitfalls to avoid.

B Google Fonts is a popular free web font service. You will learn how to use it at the end of the chapter, in "Using Web Fonts from Google Fonts."

Web font services

Web font services typically offer a subscription approach to web fonts. Instead of buying the fonts outright, you pay monthly or annually for the rights to use the fonts. Typekit was the pioneer in this space, and now several services exist.

These services host the fonts and give you a small piece of code to put into your webpages. Depending on the service, this code is JavaScript or CSS. It includes all the necessary code for the font files to be served up from a remote server. Many favor this approach because it's usually cheaper than purchasing fonts individually and it lets you try many different fonts. It can be easier to implement a font as well.

A few of the more popular web font services are:

- Cloud.typography (www.typography.com/cloud/welcome/)

- Edge Web Fonts (www.edgefonts.com) free

- Fontdeck (http://fontdeck.com)

- Fonts.com (www.fonts.com/web-fonts)

- Fontspring.com (www.fontspring.com)

- Google Fonts (www.google.com/fonts) free **B**

- Typekit (https://typekit.com)

- WebINK (www.webink.com)

By nature, web font services are able to offer more features than self-hosting. If better font files or improved code for serving them become available, the services can easily provide it. For instance, Typekit improved their offering when they began to serve up some of their fonts using PostScript-based outlines to Windows browsers to make the rendering smoother.

continues on next page

Many of these services use JavaScript to embed the code for serving up web fonts. This comes with some benefits and drawbacks. JavaScript can help a service fine-tune web font display settings and give added control over loading the fonts. This can lead to a genuinely better experience for your site's visitors.

The cost of this luxury, of course, is that you're relying 100 percent on JavaScript, which can slow down the loading of a page. The user will have to wait for the JavaScript to load before any of the web fonts load on the page. This is worth keeping in mind as you decide how to bring web fonts to your site. But don't let this scare you away from web font services. I and untold others have used them with success.

Web font quality and rendering

Unfortunately, not all web fonts are created equal. There can be noticeable differences in how they look across web browsers. This is most apparent in some fonts that just don't look good in earlier versions of Internet Explorer.

Additionally, some fonts look better at some sizes than at other sizes. They might be too frail and become difficult to read when used for body text, or lack authority at heading size.

Icon Fonts and Where to Get Them

Icon fonts are web fonts that have icons instead of letters, numbers, and punctuation. You can style them with the same CSS you use for styling text, such as setting their **color**.

The best part is that no matter what **font-size** value you use, an icon font will scale nicely and look sharp. This makes them a better option than icon images because no extra work is required to make them look crisp on any type of display (including Retina) or when changing their size in a responsive webpage.

I used Socialico by Fontfabric (www.fontfabric.com) for the social icons you see in the masthead of the Chapter 11 and 12 example. I created the necessary web font formats for it by uploading the font to Font Squirrel's Webfont Generator.

Chris Coyier has a great roundup of where to get icon fonts (http://css-tricks.com/flat-icons-icon-fonts/) and he demonstrates how to create your own (http://css-tricks.com/video-screencasts/113-creating-and-using-a-custom-icon-font/) with IcoMoon (http://icomoon.io).

As you select your fonts, do your best to vet potential web font choices by examining how they will look in a variety of browsers. This has gotten easier because many web font companies now provide live examples of the web fonts, and some companies provide screenshots of the fonts on a variety of browsers and platforms.

If you are stuck doing these tests on your own, try out the resource that is available from the site Web Font Specimen (http://webfontspecimen.com). It's a tool that lets you test how your web fonts will look in a variety of contexts and sizes.

OK, how do I get started?

The rest of this chapter focuses on two areas: how to use self-hosted web fonts Ⓐ and how to use Google Fonts Ⓑ. Of the two, Google Fonts is more straightforward, so you might prefer to start there.

Downloading Your First Web Font

Before you can style your pages with self-hosted web fonts, you must get your hands on web font files. Downloading a free web font is quick and easy. We will be using Font Squirrel, but the steps are similar with other services that offer fonts for self-hosting.

To download a web font from Font Squirrel:

1. Go to Font Squirrel (www.fontsquirrel. com), and select a font you want to use. There are many ways to browse fonts, whether via the homepage, through the Popular or Recent sections, or by searching. I've selected PT Sans Ⓐ.

2. From the font's page, choose Webfont Kit Ⓑ.

3. Deselect the SVG option under Choose Font Formats Ⓒ. If you want visitors using Internet Explorer 8 (and prior) to see the web font when you add it to your page, leave EOT selected; otherwise, deselect it.

4. Choose the subset for the font. Usually, you will want either the default option or the language of your site's content. (I chose English Ⓓ.)

Ⓐ Select a font by activating its name (shown), not by using the blue download button at the far right (not shown). That download button is for using the font on your system, not for downloading the web font files.

Ⓑ The Specimens section gives you options for seeing the font used as regular, bold, italic, and other text styles (depending on what the font offers). You can type in your own sample text in the Test Drive section. Glyphs displays each character in the font, and the License section explains the allowed usage. If you're happy with the font, choose Webfont Kit.

Ⓒ SVG isn't recommended for web fonts anymore, so I've chosen not to include it. Deselect EOT if you don't anticipate many IE8 visitors on your site.

Ⓓ Subsetting a web font reduces the number of characters, which reduces the file sizes of font files.

 **E** Download the kit to your computer.

```
●●○            PT-Sans-fontfacekit
◀  ▶    ⊞ ▤ ▥ ▦    🔍 ✱▾  ?  ▦ »

Name                              ▲  Size
📄 How_to_use_webfonts.html          10 KB
📄 Paratype PT Sans Free Font License.txt  3 KB
▼ 📁 web fonts                        --
  ▼ 📁 ptsans_bold_english            --
    📄 PTS75F-demo.html              24 KB
    ▪ PTS75F-webfont.eot            18 KB
    📄 PTS75F-webfont.ttf            39 KB
    ▪ PTS75F-webfont.woff           19 KB
    ▶ 📁 specimen_files               --
    📄 stylesheet.css            374 bytes
  ▼ 📁 ptsans_bolditalic_english      --
    📄 PTS76F-demo.html              24 KB
    ▪ PTS76F-webfont.eot            18 KB
    📄 PTS76F-webfont.ttf            41 KB
    ▪ PTS76F-webfont.woff           20 KB
    ▶ 📁 specimen_files               --
    📄 stylesheet.css            388 bytes
  ▼ 📁 ptsans_italic_english          --
    📄 PTS56F-demo.html              24 KB
    ▪ PTS56F-webfont.eot            18 KB
    📄 PTS56F-webfont.ttf            39 KB
    ▪ PTS56F-webfont.woff           19 KB
    ▶ 📁 specimen_files               --
    📄 stylesheet.css            378 bytes
  ▼ 📁 ptsans_regular_english         --
    📄 PTS55F-demo.html              24 KB
    ▪ PTS55F-webfont.eot            18 KB
    📄 PTS55F-webfont.ttf            39 KB
    ▪ PTS55F-webfont.woff           19 KB
    ▶ 📁 specimen_files               --
    📄 stylesheet.css            380 bytes
  ▶ 📁 ptsanscaption_bold_english     --
  ▶ 📁 ptsanscaption_regular_english  --
  ▶ 📁 ptsansnarrow_bold_english      --
  ▶ 📁 ptsansnarrow_regular_english   --
```

F Holy smokes, that's a lot of files and folders! Why so many? The total varies by font and by the number of font formats you chose in step 3 **C**. If you select the Specimens tab **B** on Font Squirrel's PT Sans page and scroll down, you'll see eight fonts listed **G**. They represent the various PT Sans styles and weights. And we chose three formats, so the ZIP file has eight font folders with three format files in each to go along with demo HTML and **stylesheet.css** files. In this chapter, I'll use the font format files and part of the code from each **stylesheet.css** file shown in the four expanded font folders.

5. Click the DOWNLOAD @FONT-FACE KIT button **E**, and your download should begin immediately. The download is a ZIP archive.

6. Once the download is finished, open the archive. You should have a folder containing at least one font folder inside a folder named **web fonts** **F**.

> **FONTS**
>
> PT Sans AaBbCcDdEeFfGgHhIiJjKkLlMmN
> PT Sans Regular | 723 Glyphs
>
> *PT Sans Italic AaBbCcDdEeFfGgHhIiJjKkLlM*
> *PT Sans Italic | 724 Glyphs*
>
> **PT Sans Bold AaBbCcDdEeFfGgHhIiJjKkLl**
> **PT Sans Bold | 723 Glyphs**
>
> ***PT Sans Bold Italic AaBbCcDdEeFfGgHhIiJj***
> ***PT Sans Bold Italic | 724 Glyphs***
>
> PT Sans Caption AaBbCcDdEeFfGgH
> PT Sans Caption Regular | 723 Glyphs
>
> **PT Sans Caption Bold AaBbCcDdEeF**
> **PT Sans Caption Bold | 723 Glyphs**
>
> PT Sans Narrow AaBbCcDdEeFfGgHhIiJjKkLlMmNn
> PT Sans Narrow Regular | 723 Glyphs
>
> **PT Sans Narrow Bold AaBbCcDdEeFfGgHhIiJjKkLl**
> **PT Sans Narrow Bold | 723 Glyphs**

G PT Sans offers eight styles among three versions: PT Sans (Regular, Bold, Italic, and Bold Italic), PT Sans Caption (Regular and Bold), and PT Sans Narrow (Regular and Bold). I won't use PT Sans Caption or PT Sans Narrow in this chapter. Some other fonts are limited to a few styles, or in some cases—like Bebas Neue, for example—just one style.

To view a selected font in its demo HTML file:

Each font folder within the **web fonts** folder contains an HTML file that demonstrates the font. Its file name ends with **-demo.html**. Open the file in your browser . (See "Viewing Your Page in a Browser" in Chapter 2.)

This demo file shows that the web font does indeed work. This is very exciting! Before you declare victory and call it a day, we'll explore more about how this works in the next section, and then move on to seeing how to apply the font to your own pages.

TIP Generally speaking, you shouldn't use more than two (three at the most) web fonts in a page because that's more files for your visitor's browser to download. This slows down your page loading and rendering, especially for visitors on smartphones and the like, because connections are slower. To clarify, I mean a *total* of two or three styles or weights from one or more font families. For example, PT Sans regular, bold, and italic count as three, so if you introduce another web font family, that would count as at least a fourth font.

TIP Need some inspiration on which fonts to choose for your next project? The team at Typekit writes a wonderful blog with lots of great information on web fonts and on typography in general. Try the "Sites we like" series for starters (http://blog.typekit.com/category/sites-we-like/).

TIP Do you need to use any of these fonts to mock something up in Photoshop? Install the TrueType (.ttf) font that comes with the web font kit onto your computer. Once you install it, you can use it just like any other font on your computer.

H The **PTS75F-demo.html** file that came with the PT Sans web font kit I downloaded from Font Squirrel. This file was in the **ptsans_bold_english** folder. If I wanted to view one of the other PT Sans styles, I would open its demo file. For instance, **PTS55F-demo.html** from the **ptsans_regular_english** folder. Each demo file uses the **stylesheet.css** file found in the same folder.

The combined rules from the first four PT Sans **stylesheet.css** files. (I've changed the order to match the sequence in this chapter.) All of them are the same except for the parts I've highlighted—the **font-family** value and the prefix in each web font file name. (Note: You might notice an additional **url** that references SVG in your own **stylesheet.css**. I omitted it because I didn't download that format.)

```
@font-face {
    font-family: 'pt_sansregular';
    src: url('PTS55F-webfont.eot');
    src: url('PTS55F-webfont.eot?#iefix')
        → format('embedded-opentype'),
        url('PTS55F-webfont.woff')
        → format('woff'),
        url('PTS55F-webfont.ttf')
        → format('truetype');
    font-weight: normal;
    font-style: normal;
}

@font-face {
    font-family: 'pt_sansitalic';
    src: url('PTS56F-webfont.eot');
    src: url('PTS56F-webfont.eot?#iefix')
        → format('embedded-opentype'),
        url('PTS56F-webfont.woff')
        → format('woff'),
        url('PTS56F-webfont.ttf')
        → format('truetype');
    font-weight: normal;
    font-style: normal;
}

@font-face {
    font-family: 'pt_sansbold';
    src: url('PTS75F-webfont.eot');
    ...
}

@font-face {
    font-family: 'pt_sansbold_italic';
    src: url('PTS76F-webfont.eot');
    ...
}

...
```

Understanding the @font-face Rule

Now it's time to look under the hood and see how web fonts work. Let's look at the **stylesheet.css** files found in the first four PT Sans font folders. Each file has a rule for one of the PT Sans styles, contained in the odd-looking **@font-face { ... }** Ⓐ.

The syntax is a bit different from traditional CSS because the **@font-face** portion is not a selector of an element you wish to style. So this rule doesn't affect the style of any element by itself. Instead, it lets your style sheets know that the web font exists so you can use it to style text in other rules. (Each folder's demo HTML file loads **stylesheet.css** and contains the CSS rule that uses the font.)

The second line in each rule is for the font family. For example, **font-family: 'pt_sansregular';** or **font-family: 'pt_sansbold';**.

This establishes the name for this particular web font—the name you will use to apply it to elements, just like regular fonts. The name can be whatever you choose. Instead of **pt_sansregular**, you could choose **Banana** or **The Best Font Ever**. It's up to you. In fact, we'll change it when we apply PT Sans to a page in the next section.

The next few lines in the rule are for telling the browser where the font files live. These include the three font file formats we chose so each browser would get a format it supports. This syntax can look a little scary, but for our purposes it's not necessary to understand it completely. If you *do* want to learn the ins-and-outs, I recommend Ethan Dunham's post at www.fontspring.com/blog/further-hardening-of-the-bulletproof-syntax.

Styling Text with a Web Font

We've covered the **@font-face** syntax, but we haven't actually put the web fonts onto our own page yet. Although we will use the font downloaded from Font Squirrel, the methods you will learn here apply to using any fonts you self-host.

There are a few methods for using web fonts in a style sheet. One is the way Font Squirrel does it, as shown in each **stylesheet.css** and demo HTML file. I will show you another approach.

Neither method is inherently right or wrong, but I do recommend the way I'll demonstrate. It more closely reflects how you are accustomed to styling text with regular fonts, is easier to manage (especially if you're new to web fonts), and provides the appropriate fallback if the web font fails to load.

Luckily, the CSS required for the second method is largely the same as the first. So we are going to use the **@font-face** rules from the first four PT Sans **stylesheet.css** files in our own style sheet, modifying them as necessary. For now, we'll stick with applying the regular style of the font. We'll cover italic, bold, and bold italic styling in the next section.

We will use the sample HTML shown in **A** and add the CSS to **example.css**, which is blank at the moment. Although our example uses PT Sans, I've written the following steps in a generic manner so they may apply to any web font you use from Font Squirrel. Likewise, the **@font-face** method you will learn works with any web font you self-host.

A I'm beginning with a simple HTML page and a blank style sheet. To simplify the demo, both files live in the same folder. Note that the folder doesn't contain any PT Sans font files yet.

```
<!DOCTYPE html>
<html lang="en">
<head>
    <meta charset="utf-8" />
    <title>Styling Text with a Web Font
    → </title>
    <link rel="stylesheet"
    → href="example.css" />
</head>
<body>
<h1>Local Teen Prefers Vinyl Over Digital</h1>

<p>A local teenager has replaced all her
→ digital tracks with vinyl. "It's <em>
→ really</em> groovy," she said, on the
→ record. Without skipping a beat, she added,
→ "Besides, it's like going through a time
→ warp."</p>

<p>Some of her iPod-toting classmates aren't
→ as enthusiastic. "Yeah, they needle me
→ about it. What a bunch of ones and
→ zeros."</p>
</body>
</html>
```

B I've updated **example.css** so it contains the **@font-face** rule from **stylesheet.css** in the **ptsans_regular_english** folder.

```
/* example.css */

@font-face {
    font-family: 'pt_sansregular';
    src: url('PTS55F-webfont.eot');
    src: url('PTS55F-webfont.eot?#iefix')
        → format('embedded-opentype'),
        url('PTS55F-webfont.woff')
        → format('woff'),
        url('PTS55F-webfont.ttf')
        → format('truetype');
    font-weight: normal;
    font-style: normal;
}
```

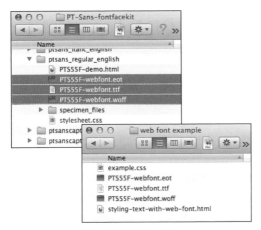

C I've copied the three PT Sans Regular font format files from the folder downloaded from Font Squirrel (top) to my example folder (bottom).

D The only modification I've made to **example.css** is changing **pt_sansregular** to **PTSans** to make the name more generic to the font.

```
/* example.css */

@font-face {
    font-family: 'PTSans';
    src: url('PTS55F-webfont.eot');
    ...
}
```

E This rule for **body** is just like your typical CSS for styling text. The **font-family** name (PTSans, in this case) in a font stack must match the one in the **@font-face** rule. The **font-size** and **line-height** styles aren't required to make a web font work.

```
/* example.css */

body {
    font-family: 'PTSans', sans-serif;
    font-size: 100%;
    line-height: 1.25;
}

@font-face {
    font-family: 'PTSans';
    src: url('PTS55F-webfont.eot');
    ...
}
```

To use a web font to style regular text:

1. Look in the **web fonts** folder from the ZIP file that you downloaded from Font Squirrel in "Downloading Your First Web Font." If you see a sub-folder for the regular text version of the font, open the **stylesheet.css** file from that sub-folder.

2. Copy the **@font-face** rule for regular text and paste it into your style sheet **B**.

3. Copy the font files (that are referenced in your style sheet **B**) from the Font Squirrel folder to the folder that contains your style sheet **C**.

4. Rename the **font-family** value so its name is generic to the font. For example, use the name of the font minus any mention of its style **D**. (The name you choose isn't important. What *is* important is that you must use the *same* **font-family** name for all flavors the font supports, such as regular, bold, italic, and bold italic. This will become clearer when you learn how to apply the other flavors in the next section.)

5. Create rules to style text elements as desired and as discussed in Chapter 10. To apply the web font, type **font-family: 'Web Font Name';** in your rules **E**, where **Web Font Name** is the name you created in step 4. Be sure to save the file.

continues on next page

If you refresh the page, it displays the web font **F**. However, we aren't quite finished. All may look good at first glance, but a closer inspection reveals that the undesirable faux bold (on the heading) and faux italic (on "really") have taken effect. I will show you how to correct those in the next section.

TIP Normally, I would write the first rule in **E** as body { font: 100%/1.25 'PTSans', sans-serif; } to take advantage of the font shorthand syntax. I listed the properties individually so it would be clear how to apply the web font by itself.

TIP For simplicity, the chapter's examples assume that the HTML, style sheet, and fonts are in the same folder. In practice, I recommend separating them. See the last tip in "Applying Italics and Bold with a Web Font" for one approach.

Local Teen Prefers Vinyl Over Digital

A local teenager has replaced all her digital tracks with vinyl. "It's *really* groovy," she said, on the record. Without skipping a beat, she added, "Besides, it's like going through a time warp."

Some of her iPod-toting classmates aren't as enthusiastic. "Yeah, they needle me about it. What a bunch of ones and zeros."

F Because I applied PT Sans to **body**, the whole page is styled with it.

Single Quotes vs. Double Quotes

The **@font-face** rules that Font Squirrel provides use single quotes around font family names instead of the double quotes shown in CSS examples throughout this book. Single quotes and double quotes work the same way in CSS, so use whichever method you prefer.

@font-face Methods

Roger Johansson has written an article summarizing two of the methods for using web fonts in your style sheets. The URL is quite long, but if you visit www.htmlcssvqs.com/8ed/face you will be redirected to the article within his site, www.456bereastreet.com. He covers Font Squirrel's method first, followed by the method I show you in this chapter.

As I said, I prefer the second method, but it does come with a potential limitation: If you use more than a total of four weights and styles of a *single* web font family—not of *all* web font families in your page—Internet Explorer 6–8 might convert certain weights to regular (normal) weight.

In practice, this isn't very limiting in the vast majority of cases. It's unlikely you will use more than four weights and styles for a single font in the first place. Remember that by using that many, you're typically requiring the browser to download more or larger font files than is desired.

On top of that, among those three versions of IE, only IE8 has a user base of any size in most parts of the world, and even that is diminishing at a decent clip. For example, at the time of this writing, IE8 is at 6.9% in Europe and 9.5% in North America. It was about 40% higher a year before that (http://gs.statcounter.com).

Local Teen Prefers Vinyl Over Digital

"It's *really* groovy,"

A In the example from the previous section, the browser artificially made the regular text a little fatter for the bold and a bit more slanted for the italic. What we want it to do is use the proper bold and italic that were designed for the font. For a refresher on faux italics and faux bold, see "Creating Italics" and "Applying Bold Formatting," respectively, in Chapter 10.

B We didn't use **font-weight: bold;** or **font-weight: italic;** anywhere in **example.css**.

```
body {
    font-family: 'PTSans', sans-serif;
    font-size: 100%;
    line-height: 1.25;
}

@font-face {
    font-family: 'PTSans';
    src: url('PTS55F-webfont.eot');
    ...
    font-weight: normal;
    font-style: normal;
}
```

C Our heading is in an **h1**, and the text we wish to stress is in an **em**.

```
...
<h1>Local Teen Prefers Vinyl Over Digital
 </h1>

<p>..."It's <em>really</em> groovy," she said,
 on the record...</p>
...
```

Applying Italics and Bold with a Web Font

A situation in which web fonts can act a little strangely is when you want to do what seems like the most basic styling of them. The thing to keep in mind is that web fonts come in only one weight and one style per font file. If you want to use bold or italic, you need to create separate **@font-face** rules for them, each referencing their own web font. Otherwise, the browser may apply faux bold or faux italic **A**. Or a double-whammy of faux bold italic, which you will see later.

In the previous section, we never specified any text to be bold or italic in our style sheet **B**. So why did those styles occur? I bet you've already figured it out. Browser default styles. The browser applied bold to the **h1** and italic to the **em C**, just as it does by default when you're not using a web font.

Fortunately, remedying this is easy. We'll follow steps that are similar to those for implementing a web font for regular text, but with a couple of changes to the CSS. As before, I'll use PT Sans as the example, but the steps can apply to any font you obtain from Font Squirrel.

To apply italic with a web font:

1. Look in the **web fonts** folder from the ZIP file that you downloaded from Font Squirrel in "Downloading Your First Web Font." If you see a sub-folder for the italic text version of the font, open the **stylesheet.css** file from that sub-folder.

2. Copy the **@font-face** rule for italic text and paste it into your style sheet **D**.

3. Copy the italic font files (that are referenced in your style sheet **D**) from the Font Squirrel folder to the folder that contains your style sheet **E**.

D Now **example.css** contains the **@font-face** rule for PT Sans Italic.

```css
body {
    font-family: 'PTSans', sans-serif;
    ...
}

/* Regular text */
@font-face {
    font-family: 'PTSans';
    src: url('PTS55F-webfont.eot');
    ...
}

/* Italic text */
@font-face {
    font-family: 'pt_sansitalic';
    src: url('PTS56F-webfont.eot');
    src: url('PTS56F-webfont.eot?#iefix')
        → format('embedded-opentype'),
        url('PTS56F-webfont.woff')
        → format('woff'),
        url('PTS56F-webfont.ttf')
        → format('truetype');
    font-weight: normal;
    font-style: normal;
}
```

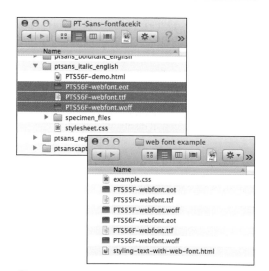

E I've copied the three font format files for PT Sans Italic from the Font Squirrel folder that I downloaded earlier (top) to my example folder (bottom).

F I've made two critical changes to the code. I've changed **font-family: 'pt_sansitalic'** to simply **font-family: 'PTSans'** to match the name in the regular text **@font-face** rule. And I've modified the **font-style** value in the italic text **@font-face** rule to reflect the style of the font.

```
body {
      font-family: 'PTSans', sans-serif;
      ...
}

/* Regular text */
@font-face {
      font-family: 'PTSans';
      src: url('PTS55F-webfont.eot');
      ...
      font-weight: normal;
      font-style: normal;
}

/* Italic text */
@font-face {
      font-family: 'PTSans';
      src: url('PTS56F-webfont.eot');
      ...
      font-weight: normal;
      font-style: italic;
}
```

"It's *really* groovy,"

"It's *really* groovy,"

G The difference between the faux italics from before (top) and the proper version that displays now (bottom) is especially evident in the "a" and "e." The real italic font is a tad smaller than the artificially slanted text, allowing it to fit naturally alongside regular text.

4. Rename the **font-family** value in the italic text **@font-face** rule so it is *the same* as in the rule for regular text **F**.

5. Change the **font-style** value in the italic text **@font-face** rule to **font-style: italic** **F**. Save your changes.

Now the italic web font will display wherever **font-style: italic;** exists in the browser default style sheet **G** or in your own **H**.

H Just to make the point, I've styled all paragraph text to display in italics. I won't leave it this way in subsequent examples.

```
body {
      font-family: 'PTSans', sans-serif;
      ...
}

p {
      font-style: italic;
}

/* Regular text */
@font-face {
      font-family: 'PTSans';
      src: url('PTS55F-webfont.eot');
      ...
      font-weight: normal;
      font-style: normal;
}

/* Italic text */
@font-face {
      font-family: 'PTSans';
      src: url('PTS56F-webfont.eot');
      ...
      font-weight: normal;
      font-style: italic;
}
```

To apply bold with a web font:

Applying bold is much the same as applying italic.

1. Follow steps 1–3 in "To apply italic with a web font," but use the files from the sub-folder for the *bold* version of the font. Paste the **@font-face** rule for *bold* text into your style sheet (step 2 from that section) 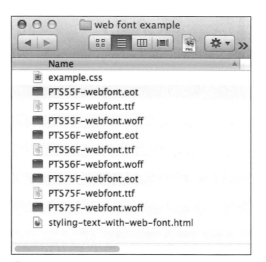 and copy the *bold* font files to your folder (step 3 from that section) 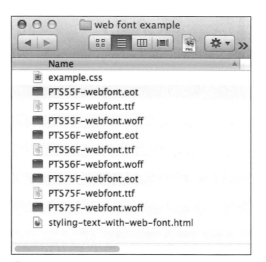.

 Now **example.css** contains the **@font-face** rule for PT Sans Bold.

```
...

... Regular and Italic @font-face rules ...

/* Bold text */
@font-face {
    font-family: 'pt_sansbold';
    src: url('PTS75F-webfont.eot');
    src: url('PTS75F-webfont.eot?#iefix')
        → format('embedded-opentype'),
        url('PTS75F-webfont.woff')
        → format('woff'),
        url('PTS75F-webfont.ttf')
        → format('truetype');
    font-weight: normal;
    font-style: normal;
}
```

 I've copied the three PT Sans Bold files from my Font Squirrel folder (not shown) to my example folder. The file names begin with **PTS75F**.

K I've changed `font-family: 'pt_sansbold'` to simply `font-family: 'PTSans'` to match the name in the other `@font-face` rules. Secondly, I've modified the `font-weight` value in the bold text `@font-face` rule to reflect the style of the font.

```
body {
     font-family: 'PTSans', sans-serif;
     ...
}

/* Regular text */
@font-face {
     font-family: 'PTSans';
     ...
     font-weight: normal;
     font-style: normal;
}

/* Italic text */
@font-face {
     font-family: 'PTSans';
     ...
     font-weight: normal;
     font-style: italic;
}

/* Bold text */
@font-face {
     font-family: 'PTSans';
     src: url('PTS75F-webfont.eot');
     ...
     font-weight: bold;
     font-style: normal;
}
```

2. Rename the `font-family` value in the bold text `@font-face` rule so it is *the same* as in the other rules for the font **K**.

3. Change the `font-weight` value in the bold text `@font-face` rule to `font-weight: bold` **K**. Save your changes.

Now the bold web font will display on whatever elements browsers make bold by default (like the **h1** in **L**) or that you specify in your own style sheets. For example, adding **p { font-weight: bold; }** to **K** would make all paragraph text bold (with a side effect on **em**, mentioned shortly).

L If you compare the faux bold from before (top) to the proper version (bottom), you can see that the letters are cleaner and spaced more appropriately in the latter. Furthermore, we now have proper bold for the heading, proper italic for the **em** text, and regular text for everything else.

To apply bold italic with a web font:

Previously, we saw how to apply a web font for regular (normal), italic, or bold text. This leaves us with one unaccounted for combination: Making text both bold *and* italic.

Remember, each web font handles only one weight and one style. Of the three PT Sans fonts we've implemented **K**, none is for **font-weight: bold** *and* **font-style: italic**. Just one or the other, or neither in the case of regular text. This is why the code in **M** doesn't work as you might expect. (Incidentally, it's also why **em** would get fake styling from **p { font-weight: bold; }**—it would inherit the bold from **p**.)

Let's add Bold Italic to our page:

1. Follow steps 1–3 in "To apply italic with a web font," but use the files from the sub-folder for the *bold italic* version of the font. Paste the **@font-face** rule for *bold italic* text into your style sheet (step 2 from that section) **N** and copy the *bold italic* font format files to your folder (step 3 from that section) **O**.

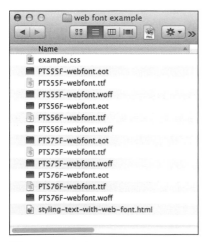

O I've copied the three PT Sans Bold Italic files from my Font Squirrel folder (not shown) to my example folder. The file names begin with **PTS76F**.

M I've added a rule to the style sheet from **K** in an attempt to make **em** text both italic (the default) and bold. Except there's a problem: We haven't loaded the PT Sans Bold Italic font, so the **em** has fake styling (admittedly, it's harder to detect).

```
body {
    font-family: 'PTSans', sans-serif;
    ...
}

em {
    font-weight: bold;
}

... @font-face rules ...
```

"It's *really* groovy,"

N Building off **M**, now **example.css** contains the **@font-face** rule for PT Sans Bold Italic.

```
...

em {
    font-weight: bold;
}

... other @font-face rules ...

/* Bold Italic text */
@font-face {
    font-family: 'pt_sansbold_italic';
    src: url('PTS76F-webfont.eot');
    src: url('PTS76F-webfont.eot?#iefix')
        → format('embedded-opentype'),
        url('PTS76F-webfont.woff')
        → format('woff'),
        url('PTS76F-webfont.ttf')
        → format('truetype');
    font-weight: normal;
    font-style: normal;
}
```

P I've changed **font-family: 'pt_sansbold_ italic'** to simply **font-family: 'PTSans'** to match the name in the other **@font-face** rules. I've also modified the **font-weight** and **font-style** values in the new rule to reflect the style of the font.

```
body {
    font-family: 'PTSans', sans-serif;
    ...
}

em {
    font-weight: bold;
}

/* Regular text */
@font-face {
    font-family: 'PTSans';
    ...
    font-weight: normal;
    font-style: normal;
}

/* Italic text */
@font-face {
    font-family: 'PTSans';
    ...
    font-weight: normal;
    font-style: italic;
}

/* Bold text */
@font-face {
    font-family: 'PTSans';
    ...
    font-weight: bold;
    font-style: normal;
}

/* Bold Italic text */
@font-face {
    font-family: 'PTSans';
    src: url('PTS76F-webfont.eot');
    ...
    font-weight: bold;
    font-style: italic;
}
```

2. Rename the **font-family** value in the bold text **@font-face** rule so it is *the same* as in the other rules for the font **P**.

3. Change the **font-weight** value in the bold italic text **@font-face** rule to **font-weight: bold**. Also, change the **font-style** value to **font-style: italic** **P**. Save your changes **Q**.

continues on next page

"It's *really* groovy,"

"It's *really* groovy,"

Q The difference is subtle, but the letters in the faked effect (top) are a little fatter and are spaced farther apart than in the proper font (bottom).

TIP If a web font does not have bold, italic, or bold italic versions but you apply one of those text treatments, browsers may apply faux styling.

TIP Some fonts, like ChunkFive, are heavy by nature and don't have alternative forms. You use them at `font-weight: normal;` (their regular state) because `font-weight: bold;` would make browsers fake an even bolder rendering.

TIP Remember that each style and weight that requires a new font file adds to the file size that the browser needs to download. This can affect performance. For this reason, many designers choose to use web fonts only for headlines.

TIP With all sorts of different files in it, our folder got pretty messy **O**. Now you can see why I recommend putting your style sheets and fonts in separate folders! Figure **R** shows one way to organize them. You would need to change each `url` in your style sheet to reflect this. For example, `url('font/PTS55F-webfont.woff')`. Also, you would need to change your HTML so the `link` element looks for your style sheet in the right location: `<link rel="stylesheet" href="css/example.css" />`.

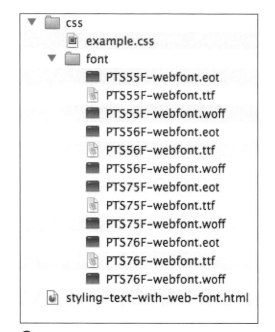

R With this structure, all font files are in the **font** folder, which is within the **css** folder.

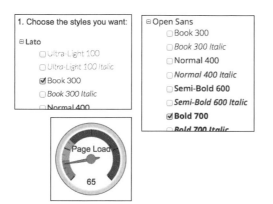

A I'm adding Lato to my collection of web fonts. Though not shown, I also added Open Sans. These are the fonts I used for the headings in the page shown throughout most of Chapters 11 and 12.

B The bottom of the page lists the fonts you have chosen (top). That same area has three buttons (bottom). The Choose button is for where you are now—browsing through fonts and choosing the ones you like. Click the Review button to see more samples and other information for the fonts in your collection. Click the Use button to use the fonts in your page.

C My webpage needs only one weight for each web font. The Page Load meter indicates how much the size of the font files could affect webpages that use the fonts. I'm in pretty good shape now, but if I were to add another weight, it would take browsers even longer to load my pages.

Using Web Fonts from Google Fonts

The previous sections explained how to add self-hosted web fonts to your page, using a font from Font Squirrel as an example. Google Fonts, on the other hand, is one of several web font services that host the web fonts for you. (See "What Is a Web Font.")

Like other web font services, Google Fonts saves you the trouble of creating or modifying any `@font-face` rules. That is one clear difference (advantage, some would say) between self-hosting fonts and using a service like Google Fonts.

Google Fonts has become a popular choice because it's free (unlike most of these services), has hundreds of fonts, and allows you to add a web font to your page in less than a minute once you know how it works. Once you've selected a font, all you have to do is drop one line of Google Fonts code into your HTML page, and then style your text as you please with CSS.

To use a web font from Google Fonts:

1. Browse www.google.com/fonts. When you find a font you like, click Add to Collection **A**.

2. Scroll to the bottom of the page and click Use **B**.

3. Select only the weights and styles you intend to use. This helps keep the size of your font files as small as possible **C**.

continues on next page

4. Select only the character sets your content requires **D**. This also affects the size of your font files.

5. Copy the `link` element code **E** and paste it into the `head` of your webpage **F**.

---

2. Choose the character sets you want:

☑ Latin (latin) ☐ Cyrillic Extended (cyrillic-ext)

☐ Greek Extended (greek-ext) ☐ Greek (greek)

☐ Vietnamese (vietnamese)

☐ Latin Extended (latin-ext) ☐ Cyrillic (cyrillic)

D Subset your fonts to the characters your content needs. Latin is the default.

Standard	@import	Javascript

3. Add this code to your website:

```
<link href='http://fonts.googleapis.com/css?family=Lat
```

E Copy the `link` code in the Standard tab.

F I've pasted the `link` code from Google Fonts before the `link` for my own style sheet (**style.css**). Note that the `href` URL in the Google Fonts `link` contains the font families and weights I selected earlier (**B** and **C**). This will load all the web font files and the **@font-face** rules needed to use them.

```
<!DOCTYPE html>
<html lang="en">
<head>
     <meta charset="utf-8" />
     <title>Le Journal</title>
     <link href="http://fonts.googleapis.
      → com/css?family=Lato:300|Open+
      → Sans:700" rel="stylesheet" />
     <link rel="stylesheet" href="style.css"
/>
</head>
<body>
...
<h1>Sunny East Garden at the Getty Villa</h1>

<p>It is hard to believe, but there are
 → about...</p>


...

<h2>Popular Posts</h2>
...
</body>
</html>
```

G Google Fonts (at bottom) shows you how to reference the font families. I've applied **Lato** at a weight of **300** to **h1** elements and **Open Sans** at a weight of **700** to **h2** elements. Those `font-weight` numbers match the numbers in the `link` element **F**, which match the weights I selected **C**. The other CSS shown here is not required to make the web fonts work.

```
body {
    font: 100%/1.2 Georgia, 'Times New
Roman', serif;
}

h1 {
    color: #333;
    font-family: 'Lato', sans-serif;
    font-size: 3.25em; /* 52px/16px */
    font-weight: 300;
    letter-spacing: -2px;
    line-height: .975;
    margin-bottom: .4125em;
}

h2 {
    border-bottom: 1px solid #dbdbdb;
    font-family: 'Open Sans', sans-serif;
    font-size: .875em;  /* 15px/16px */
    font-weight: 700;
    text-transform: uppercase;
    padding-bottom: .75em;
}

... more CSS for the page ...
```

---

4. Integrate the fonts into your CSS:

The Google Fonts API will generate the necessary browser-specific CSS to use the fonts. All you need to do is add the font name to your CSS styles. For example:

```
font-family: 'Lato', sans-serif;

font-family: 'Open Sans', sans-serif;
```

6. Style your text with the web font by using the `font-family` name specified by Google Fonts. Set the `font-weight` to one of the weights you selected in step 3 **G**. If you are using an italic web font, set `font-style: italic;` in your CSS rule as well.

7. Save your HTML page and style sheet.

Checking the page in a browser **H** reveals the glory of web fonts!

> **TIP** If you want to style any of your text in italic, make sure you choose the italic version of the font when selecting your styles (step 3) and specify the proper `font-weight` value and `font-style: italic` in your CSS (step 6). Otherwise, the font might render in faux italic. Similarly, browsers might display faux bold if you don't account for the bold version of the font. See examples and further discussion of these faked text treatments in "Applying Italics and Bold with a Web Font" (this chapter), and "Creating Italics" and "Applying Bold Formatting" in Chapter 10.

Sunny East Garden at the Getty Villa

It is hard to believe, but there are about 300 varieties of plants at the East Garden at the Getty, making the experience truly remarkable. This area is one of the most tranquil spaces at the

POPULAR POSTS

The City Named After Queen Victoria »

Heaven on Earth? Let's Have

H The big heading is Lato, and the small bold one is Open Sans.

Enhancements and Effects with CSS

One of the challenges faced by website authors until a few years ago was the limited number of options for producing rich designs using CSS. In most cases, it meant using additional HTML and CSS and a lot of images. Combined, this resulted in pages that were more complicated, took longer to download and display in the browser, and were simply more fragile and difficult to maintain.

Browsers' rapid adoption of many new CSS3 properties changed things for the better. Today, it's possible to create rounded corners, gradients, and drop shadows, to adjust transparency, and to do much more by using only CSS. You will see how in this chapter while also learning how to approach older browsers that do not support these features.

The result is webpages that use less markup and fewer images, and that typically download and display faster as a result. This benefits all users, but especially those on less powerful devices such as smartphones.

Browser Compatibility, Progressive Enhancement, and Polyfills

Because the pace at which browsers are evolving has increased significantly in recent years, it's important to understand when you can expect reliable support for these new CSS properties. Here's a snapshot of when browsers began providing basic support for each property covered in this chapter Ⓐ.

The versions listed for most browsers are ancient history, but IE8 is still hanging on a bit. It's about 8.5 percent of the worldwide market and trending downward at the time of this writing. Its users can't enjoy most of the features discussed in this chapter, but that's OK, as you will see.

Progressive enhancement

At various times you've heard me mention progressive enhancement. I discussed it first in the book's introduction. Briefly, it emphasizes creating content and functionality that is accessible to all users regardless of web browser while providing more-capable browsers an enhanced experience. In simpler terms, it means that it's perfectly acceptable for websites to look and behave differently in different web browsers as long as the content is accessible.

An example of this in practice is Dribbble (http://dribbble.com) Ⓑ, which uses CSS3 to provide a richer experience in modern browsers. Older browsers, such as Internet Explorer 8 Ⓒ, are presented a slightly different visual experience but with no loss of functionality.

	🦊	ⓔ	🌐	🧭	🅞
border-radius	3.0	9.0	1.0	3.1	10.5
box-shadow	3.5	9.0	1.0	3.1	10.5
text-shadow	3.5	10.0	1.0	3.1	9.5
multiple backgrounds	3.6	9.0	1.0	3.1	10.5
gradients	3.6	10.0	2.0	4.0	11.1
opacity	1.0	9.0	1.0	3.1	9.0
:before and :after	1.0	8.0	1.0	3.1	9.0

Ⓐ This table focuses on desktop browsers, but let's not forget mobile, which grows in importance every day. For mobile support information and more details about desktop browsers, look up each property on Alexis Deveria's indispensable site Can I Use (www.caniuse.com). It is the source of most of the information in the table. You can find a nice, but less detailed, support summary at http://fmbip.com/litmus/.

Ⓑ The Dribbble site uses **border-radius** and **box-shadow** to provide an enhanced experience for users with modern browsers, but it is built with less-capable browsers in mind Ⓒ.

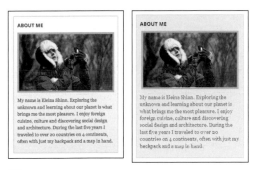

C When viewed in older browsers (such as IE8) that do not support **border-radius** or **box-shadow**, the experience differs. The slight shadow on the drop-down menu is missing, and rounded corners are simply squared off. Everything still works. This is one example of progressive enhancement.

D On the left is what modern browsers display. IE8 (right) and other older browsers show a simpler version.

More CSS3 Effects

Alas, CSS3 provides more effects than could fit in these pages. Chief among them are transforms, transitions, and animations. For example, you can create a gradual hover effect:

```
a { /* removed prefixes for brevity */
    color: #007c21;
    transition: color .4s ease;
}
a:hover { color: #00bf32; }
```

See www.htmlcssvqs.com/resources/ for links to learn more.

Later in the chapter, you'll learn how to apply a subtle gradient and drop shadow to the About Me box from Chapters 11 and 12 **D**. IE8 displays a solid background and no drop shadow, but the content is still legible.

Using polyfills for non-supporting browsers

There may be times when you want to bridge the gap between a less-capable browser and modern ones by using *poly-fills* (or *shims*, as they're often called).

Typically implemented using JavaScript, polyfills enable a degree of support for HTML5 APIs and CSS3 properties in less-capable browsers while silently falling back to official support when the capabilities exist natively in a browser. It's important to note that these generally incur a perfor-mance penalty, because JavaScript is measurably slower in less-capable brows-ers (particularly in older versions of IE).

Speaking of IE, Jason Johnston's CSS3 PIE (http://css3pie.com) is one of the best-known polyfills. It provides support to Internet Explorer 6 through 9 for most of the CSS3 effects discussed in this chapter. (Of them, IE9 requires PIE to display linear gradients only; it has native support for the others.)

TIP HTML5 Please (http://html5please.com) is a great resource for finding out which HTML5 and CSS3 features are safe to use and which polyfills are best for filling the gaps.

TIP Modernizr (www.modernizr.com) is a JavaScript library that detects whether a browser supports various HTML5 and CSS3 features. You can use the information it pro-vides to customize your scripts and styles.

Understanding Vendor Prefixes

It takes years for a CSS3 specification to reach the W3C's Recommendation status (meaning that it's final). Browsers typically implement features prior to this as part of the W3C process for developing specifications. It informs where the standards can be improved before being locked down.

In the initial stages of including a feature, browsers routinely used to implement them with what are called *vendor prefixes* 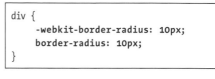. These allowed each browser to introduce its own support for a property in order to get feedback and as a safeguard in case the specification changes.

However, this approach got messy, so most browsers are moving away from using vendor prefixes. As you will see in this chapter, there remain some instances in which you may want to use them, at least until the older browsers that rely on them have an insignificant user base.

Each of the major browsers has its own prefix: `-webkit-` (Webkit/Safari/older versions of Chrome), `-moz-` (Firefox), `-ms-` (Internet Explorer), and `-o-` (Opera). They are used by placing the prefix before the CSS property name 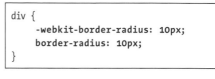. Nowadays, you'll need only `-webkit-` in most cases.

> **TIP** Not all CSS3 properties, such as `text-shadow` and `opacity`, require the use of prefixes for any browser, as you will see.

> **TIP** Several tools that create CSS3 code (including prefixes) for you are available online 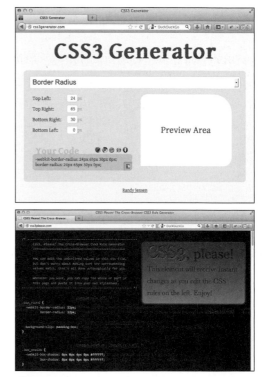. CSS3 Please! also indicates which browsers support the non-prefixed syntax and which ones require a prefix. This is very helpful when determining whether to include a prefix—you may decide it's fine that those browsers won't show the effect.

A An example of the **border-radius** property, which requires using the **-webkit-** prefix to support older versions of Android, iOS, and Safari browsers. More recent versions of those browsers no longer use the prefixed property and instead use the proper property (that is, simply **border-radius: 10px;**). As always, the last competing declaration in a rule takes precedence, which is why the non-prefixed, standard version should be last.

```
div {
    -webkit-border-radius: 10px;
    border-radius: 10px;
}
```

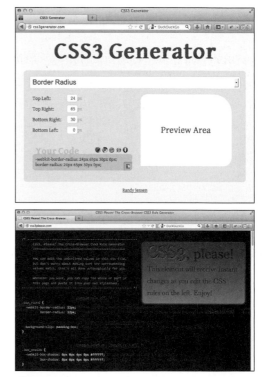

B CSS3 Generator (www.css3generator.com), by Randy Jensen, and CSS3, Please! (css3please.com), by Paul Irish and Jonathan Neal, remove the repetitious work of writing prefixed and non-prefixed CSS properties yourself. CSS preprocessors like LESS, Sass, and Stylus are even more convenient for this task. See http://css-tricks.com/how-to-deal-with-vendor-prefixes/ for more information and other vendor prefix ideas.

Ⓐ This document contains example **div**s with **class** attributes. Each is used to illustrate a different use of **border-radius** and the different syntaxes for setting all corners equally, for setting a single corner individually using the long-form syntax, for creating an elliptical corner, and for shapes such as circles.

```
...
<body>
<div class="all-corners"></div>
<div class="one-corner"></div>
<div class="elliptical-corners"></div>
<div class="circle"></div>
</body>
</html>
```

Ⓑ The CSS for the four **border-radius** examples, including the vendor-prefixed properties necessary to support older versions of Android, Mobile Safari, and Safari browsers. A value of **75px** for **.circle** would have the same effect as **50%** because the element is 150×150.

```
div {
    background: #999;
    float: left;
    height: 150px;
    margin: 10px;
    width: 150px;
}

.all-corners {
    -webkit-border-radius: 20px;
    border-radius: 20px;
}

.one-corner {
    -webkit-border-top-left-radius: 75px;
    border-top-left-radius: 75px;
}

.elliptical-corners {
    -webkit-border-radius: 50px / 20px;
    border-radius: 50px / 20px;
}

.circle {
    -webkit-border-radius: 50%;
    border-radius: 50%;
}
```

Rounding the Corners of Elements

Using CSS3, you can round the corners of most elements, including form elements, images, and even paragraphs of text, without needing additional markup or images (**Ⓐ** through **Ⓔ**).

continues on next page

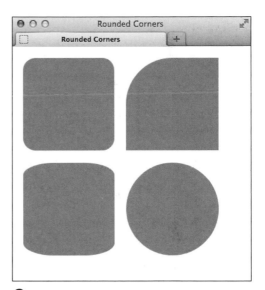

Ⓒ Browsers that support the **border-radius** property with or without vendor prefixes should render the examples similarly to these. Note that there are subtle visual differences between implementations, particularly in older versions of Safari and Firefox.

Like the **border**, `margin`, and **padding** properties, a **border-radius** can be defined in long-form or shorthand syntaxes (**F** and **G**). Include the **-webkit-** prefix only if you want the effect to show in really old versions of Android, Mobile Safari, and Safari browsers (http://caniuse.com/#feat=border-radius).

To round all corners of an element equally:

1. Optionally, type **-webkit-border-radius: *r***, where *r* is the radius value of the corners, expressed as a length (with units).

2. Type **border-radius: *r***, where *r* is the same value as in step 1 **B**. This is the standard shorthand property syntax.

To round one corner of an element:

1. Optionally, type **-webkit-border-top-left-radius: *r***, where *r* is the radius value of the top-left corner, expressed as a length (with units).

2. Type **border-top-left-radius: *r***, where *r* is the same value as in step 1 **B**. This is the standard long-form property syntax.

   Note that these steps describe how to style the top-left corner only, but you can style the other corners individually too. Here's how:

   ▸ To round the top-right corner: Replace **top-left** in steps 1 and 2 with **top-right**.

   ▸ To round the bottom-right corner: Replace **top-left** in steps 1 and 2 with **bottom-right**.

   ▸ To round the bottom-left corner: Replace **top-left** in steps 1 and 2 with **bottom-left**.

D Here's a real-world example, applying rounded corners to our familiar About Me module from earlier in the book **E**. Note that the rule for the image combines styling the **border** and the **border-radius**.

```
.about {
    background-color: #2b2b2b;
    border-radius: 10px;
    padding: .3125em .625em .625em;
}

.about img {
    border: 5px solid #bebebe;
    border-radius: 15px;
}
```

E The rounded corners on the outside are a little subtler than the 15-pixel **border-radius** applied to the image. Older browsers would show square corners for both, making this module look like it does in Chapters 11 and 12.

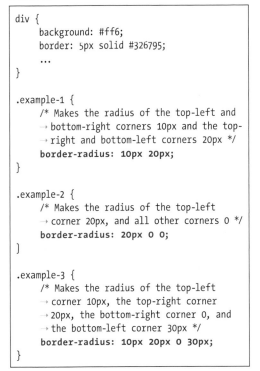 More examples of how you can use shorthand to style more than one corner rather than writing out **border-top-left-radius** and so on. I've omitted the **-webkit-** prefixed versions for brevity, but they otherwise would be the same as what is shown.

```
div {
    background: #ff6;
    border: 5px solid #326795;
    ...
}

.example-1 {
    /* Makes the radius of the top-left and
    → bottom-right corners 10px and the top-
    → right and bottom-left corners 20px */
    border-radius: 10px 20px;
}

.example-2 {
    /* Makes the radius of the top-left
    → corner 20px, and all other corners 0 */
    border-radius: 20px 0 0;
}

.example-3 {
    /* Makes the radius of the top-left
    → corner 10px, the top-right corner
    → 20px, the bottom-right corner 0, and
    → the bottom-left corner 30px */
    border-radius: 10px 20px 0 30px;
}
```

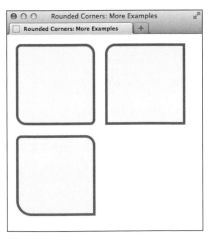

 The corners are styled just as if you'd used the long-form syntax.

To create elliptical corners:

1. Optionally, type **-webkit-border-radius: x / y**, where *x* is the horizontal radius value of the corners and *y* is the vertical radius value of the corners, expressed as a length (with units). The values should be separated by a forward slash.

2. Type **border-radius: x / y**, where *x* and *y* are the same values as in step 1 **B**.

To create a circle using border-radius:

1. Optionally, type **-webkit-border-radius: r**, where *r* is the radius value of the element (with length units). To create a circle, you can use the short-form syntax, and the value of *r* should be half the height or width of the element.

2. Type **border-radius: r**, where *r* is the same value as in step 1 **C**. This is the standard, non-prefixed syntax.

TIP Older browsers that don't support **border-radius** will simply render the element with square corners.

TIP **border-radius** rounds only the corners of the element you apply it to, not its children. So, if a child has a background, it may show in one or more of the parent's corners that you might expect to be rounded.

TIP Sometimes a bit of an element's background (not its child's in this case) can leak through its rounded corner. Add **background-clip: padding-box;** to the element's rule after the **border-radius** declaration to prevent this.

TIP Figures **D**, **E**, and **G** demonstrate combining **border** and **border-radius**.

TIP The **border-radius** property is not inherited.

Adding Drop Shadows to Text

Originally included as part of the CSS2 specification, removed in CSS2.1, and later resurrected in CSS3, the `text-shadow` property allows you to add dynamic drop-shadow effects to text in elements such as paragraphs and headings (**Ⓐ** through **Ⓓ**).

To add a drop shadow to an element's text:

1. Type `text-shadow:`.

2. Type the values for *x-offset*, *y-offset*, *blur-radius* (all three with length units), and *color* without commas separating them. For example, **-2px 3px 7px #999**. The value for *blur-radius* is optional. (See the tips for more about what values are allowed.)

To add multiple drop-shadow styles to an element's text:

1. Type `text-shadow:`.

2. Type the values for *x-offset*, *y-offset*, *blur-radius* (all three with length units), and *color* without commas separating them. The value for *blur-radius* is optional.

3. Type **,** (a comma).

4. Repeat step 2 using different values as desired.

To reset `text-shadow` to its default value:

Type `text-shadow: none;`.

Ⓐ The paragraphs and class names I'll use to demonstrate the use of `text-shadow`.

```
...
<body>

<p class="basic">Basic Shadow</p>
<p class="basic-negative">Basic Shadow</p>
<p class="blur">Blur Radius</p>
<p class="blur-inversed">Blur Radius</p>
<p class="multiple">Multiple Text Shadows</p>

</body>
</html>
```

Ⓑ These classes demonstrate some of the variety that `text-shadow` affords. The first, second, and fifth omit a blur radius value. The `.multiple` class shows it's possible to add more than one drop shadow to a single element by separating the sets of property values with a comma. This allows you to combine drop shadows to create unique and interesting effects.

```
p {
    color: #222; /* nearly black */
    font-size: 4.5em;
    font-weight: bold;
}

.basic {
    text-shadow: 3px 3px #aaa;
}

.basic-negative { /* negative offsets */
    text-shadow: -4px -2px #ccc;
}

.blur {
    text-shadow: 2px 2px 10px grey;
}

.blur-inversed {
    color: white;
    text-shadow: 2px 2px 10px #000;
}

.multiple {
    text-shadow:
        2px 2px white,
        6px 6px rgba(50,50,50,.25);
}
```

Basic Shadow

Basic Shadow

Blur Radius

Blur Radius

Multiple Text Shadows

⊙ The first paragraph has positive offsets, and the second one has negative offsets. (Offsets don't need to be either both negative or both positive.) Neither paragraph has a blur radius, but the third and fourth paragraphs do. The fourth one is inversed because I set the text color to white **ⓑ**. The last one has two text shadows, but you could add more.

TIP Vendor prefixes are not needed for the `text-shadow` property.

TIP The property accepts four values: `x-offset` with length units, `y-offset` with length units, an optional `blur-radius` with length units, and finally a `color` value. If you do not specify the blur radius, it is assumed to be zero (**ⓑ** has three examples of this).

TIP The `x-offset` and `y-offset` values can be positive or negative integers; that is, both 1px and -1px are valid. The `blur-radius` value cannot be a negative integer. All three values can also be zero.

TIP Color can be specified using hex, RGB, RGBA, or HSLA values (see "CSS colors" in Chapter 7).

TIP Although the syntax may appear similar, it's not possible to individually specify the four property values for `text-shadow` as you can for borders and backgrounds.

TIP The initial property value is `none` if not set.

TIP The `text-shadow` property is inherited.

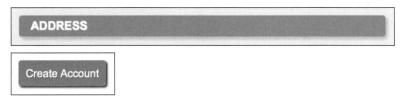

ⓓ This heading and form button from Chapter 16 use both **text-shadow** and **box-shadow** (explained in the next section). The code is available at www.htmlcssvqs.com/8ed/16.

Adding Drop Shadows to Elements

The **text-shadow** property allows you to apply shadows to an element's text, but the **box-shadow** property allows you to add shadows to the elements themselves (Ⓐ through Ⓕ). Although based on the same basic set of values, **box-shadow** allows two more optional values: the **inset** keyword and a *spread* value to expand or shrink the shadow.

Ⓐ This document contains six **div**s with classes that I'll use to demonstrate various **box-shadow** effects.

```
...
<body>
<div class="shadow">
    <p>Shadow with Blur</p>
</div>

<div class="shadow-negative">
    <p>Shadow with Negative Offsets and
    → Blur</p>
</div>

<div class="shadow-spread">
    <p>Shadow with Blur and Spread</p>
</div>

<div class="shadow-offsets-0">
    <p>Shadow with Offsets Zero, Blur, and
    → Spread</p>
</div>

<div class="inset-shadow">
    <p>Inset Shadow</p>
</div>

<div class="multiple">
    <p>Multiple Shadows</p>
</div>
</body>
</html>
```

Ⓑ Each of the first five classes applies a single, but different, shadow. The last one applies two shadows (you can add more). Browsers that don't understand **box-shadow** will simply ignore those CSS rules and render the page without the shadows.

```
div {
    background: #fff;
    ...
}

.shadow {
    -webkit-box-shadow: 4px 4px 5px #999;
    box-shadow: 4px 4px 5px #999;
}

.shadow-negative {
    -webkit-box-shadow: -4px -4px 5px
    → #999;
    box-shadow: -4px -4px 5px #999;
}

.shadow-spread {
    -webkit-box-shadow: 4px 4px 5px 3px
    → #999;
    box-shadow: 4px 4px 5px 3px #999;
}

.shadow-offsets-0 {
    -webkit-box-shadow: 0 0 9px 3px #999;
    box-shadow: 0 0 9px 3px #999;
}

.inset-shadow {
    -webkit-box-shadow: 2px 2px 10px #666
    → inset;
    box-shadow: 2px 2px 10px #666 inset;
}

.multiple {
    -webkit-box-shadow:
        2px 2px 10px rgba(255,0,0,.75),
        5px 5px 20px blue;

    box-shadow:
        2px 2px 10px rgba(255,0,0,.75),
        5px 5px 20px blue;
}
```

Supporting browsers show the sampling of **box-shadow** effects.

This element is styled with **box-shadow: 0 20px 10px -11px #999;**. The negative spread value makes the shadow narrower than the element. The **0** x-offset value means the shadow won't appear to the left or right of the element.

The **box-shadow** property also differs from its **text-shadow** counterpart in that it requires the **-webkit-** vendor prefix if you want the effect to show in older versions of the Android, Mobile Safari, and Safari browsers. See http://caniuse.com/#search=box-shadow for the latest support information. You may decide to omit the prefix.

The **box-shadow** property accepts six values: *x-offset* and *y-offset* with length units, an optional *blur-radius* with length unit, an optional *spread* value with length unit, an optional *color* value, and an optional **inset** keyword. If you do not specify the optional *blur-radius* or *spread* values, they are assumed to be zero.

To add a drop shadow to an element:

1. Type **-webkit-box-shadow:** .

2. Type the values for *x-offset*, *y-offset*, *blur-radius*, *spread* (all four with length units), and *color* without commas separating them. For example, **2px 2px 3px 5px #333**.

3. Type **box-shadow:** and repeat step 2.

To create an inset shadow:

1. Type **-webkit-box-shadow:** .

2. Type the values for *x-offset*, *y-offset*, *blur-radius*, *spread* (all four with length units), and *color* without commas separating them. For example, **2px 2px 3px 5px #333**.

3. Type a space followed by **inset**. (Alternatively, add **inset** and a space before step 2.)

4. Type **box-shadow:** and repeat steps 2 and 3.

To apply multiple shadows to an element:

1. Type **-webkit-box-shadow:** to begin the style.

2. Type the values for *x-offset*, *y-offset*, *blur-radius*, *spread* (all four with length units), and *color* without commas separating them. For example, **2px 2px 3px 5px #333**. Include the **inset** keyword as desired.

3. Type **,** (a comma).

4. Repeat step 2 using different values for each of the properties.

5. Type **box-shadow:** and repeat steps 2 through 4.

To reset box-shadow to its default value:

1. Type **-webkit-box-shadow: none;**.

2. Type **box-shadow: none;**.

TIP The *x-offset*, *y-offset*, and *spread* values can be positive or negative integers; that is, both 1px and -1px are valid. The *blur-radius* value must be a positive integer. The values for each of these attributes can also be zero.

TIP You can use a negative *spread* value to make the shadow smaller than the element to which it's applied .

TIP Color can be specified using hex, RGB, RGBA, or HSLA values (see "CSS colors" in Chapter 7).

TIP The initial property value is none if not set.

TIP The **inset** keyword puts the shadow inside the element.

TIP The box-shadow property is not inherited.

E Here's a real-world example using the About Me box from Chapters 11 and 12. I've set both offsets to zero so the subtle shadow will appear on all sides.

```
.about {
    border: 1px solid #d0d0d0;
    -webkit-box-shadow: 0 0 3px #d0d0d0;
    box-shadow: 0 0 3px #d0d0d0;
    padding: 0.313em 0.625em 0.625em;
}
```

ABOUT ME

My name is Eleina Shinn. Exploring the unknown and learning about our planet is what brings me the most pleasure. I enjoy foreign cuisine, culture and discovering social design and architecture. During the last five years I traveled to over 20 countries on 4 continents, often with just my backpack and a map in hand.

F The About Me box gets a new treatment. This time it has a one-pixel border and a subtle shadow on all four sides. (The dark background color has been replaced by the default white.)

A I'll apply multiple backgrounds to the single `div` that has `class="night-sky"`.

```
...
<body>
<div class="night-sky">
    <h1>In the night sky...</h1>
</div>
</body>
</html>
```

B First, define a **background-color** to benefit visitors with older browsers. This is optional but recommended to ensure your content is accessible. Then define the properties to load and position your background images, and declare how they should repeat, if at all.

```
.night-sky {
    background-color: navy; /* fallback */
    background-image:
        url(ufo.png), url(stars.png),
        url(stars.png), url(sky.png);

    background-position:
        50% 102%, 100% -150px,
        0 -150px, 50% 100%;

    background-repeat:
        no-repeat, no-repeat,
        no-repeat, repeat-x;

    height: 300px;
    margin: 0 auto;
    padding-top: 36px;
    width: 75%;
}
```

Applying Multiple Backgrounds

CSS3 also introduced the ability to specify multiple backgrounds on a single HTML element (**A** through **C**). This simplifies your HTML code by reducing the need for elements whose sole purpose is to attach additional images using CSS. Multiple backgrounds can be applied to just about any element.

C Browsers that support multiple backgrounds will render our example by layering the images on top of each other, with the first one in the comma-separated list at the top of the stacking order.

To apply multiple background images to a single element:

1. Type **background-color: *b***, where *b* is the color you want applied as the background for older browsers to show .

2. Type **background-image: *u***, where *u* is a comma-separated list of **url** values that point to your images.

3. Type **background-position: *p***, where *p* is a comma-separated set of positive or negative *x-offset* and *y-offset* pairs with length units or keywords (for example, **center top**). There should be one set of coordinates for each URL specified in step 2.

4. Type **background-repeat: *r***, where *r* is a comma-separated list of **repeat-x**, **repeat-y**, or **no-repeat** values. There should be one value for each URL specified in step 2.

D IE8 (shown) and other old browsers that don't support multiple background images will display the **background-color** you specify as a fallback.

E This is the same as **B** except it's written in shorthand, and IE8 and other older browsers are given both a background color and image **F**. For supporting browsers, the result is the same as **C**.

```
.night-sky {
    /* fallback color and img */
    background: navy url(ufo.png) no repeat
center bottom;

    background:
        url(ufo.png) no-repeat 50% 102%,
        url(stars.png) no-repeat 100% -150px,
        url(stars.png) no-repeat 0 -150px,
        url(sky.png) repeat-x 50% 100%;

    ...
}
```

TIP See "Setting the Background" in Chapter 10 for more information about the properties listed in the steps.

TIP You can use the standard `background` shorthand syntax with multiple background images by separating each set of background parameters with a comma **E**. As a bonus, this allows you to specify both a fallback background color and image for older browsers **F**.

TIP Vendor prefixes are not required when specifying multiple backgrounds.

F Older browsers now display a version of the page that's more representative of the enhanced version **C**.

Using Gradient Backgrounds

Gradient backgrounds, also a feature of CSS3, allow you to create transitions from one color to another without using images (Ⓐ through Ⓚ).

There are two primary styles of gradients: linear (Ⓑ through Ⓔ, Ⓙ and Ⓚ) and radial (Ⓕ through Ⓗ). Each has a different set of required and optional parameters. Browsers automatically determine the transitions between colors unless you specify the color stop position of one or more colors yourself Ⓘ.

The syntax for CSS gradients has changed during the specification process. The current syntax is stable, but unfortunately several browsers use an older syntax. Consequently, a lot of vendor-prefixed code

Ⓐ This will serve as the HTML for all CSS gradient examples except Ⓙ and Ⓚ. It contains a series of **div**s, each with a class I'll use to apply the gradients. (In case you're wondering, gradients work on most elements, not only **div**.) The complete version of this page is available on the companion website.

```
...
<body>
<div class="vertical-down"><p>default</p>
→ </div>
<div class="vertical-up"><p>to top</p></div>
<div class="horizontal-rt"><p>to right</p>
→ </div>

... rest of the divs with classes ...
</body>
</html>
```

Ⓑ A CSS gradient is a background image, so the properties used in this and the other examples could be **background-image** instead of the shorthand **background**. Always apply a baseline background for older browsers before the background with the gradient. By default, a linear gradient goes from top to bottom, so you don't have to specify **to bottom** in the property value. Making it run in the opposite direction is just a matter of including **to top**. The gradient goes from silver to black based on the direction specified.

```
.vertical-down { /* default */
    background: silver; /* fallback */
    background: linear-gradient(silver,
    → black);
}

.vertical-up {
background: silver;
    background: linear-gradient(to top,
    → silver, black);
}
```

Ⓒ Specify the direction of a horizontal gradient with either **to right** or **to left**.

```
.horizontal-rt {
    background: silver;
    background: linear-gradient(to right,
    → silver, black);
}

.horizontal-lt {
    background: silver;
    background: linear-gradient(to left,
    → silver, black);
}
```

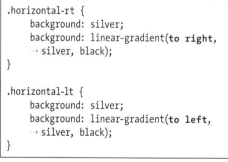

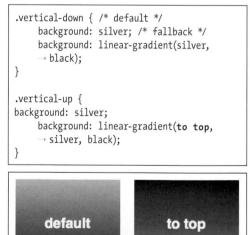

D There are two ways to angle a gradient. The first is shown here: include keywords that specify the corner the gradient should move toward. The gradient will start in the opposite (diagonal) corner.

```
.diagonal-bot-rt {
    background: aqua;
    background: linear-gradient(to bottom
right, aqua, navy);
}

.diagonal-bot-lt {
    background: aqua;
    background: linear-gradient(to bottom
left, aqua, navy);
}

.diagonal-top-rt {
    background: aqua;
    background: linear-gradient(to top
right, aqua, navy);
}

.diagonal-top-lt {
    background: aqua;
    background: linear-gradient(to top
left, aqua, navy);
}
```

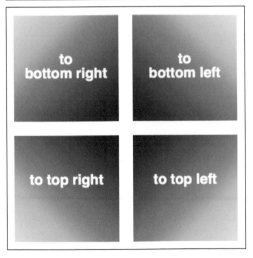

is required to support the widest array of browsers **L**. Cumbersome, to say the least!

With that in mind, I'll ease you into using gradients by demonstrating them with the correct, non-prefixed properties. Additional information can be found in the tips for this section, and you can find complete examples, including the required vendor-prefixed properties, in the code download for this chapter.

In keeping with the philosophy of progressive enhancement, it's a best practice to include a fallback background for browsers that don't support gradients. You specify it *before* the gradient in your CSS, as shown in **B** through **J**.

E The keywords **D** limit you to creating diagonal gradients that move from one corner to another. The second way to specify a gradient angle is with **deg**; for example, **90deg**. The number is the point on the circumference of a circle: 0 on top, 90 on the right, 180 on the bottom, and 270 on the left. The value you list determines the end point of the gradient. So, **0deg** is the same as **to top**, **90deg** is the same as **to right**, and so on.

```
.angle-120deg {
    background: aqua;
    background: linear-gradient(120deg,
      ⇢ aqua, navy);
}

.angle-290deg {
    background: aqua;
    background: linear-gradient(290deg,
      ⇢ aqua, navy);
}
```

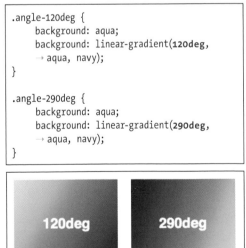

To create a fallback background:

Type **background:** *color* or **background-color:** *color*, where *color* is a hex or RGB value or any of the supported color names. (Alternatively, you may use an image.) It's generally best to avoid RGBA, HSL, or HSLA values for this because IE8 and earlier versions don't support them.

To define a linear gradient:

1. Type **background: linear-gradient(**.

2. Skip this step if you want the gradient to run from top to bottom (the default direction).

   Type *direction* followed by **,** (a comma) where *direction* specifies the direction of the gradient as **to top**, **to right**, **to left**, **to bottom right**, **to bottom left**, **to top right**, or **to top left**.

   Or type *direction* followed by **,** (a comma) where *direction* specifies the direction of the gradient as an angle value (like **45deg**, **107deg**, **180deg**, or **310deg**).

3. Define the gradient colors per "To specify the colors" or "To specify the colors and color stops," later in this section.

4. Type **);** to complete your gradient.

F Radial gradients include additional optional parameters, but the simplest example is the default, which uses the same parameters as a linear gradient. In this case, the origin for the gradient is the center of the element. You can use keywords like **at top** to specify the center's location. As always, provide a background for older browsers prior to your radial-gradient declaration.

```
.radial-center { /* default */
    background: red;
    background: radial-gradient(yellow,
     → red);
}
.radial-top {
    background: red;
    background: radial-gradient(at top,
     → yellow, red);
}
```

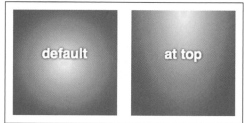

G You may also control the gradient's size. This demonstrates just a couple of your options.

```
.radial-size-1 {
    background: red;
    background: radial-gradient(100px 50px,
     → yellow, red);
}
.radial-size-2 {
    background: red;
    background: radial-gradient(70% 90% at
     → bottom left, yellow, red);
}
```

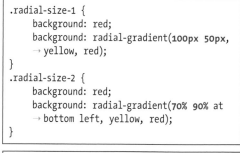

H These examples combine several parameters, including three colors. The values after the word **at** specify the coordinates of the gradient's center. In the second example, **30px 30px** marks the gradient's size. In the first example, **closest-side** determines its size by telling the gradient to stretch from the center indicated with **at 70px 60px** to the closest side of the area that contains the gradient.

```
.radial-various-1 {
    background: red;
    background: radial-gradient(closest-side
    → at 70px 60px, yellow, lime, red);
}
.radial-various-2 {
    background: red;
    background: radial-gradient(30px 30px
    → at 65% 70%, yellow, lime, red);
}
```

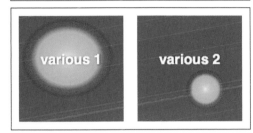

I You can specify one or more color stop positions with a percentage.

```
.color-stops-1 {
    background: green;
    background: linear-gradient(yellow 10%,
    → green);
}
.color-stops-2 {
    background: green;
    background: linear-gradient(to top right,
    → yellow, green 70%, blue);
}
```

To define a radial gradient:

1. Type **background: radial-gradient(**.

2. Specify the gradient's shape. Skip this step if you want the gradient shape to be determined automatically based on the size in step 3. Otherwise, type **circle** or **ellipse**. (Note that this declaration is ignored in some cases.)

3. Specify the gradient's size. Skip this step if you want the gradient size to be determined automatically (the default value is **farthest-corner**).

   Type *size*, where *size* is a single length representing both the width and height of the gradient (such as **200px** or **7em**) or a pair of values for the width and height (such as **390px 175px** or **60% 85%**). Note that if you use a single length, it cannot be a percentage.

   Or type *size*, where *size* is **closest-side**, **farthest-side**, **closest-corner**, or **farthest-corner**. These keywords refer to where the gradient should stretch within the space that contains it, relative to the gradient's center. The resulting boundary determines the gradient's size.

4. Specify the gradient's position. Skip this step if you want the gradient to emanate from the center of the element (the default).

   Type *pos*, where *pos* is the position of the center of the gradient as **at top**, **at right**, **at left**, **at bottom right**, **at bottom left**, **at top right**, or **at top left**.

continues on next page

Or type **pos**, where **pos** is the position of the center of the gradient as a pair of horizontal and vertical coordinates preceded by the word **at**. Examples include **at 200px 43px**, **at 33% 70%**, and **at 50% -10px**. (Specify one pair only.)

5. Type **,** (a comma) if you specified a value for any of steps 2–4. To clarify, if you did more than one of those steps, do *not* separate each one with a comma.

6. Define the gradient colors per "To specify the colors" or "To specify the colors and color stops," later in this section.

7. Type **);** to complete your gradient.

To specify the colors:

Type at least two colors, separating each with a comma. The first color you specify appears at the start of the gradient, and the last color appears at the end. For radial gradients, they are the innermost and outermost colors, respectively.

Colors can be specified using any combination of color names or hex, RGB, RGBA, HSL, or HSLA values. Browsers automatically determine where the colors shift within a gradient unless you specify one or more color stops.

To specify the colors and color stops:

Follow the instructions in "To specify the colors." As desired, include a percentage with each color value to control where the color appears within the gradient **I**. Negative percentages are allowed, as are values greater than 100%.

J What do you say we style the About Me box once more for old times' sake? You'll notice I used **background-image** instead of the **background** shorthand (the result is the same either way).

```
.about {
    /* fallback */
    background-color: #ededed;

    background-image:
    → linear-gradient(#fff, #ededed);
    border: 1px solid #d0d0d0;
    -webkit-box-shadow: 0 0 3px #d0d0d0;
    box-shadow: 0 0 3px #d0d0d0;
    padding: 0.313em 0.625em 0.625em;
}
```

ABOUT ME

My name is Eleina Shinn. Exploring the unknown and learning about our planet is what brings me the most pleasure. I enjoy foreign cuisine, culture and discovering social design and architecture. During the last five years I traveled to over 20 countries on 4 continents, often with just my backpack and a map in hand.

K Now it has a simple linear gradient to go along with the drop shadow and border applied earlier.

L Wowza. This is what's required to make the first gradient rule in **B** work across supporting browsers. It could even be worse; I left out the declaration for Safari 4–5 and Chrome prior to version 10. Most of this code was generated by CSS3 Please! (www.css3please.com), including the browser support comments.

```
.vertical-down {
    background: silver;

    /* Chrome 10-25, iOS 5+, Safari 5.1+ */
    background: -webkit-linear-gradient
    → (top, silver, black);

    /* Firefox 3.6-15 */
    background: -moz-linear-gradient
    → (top, silver, black);

    /* Opera 11.10-12.00 */
    background: -o-linear-gradient
    → (top, silver, black);

    /* Standard syntax, supported by
       Chrome 26+, Firefox 16+, IE 10+,
       → Opera 12.10+
    */
    background: linear-gradient(silver,
    → black);
}
```

Creating gradient code for older browsers

Earlier, I hinted that a veritable boatload of code is required to apply even a simple gradient across browsers. Now you can see for yourself **L**. Nobody wants to write all that by hand even if they know how. Fortunately, there are tools that can do it for you (see the tips).

On the positive side, most of the browsers that require a vendor prefix will be old enough at some point (not really far down the line) that you'll be able to safely omit most of the extra declarations.

TIP I used color keywords in most of the examples to make them easier to follow. You'll likely find yourself using hex or other values for colors most of the time.

TIP See http://caniuse.com/#search=gradient for the latest browser support information.

TIP Gradients are quite versatile. You can define multiple gradients in a single background by separating each one with a comma. By doing so, you can create many interesting effects. Check out Lea Verou's CSS3 Patterns Gallery (http://lea.verou.me/css3patterns/) to get a taste of what's possible.

TIP You can use a visual tool like Microsoft's CSS gradient background maker (http://ie.microsoft.com/testdrive/graphics/cssgradientbackgroundmaker/) to bypass the tedious work of creating CSS gradient code. It also creates all the vendor prefix properties for you to ensure the maximum level of compatibility with older browser versions. ColorZilla's gradient generator (http://colorzilla.com/gradient-editor/) is similar, but be aware that it typically generates far more code than you'll need.

TIP You should accommodate unsupported browsers by specifying either a `background-color` or a `background-image`, but you should keep in mind that images in the CSS will be downloaded by browsers whether they are used or not.

Setting the Opacity of Elements

Using the **opacity** property, you can change the transparency of elements, including images (**A** through **E**).

To change the opacity of an element:

Type **opacity: *o***, where *o* is the level of opaqueness of the element to two decimal places (without units).

> **TIP** The default value of **opacity** is 1 **B**. Values can be set in increments from 0.00 (completely transparent) to 1.00 (completely opaque). For example, **opacity: .09;, opacity: .2;,** or **opacity: .75;.** (Including a zero before the decimal point is not required.) You can write 0.00 as 0 and 1.00 as 1.

> **TIP** Text is affected by opacity too. If the **div** had (for example) white text, it would take on some brown in **D** and some red in **E**.

> **TIP** You can produce some interesting and practical effects by using the **opacity** property along with the **:hover** pseudo-property. As a basic example, **img { opacity: .75; }** would set images to 75% opacity by default and **img:hover { opacity: 1; }** would make them opaque when hovered upon. You see this effect often with thumbnail images that are linked to full-size versions. The hover effect reinforces to visitors that the images are actionable.

A This document contains a **div** element with an image enclosed.

```
...
<body>

<div class="box">
    <img src="img/sleeves.jpg" width="420"
  → height="296" alt="Record sleeves" />
</div>

</body>
</html>
```

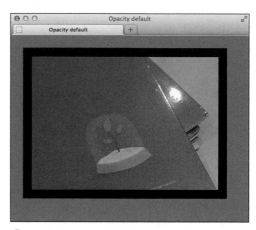

B Here's how the **div** looks like by default. As they do with other elements, browsers give it **opacity: 1;** without your having to specify that in your style sheet. The **div** has a black background, which shows around the image because of the padding. The **body** background is brown.

C By making the **opacity** value less than 1, you can make an element and its children transparent. In this case, I changed the opacity to 50 percent by using **.5 D**.

```
.body {
    background: #a2735f; /* brown */
}

.box {
    background: #000; /* black */
    opacity: .5;
    padding: 20px;
    width: 420px;
}
```

D Here's how the **div** looks with its **opacity** set to **.5**. Notice that the solid black background of the **div** element is now dark brown and that the image is semi-transparent and a little browner as well. When you set an element's opacity to less than 1, the background it sits on from a surrounding element will show through. In this case, it's the brown background from **body**. This effect is more evident with a color like red **E**.

E The **div** is still set to **opacity: .5;** but the **body** now has **background-color: red;**. The extent of the filter-through effect depends on the opacity. More red would show through if the **div** had an opacity of .35, and less would show through with it set to .8.

TIP It's easy to confuse the **opacity** property with alpha transparent background colors set with RGBA or HSLA. As you saw in **D** and **E**, **opacity** affects an entire element, content and all. But a setting such as **background-color: rgba(128,0,64,.6);** affects only the level of transparency of the background. See "A Property's Value" in Chapter 7 for a discussion of CSS colors and an example of RGBA.

TIP The **opacity** property does not natively work in Internet Explorer versions prior to IE9, but it is possible to replicate by using the proprietary filter effect **F**. Be sure not to apply a lot of these filters to a page, because they adversely affect the performance of the versions of IE that apply them.

TIP Despite how it may appear, **opacity** is not an inherited property. Children of an element with an **opacity** of less than 1 will also be affected, but the **opacity** value for those child elements will still be 1.

F This demonstrates how you can apply IE's proprietary filters for older versions. The **zoom: 1;** portion is also proprietary to IE and helps the filters take effect. Modern browsers will use the **opacity: .5;** setting, per usual. Note that the IE filters use a different number. In this case, **50** is required instead of **.5** to apply 50 percent opacity.

```
div {
    -ms-filter: progid:DXImageTransform.
    Microsoft.Alpha(opacity=50);
    filter: alpha(opacity=50);
    opacity: .5;
    zoom: 1;
}
```

Effects with Generated Content

The **:before** and **:after** pseudo-elements are incredibly handy for adding design flourishes to your pages. You can use them with the **content** property to include what is known as *generated content*. That is, content that is added to your page from CSS, not its usual spot in HTML.

Don't get the wrong idea, though—it isn't for adding paragraphs or headings to your page. Those still belong in your HTML. Instead, you can use it to add symbols (Ⓐ through Ⓓ), to create what is like a blank content element that you can style as you please (Ⓔ through Ⓗ), and to do more (see the tips).

continues on page 386

Ⓐ A simple paragraph that contains a link with a class. Notice that there are not two arrows after the words "Read More."

```
...

<pThis area is one of the most tranquil
→ spaces at the Villa. As I wandered around,
→ enjoying shade provided by sycamore and
→ laurel trees and serenaded by splashing
→ water from two sculptural fountains,
→ I couldn't help but think &hellip;
→ <a href="victoria.html" class="more">
→ Read More</a></p>

...
```

Ⓑ The paragraph with basic CSS text styling. No arrows appear after the link.

Ⓒ Here's where the magic happens.

```
...

.more:after {
    content: " »";
}
```

With Generated Content

This area is one of the most tranquil spaces at the Villa. As I wandered around, enjoying shade provided by sycamore and laurel trees and serenaded by splashing water from two sculptural fountains, I couldn't help but think ... Read More »

Read More »

Ⓓ Now, any element given **class="more"** will display double arrows after it.

Ⓔ The list of cities will be styled as a bubble with an arrow on the bottom.

```
...
<div class="travels">
    <h2>My Travels</h2>
    <img src="img/map.jpg" class="map"
    → tabindex="0" ... />

    <ul class="cities clearfix">
        <li>Victoria</li>
        <li>Los Angeles</li>
        <li>Mexico City</li>
        <li>Buenos Aires</li>
        <li>Paris</li>
        <li>Kampala</li>
        <li>Lagos</li>
        <li>Cairo</li>
        <li>Beijing</li>
    </ul>
</div>
...
```

F There are a few effects going on here. The last rule uses the **:after** pseudo-element to create and position a triangle below the list of cities. The second rule positions the list off-screen by default. The third rule puts the list back onscreen when a visitor interacts with the map (**G** and **H**). It is positioned absolutely, but relative to the **.travels div** that contains it in the HTML **E**.

```
.travels {
    /* Allows positioning .cities
       absolutely within it. */
    position: relative;
}

.map:focus + .cities,
.map:hover + .cities {
    left: 50%; /* show */
}

/* bubble */
.cities {
    background: #2B2B2B;
    border-radius: 5px 5px;
    left: -999em; /* hide */
    margin-left: -111px;
    padding: 5em 0 .9375cm .9375em;
    position: absolute;
    top: -75px;
    width: 222px;
}

/* triangle under bubble */
.cities:after {
    border: solid transparent;
    border-top-color: #2b2b2b;
    border-width: 15px;
    content: " "; /* blank space */
    height: 0;
    left: 50%;
    margin-left: -15px;
    position: absolute;
    top: 99.9%;
    width: 0;
}

...
```

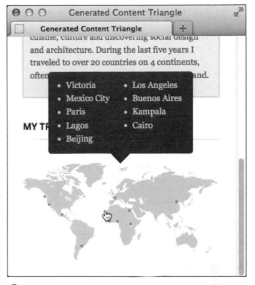

G The arrow at the bottom of the bubble is pure CSS, not an image! The cities bubble shows when you hover anywhere over the map. But that's not all...

H The **tabindex="0"** attribute on the **img** **E** allows the **:focus** pseudo-selector **F** to work so a visitor can tab to the map with the keyboard to reveal the cities instead of using a mouse to hover. Another win for accessibility! (The dotted outline shows around the map only when you tab to it.)

I could have included the arrows in the HTML of the first example Ⓐ, but they are a stylistic touch that I might want to change later. If so, I can simply modify the `.more` class Ⓑ rather than remove potentially hundreds of arrows from my HTML pages.

In the second example, I create a blank space with **content: " ";** and style it as a triangle using CSS borders Ⓕ (see the tips). You can style generated content with background colors and images (including gradients), width, height, rounded corners—you name it.

TIP **The complete code for the examples is available at www.htmlcssvqs.com/8ed/14/ gencon.**

TIP **You can apply both `:before` and `:after` to a single element, giving you two extra containers for styling. For example, you could apply multiple backgrounds in a different manner than the way shown in "Applying Multiple Backgrounds." Chris Coyier demonstrates more great uses for `:before` and `:after` at http://css-tricks.com/ pseudo-element-roundup/.**

TIP **Joel Glover goes in-depth about creating triangles with border styles at http://appendto.com/blog/2013/03/ pure-css-triangles-explained/.**

TIP **CSS Arrow Please! (http://cssarrowplease. com/) by Simon Højberg is a great tool that creates CSS triangle code for you.**

TIP **The `:focus` pseudo-class works on links and form elements by default. You do not have to add `tabindex="0"` to those elements.**

TIP **The `.clearfix` class I showed in Chapter 11 uses generated content.**

A You can leverage the file name extensions and the **.icon** class to display an icon that matches the document type. But before you do, the list shows round markers by default.

```
...
<ul class="documents">
    <li><a href="expenses.xls" class="icon">
    → Business expenses</a></li>
    <li><a href="user-manual.pdf"
    → class="icon">User Manual</a></li>
    <li><a href="story.docx" class="icon">
    → Short story</a></li>
    <li><a href="brochure.pdf" class="icon">
    → Vacation brochure</a></li>
</ul>
...
```

○ ○ ○   No sprite   ⬈
☐   No sprite   ＋

- Business expenses
- User Manual
- Short story
- Vacation brochure

B This sprite image contains three icons. Each is 16 pixels by 16 pixels and is separated from the next by two pixels.

Combining Images with Sprites

Text usually appears quickly on a page, but each image a browser has to load slows down your page load. Usually, this is even more pronounced on mobile devices. To offset this, you can combine multiple images into a single background image file (a *sprite*) and use CSS to control which part of the image displays. The secret is in the **background-position** property.

Figure **A** shows a standard unordered list (see Chapter 15). The goal is to show an icon from the sprite **B** before each document link.

continues on next page

You apply the sprite to as many elements as desired. In this case, I do so with `.icon:before` . With that, the sprite is the background image for the empty space generated by `content: " ";`. Setting that to `display: block;` allows you to set its `height` and `width` to match the size of the icon; it won't show without these three properties. You use `background-position` 🅒 to shift the right icon into place 🅓.

TIP A sprite can contain images of varying sizes and with varying distances between them. You can arrange them both horizontally and vertically.

TIP You do not have to use `:before` or `:after` to use sprites. You can apply a sprite background directly to an element instead.

TIP You can create rollover effects by changing the sprite's `background-position` in the `:hover` state of a link or other element.

TIP CSS Sprite Generator (http://spritegen. website-performance.org) by Project Fondue is one of many similar tools that create sprites and the background positioning CSS for you.

TIP The sprite icons are from the free Silk icon set by Mark James (www.famfamfam.com/lab/icons/silk/).

TIP You can create sprites for Retina and other high-pixel-density displays. See the last page of Chapter 12's "Putting It All Together."

🅒 You could apply `class="pdf"`, `class="xls"`, and so on to each relevant **a** element in the HTML 🅐. But you already know what kind of document each link points to based on its `href` value. That allows you to use `$=` to match a `href` value that ends with a specific extension.

```
...
.documents { list-style: none; }

.icon {
    display: inline-block;
    min-height: 16px;
    padding-left: 23px;
    position: relative;
    ...
}

.icon:before {
    background-image: url(sprite.png);
    content: " ";
    display: block;
    height: 16px; /* icon height */
    position: absolute;
    width: 16px; /* icon width */
}

a[href$=".xls"]:before {
    background-position: -17px 0;
}

a[href$=".docx"]:before {
    background-position: -34px 0;
}
```

🅓 The correct icon appears before each link!

Lists

HTML contains elements specifically for creating lists of items. You can create plain, numbered, or bulleted lists, as well as lists containing descriptions. You can also nest one or more lists inside another one.

All lists are formed by a parent element that specifies what sort of list you want to create, and child elements that mark the items within the list. Here are the three list types, along with the elements they are composed of:

- Ordered list: **ol** for the parent, **li** for each list item
- Unordered list: **ul** for the parent, **li** for each list item
- Description list: **dl** for the parent, **dt** marks the term to describe, and **dd** marks the description of the term. This was known as a *definition list* before HTML5.

Of these, the unordered list is used the most because it's the de facto standard for marking up most kinds of navigation (there are several examples of this throughout the book). But all three list types have their place, as you'll learn in this chapter.

Creating Ordered and Unordered Lists

An ordered list is the right choice when the order of the list items is critical to the list's meaning. For example, an **ol** is perfect for providing step-by-step instructions on how to complete a particular task (Ⓐ and Ⓑ), or for creating an outline or table of contents of a larger document—in short, any list of items for which the order is meaningful.

Unordered lists are the opposite (and are more prevalent)—use them when the order of list items isn't tied to the list's meaning (Ⓒ through Ⓖ).

Both list types are appropriate for marking up certain types of navigation (see the second tip).

To create lists:

1. Type **<ol>** for an ordered list or **<ul>** for an unordered list. For an ordered list, you can include any of the optional attributes **start**, **type**, and **reversed**. (See "Choosing Where to Start List Numbering" regarding **start**, "Choosing Your Markers" regarding **type**, and the last tip to learn about **reversed**.)

2. Type **<li>** to begin the first list item. For an ordered list, you can include the optional **value** attribute (see "Choosing Where to Start List Numbering" for details).

3. Add the content (such as text, links, or **img** elements) to be included in the list item.

4. Type **</li>** to complete each list item.

5. Repeat steps 2 through 4 for each new list item.

6. Type **</ol>** or **</ul>**, to match the start tag (from step 1) and complete the list.

Ⓐ There is no official way to format a list's title. Most of the time, a regular heading or a paragraph is the appropriate lead-in to a list like the one in this example. It's conventional, but not required, to indent list items in your HTML to indicate that they are children of an **ol** or **ul**. That doesn't make them indent when displayed, though; that's purely a function of the CSS applied to the list.

```
...
<body>

<h1>Changing a light bulb</h1>

<ol>
    <li>Make sure you have unplugged the
    → lamp from the wall socket.</li>
    <li>Unscrew the old bulb.</li>
    <li>Get the new bulb out of the
    → package.</li>
    <li>Check the wattage to make sure
    → it's correct.</li>
    <li>Screw in the new bulb.</li>
    <li>Plug in the lamp and turn it
    → on!</li>
</ol>

</body>
</html>
```

Ⓑ This list uses the default option of Arabic numerals to create a numbered ordered list. You can change this with CSS. Both ordered and unordered lists display indented by default, whether or not they are indented in the HTML itself Ⓐ.

C The **ul** element defines this as an unordered list. Each list item is marked up with an **li** element—the same as with ordered lists.

```
...
<body>

<h1>Product Features</h1>
<ul>
    <li>One-click page layout.</li>
    <li>Spell-checker for 327 languages.
    ↪ </li>
    <li>Image retouching tool.</li>
    <li>Unlimited undos and redos.</li>
</ul>

</body>
</html>
```

Product Features

- One-click page layout.
- Spell-checker for 327 languages.
- Image retouching tool.
- Unlimited undos and redos.

D Unordered lists have solid round bullets by default. You can change these with CSS.

E As you can see **D**, the default spacing between elements isn't ideal. I'll show you how to adjust that. This is the same HTML as **C** except I've added a class to the **h1** as an excuse to reinforce why classes are handy. With the styles in **F** in place, you can apply **.hdg** to any heading that immediately precedes a **ul** or **ol** and get the same results. Similarly, you could style the list with a class so the indentation and spacing rules could be used on either an **ol** or **ul**, too.

```
...
<h1 class="hdg">Product Features</h1>
<ul>
    <li>One-click page layout.</li>
    ...
</ul>
...
```

TIP Don't make the decision about which list type to use based on which marker style you want next to your content. After all, you may always change that with CSS (yes, you can even show bullets on an ordered list). Instead, think about your list's meaning—would it change if the order of the list items changed? If the answer is yes, mark up the list as an ordered list. Otherwise, use an unordered list.

TIP Use unordered lists to mark up most groups of links, such as your main navigation, a list of links to related stories or videos, or groups of links in your page footer. Meanwhile, use ordered lists to mark up breadcrumb navigation and pagination, since the links represent a distinct sequence of links (in other words, the order is meaningful). Breadcrumb navigation is often displayed horizontally above the main content area to indicate where the current page exists in the site's navigation path. Pagination is the horizontal list of links—like 1 | 2 | 3 | 4—that often appears with a list of search results or products, allowing you to jump between pages of results. I've included an example of main navigation and a bread-crumb in Figure **E** of "Styling Nested Lists."

TIP The completed sample webpage in Chapters 11 and 12 demonstrate lists used and presented in a variety of ways. It includes unordered lists for the navigation and other groups of links, and an ordered list for a list of sequential links to previous blog postings. Chapter 3 also has examples that include a **ul** as navigation.

TIP Unless you specify otherwise, items in ordered lists will be numbered with Arabic numerals (1, 2, 3, and so on) **B**.

TIP Items in unordered lists have solid round bullets by default **D**. You can choose different bullets (see "Choosing Your Markers") or even create your own (see "Using Custom Markers").

continues on next page

TIP Lists are indented from the left side by default, although you can remove or reduce the indentation ⓖ (or add more) with CSS ⓕ. "Using Custom Markers" illustrates this, too. Depending on how much you reduce the indentation, your bullets might stick outside your content or disappear beyond the left edge of the window (see the note about zero padding in ⓕ).

TIP You may create one list inside another—known as *nesting* lists—even mixing and matching ordered and unordered lists. Be sure to nest each list properly, using all the required start and end tags. See examples of nested ordered and unordered lists in "Styling Nested Lists."

TIP Be sure to place list content only within li elements. For instance, you aren't allowed to put content between the start ol or ul tag and the first li element. Various types of elements are allowed in li elements, such as any of the phrasing content elements (like em, a, cite, and so on). Nesting the likes of paragraphs and divs in list items is valid, too.

TIP If you specify your content direction as right-to-left, as you would if the page's base language were Hebrew (as an example), the lists are indented from the right margin instead of the left. To achieve this, set the dir attribute on your page's html element: <html dir="rtl" lang="he">. In this case, lang is set to he for Hebrew. You also can set dir and lang on elements (such as ol and ul) within the body to override the settings on the html element. The dir attribute defaults to ltr.

TIP At the time of this writing, browser support for the Boolean reversed attribute is less than ideal, with only Chrome 18+, Firefox 18+, and Safari 5.2+ recognizing it. The purpose of reversed is to indicate a descending ordered list (you can specify it with either <ol reversed> or <ol reversed="reversed">). Supporting browsers will reverse the list's numbering automatically.

ⓕ I've addressed the spacing between the heading and the list with the second and third rules, and the space between each list item with the last rule. The fourth rule reduces the indentation so the bullets appear near the left edge. The padding-left: 18px; portion makes room for the bullets. If it were 0, the text would line up with the left edge, and the bullets would be out of view because markers display outside list items by default. You don't have to use ems for the other values as I did; if you do, remember that they are relative to the parent element's font size.

```
body {
    font-family: sans-serif;
}

.hdg {
    font-size: 1.5em;
    margin-bottom: 0;
}

.hdg + ul,
.hdg + ol { /* works for either ul or ol */
    margin-top: .5em; /* ~8px */
}

ul { /* reduce indentation */
    margin-left: 0;  /* for <=IE7 */
    padding-left: 18px; /* ~1.125em */
}

ul li {
    /* space between each item */
    margin-top: .4em; /* ~6px */
}
```

Product Features
- One-click page layout.
- Spell-checker for 327 languages.
- Image retouching tool.
- Unlimited undos and redos.

ⓖ The page is much more presentable now.

A Here is our simple ordered list, to which we will apply capital Roman numerals (**upper-roman**). (Note that I've applied **class="hdg"** to the **h1** to take advantage of the **.hdg** rules in figure **F** of "Creating Ordered and Unordered Lists.")

```
...
<body>

<h1 class="hdg">The Great American Novel</h1>
<ol>
    <li>Introduction</li>
    <li>Development</li>
    <li>Climax</li>
    <li>Denouement</li>
    <li>Epilogue</li>
</ol>

</body>
</html>
```

B You can apply the **list-style-type** property to an **ol** (see the comment), a **ul**, or the list items themselves, as shown here. Though not shown, I also assigned a font to **body**.

```
li {
    list-style-type: upper-roman;
}

/* This would have the same effect because
→ the li elements inherit list-style-type.

ol {
    list-style-type: upper-roman;
}
*/
```

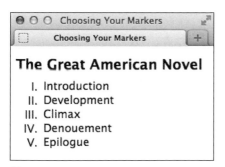

C Now the ordered list has capital Roman numerals. Note that most browsers align numeric markers to the right.

Choosing Your Markers

When you create a list, be it ordered **A** or unordered, you can also choose what sort of markers should appear to the left of each list item, or choose not to show any.

To choose your markers:

In the style sheet rule, type **list-style-type:** *marker*, where *marker* is one of the following values:

- **disc** (●)
- **circle** (○)
- **square** (■)
- **decimal** (1, 2, 3, …)
- **upper-alpha** (A, B, C, …)
- **lower-alpha** (a, b, c, …)
- **upper-roman** (I, II, III, IV, …) (**B** and **C**)
- **lower-roman** (i, ii, iii, iv, …)

To display lists without markers:

In the style sheet rule, type **list-style-type: none**.

TIP You may apply any of the marker styles to both ol and ul with **list-style-type**. In other words, an ol could have square markers and a ul decimal markers.

TIP More marker types are available, though they have varying degrees of browser support (see www.quirksmode.org/css/lists.html).

TIP You can also specify an ol's marker with the **type** attribute in your HTML, although I recommend defining it in CSS in most cases. See html5doctor.com/ol-element-attributes/ for an exception. The acceptable values for **type** are A, a, I, i, and 1 (1 is the default). For example, <ol type="I"> specifies uppercase Roman numerals.

Using Custom Markers

If you get tired of circles, squares, and discs, or even Roman numerals, you can create your own custom marker with an image. You don't have to change your HTML **Ⓐ**, just the CSS (**Ⓑ** through **Ⓖ**).

To use custom markers:

1. In the rule for the desired list or list item, type **list-style: none;** to turn off normal markers.

2. In the rule for the desired list, set the **margin-left** and/or **padding-left** properties to dictate how much the list items will be indented. Both properties are usually necessary to achieve similar results across browsers (**Ⓑ** and **Ⓕ**). Note that if you've set **dir="rtl"** for your content, you should adjust the **margin-right** and **padding-right** properties instead. See the tips in "Creating Ordered and Unordered Lists" for more details about **dir**, **lang**, and right-to-left languages in these list types.

Ⓐ This is just like any ordinary unordered list, but with a little CSS we can make it look different.

```
...
<body>

<h1 class="hdg">Product Features</h1>
<ul>
     <li>One-click page layout.</li>
     <li>Spell-checker for 327 major
     → languages.</li>
     <li>Image retouching tool.</li>
     <li>Unlimited undos and redos.</li>
</ul>

</body>
</html>
```

Ⓑ I'll show you how to use a custom marker in three steps so it's clear how various CSS properties affect the layout. First you can turn off the default markers (so you don't see both bullets and the checkmarks). If you want the list items to be flush left, you need to set both **margin-left** and **padding-left** to **0** (see the second-to-last tip). The URL to the custom marker you apply to list items will likely vary (see the first tip). It's typical to use a PNG, but a GIF or JPEG also works.

```
ul {
     /* turn off the default markers */
     list-style: none;

     /* remove indentation of list items */
     margin-left: 0;
     padding-left: 0;
}

li {
     /* show custom marker */
     background: url(../img/checkmark.png)
     → no-repeat 0 0;
}
```

Product Features

One-click page layout.
Spell-checker for 327 languages.
Image retouching tool.
Unlimited undos and redos.

C The default bullets are replaced by checkmark images, and the list items are flush left. However, the text is sitting on the new markers. Should we add left padding back into our list to make room for them? Let's try **D**.

D With `margin-left` set to **0**, we can control the amount of list item indentation for all browsers with `padding-left`. I've added temporary outlines to the `ul` and to each `li` so you can see clearly where the padding is applied **E**.

```
ul {
    list-style: none;
    margin-left: 0;
    padding-left: 30px;
    outline: 2px solid red;
}

li {
    background: url(../img/checkmark.png)
    → no-repeat 0 0;
    outline: 1px solid blue;
}
```

3. In the rule for the `li` elements within the desired list, type **background: url(*image.ext*) *repeat-type horizontal vertical*;**, where *image. ext* is the path and file name of the image you'd like to use as the custom marker; *repeat-type* is a value of **no-repeat** (typical), **repeat-x**, or **repeat-y**; and *horizontal* and *vertical* are values for the position of the background within the list items **B**.

4. Type **padding-left: *value*;**, where *value* is at least the width of the background image, in order to prevent the list item content from overlapping the custom marker.

TIP Note that relative background URLs are relative to the location of the style sheet, not to the location of the webpage **B**. (See "Setting the Background" in Chapter 10.) There should be no space between `url` and the opening parenthesis, and quotes around the URL are optional.

continues on next page

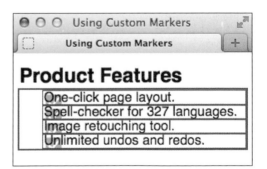

Product Features

One-click page layout.
Spell-checker for 327 languages.
Image retouching tool.
Unlimited undos and redos.

E This indented our list items, but the problem of text overlapping the markers remains because I added left padding to the list itself (the `ul`), rather than to the list items that contain the checkmarks. Time to fix that **F**.

TIP Unlike default markers, which appear outside the list items by default, custom markers display *inside* them because you apply the marker background image to the list items themselves **B**. For comparison with default markers, see **E** through **G** in "Creating Ordered and Unordered Lists." That also shows how I reduced the space below the heading and formatted the text in **G** here.

TIP Apply a class to one or more li elements and define a style rule for it if you want to apply a custom marker only to certain list items.

TIP Most browsers set the default list indentation via padding-left, but older browsers (like Internet Explorer prior to IE8) do it with margin-left. That's why it's necessary to set margin-left: 0; to achieve consistent results with padding-left. Nowadays, it's common to not worry about IE7 and older (in most countries), but there's no harm in including margin-left: 0; anyway.

TIP Another way to display custom markers is with the list-style-image property. Here's an example: li { list-style-image: url(marker.png); }. However, it never quite lived up to its promise, because browsers don't render them consistently, and you have less control over the placement of image markers than with the background image method I showed.

F I set the ul left padding back to 0 so the list is flush left again. Setting left padding on the lis allows us to see most of each marker image, and by increasing the line-height I've ensured that the images aren't cut off at the bottom. I also nudged the checkmarks down a bit to align with the text better **G**.

```
ul {
    list-style: none;
    margin-left: 0;
    padding-left: 0;
}

li {
    /* show image slightly down from top
    → of item. */
    background: url(../img/checkmark.png)
    → no-repeat 0 .1em;

    /* make line tall enough to show
    → full checkmark */
    line-height: 1.8;

    /* bump the text over to make room
    → for the checkmark */
    padding-left: 1.75em;
}
```

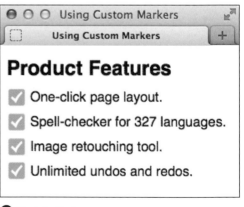

G Much better!

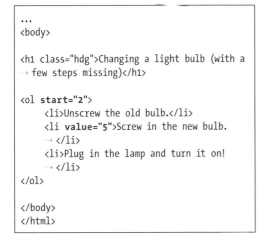 In this example, I've omitted some steps but want to maintain the original numbering of the remaining steps. So I start the whole list at **2** (with **start="2"**) and then set the value of the second item to **5** (with **value="5"**). Both attributes are optional and don't have to be used together as they are here.

```
...
<body>

<h1 class="hdg">Changing a light bulb (with a
→ few steps missing)</h1>

<ol start="2">
    <li>Unscrew the old bulb.</li>
    <li value="5">Screw in the new bulb.
    → </li>
    <li>Plug in the lamp and turn it on!
    → </li>
</ol>

</body>
</html>
```

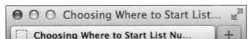

● ○ ○ Choosing Where to Start List...

☐ Choosing Where to Start List Nu...   +

Changing a light bulb (with a few steps missing)

2. Unscrew the old bulb.
5. Screw in the new bulb.
6. Plug in the lamp and turn it on!

B Notice that not only are the first and second items numbered as we specified, but the third item ("Plug in the lamp and turn it on!") is also affected. (Though the CSS isn't shown, I also styled the page a bit. Namely, I set the **body** font to Georgia, and leveraged **class="hdg"** on the **h1** **A** to take advantage of the **.hdg** rules in figure **F** of "Creating Ordered and Unordered Lists.")

Choosing Where to Start List Numbering

You might want to start a numbered list with something other than 1 **A**.

To specify the initial value of an entire list's numbering scheme:

Within the **ol** start tag, type **start="*n*"**, where *n* represents the list's initial value.

To change the numbering of a given list item in an ordered list:

In the desired **li** item, type **value="*n*"**, where *n* represents the value for this list item.

TIP If you use **start** or **type**, always give it a numeric value even if you decide to have the list display with letters or Roman numerals via **CSS** or the **type** attribute (see "Choosing Your Markers").

TIP The **value** attribute overrides the **start** value.

TIP When you change a given list item's number with the **value** attribute, the subsequent list items are also renumbered accordingly.

TIP Using **value** is handy to indicate that two or more items hold the same spot in an ordered list. Take, for example, a list with the top five finishers in a road race. Normally, they would display as 1, 2, 3, 4, 5. But if there were a tie for second, by specifying the *third* list item as <li value="2">, the list would display as 1, 2, 2, 3, 4.

TIP Your list can include more than one **li** with a **value** attribute.

Controlling Where Markers Hang

By default, lists are indented from the left side (of their parent). Your markers can either sit outside the text **Ⓐ**, which is the default, or be flush with the rest of the text (called inside) (**Ⓑ** and **Ⓒ**).

To control where markers hang:

1. In the style sheet rule for the desired list or list item, type **list-style-position:**.

2. Type **inside** to display the markers flush with the list item text **Ⓑ**, or **outside** to display the markers to the left of the list item text (the default).

TIP Because outside is the default, you don't need to specify list-style-position: outside; unless you want to override a list-style-position: inside; setting you'd made elsewhere.

TIP You can set list-style-position to ul **Ⓑ**, ol, or li. The result is the same unless you target a specific li (say, with a class), in which case your list could have both inside and outside markers if you'd like.

TIP If the text *within* your list items is cramped, as it is in the first bullet point in **Ⓐ** and **Ⓒ**, you can increase the space between each line of text with line-height. For example, li { line-height: 1.3; }. Don't confuse this with changing the space between the list items themselves, which you can do by setting either margin-top or margin-bottom on li. For example, li { margin-bottom: .5em; }.

TIP See **Ⓔ** through **Ⓖ** in "Creating Ordered and Unordered Lists" for how I reduced both the list indentation and space below the heading, and how I formatted the text.

TIP The list-style-position property is inherited.

Product Features

- One-click page layout. (This is particularly useful when you're under a heavy deadline. You just select whether you want the end product to be a book or a website, and poof, it's done!)
- Spell-checker for 327 languages.
- Image retouching tool.
- Unlimited undos and redos.

Ⓐ This demonstrates how browsers render the marker relative to wrapped text in a list item by default. The markers are outside the content.

Ⓑ Setting list-style-position to inside changes the display.

```
ul {
    list-style-position: inside;
}
```

Product Features

- One-click page layout. (This is particularly useful when you're under a heavy deadline. You just select whether you want the end product to be a book or a website, and poof, it's done!)
- Spell-checker for 327 languages.
- Image retouching tool.
- Unlimited undos and redos.

Ⓒ The markers for the lines that wrap begin at the left edge of the list item, instead of outside the content.

(A) This style rule is equivalent to setting the `list-style-type` to `circle` and `list-style-position` to `inside` on an unordered list—it's just shorter. If you want to specify a `list-style-image` in the shorthand property, this example could instead be `ul { list-style: url(arrow-right.png) circle inside; }`. But as noted in "Using Custom Markers," it's better to apply a background image on `li` rather than using `list-style-image`.

```
ul {
    list-style: circle inside;
}

/*
Use ol as the selector to style an unordered
→ list.
You may also use li instead for either.
*/
```

(B) The result is the same as in **(C)** in "Controlling Where Markers Hang," but I've switched the markers to circles.

Setting All List-Style Properties at Once

Just as CSS has shorthand properties for **background**, **border**, **font**, **outline**, and more, it has one for the `list-style` features **(A)**. It combines `list-style-type`, `list-style-position`, and the seldom-used `list-style-image` into one property.

To set all the list-style properties at once:

1. Type `list-style:`.

2. If desired, specify the type of markers that should appear next to the list items, if any (as described in "Choosing Your Markers").

3. If desired, specify whether markers should hang outside the list paragraphs or flush with the text (as described in "Controlling Where Markers Hang").

4. If desired, specify the custom image marker that should be used for list items (as described in the last tip of "Using Custom Markers").

TIP You may specify any or all of the three `list-style` properties, and in any order. **(A)** shows two. Properties not explicitly set are returned to their defaults (`disc` for `list-style-type`, `outside` for `list-style-position`, and `none` for `list-style-image`).

TIP Perhaps the most common use of `list-style` is to turn off markers quickly with `list-style: none`.

TIP The `list-style` property is inherited—just like `list-style-type`, `list-style-position`, and `list-style-image`—which is why you can apply it to the parent `ol` or `ul` (so each `li` will use it) or to `li` directly.

Styling Nested Lists

You may insert one type of list in another; the inner list is known as a nested list. You can do this with ordered and unordered lists (together or independently). There's also another kind of nested list; see "Creating Description Lists" for an example.

Nesting lists is particularly useful with an outline structured as ordered lists—where you may want several levels of items (Ⓐ through Ⓒ)—or for navigation with sub-menus structured as unordered lists (Ⓓ and Ⓔ; see the sidebar "Using Nested Lists for Drop-Down Navigation" for more details). You can style nested lists a variety of ways, as the examples demonstrate.

To style nested lists:

1. For styling the outermost list, type *toplevel* {*style_rules*}, where *toplevel* is the list type of the outermost list (for example, **ol** or **ul**) and *style_rules* are the styles that should be applied.

2. For the second-level list, type *toplevel 2ndlevel* {*style_rules*}, where *toplevel* matches the *toplevel* in step 1, *2ndlevel* is the list type of the second-level list, and *style_rules* are the styles that should be applied.

3. For the third-level list, type *toplevel 2ndlevel 3rdlevel* {*style_rules*}, where *toplevel* and *2ndlevel* match the values used in steps 1 and 2, *3rdlevel* is the kind of list used for the third nested list, and *style_rules* are the styles that should be applied.

4. Continue in this fashion for each nested list that you wish to style.

Ⓐ Note that each nested **ol** is contained within its parent start tag **<li>** and end tag **</li>**. There are four nested lists in total: one in the Introduction list item, one in the Development item, one in the Climax item, and one inside the "Boy gives Girl ultimatum" item (which is inside the Climax item).

```
...
<body>
<h1 class="hdg">The Great American Novel</h1>
<ol>
    <li>Introduction
        <ol>
            <li>Boy's childhood</li>
            <li>Girl's childhood</li>
        </ol>
    </li>
    <li>Development
        <ol>
            <li>Boy meets Girl</li>
            <li>Boy and Girl fall in love
            → </li>
            <li>Boy and Girl have fight
            → </li>
        </ol>
    </li>
    <li>Climax
        <ol>
            <li>Boy gives Girl ultimatum
                <ol>
                    <li>Girl can't believe
                    → her ears</li>
                    <li>Boy is indignant at
                    → Girl's indignance</li>
                </ol>
            </li>
            <li>Girl tells Boy to get lost
            → </li>
        </ol>
    </li>
    <li>Denouement</li>
    <li>Epilogue</li>
</ol>
</body>
</html>
```

B You can format each level of a nested ordered list separately, as shown (see the second tip for another way). If you use ems or percentages for the font size of the list text, be sure to add `li li { font-size: 1em; }` (or **100%** instead of **1em**) so that it doesn't shrink to the point of being illegible in the nested lists (see the last tip).

```
ol {
    list-style-type: upper-roman;
}

ol ol {
    list-style-type: upper-alpha;
}

ol ol ol {
    list-style-type: decimal;
}

ol li {
    font-size: .875em;
}

li li {
    font-size: 1em; /* prevent shrinking
text! */
}
```

○ ○ ○ Styling Nested Ordered Lists

Styling Nested Ordered Lists   +

The Great American Novel

   I. Introduction
      A. Boy's childhood
      B. Girl's childhood
   II. Development
      A. Boy meets Girl
      B. Boy and Girl fall in love
      C. Boy and Girl have fight
   III. Climax
      A. Boy gives Girl ultimatum
         1. Girl can't believe her ears
         2. Boy is indignant at Girl's indignance
      B. Girl tells Boy to get lost
   IV. Denouement
   V. Epilogue

C The first-level lists (**ol**) have capital Roman numerals. The second-level lists (**ol ol**) have capital letters. The third-level lists (**ol ol ol**) have Arabic numerals.

You may include `li` at the end of each selector to target the list items directly. For instance, step 3 could be *toplevel 2ndlevel 3rdlevel* `li` *{style_rules}*. The sample code **B** has examples of both.

TIP Your selectors should reflect the types of nested lists in your document; that is, you might need something like `ul ul ol` (or `ul ul ol li` to target the list items directly in this case).

TIP Alternatively, you could add a class to each nested list and style it accordingly. The method shown in **B** allows you to control the styling without changing the HTML.

TIP Ordered lists always use Arabic numerals (1, 2, 3) by default, regardless of their nesting position. Use `list-style-type` to specify other numbering schemes (see "Choosing Your Markers"). In traditional writing terms, according to *The Chicago Manual of Style*, the correct nesting order for list markers is I (that's a Roman numeral), A, 1, a (and the 1 and a levels are repeated from then on).

TIP By default, unordered lists use discs for the first level, circles for the first nested level, and squares for the third and subsequent level lists. Again, use `list-style-type` to specify the type of bullets you want (see "Choosing Your Markers").

TIP Since list items (`li` elements) can be nested within other list items, you have to be a bit careful with font sizes specified in relative values. If you use something like `li {font-size: .75em; }`, the font size of the outermost list item will be 75 percent of its parent element; so if the parent is a default 16 pixels, the outermost list item will be 12 pixels. However, the font size of the first *nested* list item will be 75 percent of *its* parent (the first list item, which is 12 pixels) and thus will be only 9 pixels. Each level gets worse quickly, making the text inconsistent and hard to read. One solution is to add `li li {font-size: 1em; }` **B** (or 100% instead of 1em). Now nested list items will always be the same size as top-level ones **C**. (Thanks to Eric Meyer, www.meyerweb.com, for the tip.)

D Here's another example of nested lists. In this case, a navigation menu (which has **class="nav"**) is structured as an unordered list with two nested unordered lists for sub-navigation (each has **class="subnav"**). With a little CSS, you can display the navigation horizontally, hide the sub-navigation by default, and show them based on the visitor's interaction **E**.

```
...
<body>
<nav role="navigation">
    <ul class="nav">
        <li><a href="/">Home</a></li>
        <li><a href="/products/">Products</a>
            <ul class="subnav">
                <li><a href="/products/phones.html">Phones</a></li>
                <li><a href="/products/accessories.html">Accessories</a></li>
            </ul>
        </li>
        <li><a href="/support/">Support</a>
            <ul class="subnav">
                <li><a href="/support/forum/">Community Forum</a></li>
                <li><a href="/support/contact-us.html">Contact Us</a></li>
                <li><a href="/support/how-to-guides.html">How-to Guides</a></li>
            </ul>
        </li>
        <li><a href="/about-us/">About Us</a></li>
    </ul><!-- end .nav -->
</nav>
...
</body>
</html>
```

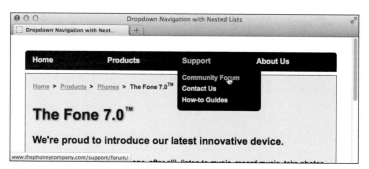

E Both the Products and Support list items contain sub-navigation in nested **ul**s, but neither shows by default because of the CSS I've applied. In this case, the Support sub-navigation displays because I've hovered over the list item that contains both the Support link and its sub-navigation nested list **D**. This screenshot also shows an example of breadcrumb navigation (below the black bar), marked up as an ordered list to reflect where the current page sits in the site's hierarchy. Each item in the list except the last is linked, since the visitor is on the page for The Fone 7.0. The complete code for this page is available on the book site.

Using Nested Lists for Drop-Down Navigation

One use for nested lists is to structure drop-down (or fly-out) navigation menus **D**. You can style the navigation with CSS so that each sub-navigation shows only when the visitor hovers over the parent list item **E** and hides again when the visitor moves the pointer away.

You can implement this effect a few ways, but it always involves leveraging the **:hover** pseudo-class as part of the selector that reveals the sub-navigation. Here's one such approach to hide the nested lists by default and then reveal them when the visitor hovers:

```
/* Default state of sub-navigation */

.nav .subnav {
    left: -999em; /* moves subnav off screen */
    position: absolute;
    z-index: 1000;
}


/* State of sub-navigation when parent li hovered upon */

.nav li:hover .subnav {
    left: auto; /* puts subnav back in natural spot */
}
```

The corresponding HTML is shown in **D**. You'll need more CSS than this to implement the horizontal layout, remove the bullets from the list items, and otherwise adjust the presentation to meet your needs. The complete HTML and CSS for the page shown in **E** is available on the book site at www.htmlcssvqs.com/8ed/15/dropdown-nav. I've also included several comments in the code to explain various parts.

You can use a similar approach for a vertical navigation with fly-out sub-menus that appear to the side.

Creating Description Lists

HTML provides a type of list specifically for describing an association between names (or terms) and values in groups. Dubbed *description lists* in HTML5, they were known as *definition lists* in previous versions of HTML.

According to the HTML5 specification, "Name-value groups may be terms and definitions, metadata topics and values, questions and answers, or any other groups of name-value data." Each list is contained in a **dl**, and each name-value group within it has one or more **dt** elements (the names or terms) followed by one or more **dd** elements (their values). **A** shows a basic description list example. Aside from some boldfacing applied with a simple style rule **B**, it renders by default as **C**.

B You may want to add formatting to the terms in the **dt** elements to help them stand out **C**.

```
dt {
    font-weight: bold;
}
```

C By default, the name (the **dt**) is aligned to the left, and the value (the **dd**) is indented. The names are in bold thanks to the simple rule in **B**. Otherwise they'd appear as normal text.

A This is the most basic type of description list, with one **dt** matched with one **dd** in each name-value group. Each group is separated by a blank line merely for legibility; the space between groups isn't required, doesn't change the meaning of the content, and doesn't affect its display.

```
...
<body>
<h1>List of Horror Movie Legends</h1>

<dl>
    <dt>Boris Karloff</dt>
    <dd>Best known for his role in <cite>Frankenstein</cite> and related horror films, this
    → scaremaster's real name was William Henry Pratt.</dd>

    <dt>Christopher Lee</dt>
    <dd>Lee took a bite out of audiences as Dracula in multiple Hammer horror classics.</dd>

    ... [more scary legends] ...
</dl>

</body>
</html>
```

D This example includes multiple **dt**s paired with a single **dd** in each name-value group because the defined terms have more than one spelling but share the same definition.

```
...
<body>

<h1>Defining words with multiple spellings</
h1>

<dl>
    <dt><dfn>bogeyman</dfn>, n.</dt>
    <dt><dfn>boogeyman</dfn>, n.</dt>
    <dd>A mythical creature that lurks under
  → the beds of small children.</dd>

    <dt><dfn lang="en-gb">aluminium
  → </dfn>, n.</dt>
    <dt><dfn>aluminum</dfn>, n.</dt>
    <dd>...</dd>
</dl>
</body>
</html>
```

E This will add more space between the name-value groups than they have by default.

```
dd + dt {
    margin-top: 1em;
}
```

Defining words with multiple spellings

bogeyman, n.
boogeyman, n.
    A mythical creature that lurks under
    the beds of small children.

aluminium, n.
aluminum, n.

F Now you can tell where one group of descriptions stops and the next starts. The rule in **E** works because "aluminium, n." is contained in a **dt** right after the **dd** from the previous name-value group.

All the following arrangements are valid for a group of **dt** and **dd** elements within a **dl**:

- A single **dt** grouped with a single **dd** **A**. (Also, see Director and the nested description list under Cast in **G**.) This is the most common occurrence.

- A single **dt** grouped with multiple **dd** elements. See Writers in **G**.

- Multiple **dt** elements grouped with a single **dd** **D**. (With sample styling adjustments shown in **E** and **F**.)

- Multiple **dt** elements grouped with multiple **dd** elements. An example of this would be if bogeyman/boogeyman in **D** had more than one definition.

Use the **dfn** element around the names in the **dt**s to indicate that the list is defining terms, such as in a glossary **D**. (See "Defining a Term" in Chapter 4 for more about **dfn**.)

continues on next page

You may also nest description lists **G** and style them with CSS as you please **H**. When a **dl** is nested in another one, it automatically indents another level by default **I** (you can also change that with CSS, of course).

To create description lists:

1. Type **<dl>**.

2. Type **<dt>**.

3. Type the word or short phrase that will be described or defined, including any additional semantic elements (such as **dfn**).

4. Type **</dt>** to complete the name or term in the name-value group.

5. Repeat steps 2 through 4 as necessary if the group has more than one name or term **D**.

6. Type **<dd>**.

7. Type the description of the name or term that was entered in step 3.

8. Type **</dd>** to complete the description (the value) in the name-value group.

9. Repeat steps 6 through 8 as necessary if the group has more than one value to define (see the Writers group in **G**).

10. Repeat steps 2 through 9 for each group of terms and descriptions.

11. Type **</dl>** to complete the description list.

G Here's an example of a description list that describes a film's director, writers, and cast, with the cast member names and their characters in a nested description list. You can style the nested list differently, as desired **H**.

```
...
<body>

<h1>Credits for <cite>Amélie</cite></h1>

<dl>
        <dt>Director</dt>
        <dd>Jean-Pierre Jeunet</dd>

        <dt>Writers</dt>
        <dd>Guillaume Laurant (story,
    → screenplay)</dd>
        <dd>Jean-Pierre Jeunet (story)</dd>

        <dt>Cast</dt>
        <dd>
          <!-- Start nested list -->
          <dl>
            <dt>Audrey Tautou</dt>
            <dd>Amélie Poulain</dd>

            <dt>Mathieu Kassovitz</dt>
            <dd>Nino Quincampoix</dd>

            ... [rest of Cast] ...
          </dl>
          <!-- end nested list -->
        </dd>

        ... [rest of Credits] ...
</dl>

</body>
</html>
```

H I want to distinguish the terms in the main list from those nested within it, so I style **dt** elements with uppercase text and then return any **dt** elements in a nested **dl** back to normal (the **text-transform: none;** declaration). However, note that all terms display as bold **I** because the declaration in the first rule applies to all **dt** elements, and I didn't turn that off in the nested list.

```css
body {
    font-family: Verdana, Geneva, sans-serif;
}

h1 {
    font-size: 1.75em;
}

dt {
    font-weight: bold;
    text-transform: uppercase;
}

/*
    style the dt of any dl
    within another dl
*/
dl dl dt {
    text-transform: none;
}

dd + dt {
    margin-top: 1em;
}
```

TIP By default, browsers generally indent descriptions (values) on a new line below their terms (names) **C**. You can change the indentation by defining your own **margin-left** value on dd elements. For example, dd { **margin-left: 0;** } makes them display flush left.

TIP You'll notice from the examples (**A**, **D**, and **G**) that you don't have to—or more to the point, *shouldn't*—mark up single paragraphs of text as p elements within the dd elements. However, if a *single* description is more than one paragraph, *do* mark it up with p elements inside one dd instead of splitting up each paragraph (without p elements) into its own dd.

Credits for *Amélie*

DIRECTOR
Jean-Pierre Jeunet

WRITERS
Guillaume Laurant (story, screenplay)
Jean-Pierre Jeunet (story)

CAST
Audrey Tautou
Amélie Poulain

Mathieu Kassovitz
Nino Quincampoix

I When a **dl** is nested in another one, it automatically indents another level by default. With the styles from **H** applied, the first-level **dt** elements are in uppercase letters, while the ones in the nested list are normal. All are bold.

16

Forms

The HTML you have learned so far has helped you communicate your ideas to your visitors. In this chapter, you'll learn how to create forms that enable your visitors to communicate with you.

There are two basic parts of a form: the collection of controls, labels, and buttons that the visitor views on a page and hopefully fills out or activates; and the processing script that takes that information and converts it into a format that you can read or tally. This chapter focuses on the first part—building forms. I've provided a couple of sample processing scripts on the companion website, at www.htmlcssvqs.com/8ed/form-scripts.

As you'll see, constructing a form is straightforward and similar to creating any other part of a webpage. Some of the form controls include text boxes, radio buttons, checkboxes, drop-down menus, and larger text areas. If you've ever purchased items online, been on a social network, or composed web-based emails, the form elements you'll learn about here will look familiar. I'll also show you how to style forms with CSS.

In This Chapter

Improvements to Forms in HTML5

If you're new to forms, you might want to revisit this section after getting familiar with the rest of the chapter.

One of HTML5's most helpful features is the improvement to forms. In the past, we often had to spend extra time writing JavaScript to enhance a form's behavior—for example, to require a visitor to fill out a field before submitting a form. HTML5 makes this a breeze by adding new form elements, input types, and attributes, as well as built-in validation of required fields, email addresses, URLs, and custom patterns. These additions don't just help us as designers and developers; they improve the experience for your site's visitors, too.

Better still, older browsers that don't support the new features won't choke. They'll simply ignore attributes they don't understand, and the form fields will otherwise work as expected. And if you want them to mimic the HTML5 behavior, you can use JavaScript to bridge the gap, just like in the old days (see the last tip).

Tables **16.1** and **16.2** summarize most of the features HTML5 has brought to forms and tell you where you can learn more about them. As you'll see, we'll focus our efforts on covering those features that are used most widely.

continues on page 412

TABLE 16.1 Inputs and Elements

Input or Element	Abbreviated Code	More Info
Email	`<input type="email">`	"Creating Email, Search, Telephone, and URL Boxes"
Search	`<input type="search">`	
Telephone	`<input type="tel">`	
URL	`<input type="url">`	

The following have limited browser support.

Date	`<input type="date">`	Learn more: www.wufoo.com/html5
Number	`<input type="number">`	Browser support:
Range	`<input type="range">`	caniuse.com/#feat=input-datetime
		caniuse.com/#feat=input-number
		caniuse.com/#feat=input-range

Data List	`<input type="text" name=` ⟶ `"favfruit" list="fruit" />`
	
	`<datalist id="fruit">`
	`  <option>Grapes</option>`
	`  <option>Pears</option>`
	`  <option>Kiwi</option>`
	`</datalist>`
		Learn more: www.wufoo.com/html5

The following also have poor support, and the W3C has declared them as at risk of not being part of HTML5 when it is finalized in 2014.

Color	`<input type="color" />`	www.w3.org/html/wg/wiki/ HTML5.0AtRiskFeatures
Global date and time	`<input type="datetime" />`	
Local date and time	`<input type="datetime-local" />`	Learn more: www.wufoo.com/html5
Month	`<input type="month" />`	Browser support:
Time	`<input type="time" />`	caniuse.com/#feat=input-color
Week	`<input type="week" />`	caniuse.com/#feat=input-datetime
Output	`<output></output>`	

TIP The browser support information at caniuse.com is typically more current than that at www.wufoo.com/html5, but the latter is still a great resource for information about HTML5 forms.

TIP It's possible—but not certain—that some of the form elements dubbed as at risk for HTML5 could be included in the final version of 5.1, which is currently targeted for 2016.

TIP One JavaScript solution for providing many HTML5 form features to older browsers is Ryan Seddon's H5F (https://github.com/ryanseddon/H5F).

TABLE 16.2 Attributes

Attribute	Summary	More Info
`accept`	Limits file types user can upload.	www.wufoo.com/html5
`autocomplete`	When **autocomplete="off"** is applied to a **form** element or specific field, disables browser's ability to auto-fill a field as user types. Default value is **on**.	"Creating Text Boxes"
`autofocus`	Places focus in a field when webpage loads.	"Creating Text Boxes"
`multiple`	Allows multiple emails or file uploads.	"Creating Email, Search, Telephone, and URL Boxes"
`list`	Links a **datalist** to an **input**.	www.wufoo.com/html5
`maxlength`	Specifies maximum number of characters in a **textarea** (text boxes have supported it since before HTML5).	"Creating Text Areas"
`pattern`	Defines a format that the text entered in a field must conform to for form to submit.	"Creating Email, Search, Telephone, and URL Boxes"
`placeholder`	Specifies hint text that appears in a field until visitor enters a value.	"Creating Text Boxes"
`required`	Requires visitor to complete field for form to submit.	"Creating Text Boxes"
`formnovalidate`	Turns off browser's HTML5 automatic validation features. Applied to submit buttons.	"Creating a Submit Button"
`novalidate`	Turns off browser's HTML5 automatic validation features. Applied to form element.	"Creating Forms"

Creating Forms

Each form begins with the **form** start tag and ends with the **form** end tag. In between are all the labels, controls, and buttons that make up the form **Ⓐ**. (Note: I'll use the words *control* and *field* interchangeably.) Each of those controls has a **name** attribute that will serve to identify the data once the form is submitted. Visitors submit a form via a submit button that you provide—when they trigger it, the data they've entered in the form is sent to the script on the server that handles the data.

Ⓐ Every form includes the **form** element itself, the other form elements inside that where the visitor enters information, and a submit button that sends the collected information to the server.

```
...
<body>
<h1>Create a New Account</h1>
<form method="post" action="show-data.php">
    <!-- Various form elements -->
    <fieldset>
        <h2 class="hdr-account">Account</h2>

        <div class="fields">
            <p class="row">
                <label for="first-name">First Name:</label>
                <input type="text" id="first-name" name="first_name" class="field-large" />
            </p>
            <p class="row">
                <label for="last-name">Last Name:</label>
                <input type="text" id="last-name" name="last_name" class="field-large" />
            </p>
            ...
        </div>
    </fieldset>
    ... more form elements ...

    <!-- Submit Button -->
    <input type="submit" value="Create Account" class="btn" />
</form>
</body>
</html>
```

Now that you know the big picture of a form, let's look a little closer. The **form** start tag allows a few attributes, the most important of which are **action** and **method** Ⓐ.

You set the **action** attribute to the URL of the script that will process your form when a visitor submits it. For example, **action="save-info.php"**.

The **method** attribute may have a value of either **get** or **post**. You will use **post** most of the time, but each method has a purpose, so it helps to understand them; please see the sidebar for more details.

To create a form:

1. Type **<form method="*formmethod*"**, where *formmethod* is either **get** or **post**.

2. Type **action="*script.url*">**, where *script.url* is the location on the server of the script that will run when the form is submitted.

3. Create the form's contents (including a submit button), as described in the sections starting with "Creating Text Boxes."

4. Type **</form>** to complete the form.

Ⓑ Here is a portion of the style sheet used to format the form. You can find the full style sheet on the book's website.

```
fieldset {
    background-color: #f1f1f1;
    border: none;
    border-radius: 2px;
    margin-bottom: 12px;
    overflow: hidden;
    padding: 0 .625em; /* 10px */
}

.fields {
    background-color: #fff;
    border: 1px solid #eaeaea;
    margin: .75em; /* 12px */
    padding: .75em;
}

.fields .row {
    margin: 0.5em 0;
}

label {
    cursor: pointer;
    display: inline-block;
    padding: 3px 6px;
    text-align: right;
    width: 150px;
    vertical-align: top;
}

input, select, button {
    font-size: inherit;
}

/* Various form field widths */
.field-small {
    width: 75px;
}

.field-medium {
    width: 150px;
}

.field-large {
    width: 250px;
}
```

Create a New Account

ACCOUNT

First Name:
Last Name:
Email: yourname@example.com
Password:
Re-enter Password:

ADDRESS

Street Address:
City:
State: Alabama
ZIP Code:

PUBLIC PROFILE

Picture: Browse...
Maximum size of 700k. JPG, GIF or PNG.
Screen Name:
Website URL: http://www.example.com
Have a homepage or a blog? Put the address here, beginning with http:// or https://.
Bio:
Gender: ○ Male ○ Female

EMAILS

☐ It is okay to email me with messages from other users.
☐ It is okay to email me with occasional promotions about our other products.

Create Account

⊙ Here is the complete form discussed in this chapter.

TIP You can use CSS to lay out your form elements **Ⓑ**. The form example that I demonstrate throughout this chapter is shown in **⊙**.

TIP The complete HTML and CSS for the code in **Ⓐ** and **Ⓑ** is available at the book's website (www.htmlcssvqs.com/8ed/16). You'll also see parts of the code throughout this chapter. Additionally, the companion site includes the show-data.php script that the form references in its action attribute. Feel free to use it to test your form as you go through this chapter. Keep in mind that it won't work unless PHP is installed on your server (see "Processing Forms").

TIP You can disable a form's HTML5 validation features (shown later in the chapter) by applying the novalidate attribute to the form element. For example, <form method="post" action="show-data.php" novalidate>.

The Differences Between method="get" and method="post"

As noted, the **form** element's **method** attribute may be to set to either **get** or **post**.

If your form uses **method="get"**, your form data will show in your browser's address bar after the form is submitted. Generally speaking, use **get** whenever you want to *get* information from the server after the form is submitted. For instance, most search engines use it in their search forms—you type in "Kermit meets Yoda," submit the form, and the search engine gets results. Because the data appears in the URL, you can save a search query or send it to a friend.

If your form uses **method="post"**, the information in your form is *not* shown in the URL after the form is submitted, making it more secure. Also, you can send more data to the server with **post** than with **get**. Generally speaking, **post** is for putting—or *posting*, as it's called—data on your server rather than getting data from it. So if you're saving, adding, and deleting data in a database, **post** is the correct choice. For example, e-commerce sites use **post** to save the credit card, mailing address, and other information you enter.

As a (very) general rule, when in doubt, use **post** so the data isn't exposed in the URL.

Processing Forms

A form gathers the information from your visitor, and the script on your server processes that information. The script can log the information to a database on the server, send the information via email, or perform any number of other functions.

There are several languages you can use to write your form processing scripts. PHP is a popular choice by those just getting started because it's simple to use for many common tasks. Plus, there are oodles of books, online tutorials, and forums to help you learn it. Explaining PHP is beyond the scope of this book, but I have provided two basic sample scripts at www.htmlcssvqs.com/8ed/form-scripts **A**.

There are many alternatives to PHP, such as Django (a framework that uses Python), Ruby on Rails, ASP.NET, JSP (JavaServer Pages), and more.

Field Name	Value(s)
first_name	Rose
last_name	Wood
email	rose_wood@testemail.com

A One of the scripts on the companion website is **show-data.php**. As you can see in part here, it displays the name and values for each form field after you fill it out and submit it. The other file (**email-data.php**) sends the submitted form data to an email address you specify in the script.

Form Security

You need to be very careful with regard to security when you're receiving form data on your server. Never assume anything about data. Just because you build safeguards into your form doesn't mean fiends won't create their own form that calls your script to send out millions of spam emails. They may also submit nefarious text that can compromise data on your server. Securing forms is an advanced topic, but I've provided some links at www.htmlcssvqs.com/8ed/form-security.

Server-side vs. Client-side

PHP (and others like it) is a *server-side* language, which means it runs on the computer that serves your webpages (aptly called a server), not on your visitor's computer where the page is viewed. Your script must be uploaded to a server to work; typically it's the same one that hosts your webpages, images, and so on (see Chapter 21 regarding finding a webhost and transferring files). In addition, that server must have PHP installed for the script to be interpreted. The vast majority of web hosts install PHP for you, so you should have no difficulty finding one that supports it. Server-side languages are needed for many functions of a professional website, such as storing data and sending emails.

As you've seen, *client-side* languages, like HTML and CSS, work inside the browser. JavaScript is another client-side language (you can also use it server-side). It can do many tasks without interacting with the server at all. For example, you can use JavaScript to check that all form data has been entered before a form is submitted, among a multitude of other tasks and behaviors unrelated to forms.

Form validation

To validate a form means to check that the visitor has completed each necessary field and that the submitted data is in the format you expect (for example, an email address format for an email field). As noted earlier, some form elements have built-in validation features. Some sites use JavaScript to perform validation as well (tutorials and scripts are available online). These are not replacements for server-side validation, because older browsers or browsers with JavaScript disabled will not perform client-side validation. There are also security concerns to consider as part of proper server-side validation (see the "Form Security" sidebar). In short, server-side validation is one crucial task you should always perform with your processing script.

Organizing the Form Elements

You can use a **fieldset** element to group related elements and make the form easier to follow. The easier it is for your visitors to understand the form, the more likely they are to fill it out correctly. You can also use the **legend** element to give each fieldset a caption that describes the purpose of each grouping, or in some cases, you can provide those descriptions with an **h1–h6** heading Ⓐ. The **legend** element is particularly important for any group of radio

Ⓐ I organized each of the four form sections in its own **fieldset**, and I grouped the Gender radio buttons in a **fieldset** within the Public Profile area. Notice that I added a class named **radios** to style that nested **fieldset** differently, and I included a **legend** element to describe the radio buttons. (I removed a couple of **div**s to keep this example simple; see "Creating Radio Buttons" for the full code of this nested **fieldset**.)

```
...
<h1>Create a New Account</h1>
<form method="post" action="show-data.php">
    <fieldset>
        <h2 class="hdr-account">Account</h2>
        ... Account fields ...
    </fieldset>

    <fieldset>
        <h2 class="hdr-address">Address</h2>
        ... Address fields ...
    </fieldset>

    <fieldset>
        <h2 class="hdr-public-profile">Public Profile</h2>
        ... Public Profile fields ...

        <div class="row">
            <fieldset class="radios">
                <legend>Gender:</legend>
                <input type="radio" id="gender-male" name="gender" value="male" />
                <label for="gender-male">Male</label>

                <input type="radio" id="gender-female" name="gender" value="female" />
                <label for="gender-female">Female</label>
            </fieldset>
        </div>
    </fieldset>

    <fieldset>
        <h2 class="hdr-emails">Emails</h2>
        ... Emails fields ...
    </fieldset>

    <input type="submit" value="Create Account" class="btn" />
</form>
...
```

B With no CSS applied to the page, you can see that browsers apply a thin border around each fieldset by default, including the one for Gender nested in the Public Profile fieldset.

buttons (see "Creating Radio Buttons"), which often wouldn't have an obvious context for visitors otherwise.

Browsers make it clear which form controls belong to a fieldset even when you don't style the page with CSS **B**. But of course, you can style `fieldset` and `legend` (as well as headings) yourself to make your form more appealing and easier to use (**C** and **D**).

C I gave all the `fieldset` elements a margin, a background color, and padding, along with special background colors for each heading.

```
fieldset {
    background-color: #f1f1f1;
    border: none;
    border-radius: 2px;
    margin-bottom: 12px;
    overflow: hidden;
    padding: 0 .625em;
}

.radios { /* nested fieldset */
    background-color: transparent;
    position: relative;
    margin-bottom: 0;
}

h2 {
    background-color: #dedede;
    border-bottom: 1px solid #d4d4d4;
    border-top: 1px solid #d4d4d4;
    border-radius: 5px;
    box-shadow: 3px 3px 3px #ccc;
    color: #fff;
    font-size: 1.1em;
    margin: 12px;
    padding: 0.3em 1em;
    text-shadow: #9FBEB9 1px 1px 1px;
    text-transform: uppercase;
}

.hdr-account { background-color: #0b5586; }
.hdr-address { background-color: #4494c9; }
.hdr-public-profile { background-color:
↦ #377d87; }
.hdr-emails { background-color: #717f88; }
```

To organize the form elements:

1. Below the **form** start tag but above any form elements that you wish to have contained in the first group, type **<fieldset>**.

2. If desired, type **<legend>**. (If you include a **legend**, it must be the first element inside the **fieldset**.)

3. Type the text for the legend.

4. Type **</legend>** to complete the legend.

5. If you didn't include a **legend**, create a heading (**h1–h6**) that identifies the group of form controls in the fieldset. (See the sidebar "The **legend** Element, Headings, Screen Readers, and Styling.")

6. Create the form elements that belong in the first group. For more information, see the sections beginning with "Creating Text Boxes."

7. Type **</fieldset>** to complete the first group of form elements.

8. Repeat steps 1 through 7 for each group of form elements.

D With a little CSS applied, each major group of form fields is clearly distinguished.

The legend Element, Headings, Screen Readers, and Styling

The **legend** element can help make your forms more accessible. Screen readers may announce the **legend** text for each form field associated with it, giving it additional context. This behavior varies by screen reader and browser, as well as by mode (screen reader modes allow users to listen to and navigate webpages a variety of ways).

In many cases, the legend is read just as you would hope. In others, the text is not read, and in others still, a screen reader may go overboard by announcing the legend multiple times for each control. Secondarily, some browsers limit how you can style **legend** or make it more difficult to do so.

Considering all these factors, using an **h1–h6** heading element as I did to identify some (but not all) **fieldset**s Ⓐ can be a sensible alternative to using **legend**. JAWS—the screen reader with the largest user base—reads the heading in conjunction with related form fields as if it were a **legend** element, so the accessibility benefit remains for its users. And all screen readers allow users to navigate a page via headings. As a bonus, you can style headings easily.

Not all forms are alike, so you can vary your approach. Regardless, I encourage you to you always use **fieldset** and **legend** for radio buttons.

TIP Organizing your form into `fieldset` elements is optional, as is using a `legend` (though that does require a `fieldset`). But I highly recommend you use `fieldset` and `legend` to group and identify related radio buttons at the least.

TIP There are some limits to how much the `legend` element can be styled in browsers, particularly regarding positioning. Search online for help if you get stuck, because there are some workarounds.

Creating Text Boxes

Text boxes can contain one line of freeform text—that is, anything that the visitor wants to type—and are typically used for gathering names, addresses, and the like.

Each text box is represented by an **input** tag with **type="text"** assigned. Several other attributes are available in addition to **type**, the most important of which is **name** Ⓐ. Server-side scripts use the **name** you assign to retrieve the value a visitor enters in the text box or that you prepopulate with the **value** attribute. In fact, **name** and **value** are essential to other form field types, too, as you'll see throughout the chapter.

To create a text box:

1. If desired, type the label that will identify the text box to your visitor. For example, **<label for="*idlabel*">Last Name:</label>**, where *idlabel* matches the label in step 4. (I explain this more in the next section, "Labeling Form Parts.")

2. Type **<input type="text"**.

3. Type **name="*dataname*"**, where *dataname* is the text that will identify the input data to the server (and your script).

Ⓐ While it's essential to set the **name** attribute for each text box, you only have to set the **value** attribute when you want to add a default value for a text box. The third text input uses the **placeholder** attribute Ⓑ, and the first uses the **required** attribute Ⓒ. Note that I also set **aria-required="true"** (see the tips). This example also demonstrates that **name** can be different than **for** and **id**, or the same as them (see the sidebar in "Labeling Form Parts").

```
...
<form method="post" action="show-data.php">
<fieldset>
     <h2 class="account">Account</h2>
     <div class="fields">
        <p class="row">
           <label for="first-name">First Name:
           → </label>
           <input type="text" id="first-
           name" name="first_name"
           → class="field-large" required
           → aria-required="true" />
        </p>
        <p class="row">
           <label for="last-name">Last Name:
           → </label>
           <input type="text" id="last-
           → name" name="last_name"
           → class="field-large" />
        </p>
        <p class="row">
           <label for="email">Email:</label>
           <input type="email" id="email"
           → name="email" placeholder=
           → "yourname@example.com"
           → class="field-large" />
        </p>
        ... more fields ...
     </div>
</fieldset>
...
```

Separating Your Form Elements

There are many ways to separate your form elements from each other. In these examples, we are using the **p** element in most cases and **div**s in others (like when nesting a **p**) Ⓐ. In each case, I apply **class="row"** as a styling hook. Alternatively, some choose to structure form elements in an **ol** or **ul**. Generally, lists can be quite helpful to screen reader users. But some screen readers can be a little verbose when announcing forms that are in a list, which could distract some users. So I've opted for **p**s and **div**s instead.

B Placeholders are a great way to give users a hint for filling out a text box, like this email address field. The **placeholder** attribute will put text in a lighter color inside your text box. When the user begins to input text in the field, the placeholder text will disappear. (One exception: IE10 hides the placeholder text when the field gains focus, not when a user starts typing.) The text will come back if the user leaves the field without entering any information. This is another feature found only in HTML5, and older browsers will simply ignore it.

C If the user submits a form before completing a field that has the **required** attribute, the browser displays a message like the one shown. The visual treatment varies in supporting browsers. This feature is specific to HTML5, so older browsers will ignore **required** (the form will still work, though). As noted in "Processing Forms," you can use JavaScript to validate the field in older browsers, and you should *always* validate your form on the server regardless of the browser used.

D When your page loads, it's helpful to have a field focused automatically so the user can begin typing right away. Use the **autofocus** attribute to achieve this.

```
<input type="text" id="first-name"
→ name="first_name" class="field-large"
→ required aria-required="true" autofocus />
```

4. If you created a **label** in step 1, type **id="*idlabel*"**, where ***idlabel*** is the same text assigned to the **for** attribute in step 1. This associates the **label** element with the text box explicitly. Although it's not required, many (perhaps most) coders make the **for** and the **id** the same as the **name** (**A** shows both approaches).

5. If desired, type **value="*default*"**, where ***default*** is the data that will initially be shown in the field and that will be sent to the server if the visitor doesn't type something else.

6. If desired, type **placeholder= "*hinttext*"**, where ***hinttext*** is the data that will initially be shown in the field as a hint to the user of what to enter **B**. The text will disappear if the input has focus or if the user types in the field (browsers do one or the other).

7. If desired, type **required** or **required="required"** (either is fine in HTML5) to ensure that the form will not submit unless the field has a value **C**.

8. If desired, type **autofocus** or **autofocus="autofocus"** (either is fine in HTML5) **D**. If it's the first form control to have this attribute, the input element will have focus when the page loads.

9. If desired, define the size of the box on your form by typing **size="*n*"**, where ***n*** is the desired width of the box, measured in characters. You can also use CSS to set the width on an input box **E**.

10. If desired, type **maxlength="*n*"**, where ***n*** is the maximum number of characters that can be entered in the box.

11. Finish the text box by typing a final **>** or **/>**. (See the last tip.)

continues on next page

TIP Although `labels` are optional, I strongly recommend using them. They are crucial to making your forms accessible and easy to use.

TIP If your visitor skips a field and you haven't set the default value with the `value` attribute, the `name` attribute is sent to the server with an undefined, empty `value` when the visitor submits the form.

TIP Don't confuse the `placeholder` attribute (Ⓐ and Ⓑ) with the `value` attribute. It's true that they both can cause text to appear in a text box by default. However, the text you assign to `placeholder` is merely a hint to users of what to enter in the field, and—unlike `value`—is not sent to the server. In this vein, if a text box has both a `placeholder` and a non-empty `value`, the latter will show in the box.

TIP By default, most browsers store text you enter so they can save you time when filling out similar fields later Ⓕ. You can disable this by including `autocomplete="off"` on the `input`. This is useful if a field asks for sensitive information such as a credit card number. If you apply it to the `form` element, it applies to every field in the form. For example, `<form method="post" action="process.php" autocomplete="off">`.

TIP When we say a text box "gains focus" or "has focus," we mean the cursor is in the box, ready for the visitor to type a value.

TIP The default for `size` is 20. However, visitors can type up to the limit imposed by the `maxlength` attribute. Still, for larger, multi-line entries, it's better to use a `textarea` element (see "Creating Text Areas").

TIP As it does with other self-closing elements (like `img`), HTML5 allows you to finish an input with either > or />. So, `<input type="text" name="city">` and `<input type="text" name="city" />` are equally valid. Whichever way you go, I recommend you be consistent.

Ⓔ Text boxes can be different sizes to accommodate different types of fields. In our example, we're using CSS to set the width with classes.

Ⓕ When I type "Ma," Firefox suggests text from previous form entries that contain the same sequence of letters. I can choose from the list or continue typing. If the entire form or this specific input had `autocomplete="off"` set, the suggestions wouldn't appear and the browser wouldn't store what I type.

A The for attribute of each label matches the id attribute of its corresponding form element, associating the label and field explicitly.

```
...

<fieldset>
    <h2 class="account">Account</h2>
    <div class="fields">
        <p class="row">
            <label for="first-name">
            → First Name:</label>
            <input type="text"
            → id="first-name"
            → name="first_name"
            → class="field-large" />
        </p>
        <p class="row">
            <label for="last-name">
            → Last Name:</label>
            <input type="text"
            → id="last-name"
            → name="last_name"
            → class="field large" />
        </p>
        ... more fields ...
    </div>
</fieldset>

...
```

B If a visitor interacts with a text box label, the cursor is placed in the box, ready for typing. Meanwhile, labels for checkboxes and radio buttons allow the user to click the label as well as the form control to modify the state. Here, a checkbox is selected.

Labeling Form Parts

A *label* is the text that describes the purpose of a form field. For example, you might have "First Name" next to the text field where the visitor should type his or her first name. You mark up these text labels with—surprise—the label element. You may have noticed them in the earlier examples.

The label element has a special attribute, for. When for has the same value as a form field's id, the label and field are associated explicitly A. This improves the usability and accessibility of your forms. For instance, if a visitor interacts with a label (such as clicking it with a mouse), its corresponding form field gains focus B. This association also allows screen readers to announce text labels in conjunction with their respective fields. Imagine how critical that is to a vision-impaired visitor who might not know what the form fields are for otherwise. For those reasons, I strongly recommend you include the for attribute in your labels.

To formally label form parts:

1. Type `<label`.

2. Type `for="idlabel">`, where *idlabel* matches the value of the id attribute in the corresponding form element.

3. Type the label text that describes the form field.

4. Type `</label>`.

5. When you create the form element, be sure to include an id that matches the for attribute specified in step 2.

continues on next page

TIP You can format your labels with CSS. The example in **C** allows each label to align nicely next to its field **B**.

TIP The `for`, `id`, and `name` attributes can have any values as long as they don't have spaces. See the sidebar on this page for related information.

TIP You may also place a form field *inside* a `label` with the `label` text. For example, `<label>First Name: <input type="text" name="first_name" /></label>`. (Note that `for` and `id` aren't necessary in these cases.) However, it's more common to separate the `label` and field **A**, in part because it gives you more control over styling.

TIP The `placeholder` attribute is sometimes incorrectly used as a replacement for a `label`. Be sure to use the `placeholder` as a hint only.

C Styling `label`s is a great way to make your form easier to use and more appealing to visitors. The `cursor: pointer;` style displays a hand instead of the default arrow when a user points the cursor at a label—a good visual cue that the label is actionable. The `vertical-align: top;` style aligns the label relative to the form field next to it.

```
/* Labels that precede form fields */
label {
    cursor: pointer;
    display: inline-block;
    padding: 3px 6px;
    text-align: right;
    width: 150px;
    vertical-align: top;
}

/* Labels after checkboxes */
.checkboxes label {
    text-align: left;
    width: 475px;
}
```

Naming Convention for `id`, `for`, and `name` Attributes

As noted earlier, it's common but not required for coders to make the **for**, **id**, and **name** attributes identical. (Radio buttons and checkboxes are the exception, because the **name** is shared by a group of inputs but the **id** needs to be unique for each input.) I've done this throughout the chapter for single-word values. For example, **for="email"**, **id="email"**, and **name="email"**.

For multi-word values, I've separated each word with a hyphen ("-") in **for** and **id** and with an underscore ("_") in **name** **A**. For example, **for="first-name"**, **id="first-name"**, and **name="first_name"**. I made **name** different for these to demonstrate that it *can* be different, and because it's common to use underscores in the multi-word names passed to form processing scripts.

Regardless of your approach, remember that **for** and **id** *have* to be the same.

Ⓐ Create a password box by using
type="password" instead of **type="text"**.

```
...
<p class="row">
    <label for="password">Password:</label>
    <input type="password" id="password"
    → name="password" />
</p>
<p class="row">
    <label for="password2">Re-enter
    → Password:</label>
    <input type="password" id="password2"
    → name="password2" />
</p>
...
```

Ⓑ When the visitor enters a password in a form,
the password is hidden with bullets or asterisks.
But the real value (what the visitor typed) is passed
to the server when the form is submitted. The
information is not encrypted when it is sent.

Creating Password Boxes

The only difference between a password
box and a text box is that whatever is
typed in the former is hidden by bullets or
asterisks (**Ⓐ** and **Ⓑ**).

To create a password box:

1. Create a **label** to identify the password
   box to your visitors, as described in
   "Labeling Form Parts."

2. Type **<input type="password"**.

3. Type **id="*idlabel*"**, where ***idlabel*** is
   the same as the **label**'s **for** attribute
   value in step 1.

4. Type **name="*dataname*"**, where
   dataname is the text that will identify the
   input data to the server

5. If desired, define the form box's size by
   typing **size="*n*"**, where ***n*** is the width of
   the box, measured in characters.

6. If desired, type **maxlength="*n*"**, where ***n***
   is the maximum character count.

7. If desired, type **required** or
   required="required". (See "Creating
   Text Boxes.")

8. If desired, type **autofocus** or
   autofocus="autofocus". (See "Creating Text Boxes.")

9. Finish the password box by typing a
   final **>** or **/>**. (See the last tip in "Creating Text Boxes.")

TIP Even if nothing is entered in the password box, the **name** is still sent to the server
(with an undefined **value**).

TIP A password box only keeps onlookers
from seeing a user's password as it's typed.
To really protect passwords, use a secure
server (https://).

Creating Email, Search, Telephone, and URL Boxes

The email, telephone, and URL input types **A** are among the new features in HTML5. They look exactly like text boxes but have helpful features for validating the text your visitors enter (**B** through **D**). In the past, we've had to rely on JavaScript to create this functionality in browsers.

Search boxes are also new in HTML5 **E**. They are just like text boxes except that some browsers make them appear like the default search boxes on their operating system **F**.

B When the visitor submits the form in a modern browser, it checks to make sure that the Email field text (if any) is in the valid email address format. If the format is invalid, a message displays and the cursor is placed in the field so the visitor can change the text.

A The appropriate **type** attribute value specifies the email, URL, and telephone boxes. The **pattern** attribute is for custom validation. It uses what are known as *regular expressions* to restrict the content that a user puts into the box. In the case of the telephone **input** shown here, the **pattern** says, "Only accept entries in this format: three digits, a dash, three more digits, another dash, and then four digits" (like many phone numbers). Don't worry about the unusual syntax of regular expressions; at http://html5pattern.com you can find common ones that you can copy and paste into your own **pattern** attributes.

```
...
<p class="row">
    <label for="email">Email:</label>
    <input type="email" id="email" name="email" class="field-large" />
</p>
<div class="row">
    <label for="website">Website URL:</label>
    <input type="url" id="website" name="website" class="field-large"
    → placeholder="http://www.example.com" />
    <p class="instructions">Have a site or a blog? Put the address here, beginning with
    → <kbd>http://</kbd> or <kbd>https://</kbd>.</p>
</div>
<p class="row">
    <label for="phone">Phone:</label>
    <input type="tel" id="phone" name="phone" class="field-large" placeholder="xxx-xxx-xxxx"
    → pattern="\d{3}-\d{3}-\d{4}" />
</p>
...
```

Browser support for all of these is pretty strong (see the first tip). And non-supporting browsers will treat the fields as normal text boxes, so they'll still work, just without the extra features. This means it's safe to use these input types today.

To create email, search, telephone, and URL boxes:

1. Create a `label` to identify the input box to your visitors, as described in "Labeling Form Parts."

continues on next page

C When the visitor submits the form, the browser checks to make sure that the Website URL field text (if any) is in the valid URL format. Notice that www.wikipedia.org is not a valid form URL, because a URL must begin with http:// or https://. This is a good place to use a `placeholder` to help the visitor. For good measure, I also mention the accepted format in the instructional text below the field, as you can see unobstructed in **D**.

D When the visitor submits the form, the browser checks to make sure that the Phone field text (if any) matches the format specified in the `pattern` attribute. Telephone fields are also handy in Safari on iOS (iPhones and iPads), because it will bring up the number keyboard instead of the normal QWERTY format.

E Search boxes are perfect candidates for a `placeholder`. Also, note the use of `method="get"` rather than `method="post"` on the `form`. This is customary for search fields (whether created via `type="search"` or `type="text"`). See the tip regarding `role="search"`.

```
<form method="get" action="search-results.php"
→ role="search">
    <label for="search">Search:</label>
    <input type="search" id="search"
    → name="search" size="30"
    → placeholder="e.g., a book or
    → magazine" />
    <input type="submit" value="Find It!" />
</form>
```

F Browsers such as Chrome (shown in the top two images) and Safari on OS X and Mobile Safari on iOS make the search box look like the rounded search boxes on their operating systems. When you start typing in it, an "x" button that clears the field appears at the right. In other browsers, it looks like a normal text box (shown in the bottom image). (See the tips for more on styling options.)

2. Type `<input type="email"` for an email box, `<input type="search"` for a search box, `<input type="tel"` for a telephone number box, or `<input type="url"` for a URL box.

3. Type `id="idlabel"`, where *idlabel* is the same as the **label**'s **for** attribute value in step 1.

4. Type `name="dataname"`, where *dataname* is the text that will identify the input data to the server.

5. If desired, type `value="default"`, where *default* is the data that will initially be shown in the field and that will be sent to the server if the visitor doesn't type something else.

6. If desired, type `placeholder="hinttext"`, where *hinttext* is the data that will initially be shown in the field as a hint to the user of what to enter. (See "Creating Text Boxes.")

7. If desired, type `required` or `required="required"`. (See "Creating Text Boxes.")

8. If desired, type `autofocus` or `autofocus="autofocus"`. (See "Creating Text Boxes.")

9. If desired, define the size of the box on your form by typing `size="n"`, where *n* is the desired width of the box, measured in characters. You can also use CSS to set the width on an input box (see "Creating Text Boxes").

10. If desired, type `maxlength="n"`, where *n* is the maximum number of characters that can be entered in the box.

11. Finish the text box by typing a final `>` or `/>` (either is fine in HTML5).

TIP At the time of this writing, Chrome, Firefox, IE10, and Opera 10+ provide the automatic validation features of email and URL boxes and the `pattern` attribute. Keep in mind that these features are conveniences for both you and your visitors only; server-side validation is still *strongly* recommended (see "Processing Forms"). This is true even if you've used a JavaScript solution like the aforementioned H5F (https://github.com/ryanseddon/H5F) to provide these HTML5 features to older browsers.

TIP An empty email, telephone, or URL box will pass validation unless you add the `required` attribute. However, if you add `required` to a telephone box but not a suitable value for the `pattern` attribute, the browser will require the field to have content but will allow any text (numbers, letters, and characters).

TIP Email boxes also allow the `multiple` attribute, which specifies that more than one email address may be entered as long as a comma separates each one.

TIP Browsers don't check whether an entered email address or URL exists in the wild, just that it follows the proper format.

TIP These input types also support the `autocomplete` attribute. See the tips in "Creating Text Boxes" for more information.

TIP By default, styling options are limited for search boxes in browsers like Chrome, Safari, and Mobile Safari **F**. Use the proprietary `-webkit-appearance: none;` declaration to override this and gain more CSS control. For example, `input[type="search"] { -webkit-appearance: none; }`. More information (including Firefox support) is available at http://css-tricks.com/almanac/properties/a/appearance/, but please remember that the `appearance` property is not an official part of CSS, so browser behavior can vary.

TIP If you look closely at **E**, you'll see that I included the ARIA landmark role `role="search"` on the form. This improves accessibility by letting screen readers announce when a search area exists in a webpage. If your form includes more controls than just for search, put the ones related to search in a `fieldset` or `div` and apply `role="search"` to that rather than to the `form` element itself. See Chapter 3 for more about ARIA landmark roles.

TIP WebKit browsers support two attributes that are not part of HTML5: `autosave` and `results`, which apply additional behavior and visual elements to search boxes. You can learn more about them at www.wufoo.com/html5/types/5-search.html.

TIP If you include a `pattern` attribute, be sure to clearly state to visitors what pattern you want them to follow. If you're not careful, visitors might give up and never submit the form.

TIP Regular expressions are outside the scope of this book, but there are many online resources (search for "regex tutorial"), and you can find useful patterns at http://html5pattern.com.

Creating Radio Buttons

In the "old" days, car radios had big black plastic buttons—push one to listen to WFCR; push another for WRNX. You could never push two buttons at once. Radio buttons on forms work the same way. Create a radio button by setting **type="radio"** on an **input** (Ⓐ and Ⓑ).

To create radio buttons:

1. If desired, type the introductory text for your radio buttons. You might use something like **<p>Select one of the following:</p>**.

2. Type **<input type="radio"**.

3. Type **name="*radioset*"**, where *radioset* identifies the data sent to the server and also links the radio buttons together, ensuring that only one per set can be selected.

4. Type **id="*idlabel*"**, where *idlabel* matches the **for** attribute value of the **label** you'll create in step 8. Unlike the **name** value, which must be the same for *all* radio buttons in a set, the **id** for *each* radio button on the page must be unique.

Ⓐ The **name** attribute must be the same on all radio buttons in a given set so that only one can be selected at a time. The **value** attribute is crucial, since the visitor has no way of typing a value for a radio button.

```
...

<fieldset class="radios">
    <legend>Gender:</legend>

    <p class="row">
        <input type="radio"
        → id="gender-male" name="gender"
        → value="male" />
        <label for="gender-male">Male</label>
    </p>
    <p class="row">
        <input type="radio"
        → id="gender-female" name="gender"
        → value="female" />
        <label for="gender-female">Female
        → </label>
    </p>
</fieldset>

...
```

B I positioned the **legend** absolutely within the context of the **.radios div**, which is set to **position: relative** (**position** works better than **margin** for **legend**s). Giving the elements with the **.row** class a large **margin-left** moves them to the right of the Gender **legend**. The **vertical-align: middle;** setting on the **label** elements helps the label text align vertically with the radio buttons to their left.

```
.radios {
    background-color: transparent;
    position: relative;
    margin-bottom: 0;
}

.radios .row {
    margin: 0 0 0 150px;
}

.radios legend {
    left: 0;
    padding: 0 6px;
    position: absolute;
    text-align: right;
    top: 2px;
    width: 148px;
}

.radios label {
    padding-left: 2px;
    margin-right: 5px;
    vertical-align: middle;
    width: auto;
}
```

C Because the labels (Male and Female) are **label** elements, interacting with one will select the corresponding radio button.

5. Type **value="*data*"**, where ***data*** is the text that will be sent to the server if the radio button is selected, either by you or by the visitor **C**.

6. If desired, type **checked** or **checked="checked"** (HTML5 allows either) to make the radio button active by default when the page is loaded. You can do this to only one radio button in the set.

7. Type the final **>** or **/>** (either is fine in HTML5).

8. Type **<label for="*idlabel*">*radio label*</label>** where ***idlabel*** matches the **id** value in your radio button from step 4, and ***radio label*** identifies the radio button to the visitor. This is often the same as **value**, but it doesn't have to be.

9. Repeat steps 2 through 8 for each radio button in the set.

TIP I recommend nesting each group of radio buttons in a **fieldset** and describing it with a **legend A**. See "Organizing the Form Elements" for more details.

Creating Checkboxes

Whereas radio buttons can accept only one answer per set, a visitor can select as many checkboxes in a set as they like. Like radio buttons, all checkboxes in a set have the same **name** attribute **A**.

To create checkboxes:

1. If desired, type the introductory text (something like **<p>Select one or more of the following:</p>**) for your checkboxes.

2. Type **<input type="checkbox"**.

3. Type **name="*boxset*"**, where *boxset* identifies the data sent to the server and also represents the checkboxes as a group. (Use the same **name** for all.)

4. Type **id="*idlabel*"**, where *idlabel* matches the **for** attribute value of the **label** you'll create in step 8.

A Notice that the label text (not highlighted) does not need to match the **value** attribute. That's because the label text identifies the checkboxes to the visitor in the browser, whereas the **value** is part of the data sent to the server-side script. The empty brackets in the **name** are for PHP (see the tip). I created a **.checkboxes** class to limit **label** styling to groups of checkboxes **B**.

```
<div class="fields checkboxes">
    <p class="row">
        <input type="checkbox" id="email-ok-msg-from-users" name="email_signup[]"
        → value="user-emails" />
        <label for="email-ok-msg-from-users">It is okay to email me with messages from other users.
        → </label>
    </p>
    <p class="row">
        <input type="checkbox" id="email-ok-occasional-updates" name="email_signup[]"
        → value="occasional-updates" />
        <label for="email-ok-occasional-updates">It is okay to email me with occasional promotions
        → about our other products.</label>
    </p>
</div>
```

B For checkboxes, it is often the case that you need to style the **label** differently, since by convention it comes after the checkbox input itself **C**.

```
.checkboxes label {
    text-align: left;
    width: 475px;
}
```

C The visitor can select as many boxes as they wish. Each corresponding value will be sent to the server-side script, along with the **name** of the checkbox set.

5. Type **value="*data*"**, where *data* is the text that will be sent to the server if the checkbox is marked (either by the visitor, or by you as described in **A**).

6. If desired, type **checked** or **checked="checked"** (either is fine) to make the checkbox selected by default when the page opens. You (or the visitor) may select as many checkboxes as desired.

7. Type **>** or **/>** to complete the checkbox.

8. Type **<label for="*idlabel*">*checkbox label*</label>**, where *idlabel* matches the **id** value in your checkbox element from step 4, and *checkbox label* identifies the checkbox to the visitor.

9. Repeat steps 2 through 8 for each checkbox in the set.

TIP If you use PHP to process your form, you can automatically create an array (named $_POST['*boxset*']) that contains the checkbox values by using name="*boxset*[ ]" in the HTML, where *boxset* represents the data sent to the script. For the example in **A** the PHP would be $_POST['email_signup'].

Creating Text Areas

If you want to give visitors room to write questions or comments, use text areas **A**.

To create text areas:

1. Create a **label** to identify the text area to your visitors, as explained in "Labeling Form Parts."

2. Type **<textarea**.

3. Type **id="*idlabel*"**, where ***idlabel*** is the same as the **label**'s **for** attribute value in step 1.

4. Type **name="*dataname*"**, where ***dataname*** is the text that will identify the text area data to the server (and your script).

5. If desired, type **maxlength="*n*"**, where ***n*** is the maximum number of characters that can be entered in the box.

6. If desired, type **cols="*n*"**, where ***n*** is roughly the number of characters visible per line (the text area's width).

7. If desired, type **rows="*n*"**, where ***n*** is the number of visible lines of text (the text area's height).

8. Type **>**.

9. Type the default text, if any, for the text area. (This displays in the text area.)

10. Type **</textarea>** to complete the text area.

> **TIP** Include text between the start and end **textarea** tags if you'd like to prepopulate a text area with a value (there is not a **value** attribute). As usual, include the **placeholder** attribute to define placeholder text.

> **TIP** The **maxlength** attribute is new to text areas in HTML5, so its behavior varies across browsers (www.wufoo.com/html5/attributes/03-maxlength.html). Older browsers ignore it.

> **TIP** You have more control over the size of a text area with CSS.

A The **rows** and **cols** attributes control the respective height and width of the text area unless CSS overrides one **B** or both settings. Even if you do set the dimensions in CSS, **rows** and **cols** are helpful to include in the off chance that a user visits your page with CSS turned off in their browser.

```
<label for="bio">Bio:</label>
<textarea id="bio" name="bio" cols="40"
→ rows="5" class="field-large"></textarea>
```

B The font properties do not always get inherited by a text area by default, so you must explicitly set **font: inherit;** for the element. If desired, you can dictate the width of a text area with the same class (**.field-large** in this case) you use for other inputs, such as text and URL boxes. In the absence of a CSS **height** property, the text area's height **C** is determined by the **rows** attribute in the HTML **A**.

```
textarea {
    font: inherit;
    padding: 2px;
}

.field-large {
    width: 250px;
}
```

C Visitors can enter up to 32,700 characters in a text area unless you limit the number with the **maxlength** attribute. Scroll bars will appear inside the text area when necessary (not shown). Visitors can change the size of a text area by dragging the slanted lines in the lower-right corner. You can prevent them from doing that by setting **textarea { resize: none; }**.

A Select boxes are made up of two HTML elements: **select** and **option**. You set the **name** attribute in the **select** element, and you set a **value** attribute in each of the **option** elements. You can style **select** B and **option** elements, with some limitations.

```
<label for="state">State:</label>
<select id="state" name="state">
    <option value="AL">Alabama</option>
    <option value="AK">Alaska</option>
    ...
</select>
```

B This CSS rule makes the menu text the same size as its parent; it may otherwise be noticeably smaller by default. You also can adjust the **width**, the **color**, and other properties, but different browsers display drop-down lists slightly differently.

```
select {
    font-size: inherit;
}
```

Street Address:	
City:	
State:	Alabama
ZIP Code:	Alabama / Alaska / California

C The default selection is either the first option in the menu (as shown) or the one you've set as **selected** in the HTML. (Note that a visitor will not be able to avoid making a selection in a menu unless you include the **size** attribute.)

Creating Select Boxes

Select boxes are perfect for offering your visitors a choice from a given set of options **A**. They are most often rendered as drop-down lists **C**. If you give the user the option to select multiple answers, the select box will render as a box of items with a scroll bar.

To create select boxes:

1. Create a **label** to describe your menu, as explained in "Labeling Form Parts."

2. Type **<select**.

3. Type **id="*idlabel*"**, where ***idlabel*** is the same as the **label**'s **for** attribute value in step 1.

4. Type **name="*dataname*"**, where ***dataname*** will identify the data collected from the menu when it is sent to the server.

5. If desired, type **size="*n*"**, where ***n*** represents the height (in lines) of the selectbox.

6. If desired, type **multiple** or **multiple="multiple"** (HTML5 accepts either) to allow your visitor to select more than one menu option (with the Control or Command key).

7. Type **>**.

8. Type **<option**.

9. Type **value="*optiondata*"**, where ***optiondata*** is the data that will be sent to the server if the option is selected. (Note: If you omit **value**, the text you type in step 12 is the option's value.)

10. If desired, type **selected** or **selected="selected"** (HTML5 accepts either) to specify that the option be selected by default.

continues on next page

11. Type **>**.

12. Type the option text as you wish it to appear in the menu.

13. Type **</option>**.

14. Repeat steps 8 through 13 for each option.

15. Type **</select>**.

If you have a particularly large menu with many options, you may want to group the options into categories (**D** and **E**).

To group select box options:

1. Create a select box as described in "To create select boxes."

2. Before the first **option** element (see step 8 of "To create select boxes") in the first group that you wish to place together in a sub-menu, type **<optgroup**.

3. Type **label="*submenutitle*">**, where ***submenutitle*** is the heading for the sub-menu.

4. After the last **option** element in the group, type **</optgroup>**.

5. Repeat steps 2 through 4 for each sub-menu.

TIP If you add the **size** attribute, the select box appears more like a list, and there is no automatically selected option **F** (unless you use **selected**).

TIP If **size** is bigger than the number of options, visitors can deselect all values by clicking in the empty space.

TIP The **option** element allows a **label** attribute for specifying the text that should display in the menu instead of the text between the **option** tags (see step **12** in "To create select boxes"). However, Firefox doesn't support it, so it's best to avoid it.

D Each sub-menu has a title—specified in the **label** attribute of the **optgroup** start tag—and a series of options (defined with **option** elements and regular text).

```
<label for="referral">Where did you find out
→ about us?</label>
<select id="referral" name="referral">
    <optgroup label="Online">
        <option value="social_network">Social
        → Network</option>
        <option value="search_engine">Search
        → Engine</option>
    </optgroup>
    <optgroup label="Offline">
        <option value="postcard">Postcard
        → </option>
        <option value="word_of_mouth">Word of
        → Mouth</option>
    </optgroup>
</select>
```

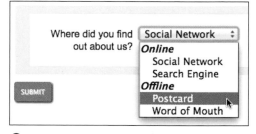

E Browsers typically indent each **option** within an **optgroup** to distinguish them from the **optgroup label** attribute text.

F Because the **size** attribute is set, the menu displays as a scrollable list and no option is selected by default. The code in this example is **<select id="state" name="state" size="3">**, making the menu three lines high.

A To allow visitors to upload files, you must set the proper **enctype** attribute and create the **input type="file"** element. Although it's not used here, include the **multiple** attribute on the **input** to allow uploading multiple files. This is new in HTML5 and is supported widely across browsers except for mobile browsers and IE (only IE10 supports it), which ignore it.

```
<form method="post" action="show-data.php"
enctype="multipart/form-data">
    ...
    <label for="picture">Picture:</label>
    <input type="file" id="picture"
  ↪ name="picture" />
    <p class="instructions">Maximum size of
  ↪ 700k. JPG, GIF or PNG.</p>
    ...
</form>
```

B The file upload area provides a way for the user to select a file on their system. Browsers create the Browse button automatically for a **type="file"** input element. Chrome and Safari don't show a box, just a button. Browsers don't allow you to style this type of input like they do for many form elements.

Handling File Uploads

You'll need a special script to handle uploads. Search online for "file upload script." Also, your web server may need to be properly configured to store files before it can accept them. Contact your web host for help as needed.

Allowing Visitors to Upload Files

Sometimes you might want your users to upload a file, such as a photograph or a résumé, to your server **A**.

To allow visitors to upload files:

1. When you begin your form, type **<form method="post" enctype= "multipart/ form-data"**. The **enctype** attribute ensures that the file is uploaded in the proper format.

2. Type **action="*upload.url*">**, where ***upload.url*** is the URL of the script that processes incoming files.

3. Create the **label** for the file upload area so your visitors know what to upload (see "Labeling Form Parts").

4. Type **<input type="file"** to create a file upload box and a Browse button **B**.

5. Type **id="*idlabel*"**, where ***idlabel*** is the same value as the **label**'s **for** attribute value in step 3.

6. Type **name="*dataname*"**, where ***dataname*** identifies the file or files being uploaded.

7. If desired, type **size="*n*"**, where ***n*** is the width of the field in which the visitor will enter the path and file name.

8. If desired, type **multiple** or **multiple="multiple"** (HTML5 accepts either) to allow visitors to upload more than one file (see caption in **A**).

9. Type the final **>** or **/>**.

10. Complete the form as usual, including the submit button and **</form>** end tag.

TIP You can't use the **get** method for forms that allow uploading.

Creating Hidden Fields

Hidden fields are used to store data in the form without showing it to the visitor (Ⓐ and Ⓑ). You can think of them as invisible text boxes. They are often used by processing scripts to store information gathered from an earlier form so that it can be combined with the present form's data Ⓑ.

To create hidden fields:

1. Type `<input type="hidden"`.

2. Type `name="dataname"`, where *dataname* identifies the information to be submitted to the server.

3. Type `value="data"`, where *data* is the information itself that is to be submitted. It is often a variable from the form processing script Ⓐ.

4. Type the final `>` or `/>` (HTML5 allows either one).

TIP It doesn't matter where the hidden fields are located in your form markup, because they won't be visible in the browser.

TIP Don't put sensitive information like a password or credit card number in a hidden field. Even though it won't show in your webpage, visitors can see it if they view your HTML source code (see "The Inspiration of Others" in Chapter 2).

TIP There are two ways to create a *visible* form element with a value that visitors cannot change. One is with the `disabled` attribute (see "Disabling Form Elements"). The other is with the `readonly` attribute. Unlike a disabled field, a field with `readonly` can have focus, and visitors can select and copy—but not change—the text inside it. It applies only to text inputs and text areas. For example, `<input type="text" id="coupon" name="coupon" value="FREE" readonly />`. You also can specify the attribute as `readonly="readonly"` (the result is the same).

Ⓐ Visitors can't see this input, but when they submit the form, the **step** name with a value of 6 is passed to the server along with the form data gathered from the visitor in other fields.

```
<form method="post" action="your-script.php">
    <input type="hidden" name="step"
    → value="6" />

    ... other form fields ...

    <input type="submit"
    → value="Submit Form" />
</form>
```

Ⓑ When you create a hidden field, you can use the variables from your script to set the value of the field to what the visitor originally entered in a previous form. (This example uses PHP syntax.)

```
<form method="post" action="your-script.php">
    <input type="hidden" name="email"
    → value="<?= $email ?>" />

    ... other form fields ...

    <input type="submit"
    → value="Submit Form" />
</form>
```

When to Use a Hidden Field?

Here is one case when hidden fields can be handy. Imagine you have a form and want to be able to give your visitors a chance to review what they've entered before they submit it. Your processing script can show them the submitted data and at the same time create a form with hidden fields containing the same data. If the visitor wants to edit the data, they simply go back. But if they want to submit the data, the hidden fields will already be filled out, saving them the task of entering the data again.

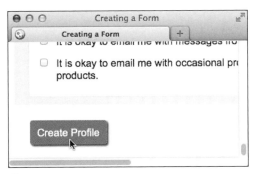

A If you leave out the **name** attribute, the name-value pair for the submit button will not be passed to the script. Since you usually don't need this information, that's a good thing.

```
<input type="submit" value="Create Profile"
→ class="btn" />
```

B I apply a background, font formatting, spacing, and some CSS3 features to the submit button by using a class. Because it's a class, I can reuse the styles on other buttons.

```
.btn {
    background-color: #da820a;
    border: none;
    border-radius: 4px;
    box-shadow: 2px 2px 2px #333;
    color: #fff;
    mmargin: 12px 0 0 26px;
    padding: 8px;
    text-shadow: 1px 1px 0px #777;
}
```

C I used Create Profile as the button's **value** because it's more meaningful to visitors for this form than the default button text (see the first tip). Activating the submit button sends the form data to the script on your server so you can use the information.

Creating a Submit Button

None of the information that your visitors enter will be any good to you unless they send it to the server. You should always create a submit button for your forms so that the visitor can deliver the information to you. Submit buttons may be text (**A** through **C**), an image (**D** and **E**), or a combination of both (**F** and **G**).

To create a submit button:

1. Type **<input type="submit"**.

2. If desired, type **value="*submit message*"**, where ***submit message*** is the text that will appear in the button.

3. Type the final **>** or **/>**.

To create a submit button with an image:

Sometimes the designer creates a button that is beyond the capabilities of CSS3, even with its fancy gradients, shadows, and rounded corners. In this case, you may use an image alone as an input element to submit a form (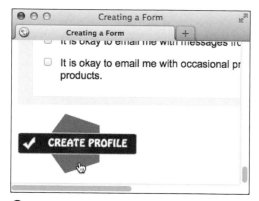 **D** and **E**).

1. Create a PNG, GIF, or JPEG image. (PNG is usually best for this because of the small file size.)

2. Type **<input type="image"**.

3. Type **src="*image.url*"**, where ***image.url*** is the location of the image on the server.

4. Type **alt="*description*"**, where ***description*** is what will appear if the image does not.

5. Type the final **>** or **/>** to finish the image submit button.

To create a submit button with text and an image:

The **button** element lets you create buttons that contain other HTML elements instead of just using a simple text value or image (**F** and **G**). (In case they are of concern, versions of IE prior to IE8 have some **button** quirks. Search online for details.)

1. Type **<button type="submit">**.

2. Type the text, if any, that should appear on the left side of the image in the button.

3. Type **<img src="*image.url*"**, where ***image.url*** is the name of the image that will appear on the button.

D With **type="image"**, you can create a submit button from an image instead of text. The **width** and **height** are optional.

```
<input type="image" src="button-submit.png"
→ width="188" height="95" alt="Create Profile"
→ />
```

E Browsers may show a hand instead of an arrow when you hover the cursor over an image submit button.

F The **button** element gives you more flexibility regarding the content of your submit buttons. This one contains both an image and text. The **button** element allows other HTML elements as well.

```
<button type="submit" class="btn">
→ <img src="check.png" width="21" height="21"
→ alt="" /> Create Profile</button>
```

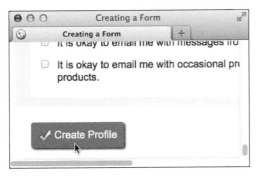

G Aside from the checkmark image, this button looks like the one in **C** because they both have the **.btn** class **B**. Browsers show an arrow when you hover the cursor over a button **C**.

4. Type **alt="*alternate text*"**, where *alternate text* is what appears if the image doesn't.

5. If desired, add any other image attributes.

6. Type **>** or **/>** to complete the image.

7. Type the text, if any, that should appear on the right side of the image in the button.

8. Type **</button>**.

TIP If you leave out the **value** attribute, the submit button will be labeled Submit or Submit Query by default, depending on the browser.

TIP If you have multiple submit buttons, you should give a **name** attribute and a **value** attribute to each one so that your script can tell which one was pressed. Otherwise, it's generally best to omit the **name** attribute.

TIP You can also use the **button** element to create a submit button without an image. In any case, you may want to avoid using **button** if your form requires more than one submit button because browser behavior can vary.

TIP Forms can have a reset button that resets all form controls back to how they were when the page loaded (before the visitor filled them out). You can create a reset button with **<input type="reset" />** or **<button type="reset">Reset</button>**. Reset buttons may be styled, too.

TIP You can turn off the browser's automatic validation of HTML5 inputs like **type="email"** and **type="URL"** by placing the **formnovalidate** attribute on the submit button: **<input type="submit" formnovalidate />**.

Disabling Form Elements

You can disable parts of your form if you don't want visitors to use them. For example, a text area could be disabled unless the visitor answers another part of a form Ⓐ.

The value of a disabled form element is not submitted to the server with the form, and it is skipped if you navigate the webpage with a keyboard.

Ⓐ Here, I apply the **disabled** attribute to the **textarea** and load a JavaScript file at the very bottom of the page. The file contains a script that enables the **textarea** only if a visitor selects the Other radio button (Ⓑ and Ⓒ). Selecting any of the remaining radio buttons disables it. (Note: In practice, I would apply the **disabled** attribute with JavaScript instead of in the HTML in this case, allowing visitors without JavaScript to fill out the text area, too. The **toggle-textarea.js** file in Chapter 19 does this.)

```
...
    <div id="choices">
        <p>
            <input type="radio" name="how" value="advertisement" id="advertisement" />
            <label for="advertisement">Advertisement</label>
        </p>
        ...
        <p>
            <input type="radio" name="how" value="other" id="other" />
            <label for="other">Other</label>
        </p>
        <p>
            <textarea id="other-description" cols="35" rows="5" placeholder="TV, school, bingo game,
            → etc." title="Please describe how you heard about us." disabled="disabled"></textarea>
        </p>

        <input type="submit" value="Submit" class="btn" />
    </div>
...
</form>

<!-- This goes at the very end, right before </body> -->
<script src="js/toggle-textarea.js"></script>
</body>
</html>
```

B When the Other radio button is not selected, the text area is grayed out and disabled, so the user cannot select the box and enter text.

C When the visitor chooses the Other radio button, the text area turns white and the user can enter text to be submitted to the server—thanks to the JavaScript.

To disable a form element:

In the form element's start tag, type `disabled` or `disabled="disabled"` (either is fine in HTML5).

TIP You can change the state of a form element from disabled to enabled (and vice versa) with JavaScript. Explaining JavaScript is beyond the scope of this book, but I've provided the `toggle-textarea.js` script referenced in **A** in Chapter 19 ("Loading an External Script"). The file includes several comments that shed some light on how it works. If you'd like to learn more about JavaScript, one respected resource is eloquentjavascript.net.

TIP See Chapter 19 for more about the `script` element.

TIP See the last tip in "Creating Hidden Fields" to understand the difference between the `disabled` and `readonly` attributes.

Styling Forms Based on Their State

Sometimes you may want to style a form element differently if it has a certain state or a particular attribute. For instance, perhaps you'd like to distinguish required fields from normal ones for your visitors.

You might recall seeing pseudo-classes elsewhere in the book, including in "Selecting Links Based on Their State" in Chapter 9. Well, CSS provides several more of them for styling form elements in a given state. Most of these are new in CSS3. I've summarized the ones with the best browser support in **Table 16.3**. Peter-Paul Koch lists the others, with support information, at www.quirksmode.org/css/selectors/ (scroll to "UI state pseudo-classes").

A This rule applies a background color to any **input** (including submit buttons) or **textarea** that has focus. To target specific input types, include an attribute selector. For example, **input[type="submit"]:focus { background-color: #ff8c00; }** would style focused submit buttons only.

```
input:focus,
textarea:focus {
    background-color: greenyellow;
}
```

| Street Address: | 27 Carpenter |
| City: | |

B The first field has focus, so its background is light green (not the most pleasant of colors, but it makes the point).

TABLE 16.3 Pseudo-classes

Selector	Applies To	Browser Support
:focus	Field that has focus (**A** and **B**).	All, IE8+
:checked	Checked radio button or checkbox (**C** and **D**).	All, IE9+
:disabled	Field with **disabled** attribute **E**.	All, IE9+
:enabled	Opposite of :disabled.	All, IE9+
:required	Field with **required** attribute (**F** and **G**).	All, IE10+, Safari 5+
:optional	Opposite of :required.	All, IE10+, Safari 5+
:invalid	Field with value that doesn't match pattern attribute; or an email or URL box when value isn't in proper format. It also applies to any empty field marked with **required** (see the tips for a caveat) (**H** and **I**).	All, IE10+, Safari 5+
:valid	Opposite of :invalid (**H** and **I**).	All, IE10+, Safari 5+

[Notation like "All, IE9+" means that, for example, Internet Explorer 9 and subsequent versions support the selector, as do all other modern browsers.]

C This rule styles the label that follows a chosen radio button or checkbox **D** (or the one you've given the **checked** attribute).

```
input:checked + label {
    color: green;
}
```

D Only the labels for the selected radio button and checkbox are green.

E This is the rule I applied to **B** in "Disabling Form Elements."

```
textarea:disabled {
    background-color: #ccc;
    border-color: #999;
    color: #666;
}
```

F All required **input** and **textarea** elements will have a more prominent border.

```
input:required,
textarea:required {
    border: 2px solid #000;
}
```

G As you can see, only the First Name field is required. The red asterisk is not a result of the CSS in **F**. It's common to note required fields with an asterisk or "(required)" in the label text, so I added it. This way browsers that don't support **:required** will also indicate the required fields in some manner.

To style form elements in a particular state:

1. Type *selector*, where *selector* includes one or more of the states shown in the table, followed by **{** to begin the declaration block.

2. Type the **property: value;** declarations you'd like to use to style your states. Descriptions of CSS properties and values begin in Chapter 8.

3. Type **}** to complete the declaration block and the style rule.

H The text in an email box will be red if it isn't in the accepted email address format.

```
input[type="email"]:invalid {
    color: red;
}

input[type="email"]:valid {
    color: black;
}
```

I The text is red until you finish typing a valid email address, at which point it turns black.

TIP The `:invalid` state applies as soon as your webpage loads, which may, depending on your styles, cause some unexpected results. For example, if your rule is `input:invalid { background-color: pink; }`, a required `input` field will have a pink background even before your visitor has tried to fill it out. (Empty required fields are deemed invalid.) To exclude required fields, you could use the `:not` pseudo-class; for example, `input:invalid:not(:required) { border: 2px solid red; }`. The `:not` pseudo-class is supported by all browsers except Internet Explorer prior to IE9.

TIP As an alternative to the previous tip, when a form is submitted, you could apply a class to the `form` element with JavaScript and use that class in your selector to style invalid fields. For example, `.submitted input:invalid { background-color: red; }`. See Peter Gasston's article at html5doctor.com/css3-pseudo-classes-and-html5-forms for sample JavaScript code as well as other tips.

TIP Browsers will ignore a style rule if it contains a selector it doesn't support. Web designers and developers often find this acceptable; visitors with more capable browsers will get the enhanced experience. Keith Clark's Selectivzr (http://selectivizr.com/) is a JavaScript file you can include in your pages if you'd like older browsers to understand these selectors.

Styling Forms with Attribute Selectors

Don't forget you also can use attribute selectors to target form fields with certain attributes, such as:

- `[autocomplete]`
- `[autofocus]`
- `[multiple]` (Limited to email boxes and file uploads)
- `[placeholder]`
- `[type="email"]` **H**, `[type="url"]`, and so on for the other input types

Video, Audio, and Other Multimedia

The addition of movies, sound, graphics, and animations to webpages can enhance your visitors' experience. Prior to HTML5, the only method of adding multimedia to your webpages was through third-party plugins such as Adobe Flash Player or Apple's QuickTime. HTML5 changes all that with the introduction of native multimedia—where the browser takes care of it all.

Not all HTML5-capable browsers support the same video and audio formats. You'll learn how to accommodate your visitors by providing various formats, including a Flash fallback for browsers that don't support HTML5 media at all.

Please note that this chapter is meant to be an introduction to adding multimedia to webpages, with a strong emphasis on the HTML5 code you need. It does not teach you how to create the multimedia content, only how to make it available to your visitors.

In This Chapter

Third-Party Plugins and Going Native

The third-party plugins I spoke of in the introduction allowed for adding audio and video to pages before HTML5, but there were problems. The code for embedding a Flash video in one browser didn't necessarily work in another, and there weren't any elegant ways around it. More importantly, the experience of visiting a site sometimes suffered because plug-ins like Flash demand a lot of a computer. In some cases, browsers would slow down or crash.

With such things in mind, native multimedia was added to the HTML5 specification. This brings a number of benefits: improved performance and stability (because browsers can manage them better than plug-ins), the media player buttons and other controls are built into the browser, and the reliance on plug-ins is drastically reduced (but not entirely gone—as you'll see later).

As with any set of standards, there are issues with HTML5's native multimedia. Despite efforts by many to standardize on one file format for audio and one for video, not all browsers and related vendors wanted to be told what to do. This means that you need to provide your media in more than one format for it to be playable by HTML5-capable browsers. We'll look at this in detail later.

The usefulness of HTML5 and native media was enhanced when Apple announced that they were not going to support Flash on their mobile devices, including the iPhone and iPad. This showed that the past near-universal reliance on Flash for playing media files was diminishing and that the day for HTML5's native multimedia was at hand. This is where HTML5 native multimedia stepped in and showed its strength, because the browser on Apple's mobile devices does indeed support HTML5. Other mobile devices have followed suit.

Digital Rights Management (DRM)

One thing you'll notice about embedding audio and video files is that the URLs to the source files are available for anyone who wants to download and "steal" your content—just as embedded images and HTML, JavaScript, and CSS source files are. There's nothing you can do about this.

HTML5 doesn't provide any method to protect your media content in any way, although there are discussions underway that might change this. So if you are concerned about protecting your media files, for now don't use HTML5 native multimedia.

What's a Codec?

A *codec* is a computer program that uses a compression algorithm to encode and decode a digital stream of data, making it more suitable for playback.

The objective of the codec is usually to maintain the highest audio and video quality it can while aiming for a smaller file size.

Of course, some codecs are better than others at performing this.

Setting the MIME Type

Some browsers may not play your media files unless they are served as the proper MIME type. If your site is running on the Apache web server—and it probably is—you can configure the MIME types in what is known as the **.htaccess** file. It's a text file that typically resides in the root directory of your site, alongside your Home page.

Here are the MIME types to add to your **.htaccess** file with any text editor:

```
AddType video/ogg .ogv
AddType video/mp4 .mp4
AddType video/webm .webm
AddType audio/ogg .ogg
AddType audio/mp3 .mp3
```

If your site already has the file, rename it **a.htaccess**, download it from your web server, add the MIME types above, upload it to your server, and rename it back to **.htaccess**. If your site doesn't have it, you can create it from scratch.

Ask your web host about updating your **.htaccess** file if you need help.

Video File Formats

Three different video file formats, or codecs, are supported by HTML5:

- Ogg Theora uses either the .ogg or .ogv file extension and is supported by Firefox 3.5+, Chrome 4+, Opera 10.5+, and Firefox for Android.

- MP4 (H.264) uses the .mp4 or .m4v file extension and is supported by Safari 3.2+, Chrome 4-? (see tips), Internet Explorer 9+, iOS (Mobile Safari), Android 2.1+, Chrome for Android, Firefox for Android, and Opera Mobile 11+.

- WebM uses the .webm file extension and is supported by Firefox 4+, Chrome 6+, Opera 10.6+, Android 2.3+, Chrome for Android, Firefox for Android, and Opera Mobile 14.

TIP You need to provide your video in at least two different formats—MP4 and WebM—to ensure that all HTML5-compatible browsers are supported.

TIP Google has said they will drop support for MP4 in Chrome, but haven't yet. Firefox is rolling out MP4 support gradually. On desktops, Windows 7+ is getting it first, although it requires users to have the codec installed on their machine.

TIP WebM will work in IE 9+ or Safari if a visitor has WebM installed on their machine.

Converting Between File Formats

If you already have a video resource and wish to convert it to any or all of the file formats listed, there are a number of free tools that can help you with this. Here are two:

Miro Video Converter, at www.mirovideoconverter.com

HandBrake, at http://handbrake.fr

Adding a Video to Your Webpage

In order to add a video to your webpage, you need to use the **video** element. Doing so couldn't be simpler . Browsers will figure out your video's dimensions when it loads the file and display it at that size **Ⓑ**, or you can set them yourself **Ⓒ**.

The video isn't displayed if the browser doesn't understand the video format you specified **Ⓓ**.

To add a single video to your webpage:

1. Obtain your video resource.

2. Type **<video src="*my-video.ext*"></video>**, where *my-video.ext* is the location, name, and extension of the video file.

   And that's it! Well, almost (**Ⓑ** and **Ⓓ**).

Ⓒ The dimensions I set here match the video's normal size, so this would look the same as **Ⓑ**. But, as with images, you can use **width** and **height** values that are a different size, and the browser will scale the video the best it can.

```
...
<body>
    <video src="paddle-steamer.webm"
  → width="369" height="208"></video>
</body>
</html>
```

Ⓐ Specifying a single WebM video with no controls.

```
...
<body>
    <video src="paddle-steamer.webm"></video>
</body>
</html>
```

Ⓑ Video pauses on the first frame by default. You now have a video without a play button, meaning visitors can't watch it! We'll correct that in the next section.

Ⓓ Browsers, like Safari, that don't support WebM display a whole lotta nothin'. Not good! Later, I'll show you how to specify more than one video format so all browsers are happy.

Exploring video attributes

What other attributes, besides **src**, can you use with the **video** element? As you can see in **Table 17.1**, there are quite a number of them, which gives you a lot of flexibility with your video.

TABLE 17.1 Video Attributes

Attribute	Description
src	Specifies the URL to the video file.
autoplay	Automatically starts playing the video as soon as it can.
controls	Adds the browser's default control set to the video so visitors can control playback.
muted	Mutes the video's audio.
loop	Plays the video in a loop.
poster	Specifies an image file to display (instead of the first frame of the video) when the video loads. Takes a URL to the required image file.
width	The width of the video in pixels. Default is generally 300.
height	The height of the video in pixels. Default is generally 150.
preload	Hints to the browser how much of the video it should load. It can take three different values: **none** — don't load anything. **metadata** — load only the video's metadata (e.g., length and dimensions). **auto** — let the browser decide what to do (this is the default).

Adding Controls and Autoplay to Your Video

So far, I've shown you the simplest possible method for adding video to your webpage. The video in that example will not even start playing, because we haven't told it to. Furthermore, your visitors can't start the video themselves because the player doesn't display any controls.

You can change that easily enough Ⓐ. The **controls** attribute tells the browser to add a set of default controls to the video. Each browser has its own set of default controls, which look very different from each other (Ⓑ through Ⓕ).

Normally, a video doesn't play unless the visitor uses the play button. You may set it to play automatically by including the **autoplay** attribute Ⓖ.

Ⓐ Adding a single WebM video file, this time with controls.

```
...
<body>
    <video src="paddle-steamer.webm"
    → width="369" height="208" controls>
    → </video>
</body>
</html>
```

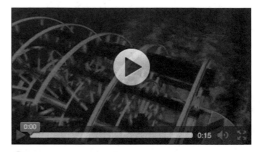

Ⓑ The video controls in Firefox. You see here that the video is a second longer in Firefox than in the other browsers.

When a Video Format Isn't Supported

If the browser you use to view the code samples (Ⓐ and Ⓖ) doesn't support the video file format you're using, it will show its controls bar and either an empty, white rectangle (in most cases) or the poster image, if one is indicated via the **poster** attribute.

For example, Internet Explorer and Safari do not support WebM but do support MP4. To show you their controls in Ⓓ and Ⓕ, respectively, I skipped ahead and created a separate webpage that uses both the MP4 and WebM formats. You'll learn how to do this in "Using Video with Multiple Sources and a Text Fallback."

The empty rectangle is generally 300x150 if video dimensions haven't been specified with **width** and **height**. If you include **controls** but use a format IE10 doesn't support, it will display a black empty rectangle and "Invalid Source."

C The video controls in Chrome

D The video controls in Internet Explorer 10

E The video controls in Opera

F The video controls in Safari

To add controls to a video:

Type `<video src="`*my-video.ext*`" controls></video>`, where *my-video.ext* points to your video file.

To add autoplay to a video:

Type `<video src="`*my-video.ext*`" autoplay controls></video>`, where *my-video.ext* points to your video file.

G Now the video element includes three attributes from Table 17.1. Thanks to `autoplay`, this video will play automatically. With `controls` set as well, visitors will have a pause button they can use at any time. The attributes may appear in any order.

```
...
<body>
    <video src="paddle-steamer.webm"
    → width="369" height="208" autoplay
    → controls></video>
</body>
</html>
```

Boolean Attributes

As you might recall from Chapter 1, Boolean attributes, such as `controls` and `autoplay`, don't need to have a value specified for them (it's optional). Either way, their presence on a **video** or **audio** element yields the same result.

The examples in this chapter don't specify values for these Boolean attributes, but **G** could also be written as

`<video src="paddle-steamer. webm" controls="controls" autoplay="autoplay"></video>`.

Looping a Video and Specifying a Poster Image

In addition to setting your video to play automatically, you can set it to play continuously until stopped  Ⓐ. (This isn't recommended, though—think of your poor users!) You simply use the **autoplay** and **loop** attributes.

If you don't include **autoplay**, normally the browser will display the first frame of the video in still mode once it has loaded. You may want to change this and specify your own image, which you can do via a poster image (Ⓑ and Ⓒ).

To add autoplay and loop a video:

Type **<video src="*my-video.ext*"** **autoplay loop></video>**, where *my-video.ext* points to your video file.

To specify a poster image for a video:

Type **<video src="*my-video.ext*"** **controls poster="*my-poster.jpg*">** **</video>**, where *my-video.ext* points to your video file and *my-poster.jpg* points to the image that you want to use as the poster image.

Ⓐ A single WebM video set to play automatically and then loop. With no **controls** included here, your visitors won't be able to stop the video! So, if you include a loop, it's best to include **controls**. Even so, an auto-playing video that loops might drive visitors batty.

```
...
<body>
    <video src="paddle-steamer.webm"
    → width="369" height="208" autoplay
    → loop></video>
</body>
</html>
```

Ⓑ A single WebM video with controls and a specified poster image that will display when the page loads and displays the video.

```
...
<body>
    <video src="paddle-steamer.webm"
    → width="369" height="208"
    → poster="paddle-steamer-poster.jpg"
    → controls></video>
</body>
</html>
```

Ⓒ A video displaying a poster image (until a visitor plays the video). In this case, the image is a screenshot taken from within the video itself.

 A single WebM video that won't load when the page fully loads. It begins to load when the user attempts to play it. Note that I omitted the **width** and **height** attributes.

```
...
<body>
        <video src="paddle-steamer.webm"
        → preload="none" controls></video>
</body>
</html>
```

Preventing a Video from Preloading

If you think it unlikely that a user will view your video (for example, it's not the main content on your page), you can ask the browser to not bother preloading it . This saves on bandwidth so is particularly good for visitors on mobile devices.

Browsers vary in the way they display a video set to **preload="none"** before play-back is initiated (B and C).

B A video with **preload** set to **none** in Firefox. It displays a generic box above the controls because it has no information about the video (not even the dimensions) and no poster image was specified. When you play the video, the browser obtains its dimensions and resizes the video accordingly.

C Chrome (top) displays an empty rectangle above the controls. That version of the player may be narrower than what appears when a visitor plays the video (bottom).

To instruct the browser to not preload a video:

Type `<video src="my-video.ext" preload="none" controls></video>`, where *my-video.ext* points to your video file.

TIP Include a poster image with the `poster` attribute if you want to set `preload="none"` but don't want a blank space to display.

TIP If you don't want to show a poster but do want the empty rectangle to match the video's size, include the `width` and `height` attributes on the `video` element, setting their values to the video's dimensions. This will prevent the jarring effect of the video resizing when play begins (Ⓑ and Ⓒ).

Other preload Settings

The default value of **preload** is **auto**. This suggests to the browser to "get a running start" in downloading the video in anticipation of the user choosing to watch it. Browsers will preload much or even all of the video. As a result, the video should be less prone to potential stops and starts during playback while the browser tries to download more for the visitor to watch.

A happy medium between **none** and **auto** is `preload="metadata"`. This asks the browser to retrieve basic information about the video, such as its dimensions, duration, and possibly a few frames of video. Browsers won't display an empty rectangle and will size the video properly before playback begins.

The **metadata** setting also hints to browsers that the user's connection is limited so it should make every effort to conserve bandwidth without interrupting playback.

Ⓐ Two sources are defined here for the video: an MP4 file and a WebM file. (Note that the **video** start tag does *not* have a **src** attribute like it did in earlier examples when specifying a single video source.) Only older browsers will display the linked text contained within the **p** element Ⓓ. Make sure your fallback link or text is *inside* the **video** element, otherwise all browsers will show it.

```
...
<body>
    <video width="369" height="208" controls>
        <source src="paddle-steamer.mp4"
        → type="video/mp4">
        <source src="paddle-steamer.webm"
        → type="video/webm">
        <p><a href="paddle-steamer.mp4">
        → Download the video</a></p>
    </video>
</body>
</html>
```

Ⓑ Browsers like IE10 that support MP4 will load **paddle-steamer.mp4**.

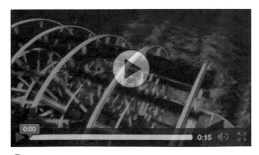

Ⓒ Browsers that don't support MP4 but do support WebM will load **paddle-steamer.webm**.

Using Video with Multiple Sources and a Text Fallback

This is all great, but all the preceding examples use only one video file and therefore one format. You've already seen that to support all HTML5-capable browsers, you need to supply video in at least two different formats: MP4 and WebM.

So how do you do that? The **source** element allows you to define more than one source for a media element, in this case **video**.

Any number of **source** elements can be contained within a **video** element, so defining two different formats for our video example is easy Ⓐ. Browsers will load the first file format referenced in a **source** element that they support and ignore the rest (Ⓑ and Ⓒ). Browsers that cannot play HTML5 video will display the fallback link Ⓓ or a message you provide Ⓐ.

To specify two different video sources with a fallback:

1. Obtain your video sources (two this time).

2. Type **\<video controls\>** to open the **video** element with the default control set.

3. Type **\<source src="*my-video.mp4*" type="video/mp4"\>**, where *my-video.mp4* points to your MP4 video source file.

4. Type **\<source src="*my-video.webm*" type="video/webm"\>**, where *my-video.webm* points to your WebM video source file.

5. Create a fallback link or message for older browsers **D**.

6. Type **\</video\>** to close the **video** element.

D IE8 ignores the **video** and **source** elements and simply displays the download link. I have chosen to include a link to the MP4 version of our video **A**, but I could just as easily have linked to the WebM file or to both.

More about multiple media sources

We'll go into the various attributes available for the **source** element in a moment, but let's quickly look at why specifying multiple sources for the same media actually works.

When the browser comes across the **video** element, it first looks to see if there's a **src** defined in the **video** element itself. Since there isn't, it then checks for **source** elements. It goes through each one in turn looking for one that contains something it can play. Once it finds one, it plays it and ignores the rest.

In our previous example, Safari will play the MP4 file **B** and won't even see the WebM file, whereas Firefox will note that it can't play the MP4 source and move on to the WebM one, which it can play **C** (Firefox is working on adding MP4 support to all versions, so this might have changed by the time you are reading this.)

Any browser that recognizes neither the **video** element nor the **source** element (that is, a browser that is not HTML5 capable) will ignore those tags entirely when parsing the document; it will simply display the fallback message just before closing the **video** element **D**.

See **Table 17.2** for the **source** element attributes.

> **TIP** Instead of a link (or links), the fallback you provide in **A** could be an **img** taken from the video or something like `<p>Sorry, your browser doesn't support HTML5 video.</p>`, followed by the link.

> **TIP** Some free videos you can use for trying out the **video** and **source** elements are available at www.bigbuckbunny.org/index.php/download/. That site doesn't provide WebM videos, but you could output your own with one of the tools listed in "Video File Formats."

TABLE 17.2 source Attributes

Name	Description
src	The URL to the video source.
type	Specifies the type of the video, which aids the browser in deciding whether it can play the video or not. As **A** shows, the value of this attribute reflects the format or codec of the video (e.g., **video/mp4**, **video/webm**, or **video/ogg**).
media	Allows you to specify a CSS3 media query for the video source, thus allowing you to specify different (e.g., smaller) videos for devices with different screen capabilities.

Providing Accessibility

Another advantage of having native multimedia is that the content can be made more keyboard accessible by taking advantage of the natural accessibility of modern browsers.

The keyboard accessibility of HTML5 video and audio is good in Firefox, Internet Explorer, and Opera. But for Chrome and Safari at the time of this writing, the only way to have an accessible media player is by creating your own control set. That requires using the JavaScript Media API (also part of HTML5), which is outside the scope of this chapter.

HTML5 also specifies a new file format—WebVTT (Web Video Text Tracks)—that allows you to include text subtitles, captions, descriptions, chapters, and so on in video content. Further discussion of WebVTT and captioning is also outside the scope of this chapter, but you can find out more at www.iandevlin.com/blog/2011/05/html5/webvtt-and-video-subtitles (including an update in 2012 to match specification changes).

TIP Ian Devlin's *HTML5 Multimedia: Develop and Design* (Peachpit Press, 2011) has chapters dedicated to showing you how to create your own accessible control set and how to use WebVTT. An excerpt is available at http://net.tutsplus.com/tutorials/html-css-techniques/an-in-depth-overview-of-html5-multimedia-and-accessibility/.

TIP Terrill Thompson compares HTML5 video accessibility among browsers at http://terrillthompson.com/blog/366.

TIP The WebVTT spec is still in development, so the means by which to implement captions and the like is subject to change.

Audio File Formats

Now that you can add video to your webpage using HTML5 native media, let's take a look at how to add audio. As with HTML5 video, there are a number of different file formats (codecs) that are supported:

- Ogg Vorbis uses the .ogg file extension and is supported by Firefox 3.5+, Chrome 5+, and Opera 10.5+.

- MP3 uses the .mp3 file extension and is supported by Safari 5+, Chrome 6+, Internet Explorer 9+, and iOS.

- WAV uses the .wav file extension and is supported by Firefox 3.6+, Safari 5+, Chrome 8+, and Opera 10.5+.

- AAC uses the .aac file extension and is supported by Safari 3+, Internet Explorer 9+, iOS 3+, and Android 2+.

- MP4 uses the .mp4 file extension and is supported by Safari 3+, Chrome 5+, Internet Explorer 9+, iOS 3+, and Android 2+.

- Opus uses the .opus file extension. It is a new audio format that only Firefox supports at the time of this writing.

You will remember that MP4 was listed as a video codec, but it can also be used to encode audio data only.

TIP As with video, your content needs to be in two different formats to ensure support across all HTML5-capable browsers. The two best formats in which to provide your content are Ogg Vorbis and MP3.

TIP The Miro Video Converter application mentioned earlier in the "Converting Between File Formats" sidebar can also be used for converting audio.

Adding an Audio File with Controls to Your Webpage

Let's move on to actually placing an audio file in your webpage. The process is very similar to adding a video, but this time you'll use the **audio** element . Of course, as with the video controls, each browser has its own idea of how audio controls should look (**B** through **F**).

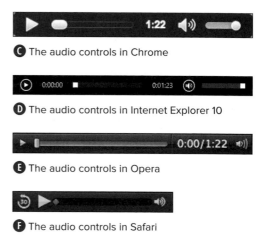

A A simple Ogg-encoded audio file with the default control set specified. You could omit the **controls** attribute, but nothing would display since an audio file is not visual.

```
...
<body>
    <audio src="piano.ogg" controls></audio>
</body>
</html>
```

B The audio controls in Firefox. As it did with the video, Firefox (and IE10 **D**) marks this audio file as a second longer than the other browsers do.

C The audio controls in Chrome

D The audio controls in Internet Explorer 10

E The audio controls in Opera

F The audio controls in Safari

When an Audio Format Isn't Supported

Browsers vary in what they display when they don't support an audio format. For instance, when you specify an Ogg file only Ⓐ IE10 shows a message Ⓖ and Safari shows the controls bar and "Loading...." Figures Ⓓ and Ⓕ shows their controls when they *do* support the file format, such as MP3.

Error: Unsupported audio type or invalid file path

Ⓖ IE10 when it doesn't support the audio file format you specify in **src** Ⓐ

See **Table 17.3** for the attributes you can use with the **audio** element.

To add an audio file with controls to your webpage:

- Obtain your audio file.

- Type **<audio src="*my-audio.ext*" controls></audio>**, where ***my-audio.ext*** is the location, name, and extension of the audio file.

TABLE 17.3 Audio Attributes

Name	Description
src	Specifies the URL to the audio file.
autoplay	Automatically starts playing the audio as soon as it can.
controls	Adds the browser's default control set to the audio.
muted	Mutes the audio.
loop	Plays the audio in a loop.
preload	Hints to the browser how much of the audio it is to load. It can take three different values: **none** — don't load anything. **metadata** — load only the audio's metadata (for example, length). **auto** — let the browser decide what to do (this is the default).

Autoplaying, Looping, and Preloading Audio

The attributes in this section work just as they do with video. The **autoplay** attribute makes it a snap to make an audio file start playing when the page loads (**A** and **B**). You can indicate that you want the audio to play in a loop by using the **loop** attribute **C**. And you can request that the browser preload the audio file in different ways by using the preload attribute values in Table 17.3 **D**.

To start the audio playing automatically:

Type **<audio src="***my-audio.ext***"** **autoplay controls></audio>**, where ***my-audio.ext*** points to your audio file. If you omit **controls**, the audio will play automatically but nothing will show in the browser.

A An Ogg audio file (with the default control set) that will automatically start playing when the page loads

```
...
<body>
    <audio src="piano.ogg" autoplay
    → controls></audio>
</body>
</html>
```

B An audio file (with controls) that began to play automatically on load

C An Ogg audio file (with the default control set) that will loop

```
...
<body>
    <audio src="piano.ogg" loop controls>
    → </audio>
</body>
</html>
```

D This Ogg audio file should have only its metadata (for example, length) loaded when the page loads.

```
...
<body>
    <audio src="piano.ogg" preload=
    → "metadata" controls></audio>
</body>
</html>
```

To play an audio file in a loop:

Type `<audio src="my-audio.ext" loop controls></audio>`, where *my-audio.ext* points to your audio file.

To ask the browser to preload only the audio's metadata:

Type `<audio src="my-audio.ext" preload="metadata" controls></audio>`, where *my-audio.ext* points to your audio file.

TIP You can include any combination of the autoplay, loop, and preload attributes on an audio element. Be aware that including the autoplay attribute overrides any preload attribute setting, because the audio file must load in order to play.

TIP The information about the auto, none, and metadata values in "Preventing a Video from Preloading" also applies to using them on the audio element. (The parts about determining dimensions don't pertain to audio.) Remember that a value for the preload attribute does not guarantee the browser's behavior; it's merely a request.

Providing Multiple Audio Sources with a Fallback

In order to support all HTML5-capable browsers, you need to provide your audio in more than one format. This is achieved in exactly the same way as it is with the **video** element: using the **source** element. The fallback method for audio is also the same Ⓐ. As you would expect, the browser ignores what audio formats it can't play and plays what it can (Ⓑ and Ⓒ). Browsers that don't support the **audio** element display the fallback Ⓓ.

Ⓐ Two audio sources are defined for this **audio** element (which also has a default control set defined): one encoded as Ogg and the other as MP3. They are followed by the fallback information. When including a fallback link, you may want to provide the file type and size to help a visitor decide whether to download it.

```
...
<body>
    <audio controls>
        <source src="piano.ogg"
        ⇥ type="audio/ogg">
        <source src="piano.mp3"
        ⇥ type="audio/mp3">
        <p>Your browser doesn't support
        ⇥ HTML5 audio, but you can
        ⇥ <a href="piano.mp3">download the
        ⇥ audio file</a> (MP3, 1.3 MB).</p>
    </audio>
</body>
</html>
```

Ⓑ Browsers like Firefox that support Ogg will load **piano.ogg**. Chrome (not shown) understands both Ogg and MP3, but will load the Ogg file because it appears before the MP3 file in the **audio** element code Ⓐ.

Ⓒ Browsers, like IE10, that don't support Ogg but do support MP3 will load **piano.mp3**.

Your browser doesn't support HTML5 audio, but you can download the audio file (MP3, 1.3 MB).

Ⓓ Older browsers, like IE8, display the fallback message.

The type Attribute

The **type** attribute helps the browser decide whether it can play the audio file. For audio formats, the value is always **audio/** followed by the format itself, as in **audio/ogg**, **audio/mp3**, **audio/aac**, **audio/wav**, and **audio/mp4**.

To specify two different audio sources with a fallback:

1. Obtain your audio files.

2. Type **<audio controls>** to open the **audio** element with the default control set.

3. Type **<source src="*my-audio.ogg*" type="audio/ogg">**, where *my-audio. ogg* points to your Ogg Vorbis audio file.

4. Type **<source src="*my-audio.mp3*" type="audio/mp3">**, where *my-audio. mp3* points to your MP3 audio file.

5. (Optional but recommended) Create a fallback message or audio download link for browsers that don't support HTML5 audio.

6. Type **</audio>** to close the **audio** element.

Adding Video and Audio with a Flash Fallback

As well as providing a fallback download link, you could—and probably should—provide a Flash fallback player that can play the MP4 video file. Yes, despite all this great work with HTML5 and native multimedia, Flash is necessary for those older browsers that can't cope, like Internet Explorer before version 9. That said, you want to reach as many users as possible, so at least there's an option!

I will show how to do this using Media-Element.js (http://mediaelementjs.com) by John Dyer. It is not the only such solution, but it's very well regarded and has been adopted by the likes of WordPress, the omnipresent blogging and CMS software. I've listed some alternatives in the tips.

MediaElement.js requires a little extra work than going with native video or audio only. First, you must obtain the MediaElement.js files and put them with your site's other files (**A** through **C**). Then you add a few of those files to your webpage (**D** and **E**). Those steps are required for both video and audio.

From there, you may add a video (**F** and **G**) or an audio file (**H** and **I**) to your page. When MediaElement.js is initialized by the script in **F** and **H**, it automatically determines whether the browser should use HTML5 native playback or the Flash player.

▶ 📁 johndyer-mediaelement-2601db5

A The name of the folder from the ZIP file might be different for you, reflecting a newer version.

▼ 📁 johndyer-mediaelement-2601db5
  ▶ 📁 build
  ▶ 📁 demo
  ▶ 📁 media
     📄 README.md
  ▶ 📁 src
  ▶ 📁 test

B You only need the **build** folder to make MediaElement.js work on your site.

📁 website

Name
▶ 📁 build
  🎬 paddle-steamer.mp4
  📄 paddle-steamer.webm
  🎵 piano.mp3
  📄 piano.ogg

C The **build** folder is pasted into the folder for my site (yours may have a different name than **website**). To keep things simple for the example, I've put **build** in the same folder as the media files. Normally, I would place the latter in a separate folder named **media** or the like.

D These files help the make the media player work and style it so it will look the same in every browser.

```
<!DOCTYPE html>
<html lang="en">
<head>
    <meta charset="utf-8" />
    <title>HTML5 Media with Fallback Flash
    → Player</title>
    <script src="build/jquery.js">
    → </script>
    <script src="build/mediaelement-and-
    → player.min.js"></script>
    <link rel="stylesheet" href="build/
    → mediaelementplayer.min.css" />
</head>
<body>

</body>
</html>
```

E Now you have the **build** folder, your webpage, and your media files.

To get the MediaElement.js files and include them in your site's directory:

1. Go to http://mediaelementjs.com. Click the Download Latest button to download the ZIP package.

2. Locate the ZIP file on your computer. It's common for files to be saved in the Downloads folder unless you specified a different location. Extract the files (usually by double-clicking the ZIP file name). You will see a folder with a name similar to the one in **A**.

3. Open the folder to reveal the subfolders. Copy the **build** folder **B** and paste it into your website folder **C**.

To add MediaElement.js files to your webpage:

Your page needs to load set of specific files, whether you want it to have a fallback player for video, audio, or both.

1. Create a new HTML page, or open an existing one.

2. Add the highlighted code in **D** so your page will load the required style sheet and JavaScript files.

3. Save the page in the same directory where you placed the **build** folder **E**.

To add a Flash fallback to a video:

1. Obtain your video files.

2. Type **<video controls>** to open the **video** element and include controls. Specify other attributes, like **width**, **height**, **poster**, and more, as desired.

3. Type **<source src="*my-video.mp4*" type="type/mp4">**, where *my-video. mp4* points to the MP4 video source file.

4. Type **<source src="*my-video.webm*" type="video/webm">**, where *my-video.webm* points to the WebM video source file.

5. Create a message and link as desired for browsers that support neither HTML5 video nor Flash.

6. Type **</video>** to close the **video** element.

7. Initialize the video player by adding the code highlighted in to your webpage. Put the **script** right before **</body>** even if your page has more content than just the video.

Now your video reaches the widest audience possible .

 The video code should be familiar; it's the same method we used earlier to list multiple sources. Add or remove other attributes to match your needs. The **script** at the bottom tells MediaElement.js to work its magic.

```
<!DOCTYPE html>
<html lang="en">
<head>
    <meta charset="utf-8" />
    <title>HTML5 Media with Fallback Flash
    → Player</title>
    <script src="build/jquery.js"></script>
    <script src="build/mediaelement-and-
    → player.min.js"></script>
    <link rel="stylesheet" href="build/
    → mediaelementplayer.min.css" />
</head>
<body>
<video width="369" height="208"
→ preload="metadata" controls>
    <source src="paddle-steamer.mp4"
    → type="video/mp4">
    <source src="paddle-steamer.webm"
    → type="video/webm">
    <p>Your browser doesn't support HTML5
    → video or Flash, but you can <a href=
    → "paddle-steamer.mp4">download the
    → video</a> (MP4, 2.4 MB).</p>
</video>

<!-- Below all your content -->
<script>
$('video').mediaelementplayer();
</script>
</body>
</html>
```

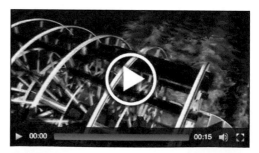

 The video controls will look the same regardless of the browser or whether the Flash version is used to fill the gap in browsers that don't support HTML5 video.

H The only difference between the `script` here and in **F** is that this one specifies `audio` instead of `video`. The `audio` element code also looks familiar.

```
... top of page same as Figures D and F ...

<body>
<audio controls>
    <source src="piano.ogg" type="audio/ogg">
    <source src="piano.mp3" type="audio/mp3">
    <p>Your browser doesn't support HTML5
    → audio or Flash, but you can <a href=
    → "piano.mp3">download the audio file
    → </a> (MP3, 1.3 MB).</p>
</audio>

<!-- Below all your content -->
<script>
$('audio').mediaelementplayer();
</script>
</body>
</html>
```

```
▶ 00:00 ▬▬▬▬▬▬▬▬▬▬▬▬▬▬▬  01:23 🔊 ▬▬▬▬
```

I Just as with video, the audio controls will look the same regardless of the browser or whether the Flash version displays.

J This initializes all audio and video players on your page.

```
...

<script>
$('audio,video').mediaelementplayer();
</script>
</body>
</html>
```

To provide a Flash fallback for your audio:

1. Obtain your audio files.

2. Type **`<audio controls>`** to open the `audio` element with the default control set. Specify other attributes as desired.

3. Type **`<source src="`*my-audio.ogg*`"`** **`type="audio/ogg`**, where *my-audio.ogg* points to your the Ogg Vorbis audio file.

4. Type **`<source src="`*my-audio.mp3*`"`** **`type="audio/mp3">`**, where *my-audio. mp3* points to your MP3 audio file.

5. Create a message and link as desired for browsers that support neither HTML5 audio nor Flash.

6. Type **`</audio>`** to close the `audio` element.

7. Initialize the audio player by adding the code highlighted in **H** to your webpage. Put the `script` right before **`</body>`** even if your page has more content than just the audio.

And now your audio reaches the widest audience possible **I**. Two victories in one day!

TIP If your page includes video *and* audio, change the script at the bottom of the page to match **J**.

TIP A browser such as Internet Explorer 8 will use the Flash fallback player that Media-Element.js creates. As long as the user has Flash installed and enabled, the video or audio content will play.

continues on next page

TIP The Flash version might show a black rectangle instead of a still of the video if you don't specify `preload="metadata"`, as I did in **F**, or a poster image with `poster`. Regardless, the black area is replaced by the video once playback begins.

TIP If you specify the `width` and `height` in your `video` start tag, the Flash version might letterbox the video (that is, put black bars on the sides or top and bottom). However, if you *don't* specify the dimensions, the video might appear larger than normal for an instant before it snaps down to its proper size.

TIP Video.js (www.videojs.com), JW Player (www.longtailvideo.com/jw-player/), and Flowplayer (http://flowplayer.org) are among the other Flash fallback solutions. The free versions of JW Player and Flowplayer display their logo on the media player.

Troubleshooting Flash Playback

Flash has security settings that may prevent your media files from working while testing your webpage on your computer—that is, when all files are located on your computer rather than on your web server.

One way around this is to upload your MP3 and MP4 files to your web server and then reference those files with absolute paths in the HTML.

Let's say you upload the files from **F** to a folder named **media** on your server. You would change the first **src** value to this (replacing www.yourdomain.com with your actual domain):

```
<source src="http://www.
→yourdomain.com/media/paddle-
→steamer.mp4" type="video/mp4">
```

You would then save your HTML page and test it from your computer (it doesn't need to be on the server). You can also change the Flash security settings to allow your local directory to work with Flash. See http://mediaelementjs.com/#installation.

If you're still having trouble, see the sidebar "Setting the MIME Type," earlier in this chapter.

Advanced Multimedia

Another great thing about having native multimedia with HTML5 is that it can work with a lot of the other new features and functionality that either come with or are related to HTML5. This section briefly discusses two of them: the **canvas** element and SVG.

Using video with **canvas**

The **canvas** element and its corresponding JavaScript API allow you to draw and animate objects on your webpages.

You can also use the API in conjunction with HTML5 video, because the **video** element can be treated just like any other HTML element and is therefore accessible to **canvas**.

With the JavaScript API, you can capture images from a playing video and redraw them in the **canvas** element as an image, thus allowing you to, for example, take screenshots from the video.

You can manipulate individual image pixels via the API, and since you can create images in **canvas** from your video, this allows you to also manipulate the video pixels. For example, you could convert them all to grayscale.

This gives you only a small idea of what **canvas** can do with the **video** element, but a thorough discussion of it is outside the scope of this book.

Coupling video with SVG

SVG (Scalable Vector Graphics) is another technology that people have begun to take more notice of with the dawn of HTML5.

SVG has been around for ages (since 1999), but HTML5 brings with it the **svg** element, which allows SVG definitions to be embedded within the webpage itself.

SVG allows shapes and graphics to be defined in XML, which the browser interprets and uses to draw the actual shapes. All that the SVG definition contains is a bunch of instructions on how and what to draw.

The graphics produced by SVG are also vector-based rather than raster-based. This means that they scale well, because the browser simply uses the drawing instructions to draw the shape to the required size. By comparison, raster graphics, like GIF, PNG, and JPEG files, contain pixel data. If you want browsers to redraw an image at a greater size than the original, there is not enough pixel data for the new size. This leads to a loss in picture quality.

A complete discussion of SVG is also well outside the scope of this chapter, but it's mentioned here so you know that video can be used in conjunction with SVG definitions. Shapes created by SVG can be used to mask videos—that is, to show only the underlying video through the shape (a circle, for example). You could also create custom video controls that scale to any size.

There are also a number of SVG filters that you can apply to HTML5 video, such as black and white conversion, Gaussian blurs, and color saturation.

Further Resources

This chapter covered the basics of HTML5 multimedia. There's a lot more to learn, so here are a number of resources that you can check out at your leisure.

Online resources

- "Video on the Web" (http://diveinto. html5doctor.com/video.html)

- "WebVTT and Video Subtitles" (www.iandevlin.com/blog/2011/05/ html5/webvtt-and-video-subtitles)

- "An In-depth Analysis of HTML5 Multimedia and Accessibility" (http://net.tutsplus.com/tutorials/html-css-techniques/an-in-depth-overview-of-html5-multimedia-and-accessibility/)

- "HTML5 Canvas: The Basics" (http://dev.opera.com/articles/view/ html-5-canvas-the-basics)

- "Learning SVG" (http://my.opera.com/ tagawa/blog/learning-svg)

Books

- Ian Devlin. *HTML5 Multimedia: Develop and Design*. Peachpit Press, 2011. (http://html5multimedia.com)

- Shelley Powers. *HTML5 Media*. O'Reilly Media, 2011.

- Silvia Pfeiffer. *The Definitive Guide to HTML5 Video*. Apress, 2010.

Tables

We're all familiar with tabular data in our daily lives. It takes many forms, such as financial data, event calendars, transit schedules, and TV schedules. In most cases, this information is presented in one or more rows, with headers above the columns or alongside the rows.

The **table** element—along with its child elements—is described in this chapter. I'll focus on basic table structuring and styling. HTML tables can get quite complex, though you'll likely have few occasions to implement them unless you have a data-rich site. For advanced examples, see the following URLs:

- "Bring On the Tables" by Roger Johansson (www.456bereastreet.com/archive/200410/bring_on_the_tables/)

- "Accessible Data Tables" by Roger Hudson (www.usability.com.au/resources/tables.cfm)

- "Creating Accessible HTML Tables" by Stephen Ferg (http://accessiblehtml.sourceforge.net/)

In This Chapter

Structuring Tables

The kind of information you put in a spreadsheet is usually suitable for structuring as an HTML table.

At the most fundamental level, a **table** element is made up of rows of cells. Each row (**tr**) contains header (**th**) cells, data (**td**) cells, or both. You may also provide a **caption** element if you think it'll help your visitors better understand the table. The caption typically displays above the table in a browser and serves to describe its purpose. Furthermore, the **scope** attribute—also optional, but recommended—informs screen readers and other assistive devices that a **th** is the header for a table column (when **scope="col"**), a table row (when **scope="row"**), or a group of columns or rows (see the last tip) **A**.

By default, browsers display tables only as wide as their information demands within the available space on the page **B**. As you would expect, you can change table formatting with CSS, as I'll demonstrate shortly.

A Each row is marked by a **tr** element. This very simple table has one row that contains the headers (the **th** elements) and three more rows with cells of data (the **td** elements). I've also included a **caption**, although this is optional (see the first tip).

```
...
<body>

<table>
    <caption>Quarterly Financials for
    → 1962-1964 (in Thousands)</caption>
    <tr>
        <th scope="col">1962</th>
        <th scope="col">1963</th>
        <th scope="col">1964</th>
    </tr>
    <tr>
        <td>$145</td>
        <td>$167</td>
        <td>$161</td>
    </tr>
    <tr>
        <td>$140</td>
        <td>$159</td>
        <td>$164</td>
    </tr>
    <tr>
        <td>$153</td>
        <td>$162</td>
        <td>$168</td>
    </tr>
    <tr>
        <td>$157</td>
        <td>$160</td>
        <td>$171</td>
    </tr>
</table>

</body>
</html>
```

Quarterly Financials for 1962-1964 (in Thousands)

1962	1963	1964
$145	$167	$161
$140	$159	$164
$153	$162	$168
$157	$160	$171

B By default, **th** text is bold, **th** text and **caption** text are centered, and the table is only as wide as its content demands.

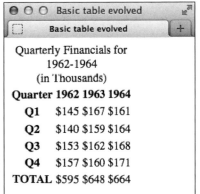

The table in Ⓐ is missing something. How do you know what each row of data represents? It would be easier to tell if the table also had headers alongside each row. Adding those is simply a matter of adding a **th** as the first element in each row. And whereas the column headers have **scope="col"**, each row **th** that precedes a **td** is given **scope="row"** Ⓒ.

I also used Ⓒ as an opportunity to introduce a few other elements that are specific to defining tables: **thead**, **tbody**, and **tfoot**. The **thead** element explicitly marks a row or rows of headers as the table head section. The **tbody** element surrounds all the data rows. The **tfoot** element explicitly marks a row or rows as the table foot section. You could use **tfoot** to include column calculations, like in Ⓒ, or to repeat the **thead** headings for a long table, such as in a train schedule (some browsers may also print the **tfoot** and **thead** elements on each page if a table is multiple printed pages long). The **thead**, **tbody**, and **tfoot** elements don't affect the layout and are not required—although I recommend using them to mark those sections explicitly when they exist—but **tbody** *is* required whenever you include a **thead** or **tfoot**. You can also target styles to all three of them.

Ⓒ I defined the table's sections explicitly with **thead**, **tbody**, and **tfoot**. Next, I added a **th** at the beginning of each row; the ones in the **tbody** and **tfoot** have **scope="row"** to indicate that they are row headers. The table now displays as shown in Ⓓ.

```
...
<body>

<table>
    <caption>Quarterly Financials for
  → 1962-1964 (in Thousands)</caption>
    <thead> <!-- table head -->
        <tr>
            <th scope="col">Quarter</th>
            <th scope="col">1962</th>
            <th scope="col">1963</th>
            <th scope="col">1964</th>
        </tr>
    </thead>
    <tbody> <!-- table body -->
        <tr>
            <th scope="row">Q1</th>
            <td>$145</td>
            <td>$167</td>
            <td>$161</td>
        </tr>
        <tr>
            <th scope="row">Q2</th>
            <td>$140</td>
            <td>$159</td>
            <td>$164</td>
        </tr>
        ... [Q3 and Q4 rows] ...
    </tbody>
    <tfoot> <!-- table foot -->
        <tr>
            <th scope="row">TOTAL</th>
            <td>$595</td>
            <td>$648</td>
            <td>$664</td>
        </tr>
    </tfoot>
</table>

</body>
</html>
```

Ⓓ The table has both column and row headers. The caption is wider than it was in Ⓑ because the table itself is wider with the new column.

To structure a table:

1. Type **<table>**.

2. If desired, type **<caption>***caption content***</caption>**, where *caption content* describes your table.

3. If desired, before the first **tr** element of the section you want to create, type **<thead>**, **<tbody>**, or **<tfoot>**, as appropriate. (To clarify, a **<tbody>** cannot precede **<thead>**.)

4. Type **<tr>** to define the beginning of a row.

5. Type **<th scope="***scopetype***">** to begin a header cell (where *scopetype* is **col**, **row**, **colgroup**, or **rowgroup**), or type **<td>** to define the beginning of a data cell.

6. Type the contents of the cell.

7. Type **</th>** to complete a header cell, or type **</td>** to complete a data cell.

8. Repeat steps 5 through 7 for each cell in the row.

9. Type **</tr>** to complete the row.

10. Repeat steps 4 through 9 for each row in the section.

11. If you started a section in step 3, close the section with **</thead>**, **</tbody>**, or **</tfoot>**, as appropriate.

12. Repeat steps 3 through 11 for each section. Note that a table may have only one **thead** and **tfoot** but may have multiple **tbody** elements.

13. To finish the table, type **</table>**.

E This simple style sheet adds a border to each data cell, and padding within the header and data cells. It also formats the table caption and content. Without **border-collapse: collapse;** defined on the table, a space would appear between the border of each **td** and the border of its adjacent **td** (the default setting is **border-collapse: separate;**). You can apply borders to **th** elements too, as shown in the next section.

```
body {
    font: 100% "Courier New", Courier,
    → monospace;
}

table {
    border-collapse: collapse;
}

caption {
    font-size: .8125em;
    font-weight: bold;
    margin-bottom: .5em;
}

th,
td {
    font-size: .875em;
    padding: .5em .75em;
}

td {
    border: 1px solid #000;
}

tfoot {
    font-style: italic;
    font-weight: bold;
}
```

Basic table evolved and styled

Quarterly Financials for 1962-1964 (in Thousands)			
Quarter	1962	1963	1964
Q1	$145	$167	$161
Q2	$140	$159	$164
Q3	$153	$162	$168
Q4	$157	$160	$171
TOTAL	$595	$648	$664

F Now the table has headers for the columns and rows, and it has a row with column totals, which are enclosed in a **tfoot** element. HTML isn't smart enough to calculate those totals for you, so be sure to enter the correct numbers in your code!

Tables can appear a little squished by default **D**. By applying some basic CSS **E**, you can add space in the cells to spread things out (via **padding**), add borders to indicate cell boundaries (via **border**), and format text, all of which will improve your table's legibility **F**.

TIP If you include the **caption** element, it must be the first element inside the **table** **A** (**caption** may also include p and other text elements).

TIP A **tbody** is required whenever you include a **thead** or **tfoot**. A **tbody** cannot precede **thead**. A **table** may have only one **thead** and **tfoot** but may have multiple **tbody** elements.

TIP If **table** is the only element other than **figcaption** nested in a **figure** element, omit the **caption** element and describe the **table** with **figcaption** instead (see "Creating a Figure" in Chapter 4). To clarify, don't nest **figcaption** in **table**, but in **figure** (as you usually would).

TIP Although not shown in the CSS example **D**, you can define a **background**, a **width**, and more in your style sheet for the **table**, **td**, or **th** elements. In short, most of the text and other formatting you use to style other HTML elements applies to tables too (see the next section for an example). You may notice slight display differences among browsers, especially Internet Explorer.

TIP You can assign the **scope** attribute to a **th** that is the header for an entire group of columns (**scope="colgroup"**) or an entire group of rows (**scope="rowgroup"**). See an example of the latter in the next section.

Spanning Columns and Rows

You may span a **th** or **td** across more than one column or row with the **colspan** and **rowspan** attributes, respectively. The number you assign to the attributes specifies the number of cells they span (**Ⓐ** and **Ⓑ**).

To span a cell across two or more columns:

1. When you get to the point at which you need to define the cell that spans more than one column, type **<th** followed by a space if the cell is a header, or type **<td** followed by a space for a data cell.

2. Type **colspan="*n*">**, where *n* equals the number of columns the cell should span.

3. Type the cell's contents.

4. Type **</th>** if you started a header cell in step 1, or type **</td>** if you started a data cell.

5. Complete the rest of the table as described in "Structuring Tables." If you create a cell with a **colspan** of 2, you will need to define one cell fewer in that row; if you create a cell with a **colspan** of 3, you will need to define two cells fewer in that row; and so on.

Ⓐ I've indicated that *Celebrity Hoedown* runs on both Tuesday and Wednesday at 8 p.m. by applying **colspan="2"** to the **td** that contains the show. Similarly, I added **rowspan="2"** to the **td** containing *Screamfest Movie of the Weak*, because it runs for two hours. Note that the Time **th** has **scope="rowgroup"** because it is the header for every header in the group of row headers directly beneath it.

```
...
<body>

<table>
    <caption>TV Schedule</caption>
    <thead> <!-- table head -->
        <tr>
            <th scope="rowgroup">Time</th>
            <th scope="col">Mon</th>
            <th scope="col">Tue</th>
            <th scope="col">Wed</th>
        </tr>
    </thead>
    <tbody> <!-- table body -->
        <tr>
            <th scope="row">8 pm</th>
            <td>Staring Contest</td>
            <td colspan="2">Celebrity
            ⇢ Hoedown</td>
        </tr>
        <tr>
            <th scope="row">9 pm</th>
            <td>Hardy, Har, Har</td>
            <td>What's for Lunch?</td>
            <td rowspan="2">Screamfest Movie
            ⇢ of the Weak</td>
        </tr>
        <tr>
            <th scope="row">10 pm</th>
            <td>Healers, Wheelers &amp;
            ⇢ Dealers</td>
            <td>It's a Crime</td>
        </tr>
    </tbody>
</table>

</body>
</html>
```

B It may have been hard to tell by glancing at the code, but in the browser it's clear how `colspan` and `rowspan` affect the table's display. The CSS style sheet I used for this table is available at www.htmlcssvqs.com/8ed/18.

To span a cell across two or more rows:

1. When you get to the point at which you need to define the cell that spans more than one row, type `<th` followed by a space if the cell is a header, or type `<td` followed by a space for a data cell.

2. Type `rowspan="n">`, where *n* equals the number of rows the cell should span.

3. Type the cell's contents.

4. Type `</th>` if you started a header cell in step 1, or type `</td>` if you started a data cell.

5. Complete the rest of the table as described in "Structuring Tables." If you define a cell with a `rowspan` of 2, you will not need to define the corresponding cell in the next row; if you define a cell with a `rowspan` of 3, you will not need to define the corresponding cells in the next two rows; and so on.

TIP Each row in a table must have the same number of cells defined. Cells that span across columns count for as many cells as the value of their `colspan` attribute.

TIP Each column in a table must have the same number of cells defined. Cells that span across rows count for as many cells as the value of their `rowspan` attribute.

Adding JavaScript

While HTML defines your webpage's content and CSS defines the way it looks, JavaScript defines special behavior. You can't build a site without HTML (or CSS if you want it to look appealing), but JavaScript is not required. In most cases, JavaScript features enhance your visitor's experience—they add to the core experience defined by your HTML and CSS. (See "Progressive Enhancement: A Best Practice" in the book's introduction.)

In This Chapter

You can write simple JavaScript programs to show and hide content, and you can write more complicated ones that load data and update your page while your visitor is viewing it. You can build carousels and slideshows like those on news sites, drive custom HTML5 `audio` and `video` element player controls, and create games that use HTML5's `canvas` element. You can use geolocation to customize your visitor's experience based on where they are, or allow them to drag and drop files onto the browser window for uploading (Dropbox's website is one example that does this). And you can write full-blown web applications with JavaScript that leverage some of the most powerful features in HTML5 and related technologies (they're advanced topics, so they aren't covered in this book).

As you can see, JavaScript has quite a range of possibilities, and its use has exploded. JavaScript libraries like jQuery (jquery.com) have made it easier to add simple interactivity and sophisticated behavior to pages. Although there are other libraries with similar goals, jQuery enjoys the most widespread use by far, largely because beginners find it easier to learn, it has good online documentation, and it has a large community behind it. Beyond the likes of jQuery, various JavaScript frameworks have surfaced that help you build and maintain large web applications. Heck, using `Node.js` (http://nodejs.org), you can even create a web server with JavaScript.

Browser vendors have spent considerable time making their browsers process JavaScript significantly faster than their versions of even just a few years ago. JavaScript also works in tablet and modern mobile browsers, though for performance reasons you'll want to be smart about how much you load in pages for these devices.

Alas, JavaScript is its own large topic, so we won't cover it in this book. In this chapter, I'll stick primarily to explaining how to insert created scripts into your HTML documents. I'll also pass along some advice about how to do that in a way that minimizes the impact on your page's display time. And I'll show you a sample script, as well as a tiny look at JavaScript event handlers.

I encourage you to learn JavaScript (and also jQuery) once you feel comfortable with HTML and CSS. *Eloquent JavaScript* by Marijn Haverbeke is one good place to start. The original version is available for free at http://eloquentjavascript.net; there is also a revised printed edition. JavaScript Garden (http://bonsaiden.github.io/JavaScript-Garden/) by Ivo Wetzel and Zhang Yi Jiang is a free, concise resource for learning some of JavaScript's quirks and finer points once you have a general understanding of the language.

JavaScript is more complicated than HTML and CSS, so don't be discouraged if it takes you longer to learn it. As with anything, the more you work with it, the more you'll get a feel for it.

Loading an External Script

A The `src` attribute of the `script` element references the script's URL. Most of the time, it is best to load scripts at the very end of your page, just before the `</body>` end tag. You may also load scripts in your page's **head** element **B**, but it can affect how quickly your page displays. See the "Scripting and Performance Best Practices" sidebar for more information.

```
<!DOCTYPE html>
<html lang="en">
<head>
    <meta charset="utf-8" />
    <title>Loading an External Script</title>
    <link rel="stylesheet"
    → href="css/global.css" />
</head>
<body>
... All of your HTML content is here ...

<script src="behavior.js"></script>
</body>
</html>
```

B This example shows a script loaded in the **head** instead. It is after the `link` element, so it won't block the CSS file from beginning to load sooner. See the "Scripting and Performance Best Practices" sidebar to learn why you want to minimize how often you load scripts from the **head**.

```
<!DOCTYPE html>
<html lang="en">
<head>
    <meta charset="utf-8" />
    <title>Loading an External Script</title>
    <!-- Load style sheets before any JS
    → files -->
    <link rel="stylesheet" href="css/
    → global.css" />
    <script src="behavior.js"></script>
</head>
<body>
... All of your HTML content is here ...
</body>
</html>
```

Loading an External Script

There are two primary kinds of scripts: those that you load from an external file (in text-only format) and those that are embedded in your page (covered in the next section). It's the same concept as external and embedded style sheets.

And just as with adding style sheets to your pages, it's generally better to load scripts from an external file **A** than to embed them in your HTML. You reap some of the same benefits, in that a single JavaScript file can be loaded by each page that needs it. You can edit one script rather than updating similar scripts in individual HTML pages.

Whether loading an external script or embedding a script, you use the `script` element.

To load an external script:

Type `<script src="script.js"></script>`, where `script.js` is the location on the server and the file name of the external script. Place each script element directly before the `</body>` end tag whenever possible **A**, instead of in the document's **head** element **B**.

continues on next page

C As you can see, JavaScript is very different than HTML and CSS! This is nearly identical to the **toggle-textarea.js** script I reference in the Chapter 16 section "Disabling Form Elements." The example on the companion website contains additional comments that explain more about how the script works (www.htmlcssvqs.com/8ed/19). Even so, I don't attempt to explain every facet of the code, and it's a lot to digest if you're new to JavaScript. I provide the example primarily to give you a glimpse of the language.

```javascript
/*
 * If visitor chooses the Other radio
 * button, the textarea is enabled
 * and the cursor is placed in it so
 * visitor can start typing. Choosing
 * any remaining radio button
 * disables the textarea.
 */

(function (window, document) {
    'use strict';

    var choices = document.getElementById('choices'),
        textarea = document.getElementById('other-description');

    if (!choices || !textarea) {
        return;
    }

    // Disable textarea by default
    textarea.disabled = true;

    // Add behavior to radio buttons
    choices.onclick = function(e) {
        var target,
            e;

        if (!e) {
            e = window.event;
        }

        target = e.target || e.srcElement;

        // Toggle textarea based on
        //    radio button chosen
        if (target.getAttribute('type') === 'radio') {
            if (target.id !== 'other') {
                textarea.disabled = true;
            } else {
                textarea.disabled = false;
                textarea.focus();
            }
        }
    };
}(window, document));
```

D Yep, this is the same script as **C**, just minified. It might look like a cat ran over your keyboard, but browsers understand it just fine.

```
(function(e,c){var d=c.getElementById
→ ("choices"),b=c.getElementById("other-
→ description");d&&b&&(b.disabled=!0,d.
→ onclick=function(a){a||(a=c.event);a=
→ a.target||a.srcElement;"radio"===
→ a.getAttribute("type")&&("other"!==
→ a.id?b.disabled=!0:(b.disabled=!1,
→ b.focus())))})})(window,document);
```

TIP To keep your files organized, it's common to place your JavaScript files in a sub-folder (js and `scripts` are popular names); see "Organizing Files" in Chapter 2. Your `src` attribute values would need to reflect this, just like any URL that points to a resource. For instance, if the JavaScript file referenced in **A** were in a folder named js that is itself in a folder named `assets`, you could type `<script src="assets/js/behavior.js"></script>`. (That's just one example; there are other ways to represent the URL. See "URLs" in Chapter 1.)

TIP A sample piece of JavaScript is shown in **C**. Because JavaScript is just text, you can write it in the same editor you use to create your HTML and CSS. If this example were saved in a file named behavior.js, it would load into the pages shown in **A** and **B**.

TIP Your page may load multiple JavaScript files and contain multiple embedded scripts (see **A** in "Adding an Embedded Script"). By default, browsers will load scripts (when necessary) and execute scripts in the order in which they appear in your HTML. See the "Scripting and Performance Best Practices" sidebar to learn why you should avoid multiple scripts when possible and how to minify them **D**.

TIP You can specify any valid file names you'd like for your external scripts as long as they have the .js extension. It's customary to give minified scripts a .min.js extension so you can distinguish easily between the normal files and the condensed ones. Keep both files on hand— update your scripts in the normal file (because it's easier for you to read), but use the minified version on your site (because it's faster for the browser). And don't forget to generate a new minified file when you update your script; otherwise, visitors will get the old version.

continues on next page

TIP If you create a minified file, be sure to change the reference to your script in your HTML. For example, `<script src="behavior.min.js"></script>`. Otherwise, your page will continue to load the normal file and your visitors won't reap the benefits of the smaller file. You can change the `src` back to the normal file name while you're working on changes to your script.

TIP Browsers that don't understand JavaScript (these are admittedly rare) or that have it disabled by the user will ignore your JavaScript file. So be sure that your page doesn't rely on JavaScript to provide users access to its content and basic experience. (Web applications that rely heavily on JavaScript are often an exception.)

Scripting and Performance Best Practices

A full discussion of best practices pertaining to scripts and page performance is beyond the scope of this book, but I'll touch on a few points that are high impact.

First, it helps to understand how a browser handles scripts. As a page loads, by default the browser downloads (for external scripts), parses, and executes each script in the order in which it appears in your HTML. As it's processing, the browser neither downloads nor displays any content that appears after the **script** element—not even text. This is known as *blocking behavior*.

This is true for embedded and external scripts, and as you can imagine, it can really affect how quickly your page displays, depending on the size of your script and what actions it performs.

Most browsers do this because your JavaScript may include code on which another script relies, code that generates page content immediately, or code that otherwise alters your page. Browsers need to take all of that into account before they finish rendering your webpage.

So how do you avoid this? The easiest technique to make your JavaScript *non*-blocking is to put all **script** elements at the end of your HTML, right before the **</body>** end tag Ⓐ.

If you've spent even a little time viewing HTML source on others' sites, no doubt you've also seen scripts loaded in the **head** element. Outside of the occasional instance where that may be necessary, it's considered a dated practice that you should avoid whenever possible. (One case in which it is necessary is loading the HTML5 shiv, as described in Chapter 11.) If you do load scripts in the **head**, place them after all **link** elements that load CSS files (again, for performance reasons).

Another quick way to speed up your script loading is to combine all your JavaScript into a single file (or into as few files as possible) and *minify* the code. Typically, minified code doesn't have line breaks, comments, or extra whitespace (among other possible differences from un-minified code). Imagine writing the code in one long line without ever pressing Return or Enter, and you'll get the idea Ⓓ.

continues on next page

TIP Technically, there is a third way to add JavaScript to a page: inline scripts. An *inline script* is a small bit of JavaScript assigned to certain element attributes directly in your HTML. I hesitate to mention them except to point out that you should avoid using them, just as you would avoid inline style sheets. Just as inline style sheets mix your HTML and CSS, inline scripts inextricably intertwine your HTML and JavaScript, rather than keeping them separate per best practices.

Scripting and Performance Best Practices *(continued)*

You may use tools such as the following to minify your scripts (the "download and documentation" links are provided primarily for advanced usage):

- Google Closure Compiler (use the second link):
  http://code.google.com/closure/compiler/ (download and documentation)
  http://closure-compiler.appspot.com (online version of tool)

- UglifyJS (use the second link):
  https://github.com/mishoo/UglifyJS2 (download and documentation)
  http://lisperator.net/uglifyjs/ (online version of tool, choose "Open demo")

- YUI Compressor (use the second link):
  http://developer.yahoo.com/yui/compressor/ (download and documentation)
  http://refresh-sf.com/yui/ (unofficial online version of tool)

Each will reduce your file size, but results will vary from script to script. Keep in mind that sometimes minifiers can be a little too aggressive and accidentally break your script, so it's important to test your page after you include a minified script. Also, it's generally faster for a browser to load one file than two (or more), even if the single file is larger than the combined size of the individual files (unless the one file is *much* larger).

Those are two common and powerful methods for reducing the impact of scripts on your page-rendering speed, but they only scratch the surface of what's possible. For in-depth discussions of script-loading methods and optimization, I highly recommend *Even Faster Web Sites* (O'Reilly Media, 2009) by Steve Souders, as well as his site, www.stevesouders.com. Be forewarned—some of the discussions get a little technical.

Adding an Embedded Script

An embedded script exists in your HTML document, much in the way an embedded style sheet does. An embedded script is contained in a **script** element **A**. Embedding a script is not the preferred method (see "Loading an External Script"), but sometimes it's necessary.

To add an embedded script:

1. In your HTML document, type **\<script\>**.

2. Type the content of the script.

3. Type **\</script\>**.

TIP Each **script** element is processed in the order in which it appears in the HTML, whether it's an embedded script or an external one (see "Loading an External Script").

TIP Even though the **script** element requires an end tag (**\</script\>**), you cannot embed code between it and the start tag when a **src** attribute is present (see "Loading an External Script"). In other words, **\<script src="your-functions.js"\>Some other functions in here\</script\>** is invalid. Any given **script** element may either load an external script with **src**, or embed a script and not have a **src**.

A An embedded script doesn't have a **src** attribute. Instead, the code is in the page. If you embed a script, do so directly before the **\</body\>** end tag whenever possible. It's also possible to embed a script in the head **B**, but it's less desirable from a performance standpoint.

```
<!DOCTYPE html>
<html lang="en">
<head>
     <meta charset="utf-8" />
     <title>Adding an Embedded Script</title>
     <link rel="stylesheet"
     ↪ href="css/global.css" />
</head>
<body>
... All of your HTML content is here ...

<script>
/*
Your JavaScript code goes here
*/
</script>
</body>
</html>
```

B This example shows a script embedded in the **head**. It appears after the **link** element so that the style sheet will load faster. See the "Scripting and Performance Best Practices" sidebar in the previous section to learn why you should minimize how often you embed scripts in the **head**.

```
<!DOCTYPE html>
<html lang="en">
<head>
     <meta charset="utf-8" />
     <title>Loading an External Script</title>
     <!-- Load style sheets before any JS
     ↪ files -->
     <link rel="stylesheet"
     ↪ href="global.css" />

     <script>
     /*
     Your JavaScript code goes here
     */
     </script>
</head>
<body>
... All of your HTML content is here ...
</body>
</html>
```

JavaScript Events

In this chapter's introduction, I noted that diving into JavaScript was beyond the scope of the book. However, I do want to give you a tiny peek at JavaScript events so you'll have a basic sense of what JavaScript can do for you.

You can write JavaScript to respond to specific, predefined events that either your visitor or the browser triggers. The list that follows is just a small sample of the event handlers (as they are known) available to you when you write scripts. HTML5 introduces numerous other ones, many of which revolve around events related to the **audio** and **video** elements. Touchscreen devices have gotten in on the action too, with special touch-based event handlers.

Please note that "mouse" in this list means "any pointing device." For example, **onmousedown** occurs if a visitor uses a digital pen, an actual mouse, or a similar device.

- **onblur**. The visitor leaves an element that was previously in focus (see **onfocus**).

- **onchange**. The visitor modifies the value or contents of the element. This is most commonly used on form fields (see Chapter 16 for more on forms).

- **onclick**. The visitor clicks the specified area or hits the Return or Enter key while focused on it (like on a link).

- **ondblclick**. The visitor double-clicks the specified area.

- **onfocus**. The visitor selects, clicks, or tabs to the specified element.

- **onkeydown**. The visitor presses down on a key while in the specified element.

continues on next page

- **onkeypress**. The visitor presses down and lets go of a key while in the specified element.

- **onkeyup**. The visitor lets go of a key after typing in the specified element.

- **onload**. The browser finishes loading the page, including all external files (images, style sheets, JavaScript, and so on).

- **onmousedown**. The visitor presses the mouse button down over the specified element.

- **onmousemove**. The visitor moves the mouse cursor.

- **onmouseout**. The visitor moves the mouse away from the specified element after having been over it.

- **onmouseover**. The visitor points the mouse at the element.

- **onmouseup**. The visitor lets the mouse button go after having clicked the element (the opposite of **onmousedown**).

- **onreset**. The visitor clicks the form's reset button or presses the Return or Enter key while focused on the button.

- **onselect**. The visitor selects one or more characters or words in the element.

- **onsubmit**. The visitor clicks the form's submit button or presses the Return or Enter key while focused on the button.

You can see a complete list of HTML5 event handlers at http://dev.w3.org/html5/spec-author-view/global-attributes.html. The touch-based event handlers that some touchscreen devices (like smartphones and tablets) contain include **touchstart**, **touchend**, and **touchmove** (www.w3.org/TR/touch-events/).

Testing & Debugging Webpages

So you are working on a page and fire it up in your browser only to find that it doesn't look anything like you expected. Or it doesn't display at all. Or maybe it looks great in one browser, but when you check it in another, something is a little off.

Between HTML, CSS, and the multitude of browsers (especially older versions of Internet Explorer) and devices, it's easy to have trouble here and there. This chapter will alert you to some common errors and will also help you weed out your own.

Some of these debugging techniques will seem pretty basic, but problems with webpages are often pretty basic too. So make sure you didn't overlook something simple before you go digging too deep in search of the problem.

Regardless, you should test your site thoroughly on a few browsers to see if each page works the way you want it to, as explained in "Testing Your Pages."

In This Chapter

Validating Your Code

Code validators point you to the source of an error  in your HTML **B** and CSS so you don't have to hunt it down on your own. An HTML validator compares your code against the rules of the language, displaying errors or warnings for any inconsistencies it finds. It will alert you to syntax errors; invalid elements, attributes, and values; and improper nesting of elements **C**. It can't tell if you've marked up your content with the elements that best describe it, so it's still up to you to write semantic HTML (see "HTML: Markup with Meaning" in Chapter 1).

You aren't required to make your pages pass the validators error-free before you put them on the web. Indeed, most sites have some errors. Also, the W3C's CSS validator will mark vendor prefixes used on property names as errors, but that doesn't mean you need to remove them from your style sheets (learn about vendor prefixes in Chapter 14).

Browsers are built to handle many types of errors (and ignore some others) and display your page as best they can. So even if your page has a validation error, you might not see the difference. Other times, the error directly affects a page's rendering **A** or behavior. So use the validators to keep your code as free from errors as possible.

See "Checking the Easy Stuff: HTML" and "Checking the Easy Stuff: CSS" for examples of errors that validators catch.

A Oops. Something is amiss—that text below the heading isn't supposed to be so big. I've already looked through my CSS to rule out that it's coming from an unintentionally large `font-size` setting. What's the problem?

B I've pasted the URL I want to check in the Address field. I also selected the Show Source option, so my HTML source code will appear underneath any errors the validator catches, with the errant parts of the HTML highlighted.

Checking HTML for Consistency

HTML5 is pretty lenient about how you format certain parts of your code. For instance, ending empty elements like `img` with either `/>` or `>` is valid. The validators don't check for consistency in these areas. If you like being sure your code *is* consistent, you can use HTML Lint (http://lint.brihten.com/html/). It has options for checking that empty elements are closed, start and end tags are lowercase, attributes are lowercase, and more.

1. **Error**: Heading cannot be a child of another heading.
   From line 10, column 40: to line 10, column 43
   n Victoria`<h1>`↵`<img`

2. **Error**: Element p not allowed as child of element h1 in this context. (Suppressing further errors from this subtree.)
   From line 12, column 1; to line 12, column 3
   alt="" />↵`<p>`An hou
   Contexts in which element p may be used:
   Where flow content is expected.

3. **Error**: End tag for body seen, but there were unclosed elements.
   From line 14, column 1; to line 14, column 7
   `</a></p>`↵`</body>`↵`</htm`

4. **Error**: Unclosed element h1.
   From line 10, column 40; to line 10, column 43
   n Victoria`<h1>`↵`<img`

There were errors. (Tried in the text/html mode.)

Source

```
1.  <!DOCTYPE html>↵
2.  <html lang="en">↵
3.  <head>↵
4.      <meta charset="utf-8" />↵
5.      <title>The City Named After Queen Victoria</title>↵
6.      <link rel="stylesheet"
    href="http://fonts.googleapis.com/css?family=Lato:300" />↵
7.      <link rel="stylesheet" href="css/victoria.css" />↵
8.  </head>↵
9.  <body>↵
10. <h1>The City Named After Queen Victoria<h1>↵
11. <img src="img/victoria.jpg" width="370" height="220" alt="" />↵
12. <p>An hour and a half aboard a comfortable car ferry is all it
    takes to transport you from the modern, urban space that is
```

C The error found on Line 10 is the problem—instead of an **</h1>** end tag, I've used another **<h1>** start tag by mistake. The other errors are caused by the first error, so once I fix that, the page will be error-free (**D** and **E**).

The document is valid HTML5 + ARIA + SVG 1.1 + MathML 2.0 (subject to the utter previewness of this service).

D Checking the page in the validator confirms that the HTML is valid.

The City Named After Queen Victoria

An hour and a half aboard a comfortable car ferry is all it takes to transport you from the modern, urban space that is Greater Vancouver to colonial Vancouver Island, seemingly stuck in the 18th century. The main town of Victoria showcases all the picturesque gems the British Empire was so proud of at the height of its spanning expansion. Representative yet inviting Victorian style

E When I refresh the page...that's more like it!

To validate your code:

1. First check your HTML with either http://html5.validator.nu (**B** and **C**) or http://validator.w3.org. See the first two tips for more information.

2. As desired, fix the HTML errors that are flagged, save the changes, and, if necessary, upload the file to your server again. Then repeat step 1.

3. Check for CSS errors with http://jigsaw.w3.org/css-validator/, similarly fixing the problems as you see fit and checking your page again.

TIP The W3C's validator (http://validator.w3.org) uses the validation engine from http://html5.validator.nu, so use whichever you prefer. The W3C's error messages are easier to read, but they don't highlight the errant portions of the HTML source code.

TIP You can validate your HTML by entering the URL **A**, uploading the HTML file, or pasting the HTML into the validator. With the file upload and copy-paste methods, you can check files without uploading them to your server.

TIP One HTML error can cause several in a validator's results. For example, a missing end tag can trigger lots of error messages **C**. Fix the end tag, and all of those subsequent errors go away **D**. Start at the top, fixing a few errors at a time, and then immediately revalidate the file to see if other problems are resolved.

TIP The CSS validator will show a couple of errors if your style sheet includes the **.clearfix** rules shown in Chapter 11. They are due to non-standard CSS required for older versions of Internet Explorer. You can ignore the errors; they won't hurt your page.

Testing Your Pages

Even if your code validates, your page still may not work the way you want it to (**A** through **C**). Or it may work properly in one browser, but not in the next. You can't be sure what browser your visitors will use, so it's important to test your page in a handful of them (see the sidebar "More About Browser Testing").

To test your webpages:

1. Validate your HTML and CSS (see "Validating Your Code"), and make any necessary changes.

2. Open your page as explained in "Viewing Your Page in a Browser" (Chapter 2).

3. Go through the whole page, and make sure it looks exactly the way you want it to. For example:

   ▸ Does the layout and formatting look correct?

   ▸ Does each link point to the proper page or asset? (Test the URLs by activating the links and seeing if the right thing happens.)

   ▸ Do all your images appear? Are they aligned properly?

   ▸ If you're checking a responsive webpage, does the layout adapt as expected at different sizes?

4. Without closing the page in the browser, open the appropriate HTML or CSS document and make any necessary changes.

5. Save the changes.

6. Switch back to the browser and refresh or reload to see the changes.

A This page validates, but it doesn't look anything like it's supposed to. What's the problem?

B The problem is the link to the CSS file—the file is named **styles.css**, and here I'm linking to **style.css**. The browser can't find the CSS and thus displays the page wrong.

```
<!DOCTYPE html>
<html lang="en">
<head>
    <meta charset="utf-8" />
    <title>Le Journal</title>
    <link rel="stylesheet"
→ href="css/style.css" />
    ...
</head>
<body>
...
</body>
</html>
```

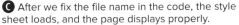

C After we fix the file name in the code, the style sheet loads, and the page displays properly.

A Testing Workflow

A common testing workflow is to check a page periodically in a couple of browsers while you are building it. Then test it across the full set of browsers when the page is finished, refining your code as necessary. When your *site* is finished, you'll want to test it thoroughly in browsers again to be sure it's all working together properly.

I recommend testing and refining your site's local version thoroughly first (per steps 1–8 in "To test your webpages"); that is, before you upload your files to your server (step 9). Once they are uploaded, test them thoroughly again, but from your server—regardless of how much testing you did of your local version during development—because that's the version your visitors will see (steps 10–11).

7. Repeat steps 3–6 until you are satisfied with your webpage. Sometimes it can take a few tries to get things right. If you're still having trouble, revalidate the code to make sure you haven't introduced any new errors.

8. Beginning with step 2, perform the same testing procedure in other browsers until you are satisfied and think your page is ready to go live on your site.

9. Upload the files to the server.

10. Return to the browser, type your page's URL in the address bar, and press Return or Enter. The page will appear in the browser.

11. Go through the page on your live site to make sure everything is all right. (It's easy to forget to upload an image or other file the page needs.) Don't forget to test it on mobile devices too, if visitors will be accessing your site on them.

TIP If your HTML code instead of your page displays in the browser, be sure your file has either the .html or .htm extension (and not one like .txt).

TIP Sometimes it's not your fault—especially with styles. Make sure a browser supports the feature you're having trouble with before assuming the problem is with your code. Can I Use (http://caniuse.com) and Quirksmode (www.quirksmode.org/css/) are two invaluable resources for browser support information.

More About Browser Testing

Generally, most people developing sites verify them in the following desktop browsers:

- Chrome (www.google.com/chrome), latest version. Chrome updates itself automatically on your computer. A new release occurs about once every six weeks.

- Firefox (www.firefox.com), latest version. Updates and new release frequency are like Chrome's.

- Internet Explorer 8+, Windows only. (IE8 is losing market share, so it will eventually drop off the list.) Various versions of IE are available at www.microsoft.com.

- Safari (www.apple.com/safari/), latest version or sometimes Safari 5+. Comes pre-installed with (and is available only for) OS X.

As good as Opera is, people are more selective about testing on it because it has a small market share in most parts of the world. Download Opera at www.opera.com.

The great news is that, with the exception of IE8 and to a lesser extent IE9, these browsers have similar levels of support for HTML and CSS features. This means you aren't likely to notice many differences in your pages, except perhaps if your page uses a particularly new HTML5 or CSS3 feature. Because IE8 is much older, it's OK if your site looks a little different on it as compared with modern browsers.

Obtaining Browsers for Testing

You can install several browsers using the download links provided above, but if you are a Mac user, how do you test on IE? If you're on Windows, how do you test Safari or multiple versions of IE? Here are some ideas:

- A virtual machine (VM) is an isolated version of an operating system that runs on your computer. Microsoft provides VMs with various versions of Windows and IE so you can test IE from a Mac, Windows, or Linux computer. They are available at www.modern.ie/en-US/virtualization-tools#downloads. You cannot run OS X in a VM to test Mac browsers from a Windows machine.

- BrowserStack (www.browserstack.com) and Sauce Labs (http://saucelabs.com) are services that allow you to test your pages on a huge range of browsers and mobile devices for a fee.

continues on next page

More About Browser Testing *(continued)*

Testing on Mobile Phones and Tablets

At the least, you'll want to test on iOS and an Android device. Testing your pages for mobile compatibility presents a special challenge because it can be difficult to get your hands on devices. Here are some options besides BrowserStack and Sauce Labs (please note that using the simulators and emulators is not the same as testing on devices):

- Use Apple's iOS Simulator to test your pages for the iPhone and iPad. The biggest drawback is that it works only on OS X, and there is no Windows equivalent. iOS Simulator is part of the free Xcode download, available at http://developer.apple.com/xcode/.

- DeviceAnywhere (www.deviceanywhere.com) provides online access to various mobile devices for testing for a fee. There is also a free version of DeviceAnywhere, which allows sessions for 10 minutes at a time.

- Use Electric Plum's iPhone and iPad simulator for Windows (www.electricplum.com). This is not affiliated with Apple, so it is not the same as Apple's iOS Simulator.

- Use emulators and simulators for other devices and mobile browsers. Mobile Boilerplate maintains a list at https://github.com/h5bp/mobile-boilerplate/wiki/Mobile-Emulators-&-Simulators.

- Look on Open Device Lab (http://opendevicelab.com) to see if there is a spot near you that has devices available to test with for free.

- If you have devices, use Adobe Edge Inspect (http://html.adobe.com/edge/inspect/) in combination with them to simplify testing and fixing bugs.

The browser market moves fast: By the time you read this, there will be newer versions of these browsers and new devices. Still, if you follow the principle of progressive enhancement, your sites can offer a simple experience in older browsers and an enhanced one in modern browsers.

Trying Some Debugging Techniques

So you've done some testing and found bugs. Here are some tried and true techniques for getting the kinks out of a webpage.

- Check the easy stuff first.

- Work incrementally. Make small changes, and test after each change. That way, you'll be able to pinpoint the source of a problem if one occurs.

- When you're debugging, start with what you know works. Then add the hard parts chunk by chunk—testing the page in a browser after each addition—until you find the source of the problem.

- Related to the previous point, use the process of elimination to figure out which chunks of your code are giving you trouble. For example, you can comment out half of the code to see if the problem is in the other half Ⓐ. Then comment out a smaller portion of the offending half, and so on, until you find the problem. (See "Adding Comments" in Chapter 3 and "Adding Comments to Style Rules" in Chapter 7.)

- Be careful about typos. Many perplexing problems can end up being simple typing mistakes—for instance, you spelled a class name one way in your HTML but a different way in your CSS.

Ⓐ I've commented out a section of this code (that is, everything between /* and */) to see if it's the culprit. On a separate note, many HTML and CSS editors include syntax highlighting, which is automatic color-coding of elements, selectors, and the like. This can aid your debugging. Mistype the name of a CSS property, for example, and the editor won't show it in the expected color: a hint that it isn't valid.

```
...

.excerpt {
    border-top: 1px dotted #ccc;
    margin: 0 .5em 2em 0;
}

.excerpt .title {
    font-size: 1.25em;
    line-height: 1.2;
}

/*
.more,
.excerpt .date {
    text-align: right;
}

.excerpt .date {
    line-height: 1;
    margin: 0 1em 0 0;
    padding: 0;
    position: relative;
    top: -1em;
}
*/

.photo {
    float: left;
    height: 300px;
    width: 400px;
}

...
```

- In CSS, if you're not sure whether the problem is with the property or with the selector, try adding a very simple declaration to your selector, like **color: red;** or **border: 1px solid red;** (or choose an uncommon site color like **pink** if **red** is part of your design). If the element turns red, the problem is with your property; if it doesn't, the problem is with your selector (assuming you don't have another selector that's more specific or that comes after the current one).

- Test changes to your HTML or CSS directly in the browser by using one or more of the developer toolbars at your disposal. Or inspect the code with these tools to try to locate the problem. (See the "Browser Developer Tools" sidebar.)

Browser Developer Tools

Browsers include invaluable tools that help you debug your pages and much more. The feature you will find yourself returning to time and again is the ability to change CSS or HTML and see it affect your page immediately. This allows you to quickly test changes before incorporating them in your code.

Following is a list of the tools used most often for each browser:

- Chrome: DevTools (http://developers.google.com/chrome-developer-tools/).

- Firefox: Firefox has built-in tools (https://developer.mozilla.org/en-US/docs/Tools), but the Firebug add-on (http://getfirebug.com) is more popular. Also, Web Developer (http://chrispederick.com/work/web-developer/) is a slightly different type of tool, but it is very handy. It's also available for Chrome at the same link.

- Internet Explorer: F12 Developer Tools (http://msdn.microsoft.com/en-us/library/hh772704(v=vs.85).aspx).

- Opera: Dragonfly (www.opera.com/dragonfly/). (This feature is in a state of transition at the time of this writing.)

- Safari: Web Inspector (http://developer.apple.com/technologies/safari/developer-tools.html).

Documentation and videos showing how to use many of these tools are available online. See an example of using Chrome DevTools in "Checking the Easy Stuff: CSS."

Checking the Easy Stuff: General

While the difference you see between browsers might be due to some obscure browser bug or some new technique you're using, often it's just something simple.

Everyone makes the occasional simple mistake that trips them up. For instance, it's easy to think the source of a problem is in the code and spend a lot of time debugging it, only to find that you're changing one file but uploading and viewing a different one from your server!

Many of the following suggestions apply to testing your site from the site's URL on your server.

To check the general easy stuff:

- Validate your code as described in "Validating Your Code." This is a great place to start, because you can eliminate coding syntax and related errors as the cause of the problem you're noticing.

- Make sure you've uploaded the file you want to test.

- Make sure you've uploaded the file to the folder where it belongs.

- Make sure you've typed the URL that corresponds to the file you want to test. Or if you've tried to browse to the page from another page, make sure the URL you coded in the link to the page matches its path.

- Make sure you've saved the file—including the very latest changes—before you upload it.

- Make sure you've uploaded any auxiliary files—CSS, images, music, videos, and so on.

- Make sure the upper- and lowercase letters in your URL exactly match the upper- and lowercase letters in your file names. (By the way, this is one reason I recommend using only lowercase letters. It reduces the room for error when typing URLs—for both you and your visitors.) And make sure you haven't used spaces in file names (use hyphens instead).

- If you disabled any browser features (such as JavaScript) during previous testing, make sure you haven't neglected to re-enable them if your page relies on them to work properly.

- Make sure the problem is not the browser's fault. The easiest way to do that is to test the page in another browser.

In the next two sections, I'll tell you how to check the easy stuff in HTML and CSS.

Still Stuck?

If you're still stuck trying to fix a problem after going through this chapter, here are some more suggestions:

- Please don't think I'm being patronizing when I suggest you take a break. Sometimes the best thing is to leave a problem alone for a bit. When you come back, the answer may be staring you in the face. Trust me, I've been there!

- Go back to the most recent version of the page that worked properly. (Related to that, make copies of your page as you progress through building it so you will have versions to go back to if necessary.) Then test the page as you add each new element bit by bit.

- For resources that your page links to, type the URL for that CSS, image, JavaScript, or media file directly in the browser's address bar to make sure it exists where you are expecting it.

- There are numerous sites where you can search for solutions or ask for guidance. Stack Overflow (www.stackoverflow.com) and SitePoint (www.sitepoint.com/forums/) are just two examples. You can find others by searching online.

Checking the Easy Stuff: HTML

Sometimes the problem is in your HTML.

To check the easy stuff in HTML:

- A simple typo or two can be easy to miss **A**. Make sure you've spelled everything correctly and that you've assigned valid values to attributes **B**. Use one of the HTML validators to expose these so you can correct them quickly (see "Validating Your Code").

- Be careful about element nesting. For instance, if you open **<p>** and then use ****, make sure the end **** comes before the final **</p>**.

- If accented characters or special symbols are not displaying properly, make sure **<meta charset="utf-8" />** (or the right character encoding if different than UTF-8) appears right after the document **head** element starts, and be sure your text editor is configured to save your HTML files in the same encoding. If you're still having trouble, try using the appropriate character reference.

A Can you see where the problems are? I've misspelled **src** and included a unit type in the **width** and **height** values. The HTML validators will flag these types of errors, saving you the time of trying to hunt them down elsewhere if you don't notice your typos.

```
<img scr="woody.jpg" width="200px"
→ height="150px" alt="Woody the cat" />
```

B The corrected version shows the **src** attribute spelled correctly, and I've removed the **px** from the **width** and **height** values.

```
<img src="woody.jpg" width="200" height="150"
→ alt="Woody the cat" />
```

C If an attribute's value contains a *single* quote, you can just enclose it in double quotes as usual.

```
<img src="jungle.jpg" width="325" height="275"
→ alt="Llumi's jungle" />
```

D If an attribute's value contains *double* quotes, use character references around the quoted text within the value.

```
<img src="cookie the-cat.jpg" width="250"
→ height="200" alt="Cookie's saying,
→ &quot;Enough!&quot;" />
```

E Don't include an end tag on void elements, like **img**. The HTML validators will flag this as an error.

```
<img src="jungle.jpg" width="325" height="275"
→ alt="Llumi's jungle"></img>
```

- Be sure attribute values are enclosed in straight, not curly, quotes. An attribute's value can contain single quotes if the value is enclosed in double quotes **C**, which is the norm. If the value itself contains double quotes, use character references for the inner quotes **D**.

- Don't use separate start and end tags for void (empty) elements **E**. (Technically, browsers may render elements correctly anyway, but play it safe.)

Checking the Easy Stuff: CSS

While CSS syntax is pretty straightforward, it has some common pitfalls, especially if you're more accustomed to writing HTML. A CSS validator will flag syntax errors like the ones discussed in this section, so validate your style sheets before you go digging through your CSS looking for errors (see "Validating Your Code").

To check the easy stuff in CSS:

- Make sure you separate properties from their values with a colon (:), not an equals sign (as you do in HTML) (**Ⓐ** and **Ⓑ**).

- Be sure to complete each property/value pair (a declaration) with a semicolon (;). Make sure there are no extra semicolons (**Ⓒ** and **Ⓓ**).

- Don't add spaces between numbers and their units (**Ⓔ** and **Ⓕ**).

- Don't forget to close your curly braces.

- Make sure you're using an accepted value. Something like **font-style: none;** isn't going to work, since the "none" value for this property is called **normal**.

- Don't forget the **</style>** end tag for embedded style sheets (which you should avoid in most cases anyway).

- Make sure the path to the desired CSS file is correct in your HTML.

- Watch the spaces and punctuation in and between the CSS selectors.

- Make sure the browser supports what you're trying to do, particularly with the latest features, because browser support continues to evolve as CSS

Ⓐ It can be hard to break the habit of separating properties and values with the equals sign.

```
p {
    font-size=1.3em;
}
```

Ⓑ Much better. Always use a colon between the property and the value. It doesn't matter if you add extra spaces before and after the colon, but it's common to include one after the colon.

```
p {
    font-size: 1.3em;
}
```

Ⓒ Another error. You must put one and only one semicolon between each property/value pair. Here, there's one missing and one extra.

```
p {
    font-size: 1.3em font-style: italic;;
    → font-weight: bold;
}
```

Ⓓ The error is easier to spot when each property/value pair occupies its own line, because the semicolons aren't lost in a sea of properties, values, and colons.

```
/* Still wrong, but easier to spot */
p {
    font-size: 1.3em
    font-style: italic;;
    font-weight: bold;
}

/* Here's the correct version */
p {
    font-size: 1.3em;
    font-style: italic;
    font-weight: bold;
}
```

E And yet another error. Never put spaces between the number and the unit.

```
p {
    font-size: .8275 em;
}
```

F This will work. Note that the space between the colon and the value is optional but common.

```
p {
    font-size: .8275em;
}
```

matures. Check browser support on Can I Use (http://caniuse.com) or Quirksmode (http://www.quirksmode.org/css/). The CSS validator won't tell you if a particular browser supports a feature, but it will indicate that you've typed a selector, property, or value that doesn't exist in CSS.

- Use the browser developer tools to inspect the style rules to quickly highlight which code isn't being interpreted as expected or to see how specificity rules have been applied **G**. (See the sidebar "Browser Developer Tools" earlier in the chapter.)

G I've inspected the code for `<h1>The City Named After Queen Victoria</h1>` with Chrome's DevTools. The HTML is on the left, and the CSS applied to the highlighted HTML element displays in the panel on the right. The tools in other browsers are configured similarly. The CSS portion shows a line through a **font-size** setting to indicate that it has been overridden by another rule (the one in the media query above it). This result is what I wanted in this case, but you can use this technique to track down why a style might not have been applied as expected. You can also edit the HTML or CSS rules to test changes directly in the browser. All browser developer tools allow this. If you like the results, you can make the same changes in your actual HTML and CSS files.

When Images Don't Display

Alternate text, little red x's, broken image icons, or nothing at all—these are all signs that your images aren't loading properly (**A** and **B**).

To fix missing images:

- First, check that the file name of the image on the server exactly matches the name you've referenced in the **img** element, including upper- and lowercase letters and the extension **A**. (Don't include spaces in file names. See "File and Folder Names" in Chapter 1.)

- Make sure the image's URL is correct in the **img** element's **src** attribute. One easy test is to put an image in the same directory as the HTML page. Then you'll just need the proper file name in the **src**, but no folder name or additional path information. If the image shows up, the problem was probably in the **src**. However, it isn't good practice to keep images in the same directory as HTML files, because your site will quickly become disorganized. So after your test, remove the image from the HTML page folder, and fix the **src** path that points to it. See "URLs" in Chapter 1.

- If the image shows up when you view your page on your computer but not when you upload the page to the server, make sure you've uploaded the image to the server.

- Have you saved the image as a PNG, JPEG, or GIF? If so, all browsers will display it, which is not true of other formats. See Chapter 5 for more information.

A The file name for the image is **victoria.jpg**, but in the HTML, it is incorrectly referenced as **Victoria.jpg** (with a capital *V*). As result, it doesn't display when you check the page from your server.

```
...
<body>
<h1>The City Named After Queen Victoria</h1>

<img src="img/Victoria.jpg" width="370"
→ height="220" alt="A weathered life ring
→ indicates you're headed toward another time
→ and place." />

<p>An hour and a half aboard ...</p>
</body>
</html>
```

B The page may look fine on your computer if it isn't picky about upper- and lowercase letters. But when the page is published to the server, which is case sensitive, the image cannot be found. Browsers like Chrome show a broken image icon instead.

Publishing Your Pages on the Web

Once you've finished your masterpiece, it's time to put it on the web for all to see. This chapter covers the steps required to do so: getting a domain name, finding a web host, connecting your domain and web host, and transferring your files to your host's server.

If you ever decide to change your web host, you can move your site to another web host's server. Your domain name and all of your site's URLs will stay exactly the same.

Also, be sure to test your pages thoroughly both before and after publishing them. Chapter 20 shows you how.

In This Chapter

Getting Your Own Domain Name

Before others can visit your site, you need a domain name to associate with it **A**. Then, once you've followed the steps in this chapter, your web host will serve your site to anyone who visits the domain in a browser.

To get your own domain name:

1. In a browser, go to a domain registrar to see if the domain name you want is available **B**. (See the first tip.) Nowadays, it can be hard to find a name that isn't taken, so you might need to search a few variations of the name you like.

2. Register the available domain you found. Charges vary from registrar to registrar, but about $10 a year for a .com domain is not uncommon (other extensions may have a different price).

> **TIP** Namecheap (www.namecheap.com) and Hover (www.hover.com) are just two of the places where you can register a domain name. (No endorsement is implied for either.) Others may be found by searching online for "domain registrars." Also, many web hosts allow you to register available domains on their sites; conversely, many registrars provide hosting services. You may prefer to use different companies for registering domains and hosting sites, as do I and many others.

> **TIP** See the sidebar "Connecting Your Domain and Your Web Host" in the next section for an important configuration that's required to make your site display when someone visits your URL.

A Only certain companies are accredited registrars of domain names (this view and the one below are from Namecheap). You can use one of their sites to see if a desired domain name is available, or you can check through a web host's site.

Popular Extensions		
☑ ☆	catalancats.com	Available
☐ ☆	catalancats.net	Available
☐ ☆	catalancats.biz	Available
☐ ☆	catalancats.org	Available
☐ ☆	catalancats.pw	Available
☐ ☆	catalancats.co	Available
☐ ☆	catalancats.co.uk	Available
☐ ☆	catalancats.in	Available
☐ ☆	catalancats.us	Available
☐ ☆	catalancats.me	Available
☐ ☆	catalancats.info	Available
☐ ☆	catalancats.us.com	Available
☐ ☆	catalancats.ca	Available
☐ ☆	catalancats.mobi	Available
☐ ☆	catalancats.com.au	Available
☐ ☆	catalancats.es	Available

Add to Cart

B If the name is available, you can register it either through a registrar site or through a web host. (And now you know that the very useful catalancats.com domain can be yours!)

Your ISP as Web Host

If you have Internet access (and I bet you do), you may already have a small amount of web space through your Internet service provider (ISP). It might not be enough for your entire website, but it's certainly enough to get used to putting pages on the web. Ask your ISP for details.

However, keep in mind that these types of hosting spaces typically don't allow you to put your site at a unique domain name. Instead, they are in a sub-domain or sub-directory of the ISP's domain, like www.*someisp*.com/*your-site*/ instead of www.*yourdomain*.com. In other words, if you have professional ambitions for your site, you wouldn't want it to be hosted on the free space your ISP may provide.

Web Analytics

Web analytics are reports that let you know how many people have visited your site, which browsers they have used, which pages are the most (and least) popular, and other useful data.

Web hosts may provide this information, but in many cases you will get richer reports by adding Google Analytics or a similar service to your site. It's pretty easy to implement—you add a snippet of code they provide to each of your pages. See www.google.com/analytics/ for more information.

Finding a Host for Your Site

Web hosts provide space on one of their web servers for your site's files. They provide other services too, like allowing you to create email addresses that are associated with your domain name (such as *yourname@yourdomain*.com).

There are hundreds of companies that provide website hosting. Most charge a monthly fee that depends on the services you choose. Some offer free web hosting in exchange for placing ads on your site (generally not recommended).

Although you can search the Internet for a web host, I recommend talking to friends to see if they use a host that they like. Or maybe the author of a blog you trust has noted what company he or she uses as a host; check in the site's footer or sidebar.

When considering a host, there are a number of things—besides price—to keep in mind.

- Does the account allow you to host more than one domain, or do you have to pay extra for each site? You should be able to find a host that provides the former if planning for the future is important to you.

- How much disk space will they let you have for your website? Don't pay for more than you need. Having said that, usually even the most basic accounts will have *plenty* of space for your site, with room to spare. Remember that HTML files take up very little space, whereas images, audio files, and videos take up successively larger amounts. You can always upgrade to an account with more space later if necessary.

continues on next page

- How much data transfer (bandwidth) per month do their accounts allow? This represents the total size of data—the HTML, CSS, images, media files, and so on—they will serve to your visitors, rather than how much they'll allow you to *store* on their server. So if you expect visitors to access a lot of large files from your site, you'll need a larger monthly transfer allotment. But just as with storage, basic accounts usually provide more than enough bandwidth when you're getting started, and you can upgrade later.

- How many mailboxes can you create for your domain? (Hosting companies often allow dozens.)

- Do they have plans that cater to sites with a lot of traffic, to ensure the site won't crash?

- What kind of technical support do they offer? Is it by phone, by email, or by online chat? How long will it take them to get back to you? Also, do they have a lot of support information available on their site? (You can probably check the quality of that content before becoming a customer.)

- How often do they back up data on their servers (in case there's a problem)?

- What kind of server-side languages and software packages come with the account? (You don't need these for a basic site.) Most provide PHP and MySQL at a minimum, and many also support WordPress and other features. Some features require a more expensive plan.

Connecting Your Domain and Your Web Host

Once you've registered a domain and found a web host, an important step is required to tie them together: You must point your domain to your web host so that your site loads when visitors type in your site's URL.

To make this work, you configure what are known as the name servers or DNS Servers associated with your domain. Your web host provides you the DNS information to use in the configuration.

The actual configuration is done in one of two places, depending on where you registered your domain (see "Getting Your Own Domain Name"). If you registered it with a domain registrar, log in to your account with them and set the DNS information for your domain (your domain registrar will provide instructions). If you registered your domain through your web host, you would log in to your account there to update the settings.

Don't worry if all this sounds a little confusing. Your web host and domain registrar (if different) will provide instructions on how to do this, and they will usually provide hands-on help if you need it.

One other point to keep in mind: When you change the name server settings, it usually takes 24 to 48 hours (72 at the very most) for the update to propagate across the web. But this change doesn't take hold at the same time everywhere. So if you've updated your domain's name server (and uploaded your site's files, as described in the next section), your friends might be able to access your site fine from where they live, even though you don't see it right away (or vice versa). Your site should show for everyone before too long.

Transferring Files to the Server

For other people on the Internet to see your pages, you have to upload them to your web host's server. One easy way to do that is with an FTP client such as FileZilla (http://filezilla-project.org), which is free for Windows, OS X, and Linux. (See the tips for other FTP clients.) Many web-page editors also include FTP capabilities, so you can publish pages right from there instead of using a program like FileZilla.

Typically, your web host emails FTP connection information to you after you sign up for a hosting account. Contact them if you didn't receive it or log into your account with them in a browser; the information is usually available there. Once you have that information, you can configure your server connection and save it under a name (Ⓐ through Ⓒ) for easy access anytime you want to publish files or download them from your site's server.

continues on next page

Ⓐ To enter information about a new server, select File > Site Manager from the main FileZilla window. Site Manager is where you configure the FTP connection details for each site.

Ⓑ When you click the New Site button, a temporary name appears under My Sites.

Ⓒ Replace the temporary name with a name of your choice, and then configure the connection details in the General tab. Don't forget to save the information by clicking either Connect or OK.

Then, connecting to your server  and transferring files (**E** and **F**) are straightforward.

Note that FileZilla looks a little different on OS X and Windows, but the interfaces are configured very similarly. Except where noted, the steps for using them are identical and the figures show OS X.

To define a new FTP site's properties:

1. Choose File > Site Manager from FileZilla's main menu **A**, or click the server icon (shown in **D**), to display the Site Manager window.

2. In the Site Manager window, click the New Site button **B**.

3. Type a name for the site (replacing the temporary name). It doesn't have to be the same as your domain name; it's just a label. Follow the information provided by your web host to complete the appropriate fields under the General tab. At a minimum, this usually involves entering the host URL, choosing Normal for the Logon Type option, and entering your user name and password (usually created when you set up the account with your host) **C**.

4. Once you've finished entering the connection details, either click the Connect button to save the information and connect to your server right away or click the OK button to save the information and connect later **C**.

D Now that your site's connection information is saved in the Site Manager, you can connect to your web host's FTP server without retyping everything each time. On Mac or Windows, return to the Site Manager via the server icon shown here or via the menu in **A**. Alternatively on Windows, as shown in the bottom image here, you can activate the down arrow next to the server icon and then choose your site's name from the menu that displays.

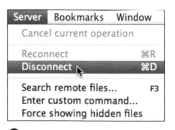

E The left pane shows a folder on your computer. The right pane shows a folder on your web server. Choose Upload to copy the selected file or folder to your web server **F**.

F The newly transferred folder appears in the pane on the right side of the window. Follow the same process for all the files and folders you want to transfer to your site. Or, to transfer several at once, select multiple files or folders and then right-click to select Upload.

G Disconnect from the server once you're finished transferring files.

To transfer files to the server with FileZilla:

1. Open FileZilla.

2. Click the server icon (on the far left) **D** to display the Site Manager window **C**. Then choose your site from under My Sites, and click the Connect button. (The Windows version has a shortcut **D**.) FileZilla will establish a connection with your server.

3. On the right side of the window, navigate to the server directory to which you want to upload files.

4. On the left side of the window, navigate to the directory on your computer that has the files you want to upload.

5. Right-click the desired file or folder in the left pane, and choose Upload from the context menu **E**. The files are transferred **F** (this will take longer for large files, like videos). You may also transfer files in the other direction (see the first tip), as well as drag and drop files from one side to another instead of using the right-click option.

6. Your site updates are live now. Visit your site at www.*yourdomain.tld*, where *yourdomain.tld* is the domain you registered (*.tld* is the top-level domain, which will be .com unless you registered a domain with a different extension). Browse around to make sure everything is working properly. Edit any of the files on your computer as necessary, and upload them to your server by following steps 3–5 (you may need to repeat step 2 to reconnect if a lot of time has passed). Repeat this step until the site is as you intend it.

7. Close FileZilla, or choose Server > Disconnect from the main menu **G**.

continues on next page

TIP You can also transfer files from your site's server to your computer. To do so, right-click files or folders in the right pane **E** and choose Download from the context menu.

TIP FileZilla is just one of many FTP clients available. CyberDuck (free, http://cyberduck.ch) is available for both OS X and Windows. Some other popular ones for OS X are Transmit (www.panic.com/transmit) and Fetch (http://fetchsoftworks.com). OS X also has built-in FTP capability (see http://osxdaily.com/2011/02/07/ftp-from-mac/). Search online for "FTP client" to find more for both Windows and OS X. They all work similarly, but some have more features than others.

TIP When you transfer files and folders, they are copied to the destination folder. The source location retains its version of the assets.

TIP Your FTP program might prompt you (as FileZilla does) to be sure you want to overwrite a file or folder if you transfer one that the destination already contains. Each FTP client is different, though, so it's possible it won't ask for your permission. Try it on a test file to learn how your FTP client handles such a situation.

TIP Relative URLs in your code are maintained when you transfer a folder to the server.

TIP If your site doesn't load when you visit its URL, it could be a few things. First, double-check that you uploaded the files to the proper directory. Often, your pages belong in a directory called *public_html*, *www*, or something similar. Your web host's instructions should specify the proper location; ask them if you aren't sure. If you've got the files in the right place and the site still doesn't show, the problem might be your domain's name server settings (see the sidebar "Connecting Your Domain and Your Web Host").

TIP If you have uploaded a new version of a file to your server but don't see the change when you visit your site, clear your browser's cache and check the page again. Search the browser's Help section if you aren't sure how to clear the cache. You can also search for instructions to disable the cache.

HTML Reference

This appendix contains a nearly complete list of HTML elements and attributes, including some that are not covered in the book. (In most cases, that's because it is a little-used or an advanced feature.) Each element has a short description and an annotated list of its associated attributes.

The Page column indicates the primary page that explains the element or attribute so you can learn more. Sometimes an attribute's page number points to where it is used on a different element—the explanation on that page is relevant to using it on all allowed elements.

Additionally, some items are marked with one of the following:

(5) An element or attribute that is new in HTML5.

(*) An element or attribute that existed in HTML before but which has been redefined in HTML5.

The new features in HTML5 are unsupported in some older browsers, such as IE8. For the latest browser support information, please see http://caniuse.com, which is updated regularly.

CSS Reference

Unfortunately, due to space limitations, we could not include the CSS Reference in these pages. But both the CSS and HTML References are available on the book site (www.htmlcssvqs.com).

TABLE A.1 HTML Elements and Attributes

Element/Attribute	Description	Page
—Most ELEMENTs—	The following attributes may be used with *most* HTML elements	
`accesskey`	For adding a keyboard shortcut to an element	
`aria-*`	For associating accessibility attribute values specified by WAI-ARIA	422
`class`	For identifying a set of elements in order to apply styles to them	82
`contenteditable` (5)	For making the content of an element editable	
`data-*` (5)	For storing custom data that is private to the page or application	
`dir`	For specifying the element's text direction	125
`draggable` (5)	For making an element draggable	
`dropzone` (5)	For identifying an element as a place where draggable elements can be dropped	
`hidden` (5)	For indicating that an element is not yet relevant or is no longer relevant	
`id`	For identifying a particular element so that it can be linked to, styled, or scripted with JavaScript	82
`lang`	For specifying the language an element is written in	44
`role`	For providing additional information to assistive devices about the role of an element as defined by WAI-ARIA	78
`spellcheck` (5)	For indicating whether the content of an element should have its spelling and grammar checked	
`style`	For adding local style sheet information	196
`tabindex`	For defining the order in which the Tab key takes the visitor through elements	158
`title`	For labeling elements with tool tips	84
a	For creating links and anchors	158
`href`	For specifying the URL of a page or the name of an anchor that a link goes to	158
`hreflang` (5)	For specifying the language of the linked resource	
`download` (5)	For specifying that the link points to an asset for download. Set the `download` value to be equal to the file name.	
`rel`	For identifying the nature of the link	160
`target` (*)	For specifying the window or iframe where a link should open	163
`type`	For noting a resource's MIME type	
abbr (*)	For explaining the meaning of abbreviations and acronyms	101
address	For identifying contact information for the nearest **article** or **body** element ancestor	106

continues on next page

Element/Attribute	Description	Page
area	For specifying the coordinates of image maps	
`alt`	For giving information about an area	
`coords`	For giving the coordinates of an area in an image map	
`href`	For specifying the destination URL of a link in an area of an image map	
`hreflang` (5)	For specifying the language of the linked resource	
`download` (5)	For specifying that the link points to an asset for download. Set the `download` value to be equal to the file name.	
`rel`	For identifying the kind of link	
`shape`	For specifying the shape of an area in an image map	
`target` (*)	For specifying the window or iframe where a link should open	163
article (5)	For identifying a self-contained composition in a page that is in principle independently distributable or reusable	60
aside (5)	For identifying a section of a page that consists of content that is tangentially related to the content around it	65
audio (5)	For embedding audio in a page	464
`autoplay` (5)	For telling the browser to start playing the audio file as soon as it can	466
`controls` (5)	For telling the browser to display controls for the **audio** element	464
`loop` (5)	For telling the audio file to start over without interruption upon reaching its end	466
`muted` (5)	For controlling the default state of audio output	
`preload` (5)	For suggesting whether the browser can begin downloading the audio file before the visitor starts playing it	466
`src` (5)	For identifying the URL of the audio file to play	464
b (*)	For identifying a span of text to which attention is being drawn for utilitarian purposes, without conveying any extra importance and with no implication of an alternate voice or mood	91
base	For specifying the base URL of the page	
`href`	For specifying the URL to be used to generate relative URLs	
`target` (*)	For specifying the default target for the links on the page	163
bdi (5)	For identifying a span of text that is to be isolated from its surroundings for the purposes of bidirectional text formatting	125
`dir`	For specifying text direction	125
bdo (5)	For explicitly formatting the text direction of its content	125
`dir`	For specifying text direction	125

continues on next page

Element/Attribute	Description	Page
blockquote	For identifying a section quoted from another source	95
`cite`	For giving the URL of the source	95
body	For enclosing a page's entire content	44
br	For creating a line break	118
button	For creating buttons	442
`autofocus` (5)	For specifying that the button is to be focused as soon as the page is loaded	423
`disabled`	For indicating that the element is not available in the current state	444
`form` (5)	For associating the element with a form that it is not a part of. Set it to the form's `id`.	
`formaction` (5)	For overriding the form's `action` attribute	
`formenctype` (5)	For overriding the form's `enctype` attribute	
`formmethod` (5)	For overriding the form's `method` attribute	
`formnovalidate` (5)	For overriding the form's `novalidate` attribute	443
`formtarget` (5)	For overriding the form's `target` attribute	
`name`	For identifying the data sent with a button	443
`type`	For specifying the type of button. Set value to `button`, `reset`, or `submit`. The latter two act like their form `input` counterparts.	442
`value`	For specifying the data that should be submitted when the button is activated	443
canvas (5)	To provide JavaScript a resolution-dependent bitmap canvas for rendering graphics on the fly	475
`width, height` (5)	For specifying the size of the canvas	
caption	For creating a caption for a table	478
cite	For marking text that is the title of a book, song, painting, play, and so on	94
code	For marking text that is computer code or a file name	112
col	For joining columns in a table into a non-structural group	
`span`	For specifying the number of columns in a column group	
colgroup	For joining columns in a table into a structural column group	
`span`	For specifying the number of columns in a column group	
datalist (5)	To contain a group of option elements that represent a predefined set of options for another form control	411
dd	For marking a description (value) in a description list (`dl`)	404
del	To mark deleted text	108
`cite`	For referencing a URL that explains the change	110
`datetime`	For specifying the time and date of the change	100

continues on next page

TABLE A.1 HTML Elements and Attributes *(continued)*

Element/Attribute	Description	Page
details (5)	For creating a widget that can open and close and which can obtain additional information or controls	
open (5)	For specifying whether the element is open or closed by default	
dfn	For specifying the defining instance of a term	103
`title`	For providing the definition of the term	103
div	For enclosing a portion of a page for styling or scripting purposes (it has no meaning)	73
dl	For creating a description list	404
dt	For marking a term (name) in a description list (**dl**)	404
em (*)	To mark text with stress emphasis	90
embed (*)	For adding multimedia	
`src`	For specifying the URL of a multimedia file	
`type`	For identifying the MIME type of the multimedia file	
`width, height`	For specifying the size of the embedded multimedia player	
fieldset	For grouping a set of form elements together	418
`disabled` (5)	For disabling all form controls within the fieldset	444
`form` (5)	For associating the element with a form that it is not a part of. Set it to the form's **id**.	
figcaption (5)	For identifying a caption or legend for the contents of its parent **figure** element	92
figure (5)	For identifying content that is referenced within the main flow of the page but that could be moved elsewhere without affecting the flow	92
footer (5)	For identifying a footer for the nearest ancestor **body**, **section**, **article**, or **aside** element	70
form	For designating a form to collect data for submission	413
`accept-charset`	For identifying the character encoding to be used with the form submission (defaults to the page's character set)	
`action`	For giving the URL of the script that will process the form data	414
`autocomplete` (5)	For preventing the browser from providing/remembering autocompletion values when the attribute is set to "off" (the default is "on"; that is, autocompletion is allowed by default).	424
`enctype`	For making sure files are sent to the server in the proper format	439
`method`	For specifying how data should be sent to the server	414
`name`	For providing the form with a name for use later	413
`novalidate` (5)	For allowing the form to be submitted without validation	415
`target` (*)	For identifying the target window or iframe of the form's submission	163
h1, h2, h3, h4, h5, h6	For creating the hierarchy of headings in a page	50

continues on next page

Element/Attribute	Description	Page
head	For creating the **head** section, which contains information about the page, including the title, author, keywords, style sheets, and scripts	45
header (5)	For identifying a group of introductory content or navigational aids	54
hr (*)	For identifying a paragraph-level thematic break	
html	For identifying a text document as an HTML document	44
`manifest` (5)	For specifying an application cache manifest that is used when the page is offline	
i (*)	For marking a span of text that is in an alternate voice or mood or that is otherwise offset from the normal prose in a manner indicating a different quality of text	91
iframe	For loading a webpage within another webpage	
`name`	For specifying the name of the iframe, to be used as a target	
`sandbox` (5)	For specifying additional restrictions on the content of the iframe, for security purposes	
`seamless` (5)	For specifying whether the iframe should appear to be part of the containing page	
`src`	For specifying the URL of the initial page	
`srcdoc` (5)	For specifying the URL of the initial page	
`width, height`	For specifying the size of the iframe	
img	For inserting images on a page	145
`alt`	For offering alternate text that is displayed if the image is not and that is for users of assistive devices	147
`ismap`	For indicating that the element provides access to a server-side image map (the element must be a descendant of an **a** element)	
`src`	For specifying the URL of an image	145
`usemap`	For specifying the client-side image map that should be used with the referenced image	
`width, height`	For specifying the size of an image so that the page is loaded more quickly, or for scaling	150
input	For creating form controls of various types	411
`accept`	For informing the browser what file types will be accepted if the input type is "file"	412
`alt`	For providing a textual alternate if the input type is "image"	442
`autocomplete` (5)	For preventing the browser from providing/remembering autocompletion values when the attribute is set to "off" (the default is "on"; that is, autocompletion is allowed by default).	424
`autofocus` (5)	For specifying that the input is to be focused as soon as the page is loaded	423
`checked`	For marking a radio button or checkbox by default	433

continues on next page

Element/Attribute	Description	Page
`dirname` (5)	For identifying the direction of the entered text	
`disabled`	For indicating that the input is not available in the current state	444
`form` (5)	For associating the element with a form that it is not a part of. Set it to the form's `id`.	
`formaction` (5)	For overriding the form's `action` attribute	
`formenctype` (5)	For overriding the form's `enctype` attribute	
`formmethod` (5)	For overriding the form's `method` attribute	
`formnovalidate` (5)	For overriding the form's `novalidate` attribute	443
`formtarget` (5)	For overriding the form's `target` attribute	
`list` (5)	For associating the input with a datalist	411
`max, min` (5)	For indicating the input element's allowed range of values	
`maxlength`	For specifying the maximum number of characters that can be entered in an input element	423
`multiple` (5)	For specifying whether the user is allowed to enter more than one value	431
`name`	For identifying data collected by an element	413
`pattern` (5)	For providing a regular expression against which the input element's value is checked	428
`placeholder` (5)	For providing a hint to aid in data entry	423
`readonly`	For keeping visitors from changing certain form elements	440
`required` (5)	For identifying that the element must not be blank to submit the form (not allowed when the input type is "hidden," "image," or some button types)	422
`size`	For specifying the length of a text or password box	423
`src`	For specifying the URL of an image submit button	442
`step` (5)	For controlling the granularity and specificity of allowed values	
`type` (*)	For specifying if a form element is a text box, password box, radio button, checkbox, hidden field, submit button, reset button, active image, date/time box, number box, or color box; for selecting from a range of values; or for entering a telephone number, email address, or set of search terms	411
`value`	For specifying the default data in a form element	422
`width, height`	For specifying the dimensions of the input (only allowed when the input type is "image")	442
ins	For marking an addition to a webpage's contents	108
`cite`	For referencing a URL that explains the change	110
`datetime`	For specifying the time and date of the change	100
kbd	For marking user input, such as the keys to press to complete an action	113

continues on next page

Element/Attribute	Description	Page
keygen (5)	For generating a public and private key pair	
`autofocus` (5)	For specifying that the **keygen** element is to be focused as soon as the page is loaded	423
`challenge` (5)	For generating a challenge to go along with the key pair	
`disabled` (5)	For indicating that the element is not available in the current state	444
`form` (5)	For associating the element with a form that it is not a part of	
`keytype` (5)	For identifying the kind of key pair to be generated	
`name` (5)	For identifying the data that is gathered	413
label	For labeling form elements	425
`for`	For specifying which form element the label belongs to	425
`form` (5)	For associating the element with a form that it is not a part of	
legend	For labeling fieldsets	418
li	For creating a list item in an ordered (**ol**) or unordered list (**ul**)	390
`value`	For determining the initial value of the list item (if it is the child of an **ol**) *	397
link	For linking to an external style sheet or other external resource	192
`href`	For specifying the URL of the resource	192
`hreflang` (5)	For specifying the language of the linked resource	
`media`	For defining a style sheet's targeted media types and/or media features	200
`rel`	For identifying the kind of link	192
`sizes` (5)	For identifying the size of the referenced icon (for use only when the **rel** attribute is "icon")	
`title`	For labeling an alternate style sheet	
`type`	For noting a resource's MIME type (only required if the link type is not "text/css")	
main (5)	For indicating the main content area of a page	59
map	For creating a client-side image map	
`name`	For naming a map so it can be referenced later	
mark (5)	For highlighting text for reference purposes due to its relevance in another context, like search results	116
menu (*)	For containing a list of commands	
`label` (5)	For labeling the menu	
`type` (5)	For identifying the kind of menu being used: "context," "list" (default), or "toolbar"	

continues on next page

TABLE A.1 HTML Elements and Attributes *(continued)*

Element/Attribute	Description	Page
meta	For associating various kinds of metadata with the page	45
`charset`	For identifying the character encoding of the page itself	45
`content`	For adding extra information about the page itself	
`http-equiv`	For creating automatic jumps to other pages, setting the default scripting language, and declaring the character encoding	
`name`	For identifying extra information about the page	
meter (5)	For representing a measurement within a known range	128
`high, low` (5)	For specifying a range of values as being "high" or "low"	128
`max, min` (5)	For identifying the maximum and minimum allowable values	128
`optimum` (5)	For identifying the optimum value	128
`value` (5)	For indicating the current value of the meter (required)	128
nav (5)	For identifying a section of a page that links to other pages or to parts within the page	56
noscript	For providing an alternative when JavaScript is disabled	
object	For embedding objects in webpages	
`data`	For identifying the source of the multimedia file to be embedded	
`form` (5)	For associating the element with a form that it is not a part of. Set it to the form's **id**.	
`name`	For identifying the object (e.g., so it can be scripted)	
`type`	For noting the object's MIME type	
`typemustmatch`	For indicating that the resource specified in the object's **data** attribute must have the same MIME type as identified in the object's **type** attribute (allowed only if the object's **data** and **type** are both specified)	
`usemap`	For indicating whether the object has an associated image map	
`width, height`	For specifying the dimensions of the object's box	
ol	For creating ordered lists	390
`reversed` (5)	For specifying whether the list is descending (…, 3, 2, 1)	392
`start` (*)	For specifying the initial value of the first list item	397
`type` (*)	For specifying the kind of numerals that should begin each list item	393
optgroup	For grouping a set of option elements under a common label within a **select** element	438
`disabled`	For indicating that the element is not available in the current state	444
`label`	For labeling the group of options	438

continues on next page

Element/Attribute	Description	Page
option	For creating the individual options in a **select** or **datalist** element	437
`disabled`	For indicating that the element is not available in the current state	444
`label`	For specifying how the option should appear in the menu	438
`selected`	For making a menu option be selected by default in a blank form	437
`value`	For specifying the initial value of a menu option	437
output (5)	For representing the result of a calculation	411
`for` (5)	For creating an explicit association between the result of a calculation and the values that went into the calculation	
`form` (5)	For associating the element with a form that it is not a part of. Set it to the form's **id**.	
`name` (5)	For identifying the data that is gathered	413
p	For creating a paragraph	88
param	For setting properties of an **object** element	
`name`	For identifying the kind of property	
`value`	For setting the value of the named property	
pre	For representing a block of preformatted text	114
progress (5)	For identifying the completion progress of a task	130
`max` (5)	Must be a valid floating-point number greater than zero (if present)	130
`value` (5)	Must be a valid floating-point number equal to or greater than zero (and less than or equal to the value of the **max** attribute, if it is present)	130
q	For quoting short passages from another source	95
`cite`	For giving the URL of the source of the quote	95
rp (5)	For providing parentheses around a ruby text component of a ruby annotation in browsers that don't support ruby annotations	124
rt (5)	For marking the ruby text component of a ruby text annotation	124
ruby (5)	For allowing text to be marked up with ruby annotations	124
s (*)	For identifying text that is no longer accurate or no longer relevant	108
samp	For representing sample output from a program or computing system	113
script	For adding JavaScript (primarily) to a page	487
`async` (5)	For influencing script loading and execution	
`charset`	For specifying the character set an external script is written in	45
`defer`	For influencing script loading and execution	
`src`	For referencing an external script	487
`type` (*)	For specifying the scripting language the script is written in (only required if the script type is not **"text/javascript"**)	

continues on next page

TABLE A.1 HTML Elements and Attributes *(continued)*

Element/Attribute	Description	Page
section (5)	For identifying a section of a page (a thematic grouping of content)	63
select	For creating a form control for selecting from a set of options	437
autofocus (5)	For specifying that the **select** element is to be focused as soon as the page is loaded	423
disabled	For indicating that the element is not available in the current state	444
form (5)	For associating the element with a form that it is not a part of. Set it to the form's **id**.	
multiple	For allowing users to choose more than one option in the menu	437
name	For identifying the data collected by the menu	437
required (5)	For identifying that the user must select one of the options in order to submit the form (the first child option element must be a placeholder or an empty value)	422
size	For specifying the number of items initially visible in the menu (and for displaying the menu as a list)	437
small (*)	For representing side comments such as legal print (small print)	89
source (5)	For identifying multiple alternative media resources within an **audio** or **video** element	468 459
media (5)	For identifying the intended media type of the resource	319
src (5)	For identifying the URL of the audio or video file to play	459
type (5)	For noting a resource's MIME type	461
span	For wrapping text that has no semantic meaning (often for styling)	120
strong (*)	For indicating content of strong importance	90
style	For embedding style information in a page	194
media	For indicating a style sheet's purpose	319
title	For labeling an alternate style sheet	
type (*)	For indicating a style sheet's MIME type (only required if the type is not "text/css")	
sub	For marking subscripts	104
summary (5)	For identifying a summary, caption, or legend for the contents of its parent **details** element	
sup	For marking superscripts	104
svg (5)	For embedding Scalable Vector Graphics in the page	475
table	For representing tablular data	478
tbody	For identifying the body of the table; in contrast with the header (**thead**) or footer (**tfoot**)	479

continues on next page

TABLE A.1 HTML Elements and Attributes *(continued)*

Element/Attribute	Description	Page
td, th	For creating regular and header cells, respectively, in a table	478
`colspan`	For spanning a cell across more than one column	482
`headers`	For explicitly associating a **td** or **th** with another **th** by including that **th**'s **id** value in the value of **headers** (separate each value with a space).	
`rowspan`	For spanning a cell across more than one row	482
`scope`	For identifying to which rows, columns, rowgroups, or columngroups a **th** applies (valid for **th** only)	478
textarea	For creating text block entry areas in a form	436
`autofocus` (5)	For specifying that the text area is to be focused as soon as the page is loaded	423
`dirname` (5)	For identifying the direction of the entered text	
`disabled`	For indicating that the element is not available in the current state	444
`form` (5)	For associating the element with a form that it is not a part of. Set it to the form's **id**.	
`maxlength`	For specifying the maximum number of characters that can be entered in a **textarea**	436
`name`	For identifying the data that is gathered with the text block	436
`placeholder` (5)	For providing a hint to aid in data entry	423
`readonly`	For protecting a text area's contents	440
`required` (5)	For indicating that the element must not be blank in order to submit the form	422
`rows, cols`	For specifying the number of rows and columns in the text block	436
`wrap` (5)	For specifying the use of soft or hard wraps when content of field is submitted	
tfoot, thead	For identifying the footer and header area of a table	479
time (5)	For specifying a date, a time, or both	98
`datetime` (5)	For providing a machine-readable version of the time or date expressed in the element's text	100
title	For creating the title of the page (required)	48
tr	For creating rows in a table	478
track (5)	For specifying external timed text tracks for the parent **audio** or **video** element	462
`default` (5)	For indicating which track is the default	
`kind` (5)	For identifying whether the track is "subtitles," "captions," "descriptions," "chapters," or "metadata"	
`label` (5)	For providing a user-readable name for the track	
`src` (5)	For identifying the URL of the track's data	

continues on next page

TABLE A.1 HTML Elements and Attributes *(continued)*

Element/Attribute	Description	Page
`srclang` (5)	For identifying the language of the track's data	
u (*)	For displaying a span of text with an unarticulated, though explicitly rendered, non-textual annotation	122
ul	For creating unordered lists	390
var	For marking text as a variable name	113
video (5)	For embedding videos, movies, and captioned audio files	452
`autoplay` (5)	For telling the browser to start playing the video file as soon as it can	454
`controls` (5)	For telling the browser to display controls for the video element	454
`loop` (5)	For telling the video file to start over without interruption upon reaching its end	456
`muted` (5)	For controlling the default state of audio output	
`poster` (5)	For specifying the URL of an image to use as a placeholder while media loads, or in case of an error loading	456
`preload` (5)	For suggesting whether the browser can begin downloading the media file before the visitor starts playing it	457
`src` (5)	For identifying the URL of the video file to play	452
`width, height` (5)	For specifying the dimensions of the video	452
wbr (5)	For identifying an appropriate place to insert a line-break into a word without hyphenation	123

Index

browser developer tools
    Chrome, 503
    Firefox, 503
    Internet Explorer, 503
    Opera, 503
    Safari, 503
browser support resources, 499
browsers. *See also* polyfills
    default display of webpages, 24–25
    explained and version numbers, xvii
    inline, 24–25
    modern browsers, xxv
    -moz- prefix, 364
    -ms- prefix, 364
    -o- prefix, 364
    obtaining for testing, 500
    prefixes, 364
    support for gradients, 381
    testing sites in, 500
    viewing pages in, 38–39
    VMs (virtual machines), 500
    -webkit- prefix, 364
bulleted lists, creating, 391, 393
button element, 442
    using with forms, 442–443

C
canvas element, 475
    using with video, 475
capitalize value, limitations of, 260
caption element, 478
captions, creating for figures, 92–93
challenge attribute, 526
character encoding, specifying, 12
characters
    accenting, 12
    dir attribute, 126
    left-to-right, 125
    right-to-left, 125
charset attribute, 45
checkboxes, creating for forms, 434–435
checked attribute, 433
checking for errors. *See also* debugging
        techniques
    CSS (Cascading Style Sheets), 508–509
    general, 504–505
    HTML (Hypertext Markup Language), 506–507
child element
    explained, 11, 212
    first and last, 216–217
Chrome
    developer tool, 503
    refreshing pages in, 39
    undocking Developer Tools, 39
    testing sites in, 500

Chrome's cache, disabling, 39
circles, creating using **border-radius**, 367
citations, indicating, 94
cite attribute, 94, 95, 110
    using with **blockquote**, 97
cite element, 87, 94–95, 522
    using for names, 94
class attributes, 82
    applying, 82–83
    implementing microformats, 83
    naming, 83
class names, assigning to elements, 82
class selectors. *See also* pseudo-classes
    vs. ID selectors, 211
    multiple classes on one element, 177, 210
    using with inline styles, 197
clearfix method, using with **float** property, 299
clearing floats, 297–300
"click here" labels, avoiding, 162
Cloud.typography web font service, 339
Coda text editor, 31
code
    displaying **<** and **>** signs, 112
    marking up, 112
    validating, 496–497
code editor, funny characters in, 47
code element, explained, 87, 112
codec, explained, 451
col element, 522
colgroup element, 522
colors. *See also* background color
    per image formats, 136
    CSS color options, 182–188
    declared with hexadecimal, 183
    declared with keywords, 182
    declared with HSL and HSLA, 186–188
    declared with RGB and RGBA, 183–185
    setting for text, 248–249
    specifying for borders, 288
colspan attribute, 482
"commenting out" declarations, 173
comments
    /* and ***/** for CSS, 172
    <!-- and **-->** for HTML, 86
    adding to HTML, 85–86
    adding to CSS, 172–173
complementary landmark role, 79–80
conditional comments, using with responsive
        pages, 333
consistency, checking HTML for, 496
contact info, adding, 106–107
containers, creating, 73–75
content, adding to webpages, 6–7
content attribute, 527
contenteditable attribute, 520

displays, media queries for, 332
div element, 73, 125
 adding around whole pages, 73
 containing pages in, 77
 vs. **section** element, 63
 surrounding content, 74
 using in HTML5, 76
dl (description list) element, 404
 creating, 404–407
 explained, 389, 523
 nesting, 407
DOCTYPE declaration
 including in webpages, 4–5, 44
document flow, explained, 278
document head, explained, 5, 46
document headings structure, defining, 50
domain, connecting with web host, 514
domain name, getting, 512
double vs. single quotes, 348
download attribute, 520
draggable attribute, 520
DRM (digital rights management), 450
drop shadows, adding to text, 368–369
dropzone attribute, 520
dt element, 389, 404
duration, specifying, 98

E

Edge Web Fonts service, 339
editing webpages, 36
edits, noting, 108–111
elements. *See also* alphabetical list of HTML
  elements in Appendix; pseudo-elements;
  selecting elements
 aligning vertically, 306–307
 ancestors, 212
 assigning classes to, 82
 attributes of, 9
 block-level, 24
 components, 8
 contents, 8
 descendants, 212
 display type, 278–281
 document flow, 278
 empty, 8
 floating, 295–300
 inline, 24
 naming with unique IDs, 82
 nesting, 11
 number available, 22
 offsetting in natural flow, 301
 parents, 11
 phrasing content, 21
 positioning absolutely, 302–303
 positioning in stacks, 304

relative positioning, 301
rounding corners of, 365–367
selecting based on attributes, 222–225
selecting by class, 208–210
selecting by context, 212–215
selecting by ID, 208–210
selecting by name, 206–207
selecting when first child, 216–217
selecting when last child, 216–217
specifying groups of, 226
visibility, 278–281
void, 8
wrapping text around, 295–296
em (stress emphasis) element, 90
 explained, 87, 523
 vs. **i** element, 90
 and percentage font sizes, 241–243
 using, 21–22, 90
em values for padding and margin, 294
email boxes, creating for forms, 428–431
embed element, 523
embedded style sheets, 194–195. *See external*
  style sheets; style sheets
empty elements, 8
ems, using in media queries, 322
emulators, using for testing, 501
enctype attribute, 439
Espresso text editor, 31
event handlers, 494
extensions. *See* file extensions
external style sheets. *See also* embedded style
  sheets; style sheets
 benefits, 192
 creating, 190–191
 importing, 191
 linking to, 191–193
 loading multiple, 193
 media attribute, 200–201, 319–322
 naming, 191
 saving with .css extension, 190
 URLs in, 193
 UTF-8 encoding, 190

F

fallback backgrounds, creating, 378
favicons, 155–156
fieldset element, 418
 using with forms, 418–421
figcaption element, 92–93
figure element, 92–93
file extensions, using consistently, 32–34
file names
 extensions, 14
 lowercase, 14, 26
 separating words with dashes, 14

placeholder attribute, 412
processing, 416–417
pseudo-classes, 446
radio buttons, 432–433
range input type, 411
regular expressions, 431
required attribute, 412
search boxes, 428–431
security, 416–417
select boxes, 437–438
server-side vs. client-side, 417
start and end tags, 413–414
styling based on states, 446–448
styling with attribute selectors, 448
submit button, 441–443
telephone boxes, 428–431
text areas, 436
text boxes, 422–424
URL boxes, 428–431
validating, 417
week input type, 411
fractional values, representing, 128–129
FTP client, using, 515–517
FTP site, defining properties for, 516

G
generated content, 384–386
generic containers, creating, 73–75
GIF image format, 134–135, 138
Gimp image editor, 141
Google Fonts web font service, 339, 357–359.
        See also fonts
Google Usage Rights, 140
gradient backgrounds, 376–380
gradient code, creating for old browsers, 381
groups of elements, specifying, 226

H
h1–h6 elements, 50
hCard microformat, 119
head element, 45
        adding to webpages, 4, 45–46
        indenting code nested in, 47
header attribute, 530
header element, 54–55
        multiple, 55
        with nav element, 55
        page-level with navigation, 54
headers, creating, 55
headings
        describing groups of form fields with, 418–421
        for defining document structure, 50
        importance of, 21, 50–51
        levels h1–h6, 21, 50
        navigating with a screen reader, 23

organizing webpages with, 51–52
proper use of, 52
using, 50
using all levels of, 51
height, setting for elements, 282–285
height vs. min-height, 284
Helvetica, showing on OS X, 235
hgroup element, removal of, 52
hidden attribute, 520
hidden fields, creating for forms, 440
high, low attributes, 128
highlighting text, 116–117
homepage, specifying default, 35
hr element, 524
href attribute
        contents, 10
        explained, 162
        including for links, 158–159
href values, including on webpages, 6, 158, 192
hreflang attribute, 520
HSL (hue, saturation, light) and HSLA, 186–188
HTML (Hypertext Markup Language), 26
        checking for consistency, 496
        debugging techniques, 506–507
        history and relationship to HTML5, xvi
        indenting, 7
        rendering by browsers, 12, 24–25
        semantics, 20–23
        thinking in, 3
        validating, 497
        viewing others' code, 40–41
        writing in lowercase, 26
.html and .htm extensions, 32
html element, 44
        basic usage, 4–5
        including in webpages, 44–46
HTML elements. See elements
HTML markup. See markup
HTML pages. See also webpages
        body element, 4, 20
        common page constructs, 53
        components, 44
        DOCTYPE, 4–5, 44, 46
        example, basic, 4
        examples, larger, 60, 230–231, 269–270
        head element, 4, 45
        html element, 4, 44
        indenting code, 7, 44
        semantics, 20–23
        structure, 44–46, 50–52
HTML5
        DOCTYPE, 46–47
        differences with HTML4, xix
        document outline, 52
        empty elements, 9

lists *(continued)*
    indentation, 392, 396
    `li` (list item), 389, 392, 396
    nesting, 392
    `ol` (ordered list), 389–392
    `padding-left` indentation, 396
    right-to-left, 392
    styling nested, 400–403
    `ul` (unordered list), 389–392
`list-style` properties, setting at once, 399
`list-style-position` property, setting, 398
`loop` attribute, 456, 466
lowercase
    files and folders, 26
    writing HTML in, 26
`lowercase` value, using, 260

M
`main` element, 59
`main` landmark role, 79–80
`manifest` attribute, 524
`map` element, 526
Marcotte, Ethan, 267
margins
    em values for, 294
    percentage-based values for, 318
    setting around elements, 292–293
`mark` element, 116–117
markers
    choosing for lists, 393
    custom vs. default, 396
    customizing, 394–396
marking up
    code, 112
    file names, 112
markup
    attributes, 9–10
    children, 11
    components, 26
    elements, 8–9
    parents, 11
    values, 9–10
mathematical markup, 113
`max` attribute
    for `meter` element, 128–129
    for `progress` element, 130–131
`maxlength` attribute, 423, 436
`max`, `min` attributes for input range, 525
`max-width`, relative, 318. *See also* width
`media` attribute, 200, 319
`@media` at-rule, using in style sheets, 201
MediaElement.js, 470–471
media queries
    base style rules outside of, 323
    examples, 320–322

media features, 319–320
    for Retina displays and other high-pixel-density
      displays, 332
    in style sheets, 323
    for style sheet for responsive webpage,
      329–330
    syntax, 320–322
    targeting viewport widths, 330
    using ems in, 322
media-specific style sheets, 200–201, 319–323
megapixels, 136
`menu` element, 526
`meta` element, 45, 324–325
`meter` element, 128–130
`method` attribute, 414
`method="get"` vs. `method="post"`, 415
microformats, implementing, 83
MIME type, setting, 451
`min-height` vs. `height`, 284
Miro Video Converter, 451
missing images, fixing, 510
misspelled words, noting, 122
mobile compatibility, testing for, 501
mobile devices resources, 332
mobile first approach, following, 327
Modernizr website, 363
multimedia
    native, 450
    resources, 476
`multiple` attribute, 431, 437
`muted` attribute, 453, 465

N
`name` attribute, 413, 436, 437, 522
Namecheap website, 512
native multimedia
    accessibility, 462
    explained, 450
`nav` element, 56
    links in, 56–58
    with `ul` and `ol`, 57
navigation
    including on pages, 162
    marking, 56–58
`navigation` landmark role, 79–80
nested lists
    styling, 400–403
    using for drop-down navigation, 403
nesting elements, 11
nh nm ns duration format, 100
Node.js, 486
`normalize.css`, 105
`noscript` element, 527
Notepad text editor
    displaying files in, 36

Q

q element, 95
    cross-browser issues, 97
    using with **lang** attribute, 95–96
Quirksmode website, 499
quotes, single vs. double, 348
quoting text, 95–97

R

radial gradients
    defining, 379–380
    explained, 376
radio buttons
    creating for forms, 432–433
    nesting, 433
readonly attribute 440
references, citing, 94
regular expressions resource, 431
rel attribute, 192
    rel values, resource, 160, 162
    using with external links, 160
    using when linking to external style
        sheets, 192
relative positioning of elements, 301
relative URLs
    vs. absolute URLs, 19
    referencing files, 17–18
    root, 18
rem (root em), sizing fonts with, 243
rendering webpages, 7, 24–25
required attribute, 422
resizing background images, 256, 332
resizing images, 154
Respond.js, downloading, 334
responsive webpages. *See also* webpages
    base styling, 326
    building, 331–332
    components, 311
    conditional comments, 333
    content and HTML, 326
    evolving layouts, 328–331
    explained, 266–267
    flexible images, 312–314
    flexible layout grid, 315–318
    images conundrum, 314
    main navigation, 328
    media queries, 319–322
    media query for style sheet, 329
    mobile first approach, 327
    picture element, 314
    scaling in proportion, 318
    srcset attribute, 314
    testing, 332
    width, 328

Retina displays and other high-pixel-density
    displays
    creating images for, 153
    icon fonts, 153
    media queries for, 332
    scaling images for, 152
    sizing images for, 153
    SVG (scalable vector graphics), 153
reversed attribute, 392
right-to-left languages, incorporating, 127
role attribute, 78,
root relative URLs, 18
rows, **cols** attributes, 436
rowspan attribute, 482
rp element, 124–125
rt element, 124–125
ruby element, explained, 124–125
rules. *See* style rules

S

s element, 108, 110–111
Safari
    developer tool, 503
    testing sites in, 500
samp element, 113
sandbox attribute, 524
saving
    animated images, 139
    external style sheets, 190
    images, 139, 142–144
    images with alpha transparency, 144
    photographs, 139
    source code, 41
    webpages, 32–36
scope attribute, 478
screen readers, xxi, 23, 49, 50, 78
Screen Sizes website, 332
script element, 487
seamless attribute, 524
search boxes, creating for forms, 428–431
section element, 63–64
    vs. **article**, 271
    considering use of, 64
    vs. **div** element, 63
    nesting in **article** element, 64
section (the word) vs. **section** element, 46
select boxes, creating for forms, 437–438
select element, 437
selected attribute, 437
selecting
    first letter of elements, 218–219
    first line of elements, 218–219
    links based on states, 220–221

WITHDRAWN

39.99

4/27/15.